I Was There

A Century of Alumni Stories about the University of Alberta, 1906–2006

ELLEN SCHOECK

I Was There

A CENTURY OF ALUMNI STORIES ABOUT THE UNIVERSITY OF ALBERTA, 1906–2006

THE UNIVERSITY OF ALBERTA PRESS

Published by
The University of Alberta Press
Ring House 2
Edmonton, Alberta, Canada T6G 2E1

LIBRARY AND ARCHIVES CANADA CATALOGUING IN PUBLICATION DATA

Schoeck, Ellen, 1949–
 "I was there" : a century of alumni stories about the University of Alberta, 1906–2006 /
Ellen Schoeck.

(University of Alberta centennial series)
Includes bibliographical references and index.
ISBN 10: ISBN 0-88864-464-7   ISBN 13: ISBN 978-0-88864-464-0

 1. University of Alberta—Anecdotes. 2. University of Alberta—Alumni and alumnae—
Anecdotes. I. Title. II. Series.

LE3.A619S35 2006   378.7123'34   C2006-904595-X

Printed and bound in Canada by Friesens, Altona, Manitoba.
First edition, first printing, 2006

The University of Alberta Press is committed to protecting our natural environment. As part of
our efforts, this book is printed on Enviro Paper: it contains 100% post-consumer recycled fibres
and is acid- and chlorine-free.

The University of Alberta Press gratefully acknowledges the support received for its publishing
program from The Canada Council for the Arts. The University of Alberta Press also gratefully
acknowledges the financial support of the Government of Canada through the Book Publishing
Industry Development Program (BPIDP) and from the Alberta Foundation for the Arts for our
publishing activities.

*Title page: The university crest from the convocation table presented to the University by the 1936
graduating class (University of Alberta Art Collection, Museums and Collections Services).*

This book is affectionately dedicated to a master raconteur, Hugh Whitney Morrison (BA '30), who during his 99 years lived a life filled with learning, wit, and humanity.

And to my mother and father, Vivian and Robert, who gave me a love of language, history, and storytelling.

Contents

Foreword

As the University of Alberta looks forward to its centennial in 2008, it is time also to look back at the history of this campus. The University of Alberta Centennial Series will celebrate the University's 100 years of academic excellence with a variety of books about the people and events that have shaped this institution.

The first book in the Centennial series is Donald G. Wetherell's *Architecture, Town Planning and Community: Selected Writings and Public Talks by Cecil Burgess, 1909–1946*. Cecil Burgess was appointed by Henry Marshall Tory as Resident Architect and Professor of Architecture in 1913. Burgess influenced the planning and development of our campus for many years, and he would be proud to know that his work remains highly valued to this day.

Commissioned specifically for the University's centennial, Professor Rod Macleod's *All True Things: The University of Alberta, 1908–2008*, the third book in the series, will delve into the community of scholars, researchers, and students at the University of Alberta over the past century. Dr. Macleod states that to be able "to reflect on the history of your own institution is a real privilege."

I Was There: A Century of Alumni Stories about the University of Alberta, 1906–2006 is oral history at its best. But it is much more than oral history. In this, her labour of love, Ellen Schoeck has captured the spirit and soul of a century-old institution. She has done so with a rigour for accuracy and with a passion for its people.

In my four years as Board Chair, I soon came to know this energetic woman with the sparkling eyes as the corporate and personal memory of the University of Alberta. I had been on the job scarcely weeks when she announced her "book project." When I asked her if there existed anywhere a list of the first members of Convocation, Ellen produced (within minutes) a photo of the March 1908 pre-convocation group, including my own grandfather, Lt. Col. E.B. Edwards. This drove me to a search of our own family records, from which I managed to extract the very list I'd asked about, contained in the official program for the October 1908 Convocation!

Obviously, not all interviews appearing in this delightful book were conducted by Ellen Schoeck in the 21st century. She has made full use of earlier interviews recorded in the 1960s, including first-hand accounts of the founding of the University. Yet the most vivid chapters are those in which Ellen has herself spend hours lovingly and patiently drawing out memories many decades old.

Central to these reminiscences is the saga of Hugh Morrison (BA '30): "Journalist, Scholar, Spy." Hugh Morrison died just as this book was going to press, but not before he related, in riveting detail, his journey from Vegreville, Alberta, through undergraduate days at U of A, to Oxford as a Rhodes Scholar, to man of the world and man of letters.

Along with the founding giants, Premier A.C. Rutherford and President H.M. Tory, Ellen Schoeck brings to life Reg Lister, Agnes Wilson, Marjorie Montgomery Bowker, Albert Ottewell, and dozens more. They help us relive the past of a great university in their own words. In fact, it was Her Honour Marjorie Bowker, retired judge, who gave Ellen the title for her book when she said, "I know, Ellen: I was there."

This book will appeal to two broad readerships: University of Alberta alumni (in the broad sense, encompassing students, professors, and support staff); and those who are curious about universities in general, and about ours in particular.

For years Ellen Schoeck conducted an orientation course for new faculty, support staff, Senators, and Board members: "Governance 101." She led "Magical Mystery Tours" to all the significant historical sites on campus. Her joy and pride in the University of Alberta inspired me when I under-took my most important task as Board Chair: recruiting a new president. I was able to brief the candidates on what made ours a very special, colle-gial, even familial institution, in spite of its growth in under a century from 46 students to almost 40,000, and from a budget of $27,489 to almost $1,200,000,000.

Finally, this book looks forward to the next century. It concludes with two special messages on "What the Future Holds" from two alumni: Dr. Richard Taylor, Nobel Laureate in Physics, and Dr. Juliet McMaster, world-renowned specialist in the English novel. You might even want to start with them.

As series editor of the University of Alberta Centennial Series, I am delighted to present our collective history to our alumni, students, and staff in these and other new books planned in this series over the next three years as we lead up to our celebrations in 2008.

HON. JIM EDWARDS, P.C.
Chair Emeritus, University of Alberta Board of Governors

Preface

I WAS THERE is a simple book of stories from alumni. They will tell you why they decided to come to university, what everyday life was like for them, and where their degrees took them after graduation. You will also hear from professors who were at the U of A in the early days and from an early staff member, Reg Lister. Their stories pluck the University's history down off the bookshelf, and make it live all over again. For instance...

Agnes Wilson (BA '12) will describe her first day of class in 1908, and you'll be with her as she twice fails English, her major, under the scrutiny of the inspiring but unrelenting taskmaster, Dr. Broadus. The first professor hired at the U of A, William Hardy Alexander ("Doc Alik") will tell you about the University's traditions. Then, in 1927, you'll be tossed off the roof of Athabasca Hall with Hugh Morrison (BA '30) during freshman initiation. Fast forward to 1966, and Myra Davies, (BA '69), will describe the first SUB, the Tuck Shop, and the radical 1960s. Finally, eight students describe life on campus in 2004. Along the way you will meet a century's worth of teachers, actors, scientists, journalists, politicians, diplomats, researchers, public servants, engineers, artists, and playwrights. You'll even meet a ghost or two.

At the core of *I Was There* are interviews with alumni who attended the U of A from 1926–2004. For earlier years, I drew from interviews of the first students and professors conducted by Ruth Bowen (BA '31).

I was inspired to tell these stories after meeting Hugh Whitney Morrison (BA '30) at an alumni function in 2000. The next day, I took Hugh and two students for lunch. We were entranced by Hugh's accounts of student life in the 1920s. Soon after, I took a year off from work to begin writing this book. If you have a story to tell, click on to the book's website: I Was There at U of A (www.iwasthereatuofa.com.)

Acknowledgements

I WAS THERE BELONGS to U of A alumni and to students. Open up this book—on any page—and share in a century of stories about life at the University of Alberta.

Most of this book was written in 2002–2003, as a personal project, during a year's professional leave from my job as director of the University Secretariat at the U of A. I am grateful to my staff, especially Garry Bodnar, for taking over my duties during that time, and to the Leighton Artists Colony at the Banff Centre, where I had uninterrupted time to write. My husband Ivan Ivankovich stood by me the entire time. Kevan Warner at the University of Alberta Archives helped me burrow into old records for two decades. And one person made sure I finished: Provost Carl Amrhein.

Courtney Thomas (BA '03, MA '05, PhD candidate at Yale 2006), critiqued the manuscript, conducted research, and proofed many drafts; she was my mainstay. Scott Davies (BA '04) scoured archival records, especially on the physical campus, researched, collected, and organized photos, and wrote several pieces for the book. The list of presidents is his. Sarah Kelly (BA '02) did an initial edit of the first eight chapters and researched and wrote several stories. The U of A Press—Peter Midgley, Alan Brownoff, Linda Cameron, Cathie Crooks, and Yoko Sekiya—patiently made it all into a book and Judy Dunlop compiled the index.

The Senate's Emil Skarin Fund, and Bruce Bentley, past president of the Alumni Association, believed in this project from the beginning. Unforgettable.

There was also some magic involved. Raymond Frogner and Alan Brownoff made fading photographs and fragile negatives leap off the page, and Dennis Weber created the digitized map of the 1940s.

Many archivists opened their treasures to me: Kevan Warner, Raymond Frogner, Bryan Corbett, Jim Franks, Ray Au, and Michael Holly at the U of A; Jane Atkinson at the Banff Centre; and archivists at the City of Edmonton, the University of Calgary and the University of British Columbia. I am indebted to generations of *Trail*, *New Trail*, *Evergreen and Gold*, and *Gateway* writers and photographers, and to U of A historians, including Michael Ford. At the U of A Faculty Club, Peter Graff, Erika Zurawski, and Debbie Hooper always gave me a quiet spot for an interview.

Rob Desjardin was the first to read a draft, and many others critiqued early versions: Hugh Morrison, Marjorie Bowker, Myer Horowitz, Carole Byrne, Heather Zwicker, Jeanette Buckingham, Adam Rozenhart, Harwood McCuaig, Catherine Eddy, Daniel Kaszor, and David Hall. Many alumni lent me photographs, including Pat Bates and Fran Olson.

My daughter, Becky Solomon, helped to organize masses of material electronically. Jeff Albert, Robin Sawh, Andy Yan, and Charles Lam rescued me from computer glitches. Warmest thanks also to the many friends and colleagues whose advice shaped the book and who know that any errors are mine.

I am deeply grateful to Her Honour Lois Hole who, each and every time I saw her, always sat me down to hear how the book was progressing. When I needed that last push in order to finish, she sent me a letter of encouragement in November 2004, when she was very ill.

The Alberta Historical Resources Foundation provided financial assistance for the publication of the book; its support is gratefully acknowledged.

Open up *I Was There* and share in a century of life at the U of A that so many helped to create.

"Tomorrow night I'll be Alberta bound."

—GORDON LIGHTFOOT

Timeline

1876–1898

- Alexander Graham Bell makes the first telephone call (1876)
- Telegraph line to Edmonton is completed (1878)
- *Edmonton Bulletin* is established by Frank Oliver (1880)
- Bell telephone operators wear headsets weighing 6.5 lbs (1880)
- CPR mainline goes to Calgary, by-passing Edmonton (1881)
- Alberta is created by a division of the North-West Territories (1882)
- First professional theatre group comes to Edmonton (1882)
- The CPR tracks reach Calgary (1883)
- The first three women students enrol at the University of Toronto (1884)
- Lord Strathcona drives in the last spike in the CPR at Craigellachie, B.C. (1885)
- Louis Riel hanged in Regina after the second Métis uprising (1885)
- Treaty 7 is signed between the Blackfoot Confederation and Canada, ceding to Canada land from the Cypress Hills to the Rocky Mountains (1887)
- The Edmonton-to-Calgary stagecoach takes five days each way (1889)
- Strathcona incorporates as a town (1889)
- CPR terminus promised to Edmonton goes instead to Strathcona (1891)
- Strathcona Hotel built across from the new CPR station (1891)
- First transatlantic radio transmission received at Signal Hill, Newfoundland (1891)
- Sir John A. Macdonald, Canada's first prime minister, dies in office (1891)
- Edmonton incorporates as a town (1892)
- Sir Wilfrid Laurier, a Liberal, ousts Sir John A. Macdonald's Conservative successors (1896)
- Frederick Haultain recognized as premier of the North-West Territories (1897)
- Klondike gold rush (1898)

1900–1902

- Alberta's population in 1900 is 73,000 and leaps to 374,000 by 1910
- A 12-year recession ends (1900)
- Queen Victoria dies and Edward VII ascends the throne (1901)
- Population of Calgary is 4,091, Edmonton 2,626, and Strathcona 1,550 (1901)
- Construction of Low Level Bridge completed, connecting Edmonton to the CPR in Strathcona (1902)
- Calgary's Western Canada College created (1902)
- The town of Edmonton buys Edmonton Power and two years later buys the district telephone company (1902)

THEY CAME WEST

"WHEAT. Free homes for millions. Good schools. Magnificent climate. Homesteads of 160 acres for a $10 entry fee."[1] So said the seductive ads that lured immigrants to Alberta.

"Come West."

And they did. They came from Ukraine, Great Britain, the United States, the Balkans, every corner of Europe, from Russia, from China, and from

Ontario and the Maritimes. As *The Calgary Herald* inelegantly informed its readers in 1907, a "Big Bunch of Immigrants" had arrived in Winnipeg in just 11 hours.[2] William Whyte, vice-president of the CPR, told Albertans that "Winnipeg and Regina were filled already with settlers and their effects, and the rush West has already commenced."[3]

Immigrants who settled in the rural districts, far beyond the towns and tracks, faced the isolating reality behind the enticing ads. Once they reached the end of the rail line in Calgary or Strathcona after a long overland journey, there was still no rest. A rugged trip by ox cart or horse-drawn wagon took settlers to a plot of land somewhere out on the vast prairie. Then came the hard work of homesteading to secure title to the land—busting 30 acres of tough sod, building a house, putting up miles of fencing, and establishing herds of farm animals. At the same time, settlers were also making a home for their families, with all the attendant risk, worry, and work undertaken in a foreign country, on raw land, with no neighbours in sight.

The isolation and homesickness were overwhelming for most. "There was no communication whatsoever in the country districts in those days," remembers one settler who later, as minister of education, opened the building we know today as Corbett Hall. In those early days, "there were no roads, no cars, no newspapers. It was long before the days of radio," much less dedicated phone lines, cars, and computers.[4] It was settlers like these, both rural and urban, who sent their sons and daughters to the University of Alberta when it opened its doors in 1908. In turn, the University would soon reach out to the pioneers, with night classes, part-time degrees, and a travelling Extension Department.

Agnes Wilson (BA '12)

AGNES WILSON was the first woman from Strathcona to register at the University.[5] Her parents came west in 1892, the year after the railroad linked South Edmonton to Calgary. With the spur line between Calgary and South Edmonton open for business, it was a mere 12-hour trip by train between the two towns—12 hours of "being jolted about on slat seats." But the train trip was a cakewalk compared to the five-day journey by ox cart through "a strange and wild environment."[6]

When you arrived at the South Edmonton CPR station, says Agnes, there were dozens of horse-drawn buggies from the north side lined up to meet the train. "The shouts of the drivers calling out the names of the four north side hotels in Edmonton made my mother think that she had arrived in some sort of civilization. But when the shouting died down and the buggies were gone, then there was nothing except for the Strathcona Hotel and the station, a few shacks, muddy streets, and no sidewalks." The South Edmonton of 1892—called Strathcona by 1898—was barren and quiet.

Agnes's father Harry opened a general store and set up shop as the first postmaster. Years later, when Agnes was 18, Harry and his wife sent their daughter down the street to the University of Alberta to study English. Only a handful of other families would make that same decision about their daughters' education. Agnes graduated, and then married another early alumnus, D.J. Teviotdale. Agnes lived near the University for most of her life, watching it evolve from a wilderness to a high-rise campus.[7]

GRADUATING CLASS '12 — GRADUATING CLASS '12

J. ADAM — MISS E.C. ANDERSON — L.Y. CAIRNS
MISS M.E. LLOYD — F.S. McCALL — G.D. MISENER

A.L. CARR — T.C. COLWELL — J.R. DRYSDALE
E.T. MITCHELL — A.E. OTTEWELL — MISS S.E. RUTTAN

R.C. HARGRAVE — MISS W. HYSSOP — G.A. KETTYLS
J.M. WAGGETT — J.G. WHITE — MISS A.K. WILSON

Edwin Mitchell, BA 1912.
Middle row, fourth from left.
(UAA 69–12–28)

Edwin Mitchell (BA '12)

EDWIN MITCHELL was president of the 1912 graduating class.[8] He had emigrated with his parents from England to Ontario, and then in 1889 the family headed west. The Mitchells travelled to Edmonton before it had a CPR connection, and so after an exhausting trip to Calgary by rail, they hired a horse and wagon and continued their journey over rutted, muddy roads.

Edwin was schooled in Edmonton, moved to Regina for teacher training at the Normal School, taught briefly, and then went east to Queen's for his degree.[9] There he met Dr. John MacEachran, soon to be a U of A professor of philosophy and first provost. MacEachran persuaded Edwin to transfer to the U of A, which he did in 1909, just as MacEachran started his professorship. Edwin now had the financial luxury of attending university right here at home and was the first student to graduate with an honours in philosophy. He married Decima Robinson (BSC '11, MSC '12), a stellar mathematician who taught at the U of A after she graduated. When Edwin was offered a professorship in philosophy at the University of Texas, he and Decima moved to Austin.

Edwin stayed in touch with Professor MacEachran and his U of A friends. He wrote a eulogy for his classmate Lee Carr in 1942, and travelled to Edmonton in 1946 to sit vigil at the bedside of his dying friend from his student days, Albert Ottewell.

Albert Ottewell (BA '12, MA '15)[10]

Albert Ottewell, BA 1912.
(UAA 70-69-006)

IN THE ONE INFORMAL PHOTOGRAPH we have of the 1912 graduating class, Albert Ottewell is standing with a small group of his classmates, wearing a victorious, almost defiant, "I-told-you-so" look on his face. He has one foot firmly planted on an upturned chair, arms folded across his chest, and his chin tilted up.

Albert Edward Ottewell had every reason to feel proud of his degree. As the youngest of 13 siblings born over a span of 45 years, he was a long shot for university. His father had emigrated from England in 1852, eventually settling in Wiarton, Ontario. Richard Ottewell had ten children with his first wife and when she died, he remarried and had three more children—two girls and Albert.

Albert's older brothers left home long before he was born. Phillip, the oldest, travelled west in 1869 and, while working with a government survey group, was captured by Louis Riel's provisional government. Phillip was court-martialled and given three options: "Join the rebels, stand up before a firing squad, or leave the 'country' within six hours. He chose the latter, a bitter experience in 40 below zero weather." Phillip arrived in Edmonton and prospered, earning his homesteading stake from a profitable potato crop he planted on Jasper Avenue. Phillip settled in the Clover Bar area, built a sod house, and cleared the land on what is now Edmonton's Ottewell district. Phillip's brother Sid joined him in Clover Bar, returning to Wiarton for a visit when Albert was an impressionable eight years old. Albert had grown up hearing tales of his adventurous older siblings, and now he finally heard first-hand about the rich farmland in Alberta and Phillip's growing threshing and coal businesses. In 1895, young Albert came west with his parents and his sister Alice.

Albert's parents settled near Phillip's farm, and 13-year-old Albert went right to work in Phillip's coal mines and on the farm. He had excelled in school back in Wiarton, but had had to drop out after Grade 8, which he finished when he was just ten years old. Now in 1895, as a 13-year-old labourer, Albert watched his nephews leave the homestead each day to walk to the local school in Mrs. Jellett's home. Albert would also watch his big brother Philip organize the Clover Bar school district and help build the first schoolhouse in the area. Albert had a deep love of the land, but he hungered to be back in school. He would later write that westerners were long denied post-secondary educational opportunities.

In 1906, Albert saw his chance. The *University Act* had been passed, and, in nearby Strathcona, a university would open in two years. And so, at age 26, Albert enrolled in the Methodist-run Alberta College, an affiliate of McGill, to finish high school and to consider preparing for the ministry. But in 1908, the principal of Alberta College, Dr. J.H. Riddell, and U of A president, Henry Marshall Tory, decided to transfer all ten ministerial students to the new university. Albert Ottewell didn't know it then, but he would spend the rest of his life at the University of Alberta.

Al Ottewell graduated in 1912 with a BA, *summa cum laude* in Classics, and then went on to a Master's degree. Right after his graduation, President Tory hired Albert to be the first director of extension. Who understood better than Albert the hunger of isolated settlers for culture and companionship? For 16 years, Al Ottewell traversed the far-flung country districts of Alberta in a Model T with his travelling library and glass lantern slides, packing up favourites like *Ben Hur* and *A Tale of Two Cities*. He gave slide shows and lectures, sang songs, and told jokes. And Albert brought news about the young university to rural Albertans. In 1928 Albert, the Grade 8 dropout, became registrar, a position he held until his death in 1946.

Rivalry over the Railroad

AGNES WILSON, the "first white child born in Strathcona," was interviewed about the U of A's early days in 1969, at age 75.[11] She also spoke to community groups about the University's first years as a public institution, telling her audiences that to understand the University's birth, they first had to know about the long-standing rivalry between the north bank town of Edmonton and its sister settlement across the river, then called South Edmonton. South Edmonton, today's popular Old Strathcona, was the site of the first U of A campus, and the "two Edmontons," North and South, jousted over access to the railroad and the consequent economic prosperity that it would bring.

As the year 1900 approached, Edmonton was in an economic quagmire: not yet incorporated as a city, and with no foreseeable hope of becoming

The first train into South Edmonton, November 25, 1891.
(COEA 10–2760)

Jasper Avenue would become a much busier road once Edmonton was linked by rail to the South Edmonton (Strathcona) CPR station.
(COEA 10–196)

one soon. But the little settlement of Strathcona across the river? It was a bustling, growing town. At the heart of this sad state of affairs lay the business monopoly of the century, the Canadian Pacific Railroad. Front-door access to the railroad, be it the CPR or the CN, could make or break a settlement. One U of A grad remembers that when the CN finally neared his hometown of Vegreville, the tracks by-passed the town by a few miles. So Vegreville pulled up stakes and moved every single building right next to the new railway.[12]

The railroad connected people in every way to the outside world. It meant moving your goods to market without an ox cart. It meant settlers could arrive on your doorstep, buy homesteading supplies, and then bring wheat to market through your city. Better yet, the railroad meant you could leave the horse and buggy at home and travel to other parts of the world.

When the CPR tracks headed west from Winnipeg in 1881, the route to British Columbia was slated to pass through Edmonton. Instead, the CPR tracks veered south to Calgary, leaving Edmonton in the dust with only a

stagecoach connection to Calgary and its coveted CPR station. Calgary prospered and Edmonton trailed behind.

But there was hope: the CPR promised Edmonton that it would build a spur line, the C&E, to connect Edmonton with Calgary. At the end of the day, however, the last railway tie of the C&E line was spiked down in South Edmonton. Why? Building a bridge over the North Saskatchewan River was simply too expensive. South Edmonton could now lay claim to the train station where thousands of settlers first set foot in Northern Alberta. It blossomed while Edmonton wilted.

Just how *did* Edmontonians get to the South Edmonton train station? Until the turn of the century, there was only one way. For a small fee you could board one of two cable ferries operated by John Walter. His upper ferry could handle a few foot passengers and one horse and buggy at a time, but to reach the ferry in the first place, you had to slither down the south bank of the river to get to the dock. And if that wasn't bad enough, when the river started to ice up in the fall or break up in the spring, a basket was attached to the ferry cable and, one by one, people could be

Before any bridges spanned the North Saskatchewan River, John Walter's ferry offered a way to cross the river at 5 cents per passenger. The fee was waived on Sundays for churchgoers. (COEA 10 2810)

transported to the other side, swaying back and forth over the frigid waters.[13] There was one other way to cross the river to catch the CPR at the South Edmonton station—as long as it was winter. Edmontonians could walk across the frozen North Saskatchewan, or drive a horse and buggy across the ice. U of A students walked across the frozen North Saskatchewan to get to classes as late as the 1930s.

South Edmonton Becomes Strathcona

AGNES WILSON and other early U of A grads were ringside when the simmering rivalry between Edmonton and South Edmonton burst through the surface. Back then, says Agnes, South Edmonton "was strictly a pioneer community" that depended on the new railroad.[14] Edmonton, on the other hand, relied on its history as a trading post. The "Twin Cities" were poised for a face-off.

The first showdown occurred when "Timber Tom" tried to move the land titles office from Edmonton to South Edmonton in 1892. As Agnes Wilson recalls, "One of the largest property owners on the railway right-of-way was 'Timber Tom' Anderson, so called because he was the Dominion Land and Timber agent. His office was on the north side of the river and after the arrival of the railroad to the south side in 1891, he used to jog over each morning via the ferry in a little pony cart to interview new settlers at the immigration hall. He was a Scot with a full beard and wore a Scotch tam. With the seeming upsurge in the fortunes of South Edmonton, he decided to move his offices to the south side of the river, and claims to have got permission from Ottawa to do so. News of this move soon spread to the northside citizens, and they were prepared to block the move by force if necessary. Inspector Griesbach, in charge of the North West Mounted Police detachment at Fort Saskatchewan, was alerted to the situation and he sent [another] detachment to the outskirts of the town. He also ordered a detachment all the way from Fort MacLeod, which arrived and set up its tents on the south side just opposite the Strathcona Hotel. The day of the move arrived. Records, books, and furniture were loaded on wagons. Edmonton Mayor McCauley ordered the Town Hall bell rung, the Home Guard turned out, ammunition and guns were distributed, and a party went to the scene. Meanwhile, the south side citizens armed themselves with any kind of gun they could muster...."[15]

Griesbach, in full uniform and on horseback, went into town on his own, just one man facing an armed mob led by the mayor of Edmonton, Matt McCauley, who threatened to shoot. Griesbach backed off. Later that day, Ottawa sent a telegram forbidding the move, and so it ended, with the land titles office remaining in Edmonton. When tempers settled, however, Ottawa made an interesting decision when it approved a satellite immigration office for South Edmonton.

South Edmonton was outraged by the vigilante action. The community disassociated itself from North Edmonton and searched for a new name as it sought incorporation as a town. The choice of a new name was easy: The CPR was Edmonton's economic lifeline, and so the town named itself after the czar of the CPR, Lord Strathcona. We all know him from his famous top-hat-and-tails photograph, driving the last spike into the CPR at Craigellachie, British Columbia.

Lord Strathcona, born in Scotland as Donald Smith, spent 30 years living in CPR cabins in Labrador and the hinterlands as a fur trader.[16] He emerged to become a master of corporate intrigue, a railway giant, a powerful politician, and an interesting husband. Smith was a crafty schemer who was on the scene when the Hudson's Bay Company transferred its land to the new Dominion of Canada. He underplayed the land values and then made his move and bought stock, thus becoming the nineteenth-century version of a dot-com millionaire. His decisions about CPR routes ensured either boom or bust for local economies. On the political scene, he was a member of parliament from Manitoba and a negotiator in the Riel rebellions.

Smith softened as he aged, transforming into a generous philanthropist. Over the years, this powerful financier married his Métis wife four times to make sure it was legal. When she died, the crusty Donald Smith, Lord Strathcona, mourned so deeply that within weeks, he too was dead. And so by 1899, the rival towns facing each other across the North Saskatchewan River were "Strathcona" and "Edmonton." But students at the University of Alberta, until the 1920s, would still identify their place of origin as South Edmonton.

First train crossing the Low Level Bridge in 1902, giving Edmonton access to the CPR.

(UAA 73–111)

Showdown in Strathcona

THERE WAS ONE MORE SHOWDOWN to come between Edmonton and the newly incorporated town of Strathcona. Ever since the C&E spur line had stopped south of the river, Edmontonians had planned and schemed to get a railway connection. In 1897, the Edmonton business community called Ottawa's bluff and financed the construction of the first bridge to cross the North Saskatchewan River. The Low Level Bridge took five years to construct and was at first opened only to wagon traffic.[17] In 1902, an eight-mile railway was built through the Mill Creek ravine and over the Low Level Bridge to connect Edmonton to the CPR in Strathcona. Only one thing remained to be done—install a switch at the Strathcona station. When the Edmonton crew arrived, the Strathcona police threatened to arrest them, and for good measure, in order to block the Edmontonians, Strathcona supporters moved a train engine over the spot where the switch was to be set. Later in the day, after a little sleight of hand, and swift mob action by a group of Edmontonians who swarmed over the tracks as a protective human shield for the switching crew, the deed was done and the switch installed.[18] Edmonton was finally connected to the outside world by rail. The old stagecoach line that ran between Edmonton and Calgary would become a thing of the past.

Ten years later the "two Edmontons" saw the economic folly of their divorce, reconciled amiably, and amalgamated. In 1912, students at the U of A could say that their university was in the City of Edmonton. But from 1908, when the U of A's doors opened, until 1912 when the first class graduated, the U of A's home was the City of Strathcona and, according to Albert Ottewell, Strathcona "had few dealings with Edmonton."[19]

Agnes Wilson, Edwin Mitchell, and Albert Ottewell were keen observers of the rivalry between the sister cities, but there were bigger fireworks to come as the new province of Alberta had to decide the location of its capital city and its new university.

*An Act to Establish and Incorporate a University
for the Province of Alberta*

43. *The university shall be strictly non-sectarian in
    principle and no religious dogma or creed shall
    be taught....*
44. *The senate shall make all provision for the
    education of women in the university...{and}
    no woman shall by reason of her sex be deprived
    of any advantage or privilege accorded to male
    students of the university.*

—ASSENTED TO MAY 9, 1906

Timeline

1903

- Frederick Haultain, premier of the Territorial government, introduces the University Ordinance (the first University Act)
- 274 new subdivisions created in Edmonton between 1903 and 1914
- *The Edmonton Journal* begins publication
- Wright brothers make the first airplane flight
- Marquis wheat revolutionizes agriculture on the prairies
- Alberta College is founded as a Methodist mission and then as a transfer institution to McGill University
- First water treatment plant built at Rossdale

1904

- Edmonton incorporates as a city
- Final session of the Territorial Assembly before Alberta becomes a province
- First recorded car trip between Edmonton and Calgary
- Edmonton city limits are extended to 127 Street

1905

- Alberta and Saskatchewan become provinces
- Alexander Cameron Rutherford is named premier of Alberta
- The federal government names Edmonton as the provisional capital of Alberta
- The Canadian Northern Railway connects Edmonton and Winnipeg

1906

- In the first sitting of the Alberta legislature, the *University Bill* is passed, establishing the U of A
- A motion to move the provisional capital from Edmonton to Calgary is defeated, 16–8
- The first Normal School opens in Calgary
- First speed limits for cars introduced
- Edmonton's first opera house opens
- First patient at the Strathcona Cottage Hospital—which later becomes the U of A Hospital

1907

- South Edmonton incorporates as the city of Strathcona
- Strathcona named as the site for the University of Alberta
- One-fifth of Edmonton's population is living in tents
- Twice-daily mail delivery is established

ALBERTA BECOMES A PROVINCE

In 1905–1906, three pieces of legislation were enacted in rapid succession in Ottawa and Edmonton. *One:* Alberta was carved out of the old North-West Territories and became a province. *Two:* Edmonton was named the capital. *Three:* the University of Alberta was born and sited in Strathcona. A quick hat trick achieved in less than two years.[1]

Sir Frederick Haultain—
Premier and Father of the University Ordinance

He was the dapper bachelor premier of the Territories, a devastating debater, and widely admired for doing the right thing. He branded the West with one word: *independence.* His name was Frederick Haultain,[2] and he led the charge for provincial status, including control of natural resources and equality with the existing provinces. It's an issue that still makes headlines today. "What we want in the West," Haultain said, "and what we have a right to expect, is to be established as a province with equal

The Simpson farm on River Lot 5, future home to the University of Alberta.
(UAA 82–155–84)

Sir Frederick Haultain.

(Courtesy of the Legislative Assembly of Alberta)

rights with the rest of the Dominion. We do not ask more, and we will not be willing to take less."[3] When Haultain was awarded an honorary degree in 1915, *The Gateway* called him a "true westerner."[4]

Haultain was born in England and headed to Alberta from Ontario in 1884 to practice law. He was thorough and deliberate in preparing the Territories for eventual entry into Confederation as a full-fledged province or provinces. Haultain's vision for dividing the four districts of the North-West Territories centred on creating one vast province called "Buffalo," stretching from Manitoba in the east to British Columbia in the west, and from the U.S. border north to the 57th parallel. Under his watch, the Territorial Assembly set in motion all the legislation and developed the structure that would be needed when Alberta and Saskatchewan were created in 1905. Retired judge Marjorie Montgomery Bowker (BA '38, LLB '39, LLD [Hon] '91) says that a hallmark of this Assembly was its "significant legislative activity, much of it forming part of the present provincial laws."[5] When Alberta became a province, the new legislature merely had to look to the solid legislation passed by the Haultain Assembly to secure its legal footing.

For Francophone Albertans, Haultain is remembered as the premier whose government legislated away, in 1887 and 1901, their right to have a viable separate school system where their children could be taught in French. For most Anglophone Albertans, he is a forgotten man. And yet Haultain's vision for higher education lives with us still. He wanted a state-supported university, free from denominational control. Haultain's university would thus be freed from simply preserving the past, and would be unleashed to teach as it saw fit, and to discover, create, and transmit new knowledge. Haultain's university would also include women.

Haultain named himself the minister of education for the Territories and saw to it that an Act was passed to enable the establishment of a university. In 1906, when the first Alberta premier, Alexander Cameron Rutherford, decided that a university should be established during the first sitting of the new provincial legislature, Haultain's Act came off the shelf and the University of Alberta was born. In fact, when the legislation was introduced in April 1906, the bill "repeated almost word for word the text of the bill passed by the...Legislative Assembly of the Northwest Territories...in 1903."[6]

Haultain's vision for a non-denominational, co-educational university distinguished the U of A from most universities in other provinces. The non-denominational provision in Haultain's Act meant Alberta wouldn't end up like Manitoba and Ontario, with several small, competing religious colleges, all with preconceived ideas about what constituted post-secondary education. And the equality provision sounds tame now, but back then women didn't have the vote, some provincial universities were restricted to men, and in some Canadian co-educational universities, certain academic programs, like mathematics at McGill, had long been off-limits to women.

Haultain was a thorough, no-nonsense leader, but he knew how to have fun. After a long day of debate at the Assembly in Regina, he hosted the group at the Palmer House for oysters, drinks, and a boisterous sing-along. There was only one person who didn't join in. It was R.B. Bennett, the Conservative leader from Calgary, lawyer for the CPR, and somewhat of a recluse. During his career, Bennett worked at making a fortune (he succeeded), manoeuvred for power on the provincial scene (he failed at first), and then played his political hand on the federal stage (he became prime minister during the Depression).[7] Bennett would come back to haunt the young University in the provincial legislature.

Wilfrid Laurier and Clifford Sifton Square Off—Alberta and Saskatchewan are Born

HE WAS THE SILVER-TONGUED ORATOR, always impeccably attired in a morning coat, and always the practical politician.[8] "He could lift audiences to rapture with his elegant, classically structured, and passionately delivered speeches," and in 1896 he swept to power, ousting the Conservatives.[9] His name was Sir Wilfrid Laurier, a Francophone, an Anglophile, and the second Liberal prime minister. Laurier had to straddle the French-English fault line to gain, and then maintain, power.[10] Ever the careful navigator between the desires of the brash new West and the perennial problems of the established, industrial East, he knew he needed Québec on side to stay in office.

Laurier's powerful minister of the interior and trusted Western adviser was Clifford Sifton. Sifton and the prime minister agreed on most policy matters, but as Alberta was being born, they parted ways over one hot issue: should separate schools be controlled by the state, or by the Catholic Church? Embedded in the so-called "schools question" were issues related to the minority rights of Francophones in the Territories. Sifton had staked his career on having state-controlled public schools in Manitoba and wanted the same for the new provinces.

In 1904, the Laurier government was re-elected. On the legislative agenda was the question of creating a province or provinces from the North-West Territories. Would these provinces control their own natural resources? Haultain emphatically said yes; the Laurier government said no. What would the physical boundaries be? Haultain wanted one big province, but that posed a threat to the powerhouses of Ontario and Québec. Laurier decided that there would be two provinces. Would there be only state-

supported schools, or, in addition, Catholic schools supported by the state? Would children be taught in both French and English? These were questions that cut to the core.

In the months before the 1904 election, Laurier had been in secret correspondence with the papal delegate to Ottawa, and was pressured to agree that the rights of the Francophone minority to separate schools would be entrenched in any bill establishing a province or provinces. As Laurier saw it, if the Church could deliver the Québec vote in the federal election, the Liberal reign would continue. And so it did, with an increased number of Liberal seats.

In February 1905, Sifton travelled to Indiana for a month for health reasons—ostensibly for hot-bath therapy, although there was speculation he was with a mistress. While Sifton was away, Laurier introduced legislation to create the provinces of Alberta and Saskatchewan—Bills 69 and 70—with provision for separate schools controlled by the Church. These provisions set the clock back, restoring to the Territories the minority rights that had been legislated away in 1887 and 1901 by the Haultain

Above the Rossdale Flats lies the McKay Avenue School, where the first provincial legislature meetings were held and where the University Act was passed.
(PAA B–882)

government. Unbeknownst to either Haultain or Sifton, however, the papal delegate asked for, and was sent, a draft of the legislation.

Sifton was furious. Shortly after his return to Ottawa, he resigned as minister of the interior and then caused such havoc in the caucus that Laurier backed down. Sifton drafted an amendment to the Bills so that separate schools would exist in the new provinces, but with a large measure of state control over such matters as teacher certification and curriculum. The amendment mirrored the earlier, restrictive legislation of the Haultain Territorial government and ensured that English would, in effect, be the language of instruction in the schools. The minority rights Laurier had promised to the papal delegate disappeared from the Bills.[11]

Bills 69 and 70 were debated in Parliament for five months, daily, until well past midnight. No bills had ever been debated for longer. They passed third reading on July 5, 1905. Alberta and Saskatchewan were born in the midst of acrimony, and as one powerful French Canadian put it, the bills "opened a gulf between Eastern and Western Canadians which nothing will fill."[12] Once Bills 69 and 70 were signed into law, Laurier named two lieutenant-governors for the new provinces, George Bulyea in Alberta and Amadee Forget in Saskatchewan. Laurier then set about deciding whom Forget and Bulyea would name as interim premiers.

Would Haultain be one of those so named? The *Edmonton Bulletin,* Liberal to the core, thought he had a chance. "Premier Haultain is placed in the unique position of being able to choose from two future provinces," said the *Bulletin.* "He has the opportunity to continue his political career in either—a very rare position for a politician."[13] But Haultain had determined his own fate some four months earlier during two Ontario by-elections held in the spring of 1905. Haultain, who as Territorial premier had largely avoided partisan politics, allied with the R.B. Bennett, the Conservative leader from Calgary, and went head-to-head with Laurier by aggressively supporting Conservative candidates in the by-elections. As Laurier wrote to Bulyea on July 25, 1905, Haultain had "openly take[n] side[s] with the opposition." Haultain's active support of the Tories in Ontario, Laurier said, "left us no alternative but to accept the declaration of war."[14] Laurier selected two Liberals as interim premiers of the new provinces—Alexander Rutherford in Alberta and Walter Scott in Saskatchewan.

The two interim premiers had a decided advantage in the upcoming elections. In August 1905, Haultain announced that he would run in Saskatchewan as leader of a Provincial Rights Party. He won only eight seats to Scott's 17. In Alberta, on November 9, 1905, Rutherford's Liberals won 23 of the 25 seats. Of note is the fact that R.B. Bennett lost his seat by 25 votes.[15] As for Haultain's Provincial Rights Party, it hung on for two more elections, and then became the Conservative Party of Saskatchewan.

Haultain was left in the wings politically. He was not invited to the inauguration of either interim premier, and when it came time for the rip-roaring, glorious parties that celebrated the birth of the two provinces, Haultain was not invited to either event. But his ideas about what a university should be, embedded in his territorial university ordinance, would live on to define the essential character of both the University of Alberta and the University of Saskatchewan. In 1912, Haultain was named chief justice of Saskatchewan. In 1917, he was knighted and began a 21-year tenure as chancellor of the University of Saskatchewan.

Haultain's brilliant career had a tragic personal twist. During most of his public life, Sir Frederick secretly provided financial support for a young Saskatchewan woman he adored, Marion Mackintosh.[16] Marion's husband had abandoned her after their first child was born, and she was left alone in England, where she and her husband lived. It was Frederick Haultain who came to her rescue financially. Marion faced difficult personal and health problems throughout her life, and in 1905 she returned to Canada in the midst of the political wrangling over the creation of the new provinces. She was now divorced, and Haultain considered marrying her, even though marrying a divorcée would likely end his career. They did marry, in Ontario in 1906, but Marion immediately moved back to England in an attempt to recover her health. People in Alberta and Saskatchewan had no inkling about Haultain's personal problems, and it was not until 1970 that his relationship with Marion came to light.

Frank Oliver Gets the Capital for Edmonton

HE WAS A MASTER OF POLITICS, and made sure his hometown would be the capital of the new province. His name was Frank Oliver, long-serving member of the Territorial Assembly, and known in the West as the Liberal founder and publisher of the *Edmonton Bulletin*.

Frank Oliver. (COEA EB 7 106)

Frank Oliver was named minister of the interior after the resignation of Clifford Sifton, thus gaining the prime minister's ear just at the moment when electoral districts for the new Alberta legislature were determined, and just as a provisional capital had to be named for Alberta. There was already a rivalry between Edmonton and Calgary, and a distinctiveness to northern and southern Alberta: northern Alberta had a more ethnically diverse population and was decidedly Liberal, while southern Alberta was ranching territory and decidedly Conservative. As a region, northern Alberta had the larger population. But Calgary's population outstripped Edmonton's, and Calgary was on the main line of the CPR. These were surely advantages for a capital city.

Nonetheless, Oliver favoured Edmonton and used his considerable power as interior minister to get his wish. At a critical moment, he wrote to Laurier: "I submit that your government is still in honour bound to give the preference to where your friends are in the large majority, as compared with the place where your opponents are in the majority."[17]

The city to the south had little chance of success. At the eleventh hour a group of Calgarians saw the writing on the wall and floated nearby Banff, at the time Canada's only national park, as an alternative site for the capital.[18] Banff, after all, had no facilities to support the machinery of a provincial government and thus nearby Calgary would *de facto* become the government's headquarters. But it was simply too late. When Laurier introduced Bill 69, the *Alberta Act*, on February 21, 1905, Edmonton got the plum.

Uproar in Calgary

THE REACTION IN CALGARY WAS INTENSE. One newspaper characterized the decision as "unfair...unpatriotic...cowardly...traitorous," while another commented, "Edmonton now estimates that it has a population of over 4,000. Estimates are easy to make. Calgary with her *bona fide* population of 11,000 is seriously thinking of estimating her population at 25,000 just to prove that its imagination is not inferior to Edmonton's."[19] At the peak of the Edmonton-Calgary rivalry, one reporter wrote that "Edmonton says Calgary wants to hog everything and Calgary replies that accusations of swinish proclivities come with bad grace from one who has had all four feet in the trough and is continually squealing for more."[20]

Calgarians knew that only an act of the new provincial legislature could change the provisional capital's location and started lobbying for support. Faced with the problem of ensuring that the legislature would endorse Edmonton, Oliver simply gerrymandered the electoral districts for the new legislature to ensure that Edmonton would garner more votes than Calgary.[21] When he arrived in Alberta in January 1908, Henry Marshall Tory wrote about the manoeuvre: "When the Province had been organized under an Act of the Dominion Parliament, in 1905, the selection of the site of the Capital was left to the Legislature of the Province, but it is only the truth to say, that the constituencies had been so arranged that the majority would favour Edmonton rather than Calgary as the site. Doubtless if a Conservative government had had the task of arranging the Province into constituencies, they would have been planned in such a way as to place the capital in the City of Calgary."[22]

As soon as the electoral map was unveiled, there was another storm of protest. Calgary Liberals Charles Stuart and C.J. Stewart telegraphed

Laurier, urging him to form an independent commission to decide the electoral boundaries. "We warn the government that unless changed, long continued soreness and ill feeling between north and south will be [engendered] and party interests in this region totally destroyed."[23] The electoral map remained unchanged, the Liberals under Alexander Cameron Rutherford won, and on April 25, 1905, members of the new legislature voted on a motion to move the capital from Edmonton to Calgary. The motion was defeated, 16–8, "with three southern Alberta MLAs voting for Edmonton."[24] Edmonton is *still* the provisional capital, subject to any change enacted by the provincial legislature.

The rivalry between Edmonton and Calgary was now set in cement. Past rivals over the CPR, rivals over a new depot for immigrants, and competitors over the capital, the two cities would soon face off over the location of the University of Alberta.

Alexander Cameron Rutherford— Founder of the University of Alberta

THE *MONTREAL HERALD*, the *Winnipeg Free Press* and the *Toronto Globe* described Alexander Cameron Rutherford as "a gentleman, a man of fine ability who pushed forward the perimeters of education. He was an honest, upright figure in politics—not a politician characterized by guile, but rather a man of action. He was a big man, physically and mentally, with a radiant humour in his eyes and lines of stubborn strength finely blended in his genial face."[25] To his closest friends, he was "Ruthy";[26] to his fellow citizens in Strathcona, he was simply "Uncle Sandy." To early U of A students, he was the premier with the stunning red Packard who, when being driven by his son Cecil or his daughter Hazel, would take the time on his way to work to pick them up and give them a ride to the University. Rutherford was the model Strathcona citizen, a family man with a loving home life. A wonderful personal trait, but fatal political flaw, was his lack of a political killer instinct.

After a quick reconnaissance trip to Strathcona on the CPR in 1894, Rutherford came west with his family in 1895 to try his hand as an urban settler on the raw frontier.[27] He established a law practice in Strathcona and quickly became a leading citizen, serving on more than a dozen boards and community groups. He was elected to the Territorial Assembly,

where he served as Speaker. "Uncle Sandy" also had superb financial and forecasting instincts, and invested in large tracts of land in Mill Creek. He built an office block at Whyte Avenue and 104 Street, and started the company known as GWG Jeans.[28] When the time came for Prime Minister Laurier to select an acting premier for the new province, Rutherford was the choice.

The University of Alberta Is Born

WHEN RUTHERFORD CAME TO STRATHCONA, one of his first actions was to join the school board.[29] And when he became premier, one of his first actions was to make himself minister of education. Rutherford was determined to avoid the proliferation of denominational colleges that characterized other provinces. He wanted a single, state-supported, coeducational institution in the province, something he and Haultain had both advocated in the Territorial government.

He was quick. He was quietly confident. He was in control. And he thought big.

Rutherford introduced the bill to create the University of Alberta on April 23, 1906, in the McKay Avenue School, temporary site of the new legislature. Many members of the public felt the province should wait a few years before establishing a university, and there were some who advocated an agricultural college instead of a university. There was already a Methodist college in Edmonton, and a Presbyterian college in Calgary. And that was Rutherford's biggest worry—that Alberta would go the way of other provinces and have a number of small competing denominational colleges instead of a single, state-supported university. So Rutherford persisted, and the Act to establish the University of Alberta was proclaimed on May 9, 1906.

A university now existed on paper. To make it come alive, it needed a home, a physical site. That was Rutherford's next move. He wrote to Prime Minister Laurier, asking for a land grant for the new institution. Laurier gave him the brush-off, reminding the just-named premier that Ottawa had already given the new provinces financial assistance as part of the birthing process. The new provinces, Laurier told Rutherford, were now "richer than Ottawa."[30] In other words, you're on your own. Rutherford was undaunted. He sized up the real estate market in 1906, a market he knew intimately, and settled on River Lot 5 as the University's future home. It was the Simpson farm, directly across from the government he headed. Rutherford negotiated a good price—$150,000—and had the provincial treasurer seal the deal. A few months later, the land was assessed at $258,000.[31] The University and the new legislature building, not yet built in 1906, would eventually face each other, one on the north bank and the other on the south.

In the meantime, Calgarians were convinced that, having just lost the capital to Edmonton, they would get the University. The newspapers were full of reports about what a fine site for a university Calgary would be. "Calgary," said one, "is destined to become a seat of learning second to none in the West. The location of the provincial university is assured for the city."[32] Rutherford, in fact, when campaigning in Calgary, had told Calgarians that the University would be built *south* of the North Saskatchewan River. Calgarians thought that meant the University would go to their city. But it was not to be. Not only had Premier Rutherford quietly manoeuvred behind the scenes so that Strathcona, his home riding, would be the site of the new University, he also bought a half-hectare plot of land, from Laurent Garneau, right next door to River Lot 5. On that land, Rutherford would build a home for his family and watch his post-secondary creation grow.

Backlash in Calgary

THE CHOICE OF STRATHCONA as the site of the new University ignited a firestorm in Calgary and on the floor of the legislature. Strathcona was confirmed as the University's location, but bitterness festered in Calgary. A *Calgary Herald* editorial in 1909 reported that "Calgary has been robbed of the capital and Calgary has been robbed of the University."[33]

Over the next few years, Calgarians fumed at what they saw as an unfair decision, and key citizens rallied local support for a second university in the province.[34] Calgarian W.J. Tregillis offered 160 acres for the "Calgary University." Dr. T.H. Blow offered new buildings in which to hold classes and lobbied for funds from the Alberta government and local citizens. The federal government was asked for land. Blow served as a sort of registrar, advertising for applicants in the September 8, 1910 edition of the *Calgary Herald*. On November 5, 1910, a president for the fledgling institution was named.[35]

One of the most aggressive advocates for a second university was R.B. Bennett. On November 18, 1910, Bennett sponsored a piece of legislation to establish the "University of Calgary." The legislation covered every aspect of university infrastructure, from curriculum to residences, and decreed that the new school would be co-educational and non-denominational. It would open in the fall of 1912, just after the University of Alberta graduated its first class. Bennett's bill did in fact pass in the legislature, but with a provision that the "Calgary College" could not grant degrees. The fight for a rival university was over before it started.[36]

R.B. Bennett, the Conservative MLA for Calgary who was Premier Rutherford's nemesis.

Rutherford's Demise

IN 1910 RUTHERFORD WAS EMBROILED in a scandal involving the financing of a northern railway. Leading the charge on the floor of the legislature, once again, was R.B. Bennett, who was still smarting over the University's location. Debate in the legislature translated into banner headlines across the province, and culminated in a five-hour speech by Bennett in which he "heaped scorn and suspicion on the government."[37] Bennett's attack was supported by a group of discontented MLAs from within Rutherford's own party, but Rutherford never saw it coming. On May 10, 1910, he resigned as premier. An investigative commission soon absolved Rutherford of any wrongdoing, but questioned his judgement for not consulting Cabinet.[38] But by that time, Rutherford was already out of office and Arthur Sifton, brother of Clifford Sifton, was premier.

In 1911, Rutherford moved his family into "Achnacarry," their new home beside the University of Alberta and concentrated on his business interests and civic volunteering. In 1927, Rutherford became chancellor of the University, serving in that position for 15 years.

This pioneer, this principled gentleman, had the University of Alberta first in his heart, and first in his mind, for four decades. In 1905, we were a glimmer in his eye. When he retired as chancellor in 1941, we had some 2,000 students and 140 staff, an operating budget of $1.2 million, and a dozen buildings. River Lot 5 was a good deal indeed.

*"There is wine in the air;
a feeling of excitement;
of expectancy....great things
are about to happen."*

*—HENRY MARSHALL TORY
to his wife Annie
during an early visit to Alberta*

Timeline

Enrolment and Finance, 1908
- Fall student head count: 45
- Operating budget from the Province of Alberta: $27,489.29
- Full-load undergraduate Arts tuition: $20.00
- SU membership fee: none

Key Dates, 1908–1911
- Dr. Tory starts work on January 1, 1908
- The first governing body, called the Senate, has its inaugural meeting on March 30, 1908, with Chancellor Stuart in the Chair (1908)
- Senate establishes the Faculty of Arts and Science as the first faculty (1908)
- Senate confirms the hiring of the first four professors (1908)
- Eugenie Archibald serves as the first librarian (1909–1911)
- Cecil Race hired as the first registrar and also serves as librarian (1911)

Selected Campus Buildings, 1908–1910
- The U of A holds classes in rented quarters in Strathcona (1908–1910)

Beyond Campus, 1908–1910
- Strathcona Collegiate Institute, later called Old Scona High School, is built (1908)
- The first streetcar appears on Jasper Avenue, courtesy of the Edmonton Radial Railway (1908)
- Wilbur Wright flies 30 miles in 40 minutes (1908)
- The Ford company produces the first Model T (1908)
- "Bakelite" is invented, inaugurating the Plastic Age (1909)
- Architect Frank Lloyd Wright is at his peak, the tango is popular, and Marie Curie publishes her work on radiography (1910)

Henry Marshall Tory.
(UAA 69–152–003)

HENRY MARSHALL TORY

THEY HAD ALREADY MET. The new premier, Alexander Cameron Rutherford, and the soon-to-be University of Alberta president, Henry Marshall Tory,[1] were both McGill graduates. Rutherford knew about Tory's work in British Columbia to establish an affiliate of McGill, and they had met in Edmonton to discuss it. The "affiliate" would grow up to be the UBC we know today. Rutherford, Founder of the U of A, knew that in Tory he had found his Builder. Rutherford likely also knew that his choice for president had resigned as a Methodist minister after criticism that Tory was advocating a state-supported college in British Columbia rather than a Methodist-run institution. The two men shared the same belief on the key point of state-supported education. And they were both indomitable optimists, with wide-screen vision and incomparable energy.

Rutherford chose as the first U of A president a visionary and doer, just like himself.

The various designs for the University crest, from left to right: The first crest, designed by Jimmy Adam, 1908; First crest approved by the Board of Governors, 1911; Henry Glyde's redesigned crest, 1950; Walter Jungkind's redesign, 1984. The University's current crest (bottom) forms part of the official Coat of Arms. It was designed in 1994 by Joan Boumeester at the behest of then Chancellor Sandy Mactaggart. (Creative Services)

The premier travelled to Montréal to entice Tory away from the comforts and traditions of McGill to the vast new West. On January 1, 1908, Tory started work as president of an institution that existed only on paper, with no staff or students, no buildings, and in a province divided over the University's location and role.

Tory Navigates Past Calgary's Wrath

TORY WAS AN EARLY MASTER of the newspaper interview. He had to be. The *Calgary Herald* caught Tory on his arrival in that city, on the train bound for Edmonton, just as he assumed the presidency. Tory knew perfectly well that he had walked into the bitterness surrounding the choice of Strathcona as the site for the University and that Calgary still smarted badly. In fact, two years before, he had suggested to Calgarians that they just "get over" not being named as the capital, and ask for the University. His message, now that the University had gone to Strathcona, was simple: "The University will belong to the *province*" and not to any one location.[2] He tied the success of the infant university to the economic and cultural success of the province as a whole, and not to any one region.

Tory was more than smooth talk. Savvy and practical in his early honeymoon months, he travelled the entire province to woo prospective students and drum up support for the new University. He moved quickly to get to know Calgary, Edmonton, and Strathcona. But he staked out the entire province as his territory and, everywhere, he consolidated support and sought out the key players in rural Alberta and in the cities. All the while he stayed in close touch with Rutherford. For 20 years they had a comfortable professional and personal relationship. They enjoyed each other's company, and when the Mayfair Club opened, they golfed there regularly, laughing over their game, and counting only the "happy strokes."[3]

Claiming the entire province as U of A territory was a smart, tactical move. But Calgary was still angry. Within two years, R.B. Bennett would be elected to the legislature and propose that a rival university be established in Calgary. However persuasive Bennett's arguments were, the authorities saw clearly that "the province could not sanction two degree-granting institutions, with the inevitable tug of war for public support."[4]

Annie Tory—The Person Behind the Human Dynamo

EVERY SINGLE ACCOUNT tells of her warm personality and constant entertaining, and she was especially welcoming to the new faculty brides brought to the fringe of civilization by her husband's young professors. "Every kindness surrounds her memory," said math professor Ernest Sheldon, whose New York City wife, Helen McHugh Sheldon, was the first faculty bride.[5]

There was only one peculiar aspect to Annie Tory's life: she was the wife of a human dynamo. But she was the one who, in many ways, made it possible for him to be who he was. Tory founded four Canadian universities and had a long resume. But to Annie, President Tory was just "Marsh." The Torys lived "overtown" in Edmonton, and whenever "Marsh" couldn't make the trek home for lunch, Annie made sure one of the faculty wives over the river in Strathcona fed him.

You can tell from Mrs. Tory's concern about her husband that she was warm-hearted and caring. "Auntie Tory," as campus children called her, was the person who delivered home-baked buns when someone was in hospital, and always arrived back from far-off travels with gifts for the neighbourhood children in the Ring Houses where senior faculty lived.

(UAA 86–41–15)

scribed Tory as a human dynamo. One

who "could see ahead to things that

ility to inspire to action."[6] According

olvement in students' lives and activi-

rs, long-time English professor R.K.

ld see him hurrying across campus,

morning coats back then—sturdy,

t for anything and everybody. He did

esk."[8]

unched the institution that became

ed the World War I Khaki University,

of which he served as president from

ne organized Carleton University and

es? Nine. Memberships on national

ght. On his first day of work as presi-

partment. On his last day of work in

chools, and 43 departments.[9]

"There is so little time, so little time," he would bemoan.[10] He just never stopped. "He was everywhere, out and around campus," his staff said, and he would "get things done." He was the "heart of the machine," who "made things go." And as he went about his daily survey of the campus, Tory could be heard humming Methodist hymns under his breath.[11]

FACULTY AND STUDENT STORIES ABOUT PRESIDENT TORY

A Visionary

TORY'S FACULTY MEMBERS admired him for his vision, energy, enthusiasm, and steel. To English professor R.K. (Rob) Gordon, Tory was "the chief inspirer of hopes and dreams, the eager encourager of great expectations, the incorrigible believer in progress.... A strange mixture of idealist and politician, he was a good man to build up a university in a community which had just said goodbye to its pioneer days."[12]

But he *was* human, remembered Rob Gordon: "Anyone who was there at the time would not deny his faults, and at the same time, praise him....

West Lab, 1930 and Cameron Library

ONE DAY *Dr. Tory came upon a group of workmen clearing brush for the new Plant Pathology lab (the "West Lab"), which was to be a temporary stucco structure with an attached greenhouse. Along came D.E. Cameron, the librarian, who, upon discovering that this choice spot was destined to be a laboratory, protested vigorously, arguing that this site should be reserved as the location of the future library.*

Dr. Robert Newton, then dean of agriculture, later recalled how "Dr. Tory promptly walked off further west and, pointing to a knoll south of Pembina Hall,...told the workmen to put the lab there." Dean Newton was not pleased with the location of his new temporary building—it was too far from the other agriculture offices and really, as a prime site, should have been saved for a more permanent building. "But Dr. Tory's word was law," and the West Lab went up on the site Tory chose. Today, Cameron Library stands on the site advocated by D.E. Cameron in his chance meeting with Dr. Tory. Dean Newton went on to be president from 1941–1950. In 1966, the "temporary" West Lab was demolished to make way for today's Students' Union building.[13]

West Lab, 1930 (UAA 69–19–39–46) and Cameron Library (Courtesy of Alumni Affairs)

The President was a remarkable man." Although the faculty at one time or another could be critical of Tory, they "were also proud to be his men."[14]

The first dean of Dentistry, Dr. Bulyea, thought "he was a great man to work with if you took him right." Tory's penchant for dealing with detail was probably a difficult trait for strong faculty and deans to deal with. But Bulyea also had this to say about Tory's attempts to convince him to organize a course of studies in dentistry: "Dr. Tory was persuasive. He put it in such a way that you had faith in him. He told me, 'There is no money for the course, but I will get it for you.' And he never went back on anything."[15]

Early faculty told many stories about their salaries, which they felt were terribly low. Rob Gordon comments that "nobody could make dollars go farther than Dr. Tory. Whatever mistakes he made…he certainly never made the mistake of overpaying his staff." Professor Edouard Sonet remembers returning to the U of A after five years of military service. "I had been there ten years. The salary they offered me was $1,500 a year. I resigned and returned to France." (The senior professors hired in 1908 made $2,500 a year.) Then a letter arrived from Tory doubling Sonet's salary. The professor of French accepted with a philosophical air: "You see, I am a *professeur* in spite of myself!"[16]

Helen Sheldon, advisor to women, remembers Tory's personal generosity to the faculty in 1910, the year Premier Rutherford resigned so suddenly: "Tory wasn't a wealthy man, although he had two wealthy brothers. Tory was personally underwriting the salaries of the professors when we came—this was after the Government's trouble when the Premiers changed and the advance to the University was withheld."[17]

In the opinion of Rob Gordon, Tory was not a memorable public speaker, but "his drive and warmth and the rich humanity in him more than made up for all defects. Where he spoke really well was at his own fireside, recalling his boyhood days in Nova Scotia, or giving his comments, humorous, shrewd and racy, on men and women."[18]

A Micromanager

AGNES WILSON remembers Tory having a "finger in *every* pie," but when interviewed at age 75, she quickly added that "today, there would be too many pies."[19] After her graduation, Agnes subbed for Dr. Tory's secretary,

"Take a letter, Miss Ockley . . . "

Illustration courtesy of Juliet McMaster.

Miss Beatrice Ockley, when she went on vacation. "I often wonder how Miss Ockley coped," says Agnes. "Dr. Tory would come bursting in, his coat would go one way, his hat the other. He would commence dictating and it didn't stop whatever else he was doing."[20]

Helen Montgomery MacLeod (BA '14), winner of the first Academic Women's Association gold medal, remembers when university women formed the Soldiers' Comforts Club and sent parcels to the troops overseas during World War I. "One day when we were wrapping up Christmas parcels for the men, Dr. Tory came into the room and after watching for a while, interrupted us and said, 'Let me show you how to tie those parcels— I once clerked in a store and know the best way to do it.' I have used his way ever since."[21] And in this same era, when University of Alberta women would get together to knit socks for the University men who were overseas, Dr. Tory would join them. He was an excellent knitter, having learned the skill as a young boy when ill and confined to bed. The toughest part of knitting a sock was "turning the heel"—negotiating the twists and turns needed to form the heel. Tory was an expert at it, and less experienced knitters would give him their socks so that he could turn the heel for them.[22]

A Good Sport and a Convivial Host

ONE 1913 EVENING in Athabasca Hall, the students staged a mock faculty meeting, roasting all the campus luminaries with one-liners. For instance, Al Ottewell (BA '12), who was now the 300-lb. director of Extension and travelling all around the province in a Model T, was referred to as "the man spreading all over the province." Of Tory someone quipped, "Ask him what kind of fountain pen I should buy."[23] Perhaps the line hearkened back to the first week of classes in the rented quarters at Duggan School, when one of the new students burst into a sombre faculty meeting, chaired by Tory, to ask the president where he could buy a fountain pen. Clearly, there was no matter too small to capture Tory's attention—from the choice of a fountain pen to the wrapping of a parcel. Tory took the ribbing like a good sport.

On another evening in Athabasca Hall, Professor MacEachran (the provost), Dr. Boyle (future dean of Engineering) and Dr. Killam (a math professor and the resident wit) acted out an irreverent "improv" skit titled "The Professor's Dilemma or Fifi From Paris, a Tragi-Comedy in Three Parts, and Several Interludes." The president and his wife were guests, and Dr. Tory was "the butt of some sharp barbs."[24] The audience no doubt held its breath for a moment, awaiting Tory's reaction. But Tory and his wife "had a good sense of fun," said the provost. "They congratulated the actors." Tory kept the program as a souvenir.

The Torys are remembered fondly as great hosts, and in the early days they could fit all the faculty members and their spouses into the drawing room of their Ring House home, today's Museums and Collection Services. Hector MacLeod (MSC '16 and later a faculty member) says, "The warm friendship and inter-faculty co-operation at the University were due in no small measure to Dr. and Mrs. Tory."[25] Hector's wife, Helen Montgomery, remembers that at the Tory parties there was the inevitable and popular game of Charades, and she recalls "the gusto with which Dr. Tory enacted the first syllable of Madagascar."[26] Pause for a moment and imagine that.

But Tory didn't join in with the first professors on their many outings to the mountains, to fish, hunt, or just camp. One faculty member, perhaps waiting for the moment when Tory might chat casually with his new recruits, remembers a meeting of the small general faculty council when, at the end of the afternoon's decision-making, Tory reached down to a paper bag sitting at his feet. There was a glimmer of hope that perhaps Tory might offer a libation to the tired little group. Actually, he was reaching for a sack of potatoes to take home to Annie.[27]

Focused and Driven

HOW SERIOUS AND FOCUSED could Tory be? Annie Tory recalled one night when she and her husband were to go out for the evening, and Marsh had disappeared upstairs for too long. She went to check. He was in bed, in pyjamas, thinking through a problem, absolutely absorbed. He had utterly forgotten about the social engagement![28] Former President Robert Newton tells how

> Tory identified himself completely with any enterprise he under-took, and by his energy and drive usually dominated it. No one in the university ever thought of questioning his decisions, even if they had private reservations. This applied with almost equal force to the Board of Governors and even to the Provincial Government of the day. Only once, to my knowledge, did the premier of Alberta tell him he could not have his way. That time, Premier Greenfield came to the University to tell him he could not go on with his plans to establish a Faculty of Medicine, as the Province could not afford it. By a remark-able coincidence, Tory had received from the Rockefeller Foundation in that morning's mail a cheque for half a million dollars to help start the Faculty. Tory waved it before the premier, who got up without another word and never raised the question again.[29]

> Dr. Rae Chittick (LLD [Hon] '54), a pioneer nurse educator in Alberta, recalls Tory's dynamic challenge to all his new staff. It was simple: Succeed! "Tory wouldn't brook failure," Chittick says. "He had a vision that wouldn't permit failure."[30]
>
> Albert Ottewell, who observed Tory from the vantage point of a student, and later as an administrator, said, "Dr. Henry Marshall Tory was a fortu-nate choice of the first President. For twenty years his energy and vision gave the needed drive and inspiration to the staff he headed."[31]
>
> Tory *did* relax. He was an avid golfer, and there is a photograph of Tory in the Mayfair Golf and Country Club, sitting on the grass in a group

photo. Tory also curled, most often with his friend Premier Rutherford. And he loved to go to the horse races.

Tory also had a soft side. During the November 11 commemorative services held in Convocation Hall each year following the end of World War I, the names of the U of A students and staff who had perished were read aloud. Tory could never read the complete list without breaking down. One of his regrets as president was that the student population became so large that he wasn't able to know each student personally.

Tory as Architect

TORY'S ONE BLIND SPOT concerned the aesthetics of campus design. Although he was involved in every aspect of the design and construction of the first buildings, he simply couldn't read architectural blueprints, and had an unusual sense of what the campus should look like.[32] President Emeritus Robert Newton remarked,

> The mixed, and in some cases incongruous, architecture of the University must be laid in part at [Tory's] door. That the Arts building, the best one constructed during his regime, is a pleasure to look at, is due more to the influence of certain staff members than to Tory himself. [Indeed], some of Tory's initial ideas in regard to the layout of the Edmonton campus were a source of embarrassment to his collaborators. The land was covered with poplar scrub, admittedly much better than no trees at all, and he wished to save as much as possible of this. He proposed a serpentine road connecting the north half of the campus, the site of the academic buildings, and the south half, where farm buildings were to be erected, using the scrub as a screen between the two. It was not a bad idea at the time, but the farm buildings were destined soon to be moved farther afield, and the straight avenues with new plantings of better trees, to which he finally acceded, proved more practical as well as more ornamental.[33]

As for the design Tory originally chose for the proposed Arts building, it was apparently awful. In 1909, when the newly-hired Professor MacEachran and President Tory took the boat back to Canada from England, MacEachran spent hours trying to persuade Tory of just that fact. "The original design was like Alberta College (today's St. Stephen's College) and many of us wondered how Dr. Tory, who had seen so many beautiful buildings, could have chosen that one. He showed me the plans when we were returning from England. I opposed the plan from the first but it was O.M. Biggar, chairman of the Board of Governors, who forced the change of design. The excavation was adapted to accommodate the present building."[34]

Soon after this criticism, to Tory's credit, he hired a professor of Architecture, Cecil Burgess. Burgess, a shy and gentle man, seems to have found the secret to handling Tory's blind spot. Burgess would walk around campus with Tory, and Tory would ask, "What do you think?" Burgess would tell Tory his ideas. "Several weeks later," Burgess said, laughing at the memory, "Dr. Tory would say, 'I have been thinking,' and then present the ideas as if they were his own."[35]

OUR BEST RECRUITER

TORY WAS WITHOUT A DOUBT the best recruiter the U of A ever had. He persuaded many established faculty to come to the wild west and had a talent for finding young graduates at the top of their class who were ready to take a chance on a new university. Hector MacLeod, an early Engineering professor, says Tory "had the ability to make you feel that you had a part to play in the building of a great University. In so doing, he won the loyalty of his staff."[36] Tory's presidential peer, Robert Newton, remembers, "Dean Rankin (the first dean of Medicine) told us of his own first arrival at the university. Tory was showing him around the campus when they came upon a field of turnips. Tory climbed over the fence, pulled up a turnip, wiped it clean with his handkerchief, and cut off a piece with his pocket-knife, offered it to Rankin to sample, and asked him if it were not the best turnip he had ever tasted!"[37]

Pioneer on a Mission

TORY WAS DRIVEN by one thought, one goal: he wanted education to be available to the youth of Canada. How? Through the establishment of strong and unified state-run provincial universities, and not by a hodge-podge collection of small denominational colleges. Tory's resignation as a Methodist minister over this belief was one mark of his determination.

What drove him? Here is Tory's own explanation: "I have been a pioneer all my life, a pioneer in education. I came from a little section of Nova Scotia settled by revolutionary war veterans. The early pioneers were, by the very nature of their circumstance, cut off for a long time from the outside world. I was compelled to secure my education by strenuous personal effort. The early struggles left upon my mind the deep desire to see the facilities for higher education made available more broadly to the youth of Canada."[38]

In his twenty years as president, Tory was persistent in having a liberal arts basis for the U of A; persistent in controlling affiliation with denominational colleges; and persistent in making the University the locus for training and examination in all the professions. The University of Alberta would be the one central post-secondary institution in the province. This was his vision from the beginning, and he achieved it.

Tory's Official Portrait

BY THE TIME Tory retired as president of the University in 1928 to head the National Research Council, he had turned an institution that existed only on paper into one of the finest universities in Canada. Tory's official portrait was painted by the famous Group of Seven artist Frederick Varley. Varley had the knack for capturing on canvas a person's spirit, and is regarded as Canada's greatest portrait artist. Varley's portrait of Tory shows him in his brilliant red academic robes, hands clasped in front of him, with an intent, serious look on his face. But to all who saw the original, Varley had made Tory's hands far too big. Varley gave in to the criticism, and repainted the hands so that they were in "nearer proportion" to reality.

The revised portrait is still on display in the restored Senate chamber in the Arts Building and Tory's hands still clearly dominate the canvas. Former Provost MacEachran says that Varley *deliberately* left Tory's hands that way because of his conviction that "the strong hands expressed the great strength of Dr. Tory."[39] There is no doubt that Tory was a strong leader. He was in control, moment by moment, of both the big picture and the small details. The former Methodist minister had a clear vision. He was on a mission to spread the gospel of education across Canada, and he had "so little time, so little time." He defined the University of Alberta.

Luther Herbert Alexander.
(UAA 69–90–3)

William Muir Edwards—
the engineer with a deadly
drop-kick. (UAA 69–90–63)

PIONEERING PROFESSORS—THE "FIRST FOUR"

THEY CAME FROM the culture and comfort of Leipzig and Harvard, Queen's and Columbia. They left the world of established academe, with posh faculty clubs and entrenched traditions, for a university with no campus and no students. Their salaries were low, and they arrived in a raw city with a few wooden boardwalks and a lot of mud, where decent housing was virtually non-existent. They were pioneers in education, all with excellent reputations. Why did they come *here*? Perhaps Tory himself put it best in 1905: "This country fascinates me. There is wine in the air; a feeling of excitement; of expectancy. It is difficult to explain. Perhaps it is just that everything is new; the people young, and the conviction grows that great things are bound to happen in this rich new country."[40] No doubt Tory communicated that buoyancy when he recruited "The First Four": Professors Luther Herbert Alexander, William Muir Edwards, William Hardy Alexander, and Edmund Kemper Broadus.

Luther Herbert Alexander

HE WAS THE MODERN LANGUAGES EXPERT with the "New Yorker wife," a shadowy figure with a flair for music who left after one year because his wife "didn't enjoy the pioneering."[41] Luther Herbert Alexander, "L.H." for short, returned to Columbia University in 1909 to finish his PhD. But before he left, he organized a glee club so that there would be vocal music at the first Convocation. It was a modest beginning that gave rise to a world-class choral tradition in music. The students all liked L.H., and you can sense their regret that he had to leave.[42]

William Muir Edwards[43]

HE WAS THE HOMETOWN BOY with a famous mother, Henrietta Muir Edwards, and he died too young.[44] His name was Muir Edwards. He graduated at the head of his class at McGill. The next year, he graduated from the department of Civil Engineering, topping off that capstone year by winning the British Association Medal for Applied Science. Tory recruited Muir to teach Mathematics and Civil Engineering. He later headed the University's first Engineering department and as a young engineer in Edmonton Muir was "credited with eliminating the cause of a serious typhoid epidemic...by redesigning the water intake."[45]

Muir Edwards held the lofty title of "professor," but back in 1908, he wasn't much older than his students. And he was a fine athlete. Muir had played rugby at McGill and won the McGill Athletic Association silver medal, breaking the record for the two-mile race. He was a natural to teach U of A students to play rugby on the open fields in Strathcona near the CPR station off Whyte Avenue. He did this regularly, as soon as classes were out.

Clearly, students liked this man, and they asked him to be honorary president of their new Athletic Association. The affection was mutual. A few years later, during World War I, when so many students were in the trenches and homesick for news from Edmonton, Muir poured himself into a weekly publication that was sent overseas to the troops.

Muir Edwards was too soon dead. In 1918, the worldwide flu epidemic hit Edmonton hard. Thousands in the city died. Classes at the U of A were cancelled. Pembina Hall was converted into an emergency hospital and morgue. Graduate Agnes Wilson was there, and she describes Muir's role in one succinct sentence: "The nursing shortage was acute and Professor Edwards offered his services."[46]

Muir Edwards died in Pembina Hall on his 39th birthday, having nursed gravely ill students for weeks: "He tenderly bore the sick in and reverently carried the dead out, and by ready acceptance of the meanest tasks inspired in others a true sense of service."[47] When Muir died, the "Great War," World War I, had just ended. Muir left his wife Evelyn, three young children, and a campus to mourn him.[48] In the Arts Building today, you will find a plaque dedicated to Professor Edwards, recounting his service during the influenza epidemic.

It is the only plaque on campus dedicated to an individual professor from the entire community.

The Two Who Stayed—
William Hardy Alexander and Edmund Kemper Broadus

ONE WAS COUNSELLOR, guide and friend. He wrote the University Grace, selected as our motto *Quaecumque Vera,* and his wife Marion chose evergreen and gold as the University colours. He could punt a mean football and helped U of A students over the years with just about every extracurricular activity. His name was William Hardy Alexander. To his friends he

W.H. Alexander. (UAA 69–90–3)

was "Will," and the students nicknamed him "Doc Alik."[49] Will Alexander became head of Classics and then dean of Arts and Science in 1936. In 2001, the University named a teaching award in his honour.

The other was reserved and scholarly. He loved to read aloud to his classes, and students adored it when he did. He was stern, cool, and demanding, but he was not without panache. As soon as he could afford it, this professor bought a very cool car, which he named "Hotspur," after the Shakespearian character. His name was Edmund Kemper Broadus.

Broadus and Alexander were both at the University for three decades. Broadus died in 1936, and Alexander left for the University of California at Berkeley in 1938. Both came to the U of A in 1908 because they were challenged by the "independence of the new university."[50] They both set high academic standards, shaped University of Alberta traditions, and helped define who we are. Alumni from the 1920s and 1930s still look back on classes taught by Broadus and Alexander with fondness, gratitude, and instant declarations that their classes were, to quote one student, "simply inspiring!!"

William Hardy Alexander—"Doc Alik"

STUDENTS DEDICATED the first-ever yearbook to him, calling him their counsellor and friend. He was popular. Students loved his "quick wit and sparkling humour."[51] But he brooked no nonsense in the classroom and students knew it. He wasn't quick to praise, but when he did, students knew they had truly earned the accolade.[52]

Will Alexander shepherded every arts student though Horace's odes and Homer's *Iliad*—no translated versions were allowed. He taught Latin and Greek, and every student seeking a BA degree was required to take at least one of these ancient languages.

"Doc Alik" was a taskmaster in class, but after class he was a guide and mentor. He and Muir Edwards taught students to play rugby, and he encouraged students to get involved in theatre—which they did, forming a Literary Society in 1908. He wrote for the first *Gateway* in 1910 and for the first yearbooks, until both new publications found their feet. With his relaxed manner and quick smile, students took to him immediately. When Ethel Anderson had a group photo taken after her graduation in 1912, there was only one professor in it: Doc Alik.

Will Alexander came to the U of A from the University of Western Ontario. When he and his wife Marion ventured out to Canada's wild west, the first challenge was finding a house. There was little suitable housing in Strathcona in 1908, which was infamous for its rutted, muddy roads. The first streetcar had started up in that year, but service was slow. You walked everywhere, or you had one of those new-fangled inventions that had had just made their appearance in Alberta two years before—a car.

Frozen Pipes and Arctic Rooms[53]

THE ALEXANDERS rented the top floor of a house on 84 avenue and 104 street until they could "move onto campus,"[54] to Athabasca or Assiniboia Hall, or one of the Ring Houses. Their rented accommodation turned out to be frigid and draughty, and in the winter it was a "never-ending battle with frozen pipes" in rooms so cold they couldn't live in them for six months of the year.[55] The Torys had given up on Strathcona and lived over the river in Edmonton. The Alexanders dealt with the housing problem by joining forces with their new friends, the Broaduses, to buy property "far out in the country" on land that had been homesteaded only 30 years before, when the nearest railroad was still 800 miles away in Winnipeg.

The two professors researched how to build cozy, winter-proofed homes, swearing that "some day we should be warm in latitude 54." They used building paper of the "thickest felt hair" to clad the wooden frames in "a perennial coat of fur." The Broadus house was designed so that every room abutted a central chimney. Forty below, wrote our first English professor afterwards, was "not a terrible thing. It spells beauty, a beauty austere and magnificent." Despite the beautiful austerity of winter, there was, at last, warm housing. The two little brown houses they built were modest, but the view was magnificent. Their homes commanded an unimpeded view to the west, looking out over the North Saskatchewan River for miles. Today, you can drive by these two homes and have no sense whatsoever of their isolation from civilization nine decades ago. In 1910, it was wilderness; today, their homes on Saskatchewan Drive, near the intersection with Keillor Road, sit on prime real estate.

Edmund Kemper Broadus

Edmund Kemper Broadus.

(EA EB 26–63)

BROADUS WAS A HARVARD MAN who was raised in Virginia. Towards the end of his PhD studies in Boston, he was diagnosed with a tubercular gland in his neck, put in a sanatorium, and told he had to live in the West. President Tory was in the East recruiting professors for his new university, and the match was made.

One of Dr. Broadus's former students, and later a close friend, comments wryly that "Edmonton, to the Boston of that time, was almost as remote as the Yukon, and Broadus must indeed have been a dying man, in the eyes of his Cambridge friends, if the demands of his health could drive him to take up a teaching post in a university sprung out of the great plains where but a few years before buffaloes and Indians had roamed, and the Mountie had dispensed law and made order prevail."[56]

But Broadus could also have gone to Switzerland to teach. He did not. Tory was known for his persuasive ways and, judging from Dr. Broadus's later description of his recruitment meeting with Tory, it must have been quite a sales pitch. Broadus recalls that "on a day in June 1908, the president of a university not yet in being, in a province which I had never heard of, in a country which I had never visited, came to Harvard and offered me the professorship of English. The offer sounded like midsummer madness." But Broadus accepted it and, with his wife Eleanor, a Radcliffe graduate, boarded the train.[57]

English 2

THERE WAS NO AVOIDING BROADUS. Passing English 2 was a requirement, and he was its only teacher.[58] He, too, accepted no nonsense. Students were expected to be prepared, seated on time, and fully engaged in their studies. If they weren't, Broadus called them to task in no uncertain terms. Broadus's colleague, Rob Gordon, would test students on their week's lectures on Saturday mornings. On one occasion, Gordon recalls, "[Broadus] met me in the hall and asked if I would mind if he attended as an auditor. The class failed miserably that morning in answering any questions. So Dr. Broadus came down to the front and faced the class. Have you ever experienced Dr. Broadus's sarcasm? He was a master of it."[59]

Fraser Macdonald (BA '34, BED '35) describes Broadus's manner as severe and precise;[60] his fishing partner and colleague, Cecil Burgess, has said Broadus was "a master of irony. He could spit it out. I was glad I was his friend."[61] But Dr. Broadus nonetheless remains a legendary teacher in the memories of alumni—even though he had "a bite to the tongue."[62] Don Cameron (BSC Ag '29) described Broadus as "esteemed and feared."[63] Ethel Anderson went back to school after her graduation in 1912 just to take extra courses from him. She remembers fondly how Dr. Broadus would come in on snowy mornings, "a muffler wound over his cap and around his head and neck and announce with a smile, 'Well, the old man is here!'"[64]

Horatio Lovat Dickson (BA '27), known to his friends as "Rache," taught as a lecturer under Broadus after graduation. Rache remembers English 2 as "a hazardous course, designed wickedly by Broadus to trap the worthy into specialization in English.... He was like a Regimental Sergeant-Major. The square where we drilled was the whole field of literature."[65]

Forty years after Esther Miller (BA '27) took Broadus' classes, she remembered him vividly.[66] English 2 was a huge class for its days—the only Arts class that in the 1920s had to be scheduled in the amphitheatre of the Medical Building (today's Dentistry/Pharmacy Centre). "Not to have had the privilege of taking English 2 from Dr. E.K. Broadus is like omitting the main course from your dinner.... I would sit transfixed as his long finger moved over the page of his class register, pause, then, 'Miss Miller, please rescue Cordelia from the tower for us.'" This random selection of a student was Broadus's way of making sure all the required reading had been done.

"Ah! The delicious terror of it all!" says Esther. She remembers when former Registrar Alex Cairns, also in English 2, was selected during one of Broadus' roll calls, "with the stentorious voice saying, 'Alexander Duncan Cairns, EMERGE'." Let's hope Alex Cairns did his homework that day.[67]

Agnes Wilson and Rache Dickson Fail

THE UNIVERSITY "exacted scholarship" from the beginning and English Department colleague Rob Gordon remembers that Dr. Broadus "gave no quarter. He would say, 'don't be afraid of plucking people.'"[68] He was, undoubtedly, tough. But Esther Miller recalls that when she was working in the Registrar's office after graduation, Broadus came in to submit supplemental examination results: "He stood at the counter and said to himself, 'Oh, come on Broadus, be a sport—raise him from a 48 to a 50,' and before our astonished eyes, he did." The two-point raise meant the anonymous student passed the course.[69]

Broadus did fail students, and two of them have left accounts of it. Both say they were inspired, not bowed, by their failure. Agnes Wilson told Ruth Bowen, "I failed English in my second year [1909] and Dr. Broadus failed me again in the supplemental. The blow was that English was my subject. I had done well in my first year. So I went to Dr. Broadus and was informed, icily, that he accepted no odds and ends of information in the course in answer to university examination questions. It was a salutary lesson. I applied myself from then on and I earned my good marks."[70]

Rache Dickson, who went on to publish the best-selling Grey Owl books in the 1930s, was also one of Broadus's students. Rache achieved fame as editor (at age 26) of the *Fortnightly Review* and then of the *Review of Reviews.* But as a second-year student at the U of A, Rache received a failing grade on his first essay and went to Dr. Broadus to protest. "He wasted little time with me over preliminaries," Rache later wrote. "Who in God's name told you that you can write?...Get out of my sight, man, until you can hold your head up and look me in the eye, and say 'I have really tried. Goodbye.'"[71]

Rache learned the error of his ways and wrote a best-selling autobiography in the late 1950s. In it he writes, "When I look back over the years, the Professor, as much as my father, made me who I am."[72]

There is no question about the impact of these early English classes at the U of A. Proper grammar was drilled into students, and students left knowing how to parse a sentence, knowing the classics, and knowing how to think. A story is told about Bertha Laurence (BA '21, MA '37). Bertha fell and broke her hip when she was well into her 90s. She was a prisoner in her apartment until help came in the form of a worried friend, John. John knocked hard on the door, calling out, "Bertha!! It's me!!! John!" Bertha, from her prone position on the floor, instantly corrected his grammar: "No, John, it is *I*."[73]

Broadus once received some anonymous notes from students praising his teaching. He replied in the February 18, 1936 edition of *The Gateway*:

Any teacher to whom teaching is an art rather than a job cares very deeply for the appreciation of his students. What he lives for is to persuade his students to like what he likes, because (right or wrong) it is worth liking. But day after day he faces a class, and gives the best that is in him, and goes back to his office, and asks himself: 'Did they get it?'—and doesn't know.[74]

Business student Allan McTavish (BCOMM '36) sums it up. In the 1930s, Alan says, students who didn't have Broadus for English would drop in to his class, check for an empty seat, and stay for the hour. They came to listen to a lecturer who "taught you about things you had never thought about."[75]

UNIVERSITY OF ALBERTA TRADITIONS

The Glee Club and the College Yell

IN 1908 the U of A was brand new, with no established traditions, and the first big public event, Convocation, was about to take place. It was expected to be a political showcase attended by over 1,000 educators, students, and politicians from across the province.

L.H. Alexander organized a Glee Club, while Will Alexander and Edmund Broadus wrote a song for the first Convocation. Dr. Broadus's wife Eleanor, an accomplished musician, likely wrote the music. In later years when the Glee Club faltered, she was instrumental in getting it reorganized.

The students were concerned that there be a "yell." The students, Al Ottewell says, "had heard that every self-respecting university had a yell to be used in and out of season. So a sort of editorial group set to work. By the date of the first convocation, held in the now long defunct IOOF Hall, a few days after classes began, the present Alberta yell was ready. I am afraid, to the annoyance of the more staid part of the audience, it was given at frequent intervals during the program with much gusto and as much volume as the small group could produce. What was lacking in numbers was made up in enthusiasm and lung power."[76]

The Glee Club. (UAA 86-41-15)

THE UNIVERSITY CREST

THE DEBUT of the U of A Crest, or Seal, was on the first Calendar, printed in 1908, and the same crest was used for the inaugural 1908 Convocation. The Crest was drawn by an undergraduate student, James ("Jimmy") Adam (BA '12, MA '15). It was a shield within which was a simple depiction of mountains and wheat fields. Based on the provincial Coat of Arms, it included as one element the cross of St. George.

In November 1909, the faculty of the University recommended to the Senate that the provincial Coat of Arms be adopted as the university emblem, with three additions—an image of an opened book atop the shield and superimposed on the St. George's cross; the provincial motto *Lux et Lex* (Light and Law); and the University's name. In January 1911, the new University Motto, *Quaecumque Vera* (Whatsoever Things are True), chosen by Professor William Hardy Alexander, replaced *Lux et Lex*. The Crest (or emblem) is one part of the University's formal Coat of Arms, and it was redesigned in 1950 by Professor Henry Glyde, who was a contemporary of the Group of Seven and first chair of Fine Arts.

But the Crest and Coat of Arms had never been heraldically approved. Eighty-six years after its original design, Chancellor Sandy Mactaggart gave the University a proper Coat of Arms. Designed by Joan Boumeester, a BFA graduate from the U of A, the formal Coat of Arms was presented to the University by His Excellency the Right Honourable Ramon Hnatyshyn, Governor General of Canada, at Convocation on June 13, 1994. The St. George's cross was eliminated, and the open book that had appeared atop the shield was now placed within the shield itself. The Coat of Arms included a golden bear, the U of A's mascot, and a pronghorn sheep, an element taken from the provincial Coat of Arms. Both are standing on a bed of wild roses, the province's official flower. Perched atop the Coat of Arms is a Great Horned Owl, representing wisdom.[77]

Marion Kirby Alexander.

(Private Collection)

Evergreen and Gold

IT WAS Marion Kirby Alexander, Doc Alik's wife, who chose evergreen and gold as the University's colours in 1908. Marion and Will Alexander had acres of open field around their house on Saskatchewan Drive, and they often walked along the riverbank in front of their home, or golfed their way over to River Lot 5, where the campus would soon be. "One day," Will Alexander told the Edmonton Historical Society in 1959,

> Marion and I, in our first Alberta October, were wandering along the south bank of the Saskatchewan. Suddenly, she exclaimed, "There it is! I've got it!"
>
> "Got what," said I, having no lead to suppose what she had in mind.
>
> "The colours," she said. "I was discussing only yesterday with some of the girls what should be the Alberta colours. Don't you see them? Why, the whole view cries out: Green and Gold!"[78]

Marion went to the best department store in town, Johnstone Walker's, and selected two ribbons—one green and the other gold, representing the shimmering gold of the autumn leaves against the deep green of the spruces and pines. And so the U of A colours were chosen. In the formal university records, however, it was the Committee on College Colours that recommended green and gold to the Senate, which approved the colours on October 13, 1908, with the following explanation:

> The choice of this beautiful and at the same time infrequent combination was based on an appropriate symbolism—the green representing the wide stretches of verdant prairie—and flanked by the deep Spruce forests of the Province—while the gold prefigures the golden harvest fields that are Alberta's boast. Referring back to the old accepted Symbolism of Colours, the choice was still found to have been made with discerning art; for green there is the symbol of hope, of joyous optimism, and gold of the shining light of knowledge. Both are certainly particularly applicable to the new University.[79]

Green and gold banners decorated the IOOF hall for the first Convocation in 1908, and Marion Alexander's choice of colours has defined the U of A ever since. Marion's grandson, Will, now lives in the family home on Saskatchewan Drive, enjoying that unique view where the river takes a deep bend. He keeps the two green and gold ribbons from his grandmother in a special box in the attic.[80]

FIRST CONVOCATION AND SENATE [81]

THE FIRST CONVOCATION is probably not what you think. No students graduated. But without this unique Convocation in 1908, there would be no U of A. The 1906 *University Act* set up a Senate comprised of the president, premier, and other *ex officio* members, and chaired by a chancellor, as the single governing body of the new university. In addition, the Senate would have ten members appointed by the government—and five other members elected by "Convocation." That was the interesting part. The University of Alberta could not function until the Senate was established, and Senate could not be established until "Convocation" was brought into being.

What did "Convocation" mean? Clearly, the reference was not to the usual ceremony we know today. It was simple. The University didn't have any graduates of its own yet, and so it created some. The University called them, collectively, "Convocation." A "call" was published in newspapers, inviting anyone who had a degree from a British or Canadian university to pay $2 and register as part of Convocation. Three hundred and sixty-four people responded. This group, or "Convocation," was responsible for electing the chancellor and for electing five members to serve on the Senate. Not all 364 attended, but Convocation met in Edmonton in March 1908.

The Senate decided that all members of Convocation would be given *ad eundem* University of Alberta degrees. The Senate simply bestowed the U of A name on degrees already held by the members of Convocation. But it was more than that, much more. The special degrees honoured these people and bonded them to the new university. This group would be our first graduates.

Tory invited them all back to Strathcona to receive their degrees. "Convocation," the group of 364, was about to "convocate." Tory planned the event as a big party—a crucial political party. The CPR arranged for special trains to bring people in from across the entire province. Tory had invited all high school students and their principals, and asked school board members to come as well. It was an important step in securing support for the new University. The school board gave an unprecedented half-day holiday for its members to attend. With that one political move, Tory set up the University of Alberta as "the place to go once you finished high school."[82]

The October event was just the kind of success Tory envisioned. It was well attended by the public, and every political luminary gave a speech. Green and gold banners decorated the walls and the new Crest appeared on the program. Students shouted out the college yell and sang the University Song. They elected a chancellor and the five Senate members, and then dispersed across the province to their homes.

The University now had its governing body and legislative branch in place—the Senate. As Tory told them at their first meeting, "You are the founders of an institution from which the whole province will benefit."[83]

First Chancellor—Charles Stuart

THE FIRST CHANCELLOR was Charles Stuart, a judge from Calgary. As the first governing body, the Senate was responsible for both financial and academic matters—a combination of today's Board of Governors

Charles Stuart, the first Chancellor of the University. The portrait was painted in 1924 by F.H. Varley.

(UAA 69–18–73)

and General Faculties Council (GFC). In 1910, a Board of Governors was created to deal with finance and management issues, leaving academic matters to the Senate. It was the beginning of bicameral governance.

But back in 1908, the Senate did it all, and so Chancellor Stuart was, in effect, the first Board Chair, the first Senate Chair, and the first GFC Chair. Chancellor Stuart presided over some extraordinarily long and difficult meetings. One of the first touchy issues concerned whether or not President Tory should hire only local professors. When the dust settled, the clear answer was "no." Hire the best, no matter what their origin. Tory was left in charge. The other momentous question considered by the Senate was this: what should the first Faculty be?

The Senators came from a range of professions and had degrees from at least six well-known universities. Everyone had an opinion. To compound the matter, there was public pressure that the founding Faculty be Agriculture. President Tory, a scientist, led the debate, and when discussion finally ended, the sole Faculty for the new University was Arts and Science.[84]

"Arts and Science" was seen as the foundation for all other disciplines. The Calendar called it the "First Faculty." Sheltered within the Faculty of Arts and Science was Applied Science, which would grow to be the Faculty of Engineering. Tory's intention was to proceed as quickly as possible to draw all other professional training under the umbrella of the university so that there would be a single, central, integrated university in Alberta. By 1928, our faculties, schools, and departments included Arts, Sciences, several branches of Engineering, Extension, Medicine, Agriculture, Law, Nursing, Pharmacy, Dentistry, Physical Education, Accounting, Household Economics, Architecture, and Veterinary Medicine. We also had a Department of Industrial Research (forerunner of the Alberta Research Council) and a University Hospital Board. Education would come under the University's purview in the 1940s. And there was one other Faculty being born back in 1908. Way off in Pincher Creek, the forerunner of our current Faculté Saint-Jean was established as a bilingual college with the primary aim of preparing "priests to join the Order of the Oblates of Mary Immaculate."[85] In 1910, that bilingual college moved to the site presently occupied by Faculté Saint-Jean. In that same year, Augustana Faculty began life in Camrose.

Frederick Varley also painted Chancellor Stuart's portrait, and it hangs in the restored Senate Chamber in the Arts building, across from Tory's portrait. We also have formal records of the many meetings Stuart chaired during his 18-year tenure. But what was he like as a person?

Professor Rob Gordon recounts a defining story about the first chancellor. The setting is the 1916 Convocation, and most of the graduates would leave the following day for the battlefields of Europe:

The boys in the Company pretty well filled Convocation Hall in the spring of 1916....They had come partly to see their Captain, H.J.

MacLeod (of the Physics Department) go up for his MSc. One speaker, addressing the troops, said he hoped they would kill a lot of Huns and would all come back safe. I mention this only as a contrast for what followed. The Chancellor, Judge Stuart, stood up. He looked in silence at the khaki rows with his grave, kindly face, which you can see in Varley's portrait of him in the Senate Chamber. He was in no hurry to speak. At last he said: "I wish you God speed." And sat down.[86]

President Tory Sets the Agenda

TORY SPOKE AT LENGTH about the role of the new university at the October 1908 Convocation:

> The modern state university has sprung from a demand on the part of the people themselves for intellectual recognition, a recognition which only a century ago was denied them. The result is that such institutions must be conducted in such a way as to relate them as closely as possible to the life of the people. The people demand that knowledge shall not be the concern of scholars alone. The uplifting of the whole people shall be its final goal.[87]

By then, Tory had achieved gargantuan goals. In less than ten months, all the institutional machinery was humming along, and he had consolidated public support for the U of A. But that's not all Tory was doing in those first ten months. He was engaged in another enterprise. The first classes were already in session.

That's the next story.

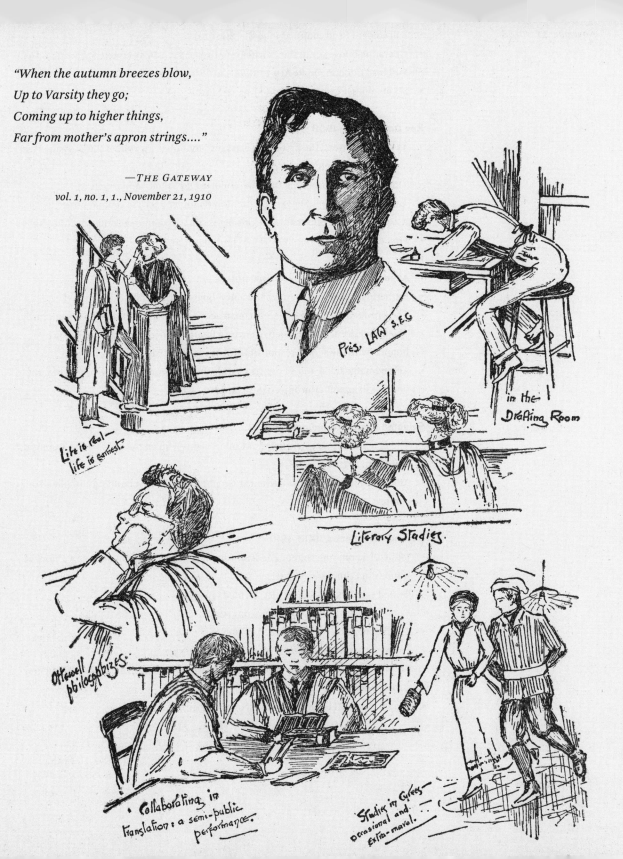

*"When the autumn breezes blow,
Up to Varsity they go;
Coming up to higher things,
Far from mother's apron strings...."*

—THE GATEWAY

vol. 1, no. 1, 1., November 21, 1910

Life is real—
life is earnest.

Pres. LAW S.E.G.

in the
Drafting Room

Literary Studies.

Ottewell
philosophizes.

Collaborating in
Translation: a semi-public
performance.

Studies in Curves—
occasional and
extra-mural.

Timeline

Overleaf: The Gateway,
November 21, 1910.

Enrolment and Finance, 1908–1910

- Fall student head count: 45 (1908); 129 (1910)
- Operating budget from the Province of Alberta: $27,489.29 (1908); $24,082.43 (1910)
- Full-load undergraduate Arts tuition: $20.00 (1908); $20.00 (1910)
- SU membership fee: none (1908); $2.00 (1910)

Key Dates, 1908–1909

- 37 students attend the first day of class on September 23, 1908 at the Duggan Street school (now Queen Alexandra)
- The U of A moves from the Duggan school to Old Scona (January, 1909)
- The Senate institutes May 9 as Charter Day (Founders' Day) to commemorate Royal Assent to the first *University Act*—this day is still part of the academic schedule (1909)
- First of two sod-turnings for the Arts Building (1909)

1910

- Augustana Faculty begins life in Camrose
- Rutherford resigns as premier and a new Board of Governors is appointed
- The University's grant is delayed; construction of Athabasca Hall stops temporarily
- The *University Act* is amended to create a Board of Governors, responsible for finance, with the Senate responsible for academic affairs
- Amendments to the *University Act* provide that the provincial government, not the board, will appoint the university president

Selected Campus Buildings, 1910

- The first building is constructed at Collège Saint-Jean on the site of today's Campus Saint-Jean (1910)
- Alberta College South, the current St. Stephen's, is the first building completed on campus (1910)

Beyond the Campus, 1908–1910

- Jessie Dickson, superintendent of Strathcona Cottage Hospital, founds a school of nursing in Edmonton (1909)
- United Farmers of Alberta (UFA) formed (1909)
- Toronto hosts the first-ever Grey Cup (1909)
- The first newsreels are produced (1909)
- Permanent waves for women's hair first appear (1909)
- Edmonton's second bridge, the 102 Avenue Bridge, opens as a trolley crossing over Groat ravine (1910)
- King Edward VII is succeeded by George V (1910)

Duggan Street School, the University of Alberta's original home. (UAA 69-12-238)

THE FIRST DAY OF CLASS[2]

Registration at the Duggan Street School

FOR UNIVERSITY OF ALBERTA STUDENTS, it all started on September 23, 1908, when the university opened its doors for registration and classes in the four rented rooms on the top floor of Duggan Street School. Ready and waiting to greet the new students when they arrived were President Henry Marshall Tory, Tory's stenographer, Miss Jennie Carmichael, and the professors Tory had hand-picked: W.H. Alexander, E.K. Broadus, W.M. Edwards, and L.H. Alexander.

The new school had all the modern conveniences of the day, including electric lights and indoor plumbing. Conveniences aside, the quarters were a bit cramped, but no one seemed to mind—least of all President Tory, who had spent ten intense months getting ready for the opening day. Part of his preparation included a trip to the east to buy the necessary books and scientific equipment. In one of the four rented rooms, a 10-volume set of Edgar Allan Poe's works and a collection of Western Canadiana donated by Premier Rutherford formed the cornerstone of the library holdings.[3] A second room had been transformed into a laboratory. The remaining rooms functioned as a classroom and Dr. Tory's office.

Libby Lloyd's registration card.
(UAA 75-68-001)

1910-1911

The University of Alberta

REGISTRATION

M̲iss Mary Elizabeth Lloyd HAS
REGISTERED AS AN UNDERGRADUATE OF THE
Third YEAR IN Arts

VERace

[OVER]   *Registrar*

Just how cramped *were* the quarters? In 1998, when our 90th anniversary celebration was held at the Queen Alexandra School (which is what the Duggan School is now called), Dr. Tory's office had been transformed into a janitor's closet.

President Tory had already met most of the 45 men and women who were expected to register—after all, he had personally recruited most of them on his travels throughout the province. To boost enrolment, he had arranged with the principal of the Methodist-run Alberta College to have 10 ministerial students transfer to the University. Some of the students had to travel along Alberta's unpaved, rutted roads by horse-drawn wagon or buggy, and only 37 of the anticipated 45 students arrived on the appointed day. Tory delayed some of the classes for a few days.

President Tory, who was also the registrar, formally enrolled the students who were able to arrive on time. Each student was given a "registration card" the size of a business card with their name, their year and the Registrar's signature on it—the first ID card. Students paid their fees, including a $5 "caution money" deposit in case any damage was done to books, furniture, or lab equipment. Then Tory and the four faculty members organized the first timetable, placing the fledgling students into their classes.

From the start, the emphasis was on providing a well-rounded education. One of the early professors, Ernest Sheldon, illustrated the point in a talk he held at Alberta College during his first month on campus in

1910. Sheldon, an engaging and poular teacher, cautioned students about becoming one-track and losing an appreciation of "the whole." As more and more University courses were being offered, he said, there was a "tendency on the part of each Faculty to hold apart from the others. The Law student should meet the Theology student; the Medical student should meet the Arts student, and in so doing, students would not only be exposed to book learning, but would learn about mankind."

The 1908 Dress Code

AT THEIR FIRST TWO MEETINGS, the Senate had set tuition, established a scholarship fund, debated hiring policy, and established Arts and Science as the founding Faculty. They also decided on an academic dress code.

Ethel Anderson. (UAA 69–12–28)

Their directive was simple. Everybody—students and professors alike—had to wear black convocation robes that could be purchased from the Library (which doubled as the bookstore) on the first day of class. Later, when students graduated, they passed their robes down to freshmen. One student's gown was so well-used that by the time of his graduation, only the yoke was left...and he proudly wore it to Convocation.

The matte-black gown announced to one and all that you were a U of A student. For the elementary students at Duggan School in 1908, it must have been a dramatic sight to see the small band of professors and students ascend the stairs with black, knee-length Convocation gowns flowing behind them.[4]

Ethel Anderson Remembers the First Classes

ETHEL ANDERSON was a first-year student in 1908, a "student counsellor," and the first woman in the Athletic Association. In 1970, when she was 79 years old, Ethel recalled her first days at university:

> For staff and students alike there was a challenge about association with the University of Alberta. Also, there was a challenge to each other. The staff met great open spaces educationally in a brand new land where students were either straight from high school or had been Methodist ministers and missionaries for a number of years—the "Theologs." Some of us were pretty young and silly, but years later Dr. Alexander told me how astonished he was to realize some of his

students were as old as, or older, than he. But we students knew it was a privilege to be taking lectures from these great scholars. We were in awe of them, especially Dr. Alexander and Dr. Broadus. True, we sat in desks, just like in school, but there was no similarity to high school in our lectures.

The great confrontation followed registration, September 23, 1908. The students donned their new black gowns and climbed three flights to four classrooms at the top of Duggan Street School. There, I took French from Professor L.H. Alexander recently of Columbia; Classics from W.H. Alexander who had come from the University of California; English from Dr. Broadus of Harvard; and Mathematics from Professor Muir Edwards of McGill.

Dr. Tory, a physicist and mathematician, pitched in to lecture in History. It was not his field, but there were a number of local teachers who were beginning university studies in 1908, and History was part of their program. So Tory scheduled the first evening course in order to accommodate those teachers, and at 5 P.M. on the appointed days, the whirlwind administrator taught history. And Tory's lectures? There are no recollections of his science lectures, but Agnes Wilson says Tory raced through the history lectures in such a rapid-fire fashion that she could barely keep up.[5]

The First "Orientation"

IN 1908, there were no senior students to welcome the 45 freshmen or show them the ropes. Members of the Class of 1912 were on their own, with a president and four professors as guides. Someone organized a masquerade party to help break the ice and that was the extent of the orientation.[6]

By 1909, when the Class of 1912 were seasoned sophomores, they hosted a reception to welcome the freshmen. Each freshman received an invitation to a reception in the Assembly Hall of Old Scona on November 4, at 8 P.M. The invitations had a green and gold stripe across the top left corner, and at the bottom of the invitation it said, "Please represent the title of a well-known book." This sophomore party soon became an established event. Gradually, it evolved into an initiation, then Freshman Introduction Week, and then First Year Orientation.

THE FIRST STUDENTS AND THE FIRST STUDENT ORGANIZATIONS

Albert Ottewell—The Farmer who Sneezed Greek[7]

AT 6 FEET 3 INCHES, Albert Edward Ottewell (BA '12, MA '15) was a giant of a man. He had worked as a farmer, lumberjack, and miner. His nickname was "Tiny."[8]

Albert Ottewell came to Alberta with his family as a young boy, taking the hard overland route from Ontario and settling in Clover Bar. He ended his education at Grade 8 and was well into his twenties when he decided to be a Methodist minister and go back to school. In 1908, when Al registered at the U of A, he was 26 years old. By the time he graduated with his BA, his classmates joked that "learning seemed to ooze from every pore—he coughs in Latin, whistles French and sneezes Greek." A star athlete, tops in his class in Greek and Classics, "Tiny" was the first editor of *The Gateway.* Albert later served as the first Extension Director before becoming Registrar in 1928. In 1940, in an article written for *The Gateway,* he looked back to 1908:

> The student body consisted of about forty-five students, seven of whom were women. We were quite an assorted lot. Three entered with advanced credits covering the work of the first year. These were Mrs. E.T. Mitchell, neé Decima Robinson, A.J. Law and R.H. Dobson. It is to their credit that all of them survived the academic seasons to graduate on time in 1911 and to receive the first earned bachelors' degrees.... The remainder of the class had for the most part matriculation deficiencies of one sort or another. A number were of mature age and had been denied educational advantages. But almost without exception they were in deadly earnest; students of today would probably say ridiculously so.

The youngest ones were the tender age of 16 and had just finished Grade 11, the entrance requirement of the day. Some were in their early twenties, and some, like Al Ottewell, were older than their professors.[9] Some had matriculation deficiencies; others had advanced standing in Physics, Mathematics, or Philosophy. Allowances were made for those who needed

to catch up on subjects like Latin or English, but the new professors set high standards, and from the start, they put their recruits through their paces. Students churned out essays, had a formal test every month, and wrote two sets of final exams in a year.[10] There was the odd failure in a course, but to a person, everyone in the first class was promoted to the next year.

A vibrant extracurricular life also began in 1908. Al Ottewell explains that "all student activities were under two divisions, a literary society and an athletic body, with the students' council as a coordinating agency." Each group had six to eight members and either President Tory or one of the professors served as honorary presidents, and mentors. As Agnes Wilson put it, "only two of us had been to another university and we depended on the professors to set the traditions."

Laurence Yeomans Cairns—First President of the Literary Society[11]

CALGARIAN LAURENCE YEOMANS CAIRNS (BA '12, LLB '15, LLD [Hon] '55), who dubbed himself "Laurence Yucalyptus," was the class "humorist and wit, the poet and cartoonist." In the days before television and radio, the piano was a great source of fun, and it was Laurence who could play any popular song by ear, getting everyone to join in. Laurence wrote the class poem for the 1912 graduation ceremony, characterizing all his classmates with pithy one-liners. And it was "L.Y.C." whose poems filled the early edition of *The Gateway*.

Laurence Cairns was 16 years old on his first day of class in 1908. Exactly 50 years later, he was named chancellor of the University. It was only one of many achievements: L.Y. Cairns was a judge, a U of A lecturer in two faculties, and president of the Alberta Law Society, the Edmonton Chamber of Commerce, and the Alumni Association.

Laurence was the first president of the Literary Society, which oversaw the activities of all non-athletic clubs. For decades, it remained the largest student organization at the University of Alberta, overseeing the Glee Club, the Debating Society, Mock Parliament and a series of talks by faculty members.

Cecil Rutherford—First President of the Athletic Association

ANOTHER MEMBER of the first class was Cecil Rutherford, the son of the premier. Cecil had wanted to follow in his father's footsteps and attend McGill, but instead he enrolled at the new university in his home city of Strathcona, where he served as first president of the Athletic Association. Cecil went on to a career as a lawyer.

With Professor Muir Edwards as their honorary president, the Athletic Association organized hockey, basketball, and rugby (in that order), despite the fact that there was neither equipment nor playing fields. They used the town's facilities, remembers Agnes Wilson: "There were two covered skating rinks, one on the south side and one on the north. McKernan Lake to the south of the town [long since drained and now built up with houses] was another spot available."[12]

The "first organized practice" for a U of A athletic game was a rugby practice on Saturday, October 22, 1910. The team had a practice match against the Edmonton Eskimos and then travelled to Calgary for their first game against Western Canada College. They lost 28–13, but rebounded on November 5, winning the first-ever home game soundly, despite the snowy conditions. The women students, who had formed a group of their own—the Wauneita Club—watched all the action. "From the time the

The first Students' Union Executive. Standing, left to right: Albert Ottewell, Ada J. Johnston, S.B. Montgomery, Ethel Anderson, Jim Law. Seated, left to right: Professor Muir Edwards, Cecil Rutherford, President Tory, Premier Rutherford, Kathleen Wilson, Stacey McCall.

(UAA 69-132-1)

fair co-eds were seen on the sidelines," reported *The Gateway*, "the final result was never in doubt. With the frantic cheers of the Wauneita Club to urge them on, the boys in green and gold overwhelmed the bunch from the banana belt by 17–2, tying the score for the series."

F. Stacey McCall—First President of the Students' Council

STACEY MCCALL was one of the ten Theologs who transferred to the new university from Alberta College. Stacey hung around Strathcona for two days before the U of A's doors officially opened, staking out his territory on Duggan Street so his name would be at the top of the matriculation list. He was older than most, a practicing Methodist minister and later president of Alberta College (now St. Stephen's). Stacey was thought of as learned and kind, and at "six feet two without his sox," he was "a sort of living breathing fishing pole." Stacey's classmates nicknamed him "Mac" and elected him as the first Students' Union president twice, making him the first of only three students ever to serve two consecutive terms in that position.[13] Stacey maintained close ties to the U of A his entire life, serving on the Senate and Board of Governors.

Stacey was a dignified college president later in life, but back in 1908, at the first Convocation, with hundreds of Albertans present, it was an effervescent Stacey who led the U of A students in shouting out the college "yell"—sometimes at quite inappropriate points in the staid program.

Jimmy Adam—The Ideal Student[14]

JIMMY ADAM (BA '12, MA '15) personified Ernest Sheldon's ideal student: he had come came from Glasgow and London Universities and "had been a headmaster of a school with an enrolment of 1,400." By all accounts, he was a character: there was always a cigarette dangling from his mouth, and he would swing his cane as he and his constant companion, a "scowling bulldog" he tied to a chair in class, strolled along. He was known for wearing brilliant green socks and "nifty college hats." Jimmy excelled in English, Philosophy, and Drawing, both artistic and scientific. He was a founding member of the Dramatic Society and, later, of the Edmonton Museum of Art. While still an undergraduate, he was hired to teach Drawing in Applied Science.

Jimmy had two Arts degrees and two passions: drawing and drama. Jimmy attended the U of A at a time when applied science—later called engineering—was part of the Faculty of Arts and Science. As a first-year student, Jimmy combined his scientific and artistic talents by designing the University of Alberta's first Crest. The Crest appeared on every official document, from the Calendar to the Convocation program. He followed up by drafting the covers for the *Trail*, predecessor of today's alumni magazine, the *New Trail*.

James Adam was an Engineering professor at the U of A from 1911 until his retirement in 1938. As a teacher, says former Dean George Ford, Jimmy took a classical approach to descriptive geometry: "Like Leonardo da Vinci, who was the last of the great empirical engineers, Jimmy Adam was the last instructor to use the classical graphical method in the solution of engineering problems."

Jimmy Adam, the undergraduate who designed the first University Crest, below Dr. MacEachran and to the left.
(UAA 69-12-065)

"We Are Seven"—The first seven women students, 1908. From left to right: Erna Roedler, Decima Robinson, Ethel Anderson, Agnes Kathleen Wilson, Ada J. Johnston, Winnifred Dorothy (Dot) Hyssop, Mary Elizabeth (Libby) Lloyd. (UAA 70-69-10)

THE FIRST SEVEN WOMEN [15]

IN 1908, women didn't have the vote; they weren't recognized as "persons" under the *British North America Act*; they could not serve on the Canadian Senate; and some universities and programs were open only to men. But the Alberta government's *University Act* of 1906 said that men and women would be able to enter the new university on an equal basis. Nonetheless, when it came to finding jobs after university, Ethel Anderson (BA '12) says that women had no doubt about the "context of their opportunities" in those days.

Seven of the 45 students who registered in 1908 were women. And in an amazingly symmetrical way, say Ethel Anderson and classmate Libby Lloyd, "for the first four years of the university, seven co-eds arrived each year." The original seven women undergraduate students were Agnes Kathleen Wilson (the first woman to register at the University), Ethel Anderson, Ada J. Johnston, Winnifred (Dorothy) Hyssop, Decima Robinson,

Mary Elizabeth Lloyd ("Libby," the class historian), and Erna Roedler. There was also one female graduate student, Jennie Storck Hill, who took special classes.

Agnes Wilson

TWO OF THE WOMEN, Agnes Wilson and Ethel Anderson, left memoirs. Agnes Wilson was a violinist, Vice-President of the first Students' Union, a *Gateway* editor, and an executive member of both the Wauneita Society (the women-only club), and the Literary Society.[16] Her fellow students described her as "full of mirth and merriment" and at the "center of the social life of the University."[17] After receiving her BA in 1912, she went on to teach, served overseas as a volunteer nurse, and then returned to the university as secretary to the meticulous and kindly Dean of Arts and Science, Dr. Kerr. She was also a temporary secretary in President Tory's office. As Mrs. D.J. Teviotdale, Agnes lived near the University all her life, watching it grow from a woodland to a jam-packed, high-rise campus.

Ethel Anderson

ETHEL ANDERSON graduated with a BA in English, taking extra courses from a professor whose classes she loved, Dr. E.K. Broadus. She had a career in teaching at Eastglen, Strathcona, and Westglen schools.

Their memoirs, along with interviews and speeches they gave about early university life, provide a glimpse of student life at the time—from the organizing of the first athletic teams to the hairstyles of the day.

Seven Independent Spinsters and Upsilon Upsilon

ETHEL RECALLS that one of the first things the women did was to organize the SIS, "a deep, dark secret finally revealed to mean Seven Independent Spinsters. When the new term arrived, the first seven plotted dire things for initiation of seven others. They rolled the innocents in a barrel down a short flight of stairs at Strathcona Collegiate Institute." Why the term "spinsters" when they were only 16–19 years old? Back then, if they were married, it was unheard of for a woman—even a woman with a degree—to work. Women tended hearth and home. Only an unmarried woman, a spinster, was independent.

The 1911 Wauneita Society. Decima Robinson (folded hands, centre) was the first woman to graduate from the University of Alberta. Surrounding Decima, l–r, are Sylvia Robertson, Libby Lloyd, Helen Montgomery, Kathleen Lavell, Agnes Wilson, and Mary Millar. Many of these women stayed in touch with each other for the rest of their lives.
(UAA 69–132–2)

A hand-painted Wauneita invitation belonging to Libby Lloyd, the 1912 class historian.
(UAA 75–68)

"At the same time as SIS was being organized," continues Ethel, "the Academic Women's Association was being formed by its founding President, Mrs. Eleanor Broadus. The AWA, the nucleus of the University Women's Club, then had the aim of developing the education scheme relating to women and, as Mrs. Broadus suggested in a letter to university women in Calgary, Red Deer and MacLeod, the AWA would provide social advantages until the university should have a residence and a Dean of Women." One of the AWA's first acts was to establish a scholarship for the female student who achieved the highest standing in her first year. It was the first scholarship offered by any person or group outside the University proper. The first recipient was Helen Montgomery.

In late 1908 or early 1909, some of the women formed a sorority called Upsilon Upsilon, also known as the "Umpty Umps." However, Tory, who viewed secret societies as elitist, was adamantly opposed to fraternities and sororities and the Umpty Umps disbanded.[18]

The Wauneita Club—Payuk Uche Kukeyow[19]

AMONG THE SEVEN new women who joined the original group in September 1910 was Stella Ruttan, one of only two women students with any experience of university traditions and mores. Ethel remembers Stella's part in launching a new women's society that would remain a focal point for women's activities for six decades: "Miss Stella Ruttan (Mrs. R.J. Russell), who happened to be one of the second seven, arrived from Queen's. She proposed that the 14 women at university should organize under the name Wauneita, meaning 'kind-hearted' in Cree. Dr. Tory was very supportive of the Wauneitas—down to the details, suggesting to them that they should publish a Co-Eds Corner in *The Gateway* to replace the social reports. The new organization adopted the everlasting motto of U of A co-eds, 'Each for all and all for each,' which fellow student Roy Taylor translated into Cree: '*Payuk uche kukeyow mena kukeyow uche payuk.*'"[20] The Cree version of the Wauneita motto is chiselled above the north and south angled entrance doors of Pembina Hall.

The Wauneitas had an ambitious program in their early years. There were social events and monthly speakers. Professor Barker Fairley, an Englishman newly arrived from a German university, "advised that co-education met some obstacles in European universities, particularly

Germany." Dr. Alexander met with the Wauneitas, advocating that women be given the vote. He told them that "one wave of social change is the emancipation of women." And he finished up by telling this small group of women who were seeking university degrees that "there has already been an intellectual emancipation."

Why a club for women and not for men? In 1909, when those first 14 women formed the Wauneita Club, there were 68 male students and for decades to come, men would outnumber women on campus. Men held all the presidential positions; such was the way of the world at the time. The Wauneita Club, with its several lounges located around campus, became a Society within the Students' Union in 1929. Until the late 1960s, when it was disbanded, it served as a social centre, a place to practise debating skills, and a source of leadership training.

VIGNETTES FROM 1908–1910

The Daily Trek from Edmonton to Strathcona

ETHEL ANDERSON and Decima Robinson had been childhood friends, and now they were two of only three students who walked to school every day from "overtown" in Edmonton, regardless of the weather. When the river was "open" they would take the ferry, and in the bitter winters, they walked across the iced-up North Saskatchewan and then "puffed and panted up the hills."[21] They could have taken the streetcar that travelled down from Jasper Avenue, over the Low Level Bridge, and up to Whyte Avenue, but service was "hourly at best," which made it "undependable for students."

Once in a while, they ran into Premier Rutherford on his way to the Legislature and he gave them a lift in his brand new red Packard. Cars were rare, though, and "we walked everywhere," says Ethel. "No parking problems on campus in those days—no cars!"[22]

Stanley Cup Fever in 1908

EDMONTON HAD A DYNAMITE HOCKEY TEAM in 1908. On December 11, the Edmonton Hockey Eskimos were set to face off against the Strathcona team in the last game of the western finals of the Stanley Cup playoffs. The winner would travel to Montréal in a bid to wrest the

Cup from the top-ranked Montréal Wanderers. It was a classic match between traditional rivals, and the savvy new manager of the Eskimos, Fred Whitcroft, was determined to win the Cup for the capital city.

The U of A women planned to be a part of the action and were set to head downtown to the Thistle Rink for the big game when Dr. Tory found out. He was not about to let his young female students go overtown alone at night. In his view, says Agnes, it was a matter of propriety that they should be chaperoned, and so the President escorted the girls to the game. Tory's penchant for propriety enabled him to watch Edmonton capture the western title 21–0.

And the Stanley Cup? The women who saw that playoff game would want you to know what happened. With the Stanley Cup now in his sights, Fred Whitcroft signed on Tom Phillips, winner of two previous Stanley Cups. Then Whitcroft did the impossible. He searched for a man who had quit hockey to help out in the family lumber mill. The man's name

The Strathcona Collegiate Institute 1912 women's hockey team. (UAA 88–93–1)

was Lester Patrick,[23] the Wayne Gretzky of his day, and former captain of the Wanderers. Whitcroft found Lester in Nelson, BC and convinced Lester's father to give his son three weeks' vacation to join the Edmonton team for the final games in Montréal. Lester Patrick made it to Montréal just in time to play for Edmonton against his old Stanley Cup team. There were two playoff games: the first went to Montréal, 7–4; the second to Edmonton, 7–6. But Montréal retained the Cup based on their overall goals in the series. There would be no Cup for Edmonton until 1984.

Hockey games were a favourite group date in those days, and so were sleigh rides, but these were also "heavily chaperoned."[24] In fact, it was hard to have a private dating moment at all. On one occasion, says Agnes Wilson, Dr. Tory learned that she had been asked out on a date to attend another hockey match. Tory phoned her. "Does your Mother know, Miss Wilson?" Imagine a University president today calling you to check out your Saturday night date.

Conversazione

BEFORE THERE WAS RAGTIME, jazz, or swing, before there was country or rock 'n roll, raves or rap, there was Conversazione.[25] The administration loved it. The students did not. For President Tory, Conversazione was an event to showcase the U of A, but for the students, it was a stuffy, stilted way to socialize. Worst of all, dancing was not allowed. As one who had to endure several evenings of Conversazione, Agnes Wilson knew all about them:

> The Conversazione played a prominent part in the early life of the University and then faded from the scene. Up until the end of the First World War the proprieties of the Victorian era were subscribed to even in the pioneer community. Along with it some strong Puritanical forces were at work. Dr. Tory, as well as being a scientist, held a Bachelor of Divinity degree and was a Methodist. Methodists of that day did not hold with dancing and in line with this thinking, the first Conversazione was born.
>
> Conversazione consisted first of a musical number—badly rendered as I remember—and then promenades on which perfectly good dance music was wasted. Couples headed by the Lieutenant Governor and

his partner solemnly walked around in a prescribed circle engaging on conversation. Conversation thus prescribed, as you can imagine, was anything but scintillating. To these "Conversats," as they came to be known, were invited the elite of the town—the Lieutenant Governor and his entourage, government officials and their wives, Board of Governors, members of Convocation.

The 14 women students in 1909 spent the entire day getting ready for a "Conversat." They were expected to prepare cakes and sandwiches for all the guests, and were obliged to borrow their parents' best china and silverware in order to put on a good show. Once all that was done, they had to be properly groomed and attired. The hardest part of the day was dealing with their long hair—no short "bobs" back then and very few hairdressers. "Many hours were spent rolling rebellious long hair into bun-like curls all over our head," says Agnes. "Our heads looked like bushel baskets when finished." It was the fashion of the day. And *no* make-up. "Make-up was not considered by 'nice' girls," says Agnes, "and the only concession to glamour was talcum powder, which at 2 o'clock in the morning took on a ghastly hue." Men wore tails and usually came equipped with an "extra collar" to replace a wilted one. The women wore long gloves—and gloves were also a must for the men.

The Barriers Against Dancing Come Tumbling Down

THE STRICTURE AGAINST DANCING at Conversazione really bothered the students, but fortunately it was only a matter of time before President Tory changed his mind. So who was first on the dance floor?

Ethel Anderson remembers that at one 1909 Conversazione, it was the "young professors and their wives" who ended one of the structured promenades by dancing. Almost 20 years later, Professor Will Alexander explained how it happened:

It was in the early weeks of 1909 that the students of the University of Alberta blazed forth into the distinction of a university "conversat," an event which it is almost useless to describe in these times (1928) when everything is a dance, but the old-timers will understand. There was a programme—my dear, can you stand it?—and a supper, and after that "promenades" on which perfectly good dance music was being wasted, just blowing off like Turner Valley gas. A few daring souls thought of putting it to use, the president smiled assent, and in a few minutes a circle of chairs about thirty feet in diameter had been formed. Inside this there entered for the next waltz four valiant hearts who gyrated softly, while the promenaders from beyond the chair-backs eyed them curiously as one might eye a new specimen in a zoological garden. From such a tiny seed has grown the great dancing industry of the University of Alberta.[26]

It's a good bet Doc Alik was first on the dance floor. Alumni from the 1930s describe him as an excellent dancer.

Once the "barriers against dancing" finally came down, dance was a popular part of Conversat, and students danced into the wee hours every chance they got. When Athabasca Hall became a residence, there were dances in the lounge where waltzing couples could "whirl in one door and out the other."[27] Students' love of dancing has not diminished over the decades, and by 2004 the U of A Dance Club had some 1,800 members—far more than any other campus club.

THE MOVE TO OLD SCONA AND THE BIRTH OF THE GATEWAY

AFTER FOUR MONTHS at the Duggan Street School, the U of A moved to larger quarters in the Strathcona Collegiate Institute, which we know today as Old Scona High School. At the time, the entire university furnishings, including all the lab equipment and the library, fit onto one truck. The U of A would stay in Old Scona for two more years until Athabasca Hall, the University's first building, opened.

Old Scona is where *The Gateway* had its rocky start under the auspices of the Literary Society. In 1909, Dr. Broadus invited Al Ottewell and Jim Law to his home for lunch to talk about starting a student newspaper. "It was there and then decided that something might be attempted," according to Al Ottewell, and a staff was organized and "copy prepared." But that is where the lofty plans ended. The first Students' Union Treasurer, Lee Carr, wouldn't let *The Gateway* operate on a deficit budget.[28] But in the

session of 1910–1911, amidst a general mood of optimism on campus, *The Gateway* finally appeared.

Typhoid

THEN, just as *The Gateway* was getting started, a typhoid epidemic broke out when an ice jam created water eddies that sent raw sewage straight into the city water main. It was Professor Muir Edwards who found the problem and fixed it. Before the water intake was moved, however, "one in ten of the entire student body was stricken" and one student died. *The Gateway*'s business editor and sports editor were both hospitalized and it looked as though *The Gateway* would fold. But L.Y. Cairns started up his "Letters to Dad" column, artist Walt Mason kept the cartoons and drawings coming, and *The Gateway* stayed afloat.

Without financial support from the Students' Union, *The Gateway* relied on advertising for its survival. In early *Gateway*s, the Strathcona Hotel advertised rooms for $2 per day; the Strathcona Pantorium would clean four suits a month for $4; a tilting desk chair was $5.40 at McCallum & Westbrook on Whyte Avenue; and Douglas Brothers Ltd. proclaimed itself the "Varsity Store...in the Varsity City...for Varsity People." There were no distribution boxes and no free copies. You could buy a copy for

L.Y. Cairns, the class wit and humorist, and a future chancellor of the University.
(UAA 69–12–28)

20c, or do without. *The Gateway's* business manager, George Misener, "worked like sixty people" to keep *The Gateway* solvent. By the time of *The Gateway's* first publication, the University had a student enrolment of 129 and had hired five more faculty. The University was a growing concern and the commercial ads in *The Gateway* targeted the University, for the first time, as a distinct market.

The Gateway published its monthly editions in November, December and January, 1910–1911, with Albert Ottewell as editor and Blanche McLaughlin (BA '14) as the "Lady Editor." *The Gateway* persuaded 27 businesses to take out paid ads, and both the U of A and Alberta College included full-page descriptions of their programs.

The Gateway was full of reports on the goings-on at Alberta College, the activities of the new Students' YMCA with its Bible study group, the plans of literary and athletic organizations, and the activities of the Wauneita Club.[29] Freshman initiation was covered, but never too thoroughly, giving tantalizing clues as to what exactly went on when the sophomores had their day with the new students, initiating them into the mysteries of university life.

Gateway Poems

EACH *GATEWAY* included short stories and silly jokes and introduced new professors. And, always, there were poems. In fact, there was a poem on the front page of each of the first three *Gateway* editions—most often authored by freshman L.Y. Cairns. Cairns was relentless and took aim at everything from Trigonometry to English. Reprints from his column, "Letters to Dad," appeared in *The Gateway* well into his term as chancellor of the University in the late 1950s.

As always, Doc Alik was at the ready to help with the students' extracurricular activities. He wrote a column, "The World at Large," for *The Gateway*. It was a sophisticated commentary on global, political events. Al Ottewell also had a regular column, "What We Think," and what he thought in the inaugural *Gateway* issue of November 1910, was this: "The University of Alberta may justly be considered as the entrance to a great opportunity. Here too is afforded the sons and daughters of Alberta, many of whom would otherwise be unable to realize it, [the opportunity] of securing a training which shall qualify them for worthy citizenship in

November, 1910

Published by the
Undergraduates of the University of Alberta

Just Smile

If you've got an English test,
Just Smile.
Wear a grin and do your best.
Just smile.
If you have a theme to do, What's the use of
*   feeling blue;*
Thank your stars you haven't two,
Just smile.
If Chemistry's obscure,
Just smile.
It's harder farther on, that's sure,
Just smile.
Don't let everybody know,
Or make the naughty language flow,
But cool your head in H_2O
Just Smile.
...
When History is dry,
Just smile.
Keep a twinkle in your eye,
Just smile.
History shouldn't bother you!
You are making history too,
That all your kids will have to do.
Just smile.
If "Trig" is pretty tough,
Just smile.
A science course is always rough
Just smile.
Dr. Sheldon when a lad,
Heard of science from his dad,
How we wish he never had,
Just smile.

L.Y. CAIRNS

The cover of the first edition of The Gateway.

Freshman: "Well, I'm trying to
get ahead."
Sophomore: "I'm very glad to
hear that. You certainly
need one."

Parent: "I should never have
thought that studying
would have cost so much
money."
Son (home from college): No
father, and if you only knew
how little I studied."

Freshman: "Well I declare, I've
forgotten all I ever knew."
Sophomore: "Never mind, old
chap, take an hour off some
time and learn it all over
again."

"Wise men hesitate; only fools
are certain," observed
Misener.
"I don't know about that,"
replied Miss Ruttan.
"Well, I am quite certain of it,"
explained Misener.
Then he wondered why she
laughed.

Prof: "Now then, what are
you doing, learning
something?"
Pupil: "No, Sir, I'm listening
to you."

The jokes are taken from the following
Gateway publications: November 1910, 22;
December 1910, 9; January 1911, 6, 13, 26.

this splendid new country." He described the University as "the gateway of the Last West and of opportunity," and with those words, he confirmed the name of the new publication. The name had been chosen as a result of a competition—many entries, but only one was chosen. *The Gateway.*

SOME SIGNIFICANT APPOINTMENTS— A PROVOST, AN ADVISOR TO WOMEN, AND A DEAN OF WOMEN

TORY RECRUITED eight professors and lecturers between 1909 and 1911. Among the new recruits were John MacEachran, Ernest Sheldon, and Margaret Keeling.[30]

John MacEachran—First Provost[31]

JOHN MALCOLM MACEACHRAN, a Philosophy professor, was supposed to be part of the original contingent of professors in 1908, but he never made it to the first day of class. In his correspondence with MacEachran, Tory had persuaded the young professor to leave Queen's University and come west for the 1908 opening session. MacEachran took Dr. Tory at his word and quit his job. His plan was to indulge in a summer of study at the Sorbonne, followed by a vacation in Leipzig before heading to the U of A. Then the bombshell dropped. Tory was only authorized to hire four professors, and MacEachran was not one of them. Left without a job, MacEachran borrowed money from one of his Queen's colleagues and set off for an extended study-vacation in Europe. Soon after, Tory came to Europe to meet him in person, to make amends, and to pin him down for the 1909 session. It was a strange encounter, MacEachran recalls:

The opera *Lohengrin* was being sung at the Paris Opera House, where I was entertaining Professor Tory. I was lost in the music but Dr. Tory was giving less than full attention. He had a mission to accomplish. To the Wagnerian background he was urging upon me the bright future of a professor's career at the University of Alberta. He was anxious to add me to the roster of four professors at the year-old university when the new term resumed in September 1909. Sixty years later, I look back on that evening with wry amusement and exasperation. I was young. I had obtained the best seats in the house. I had never heard *Lohengrin* more beautifully sung and all through the opera Dr. Tory kept talking about the University.

MacEachran had prepared a week's entertainment in anticipation of Tory's visit. But Tory came and went in only a day. "He used every moment to promote his cause. Nothing stood in the way of his goal. And nothing did. I cancelled my trip to Switzerland and returned to Canada with Dr. Tory." Always on the go, "Dr. Tory stopped over in England where he investigated new, experimental research on wheat."

The first provost and dean of men, Professor John MacEachran. (UAA 97–16)

MacEachran joined the staff in 1909. With so few professors and so many subjects to teach, MacEachran pitched in and taught German and History in addition to Philosophy. He was also assigned to oversee discipline in Athabasca Hall and was named provost simply because he was the only bachelor among the professors at the time.

These were the days of receiving lines, calling cards, Conversazione, and dressing for dinner. MacEachran was a self-described stickler for protocol, and this tendency poured over into student affairs. At Queen's, MacEachran had admired the dean of women for her emphasis on proper behaviour and so he, too, expected "courtesies and formalities" at U of A student functions. He expected no less of himself. When he and Tory were invited to share the premier's box at the horse races, they may have gotten to the track by horse and buggy, but the two professors wore evening dress and top hats.

MacEachran was a keen advocate of house rules and proper deportment for the women students. There were very few rules for the men who lived in residence, but the women were not allowed to be overtown in Edmonton past a certain hour. When the women went to see MacEachran about the curfew, he ultimately relied on the supremacy of maternal discipline: "I told them that the matter would have to be taken up with the President, then with the Students' Council and finally with each of their mothers. This would be impossible for me, so I advised them to confer with their mothers, individually, and to bring me their opinions. I never heard another word about it."

Despite his early leanings towards strict protocol and stuffy social events, MacEachran is remembered as a provost who stood behind the students when it was clear they wanted an increasing measure of control over their own affairs. By 1912, under the auspices of the Students' Union, there was a students' court "to try offences against the student body," and residence discipline was under the control of a House Committee that had a majority of student members. The Senate had approved a Committee on Student Affairs, chaired by the provost, "to deal with matters affecting students, to secure cooperation between the student body and the administration, and to be a court of appeal in cases of difficulties in matters of discipline." For the most part, discipline problems were handled without the intervention of the University, and on the occasions when the University *did* intervene, there was invariably a call for autonomy from the students. MacEachran intervened as little as possible.

MacEachran had been a member of the all-Canadian soccer team while at Queen's. His sporting abilities made him the obvious person to be in charge of men's athletics at the U of A. He travelled with the hockey team to its first out-of-province game against the University of Saskatchewan.

MacEachran was also intensely interested in music. He frequently spent his evenings at the Broadus household talking about music and literature. On one occasion when they were discussing an opera, MacEachran recalls that Eleanor Broadus "went over to the piano and played the score from memory." MacEachran and Mrs. Broadus later joined forces to revive the faltering Glee Club.

Although MacEachran was not one of the "First Four," he followed closely on their heels and left an imprint on student life for decades to come.

Helen McHugh Sheldon—First Advisor to Women Students

PRESIDENT TORY would keel over if he knew there were co-educational residences on his campus today. It was his conviction that women should be properly chaperoned to public events and that they should have their own residence, with a dean of women to oversee their activities and lives.

When Ernest Sheldon was hired as a professor of Mathematics in September 1910, Tory asked Sheldon's wife, Helen, to be the first Advisor to Women Students when Athabasca Hall opened. Helen Sheldon was "young and beautiful," and "gay and charming," with an impeccable upbringing and education. Delicate? Hardly. She could drive a team of horses and often took Mrs. Tory out for drives with Molly and Jack, who were stabled behind the Tory's Ring House residence.[32]

Helen accepted the offer. At the time, she and Ernest lived near Old Scona, in rented quarters recently vacated by the Alexanders. The Sheldons were close friends of the Torys—in fact, Tory had loaned "Shel" money to attend Yale University for his Ph.D. When Athabasca Hall opened early in 1911, the Sheldons lived on the second floor with Miss Ockley (Tory's secretary) and ten women students. Helen Sheldon was not much older than the young women entrusted to her care, but she was a stickler for protocol, just like Provost MacEachran. Helen was raised in New York City—in posh Gramercy Park—and schooled in New England at Mount Holyoke and the Northfield Massachusetts Ladies Seminary. She was born and bred to know proper behaviour for women at a university. Women were outnumbered six to one on the U of A campus, so perhaps Mrs. Sheldon had reason to insist that there be no visiting overtown in Edmonton past 9 P.M.

Helen Sheldon, the first advisor to women.

(University of Alberta Textiles Collection)

The Sheldons had the only telephone on the floor, and whenever the girls used it, "Shel" would step out into the hall and pace the floor while the girls talked to their boyfriends. "Shel" was a "paragon of courtesy and discretion" and did a lot of pacing in 1911.[33] Mrs. Sheldon chaperoned the girls on sleigh rides and at dances, and she was strict. But she was also a young bride, with a handsome, witty, and patient husband, and life in residence was happy for the ten women under Mrs. Sheldon's care. The first time Mrs. Sheldon "entertained all the ladies in residence at tea, she had no idea that her party conflicted with Dr. Tory's History class. The guests didn't mention it. They simply cut history class for tea, a fact that was not lost on their professor. Dr. Tory accepted the mistake in good humour, but he stuck his head around the door to advise the hostess, 'Next time, will you let me know when you are entertaining my History class at tea?'"

Helen Sheldon served as advisor to women for one year (1910–1911). At the end of the year, the Sheldons moved into Ring House 7. On the sidewalk leading to their new home was a slab of cement into which was carved a diagram depicting the Pythagorean Theorem. Ernest, after all, was a brilliant Math professor, and perhaps the diagram was a way to

First dean of women, Margaret Keeling Fairley. (UAA 69–90–119)

announce his academic passion. But legend tells us otherwise. Ernest Sheldon, well known as a deep thinker, would leave the Arts building and walk across campus to Ring House 7, his head bowed in thought. Thus preoccupied, he regularly walked right past his home. The solution was to install the engraved slab of cement to mark the spot where Sheldon should emerge from his deep thinking and turn to walk up the steps to his house. When the Sheldons' Ring House was demolished, the plaque bearing the Pythagorean Theorem was moved to a spot in front of today's Mechanical Engineering Building.

As for Helen, was the young bride from the privileged New York family happy in muddy, out-of-the-way Edmonton? "The University is a very human institution. The first time I returned to New York," says Helen, "I wondered if I would want to come back to Edmonton, but I couldn't wait to return. It has been a wonderful life."[34]

Margaret Adele Keeling—First Dean of Women[35]

KEELING WAS THE DAUGHTER of the Headmaster of the Bradford Grammar School in England. He encouraged Margaret's intellectual drive and supported her decision to enter Oxford. There, she was don of a women's college and attained first class honours as a brilliant literature specialist, but was denied a degree because she was a woman. That policy changed in the early 1920s—too late for Margaret.

Margaret quit her position as don and left Oxford. She travelled in England and then departed for Canada, working towards her goal of founding a girls' school. Despite discussions with deputy ministers in Canada about starting a school for girls, Margaret was stymied and returned to England. And that is where Tory discovered her. Tory offered Margaret a three-part deal: an *ad eundem* degree from the U of A to take the place of the degree Oxford denied her; a teaching post at the U of A; and the position of dean of women. Margaret would be the on-site administrator in charge of discipline and decorum for women students. Margaret Keeling was the first dean of women—a title apparently conferred solely on Dr. Tory's authority—and she served in that capacity in 1912–1913.

Soon after Margaret arrived on campus, she met Barker Fairley, a young Englishman, a Goethe scholar and a "fiery and persuasive teacher." Tory had hired him in 1910, soon after he finished his Ph.D. at Jena in

Germany. The sparks must have flown between Barker and Margaret. They were married, and had the first of their five children in 1914. Soon after, the Chancellor of the University of Toronto visited Barker on the U of A campus and offered him a professorship and an administrative position in the East. In 1914 Barker and Margaret left the U of A.

The little we know about Margaret Fairley is gleaned from books about Canadian art. Margaret's richly-coloured, shimmering portrait hangs in the Art Gallery of Ontario. It was painted by Canada's most famous portrait artist, Frederick Varley.

Why did the famous Varley paint her portrait? Soon after Margaret and Barker arrived in Toronto, Barker developed an interest in Canadian art and became an early supporter of the then controversial Group of Seven—the small band of struggling artists who turned their backs on European methods and landscapes to paint Canada, their own country. Barker founded the magazine *Canadian Forum,* which included critiques of the Group of Seven. Barker's interest in art led to a close friendship with Varley. Margaret, known for her social conscience and concern for the poor, was a strong personality with a face to match. No doubt Varley quickly saw the possibility for a great portrait.

THE FIRST GRADUATION CEREMONY [36]

DECIMA EVELINE ROBINSON, in 1911, was the first student to be awarded an undergraduate degree at the U of A. She had studied for a year at London University, England, and was one of three students in the original class of 45 who was given advanced placement. Back then, the Calendar published each student's class ranking, and there is no doubt that Decima aced her Chemistry, English, Mathematics and Astronomy exams. She received special coaching in organic Chemistry and Calculus, where she won honours. A year later, Demica completed her Masters and joined the U of A staff. Decima married Edwin Mitchell, the 1912 class president, and when Edwin was offered a job at the University of Texas, the couple moved to Austin.

The other students who had been given advanced placement were Albert James Law ("Jim," the 1911 class president) and Robert Howard Dobson. Jim Law had studied at Queen's and Robert Dobson at McGill. Both received B.A. degrees in 1911. All three students—Decima, Jim, and

Robert—graduated a full year before their classmates, in a small ceremony held at today's Old Scona.

Five other students were part of that first convocation, receiving graduate degrees. As the *Strathcona Plaindealer* put it, they were taking special classes and were not "in regular attendance" with the undergraduates, since they had all previously received degrees from "eastern universities." Jenny Storck Hill became the first student to earn a graduate degree when she received an M.A. Her husband, Ethelbert, received his M.Sc. Two other students, James Alexander Fife and Clarence Arthur Curtis, also received an M.Sc. The final graduate student at the 1911 convocation was George Frederick McNally, a future University chancellor, who was awarded an M.A.

The 1911 ceremony at the Strathcona Collegiate Institute was a simple event, but it was attended by a large crowd. The academic procession was followed by the Lord's Prayer, read by Chancellor Stuart. President Tory gave a report on the progress of the University ("splendid," said the *Strathcona Plaindealer*). The Address to Convocation was delivered by a former Queen's professor, Dr. S.W. Dyde, Principal of the Presbyterian Robertson College.[37] Scholarship and prize winners were announced, and then each graduand, with clasped hands extended in front of him or her, knelt before the Chancellor. The Chancellor enclosed each student's hands with his and said *"Admitto te"* (I admit you). The first eight graduates were "admitted" into the fold and were now a part of the University of Alberta family. Tory called them "the first fruits of our labour."

For young Albertans like Decima Robinson and Jenny Storck Hill, education was finally available at their front door. Few young Albertans could afford to leave Alberta for a degree, and having a university in their home province provided them with previously unheard of opportunities. "Many of us," said one early graduate, "had waited a long time for the chance to get an education."

By the spring of 1911, the U of A was firmly established. The first graduates had convocated, the value of the University to the province was no longer questioned, enrolment was growing, and an outstanding staff was in place. University life, however, was about to change: that September, the University would move from its rented quarters to a brand new campus.

"*In 1913, I lived in Assiniboia Hall when it was a residence. Every morning, a meadowlark sang and I gathered lady slippers in the woods behind the building.*"[1]

—CECIL BURGESS
Professor of Architecture, hired in 1913

Timeline

Enrolment and Finance, 1911–1913

- Fall student head count: 185 (1911); 434 (1913)
- Operating budget from the Province of Alberta: $34,614.68 (1911); $88,082.28 (1913)
- Full-load undergraduate Arts tuition: $20.00 (1911); $20.00 (1913)
- SU membership fee: $2.00 (1911); $5.00 (1913)

Key Dates

1911

- First issue of *The Gateway*

1912

- Department of Extension established with an office in the basement of Assiniboia Hall
- The Senate (now GFC) committee on student affairs established
- Men's Faculty Club established
- Faculty of Law established with 35 students enrolled in the LLB program

1913

- Geneva Misener, first female professor, is hired
- Faculty of Medicine established with 26 students enrolled for the first three years of the program
- Faculty of Applied Science established (renamed Engineering in 1948)
- Department of Extension initiates its travelling library and organizes debate clubs across the province
- First football grid staked out by Professor Muir Edwards
- Walter Dyde becomes the U of A's first Rhodes scholar

Campus Buildings, 1911–1913

- First U of A building, Athabasca Hall, opens (1911)
- St. Stephen's College opens for classes (1911)
- Basement of Assiniboia is excavated by 100 men using shovels (1911)
- Rutherford's home on Saskatchewan Drive is built (1911)
- Dr. Tory's residence on campus is completed (1911)
- Assiniboia Hall is partially occupied in 1912 and opens in 1913
- Athabasca Dining Hall and Gym opens in 1913
- The second sod-turning for the Arts Building (1913)
- First power plant and smokestack built behind Athabasca Hall (1913)
- Agriculture's first barn built near the current Faculty Club—it houses five cows and four horses (1913)
- Excavation started for Pembina Hall (1913)

Beyond the Campus, 1911–1913

- An economic boom begins in 1911, collapses in 1914
- Alberta MLAs move into the new Legislature Building (1911)
- Strathcona votes to amalgamate with Edmonton (1912)
- The legislature grants Strathcona a number of concessions as part of the amalgamation agreement, including a new bridge at 105 Street and a streetcar line to the McKernan's Lake area (1912)
- High Level Bridge completed (1913)
- Rutherford is narrowly defeated as an MLA and begins career of public service (1913)
- First crop failures in the west (1913–1914)
- Zippers, the fox trot, and the automotive assembly line define an era (1913)

A PLACE TO CALL HOME

IN SEPTEMBER 1911, after two-and-a-half years in rented quarters in Strathcona, with no real focal point for student life or teaching, the University of Alberta finally moved into its first permanent home on the new campus: Athabasca Hall.

Athabasca Hall was the catch-all building that housed offices, a residence, classrooms, labs, the library, the bookstore, and an infirmary. Everything was in a single location, and the University was crowded. Two professors shared an "office" that later became a washroom. There was an advantage to a single-building campus, though. It was hard to get lost.

A Farm in the Bush—River Lot 5

TODAY'S DENSELY PACKED CAMPUS started out as a simple "farm in the bush."[2] It was "a wild stretch of land," said one yearbook. One of the students, Ethel Anderson, called it a "beautiful woodland park." To Dean John Macdonald, the early campus was "coated with a growth of scrubby willows and poplars, unbroken by path or building. To the west it was a long and level expanse of poplars, the sameness of it relieved in the spring by patches of pussy willows and in June by the vivid blossoms of wild roses." In the fall, it was a "blaze of golden splendor." Reg Lister often saw "deer running across the campus in the early days."[3]

Will Alexander, the Classics professor, had spent many hours roaming River Lot 5 before any buildings appeared. He later recalled that

> probably no eye save that of Dr. Rutherford's had ever discerned the latent possibilities of River Lot number 5,...a stretch of land covered by youngish poplar and scrubby willows, rather far removed from the houses and public structures of Strathcona. Nothing on it suggested human life or work except a few sinuous trails and a much decayed log barn, and these spoke rather of an effort abandoned than of an enterprise begun. But the wild roses made it beautiful in June.

When Dr. John MacEachran, recently recruited from Queen's university, saw the campus grounds in 1909, he marvelled at how big it was. "Much bigger than Queen's," he mused, "it was a wild, wind-blown bush-

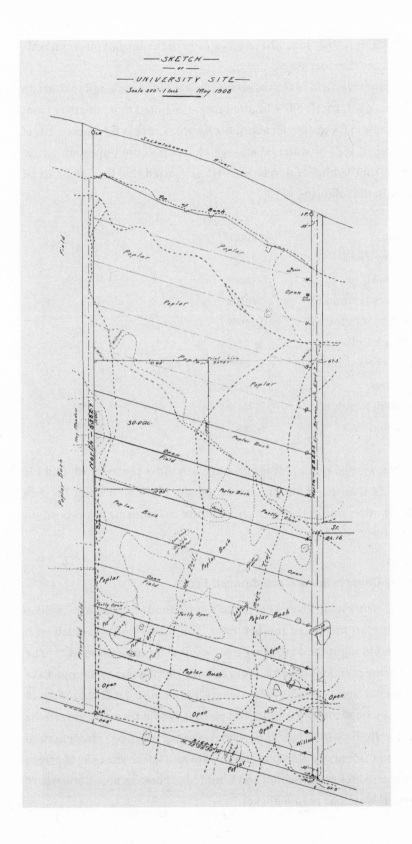

A map of River Lot 5, the original land on which the University of Alberta was built. It consisted of 258 acres of brush that Premier Rutherford had personally selected in 1905 to be the future home of the University of Alberta.

(UAA 2006–29)

land." Not only that, but "there was a *farm* in the bush! You could walk over and see the Guernseys."

The Montréal firm of Nobbs and Hyde was commissioned to draw up a campus plan. Dr. Nobbs's original proposal noted that "the river front is the position for the big façade of the future. The east side faces a street which might well be widened and which will become important as the driveway on the bluff is developed." He suggested that the 258 acres be divided in the following way:

Farm	80 acres
Playing Field	16 acres
Hospital	16 acres
University Buildings	45 acres
Professors' Houses	10 acres
Church Colleges	3 ½ acres
Powerhouse and Yard	8 ½ acres
Campus	5 ½ acres
Student Residences	9 ½ acres
Wooded Park	7 acres

Nobbs wanted the buildings grouped around a central yard, and his vision was that the "buildings crowning the bluff, which will be seen from the other side of the river, should form as imposing a composition as possible."

Howling Coyotes and a Cacophony of Frogs

TO THE SOUTH of River Lot 5 was a wasteland—a marsh or a lake, depending on the eye of the beholder. The marshland was filled with frogs, and at night their croaking was "audible for miles around."[4] "The bog," as one professor called it, soon became the popular McKernan Lake recreational area, served by the rickety Toonerville Trolley. McKernan Lake had a huge toboggan slide, and plenty of room for picnicking in the summer. In the winter, the U of A hockey team practiced on McKernan Lake, and students would skate and sled there. Today? The Lake has been drained and McKernan School and hundreds of houses now stand where the first teams once played hockey.[5]

In August 1911, the frogs that inhabited this marshland competed each evening with the mournful, echoing song of the coyotes down in the river valley. A month later, their new neighbours moved in: 129 students were about to start classes in the new, neat, trim Athabasca Hall.

Professor R.K. Gordon was able to capture the sharp contrast between the scrubby woodlot and the first two buildings on campus, Athabasca and Assiniboia Halls:

> We were a small, light-hearted company, hardly more than a score of us; and all of us were young. We lived in a clearing in the poplar bush on the south bank of the North Saskatchewan River. On the sloping sides of the great valley and on the flats below the coyotes barked and howled at night, but on the top of the bank we taught Mathematics and Physics, Greek and History, English Literature and Biology. Along with some four hundred students and two red brick buildings, we were the University of Alberta, and we felt sure that the future belonged to us, and not to the coyotes.[6]

Athabasca Hall in 1911[7]

LIFE ON THE PROSPECTIVE CAMPUS was a hive of activity. Athabasca was nearing completion, the President's residence was finished, and three other Ring House homes on the "horseshoe" were nearly ready for Professors Edwards, Kerr and Lehman. "Plumbers, steamfitters, carpenters and bricklayers worked all the summer of 1911 getting Athabasca ready for the students who arrived in the fall," according to Reg Lister. When the big day came, the U of A was again packed up and hauled across town. Athabasca Hall "stood by itself, surrounded by bush," says Reg. "There were no sidewalks or roads. The trails to Athabasca came around sloughs or across the field from 112 Street. There were no trucks or cars in those days and everything had to be hauled by horse and wagon...bricks, stone, lumber, furniture, equipment. It was quite a job and often the wagons would get stuck in the mud up to their axles." The *Strathcona Plaindealer* said that before the quad was cleared, the trees were so dense that you couldn't see Athabasca from the site of the Arts Building's foundation. Those trees have long been felled to make way for CAB and Cameron Library.

The first building on campus was to have been Arts, the main building for instruction; later would follow three residences—Athabasca, Assiniboia and Pembina. As it turned out, the sod-turning for the Arts building occurred, but construction was put off for several years. Athabasca, seen here under construction, became the first building on campus. (UAA 77–177)

The brand new Athabasca Hall was ready when classes started in the fall of 1911. Tory chose the furnishings himself, and he was undoubtedly the person responsible for the floor plan. All the administrative offices, including the President's Office, were on the third floor. Athabasca was also the "residence for 35 men and 7 women," says Reg. Every available room was snapped up by the students. Provost MacEachran, Advisor to Women Mrs. Sheldon, and her husband, Professor Ernest Sheldon, lived on the second floor with the student residents. "There were sitting rooms in the front hall, north for ladies and south for men," says Reg. "Room 26 was the pressing room for ladies….The Lounge in Athabasca was then the dining room and the suite off the lounge was the kitchen and above the kitchen were rooms for maids and kitchen help….The boilers to heat the building were under the lounges, and were two low-pressure units, fired by coal by hand. The firing was done by students who received their room and board for the work."

There was a fireplace in every room—for heat, not ambience. "In September," Reg recalled, "I helped move equipment from Old Scona into Athabasca, where I lit the first fire in the kitchen." But the fireplace didn't draw. Fortunately, the university had been careful in its precautionary measures and used only "slow burning wood" during construction. Fortunately, too, Reg was able to fix the flue.

The new residents named their rooms: Inferno, Olympus, Pandemonium, Elysium, and Angels' Roost. Very soon, the informal system of student management evolved into a "House Committee," where senior students and the provost (or dean of women) would be in charge of student discipline in the residence. There was, however, always the informal overseer of student discipline, Reg Lister, and many discipline infractions never made it to the House Committee.

Reg remembers that in "the first few years of residence we used the basement of Athabasca...for the infirmary. There was no nurse in charge; any student who fell ill was put to bed...and given a dose of castor oil, and was later seen by a doctor.... It was not until after the first war that a nurse was engaged."

Athabasca Hall *was* the campus, and the students who had registered in 1908 at the Duggan Street School would spend their fourth and last year of University in this one structure. From the basement infirmary to the top-floor presidential office, Athabasca had it all. And more, for there was something about Athabasca Hall that doesn't appear in the standard histories: the resident ghost, a little boy dressed in a plaid button-up shirt and wool pants.

The only account of the ghost appeared in *The Gateway*, and it was never substantiated by anyone other than the author of the article, Dave Alexander.[8] The sad tale goes back to the 1910 construction of Athabasca, when the men building the residence pitched a camp by the river. "Among the new immigrant families employed was a couple with a son of about eight or nine years old. The wife worked as a cook in the camp and the husband was employed as a mason." The little boy disobeyed his parents and played down by the river, and one day he forgot his coat down on the river bank. And so in the dark of night, he secretly slipped away to fetch it. He never returned. The next day his parents found their son's frozen body down by the river. Heartbroken, they immediately left the city that had brought them so much sadness. But the sobbing boy with the blue lips was said to have returned regularly to the place where his father worked, and he haunted Athabasca Hall through the 1940s.

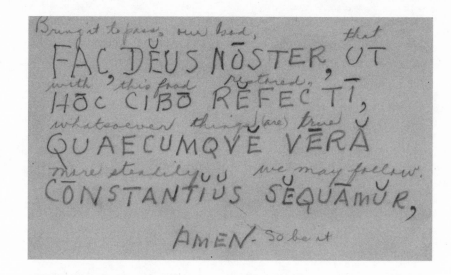

UNIVERSITY TRADITIONS

The University Grace

EVERY STUDENT in the early days of the University could recite the University Grace. It was solemnly said before meals in Athabasca, Assiniboia, and Pembina Halls, the three residences until Lister Hall was opened in the early 1960s.

The first professors, many of whom also ate in the residence dining room with the students, remember the manners as "countrified," and a professor was assigned to each table to instill decorum and order. Reg Lister, superintendent of residences, says that students would bolt their dinner in ten minutes and "throw slices of bread to one another."[9] A Grace was needed to signal civility, intelligent conversation, and end-of-day-calm.

And to be sure, the Grace written by Dr. William Hardy Alexander was Christian. But it did not come about without vigorous debate. The tenor of the day was overwhelmingly Christian—Protestant Christian. At the heart of the debate lay the ending to the proposed University Grace. As Provost MacEachran, the resident philosopher, explained, "Dr. Alexander objected to using the traditional expression 'through Jesus our Lord' because he felt it implied absolution. He wanted to omit any such phrase but I felt that the omission would offend some of the students. I suggested the expression, 'according to the spirit of Jesus Christ.'"[10] The University accepted MacEachran's argument and the official version of the Grace read:

Fac, Deus Noster, ut hoc cibo refecti, Quaecumque Vera constantius sequamur, secundum Jesu Christi spiritum. [Grant, O God, that being refreshed by this food, we may more steadfastly follow after whatsoever things are true, according to the spirit of Jesus Christ.]

But Doc Alik did not accept MacEachran's argument and he wrote his version of the Grace on a 3x5 card, which is kept in the family album by his grandson, Will Alexander. To this day, the family recites the Grace as Doc Alik originally penned it:

Fac, Deus Noster, ut hoc cibo refecti, Quaecumque Vera constantius sequamur, [Grant, O God, that being refreshed by this food, we may more steadfastly follow after whatsoever things are true.]

That last comma is not a typo. The Grace ends with a comma and omits the reference to Christ. Doc Alik would not back down on a point of principle.

In the 1970s, President Walter Johns was concerned that the Grace should reflect the University's non-sectarian nature. [11] In 1979, he therefore encouraged incoming President Myer Horowitz to rewrite the Grace. Dr. Horowitz did so, with help from former dean of education, Herbert Coutts. The original Grace is still "on the books," but the words now spoken before every formal university meal are these:

Hoc convivio firmati, praecepto nostrae universitatis parentes, constantius sequamur quaecumque vera. [Refreshed by this meal and fellowship, obeying the precept of this our University, let us pursue more steadfastly whatsoever things are true.]

The University Motto[12]

THE UNIVERSITY'S MOTTO, *Quaecumque Vera* (Whatsoever Things Are True), was selected by the same man who penned the Grace: Professor

Will Alexander. The Motto is taken from the Latin Vulgate version of the Bible, chapter 4, verse 8 of St. Paul's epistle to the Philippians. The Motto tells us to reflect on and search for the truth, to Do the Right Thing. It's a motto that St. Joseph's College later amended and adopted as *Doce Me Quaecumque Vera* (Teach Me Whatsoever Things are True). The full passage of St. Paul's epistle, from the King James version of the Bible, reads:

> Finally, brethren, whatsoever things are true, whatsoever things are honest, whatsoever things are just, whatsoever things are pure, whatsoever things are lovely, whatsoever things are of good report; if there be any virtue, and if there be any praise, think on these things.

ON THE FRINGES OF CAMPUS

Laurent Garneau[13]

ON 111 STREET, just off Saskatchewan Drive, is a tree called "Garneau's Tree," with a plaque that reads as follows: "This tree, planted about 1874, marks the homesite of Laurent Garneau (1840–1921) after whom this part of the city is named." Further up Saskatchewan Drive is a plaque commemorating Garneau as a "farmer, community organizer, and musician, who acquired the property in 1874. His original home was on the lane at the rear of 11108–90 Avenue. A maple tree planted by him still grows there."

Laurent Garneau and his wife started off in a small log cabin on River Lot 7. The log cabin was eventually replaced by a stately brick mansion. The mansion, in turn, made way for the Humanities Centre. The huge evergreens that border the Humanities parking lot were once in the back yard of the Garneau mansion.

Garneau lived to see his land subdivided and develop into a close-knit neighbourhood that now bears his name. One of the first lots he sold in 1905 was a half-hectare fronting on the bluff above the river. The buyer was the Premier.[14]

A PEN PICTURE OF THE FIRST LOG CABIN IN GARNEAU
By Nettie Burkholder

Garneau, a French half-breed from the Red River, came into this country as a Guardsman in the first Riel Rebellion. He homesteaded on the south bank of the Saskatchewan, and built his cabin just west of the present site of the University.

Top: Laurent Garneau on or near University property May 6, 1898. (PAA B6383) Bottom right: Nettie Burkholder's sketch of the first log cabin in Garneau. It is in this homestead that Laurent Garneau and his wife started out as a family. (Gateway Literary Supplement, March 22, 1935). Bottom left: The Garneau mansion. (Private Collection)

Premier Rutherford's mansion (centre), with the Pierce home to the right and the Simpson barn to the left, 1910.
(UAA 76-25-338)

The Premier Builds a Mansion[15]

TODAY RUTHERFORD HOUSE virtually disappears in the shadow of the Humanities Centre, but in 1910 Premier Rutherford's new brick home dominated a Spartan landscape. Rutherford built his gracious mansion right next door to the future campus of the university he founded, and directly across the river from the site for the Legislature—another site he had chosen personally.

To one side of the magnificent new home was a sagging barn, a relic of the former Simpson farm. The Rutherfords kept their Jersey milk cow in it—they were too far out in the country to be on a delivery route. On the other side of the Rutherford home, the Pierce family was building a modest house. There wasn't another structure in sight.

The Rutherford mansion was ultramodern for its time. It had electricity, central heating, and flush toilets. The grand driveway was a "carriage sweep," an elegant circular driveway immediately off Saskatchewan Drive. To the southeast of the main house stood an unusual outbuilding—one of the first garages in Edmonton, complete with a grease pit and a storage tank for gasoline. Inside this modern-day stable was the premier's famous

six-seater red Packard. Many of the early students remember getting a ride to campus in that Packard when the premier was driven to work by his son or daughter.

However grand it was, there was a homey feel to the new mansion. There was a large vegetable garden to the east, where some of the neighbours had plots. The rustic summer house that stood near the corner of 112 Street and Saskatchewan Drive was "used not only by the Rutherfords, but by many courting students as well."[16] Once, someone found an engagement ring in the summer house, thrown to the floor after a lovers' quarrel. Happily, the couple later reunited. The summer house illustrates the close relationship between the Rutherfords' home and the University. Generations of students were entertained here each May on Founder's Day and at Convocation receptions.

Premier Rutherford lived on River Lot 7, in the middle of nowhere, but a short distance away, on neighbouring River Lot 5, the University campus was slowly taking shape. St. Stephen's College, Athabasca Hall, and President Tory's Ring House home would soon dot the vast acreage to form the start of the new campus.

St. Stephen's College[17]

ST. STEPHEN'S WAS BUILT IN 1910, but the basement was excavated four years earlier. The answer to this rather odd bit of trivia lies in the heated battle over the location of the prospective university. It is a convoluted story filled with political intrigue. In 1903, Methodists founded Alberta College North in Edmonton. By 1906, they were planning to build Alberta College South in Strathcona, on River Lot 5. Premier Rutherford, who had already earmarked River Lot 5 in Strathcona for the new university, knew that any building activity on this site gave Strathcona an edge over Calgary. And so St. Stephen's was given a grant of land with the agreement of the government and the university. In 1908, when the U of A opened, Alberta College affiliated with the new university and the "BD,"' or Bachelor of Divinity degree, was offered as a U of A degree until the Methodist Church transferred the program to St. Andrew's College in Saskatoon in 1925. At this point, the Methodists formed a union with Presbyterians and Congregationalists, and the United Church was born. Alberta College South was renamed St. Stephen's College.

It is true that many early students started their university careers here, at a time when Alberta College was affiliated with McGill. It is true that in 1912 the U of A Convocation was held at St. Stephen's. And it is a fact that thousands of students attended church services in its tiny chapel, still a gem on today's campus. But there is a closer connection between U of A students and St. Stephen's College.

St. Steve's—as thousands fondly call it—was an undergraduate residence, a place to call home for generations of U of A students until the 1970s. Some of the best memories centre on the two spiral fire escapes that were added to the stately building just after World War I, when St. Stephen's became a convalescent home. The idea was that in case of fire, one could load a patient into the spiral fire escape and the patient would swoosh down in gentle spiralling circles to ground level safety. Students, of course, put these fire escapes to other, more creative, uses, as did the children of the professors who lived in the campus Ring Houses.

St. Stephen's also has a fascinating historical link with former Premier William Aberhart. In the 1930s, Bible Bill lived in St. Stephen's while he made some extra money grading departmental exams. It was here that

Workmen on the steps of President Tory's house during construction of the Ring Houses. (Alumni Affairs)

a fellow teacher persuaded him to read a book about the social credit economic theories of Major Douglas. Aberhart's Social Credit party would rule Alberta from 1935 to 1971, when it was ousted by the Tories, led by Peter Lougheed (BA '51, LLB '52, LLD [Hon] '86).

Today, the stately St. Stephen's College is home to Alberta Culture's Historical Resources Division. After selling the building to the government, St. Steve's constructed a small new building right beside the old College. St. Steve's still owned the land directly behind them, where there is now a parking lot. It is *their* parking lot, and not the University's. The lot is run by a private company hired by St. Stephen's, and not by University Parking Services. And that is why your university permit has no force and effect in this particular lot.

The Ring Houses

THERE WAS NO PUBLIC TRANSPORTATION to the U of A in 1910, and Strathcona suffered an acute housing shortage. The situation was so bad that the Torys had decided to risk the raised eyebrows of Strathconians by living over the river in Edmonton, where decent housing was available. Tory dealt with the housing problem by having homes built for the first professors. The ten brick and wood houses on the edge of campus, just off Saskatchewan Drive, formed what was variously described as a loop, a horseshoe, or a ring. The latter term stuck, and the homes became known as the Ring Houses.

"Marsh" and his wife Annie lived in Ring House 1, while senior faculty and deans occupied the other nine homes. In 1959, the aging Ring House 1 became Pembina House, a residence for women students, and the new President, Walter Johns, moved into the campus home we know today as Alumni House. Today, Ring House 1 is home to the university's Museums and Collections Services. Two other Ring Houses also survive, and sit just off Saskatchewan Drive, near today's Faculty Club.

THE ARTS BUILDING [18]

WHEN THE U OF A MOVED into Athabasca Hall in 1911, there was just a clutch of buildings in the vicinity—St. Stephen's College, Ring House 1, three other faculty homes in the works, and the premier's new home. There *was* one other landmark. In the middle of campus, two small shacks flanked a huge hole that marred the campus for several years. From 1909 to 1915, the "abysmal hole," as the provost called it, collected water each spring. The students dubbed it the campus swimming pool. It was, in fact, the excavation for the Arts Building—a nightmare that seemingly would not be put to pasture.

Tory's vision for the first campus was simple. He envisioned a spacious building for classes, labs, the Library and administrative offices, and three residences. The "Main Teaching Building," today's Arts Building, would be built first. The sod-turning happened amidst great fanfare in September 1909: in an often-published photograph, Premier Rutherford works the plough while Board member W.D. Ferris holds the reins of a team of horses. The proposed date of completion was 1911, but the workmen got no further than digging a basement.

Tory's First Design and the Senate's Revision

PROVOST MACEACHRAN tells us that Tory was absolutely wedded to the concept of a "Collegiate Gothic" structure similar to today's St. Stephen's College. No one liked Tory's design, and the professors, in particular, thought it was awful. But Tory was used to having the final say, and so

Top: The original and controversial design for the Arts Building, 1909. *(UAA 86–109–3)*

Bottom: A student playing tennis on the site of the Arts building, 1912. (UAA 69–10–01)

there was a stand-off. In December 1909, the University hired the firm of Nobbs and Hyde to draft a campus plan. Tory and Dr. Nobbs corresponded regularly, and Nobbs advised Tory about the best designs for campus buildings. Presumably, Tory was persuaded to change his architectural vision of the Main Teaching Building, and the Senate approved a new design.

Suddenly, in 1910, Rutherford resigned as premier. The new government was less generous and stalled the financing of both Arts and Pembina Hall. In the same year, the *University Act* was changed, creating a Board of Governors that would be in charge of finance and management, while the Senate would be in charge of academic affairs. As soon as the new board was in place, they scrapped the existing plans for the Arts building and put forward a new design.

There was only one problem. The existing foundation had been poured using the Senate design and, quite literally, the board's new design did not match up. The new government reviewed the board's plan and decided it was too costly and assigned a fourth architect, Mr. Jeffers, to the project. To compound the confusion, a member of the board executive, Oliver Mowatt Biggar, travelled to Europe and the United States to look at campus buildings and corresponded directly with the architects in Montréal. Tory was also in direct correspondence with the architects.

The Foundation of the Arts Building is Blown Up

IN 1912, Dr. Nobbs and Mr. Frank Darling, architect for the University of Toronto, presented the Board of Governors with a comprehensive campus plan. A detailed correspondence ensued over the fate of the original foundation. Eventually, Nobbs recommended privately to Tory that he hire a resident architect, and suggested a man named Cecil Scott Burgess. Tory hired him, and Burgess arrived on the scene in March 1913 as resident architect and the U of A's first and only professor of Architecture.

Burgess looked at the latest plans for Arts and studied the existing foundation. On September 11, 1913 he wrote to Hobbs: "[Regarding the existing foundation, the concrete walls are too light] to retain the 9' depth of soil outside of them and already show signs of yielding at every part... must be rebuilt...." As the student yearbook so succinctly put it years

later, "the original foundations of the Arts building were blown up and larger ones laid."

There was a quiet, second sod-turning in 1913 for the new version of the Arts Building.

Oliver Biggar worked directly with the Montréal architects on redesigning the building. Provost MacEachran credits Biggar with overruling Tory on the final design and giving us today's elegant Arts Building. But the nightmare was not quite over yet. Just as the Arts Building neared completion, with only the roof left to finish, the money ran out. World War I had begun and the economy was in a steep dive. The government and the banks turned down Tory's plea for additional funds to complete the Arts Building, so Tory travelled to New York City to meet directly with the contractors. Tory's persuasive powers worked some magic once again, and the contractors agreed to finish the Arts Building and be paid later.

The opening of the Arts Building in 1915 was a spectacular event. Eleven honorary degrees were conferred, including five to senior clergy. Luminaries from all levels of government attended. In fact, the program was so long that, as the event grew longer and longer, the last three speeches were quietly cancelled.

Reg Lister, 1914. (UAA 81–145–10)

A GUIDED TOUR OF CAMPUS WITH REG LISTER [19]

REG LISTER belonged to the U of A campus while it was still little more than a dream. He came to Canada from England as a 19-year-old in 1910, and started work the following year on a densely wooded dairy farm that would soon become the University of Alberta. For 25 cents an hour, he helped to dig the basement for President Tory's home. In his 45 years at the U of A, Reg Lister came to know every corner of campus, every underground tunnel and, as the first superintendent of residences, every student who lived on campus. For almost half a century, Reg Lister acted as "guide, counselor and friend" to students. As the undergraduate chairman of the 1949 Men's House Committee put it, "Reg Lister taught the students some of the most important things they had learned at the University, in particular, how to live together."

In 1958, when the University turned 50, Reg Lister retired. The senior students who were about to graduate inducted Reg Lister into their class, and the Alumni Association made him an honorary life member. The University itself conferred upon Reg Lister the unique honour of making him an Honorary Member of Convocation. Six years after his retirement, when the first phase of a new residence complex opened, it was named in Reg's honour—Lister Hall.

To mark both Reg's retirement and the University's 50th birthday, ex-Pembinite and renowned playwright Elsie Park Gowan sat down with Reg Lister and helped him write his memoirs. Reg told stories about campus life, outlined the physical development of the early campus, and described some of the best pranks ever pulled off by students. No one could summarize his time at the U of A better than he did himself:

> During my forty-five years in residence, I had done almost every-
> thing...undressing students and putting them to bed (when they
> had mumps), as well as dressing some (when they'd had too much
> to drink the night before and needed to get to class the next day).
> I've reported some to the Provost or other University Officials, as
> well as shielding some when it seemed necessary. I have always
> tried to be fair to the students and the University.... And I've enjoyed
> some of the parties—not all of them. I've helped some students with
> their tricks and condemned others. I've always tried to make the
> students' time in residence as pleasant as possible. Some of them
> have grown from boys to men and I've watched how they developed
> over the years. It has been a very interesting life.

There could be no better tour guide of the early campus than Reg Lister.

1910—"Number 1"

THE YOUNG MAN who dug the foundation for the university president's home was a keen, but gentle, observer of human nature. He describes

President Tory as both a micromanager and a humble and caring human being:

> Dr. Tory used to drive around every day with his chestnuts and tie them up almost any place in the bush, and then inspect the work," says Reg. "He always wore a frock coat and striped trousers. He would often stop and chat with the workmen. And he was delighted to see a good bonfire; he told me it reminded him of his younger days in Nova Scotia when he used to gather driftwood and have a fire on the beach.

There was, of course, a barn being built behind the house for Tory's horses, Jack and Molly.

1911—The Gas House

IN 1911, coal was king and fortunes were made on it. It was the fuel of the day—there was no natural gas used until 1924. So in the fall of 1911, the firm of Mansfield and Sons of Liverpool, England, built a Gas House right behind Athabasca. Here, Reg explains, coal oil was turned into gas for use in the labs and kitchen. The Gas House later became home to the Horticulture Department. Reg also remembers the first deaths during the heyday of construction: "Two of the bricklayers who built the gas house were afterwards killed while working on the Arts Building. A scaffold broke and they fell to the ground."

1912—Assiniboia

IN AN AUTOBIOGRAPHY he started but never finished, Henry Marshall Tory wrote that "it was decided...in naming [the residences] to adopt the names current in the country inherited from the old Indian population. These three residential buildings are now known as Athabasca Hall, Assiniboia Hall and Pembina Hall."[20]

Since the Arts Building project was at a standstill, Athabasca Hall, the first of these three buildings to be completed, was packed to the rafters with people. Construction of the second building could not be delayed and so, in the fall of 1911, "about one hundred men with shovels and a few horses and wagons" began excavating the basement of the second building, Assiniboia Hall. This basement would be the first home of Extension, with early graduate Albert "Tiny" Ottewell as Director.

There was an intense winter building schedule, and so brush fires burned all winter to heat the cement used for Assiniboia's foundation. In March 1912, stonemasons cut the stone for Assiniboia by hand. "The granite base was laid in April," lectures started September 27, "and the building," says Reg, "was finished by October."

Everyone except the student residents moved out of Athabasca and into Assiniboia. President Tory's office was on the centre floor, on the south side, and the Registrar's office was on the opposite end of the floor. Assiniboia had "suites for Professors Sonet...and Sheldon...and for Mr. Burrows, the...Librarian. The Wauneita Society also started in Assiniboia, and its first lounge was in the basement, Rooms 26 and 24. Student residence rooms were on the second and third floors of the north wing."

1913—A Dining Room and Gym for Athabasca

IN HIS 1912 REPORT to the Board of Governors, Tory sounded the alarm bell: the U of A needed more space. There were students sitting on the floor in some classes, a dining room was "an absolute necessity," and students needed a place where they could "exercise...in the cold weather."

During the summer of 1912, Reg helped build a dining room and gym off the back of Athabasca. The Athabasca dining hall/gym opened in 1913, and immediately there were dances, plays, skits, and games. Students were hungry for a place to get together informally after three years of struggling in cramped rented quarters in Strathcona. Dancing was the rage and, according to one professor, the students danced "endlessly." But it was not only about creating opportunities for indoor exercise. In 1913, Professor Muir Edwards staked out a football grid and the rugby games that had been played on the open fields in Strathcona near the CPR station now moved to the new campus.

The dining room ceiling was made of oak panels that were sawn in the carpenter's shop that was set up just behind Athabasca. The oak floor was "laid and scraped in one day by twenty carpenters." Each dining room table sat 12, and in order to set an example of good manners for some of the "countrified" students, senior students sat at the head and the foot of each table. Faculty members were present at meal times, the University Grace was said, and boisterous behaviour frowned on. The first meal? One student clipped a newspaper article about it—it was roast beef. But it took a while before dinner was served: First the chancellor gave a speech; then the premier and the minister of education; and finally Dr. Tory.

The campus was growing rapidly, but it was still crowded and the buildings served multiple purposes. All exams, including professional exams, were held in the Athabasca gym. Reg Lister recalls that "Miss Ruby Clements, the first woman lawyer in Alberta," wrote her examinations there.

Nearly every campus activity centred on the two new buildings and the first rugby field. Athabasca Hall was full of life. One night, while refereeing a boxing match, Dr. Broadus fell and broke his arm. Every Sunday, there were church services led by Dr. Tory, and there were constant high-jinks and pranks.

1913—The First Smokestack, Power Plant, and Barn

A SMOKESTACK was constructed behind Athabasca, and also a power plant, with a steam engineer and a crew of two "firemen" to keep it all going. Reg remembers that "the Agriculture Department's first barn was built in 1913" on the location where Reg's Ring House 11 residence was built in 1930, right behind Athabasca Hall. "The livestock at this time consisted of five dairy cows and four horses. The milk was used in the dining hall and the horses were used on the farm in the summer; in the winter they hauled coal for the power house."

The Campus is "Levelled"

BEFORE 1914, says Reg, "the campus was just a big field and not at all level. The land was high where the new administration building stands and was very low at the north end of Assiniboia Hall. In 1914 leveling began, using man and mule-power, a big leveling machine with twelve mules pulling and six mules pushing. You could hear the mule skinners swearing all over campus....An open-air shooting range for COTC [Canadian Officers Training Corps] was where the Works Department now stands."

Reg even remembers when the first trees were planted: "The maple trees around the residences arrived in 1912. They were about as thick as match-sticks, wrapped up in burlap. A furrow was ploughed behind the buildings and we stuck the seedlings in and ploughed the sod back on them. They were planted out in 1915." In 1914, "The first elms were planted by Professor Harcourt when they were about 3 feet high. They are now (1958) higher than the buildings. They were planted after the grounds were terraced and the sidewalks put in, about 1914."

Cecil Scott Burgess.
(UAA 71–213–266)

Pembina Hall—1913–2006

THE THIRD PROPOSED RESIDENCE, Pembina Hall, opened in 1914 and remained a hub of student activity and residence life through to 2004. Pembina's halls are filled with stories—that its foundation almost caved in; that the building is haunted; that the tunnel in the basement was the focal point of a great prank; or that Pembina was slated for demolition in the 1970s. Visitors may wonder why there is a propeller in the lounge, or a spacious suite amidst much smaller residence rooms. Most passers-by have no idea what the meaning is of the foreign words carved into stone on the outside the building.

Pembina Hall was designed by the new Professor of Architecture, Cecil Burgess and his version of how the residence got its name differs somewhat from the version given by Tory. Burgess was a kind and rather shy person, but he had an adventurous spirit. Widely travelled, he had discovered skiing during his days in India and he brought this curious novelty with him to Edmonton. Burgess arrived on March 15, 1913 and "set about designing Pembina Hall at once, and six houses on the loop—the Ring Houses." [21]

Burgess made sure Pembina Hall was solidly built. His first concern was the foundation. The massive piles of sand left over from the excavation had led to rumours that Pembina was sinking. To allay any fears that this might be true, Burgess called in two U of A professors, an Engineer and a Geologist, to check that the foundation was safe. They decided to remove all the sand, exposing a solid layer of clay underneath, which suggested that the rumours were unfounded and the foundation would be stable. For good measure, though, Burgess had engineer Muir Edwards

Painters and builders on steps
of Pembina, 1912. (UAA 69-12-229)

take measurements of the entire foundation as the building proceeded, and "he found not ⅛th inch difference."

Burgess saw to it that, unlike Athabasca and Assiniboia, Pembina was constructed with a steel and concrete frame—a first on campus. Burgess also made sure that Pembina incorporated the latest in fire safety, and in 1969, at age 99, he asked an interviewer how well his specially designed fire doors had stood the test of time.

When it came to the choice of building materials, it turned out that the Board of Governors was keen to use local stone. So Tory, Burgess, the board chair, and several board members headed out to Entwistle for a picnic to check out the stone on the Pembina River. Burgess decided that the stone was not suitable, but he had been "casually labeling 'Pembina stone'" on the plans, and the name stuck.

Pembina was planned as a women's residence and would be home to the Wauneita Society, the club to which all women students belonged.

Their motto, selected in 1910, was "Each for All, and All for Each." The Wauneita Society drew its initiation rites and value-set from what the women understood of Cree culture. Fellow student Roy Mitchell translated the motto into Cree, and the Cree inscription was carved in stone above the north and south entrance doors to Pembina—one half of the motto appears above each door.

But Pembina would not be a women's residence until 1919. Financial problems in 1913 slowed construction and as the building finally took shape there was another space crunch on campus. Professors, students, and administrators were moving in to Pembina even before the building was finished. Nurses took over the south wing, and there were medical labs and classrooms in another wing. There was also an anatomy lab, which provided one source for the rumour that Pembina is haunted.

Then came the First World War. Enrolment plummeted as students and staff headed off to the front. President Tory reported to the board that Pembina would probably close unless the military used the building. Assiniboia had already been rented to the Red Deer Ladies College, and Pembina served as a military billet during part of the war.

In 1916, part of Pembina was used as a men's residence, and initiation there was rough and raucous. "One night," says Reg Lister, "they pulled the large marble slabs down and smashed them to pieces. They had to pay for the damage and it cost them plenty, so they were quiet for a while."

In 1918, as the war was ending, a flu epidemic hit. Pembina was converted into a municipal hospital, and at least 72 people died there—one source of the rumour that Pembina residents shared their home with ghosts. One of the ghosts is said to be a young nurse who died during the epidemic. She haunts the halls looking for her husband or boyfriend, who also died during the epidemic.

In 1919, the women finally moved in, and Pembina was the girls' residence for some 22 years, with Classics professor Geneva Misener as the first live-in warden. Dr. Misener was followed by the indomitable, the revered, and the sometimes-feared Miss Florence Dodd, who occupied a spacious suite. Miss Dodd knew all her residents by name and was strict about behaviour and curfew. As one male student put it, "We never wanted to find out what would happen to us if we brought a girl home late. No one crossed her."

There is a story told about Miss Dodd and the boys who lived next door in Athabasca. The Pembina girls were hosting their annual dance, the "Pembina Prance." Only the girls and their male guests made it through Pembina's front door to the dance floor. But the boys next door knew about the service tunnel that connects Athabasca and Pembina. They headed down to the basement, flipped the main switch, and made use of the temporary blackout to invade the dance floor. Amidst all the confusion, someone handed Miss Dodd a candle so she could see in the dark. But Miss Dodd could only see as far as the soft glow of the candle would allow. The invaders from Athabasca, of course, made sure they stayed well beyond Miss Dodd's little circle of light, and apparently a fine time was had by all.

During World War II Pembina was taken over by the RCAF Initial Training School Number 4, or the ITS for short. When the military left Pembina in 1945, Group Captain J. Hutchinson presented the residence with an airplane propeller that still hangs in the front lounge. "The propeller," *Folio* once reported, "was said to have been taken from the first airplane to cross the hump to China."

In 1969, Athabasca, Assiniboia and Pembina were slated for demolition, "to make way for an apartment complex for graduate students."[22] It was a happy day for many when the Board reversed its decision. All three buildings, the original residences, were eventually renovated. Athabasca and Assiniboia were completely gutted, leaving only the original brick and sandstone shells. Pembina had a different fate. Since Burgess built Pembina with a "concrete frame," much of its interior remained and is vintage 1914. Pembina was condemned in 1974, but a protest saved it and instead the building was renovated and re-opened in November 1975 as a mature students' residence. In 2003 it became a residence for the graduate students. In 2005–2006 Pembina Hall was converted to academic office space.

THE NEW PROFESSORS, 1909–1913

SEVERAL NEW PROFESSORS and lecturers joined the ranks between 1909 and 1913, all recruited by Tory. One of the new recruits was a native of France, Edouard Sonet, whose vibrant memoir crackles with accounts of professorial high-jinks.

Edouard Sonet—A Zest for Life[23]

Edouard Sonet. (UAA 69-90-230)

SONET IMMIGRATED TO CANADA in 1910 after serving in Africa with the Zouaves, "that notable regiment which had come to the rescue of the British in the Crimean War." He worked as a farm labourer in Alberta for a year before looking for work as a French teacher. In 1911, he breezed into Old Scona, bounded up three flights of stairs to Tory's office, and was hired by Tory. Sonet joined the ranks of another dozen or so university staff. "We were young," he says of the new teachers; "Alexander and Broadus were 30. We were 20."

Sonet remembers that "when the unmarried professors lived in Assiniboia, every night between 7 and 8 P.M. there was bedlam. Dr. Burt, the new history teacher, had a piano in his room and he banged on it, the perspiration running down his face. Dr. Rob Gordon, the new English teacher, was studying Latin, and just rolling out the Latin. There was a sentimental German, Von Zabhensing—he was there for a year. He would recite poetry, striking his breast and throwing himself flat on his face. Rob was playing his flute and over all, the voice of Killam dominated, saying he was the only good man in his family. And I? Yes, I was scraping on my violin. I saw it in a shop window on Craig Street in Montréal, marked 'Stradivarius $5.' I bought it! But after 8 o'clock we all went to work, and we worked very hard."

Edouard Sonet, known for his zest and wit, was "a brilliant and inspiring teacher, one of the most entertaining members of the faculty...." When Sonet left to teach in California in 1947, *The Gateway* "lamented that the University is losing one of its most versatile and aggressive professors to the United States." One of Sonet's former students says that "Sonet was the professor who always made us think."

Douglas Killam—Legendary Comic

DOUG KILLAM, a Math professor under Dr. Sheldon, was another new faculty member. Killam was "legendary" among his young colleagues for his zany sense of humour. "Where Killam was, there was always fun," says Sonet, reflecting on how one night Killam dressed himself as a woman of the street, in rags, bundled up a large doll and cradled it in his arms, placed his hands "palm to palm," and walked over to the house of his boss, Dr. Sheldon. When the door opened, Killam flung himself on the startled Sheldon, crying, "You are the father of my child!"

Then there was the time Killam went hunting. "I will tell you about the time Killam shot the partridge," Sonet says. "Although he was not a very good shot, he was going shooting at 5 o'clock in the morning and he saw a partridge sitting on the President's gate. He looked at the partridge and he thought he should not shoot it off the President's gate, but then he raised his gun. He was so close, the partridge disappeared, but the President looked out of the window. 'Killam!' said Tory. 'Next time you shoot a partridge on my gate, wait until 7 o'clock!'"

Douglas Killam. (UAA 69–95–17)

228 Litres of Wine Delivered in the Dark of Night

KILLAM'S PARTRIDGE EPISODE offered Sonet a segue into his own little encounter with Tory. Sometime in 1913, Sonet and his lifelong friend, Robert Boyle, decided to smuggle some wine onto a campus where none was allowed. Most of the professors in the Ring Houses were in on the caper. It was essential to have Dr. Kerr on side since his home had large basement windows. It was also essential that Tory, a former Methodist minister who did not approve of drinking, not know about the plan. But allow Edouard Sonet to describe the ensuing events himself: "I am accustomed to drinking wine," he wrote, "and I had ordered from France a barrel of 228 litres, a grand barrique, and also some wine bottles. I asked them to deliver the barrel at night, for the President might disapprove. It was to be stored in Dr. Kerr's basement, and we were all there to lower the barrel into the basement by a rope when the President saw the lights and came over to see what we were doing."

They were caught in the act. At first no one spoke. Then Sonet looked Tory square in the eye and said, "This is my wine. I am accustomed to having wine." Tory was outnumbered five to one. And he was also a good sport. So Tory "took an end of the rope" and helped Sonet, Boyle, Killam and MacEachran lower the huge barrel of wine into Dr. Kerr's basement. Afterwards, in Kerr's basement, Sonet filled individual bottles with the wine from the grand barrique, and Boyle put on the tops. And then Sonet said to Boyle, "I will give four bottles to Dr. Tory." Boyle advised strongly against this, but Sonet balanced four bottles in his arms and walked over to the Tory's home. When Mrs. Tory came to the door, he announced to her, "I have brought you some wine."

"Mrs. Tory said, 'Thank you very much, but we do not drink wine.' I told her then, 'It is very good if you have a cold,' and she said, 'In that case, thank you very much for the wine,' and Mrs. Tory accepted the four bottles." And so every Ring House home on the horseshoe was stocked with French wine.

Who *were* these late-night wine merchants? Dr. Kerr, whose basement became the storage place for the barrique of wine, would later become the first dean of Arts and Science, and then president of the University. Dr. Boyle would soon be named as the first dean of Engineering. Dr. MacEachran, already in charge of discipline in the residence, would soon be the provost, responsible for enforcing discipline across the campus. As for Doug Killam, the resident comic, he served with distinction in World War I, but on a trip back to his native Nova Scotia shortly after demobilization, he drowned in a tragic accident. It was a sad end to a vibrant life.

INITIATION, HIGH-JINKS, AND THE HIGH LEVEL BRIDGE

BY SEPTEMBER 1912, with the 1908 pioneer class soon to graduate, a new group was taking over. The Freshman Reception in 1912 was a far cry from the uncomfortable 1908 masquerade, that informal function where students and professors first met each other. By 1912, the Freshman Reception went on into the wee hours, with a special trolley leaving campus at 1:15 A.M. to take off-campus guests home. And there was lots of dancing—waltzes, two-steps, three-steps, and one French minuet. Students were dancing out the north door of the Athabasca dining room, taking a spin in the foyer, and whirling back in through the south door.[24]

There was something else afoot to welcome freshmen. A campus-wide initiation, never formally sanctioned by the University, had quickly become a tradition, and it would become an increasingly rigorous event. Initiation had nothing at all to do with fraternities, which were not allowed on campus at the time. Initiation had become the sophomores' way of welcoming the "Freshies." One example of the welcome? One end of a wooden chute (think splinters) was secured to the lower window of a

ession of Supreme Court

The Bath

Procession on it's way to North S...

A selection of photographs depicting initiation ceremonies during the early years on campus. Outrageous clothing, a parade over the High Level Bridge, a "tubbing" or "bath," and a mock trial based on trumped-up offences all formed part of the freshman initiation rituals. (UAA 86-41-6-6-62-64)

room in Athabasca, while the other end catapulted the nervous Freshies into a horse trough filled with cold water. Of course, the water might have other "things" added to it. One by one, every fledgling undergraduate was popped into the chute and sent hurtling down into the horse trough. Everyone turned out to watch, with the professors peeking around the corners of Athabasca to see how the ride went.

The students took advantage of every opportunity or new development to break the tedium of their academic pursuits. Take that one-of-a-kind marvel, the High Level Bridge, for instance. One condition of the 1912 amalgamation of Edmonton and Strathcona was construction of a new bridge, and after three years of work and the loss of three lives, the High Level opened in 1913. The first passenger train to travel between north and south Edmonton—Edmonton and Strathcona—left the Strathcona station at 11 A.M. on June 2. There was a dual streetcar track on the top deck as well, and the lower deck was reserved for cars, with sidewalks for pedestrians. But only a student could recognize the true potential of the new bridge, and it was not long before the High Level became an integral part of high-jinks and pranks. In 1913, as part of initiation, students took down the barriers blocking the bridge and were the first people to use it. They were led by a *Gateway* staffer named Sandy Carmichael, who rode across the bridge on a donkey. Reg Lister reports that in later years, a student drove a car across the top of the bridge—no mean feat given the trolley and train tracks that traversed the surface. Students hung "bodies" from the girders and in winter hitched their toboggans to the back of the streetcars, trailing along at high speeds, a risky venture given that the High Level Bridge had no railings.

THE 1912 GRADUATION CEREMONY [25]

IN THE SPRING OF 1912, the first students who had entered in 1908 were ready for graduation. This was the group that had started together at the Duggan Street School the first day the U of A opened its doors. They spent nearly three years together at Old Scona, and their last year was on the one-building U of A campus, with Athabasca Hall as the centre of activity. Agnes Wilson, who convocated in 1912, described the week's graduation activities to Ruth Bowen in 1969:

Of the 45 who entered the University of Alberta in September day in 1908, 18 graduated in 1912. Four of the 18 were born outside Canada—one each from Scotland, England, the United States and Bohemia.... I was the only graduate born in Edmonton, or South Edmonton as it was known then. We had started with four professors and the President in 1908 and a student body of 45. After four years, by the time of our graduation, there were in excess of 180 students and 15 professors. By today's standards—1969—these were indeed small beginnings. The last memorable week began May 9, which marked Founder's Day, with a tree planting and pilgrimage.

The students visited all the buildings that held memories for them, and Ethel Anderson remembers that their pilgrimage even included the Gas House, one of the few structures on campus in 1912. Their walk concluded with tea at Dr. and Mrs. Rutherford's residence. The *Bulletin* reported that the graduates were "royally treated." Agnes, the premier, and class president Edwin Mitchell each made a speech.

The graduation ceremony was held on May 10 at St. Stephen's College. Libby Lloyd prepared a class history and Lawrence "Yucalyptus" Cairns read a poem that captured the essence of each of his classmates in rhymed couplets. The entire class spent the rest of the day at the Rutherford home.

"May 11," remembers Agnes, "was marked by a picnic; May 12, Sunday, included the baccalaureate service at the Methodist church, with Dr. Tory as the speaker, and Class '12 paraded to the church from our former quarters at Strathcona Collegiate Institute (Old Scona)." On May 13 there was a class dinner and theatre party. On May 14, the graduates held an "At Home" in Alberta College and entertained their well-wishers. Then they set off into the real world.

THE DEPARTMENT OF EXTENSION IS BORN [26]

After his 1912 Convocation, Al Ottewell decided to stay on at the University of Alberta for a graduate degree, and President Tory approached him to be the first director of Extension. Tory and the early professors had given lectures in rural areas since 1908, but by 1912 an administrative infrastructure was put in place to carry elements of the University's liberal arts curriculum to the far corners of Alberta. Tory and Ottewell, the two men who had set out earlier in their lives to be Methodist ministers, were now involved in an enterprise that would bring the University to the people.

"Contacts with the outlying areas were established and maintained by means of lectures, traveling libraries, lantern slides, moving picture films and the like," said Ottewell. There was a lending library, and books were packaged and mailed all over the province, bringing "pleasure and sustenance to thousands of people through the long, isolating winter." Extension activities in 1913–1914 touched an estimated 25,000 Albertans.

A program of high school debates was set up, with subjects pre-selected and materials for study prepared. Fifty travelling libraries serviced 44 communities and, beginning in 1913, there was a weekly press bulletin. But best of all, Al Ottewell, "a man of warm geniality, full of common sense, kindness and humour," was out there himself meeting people, talking about the University, showing slides, and giving talks. He told stories and had dozens of songs at the ready to break the ice and get an audience warmed up. For many years a one-man department, Al Ottewell travelled to every corner of the province. The "young giant" went out in all weather, by buggy, by rail, and by Model T, bringing the University to Albertans.

FOUR SHORT YEARS BEFORE THE GREAT WAR— 1910–1913

THE FOUR YEARS BEFORE the Great War were a near-perfect time for U of A students. Spirits ran high for undergraduates. For the administration, there were some terrible financial worries, especially when Rutherford resigned and a new premier and cabinet took over. But overall it was a time of growth, consolidation, and fun. Athabasca and Assiniboia were built, and the basement for Pembina Hall was excavated. Enrolment leaped from 45 in 1908 to 434 in 1913, putting administrators and staff into a controlled frenzy about how to cope without sufficient resources, residences, or classrooms. Worse yet was the new reality in 1913 that the President and 11 faculty didn't have a hope of knowing all 434 students personally. Just four years before, with only 45 students and six staff, everyone knew each other's name, hometown, and life story. There were also now several hundred graduates, and *The Gateway* launched an "alumni news" column in the fall of 1913 in an attempt to keep track of everyone.

Times had changed. And times would soon change again. The world was about to go to war.

FACULTY OF ENGINEERING

E6-050 ETLC, University of Alberta, Edmonton, AB Canada T6G 2V4
Phone: **780.492.3320** | Fax: **780.492.0500** | **1.800.407.8354**

www.engineering.ualberta.ca

They went with songs to the battle, they were young,
Straight of limb, true of eye, steady and aglow.
They were staunch to the end against odds uncounted,
They fell with their faces to the foe.

—Laurence Robert Binyon
For the Fallen (September 21, 1914)

U. BUCHANAN
TRAINER

GORDON MCGUIRE
ASSISTANT COACH

L.S. MACDONALD
OUTSIDE WING

C. RILEY
CENTER SCRIMMAGE

C. LARSON
RIGHT SCRIMMAGE

H. TRELLE
INSIDE WING

H. BEECROFT
HALF BACK

T. WILSON
FULL BACK

UNIVERSITY of ALBERTA
· RUGBY TEAM ·
PROVINCIAL CHAMPIONS
EDMONTON ◇ ALBERTA

1914

BUCK
MIDDLE WING

F. PARSON
CAPTAIN & QUARTERBACK

E.G. ANGUS
MANAGER & MIDDLE WING

G. PARR
MIDDLE WING

R. FITZGERALD
INSIDE WING

F. PERRATO
HALF BACK

Timeline

Enrolment and Finance, 1914–1919

- 438 students, alumni, and staff served in World War I
- Fall student head count: 443 (1914); 1,103 (1919)
- Operating budget from the Province of Alberta: $34,000.00 (1914); $482,693.75 (1919)
- Full-load undergraduate Arts tuition: $20.00 (1914); $20.00 (1919)
- SU membership fee: $5.00 (1914); $6.00 (1919)

Key Dates, 1914–1915

- In 1914, the Department of Pharmacy begins instruction within the Faculty of Medicine; becomes a School in 1917
- Faculty of Agriculture founded, with Dr. Howes as dean (1915)
- Committee on graduate studies set up (1915)

1916–1918

- School of Accountancy established (1916)
- "Owing to war conditions no calendar was issued for the year 1917–18"
- Department of Dentistry established within the Faculty of Medicine (1917)
- Department of Household Economics organized under the Faculty of Arts and Science (1918)
- A directress of physical education for women appointed (1918)
- The first nursing program offered (1918)

1919

- $3 SU fee for medical services is approved
- Major curriculum revisions allow more freedom to select courses
- The University acquires 600 acres for the study of animal husbandry near today's Corbett Hall
- Under President Tory's leadership, the Scientific Association of the University of Alberta (later named the Research Council of Alberta) is formed

Selected Campus Buildings, 1914–1919

- Pembina Hall opens (1914)
- Strathcona Hospital built by the City on a site donated by the University (1914)
- South Lab built (1914); North Lab follows (1919)
- Arts Building opens (1915)
- A "handsomely turfed" athletic field with a quarter-mile cinder track is built (1915)

Beyond Campus, 1914–1919

- A numbering system is adopted to identify Edmonton streets (1914)
- Elmer Rice writes *On Trial* and U of A students mount his avante garde works in the Inter-Year Play Competition (1914)
- Fort Edmonton demolished; Hotel Macdonald built (1915)
- In the USA, Margaret Sanger is jailed for advocating birth control; one year after her release, she opens the first birth control clinic (1916)
- Women in Alberta win the right to vote (1916)
- Prohibition enacted in Canada (1916)
- Women in Edmonton allowed to take evening classes in Edmonton public schools (1917)
- Katherine Stinson delivers the first airmail letters from Calgary to Edmonton (1918)
- The Spanish flu kills hundreds in Edmonton (1918–1920)
- The Prince of Wales tours Canada and the USA (1919)
- Only Jasper Avenue, 101 Street, and nearby side streets are paved (1919)
- First transcontinental telephone call (1919)
- Babe Ruth hits a 587-ft home run (1919)

WORLD WAR I—A CANADIAN IDENTITY

AFTER THE BATTLE at the Somme in 1916, it was reported that 20,000 *British* troops, including Canadians, had died on the first day of the battle, July 1.

After the battle at Vimy Ridge in 1917, it was reported that 3,598 *Canadians* died, and that 7,004 *Canadians* were wounded.

Canadian troops entered the war as part of the British forces, but emerged as Canadians. "Immigrants became Canadians in battle," says war historian Jack Granatstein, for they were "convinced that their corps, their nation-in-formation, was something special."[1] It was a brutal way to forge a national identity.

The Somme and Vimy Ridge were but two battles in this grim, bloody war. "How grim no one guessed," said Dr. Will Alexander, beloved U of A professor and co-publisher, with Muir Edwards, of a monthly newsletter that went overseas to the U of A troops[2] who fought at the front lines of the Western Front, in the trenches and from rough dug-outs, with ammunition transported to artillery locations by mule.[3]

Hip waders and gum boots were standard issue for negotiating the thick mud that filled the 8-ft deep trenches.[4] The men carefully ran their lighters up and down the seams of their clothing to kill the thousands of lice multiplying in their uniforms. At night, the rats gnawed their way into the soldiers' sleeping bags to share the warmth and look for a meal. Some days were simply boring, with little to do but await battle orders. On other days, the air was suddenly filled with the sound of shells and mortars lobbed by hand or shot by gun from the opposing German trenches that were just yards away. Soldiers nicknamed the various deadly parcels Moaning Minnies, whiz bangs, rum jars, "piss-tins," and coal boxes. Some of the shells and mortars contained phosgene or chlorine gas that exploded in poisonous yellow clouds. Some were filled with shrapnel that ripped through the air after impact. The Moaning Minnies, with their 200-lb payload, were slow but deadly. They exploded with tremendous force, leaving 10-ft craters in their wake and causing permanent deafness in many of those who survived. The whiz bangs, in contrast, were small and swift. One moment you could the hear the "whiz" as the shell was fired and in the blink of an eye came the "bang" when the shell found its target.

The boys in Montréal in their full uniform, 1915. Among them are Don Edwards (whose son James would later become Board Chair) and Francis Galbraith, a future Chancellor. Front row, left to right: F. Philip Galbraith, Harvey Beecroft, G. Stanley Fife, Robert M. Martin, A. Earl F. Robinson, F. Reg Henry. Centre row, left to right: Salteau, E.C. Peters, Earl German, J.B. McCubbin, Larry H. Crawford. Back row, left to right: Donald S. Edwards, A. Hutchinson. (UAA 71–197)

Many U of A students, faculty and staff took part in these battles. Gordon Stanley Fife, lecturer in History and English, was one of the first to head overseas. L.Y. Cairns, the class humorist who was part of the 1908 freshman class, finished his law degree and enlisted the day after he was admitted to the bar. Fife was killed in 1916 at the battle of Sanctuary Wood. Cairns, a future U of A Chancellor, was gassed during the war, but made it home. Fife's name is inscribed on a memorial plaque on the first floor of the old Arts Building. A portrait of Cairns hangs directly upstairs, on the second floor. Another portrait—a stunning work by Grandmaison—hangs in the Law Centre.

U OF A RECRUITS—REG LISTER, HEBER MOSHIER, AND THE RUGBY TEAM

Reg Lister[5]

FORTY YEARS BEFORE the U of A residence complex was named after him, Reg Lister fought at the Somme and at Vimy Ridge. When Britain entered the war, Reg itched to get to the front. Canada had no legislated draft yet, and it was up to each individual to decide whether or not to head to the battlefields of Europe. For Reg, there wasn't a moment of indecision. He immediately joined the 101st battalion, under the command of

Professor Muir Edwards's father. But when there was a delay in calling up the 101st for service, Reg looked for another way to join the troops overseas.

Heber Moshier, MD

HEBER MOSHIER was Reg's entrée to the front lines. A University of Alberta physician and Physiology professor, Moshier had aced medical school in the East, graduating at age 20. He was also one of the few professors on campus with military training. When war broke out, Major Moshier organized a field ambulance unit, and nearly the entire medical class of 1914 joined. In an instant, virtually the whole class was transformed from first- and second-year students to members of the XI Field Ambulance, a key part of the Canadian Medical Corps.

Reg knew these young medical students well since most lived in residence. They would soon be at the front, and Reg was determined to go with them. But Dr. Moshier balked, wanting only medical students in this elite ambulance corps. Reg was persistent, making a case for his inclusion in the unit at every turn, and he finally won the day.

Next, however, came a bigger stumbling block. The University of Alberta didn't want Reg to leave for war. He was too valuable at home. The University's tactic was to have Moshier deliver a "written discharge" to Reg. But for Reg there was absolutely no question about heading immediately to the front. He was English-born, and his sweetheart was in the line of fire across the sea. Come hell or high water, he was going to fight, so he joined Heber Moshier's medical unit as the batman.

Students in 1914 knew their Latin and Greek, and could tell you that the term "batman" derived from the Greek verb, "to carry." A batman was the carrier, the orderly, the right-hand man. Reg would be as indispensable in war as he was in the Athabasca and Assiniboia residences.

In his memoirs, Reg recounts many light-hearted tales about life as a soldier. In one story, the boys were up at the Vimy front and there was to be a change of command. They planned a big party to say farewell to one particular colonel and to welcome another. The liquor for the send-off was stored underneath the bed of a Captain Turnbull. By morning's light, however, every bottle had disappeared. The entire unit was turned inside out looking for the booty, and then, Reg says, "everyone was lined up and searched and even breaths smelled!" It wasn't until after the war that Reg discovered the truth. "Some of our U of A students had stolen the liquor while the Captain slept, and had sunk it in a small river at the back of the camp, suspending the bottles by strings round the necks and for months they would go and bring in a bottle or two and have a party."

Reg told many such humorous stories about his war-time service, but he never wrote a word of the horrors he saw.

Others, however, did. George Coppard, who, like Reg and Heber, fought at the Battle of the Somme, wrote about storming the opposing German trenches, which were protected by huge rolls of wire studded with five-inch barbs:

The next morning [July 2] we gunners surveyed the dreadful scene in front of us....It became clear that the Germans always had a commanding view of No Man's land. [The British] attack had been brutally repulsed. Hundreds of dead were strung out like wreckage washed up to a high water-mark. Quite as many died on the enemy wire as on the ground, like fish caught in the net. They hung there in grotesque postures. Some looked as if they were praying; they had died on their knees and the wire had prevented their fall. Machine gun fire had done its terrible work.[6]

Heber Moshier and Reg Lister survived the Somme. One of their next engagements was at Arras, where Heber was killed in action in 1918. Reg and the rest of the medical class went on to fight at Vimy Ridge. They all made it back.[7]

The Rugby Team

IN 1914, the U of A won the provincial rugby championship. There are 24 strapping young men in the victory picture. One of their coaches, Doc Alik, described them as "a perfect aggregation, that team, perfectly balanced and endowed about equally with brains and brawn."[8]

Al "Tiny" Ottewell, all 290 lbs of him, was now a graduate student and the chief steamroller on the rugby scrimmage line. After the scrimmage came the clean-up crew, the light and fleet players like Ernie Parsons and Arthur Deitz. The U of A team beat their nemesis, the Edmonton

The 1914 rugby team that won the provincial Championship. Within two years, most of the team members would be dead on the battlefields of France and Belgium. (UAA 69–114–1)

Eskimos, and then came the coup when they beat the Calgary Tigers to win the provincial crown.

A year later most of the team was at the front and by 1917 most of them were dead, including undergraduates Ernie Parsons and Arthur Deitz.[9] Al Ottewell was not able to enlist in active service because of his defective eyesight and instead joined the Foresters Battalion.

CHARLES F. REILLY (BSC '20)
TALKS ABOUT HIS WAR BUDDIES

IN 1925, Charlie Reilly (BSC '20) wrote an article in *The Gateway* to help the University raise money to install a pipe organ in Convocation Hall as a memorial to the war dead. Charlie was one of a flood of students who came back after the war to finish their degrees. He was Students' Union President in 1919–1920, then became Master of the Methodist Western Canada College, and still later was elected to serve on the University Senate. The four men he wrote about in *The Gateway* were his fellow students and his war buddies.[10]

"The boys who left the University to go the war," Charlie said, "we loved them and they must not be forgotten. Sometimes...I dream that I see them again."

G. PARR
MIDDLE WING | R. FITZGERALD
INSIDE WING | F. PERRATON
HALF BACK | C. BELL
LEFT SCRIMMAGE | E. JAMES
FLYING WING | K. AYLEN
OUTSIDE WING | PROF. W. M. EDWARDS
ASSISTANT COACH | GORDON DAVIS
HEAD COACH

*A sketch of the Memorial Organ
installed after the war.*

(1925–26 Evergreen and Gold, *p. 5)*

Ernest Howard Parsons ("Ernie") and
Robert Norman McArthur ("Tiny")

AMONG THE "BOYS" he referred to was Ernest Parsons from Edmonton, who in 1914 was a part-time student finishing his Arts degree. Ernie was a star half-back of the rugby team. His friend "Tiny" McArthur, from South Edmonton, was also in Arts, but full-time, in his third year. In the University Calendar, you will see their names recorded forever on the list of Christmas exam results. In March, they were writing those exams. In April, Ernie graduated and Norman (Tiny) finished his third year. In May, they were in the trenches of France. The next year they were both dead, along with many other recruits to the Princess Patricia's Canadian Light Infantry. As Professor Broadus wrote of them and the other members of Princess Pat's who died: "You could not call it a casualty list. It was not even decimation. It was—annihilation."[11]

Charley Reilly remembered the tiniest detail about his friends. "Old Ernie Parsons," he wrote,

> with his books under his arm, shuffling across the campus in that ambling fashion that gained him the sobriquet of "Farmer," and stopping for one last kick at the rugby ball before he left for home— the same old Ernie sitting calmly at his post on the front line trench and reading a magazine to while away the weary hours; I can hear him and Tiny McArthur planning their journey home via Bering Straits to avoid the ocean voyage and its concomitant seasickness; Tiny sitting tailor fashion of the floor on the dug out and quite talkative after his early morn tot. They were both awfully fine fellows.
>
> One day in the autumn of '15, the three of us were comfortably seated in the parlor of an old French house where the kind lady of the establishment had prepared a spread for us—real old-fashioned apple pie and milk. I had "spun the bat" for it, and Ernie, being the only one in funds, was footing the bill.

Ernie and Tiny were both killed in action on June 2, 1916 in the battle of Sanctuary Wood, also known as Hill 62, in the Ypres area of Flanders.[12] U of A students Barney Loptson and Francis Galbraith survived the battle and wrote home that "we were subjected to a very intense bombardment, following which the enemy came over and occupied a portion of our front and second line trenches. The shelling continued through June 2, 3 and 4 and was very heavy....[I was in the bay with Ernie] and he told me that he was going to see how [U of A student] Roy Stevens was getting along. Ernie hadn't been there a minute when a shell exploded, killing him instantly.... Norman McArthur was shot through the body and instantly killed....It's useless to attempt to describe it as there is nothing to compare it to....We all feel the loss of these boys very much and it will be a long time before we forget our experiences of the last few days."

J.W. Lewis, another survivor of the battle, wrote home that "...our boys fought like heroes, not one ever thinking of retreat. After being wounded so they could not shoot, they almost without exception did not leave as they were privileged to do, but carried water and ammunition to those who could shoot. German dead were piled in heaps some places. Those who stayed until things were quieted down had to crawl over dead German bodies who were killed in the attempt to capture our trenches."

Alexander Robertson McQueen ("Alex")

ALEX, SON OF REVEREND DAVID MCQUEEN and Catherine Robertson McQueen, was a part-time Arts student from Edmonton in his second-year when he went to the front.

The only course he was taking that year was Descriptive Geometry 2. There were 23 others in the class. Two of Alex's Geometry 2 classmates also died in the war: Lawrence Hotley Crawford, a second-year engineering student with three more years of school to go, and John Griffith Russell from Camrose, a special student in his first year of engineering.

Alex McQueen was the section commander of the Company Grenade Throwers. Charlie Reilly described Alex's quiet heroism:

A lad named G.B. Johnson was the first one of our Company to get killed. A trench mortar had blown in the bay where he was on sentry about 7 o'clock in the morning. He was a mangled mess of khaki but we couldn't get him in until after dark. Our trenches were only thirty yards from the Germans and the blown-in bay was completely exposed.

In spite of this, Alex McQueen was restrained only by direct command of the officer from going out to fetch him.

Alex acted like a hero that morning, and we all expected he would receive some award for his bravery. A dud mortar dropped into the trench. But Alex didn't know it was a dud when he picked it up and tried to heave it over the trench wall. I can see the sergeant yet as he turned to beat it when he saw Alex with the damned thing in his arms.

Lance Corporal Alex McQueen died on June 4, 1916, of wounds received at the battle of Sanctuary Wood.[13]

Barney Loptson and Vimy Ridge[14]

BARNEY WAS A FIRST-YEAR ARTS STUDENT from Edmonton, and he had just finished the dreaded Latin requirement. In the *Gateway* article, Charlie Reilly picked up Barney's story from the point where Alex McQueen had tossed the dud mortar out of their trench: "This was our first experience under fire, and we were awfully green and awfully frightened; all except Barney Loptson, who never seemed to know what fear was. When he saw the first of the trench-mortars coming, hurtling through the air, 'ha, ha,' says he, 'they're chucking tin cans at us.'" Barney survived the battle of Sanctuary Wood. The next news we have of him came from "somewhere in France," where he was billeted in a barn with nine other U of A students, probably on his way to Vimy Ridge, a battle he also survived. In fact, Barney almost made it home. He was killed in 1918 shortly before the Armistice.

By October 1916, Canadian troops, including Reg Lister, were heading to Vimy Ridge, a seven-mile long escarpment whose height gave it strategic importance. For three years, the Allies had tried but failed to win this German stronghold. But in April 1917 the Canadian Corps stormed and captured the Ridge "with blinding speed." They lost 3,598 men. The newspaper headlines from New York to London praised the gallantry and valour of the Canadian troops.[15]

Journalist Gord Henderson visited Vimy Ridge in 2004. "Every nation has its hallowed ground," he writes, "and Canada's sacred soil dominates a chalk ridge within binocular range of Belgium...Vimy Ridge." Henderson

An elegant side view of the Arts Building. (UAA 69–97–846D)

describes the "lush countryside" as one approaches Vimy Ridge 87 years after the battle. Then, Henderson says, come the cemeteries, with their endless white headstones standing amid "impossibly blue fields of flax in bloom...[with] streams of crimson poppies radiating out from the cemetery toward the road." One of Henderson's companions looked at a particular cemetery and immediately said, "My God, it looks like it's bleeding."[16]

There is a massive monument at Vimy Ridge, carved from some 6,000 tonnes of limestone. The names of 11,285 Canadians who were killed in France are hand-carved on its walls, including the names of Barney Loptson, Alex McQueen, Ernie Parsons, and Robert Norman (Tiny) McArthur.

BACK AT THE HOME FRONT—1915–1917

The Arts Building Opens At Last

IN THE MIDST OF WAR, the long-awaited Arts Building opened in 1915, at the time the most expensive building ever constructed in the province. The opening of the Arts Building was a grand event, complete with a

Convocation. Everyone was dressed splendidly, the lieutenant governor attended, and Premier Sifton was one of many who spoke. Eleven honorary degrees were awarded—a record. The first student function held in the building, remembers Reg Lister, was "a Red Cross dance" held in Convocation Hall.

After the Arts Building was completed, most of the classes and all the labs were moved out of Assiniboia and Pembina. For decades to come, students would take all, or nearly all, their classes here and it was now the Arts Building that became the centre of campus activity. It housed the bookstore, post office, print shop, and common rooms for the students, with library stacks in the basement. There was a Law reading room on the top floor. The building's anchor was Convocation Hall, used for everything from dances and recitals to every large, formal gathering. The plush and panelled Library reading room was on the main floor near Convocation Hall. On the second floor, the Senate Chamber, now under lock and key, has been restored to its former glory. The formal portraits of Henry Marshall Tory and Charles Stuart, both by Group of Seven artist Frederick Varley, hang there.

Tory's comfortable office was just down the hall from the Senate Chamber. Former President Robert Newton says that Tory "provided spacious offices for himself both at the U of A and later in Ottawa at the National Research Council." He had a good sense of "position" and of the need to have an office that bespoke the top job. The President's office was oak-panelled and carpeted with a beautiful Chinese rug.

Elms were planted out front, there was a sweeping, curved driveway leading to the front door, where you could park for free. There was no Tory Building, no HUB, no Business Building—you could see all the way down to the river, and looking across the quad, you could watch new houses springing up in Garneau.

The Faculty of Agriculture—Showdown in Calgary[17]

THE FACULTY OF AGRICULTURE was established in 1915, and its birth was almost as difficult as the process of bringing the Arts Building to life. No other Faculty had such a divisive beginning.

Tory's determination to have all post-secondary education, including Agriculture, under the U of A's umbrella clashed with two major forces.

First, most Albertans were familiar with the Ontario model, where there was a separate college of agriculture, and they saw no reason to change. Second, R.B. Bennett was determined to have a university in Calgary and he wanted agriculture to be part of it.

Tory did his spadework, speaking to farm groups throughout the province about the teaching of agriculture and seeking opinions in Britain and the United States. The showdown came in 1910 when he was asked to speak at the annual convention of the United Farmers of Alberta (UFA). Tory did so against a backdrop of savage attacks in the press and with a contingent in the audience who supported a rival university in Calgary.

Tory was interrupted and harangued from the moment he spoke. There was, in fact, a motion that he only be allowed five minutes to address the audience. Tory blazed with anger, marshalled all his evidence and argument, and talked to those assembled for an hour. He had an unshakeable belief that all university education belonged under one roof and should not be distributed across the province. He also believed that the work of

In 1913, three diploma schools were set up as feeders for the new Faculty. Tory served on the board that oversaw the development of these schools, which included Olds College. By 1915, there were enough students moving through this feeder system to warrant opening the University's Faculty of Agriculture. In 2005, Faculty of Agriculture, the University of Alberta and Olds College re-established their formal affiliation agreement.

(UAA 68–9–110)

the University should relate to the life of the people of the province. His message to the UFA was that the University of Alberta would not sink into an ivory tower mentality, but rather would "relate its research to practical production problems as well as the social and economic problems of farm people." The UFA voted 243 to 7 that agriculture be taught at the University of Alberta.

How difficult was that UFA meeting in Calgary for Henry Marshall Tory? The dynamo had met his match. Tory came home and spent three days in bed recovering from nervous exhaustion. And how divisive was the question of the location of an agricultural school? R.B. Bennett, the provincial conservative leader who would shortly bring down the Rutherford government and would later become prime minister, was adamant that "the day will come when the outraged citizens of Alberta will tear down the university and cast it brick by brick into the North Saskatchewan River."

The Wauneitas[18]

THE WAUNEITA CLUB was very active during the war. With an advisory committee of recent graduates, there was a full program of debates, social gatherings, dramatic and musical events, and fundraisers for the war. The Wauneitas had settled into an annual ritualistic initiation, "borrowing stereotypical imagery from native culture."[19] Thus the "Big Chief," dressed in a blanket decorated with an Indian motif, welcomed freshmen women into the tribe. During the war, the Club evolved from a social organization that bolstered women's skills in areas like debate to an organization concerned with student government. By 1920, the Wauneita Council had become a university disciplinary committee related to women's affairs.

Katie McCrimmon—First Woman to Head the Students' Union

KATHERINE ISABELLE MCCRIMMON, "Katie Mac" to her classmates, was the first woman to become president of the Students' Union. Up to this time, a man had always been president, and a woman had always been vice-president. In fact, it would be five decades before a man held the "lesser" position of vice-president. It was the war that offered Katie the opportunity to be president in 1916–1917, since most of the men were overseas.

Katie was also president of the YWCA, headed the Wauneita Club, and was a class favourite as an actress in campus drama productions. Daughter of a "pioneering railway man," she graduated in 1917, married John Russell Love in 1925, and was the first alumna to be elected to the University Senate. Katie died in 1930 from complications following the birth of her third child. In 1990, she was posthumously named as Woman of the Year by the YWCA in recognition of her role in founding the Canadian Girls-in-Training program in Alberta.[20]

During the Great War, women were moving from hearth and home into the workplace, replacing the men who were overseas. By 1915, the lobbies for prohibition and for the vote was at a peak, and by 1916, both were achieved. Dr. Will Alexander was one powerful U of A staff member who backed the woman's suffrage movement. In 1916, the western provinces granted the franchise to women. After prohibition went into effect in 1916, it was reported that alcohol consumption was reduced "by as much as 80%," and "family savings doubled."[21]

Helen Montgomery, Hector MacLeod, and the Banned One-Step

IN 1914, as the war broke out, Hector MacLeod was a brand new lecturer in Engineering. In that same year, the University Senate approved the establishment of the COTC—the Canadian Officers Training Company. Under the auspices of the COTC, male students at the university would train on campus for wartime service. And from the COTC, contingents of men would then be formed to be sent overseas for active duty.

As the fall of 1914 approached, with students about to return to campus for study, the federal government decided that a contingent of troops should be formed at the U of A. This contingent would be Company C of the 196th battalion, with Companies A and B drawn from other western provinces. At some point, whenever needed, they would be shipped to France.

Tory approached Hector to command Company C—the U of A group. Hector was reluctant, since he would be commanding men much older than himself. He told Tory that, in his opinion, someone more senior should be in charge.

"Well they are not going to get it," Tory said and according to Hector, Tory then demanded, "Will you take it?" Hector was undecided.[22]

The COTC troops under the command of Hector MacLeod, 1915. Top: G.T. Riley, J.A. Carswell, President Tory, J.S. Kerr. Middle: A. McQueen, E. Parsons, Hector MacLeod (with booted legs crossed and Captain's insignia on his hat), C. Beck. Bottom: N. McArthur, R. Stevens, A.T. Glanville. (UAA 86-41-4-9-24))

In the meantime, Hector was courting the brilliant Helen Montgomery (BA '14), winner of the first AWA Gold Medal. In some ways, Helen was typical of many U of A women. She had a fiancé going overseas, and it would be four years before she and Hector would be able to marry. During their courtship, Hector worked at his MSc studies, and Tory kept up his relentless pursuit to persuade Hector to lead the troops. In 1916, as Hector was about to graduate with his Master's degree, he finally agreed to lead the U of A men into battle.

And so Hector prepared for his 1916 convocation—and prepared, as well, to lead troops into battle. Convocation that year was attended by all of Company C, and Helen remembers what "a moving experience it was to see the men in uniform parade into Convocation Hall." When Hector got his parchment, the roof was raised by the cheering of his loyal troops. Later that night, there would be a great celebration and dance, hosted by the University. It would be the last time the troops could let loose.

But an odd undercurrent of discontent soon surfaced. President Tory and Provost MacEachran were not happy with a new dance that was popular with the students—the one-step. The University had banned this dance, and there was a $5 fine for performing it in public.[23]

Would there be a rebellion amongst the troops? Would they dance the banned one-step? After all, they were young students, and this was their last night out. But instead of leading a rebellion, Hector quietly asked the Company C troops to refrain from doing the one-step. His men were going to war, but there would be no one-step in public the night before their departure for France.

Carved By Our Students in the Trenches

HELEN WAS BUSY ON THE HOME FRONT, helping to organize what became known as the Canadian Soldiers Comforts Club. People furiously knitted socks, continually knitted, and sent them overseas along with parcels of comfort food. A weekly U of A newsletter was soon sent abroad, sometimes in conjunction with *The Gateway* publication, with Professors Muir Edwards and Will Alexander at the newsletter's helm. Will's columns on world events were popular and were sold commercially, with the proceeds donated to the Comforts Club.

The comfort parcels nearly always reached their intended destination. Helen remembers one particular thank-you letter from the boys at the front, in the form of a hand-carved plaque:

A memento of appreciation came back from 20 U of A students in the trenches with the Princess Pat's. From wood salvaged from

The World War I plaque that went missing for decades.
(CS 5809-01-009-B; Courtesy of Museums and Collections Services)

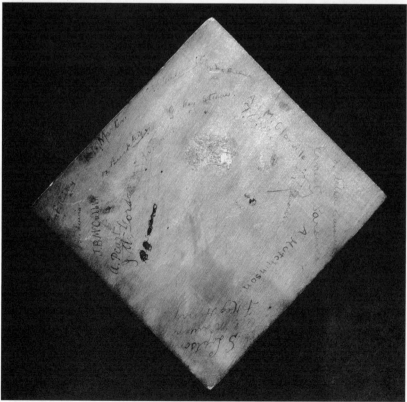

the bomb-shattered White Chateau near Ypres, the regimental crest had been carved by one of the boys in the trenches with a pen knife. On the crest were the names of battles, St. Eloi, Ypres, and Armentiers and on the back of the crest, the students' signatures.[24]

Among the signatures were the names of three men who made it back: Francis Phillip Galbraith, later Chancellor of the U of A, Don S. Edwards, whose grandson James, decades later, became chair of the Board of Governors, and Charles Reilly, Students' Union president in 1920. Also signing the plaque, along with sixteen of their friends, were Ernie Parsons, Robert Norman (Tiny) McArthur, Alex McQueen, and Barney Loptson. The plaque hung for years in the Library of the Arts Building and then disappeared after the Arts Library was incorporated into the new Rutherford Library. Helen's description of the plaque, however, endured —because she donated her memoirs to the University Archives. Her memoirs included a description of the plaque, thus leading to its rediscovery. The University plans to install the plaque in Convocation Hall in 2008 in the presence of the relatives of the students and staff who originally signed it in the trenches of France some 95 years ago.

THE KHAKI UNIVERSITY—1918

IN 1914, when the war began, everyone thought it would be over in six months. It didn't end until four years later, on November 11, 1918. Thousands of soldiers were ready to leave Europe. It was no simple task to demobilize so many people and bring them back to Canada. Quartermaster Cecil Burgess, professor of Architecture at the U of A, put it crisply: "There weren't enough ships to bring them home." There was also a calculated decision to keep troops close at hand for a while—just in case. But once the "returned men" (as they were called) came home, they were determined to make up for lost time and resume, or start, an education. They wanted to be back with their families, and they wanted normality.

And so Tory set to work feverishly once again. The "Y" was already involved overseas in setting up lectures and study groups and in 1916 Tory wrote a report for the YMCA on what he thought should be done to meet the needs of the men who would soon return home from the war. The "Y" read the report and asked Tory to draft a plan. Tory was known for his huge vision, and his plan to deal with the men stuck in Europe was a grand scheme involving hundreds of people and multiple levels of government in several countries.

Tory presented his scheme to the National Council of the YMCA, and there is no doubt that he captured the imagination of the audience, all of whom knew his reputation for relentless follow-through of seemingly impossible visions. Tory's friend Robert Newton says he loved a tough audience: "His strong figure, palpable enthusiasm, and intense purpose, all reinforced by vigorous utterance, ignited sparks in his listeners."

Tory pushed his plan forward, taking a leave from the U of A and obtaining the permission of the Canadian government to set up "what came to be known as the Khaki College at Ripon in Yorkshire." His plans were "far ahead of the thinking of the men actually engaged in the work." He faced down problem after problem. Ever the stickler for detail, he even had a crest designed for his new creation. "The Khaki University was a stroke of genius on the part of Dr. Tory," says Quartermaster Burgess. "He arranged for the education of hundreds of restless young lads left in England."

What Tory did was to save scores of soldiers from losing a year of university by placing them at colleges and universities in England. He used his persuasive powers to convince many Canadian and British educators to lend a hand with "Khaki U." Tory had professors from McGill, Oxford, New Brunswick, and Birmingham heading the "Khaki" academic departments. He recruited Drs. Killam, Sonet, and Burgess from the U of A. He had textbooks printed. He arranged for housing. And Tory received no pay except that due his rank of Colonel. Neither did others. Everyone pitched in. The result? From 1917–1919, "upwards of 650,000 men attended lectures and 50,000 were enrolled in classes." Compare that with the 2006 enrolment at the U of A of about 35,666.[25]

THE END OF THE DECADE

The Spanish Flu Epidemic

IN 1917, only 12 students graduated. In 1919, enrolment tripled as the "returned men" came home. There were special classes in the summer to help them make up for lost class time, and, for many, the "Latin 2"

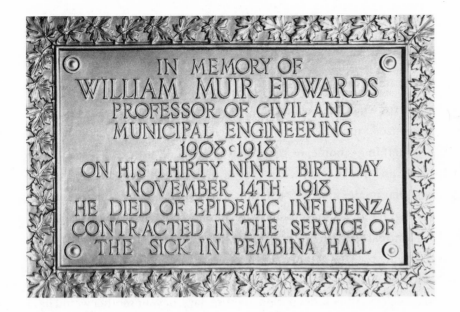

requirement was overlooked, a harbinger of major curricular reform. The requirement that students wear academic robes to class was dropped, except for senior students.

And just at the moment the war ended, the Spanish influenza made its deadly, relentless way around the world. Over 400 Edmontonians died in what was the worst world-wide epidemic since the Black Death of the 14th century. The University was shut down for two months. *The Gateway* suspended publication. Pembina was converted into an emergency municipal hospital, quickly becoming an isolation unit and morgue. "Over three hundred patients were admitted and by November 20, a total of 72 had died." One of the first deaths was a U of A student, Clara May Bell, who had edited the overseas Newsletter and who had helped Helen Montgomery organize the Comforts Club.

Helen Sheldon remembers that when the flu hit, a physician from Madras, India, Dr. Jessie Allyn, happened to be visiting. "Dr. Allyn directed the medical program in Pembina," Mrs. Sheldon says, "and Muir Edwards volunteered to help out. He was the 'admitting officer.'"

Muir Edwards died there of the flu on his 39th birthday. Muir was remembered as one of the first four professors at the U of A, the youthful McGill graduate who taught math. He was the first head of Civil Engineering, and the man who, with Doc Alik, introduced rugby football to the first students. Muir was the honorary president of the Athletics Association and the man who staked out the first football grid on River Lot 5.

Emma Read Newton

IN 1919, when Dr. Tory met the wife of one of his new professors, he recognized Emma Read Newton immediately. At a welcome reception for new staff in his home, he rushed up to her and said, "I have just discovered who your parents were!" Tory's mother and Emma's mother had been classmates together at McGill, and they were in the same graduation photograph. The same graduation photograph Emma had grown up with in Montréal was hanging right there in the Torys' Edmonton library.

Having realized who she was, Tory then told Emma, in front of all the assembled guests, "It was fortunate for me that women were not allowed to take the mathematics option in those days, or your mother would have taken my gold medal."[26] It was, of course, meant as a compliment, but the comment bespoke the times.

Emma apparently is still with us. From 1950–1959, Emma lived in Ring House 1 as the wife of President Robert Newton, and according to staff in Ring House 1, Emma's ghost visits on occasion, running up and down the stairs and opening and shutting doors. They smell cigarette smoke in a house where no one smokes or is allowed to. They believe Emma is making her presence known.

Emma is one of five ghosts said to live on campus. Besides the boy with the blue lips who occasionally appears around Athabasca Hall, there is a ghost named Emily who makes her appearance in Corbett Hall. There are two ghosts on campus without a name or identity—one lives in old St. Stephen's College and the other in the old Power Plant.

The Power Plant

A "POWER HOUSE" was built after the war as a temporary structure and was home to the "wireworms," the third- and fourth-year electrical engineering students who had lectures and labs there. Extension also had offices in the Power Plant, and there was a nutrition lab in the original building. In 1945, the Power Plant doubled in size.

The Power Plant was home to the Graduate Students' Association (GSA) in 2004. GSA President Alexis Pépin describes the ghost who haunts the

GSA's quarters: "You can hear things fall off tables in the next room," she says, "but when you go to check, no one is there. And no one *could* be there because the rooms are locked. On the weekends when only a couple of us are here working, you can hear someone running from one room to another, but again, when you go to check, no one is actually there. And lights flick on in empty rooms. It's creepy." Who's the ghost? No one knows.[27]

Armistice Day 1919—World War I Flying Ace Wop May

FOR A SHORT TIME, the U of A had a flying ace in its undergraduate ranks.

The ace had learned to fly a Sopwith Camel and came home from World War I with a Distinguished Flying Cross. He was a risk-taking barnstormer, and one student remembers when this young man flew under the High Level Bridge with just a few inches to spare on either side of his plane's wings. In 1929, he was the pilot who made a daring mercy mission to Fort Vermilion, delivering diphtheria vaccine for the town of Little Red River—600 miles in -30° Fahrenheit. Thousands of Edmontonians held their breath, waiting at the airfield for his return. For risking his own life to save others, he was awarded the Order of the British Empire. But his post-war attempt at university? It was short lived, and you won't find his name in any of the standard histories about the U of A. University just wasn't for him. His name was Wilfrid May, nicknamed "Wop" by a young cousin who couldn't pronounce his first name.

From the time he was a little boy, Wop May knew he wanted to fly. In 1918 he graduated from flight training school in England with only five-and-a-half-hours of flying time. With a little more training under his belt, he headed out on his first air mission. Instead of observing the action from afar, as he was told to do, Wop May flew into the fray, and was chased by Germany's most famous flyer, Baron Manfred von Richthofen—the Red Baron. By the end of that day's mission, the Red Baron was dead.

After Wop came home, the adventures never stopped. Wop May was the pioneering bush pilot who made the first mail flight to Aklavik. He started up Commercial Airlines (later bought out by Canadian Airways), tracked the Mad Trapper of Rat River from the air so the RCMP could catch the infamous murderer, and had a short stint in Hollywood advising Howard Hughes about a combat movie.

Top: Wop May, World War I flying ace, 1919. (Private Collection)

Bottom: Wop May's photo of the University, 1919—the first aerial of the U of A campus.

(Private Collection)

Even after losing an eye in an industrial accident—and losing his flying licence as a result—Wop May faced down the bitter disappointment at being grounded and got on with his life. He was awarded the American Medal of Freedom for his service in training World War II Commonwealth pilots and inaugurating the first search-and-rescue units.

Wop May left a wonderful, practical gift to the U of A, something that has appeared in each official U of A history: the first-ever aerial photograph of the University campus, taken in 1919, the year when he was an undergraduate at the U of A.

The photograph he presented to the University hangs today on the 6th floor of the Humanities Centre and in University Hall. It is inscribed as follows: "Presented to the University of Alberta By the May Airplanes Ltd., 1919. Photo by Captain W.R. May, DFC." The "DFC" designation stands for that rarest of honours, the Distinguished Flying Cross.

And what do we know about Wop May's time at the U of A? Reg Lister knows:

The University gave the returned men permission to have a dance in Athabasca Hall on November 11, 1919; an Armistice Ball. This was a great night for the boys to let loose....These were prohibition days...and Steen's Drug did a real business at $7.00 a bottle.

The night before was the time the boys brought a cannon on to the campus. Wop May, who was a student then, took one of his father's trucks and hauled the cannon from one of the armouries. Of course, they did not ask permission to take it. But it somehow got on to the campus in front of Athabasca Hall. I found the boys lots of old newspapers and some broom handles, and a bucket of water. They tore the newspaper and damped them down and rammed them into the barrel of the cannon with the broom handles. They fired the cannon quite a few times. The report was heard all over the city and all the windows were jarred in the University buildings. There was quite a fuss over town about the stealing of the cannon....

Reg later remembered 1919, and this prank, as the highlight of his 45-year career on campus.[28]

The Post-War New Order

PROFESSOR WILL ALEXANDER was one of some two dozen professors who remained on campus during World War I to teach students. "Victory," he said, "will hereafter be to the nation that has most successfully learned to exploit its natural endowment."[29] After the war, Dr. Will Alexander (Doc Alik) reflected on the war's impact. He called it the "new order."

Professor Robert Boyle, the man who loved art and theatre and who was the first dean of Engineering, became renowned during the war for developing sonar technologies to detect submarines. Boyle also saw the new order emerging. He wrote to Tory that "the great effect of the war will be that Applied Science will receive an immense impetus."

Boyle and Alexander, the physicist and the classicist, were right. In the next decade, the Greek and Latin Doc Alik taught would soon be on the decline, with research in physics, agriculture and engineering ascendant.

Engineer Hector MacLeod and Helen Montgomery finally tied the knot in 1920 when Hector returned from war. Hector then went to Harvard for his PhD, came back to Edmonton in 1921, and later headed the department of Mechanical and Electrical Engineering. Hector and Helen raised their family on the horseshoe, in Ring House 2, next to the Torys. In 1936, Hector was recruited by UBC as a department head. He later became UBC's dean of Applied Science and was awarded the Order of the British Empire. On today's UBC campus, there is an engineering building named in Hector MacLeod's honour and a portrait painted by the renowned Canadian artist Charles Comfort.

Conversazione

CONVERSAZIONE—the dull and stultifying social gathering of earlier days—was now *the* event to showcase the arts and the sciences. The Glee Club sang, the University Orchestra gave a concert, and a one-act play was performed. Then every department was opened up to the public, with demonstrations in all fields. There were experiments with hydrogen and carbon dioxide, a moving picture exhibit, and displays of plant collections, maps and mineral products, and much more.

Included with each Conversazione invitation was a dance card, listing each dance the orchestra would play, and numbering the dances sequen-

GENERAL PROGRAMME

RECEPTION—8:30 to 9:00

CONCERT—9:00 to 10:15

Convocation Hall. (Programme: Pages 6 and 7)

DEMONSTRATIONS—10:15 to 11:30

(Information: Pages 4 and 5)

SUPPER

(North Engineering Building)

First Sitting 10:30 to 11:00

Second Sitting: 11:30 to 12:00

DANCE—11:00

(Convocation Hall)

DANCE PROGRAMME

1. Waltz
2. One - Step
3. Fox - Trot
4. Three - Step
5. Waltz
6. One - Step
7. Fox - Trot
8. Waltz
9. Fox - Trot
10. Waltz
11. One - Step
12. Fox - Trot
13. Waltz
14. One - Step
15. Waltz
16. Fox - Trot
17. One - Step
18. Waltz
19. Fox - Trot
20. Waltz
Extra 1
2
3

Libby Lloyd's dance card.
(UAA 75–68)

tially. The idea was that the men going to Conversazione would arrange in advance with various women to be their partners for the first waltz or the fourth fox trot, the sixth "three-step" and so on. In those days, a tiny pencil was attached to each dance card, making it easy for women to write in the names of those they had agreed to dance with.

Libby Lloyd, from the Class of 1912, came back to her alma mater for the 1920 Conversazione. She kept her dance card for years, and on it you can see that there were 23 dances that night, starting at 11 P.M. Libby's dance card shows that five of the dances were the "one-step," the dance that had been banned six years before.

Remembering Those Who Died

IN NEW YORK CITY on September 11, 2002, all the names of those who died in the World Trade Center the year before were read aloud. For many years at the U of A, the names of the 82 U of A students and staff who died in World War I were also read aloud. The ceremony took place in Convocation Hall, every November 11, Armistice Day, in the Arts Building in the centre of campus, where there is a simple bronze plaque memorializing the names of those who died in World War I.

It was President Tory who recited the names. But he could never finish reading aloud the list without breaking down.

The U of A sent 324 of its 433 students and nearly half its 45 staff into the war in a battalion known as Company C, part of the 196th. One-quarter of them died. They were the rugby team, they were professors, they were future professionals and parents. But to most of us, they are now just anonymous names, young men whose names were captured on a bronze plaque affixed to a wall in Convocation Hall.

Visit the Arts Building some day, and find the two bronze plaques that list the dead from World War I and World War II. You will also see four plaques called "Active Service Rolls." Each one is about five feet high and in careful hand-lettering, they list all those from the University who served in the First World War. You will recognize the names of many people whose stories are in this book, including the only woman listed—Agnes Kathleen Wilson, a graduate whose memoirs guided us from 1905 to 1912. Charlie Reilly and Reg Lister are on the Honour Roll.

Then find the bronze plaque naming those who died in World War I. Take a moment to find Alex McQueen, Ernie Parsons, Robert Norman (Tiny) McArthur, and Barney Loptson, and remember their stories.[30]

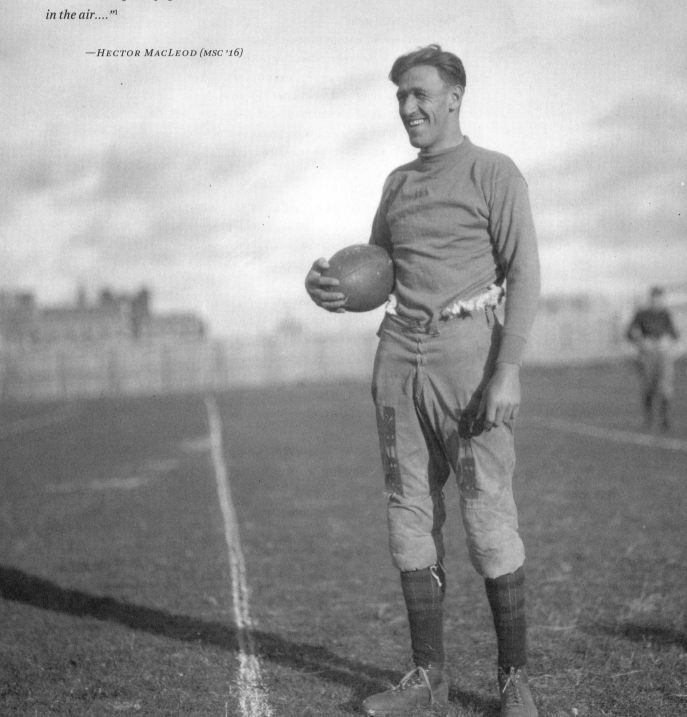

*"There was a spirit of optimism
in the air...."*[1]

—HECTOR MACLEOD (MSC '16)

Timeline

Enrolment and Finance, 1920–1929

- Fall student head count: 1,106 (1920); 1,591 (1929)
- Operating budget from the Province of Alberta: $427,825.33 (1920); $525,023.00 (1929)
- Full-load undergraduate Arts tuition: $30.00 (1920); $85.00 (1929)
- SU membership fee: $7.00 (1920); $10.00 (1929)

Key Dates, 1920–1925

- Department of Dentistry becomes a School (1920)
- First issue of the *Evergreen and Gold* yearbook (1920)
- Applied Science (Engineering) becomes a Faculty (1921)
- University acquires the Strathcona Hospital (1922)
- School of Nursing opened (1924)
- Dentistry offers the complete five-year course for the first time (1924)
- First medical students trained entirely at the U of A graduate (1925)

1926–1929

- Al Ottewell, director of Extension, has worn out seven Model Ts since 1913 (1926)
- The SU takes the lead in organizing the Canadian Federation of Students (1926)
- Former Premier Rutherford is elected as University chancellor (1927)
- First students in Dentistry and Nursing graduate (1927)
- CKUA goes on the air (1927)
- Household Economics becomes a School (1928)
- "Accountancy" becomes the School of Commerce (1928)
- School of Education established (1928)
- President Tory resigns to head the National Research Council; Dr. Robert Wallace is named president (1928)
- The University ends the ban on fraternities (1929)

Selected Campus Buildings, 1920–1929

- Medical Building completed (today's Dentistry/Pharmacy Centre) (1921)
- The first Tuck Shop opens (1924)
- St. Joseph's Catholic College opens as an affiliate of the University (1927)
- University Hospital taken over by the province; the University is represented on the board (1929)
- Today's Corbett Hall opens as the Provincial Normal School, offering teacher training courses (1929)

Beyond Campus, 1920–1929

- The first woman admitted to the bar in Alberta (1920)
- Gandhi sentenced to six years imprisonment for Civil Disobedience (1922)
- Insulin first administered to diabetics (1922)
- Prohibition ends (1923)
- First 16mm movies; first television images; first liquid rocket fuel (1925)
- Charles Lindberg (1927) and Amelia Earhart (1928) make solo flights across the Atlantic
- Alberta wins control of its natural resources (1929)
- Canadian women are legally declared "persons" and eligible for appointment to the Senate (1929)
- Drivers' licences are required in Alberta (1929)
- First Academy Awards (1929)
- The New York Stock Market crashes (1929)

VIGNETTES FROM THE 1920s

The University of Alberta Turns 21

THE 1920S BEGAN as the troops returned home from World War I. It was the decade when the U of A came of age, turning 21. Enrolment boomed, new buildings appeared, research came to the fore, the curriculum was revamped, new faculties were organized, and everyone plunged into a vibrant social life.

One professor described students in 1920 as two different streams coming together in a single great river. One stream of students came fresh-faced from the farm or the growing urban centres. The other contingent came from the brutal battlefields of World War I, from acts of war they rarely talked about. The University's enrolment more than doubled as the "returned men" resumed their studies. Both streams of students, so different in their life experiences and maturity levels, sat side by side in class. These two groups of students, however, had one thing in common: they were all ready for release from the war's grip and had headed into university life with an element of social abandon and a determined drive to succeed. As *The Gateway* editor put it in a 1920 edition, "We are now starting out on a voyage of great possibilities."[2]

The 1920s were golden years at Varsity, but beyond the boundaries of the university, life was hard. In southern Alberta there was a terrible drought; wheat prices plummeted; in 1921 the United Farmers of Alberta ousted the Liberals; and in nearby Winnipeg, there was a general strike. But at Varsity, President Tory ushered in a research council, graduate studies blossomed, and post-war students threw themselves with a vengeance into study and play.

By 1920, enrolment had grown to the point where Dr. Tory lamented that he didn't know the names of all the students. Even *The Gateway* commented that for the first time in the U of A's history, students couldn't possibly know the names of all their classmates. Tory's hope was that he could devolve upon the professors the wonderful duty of having personal contact with students, learning their first names and family situations, and taking their best interests to heart.

Marsh and Annie Tory also suddenly discovered that they were unable to entertain all the professors and their spouses in their home. For the first time, a presidential social function was held outside the president's Ring House home, in Athabasca Hall.

In the spring of 1920, students were producing the year-end edition of *The Gateway*, which commemorated graduation. The publication began with President Tory's written message to the seniors. The Winnipeg General Strike was still fresh in everyone's minds, and Tory called for social justice and equality of opportunity among the classes, bemoaning the "material craze...affecting every class of society":

> You will always find a clear conscience and a noble purpose infinitely more satisfying than material wealth. Nevertheless, let me urge you in tackling the problems of your own lives and those of the communities where your lot may be cast, not to let your vision of the things that are worthwhile be obscured by the selfish materialism that you may see in the lives of men and women around you. I am sure I can wish you nothing better than that you will always be found on the side of those who are seeking the common betterment of their fellow men.

As U of A graduate Marjorie Bowker put it, Tory's message "might be seen as an apt warning against the materialism and consumerism that overtook the world 50 years later."

The 1920 valedictory address was written by Roland Michener, an undergraduate who was the Rhodes Scholar for 1920, and who later became governor general of Canada. Michener spoke about the two purposes of a university:

> The University...lays the solid foundation of fact, shows us how to use the tools and collect the materials, and then says, "go ahead, build your own structure." The other function of a university is to produce leaders and equip them with all the essentials of good citizenship. The place that Alberta's graduates take in the future will be the conclusive test of her success in this respect. All that remains to be done is to pass on to your keeping the torch of Alberta's destiny, with the hope that in your hands we shall raise it higher and yet higher in the search for "whatsoever things are true."

Loosening Up

THE FIRST CLASSES of the decade began on September 29, 1920. By now, only the seniors were still required to wear black convocation robes to class, and *The Gateway* and the yearbook both contained advertisements for fashionable clothes aimed at the well-dressed student. In 1910, *The Gateway* had worked hard to get advertisements, but a decade later, with gowns gone, *Gateways* brimmed with advertisements—mostly to show students what to wear to class, to rugby games, or to dances.

Not all the changes were exterior: there were changes to the curriculum, too. Returning veterans balked at what they saw as outdated academic requirements and pushed for modernization. Latin was still required for matriculation, but by 1920, students working on a BA or BSc could take French and German to fulfill language requirements, thus avoiding Latin and Greek. And there were also more academic options.

The 1920s was the decade when women were freed from having to wear long Edwardian tresses and could bob their hair. They shortened their skirts and on occasion even bared their arms. There was one notable, immovable exception to the trend for short hair. Nursing students were not allowed to cut their hair and "would be confined to their rooms for this offense." In fact, they had to wear veils that covered their hair. Junior nursing "sisters," as they were called, were required, when speaking to a superior, to stand military-style, "with their hands behind their back." It would be decades before nursing students were free from such restrictive personal requirements.[3]

Skiing made its appearance in Banff at mid-decade, dancing was all the rage, and students even speculated in a *Gateway* survey about cohabitation before marriage—what was called "companionate marriage." Sophomore Wilbur Bowker, a future dean of Law, opposed the idea because "it does away with one sweep all our morals and ideals in regard to the institution of marriage." Wes Oke, president of the Students' Union, was for it: "This mated for life idea is a fragment of an outworn moral code and there is no reason why we should not experiment to find a compatible mate." The last on-the-street student who was interviewed said simply, "Fifteen years from now it will be the accepted thing."[4]

"Discipline sagged somewhat" after the war, said beloved professor Will Alexander. "It had been too much to the fore in too many students' lives during the preceding years. There was a veritable craze for social affairs. Youth felt it had been cheated out of a good deal, and was in haste to make up arrears."[5] Students had survived the war. They had survived the flu epidemic. It was time to loosen up and have fun.

There were at least 12 formal dances during the year, says Reg Lister, beginning with "the Sophomores' Reception to the Freshmen. Then came the Junior Prom before Christmas, and the Christmas Banquet and Dance. The Med Ball and Engineers' Ball were in January, followed by the Senior Spring Formal, the Under-Grad Dance...the President's reception to the staff, the Premier's Reception...And there was also a banquet a week...."[6]

A Landmark Change—Girls in Slacks

CECIL BURGESS played a role in introducing some of Edmonton's women to slacks, as one woman recalls:

I started skiing in 1925 because U of A Architecture prof Cecil Burgess had skied while in India, bringing home two pairs of skis. I chummed around with his niece. She asked me if I'd like to ski and I said, "What's ski?" She had gotten a continental magazine about the upper crust skiing in Switzerland and she showed me a picture and they were in slacks...the women! In slacks! But they were full like Dutchmen's pants. So we skied a while in our long johns, wool stockings, fleecy bloomers and pleated skirts. The skirts went out like a parachute when you went down the hill so I decided I'd like really thick slacks, just like the ones in the pictures of the "smart set" women in the European magazines.

So I went through all the Edmonton stores and asked if they had slacks. They all said, "What are slacks?" So I got the magazine and showed them and they said, "No, no. They'd never do here." So I went out and bought what was called melton cloth...and I made myself slacks. You could buy knitted cuffing for around your ankles, and I wore galoshes. The skis, you see, had no bindings—just a strap you put your toe through and you could tighten them up at the ankle.[7]

The new 1920s look was a far cry from the corseted Edwardian mode of 1908, with cinched waists and black skirts down to the ankles. One student, an excellent horsewoman, remembers having her riding pants made by the RCMP's tailor. *They* knew how to make slacks.

The Mayfair Golf Club—The Thief of Time

AND ALL THE WHILE, the professors were having fun too. The Mayfair Golf Club, nestled just below the University, opened in 1922 and soon became the social centre for U of A faculty. Professor Cecil Burgess, recently returned from the war, described what a big difference the golf club made to life on campus:

> We all joined the club. I joined because I wanted to see what they had done with the fields I used to explore to gather flowers. I was never a good golfer or tennis player but I had played golf in Scotland. I played at the Mayfair with Broadus or MacEachran....D.E. Cameron, the librarian, was the best golfer of us all. The only staff member who didn't join was Dr. Boyle, the dean of Engineering. He described golf as a thief of time.

Burgess also recalled Tory talking about his golf games with former Premier Rutherford—soon to be Chancellor of the U of A. There was one game where Rutherford had 11 strokes on the 10th hole—but he "wasn't counting his score, so he's going to win this match!" One student yearbook featured a cartoon of all the professors playing one sport or another, and their whimsical cartoon of Tory shows him at the Mayfair, looking puzzled as he tries to get out of the rough. His golfing companions said that Tory would go at it for quite a while and then say, "I got three on that!"

Hector MacLeod also remembers the Mayfair. It was a far cry from the battlefields of France, where he served throughout the war just after receiving his MSc:

> The Mayfair Golf and Country Club opened in the spring of 1922 and we became charter members by paying $100 for a share and $40 for annual fees. A large number of university people, from the President on down, became members. Some serious efforts were

made to bring down the rather high scores, but generally the game was played for pleasure. Judge Morrison, a Senate member who lived in the Garneau mansion on the edge of campus, often joined us. Most people agreed with him that "anyone whose score got below 90 ceased to be a social being."

If you look at the old photos displayed at the Mayfair, you'll find one of Tory seated on the grass in a group photo. This is a rare chance to see a relaxed Tory. You'll also find Doc Alik, Mayfair's charter member #72, posing with other members of the first Mayfair Board.[8]

On the Road

THE FACULTY OF EXTENSION was the place to find the "techies" of the day. In order to reach their rural audience and deliver a lecture, Extension staff had to be technically adept and constantly resourceful. On any one trip they might have to repair an engine, devise some missing part from the lantern slide apparatus, or haul a Model T out of a muddy rut on a back road. Students didn't come to Extension, Extension went to the students— who for the most part were isolated, lonely, homesick homesteaders.

In the 1920s, it was most often Al Ottewell who was out on the rural circuit. He was joined later in the decade by Ned Corbett (after whom Corbett Hall is named) and U of A graduate Don Cameron (later a member of the Canadian Senate). Their stock-in-trade was an evening talk given in a church or community hall. The talk would be illustrated by lantern slides—hand-painted slides, about four inches square and made of thick glass which were displayed through a projector illuminated with acetylene gas.

Ned Corbett recalls starting out on a 90-mile trip north along deeply rutted roads: "As we ploughed our way toward St. Albert, on three different occasions we had to get out and literally lift the car out of the way of traffic coming into Edmonton."[9] On another occasion he arrived in a settlement 100 miles north of Edmonton to give a lantern slide show, and found a note pinned to the door of the meeting place: "Dear Prof. The whole village has gone to the stampede. Come up and join us." He did. Ned Corbett knew the children had never seen a lantern slide show and he was not going to deny them an opportunity to do so. When the stampede was over, the homesteaders decided not to go back to town for Ned's program. Instead, they used two logs covered with boards, called "stoneboats," to slide a building from town down to the stampede site. It was not long before the building arrived at the stampede, and Ned had a place for his show.

Then there was the time Ned Corbett and Al Ottewell were stuck in a blizzard on the frozen prairie. Perrin Baker, the "homesteader" minister of education in the 1920s, describes how Al and Ned started their frigid car. "I blush to tell you," says Baker, "how Ottewell and Corbett got the Model T started in a blizzard once in southern Alberta, but Ottewell had a farm boy's know-how about how to use the body's...ummm...available warm water...to defrost the radiator."[10]

Revolution in the Air

THE MOST RESOURCEFUL of all Extension staff was, without a doubt, H.P. Brown. H.P. tinkered with anything mechanical, photographic, or electronic. In the early 1920s, he built a crystal radio set so that he could tune into the new U.S. radio stations. He was struck by the thought of putting the university "on the air" through the emerging technology of radio. H.P. knew that radio was quickly taking over in the U.S., and that in Canada it was the Montréal-based Canadian Marconi Company that led the way with test programs in 1919. "It didn't take Brown long to see the superiority of radio over mules and Model Ts in the dead of winter...."[11]

The U of A had no ready money for this risky adventure, and so the Department of Extension persuaded *The Edmonton Journal* to free up their radio station, CJCA, one night a week so that Extension could provide the programming. A broadcasting studio was set up in today's old Power Plant, complete with a grand piano, a few chairs, and burlap sacking for soundproofing. Technical help came from famed Calgary radio engineer W.W. Grant.

In an experiment "unique in Canada," CKUA, the U of A's non-commercial, educational radio station, went on the air in November 1927.[12] When the station couldn't power up to its own frequency, Mr. Grant booted his own Calgary radio station off the air and let CKUA take over his station's frequency. CKUA's 1927 inaugural broadcast preceded radio transmission

by the CBC by seven years. Emma Read Newton (BA '31), whose mother had attended McGill with Tory, played "God Save the King" on the grand piano. Dr Tory gave the very first talk.

Early programming included technical talks given by professors in Agriculture ("Care of Brood Sows and Fall Pigs" was one), selections by the University Orchestra, songs from the Glee Club, and some short educational talks.

Letters of support poured in. Over time, programming was expanded to include variety shows, French lessons, the first live broadcasts of sports shows, the first live broadcasts directly from the Legislature, and "national evenings of live story and song featuring English, Scottish, Irish, Welsh, French and Ukrainian artists, which were enjoyed by the many homesick newcomers to the province."[13]

A stylized rendering of the heart of campus in 1929, with an athletic field in the lower right, where University Hall stands today. The Plant Pathology Lab ("West Lab") stands opposite the athletic field, on the site of today's Students' Union Building.
(UAA 69–97)

THE CAMPUS IN THE 1920s

EDMONTON IN 1919 had a population of about 60,000. As the newly arrived professor of Agriculture, Robert Newton, remembers it, "Edmonton sprawled over an enormous area on both banks of the North Saskatchewan River, linked by three bridges (Low Level, High Level and Dawson—no Groat Bridge until 1955). The High Level Bridge, over the great valley, with streetcars on the top deck, commanded a magnificent view in both directions. There were plenty of great open spaces...and the many short-cut paths through poplar-covered blocks gave one the feeling of being in the country."[14]

In 1919, the campus, too, was a simple place, with room for two barns, a house for the farm manager, and experimental crop plots. The only major buildings were the three residences, Pembina, Athabasca, and Assiniboia, the Arts Building, two long, narrow engineering and agriculture buildings (the North and South Labs), and St. Stephen's College. But the campus was bursting with people; students were sitting on the floors and on window sills during classes in the Arts Building. Intensifying the space crunch was Tory's determination to introduce a medical program.

The Faculty of Medicine—Tory Outmanoeuvres the Premier[15]

PRESIDENT TORY was going to have a Faculty of Medicine. There were no two ways about it. He would require two buildings in order to establish

a medical program—a teaching building and a teaching hospital. First Tory set his sights on the Strathcona Hospital, which had started life way back in 1906 as a "Hospital Cottage." This "Hospital Cottage" later opened as a stately brick building on the University's doorstep, on the site of today's Walter Mackenzie Health Sciences Centre.

Tory made absolutely sure the hospital would be close by his university by having the Board of Governors donate university land for the new hospital to the City of Strathcona. As for the teaching building, Tory hedged his bets by lobbying both the premier and the Rockefeller Foundation in New York City for a teaching building. The day came when Premier Greenfield visited Tory to tell him that the province couldn't afford to establish a Faculty of Medicine. That same morning Tory had received a half-million dollar cheque from the Rockefeller Foundation, which he triumphantly waved in front of the premier.

The Medical Building constructed with the Rockefeller grant is the stately brick building, topped with a cupola, which is now the Dentistry/Pharmacy Centre. Walk into the lobby today, and look straight ahead to the inner door. Up above is the symbol of the Faculty of Medicine—the caduceus, flanked by a mortar and pestle on one side and a microscope on the other. The caduceus, a symbol of healing found in the Bible and Greek mythological sources, is an image of a snake wrapped in spiral fashion around a staff. In the display cases, you'll find some early medicines that are making news again today—cinnamon, red clover, and golden seal root. For decades, U of A students knew this building simply as "The Med" or "The Med Building." Its planning and construction went smoothly when compared to the seven-year saga surrounding the opening of Arts.

In 1920, the CPR built a spur line to the University to haul in gravel and brick for the new building. The contractor's estimates were perfectly accurate, and the Medical Building opened in September 1921. Suddenly, the Arts Building, which for six years had been the main teaching facility for every subject, had a rival. The pathways on campus changed overnight, and when students reached the centre of campus after their walk from the streetcar or the residences, the well-worn path to the Arts Building now had a spur line of its own, straight to the Medical Building.

By 1921, the Medical Building housed all the health sciences, the Provincial Laboratory for Public Health, Chemistry, Entomology, and University laboratories. The Med Building's classrooms doubled the University's teaching space. The only two amphitheatres on campus were located in the Medical Building, and all large classes were scheduled to meet here, including Dr. Broadus's English 2 class.

A year after the Medical Building opened its doors, the University acquired the Strathcona Hospital and Tory had met the two required conditions for a full program of study in medicine. In 1925, the first class of medical students trained entirely at the U of A graduated. Gone was a time when only the first years of the medical program were offered in Edmonton, with the final years taken at a finishing school—usually McGill or the University of Toronto.

The Faculty of Medicine's First Graduate

FIRST ACROSS THE STAGE in 1925 was Leone McGregor (Hallstedt), the only woman in the 11-member medical class of 1925. This meant that Leone laid claim to the honour of being the first University of Alberta-trained physician to convocate. Decades later, while living in Stockholm, she had a chance meeting with a young medical graduate from the U of A who was studying in Sweden. Leone told the student how she came to be the first one in the 1925 Convocation line-up. According to Leone, "there was just enough chauvinism in the men that they let me go first." The

Leone McGregor, front row centre, was the first woman to graduate from the Faculty of Medicine. When not engaged in her studies, Leone was a hockey goalie.

(UAA 70–188–3)

young student was Dr. Lorne Tyrrell, who would later discover a cure for Hepatitis B and go on to serve as dean of Medicine and Dentistry at the U of A from 1994–2004. "I met Leone McGregor purely by chance," Lorne says. "I was doing graduate work in Stockholm, where I happened to have distant relatives. These relatives asked me to pick up an old family friend and give her a ride to a dinner party."

The old family friend turned out to be Dr. Leone McGregor, but young Lorne didn't know this when he arrived to pick up the mystery guest at her magnificent apartment. "You're late," Leone scolded. And Lorne Tyrrell soon found out that he was only allowed to cross the threshold into Leone's apartment because he had passed a test of sorts—he wasn't wearing jeans and didn't sport a beard. "On the way to the party," Lorne explains,

I discovered the identity of this woman—the first physician to graduate from the Faculty of Medicine at the U of A. I had heard about her from Ralph Shaner, a professor who came to teach at the U of A in 1922 on a one-year contract. He stayed—and taught every student who graduated in Medicine between 1922 and 1976. I lived with Dr. Shaner and his wife Jean from 1965 until 1967. Before leaving for Sweden, as I said good-bye to the Shaners, Ralph said he knew of only one person in Sweden—Dr. Leone McGregor. He didn't know her married name, and he had not heard from her since 1939. Can you believe it? In a city of two million people, there I was at Leone McGregor's doorstep to escort her to a family party.

Lorne Tyrrell reminds us that the Rockefeller grant is still alive and well as a continuing budget line for the Faculty of Medicine and Dentistry: "We use the Rockefeller grant every year. It's a source of start-up funds for new faculty members, so that when we're nose-to-nose with another university in recruiting a new faculty member, those Rockefeller dollars give us an extra advantage—we can sweeten the pot with something a researcher really needs. Maybe it's extra research assistance, or possibly lab equipment." A grant made in the 1920s still remains a life-line for the Faculty in the 21st century.

The Tuck Shop[16]

IN 1924, a modest little building was constructed on campus; however, its modesty, maintained in the newer version erected in 1929, was restricted only to its looks. This little building instantly changed daily life on campus, and alumni from the 1920s through to the 1960s remember no other building with greater fondness than this one. It was called the Tuck Shop.

Privately owned and located near today's LRT station, it was the first informal gathering place for students outside their parents' homes or their campus residence rooms.

Life at Varsity would never be the same. Soon there would be a "full court press" for a covered skating rink so that students would have an arena for hockey and casual skating. Then the race would be on for a proper Students' Union Building and a gym. But for now, in 1924, the Tuck Shop was where students could relax and eat home-cooked food—without going home. Students remembered the little things, like cinnamon buns: "The mom and pop who ran the café had passed through with the coffee pot, pouring it with gusto into thick white china cups (the kind with the green stripe running under the rim) and soon would be bearing trays of fresh, hot cinnamon buns to our tables. We could smell the spices and melting brown sugar in the air."[17]

The Varsity TUCK SHOP

"Home"
The place where you grumble most
and
Are treated the best.

The Place Where You Can Get Everything You Need

Cinnamon Buns—The Tuck Shop's Recipe from the New Trail

THE VARSITY TUCK SHOP was renowned for its famous Cinnamon Bun recipe:

An electric mixer is needed for this recipe as it requires a lot of beating. If the dough is too soft to handle, add a bit more flour. However, the less flour used the better the buns will be.

Soften 2 packages instant yeast or 1 oz fresh yeast in ½ cup warm water and 2 tbsp sugar. Let mixture set until the yeast is dissolved (about 10 minutes).

In a large bowl, put 2 cups boiling water, 3 tbsp margarine, 2 tsp salt, and 3 tbsp sugar. Let the margarine melt and the mixture cool a bit. Then add 2 cups all purpose flour. Beat this mixture hard until very smooth and creamy (about 5 minutes). Then add the yeast mixture, 3 eggs, and 3 ¼ cups additional flour. Continue beating until the dough is very smooth. (Dough will be very soft.) Cover and let stand in a warm place to rise until the dough is doubled in bulk (about 1 hour).

While the dough is rising, in a flat pan melt ⅓ cup margarine and set aside to cool. In a flat dish mix 1 cup white sugar and 1 ½ tsp cinnamon. Turn the raised dough onto a lightly floured work surface. Let the dough set 5–10 minutes to "firm up."

Cut the dough into pieces about the size of an orange. Dip each piece of dough first into the melted margarine, the coat it well in the cinnamon-sugar mixture. Stretch the dough piece until it is 4–5 inches long and form it into a simple knot. Place the knots side by side in a 9" x 12" x 2" pan. (Be sure the pan is 2" deep and allow a 3" square for each bun.) Let the finished buns rise for about 45 minutes. Bake at 375 for 30 minutes. Makes 18 buns.

(1926–27 Evergreen and Gold, p. 171)

"Varsity Tuck Shop would not rank high from the point of view of an architect," said another student, but here one could find "heart-enclosed initials in some inconspicuous corner of the table or table leg." The Tuck was the spot where you could "sit for three hours with just one glass of chocolate milk," or take magazines from the racks, read them and leave them on the tables for others.

All roads, the saying goes, lead to Rome. At the U of A, all roads, it seemed, led to the Tuck Shop. Students beat pathways there from all the other buildings on campus. In old photos, you can see swarms of students decanting from the Arts Building at noon-time and heading due south to the Tuck. It was the *Tim Hortons* of its day, except that there was a cook in the kitchen, and you could get an affordable homemade meal day or night. At the till was a small convenience counter where you could buy necessities like toothpaste, candy, and safety pins. "My mother used to take me to the Tuck Shop when I was little and she was a student," says one alumnus, "and I loved it. I was allowed to pick out one comic book each time. When I became a student, the Tuck was my hang-out. It was a little beat up by then, but so friendly, and I loved it."

The demolition of the Tuck in the late 1960s caused decades of bitterness on the part of students and alumni. No one disputed the need for new quarters for Fine Arts and Law, the complex that replaced Tuck in the early 1970s, but the Tuck Shop had been home to thousands of students for more than 40 years. It was small-scale and personal—the antithesis of a corporate fast-food chain. It is still dearly remembered, and missed, by many.[18]

St Joseph's College[19]

IN 1926, excavation began down the street from St. Stephen's. With the aid of a grant from the Carnegie Corporation of New York, matching dollars from the province, and the bulk of the quarter-million-dollar tab coming from the Catholic Church, the U of A was to have a second affiliated College on campus.

It was U of A policy to encourage denominational colleges on campus as long as the U of A remained in control. The Catholic Church took up the challenge to establish St. Joseph's College. The College led many lives in the 1920s. It was, and still is, a residence for men—over 4,000 U of A

students have lived in St. Joe's while students at the U of A, including former prime minister Joe Clark and former senator Nick Taylor. In the north wing of St. Joseph's College, was a gym, and in the south wing a chapel that is still heavily used today. St. Joe's tea room and cafeteria (the "Little Tuck"), were popular spots to take a date or linger over a snack. Long before there was a SUB, Students' Council met here, in the basement library, and student clubs also booked space at the College.

Today, you can take approved classes at St. Joseph's College and transfer the credits to the U of A. On Sundays at 9 P.M., you can attend Last Chance Mass, which the current president of St. Joseph's, Father Timothy Scott, inaugurated in 1986 when he was a chaplain at the U of A. "For students," he says, "it's a perfect time for service; it's just packed. There are students just hanging out down the steps."[20] Scott adds that the most difficult part of providing the service is keeping the priests awake that late.

The Normal School—Corbett Hall

In 1921, the United Farmers of Alberta (UFA) swept to power with 39 seats in Parliament, leaving the stunned Liberals with 14 seats. UFA minister of education, Perrin Baker, interviewed at age 92 in 1969, recalls that "in 1921, the situation in rural schools was deplorable. There was a dearth of teachers and children attending school 160 days, where 200 days was the minimum. Some schools crowded as many as 70 children into a

Varsity Rink

IN THE MID-1920S, *what students really wanted was a covered skating rink. There was no SUB yet, the gymnasium in Athabasca was small and old, and there was nowhere on campus to exercise during bitter winter months. And so the Students' Union worked out a funding scheme with the University and the provincial government. In 1927 the Covered Rink was opened one block west of 112 Street, opposite 87 Avenue. The Rink was open three times a week for student use. As the 1935 yearbook put it, "most students never missed a night of skating. Many a student who is hazy about the whereabouts of the Architectural or House Ec labs, can immediately and with accuracy tell you how to reach the Covered Rink."*

The Rink was designed by Professor Cecil Burgess. "The skating rink roof had the biggest span of any roof in town," he remembers. "I saw them hoist the roof, and when it went up, it was shaped like an 'S,' and then it straightened out perfectly."[21] Students skated and played hockey in the Rink for decades, and in the 1940s double-decker bunk beds would be stacked in the dressing rooms as temporary housing for World War II veterans.

The varsity rink during construction. (UAA 71–213–281) In the picture below, the U of A takes on Saskatchewan in February 1940. (UAA 72–58–176)

room. There were 3,000 school divisions and as many school boards." He remembers how, as minister of education, he personally drove Al Ottewell from Extension throughout southern Alberta in his horse and buggy to visit schools and speak to community groups in an attempt to alleviate the problem.

Dr. Rae Chittick, a nurse educator in the 1920s and later director of the nursing program at McGill, was also interviewed in 1969 when she was in her 90s. Her recollections of early rural education in Alberta echo Baker's: "Originally in Alberta, teacher training was a four-month course at the Camrose or Calgary Normal Schools. There was a critical shortage of teachers, but even so, after World War I, the training period was extended to eight months."[22]

The way it worked was that if you finished grade 11, you could acquire a second-class teaching certificate, and if you finished grade 12, you were eligible for a first-class teaching certificate. By 1919, the University had started offering summer school classes for teachers who wanted to pursue a BA or BSc degree. "Early summer schools," says Chittick, "offered new horizons for rural teachers. Teachers in those early days led such meagre lives. They might have to go 15 miles for groceries. They had neither newspapers, books or magazines. For the most part, they had such limited social backgrounds that the picnics, dances, sports, brought them back to live in the residences year after year. Summer school created an imaginative world of things to do and teachers could gain insight into their teaching problems." Perrin Baker, the provincial government's representative in 1929 when the Normal School opened in Edmonton, finishes the story: "So in order to raise the standard of teaching in general, we raised the standard of entrance to Normal School (where all teacher training was done at the time) from grade 11 to grade 12. The Normal School was moved from Camrose to Edmonton, where according to opinion, which I strongly shared, it should have been in the first place. A fine new building was erected for it on the campus."

By the mid-1940s, all teacher training would be transferred to the University of Alberta, under the auspices of a College of Education and then a Faculty of Education. When today's Education Buildings were opened, the Normal School was re-named Corbett Hall to honour Ned Corbett, a pioneer in adult education in Canada and second director of Extension at the U of A.

A GLANCE AT THE CALENDAR—1920-1929

Elite Scholarships[23]

THERE WAS NO MORE COVETED AWARD than the Rhodes Scholarship, and during the 1920s the name of every U of A Rhodes Scholar was listed in the Calendar. Its value, both monetary and in terms of the doors it opened, was incomparable in an era when most scholarships were worth from $10 to $50. With an annual value of £350, the Rhodes was in a class of its own. At the time, the Rhodes competition was open only to single men between the ages of 19 and 25. You couldn't be just "a bookworm," as Mr. Rhodes put it. You also had to succeed in "manly outdoor sports such as cricket, football and the like." Candidates needed to show "moral force of character" and "sympathy for and protection of the weak." The scholarship award was good for two years at Oxford, with a possible third year. The competition for a Rhodes Scholarship is still fierce, and recipients are regarded as the best in their fields. The decision on a Rhodes outranked every other front-page story in a 1920s *Gateway*.

There were two other scholarships in the 1920s with a high monetary value. One was for women only, and was offered by the Federation of University Women. Valued at $1,250, it was a cross-Canada scholarship that was not often awarded in the West. The other was offered by the members of the Imperial Order of the Daughters of the Empire, the IODE. The $1,400, one-year scholarship, for study anywhere in Britain, was open to both men and women.

One of the IODE scholars during the 1920s was Marjorie Sherlock, noted for her "wit and ability to annihilate argument." A sessional in English for a year before winning the IODE, she had a long career at the U of A as a head librarian. Marjorie worked with architects to plan the Rutherford Library—the University's first free-standing library.

Regulations of the Day—"Submit Cheerfully"

THE 1929 CALENDAR listed meetings of the full Students' Union—no classes were held at that time. Every student was part of the Union and expected to attend every meeting. Whether all actually attended was another question altogether.

Registration in the 1920s was in the last week of September, and you registered and paid all on the same day. Once you were officially in, you were given "a ticket" which would let you into classes. "After that," as the Calendar put it, "regular and punctual attendance was required." There was usually a student who acted as a class monitor, taking attendance, and if you were late for class you had to take it up with the instructor afterwards. Instructors were strict about attendance and lateness usually counted as an absence. Missing more than ten classes throughout the year meant that you couldn't take the final exam and therefore failed the course.

One student remembers running at a break-neck pace to get to Professor Sonet's French 2 class on time: "Down the second floor corridor of the Arts Building would come Sonet, for an 8 A.M. class, humming a French tune. His gown snapping with energy, he outpaced a dilatory student panting to the head of the stairs. Dr. Sonet opened then closed the door of room 246. French 2 was immediately in session. The dilatory student opened then closed the door as unobtrusively as possible, slid to a seat in time to answer 'Present' for roll call. Otherwise Dr. Sonet would pronounce sentence: 'You are LATE, Ma'm'selle. Then you are absent.'"[24]

The Calendar made it clear that students were expected to "submit themselves cheerfully to the rules and regulations." The Committee on Student Affairs could expel you if your presence was deemed prejudicial to the interests of the university.

Want to book a room for student function? You had to write to President Tory for permission at least one week in advance. Want to play on a sports team? You now had to show proof that you were a *bona fide* student in good standing. How many exams in a year? In junior courses, four one-hour tests and a final exam. Want a re-read of your final exam? Appeals were allowed beginning in 1921.

THE EVERGREEN AND GOLD

IN 1921 the Students' Union produced the first edition of the *Evergreen and Gold*, the student yearbook. An outgrowth of a special, year-end edition of *The Gateway*, the *E & G* was a sumptuous, leather-bound keepsake. It was filled with photos and descriptions of student activities, student

The cover of the 1929–30 Evergreen and Gold *included an engraving of a pioneer family travelling by ox-drawn wagon across the prairie. The wife is in the back of the wagon with a baby and young boy while the husband, dressed in buckskins and a coonskin cap, is on his horse, looking off to the horizon. Far in the distance, the clouds have parted to show a shimmering building—the new Medical Building. And that is where the pioneers are headed. The yearbook's dedication? "To the undaunted spirit of our forefathers who laid the foundations of our province and who in their wisdom provided for the higher education of the youth of Alberta."*

government, and graduates. The first *Evergreen and Gold* was dedicated to Professor Will Alexander.

In the late 1920s, in the *Evergreen and Gold* sections describing student clubs, one person keeps reappearing, a volunteer named J.B. Carmichael. Mrs. Carmichael was one of the musical pioneers at the U of A, a whirlwind of musical excellence some four decades before there was a department of Music.

J.B. Carmichael[25]

J.B. Carmichael was born Beatrice Van Loon. One of five musically inclined sisters from South Bend, Indiana, she was on the stage singing by age 4. At 16, she conducted an operetta with 100 in the company and 50 in the orchestra. She was recognized as "one of the finest dramatic sopranos on the continent." After Beatrice's European tour was side-tracked by World War I, her parents agreed that she could take her orchestra to Edmonton for an eight-week contract at the Hotel Macdonald—as long as she didn't expose her face to the cold for any length of time. While performing at the Mac, Beatrice met and fell in love with an Edmonton dentist and became Mrs. J.B. Carmichael.

"She Brought Us Music"

WITH HER WARM PERSONALITY, her personal flair (her 1920s flapper outfits were stunning), and her matchless skills (she played first violin for the Edmonton Symphony Orchestra), Mrs. J.B. Carmichael ("Auntie Van" as she was affectionately known) introduced U of A students to orchestral excellence and to the magic of opera. When she lifted her baton, there was always an "encouraging smile and a sparkle in her eye" as she said, "All right, girls and boys, let's go!" Students loved her. Mrs. Carmichael was a "constant friend of university music" who always outdid herself "in patience, enthusiasm and art."

J.B. Carmichael in 1919. (COEA–10–1523A)

It was a lucky break for Edmonton. Mrs. Carmichael founded the Edmonton Opera Society, and she brought opera to the U of A. In 1927, *Maritana* was the first opera staged at the U of A, in Convocation Hall. No one thought an opera could be sucessfully produced in a community as small as the U of A campus (1,500 students), but it was a smashing success—a crowded house two nights in a row, great reviews, and a profit to boot. Helping Mrs. Carmichael was Engineering professor James Adam, who as an under-graduate had designed the University's Crest. The president of the Literary Society, which was overseeing the production, was James Adam's son Jimmy.

Mrs. Carmichael also introduced operetta to the campus. These productions were wildly popular, and the cast travelled down to Calgary for two- and three-night sold-out runs.

And that's not all. Mrs. Carmichael conducted the University Orchestra and played at every major student and university function during the year. With Physics professor L.H. Nichol, leader of the Glee Club, she blended orchestral and vocal music—the "Glee Sym." By 1933 the two clubs were combined into a Philharmonic Society, with Mrs. Carmichael at the helm. In the same year she took on the leadership of the Edmonton Symphony Orchestra. When CKUA made its debut, she organized and conducted an orchestra to play live on the air.

GLIMPSES FROM THE GATEWAY—1920-1929

IN EACH MAY EDITION, *The Gateway* published every student's name and final exam grade for the entire world to see. But it did more: *The Gateway* chronicled the life of the University in the 1920s, from club activities to research. Headlines from various editions throughout the decade provide a good sense of what life was like for students.

"Glee Club Meets"—October 10, 1924

NO ONE TOUCHED the memorial organ in Convocation Hall except Mr. Nichols, a Physics professor who was also the university organist. In the 1920s, Mr. Nichols revived the Glee Club, which had its ups and downs since the first student vocal group sang in 1908 at Convocation. The faltering Glee Club would eventually give rise to a rich choral life at the U of A.

"D.H. Rice Balks at Initiation; Then Defies Authority"—March 12, 1925

DWIGHT RICE had been a schoolteacher for four years before registering at the U of A. When the sophomores set about initiating him in their annual "rite of passage" for all freshmen, he refused to "make a clown of himself for the amusement of the Sophomores." Rice was summoned before the Student Court. He refused to appear. The Student Court, run by the Students' Union, charged him with contempt and expelled him. The University considered the matter in its Committee on Student Affairs, but declined to overrule the Student Court. Mr. Rice left the University.

"Mark Levey Retires as President of the Students' Union"— March 20, 1925

MARK CAME TO THE U OF A with a brilliant military record, having won the Military Medal for service in World War I. His student record proved to be just as impressive—he created the first reserve fund for the SU; initiated the first student handbook; started the plans for the Covered Rink; created a questionnaire for freshmen to help them decide which extracurricular activities to join; established a "central check" system for SU expenditures to stretch student fee dollars; and, as *Gateway* editor, put the newspaper on a sound financial footing. He acted in and directed campus plays, put the French Club on its feet, and was president of his class.

Mark didn't live in residence, but he had dinner in Athabasca Hall, sitting with other medical students. He noticed a silent, shy freshman, sitting alone, who had just suffered through initiation. The freshman's name was Rache (pronounced "Raysh") Lovat Dickson. Within a decade, Rache would be known throughout most of Britain and Canada because his company published the first Grey Owl book, *Pilgrims of the Wild*. The book went through eighteen printings in England in one year, and in the 1990s actor Pierce Brosnan brought Grey Owl to life on the screen. As one mark of Rache Dickson's impact on the literary world, his autobiography was later reviewed by *The New Yorker*, *The London Times* and *The New York Times*.

But as a freshman back in 1924, Rache was in a post-initiation funk.

One night Mark Levey got up from his crowded table and invited Rache to join the group. Rache never forgot it. Thirty years later he wrote about

Mark Levey, the extraordinary student leader who changed his name to Mark Marshall.
(UAA 90–126–6)

that feeling of loneliness, and about the moment Mark Levey rescued him from his freshman isolation, in part one of his autobiography, *The Ante Room.*[26]

Mark Levey was Jewish at a time when because of his religion he couldn't, for instance, become a member of the local golf club. Indeed, as late as the 1940s, even universities like McGill and the University of Toronto denied entrance to some Jewish applicants, including the famed chemist and philanthropist Alfred Bader.

Mark changed his last name, and he wasn't the only Jewish student to do so. Mark Levey became Mark Marshall. In 1936, he was hired as a professor of Ophthalmology. He soon became the department head, serving in that capacity from 1940–1962. In the 1950s, having banked all his honoraria in trust funds, he negotiated with the provincial government and used his honoraria to add an Ophthalmology annex to the Mewburn Pavillion. "It came as a complete surprise to everyone on campus, including the president and the dean of Medicine," says author Elise Corbett. Mark Marshall was also responsible for setting up the graduate training program in Medicine, something that "would in time change the basic philosophy of the school." In 1943, Mark was one of the first physicians from the U of A to sign up for active service in World War II.

"Initiation to Satisfy The Most Exacting"—October 15, 1925

FRESHMEN WERE JOLTED awake at 3 A.M.; their heads were shaved to make a "V'" for Varsity; they were dunked, paddled, and rolled down inclines out the windows of Athabasca. They were dressed in outlandish clothes, slathered with cold cream and limburger cheese—you get the idea.

"In Memoriam"—November 12, 1925

THE PIPE ORGAN in Convocation Hall was dedicated to the memory of U of A students, staff, and faculty who had died in World War I.

"The Brain Drain"—November 19, 1925

IN A "DÉJÀ VU ALL OVER AGAIN," Dr. Tory lamented the brain drain that was affecting Canada.

"Rhodes Scholars Given Send Off"—October 2, 1926

FIVE STUDENTS from across the Dominion of Canada gathered for a celebratory dinner in Montréal, on their way to study at Oxford. Clarence Campbell from the U of A was one of them. Later, he became president of the National Hockey League.

"Covered Rink to Be Rushed this Fall"—October 14, 1926

STUDENTS WEREN'T SATISFIED with plans for a SUB; they wanted an indoor skating rink. The star project of the Students' Union was moving from plan to reality, but the opening wouldn't occur for another year.

"L'art pour Canada"—October 14, 1926

"ON MONDAY EVENING the Edmonton Museum of Art was fortunate in having as their guest of Honor A.Y. Jackson, RCA, leader of the Group of Seven....The Group of Seven is the first stirrings towards a national art. They do not go to foreign countries to learn a style...." Their art was a "product of the soil" of Canada. By 1950, U of A students would dedicate their yearbook to Canadian artists. But in 1926, Canadian art, and its chief exponents, the Group of Seven painters, were very much on the fringe.

Still controversial since their first show in 1920, Group of Seven members were travelling Canada and the Territories, and painting what they saw right here at home. A.Y. Jackson had made his first sketching trip to Jasper National Park in 1924. He and his colleagues would create thousands of oil paintings of the West. "Their images captured brilliantly sunlit prairies, the rolling foothills, breathtaking mountains, the evocative coastal atmosphere, austere and barren northlands, portraits, people and abstractions."[27] Their style, as *The Gateway* put it, was "not a copy in the French manner, as their Parisian instructors taught them, "but rather something new, distinctive, and fresh." And so on October 14, 1926, *The Gateway* reported, Edmontonians heard about the birth of Canadian art.

"University Gets Myrtle's Skull"—October 7, 1927

"EVERYONE RECALLS the thrilling adventure which took place in Cranbrook, B.C. early in August," said *The Gateway*. "Five elephants travelling with the Sells-Floto circus escaped, three of them, Tillie, Myrtle and Charlie, running wild for several weeks. The attempts of Kootenay Indians, expert trackers, and elephant trainers to locate and capture them was of no avail."

Tillie was lured out of the wild with peanuts. Myrtle was found dead and her skull was sent to the University "to excite the wonder and curiosity of zoological students." Charlie's remains are still out there.

"Rutherford Elected Chancellor"—October 7, 1927

THE GATEWAY paid tribute to Charles Stuart, the first chancellor and in effect the first chair of the Board of Governors, who died in office, and welcomed the former premier, "Father of the University," as the new chancellor. This new generation of students warmed to Rutherford. "From the first," said *The Gateway*, "he had in mind an institution to care for the growing educational needs of the province which was only just out of its swaddling clothes."

"Local Symphony Commences Season" With Vernon Barford—October 20, 1927

"ON SUNDAY NIGHT the Empire Theatre was filled to capacity...to hear the Edmonton Symphony Orchestra. Mr. Vernon Barford...ably displayed his skill as a conductor...."

Vernon Barford was also at the centre of the music scene on campus, directing the Glee Club, and was in charge of music for Elizabeth Sterling Haynes's Little Theatre productions. He was a force in music in the city for sixty years. In 1908, he conducted a chorus of 250 and an orchestra of 40, with an audience of 2,000, in Edmonton's Thistle Rink. And he was a calm force—he "never ran. Nor did he walk. He strolled—with a cane for effect—and his dress and manner always suggested that he had a yacht tied up around the corner."[28] When he was well into his 90s, Vernon Barford tried to cross Jasper Avenue at rush hour. He couldn't quite make it in the "allotted time." When the cars came rushing towards him, he held up his cane to fend them off, finally "mounting the curb as though it were a podium. Then he turned, raised his cane like a baton, flashed the familiar smile and bowed to the audience."

"Tuxedos" at The Boys' Shop for $25—October 20, 1927

"TUXEDOS—In the evening the Tuxedo is the correct thing for the dinner dances, concerts, theatre parties and other evening affairs—they keep you looking your best....Every young man's wardrobe should contain one." Many students did indeed own a tuxedo, and if they didn't, they rented one for the monthly formal dances.

"Annual Application for Med Night Opposed"—November 11, 1927

ALL THE NON-ATHLETIC STUDENT CLUBS were run by the Literary Association of the Students' Union, except for the Med Club. The Med Club was "distinct," as *The Gateway* put it, and in 1927 Provost MacEachran refused to sanction the Club's proposal for Med Night.

Things could get a little out of hand at Med Night and, in fact, *The Gateway* said that the activities that went on during the day were "undignified and degrading." Although Med Night was a welcome break from classes, "the dignity and honour of the University has been abused, especially last year." *The Gateway* reported that student opinion was with the provost.

But the Students' Union was fiercely attached to the notion of self-government, and in succeeding *Gateways*, the main headlines screamed out the issue: "Student Government Ha Ha." And "Are We Not Supposed to be Independent?" A meeting of the Union was called to discuss the question. All students were required to attend. But when the time came, there was no quorum.

The following month, Wes Oke, the Students' Union president, said that the SU was "failing in all three branches of government." The Union provided for direct government by all students. Was this now too cumbersome? Did students care? Was the student body too large and diverse for direct government?

The headlines continued into the following year: "Do the SU president, the student Chief Judge and *The Gateway* editor take their orders from Dr. Tory?" "Will this SU ever be worth two hoops in Hades to anybody?" Soon there would be major revisions to the way the Students' Union governed its affairs.

"Collip Going to McGill to Chair Biochemistry"—November 24, 1927

FOUR YEARS BEFORE, in 1923, Dr. J. Bertram Collip had "received signal recognition of his share in the discovery of insulin" when Nobel Prize winners Drs. McLeod and Banting of Toronto divided the prize money with "co-discoverers Drs. Collip and Best."

On a year's leave from the University of Alberta, Dr. Collip took up an appointment at the University of Toronto and worked with the research team that had discovered insulin. His part of the project was to refine insulin so that it could be administered to diabetics without causing unexpected complications. "The problem seemed almost hopeless," he wrote to Tory,

> so you can imagine my delight when about midnight one day last week I discovered a way to get the active principle free from all the "muck" with which it appeared to be inseparably bound....I have never had such an absolutely satisfactorily experience....To be associated in an intimate way with a solution of a problem which for years has resisted all efforts was something I had never anticipated. I only wish that the various papers which will be published on this work were coming from Alberta rather than Toronto. A whole new field has been thrown open however and I will continue to work along these lines for some time no doubt.[29]

The Gateway regularly covered research-related stories, and it was front-page news when professors went off for a year to finish their PhDs. Classics professor Will Alexander made sure that U of A students understood that research marked the difference between a college and a university.

"Toronto Royal Winter Fair"—November 24, 1927

THE U OF A Animal Science Department started a breeding program in 1920 and was soon entering prize specimens in national and international shows. One of the biggest shows was the Toronto Royal Fair, where up to 10,000 animals were entered in a single classification. In 1925, Agriculture student Tom Devlin took top honours in all of Canada at the Toronto Royal Fair. In 1927, the U of A "swept the show."[30]

Matthew Halton—Gateway Editor 1928–1929

MANY *GATEWAY* EDITORS and writers have gone on to fame: Joe Clark, former prime minister and leader of the Conservative Party; Peter Lougheed, premier of Alberta from 1971 through 1985; Beverley McLachlin, chief justice of the Supreme Court of Canada. But no one can match Matthew Halton's stellar journalistic career.

Virtually every Canadian tuned in to the radio to hear Matthew Halton's daily reports from the battlefields of Europe during World War II. Canadians knew Matt Halton's name and they knew his voice. They hung on his words. Halton's reports were described as "prose poems" because of their clear language and succinct messages that conveyed both fact and emotion. Matt reported virtually all the major events of World War II— the fall of Ortona, the landing of Canadian troops at Normandy on D-Day, and the liberation of Paris. He was present as a CBC reporter when the armistice was signed. Check the Web to listen to some of his most famous reports and, when you do, remember that the sounds of war that you hear were recorded on a phonograph, not a tape recorder.

THEATRE—THE NUMBER ONE GATEWAY STORY

FOR CONSISTENT front-page coverage in *The Gateway* during the 1920s, one subject stood out. Live theatre. The place was the Convocation Hall stage in the old Arts Building. The players were university students from every faculty. *The Gateway* followed theatre stories with a dogged passion. Every aspect of theatre production was front-page news, with lavish photo spreads. The competition to select directors for the plays was covered in as much detail as were the actual plays.

The Shield

IT STARTED THE DAY YOU ARRIVED on campus and peaked in the spring. Every class competed in it—seniors, juniors, sophomores, and freshmen. Students from every discipline took part. It was the Inter-Year Play Competition, and from September to April *The Gateway* covered every detail of the competition on the front page. The Dramatic Shield was introduced in 1921, on the U of A's 15th birthday, and was awarded to the class—the freshmen, sophomores, juniors, or seniors—that presented

the best publicly performed one-act play in the Inter-Year Play Competition. Competition was fierce.

Since the days of World War I, students had put on plays, first in Athabasca Hall and later, as new buildings appeared on campus, in the ever-larger venues of Convocation Hall, Corbett Hall, and the Jubilee Auditorium. When students began mounting plays, there were no movies, no radio, no TV, and no computers. Entertainment was live theatre, and all Albertans loved it.

Down the street from campus, Garneau High School had a drama club, and so did every other high school. Overtown in Edmonton, there was the elegant, art deco Empire Theatre, where travelling professional companies put on plays and variety shows. In rural Alberta, everyone for miles around put down the plough, hitched up the buggy, and came into town for the show when the Chautauqua troop arrived with its huge tent and cast of characters.

Students from the 1920s would say that nothing, but *nothing*, animated their lives like theatre. In just one night, after months of preparation, the seniors, juniors, sophomores, and freshmen each staged a one-act play in front of a packed house and a group of adjudicators. There was no university credit to be gained, no Drama Department to guide the hopefuls, and no pressure to get involved. But nearly everyone did—on the stage, behind the scenes, or in the audience.

When the four short plays made their debut, Edmontonians flocked to campus for the competition, and they hung from the rafters. By the end of the decade, student plays (and operas) were being taken down to Calgary for a run of several days, always to sold-out theatres.

The person who made it all happen was Elizabeth Sterling Haynes. On April 25, 2004, almost half a century after her death, *The Globe and Mail* remembered her contribution as a theatre director, educator, and co-founder of the Banff School of Fine Arts. But for hundreds of students at the U of A, and for thousands of Albertans, she was simply their amazing, inspiring drama teacher.

Elizabeth was the first drama specialist in the Faculty of Extension. From the 1920s, when she arrived in Edmonton, to the 1950s, when she went home to Ontario with terminally failing health, this woman embodied theatre. Haynes never held a tenure-track position, but no other teacher in the U of A's history has affected so many students, from so many disciplines, and is remembered with such affection and reverence.

Elizabeth Sterling Haynes, the inspiring teacher who changed lives. (UAA 78–17–105)

Elizabeth Sterling Haynes—
The Drama Teacher Who Changed Lives

TORONTO-TRAINED, and a theatre star at the University of Toronto, Elizabeth Sterling Haynes came to Edmonton in the early 1920s because her husband wanted to establish his dental practice here. One day, she ran into an old Toronto friend, Classics professor W.G. Hardy, on Whyte Avenue. Hardy had seen Elizabeth's productions and he had seen her act. Right there on the street corner he urged Elizabeth to direct a play he was working on. It was that simple a beginning.

Elizabeth did not need much persuading. The theatre was akin to a religious calling for her, and the West, starting with the U of A campus, would rapidly become her missionary field. Be they students from the 1920s to the 1950s unknowingly waiting for a theatre guide, or farmers in the 1930s on the snow-locked prairies ripe for a creative release, Elizabeth led them all from the wings to centre stage.

Haynes accumulated a huge legacy during her 30-year career. From 1923 to 1930, she directed the U of A Dramatic Society, where her choice of plays and her new style of directing were revolutionary. After the late-winter, Inter-Year Play Competition, she would cherry-pick the best talent and produce the spring play. Edmontonians flocked to these productions. They were all sell-outs, with overflow audiences crowding the aisles.

In 1929, when President Wallace proposed that the U of A help start a "Little Theatre" in Edmonton, Elizabeth was the first director. Already popular in the US, the Little Theatre movement swept across Canada in the late 1920s. Little Theatres were amateur groups, but they were committed to achieving professional standards. Will Alexander was the first president of Edmonton's Little Theatre, and Jimmy Adam, the engineering student who designed the University Crest, conducted play readings.

In the late 1920s, Elizabeth founded the Alberta Drama League. The League divided the province into 14 "workshop" areas, established drama clubs, fostered their development, and sponsored festivals. In the 1930s, when Elizabeth was hired as the first Drama specialist in the Faculty of Extension, she toured dozens of rural towns, teaching theatre to thousands of eager Albertans who met her at the train station on wintry days to escort her to their schools and community halls.

From 1949 to 1954, Elizabeth taught in the new Drama Department, directing and acting in productions of the fledgling Studio Theatre. All along the way, she established and worked with dozens of theatre groups. It was Elizabeth who was the inspiration behind the first high school drama organization in Edmonton, and Elizabeth who established Theatre Workshop classes for adults and children. In 1935, she and Betty Mitchell (BSC '24) persuaded the Department of Education to make Drama an accredited course in the schools.

In 1986, the "Elizabeth Sterling Haynes Awards Celebrating Theatre in Edmonton" were established—better known as the "Sterlings." Elizabeth is one of the reasons Edmonton has such a rich theatre life. With some 14 professional theatre companies in the city and the vibrant Fringe Festival, Edmonton has "more theatres *per capita* than any other North American centre."

Those who were touched by her magic include people whose names have become synonymous with Canadian theatre, and they recall their first encounters with her vividly.[31]

Joe Shoctor (LLB '45, LLD HON '81, ORDER OF CANADA, QUEEN'S COUNSEL)[32]

JOE SHOCTOR was a Law graduate, but theatre was his passion. In his university days, Joe originated and produced the Varsity Show and was president of the Literary Association. Thirty years later, he founded Edmonton's Citadel Theatre Complex. One of his mentors was Elizabeth Sterling Haynes.

"Simply put," Joe said in 1974, Elizabeth Sterling Haynes "made me want to be in theatre. As a young boy, I acted under Mrs. Haynes' direction in *Ten Cents a Copy* (in Talmud Torah Hall), and Maxwell Anderson's war play, *The Eve of St. Mark* (in Westglen School). Theatre became as important to me as breathing."

In 1974, Joe Shoctor raised $5 million to build a new theatre in Edmonton. In 1976 a $40-million performing arts complex was built in the downtown core, complete with production facilities and a theatre school enrolling some 350 students. The Citadel's five theatres, including the Shoctor stage, now produce more than 900 performances a year.

Tom Peacocke (DIP ED '53, BED '55, BA '59)

TOM PEACOCKE, professor emeritus of Drama at the U of A, has shaped the talents and careers of hundreds of actors, including Paul Gross (BFA '97), star of the television series *Due South*. Elizabeth Sterling Haynes was Tom's mentor.

"It was the fall of 1951," Tom remembers, "and I was a History-English major in Education taking an elective course in Drama. My attention was deployed on a variety of mind-boggling problems and confusions... should I rush a fraternity? Was it morally right to buy the canned notes for History 58? How could I make the Assiniboia Hall football team? Preoccupied by these and other dilemmas, I balanced precariously atop a rickety ladder in the rickety Quonset hut that was Studio Theatre.... I was assigned to something called a light crew. 'What in God's name am I doing here?' I thought. 'Who in hell are all these creeps in Drama anyway?'

"During a quiet moment, a voice the like of which I had never heard before, floated through the auditorium, rich, resonant and vital. Pausing in my work, I eavesdropped on a conversation about some fellow named O'Casey who had written a play about a Silver Tassie. Words, thoughts, insights, passions, were uttered about the theatre, about the Irish, about

O'Casey, about actors, that were beyond my comprehension. And always that voice! I remember striving to imagine what body, what face, could produce such a sound. Purposely I dropped my wrench to the floor.... I fixed my gaze on the most statuesque figure I had ever seen.

"It was at that moment that I subconsciously began to reconsider the direction my life would take."[33]

In 1981, Tom Peacocke won a Genie as best actor.

It was not only the stars of Canadian theatre who remembered Elizabeth Sterling Haynes. At least three students from the 1920s—Gwen Pharis Ringwood, Elsie Park Gowan, and Teddy Cohen—have left us with accounts of her remarkable presence.

Gwen Pharis Ringwood (BA '34)—"Alberta's Theatrical Sodbuster"

"I FIRST SAW Mrs. Haynes directing a play in 1929," Gwen recalls. "I felt awe at the vibrancy generated as she patiently, tenderly, methodically pushed novice actors towards the playwright's vision, towards the time when the play would unfold as a flowing, united whole before an audience.

She demanded greatness.[34]

Gwen graduated from the U of A in 1934, but she started university much earlier, in the late 1920s. Raised in the southern Alberta farming community of Barons, she had to drop out of university twice in order to work to pay for her schooling. Within five years of graduation she had written a one-act play, *Still Stands the House*, which became Canada's most widely produced one-act play. Gwen wrote about the ordinary people of the West, the people she knew best. During her career, she had "over forty plays produced on stage, radio and television...socially alert dramas, comedies and musicals...." She is viewed as "the most important playwright produced by the affiliated theatre and little theatre movement of the 1930s and 1940s."

"When I arrived at the U of A in the fall of 1929," says Gwen, "I had some of the 'greats' as teachers, like Will Alexander and Dr. George Hardy. Both of them were very important to me...because of their humanistic philosophy. You began to think about how other people thought about things you thought you knew." It was Doc Alik who encouraged Gwen to apply for a Rockefeller Fellowship, and she readily acknowledges his assistance: "I got it through Elizabeth Sterling Haynes and Dr. Alexander, and I went to the University of North Carolina for a Master's, studying theatre, English and playwriting."

When Gwen met Elizabeth in her freshman year, Elizabeth did not yet have a teaching position. "Wherever Elizabeth was," says Gwen, "things began to happen. I joined the Drama Club—my husband, a medical student then, joined too and had some parts in plays. I really loved it.

"As a student, I just worshipped Elizabeth Haynes and if she ever even looked at me, I just couldn't believe it. Someone who knew so much and who was so nice and so extremely fascinating....

"It made a great difference in my life because I don't think I'd ever have tried to write for theatre of any kind if I hadn't got to know Elizabeth.... She had a great generosity about money, about time—her time—her energy, and she really expended herself—she loved theatre.

"Elizabeth Haynes was the strongest influence on me.... I learned most of the technical knowledge of the theatre I possess from Elizabeth. I acted for her, directed, adjudicated....I inherited from her a highly idealistic idea of what theatre can mean to a culture, society, country, individual."

In 1982, Gwen Pharis Ringwood was awarded an honorary doctorate by the University of Lethbridge for her contributions to theatre.

Elsie Park Gowan (BA '30, LLD HON '82)—Stagestruck[35]

BORN IN THE SAME YEAR that Alberta became a province, Elsie Park Gowan's name is famous in Alberta theatre. *The Globe and Mail* commemorated Elsie in its February 2, 2004 edition on what would have been Elsie's 99th birthday. Elsie "developed an interest in theatre from historical, economic and feminist perspectives," said the national newspaper. By 1958, Elsie had written "more than 200 radio plays for national audiences, exploring such issues as mental illness, daycare, unwed pregnancy and the changing status of women."

But back in 1926, she was just 21-year-old Elsie Young, a freshman majoring in History. Her friend Gwen Pharis recalls, "Elsie had a reputation for her wit and her sharp tongue and seemed to be so sure of everything. It was some years before I got over the awe of Elsie. But then we became friends while writing a series of plays together and it all worked out very well."

During her long career as a high school teacher, Elsie wrote dozens of plays, many of them comedies, and passed along to thousands of students the love of theatre that she developed at the U of A.

How did Elsie make the leap from serious History student to Drama enthusiast? Right after registration, she joined the Drama Club, where Elizabeth Sterling Haynes was the director. Elsie describes herself as "stagestruck."

To understand U of A students and theatre in the 1920s, says Elsie, you really must know something about the Empire Theatre and "the talkies." The New Empire Theatre, opened in 1920, was a glorious building that seated 1,500 people in its plush chairs. The walls were covered with brocades imported from France and murals painted by Italian artists. The chandeliers were exquisite. Elsie remembers that there were "goddesses on the ceiling," and when you went to the Empire, "you got dressed up to go, and it was an *occasion*."

The Empire Theatre played host to professional travelling companies until 1929. "One of the last companies to come through," says Elsie, "was an English company called Stratford on Avon. And this was the great thrill of it—they used university students for the extras, for the mob scenes.... Oh, boy! We really got to act! It was the thrill of a lifetime!"

Then the talkies arrived, seemingly out of nowhere, and the road shows died. Elsie remembers that at almost the same moment that professional theatre stopped, "Little Theatre" arrived. "There was a big meeting in the old Med Amphitheatre [on campus]," remembers Elsie, and prominent people in Edmonton were there, including some University professors, and they formed the Edmonton Little Theatre. The important thing was that we had here a woman of terrific dynamic potential: Elizabeth Sterling Haynes.

"When I was a student," says Elsie, "there was no Drama department, you understand. We had a student club, and we just did plays for the fun of it. One year, our play was *The Adding Machine*, by Elmer Rice, straight off Broadway." The Drama Club director was Elizabeth Haynes. She took the play to the Little Theatre and the play was performed on the Corbett Hall stage for the general public. For Elsie and other students who participated, they had arrived—they were "on the stage."

Elsie describes Elizabeth Haynes as "terrific," as the "high priestess of theatre," and as a "breakthrough" director, doing things no one else had ever thought of. She had them using the Stanislavsky method before there was a name for it.

The first play Elsie was in was titled *He Who Gets Slapped*, by Leonid Andreyev. It ushered in experimental theatre, it "moved the boundary posts, it signalized...a departure in the dramatic activity of this university." As the yearbook put it, in an article likely written by Doc Alik, "Non-British continental drama has been almost unknown in this country." Elsie played Zenida, the lion tamer. "He" who gets slapped was the circus clown, Eric Gibbs (BA '30). "The Gentleman," who stole Eric's wife, was Hugh Morrison (BA '30). All went on to fame in their chosen careers—drama and journalism.

Elizabeth was intense, but there were light moments, too. In one of the first Studio Theatre plays, recalls Elsie, "there was a scene in the Garden of Eden, and they had to have a tree. At 5:30 P.M. the night of the show, there was no tree. So Elizabeth and one of the boys went down to Queen Elizabeth Park and cut one down." Elsie hits one sour note. "It wasn't fair," she laments, "that Elizabeth did so much work and never got the credit."

In 1982, the U of A conferred an honorary degree on Elsie Park (Young) Gowan, and in 1993, she was inducted into the Edmonton Cultural Hall of Fame.

Teddy Cohen, the student who "took fire." (UAA 78-17-75)

Theodore Cohen (LLB '30)—"He Just Took Fire"[36]

THE YEARBOOK SAID that Teddy could easily attack "25 equity cases," but when Teddy was bit by the theatre bug, it changed his life.

In 1929, a senior student named Hugh Morrison, long involved in the Literary Society, was selected to direct the senior play. He chose a murder mystery called *Shall We Join the Ladies?* by J.M. Barrie of *Peter Pan* fame. "I chose that play," says Hugh, "because it had 15 starring roles in it, and there were so many excellent actors in the senior class that year, like Elsie Young, Walter Little and the amazing Eric Gibbs, who teetered between a career in law and acting—he was just a fabulous actor." Gwen Pharis called them the "young intellectuals."[37]

The play was a huge hit. People were turned away from the doors, and many missed the last streetcar and had to walk home. It not only won the Shield, but Elizabeth Sterling Haynes decided to take the play to the Little Theatre festival in Calgary. That's when Teddy met Elizabeth.

"Oh, I'll tell you all about Teddy," says Elsie Park Gowan. "Ted was this handsome young lawyer, who was in his second or third year at the university. In 1929 we put on *Shall We Join the Ladies*. Well, it's a very posh play with a very posh setting—you know, a table set with stemware and silverware and all that. And somebody said, 'Get Ted Cohen to do the props. He knows all the rich people in town.'" The posh props, of course, had to be borrowed.

"And you know? Ted just took fire."

When Elizabeth directed the play for the Little Theatre, "Ted became her assistant," says Elsie, "and he got more and more drawn into theatre. And finally he quit his law course, much to his family's distress, and became Elizabeth's assistant. He was at the Banff Centre with her, directing for five or six years."

Hugh Morrison continues, "When Elizabeth left for the Maritimes in 1936 to start Little Theatre there, Ted went with her. He just adored her. But she was married. And so he left for New York, changed his last name to Corday, ended up in Hollywood, and made a big name for himself in television, at NBC, and in radio."

And that—through the eyes and accomplishments of a few of her students—was Elizabeth Sterling Haynes. She made the University of Alberta pulsate with theatre for decades and had a profound effect on students enrolled in the arts, the sciences, and in the health sciences and professional faculties. There is no theatre named for her on campus and no honorary degree was ever awarded. But her legacy is all around us.

Wallace Sterling

WALLACE STERLING came to the U of A in 1928 to study for a graduate degree in History. His sister Elizabeth had already moved to Edmonton, so he would not be on his own. Shortly after Wally arrived, the U of A's professional football coach resigned. With the fall season fast approaching, the University was pressed to find a replacement and had no money to

Wallace Sterling, the substitute coach who, as a history student, led a Cinderella team to victory. (UAA 69–10–35)

hire another professional coach. Wally had played Canadian football while studying at the University of Toronto and so the U of A took a chance on the young graduate student from the History Department, and named Wallace Sterling as coach.

In 1926, the U of A had lost the Western Finals to Regina, 13–1. In 1927, they lost the Hardy Trophy again, this time to Manitoba. In 1928, hopes were high that they would win it back. *Gateway* editor Matt Halton sent the sports editor, Hugh Morrison, to Winnipeg to report on the action. "A separate telegraph line was set up from the field to *The Gateway* office," says Hugh, "and I had a telegraph man with me with a key for tapping in my reports. I did a play-by-play report and the plan was that we would do an 'extra' edition of *The Gateway*. *The Edmonton Journal* and the *Edmonton Bulletin* were also on board and were going to do 'extras' as well. We had a gang of students ready to hit the streets with all these special newspapers."

Anticipation was in the air as everyone wondered if the U of A had won. Finally, the wait was over and the answer came. Yes! Wally Sterling's Golden Bears mopped the floor. Then they beat every team in their league, and went on to beat UBC, not yet in the western league, as well. Wallace Sterling finished his degree, and shortly thereafter the Calgary Tigers recruited him as their coach. Wally later served as president of Stanford University from 1949–1968.

And what happened to Hugh Morrison's article and the special edition of *The Gateway*? "Just as we filed our story," Hugh says, "the ship Vestris sank in the Bermuda Triangle, with the loss of many lives, and took over the front page of *The Edmonton Journal*. Our biggest sports story was lost on the public."

Two years later, in 1930, Vegreville-born Hugh Morrison was named a Rhodes Scholar and set out to study at Oxford.

Hugh Whitney Morrison (BA '30) — Journalist, Scholar, Spy[38]

FLEET STREET REPORTER, spy, adventurer, United Way Director. Hugh Morrison has seen it all, from small town Alberta to the high life in London and New York City. At 96, Hugh is one of the U of A's oldest graduates, and he lives a non-stop life. In his high-rise apartment in Thornhill, Ontario, Hugh's den is jammed with the books and papers that are fodder for his latest essays, articles, and interviews.

Pioneer Beginnings

HUGH WAS BORN in Vegreville in 1908, the same year the U of A opened its doors. He grew up on the edge of campus, in the old Garneau mansion that was demolished years ago to make way for the Humanities Centre.

Mabel Whitney and Frederic Morrison, Hugh's parents, were raised with all the refinements the settled East could offer. Frederic graduated with a law degree and then a BA from Dalhousie, and American-born Mabel was a graduate of the New England Conservatory of Music. But the opportunities and risks of the Northwest Territories—soon to give birth to Alberta and Saskatchewan—lured Frederic and Mabel west at the turn of the century.

Hugh's father ventured out first, in 1902. "Dad worked initially in Winnipeg and then in Regina, with Sir Frederick Haultain's law firm," says Hugh, "but even Regina wasn't far enough west for dad."

Frederic supplemented his income from the practice of law by working the harvest on a farm. And in 1905, that's where he heard that the railroad would be going through the frontier town of Vegreville in the new province of Alberta.

Frederic knew that Vegreville would boom once the tracks were laid. He pulled up stakes and boarded the train. Two years later, his fiancée

Mabel, who had never been further afield than Boston, made the long journey west to join her intended. Over the years, they had four children, and Frederic's passion for politics saw him become the first mayor of Vegreville and friend to both Senator James Lougheed and future prime minister R.B. Bennett.

Hugh heard great adventure stories of the far north. When his father was named a judge in 1916 and the family moved to Edmonton, Hugh would travel up north on the Edmonton, Dunvegan & British Columbia (ED&BC) railroad with his dad, watching trials, and had his first beer across the border in BC, where there was no prohibition at the time. Hugh and his friends used to joke that the ED&BC railroad really stood for "Easily Damaged and Badly Constructed." But the ED&BC got him where he and his dad were headed—to Grande Prairie and the Peace River region.

"This railroad," remembers Hugh, "ran from Edmonton via Lesser Slave Lake to Grande Prairie, and never did make it to BC. The train carried no diner and, therefore, had to stop for meals at the appointed station. Departure was just before suppertime, so the supper stop was Westlock: breakfast the next morning at a small community along the line."

And when they arrived, Hugh got to hang out at Ma Brainerd's, *the* meeting place in the North in the early days. "Believe me," Hugh says, "it was an eye-opener for a young boy. Ma's stopping place was at the midpoint on the Grande Prairie–Pouce Coupe Trail, and it was always filled with characters, all travelling in the remote North. Ma and her daughter made the best roast chicken dinners you could ever hope to eat."

"Ma" was Dora Brock Brainerd, who came to the Peace River Country in 1910 to join her homesteader husband. She ran her stopping place out of abandoned buildings near Lake Sinclair until husband Lee built her a log house to accommodate the booming boarding business. Ma's biographer recounts that "sometimes 20 teams and teamsters would put up at Ma Brainerd's, with 40 or 50 eating her famous chicken dinners. The charge? Fifty cents for all you could eat....and legend has it that she gave away as many meals as she sold. Because she used a thousand birds a season, she always had 'one in the pan, one ready to put in the pan, and some handy at the door ready for the axe.'" At Ma's table were rough and tumble teamster drivers, trappers, and RCMP officers (known as the Royal

North West Mounted Police in those days). Conversation buzzed with frank language and stories of adventure—quite an experience for a young teenager like Hugh. Ten years after Hugh's railside meals at Ma Brainerd's, he was being served breakfast on a silver tray in Windsor Castle by his butler, Dawson.

School Days at Garneau Elementary and Old Scona

AT GARNEAU ELEMENTARY, Hugh won the award for best overall student, and at age 14 gave an acceptance speech in Convocation Hall. "I'd heard dad many times out on the political stump and I just copied him: 'Unaccustomed as I am to public speaking....' There were giggles in the audience but I was very proud." This would be the first of many honours for Hugh.

At Garneau, one of Hugh's teachers was the principal, Harry Ainlay, and when Hugh attended Old Scona, the principal was Ross Sheppard. Both these men have Edmonton high schools named after them, and Hugh remembers them both as strict disciplinarians. "Those were the days of the strap," says Hugh, "and the strap was whipped across the palms of your hands for various transgressions. Back then it was a great triumph if you got the strap. You would come back from the principal's office rubbing your hands and the whole class—the boys anyway, as the girls got some lighter form of punishment—would say to you in a loud whisper, 'How many did you get?' And the more you got and survived, the bigger hero you were." Hugh would be the first to tell you that he got the strap more than once.

By the time Hugh reached Old Scona, he and his friends had conquered Latin, the universal language requirement of the day. Hugh delighted in concocting word games in Latin, confounding the teacher in front of the whole class. For decades afterwards, Hugh's life would be filled with the thrill that comes from testing the limits.

But Old Scona wasn't all Latin and academics. Hugh and his pal Bill Kent were stars on the rugby team until Hugh broke his arm tossing a football around in the middle of Whyte Avenue to impress his female classmates. It wouldn't be the last time Hugh set out to impress a girl.

In the 1920s, the most daring pastime for high school students was to sneak into Strathcona's pool halls. Hugh was a regular observer of the forbidden game. He remembers that "there was always this young girl in the pool halls—we called her 'Speed' Hall. She was *good*. We could never figure out how she managed to spend so much time in the pool hall and still get through school." Hugh certainly knew how to hit the books, but he also spent his life right in the thick of the action.

LIFE ON CAMPUS WITH HUGH MORRISON

Registration and Initiation—Chamber of Horrors

HUGH LIVED ON 91 AVENUE most of his early life, observing university students from his garret room on the top floor of the old Garneau mansion.

When he was 18, Hugh registered at the U of A. Hugh's academic path was made clear by his father, a judge, and in 1926, Hugh enrolled in the six-year combined BA/LLB program. Hugh came to know every one of the 182 freshmen in his class, the Class of 1930, at least by sight. "I knew students in my freshman class from across *all* the Faculties," says Hugh, "not just Arts and Law."

The University was running a deficit in 1926, but it went unnoticed by the freshmen. If you knew what program you wanted, the choices were simple, and there was room in classes for everyone. There were no quotas. Registration was a breeze for Hugh. He hardly remembers it. But after registration came initiation.

"We lived on the edge of campus," explains Hugh, "and every fall we would come and watch this initiation spectacle. So I had some idea of what to expect, at least from the outside." But it was what happened *inside* the hallowed halls that eventually caused the University to ban hazing.

"I can't give you the chronological order exactly," Hugh says, "but first we were all corralled together—all the male freshmen. The girls had a milder form of initiation run by the Wauneita Club. It was the sophomore boys who ran the show for the male freshmen. They were the ones who had been initiated the year before and they were out to inflict the same on the incoming class. So we were herded together and given some instructions about what was going to happen."

First there was a fake operation, which felt very real because the Med students who performed it were ingenious, says Hugh. "In those days there were no electric refrigerators. Instead, there were ice boxes, with the top part being filled every week with a new block of ice. What the Med students had done was to carve sharp pieces out of the slabs of ice, thin as knife blades. They held these shards of ice over us and told us they were going to make an incision. We felt this sharp slice down our bare abdomens. As far as we were concerned, they were cutting us.

"Then we were taken over to the roof of one of the residences, I am pretty sure Athabasca, and we were still blindfolded. It seems incredible today, but we were either on one of the fire escapes on the side of the building, or up on the roof, blindfolded. I remember it as the roof. And it was nightfall by now. We were picked up by our arms and legs and heaved overboard, into the air, and down below there was a big blanket, not a regular blanket, but one of those lifesaving rescue blankets that firemen use. It was a four-storey drop. And, amazingly, no one was hurt."

But it wasn't over yet.

"At some point in all this we were taken over to St. Stephen's College, which in those days had spiral fire escapes attached to the sides of the building. We were herded over there, taken to the top floor and put into the fire escape. Buckets of cold water sloshed down after us and we were soaking wet as we spiralled down to the ground floor. Then we were liberated, and the final event of initiation was the Snake Dance. Somewhere along the way our clothes were dried out and we went downtown in trucks, and then proceeded to form a long, human chain, holding hands and walking in a single-file line all the way down Jasper Avenue, shouting cheer songs, yelling and raving as we went."

Not all students were fans of initiation, but many alumni who went through it maintain that it bonded them as a class, and they look back on their survival with pride. Certainly, no one forgot the experience.

Paying for Tuition—The Mayfair Club

HUGH REMEMBERS his tuition bill as $200. After 76 years, his recollection is close to the target. Tuition in 1926 for Arts students was $170 plus $10 for the SU fee—and then, of course, there were books. Did his father, a judge, pay? No. There were nearly five months off in the summer for students to earn the money for tuition or, in some cases, return to work on the farm.

"I got a summer job at the Mayfair Golf and Country Club," recalls Hugh. "In my first summer, I was a weeder of the greens. That meant

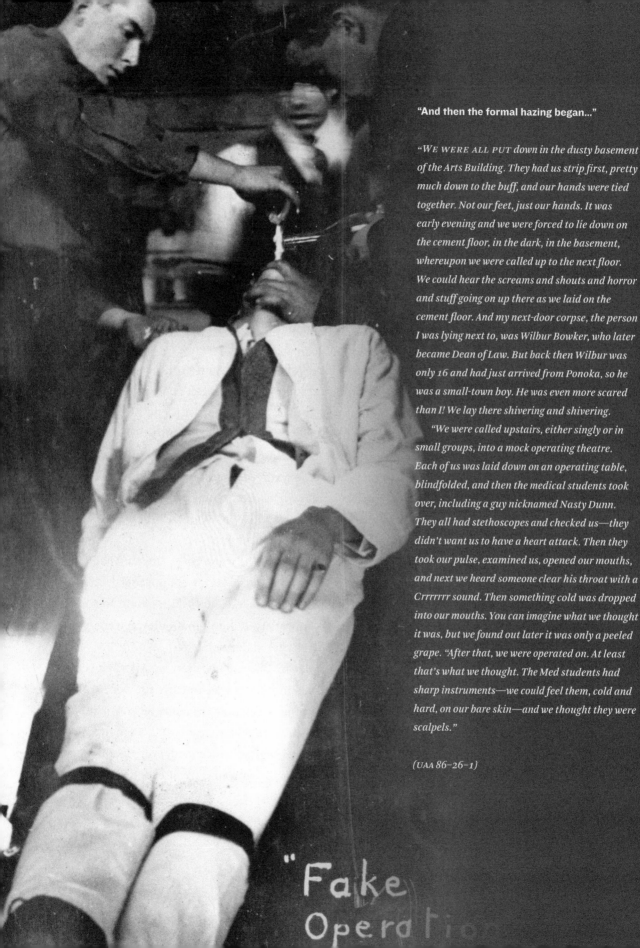

"And then the formal hazing began..."

"WE WERE ALL PUT down in the dusty basement of the Arts Building. They had us strip first, pretty much down to the buff, and our hands were tied together. Not our feet, just our hands. It was early evening and we were forced to lie down on the cement floor, in the dark, in the basement, whereupon we were called up to the next floor. We could hear the screams and shouts and horror and stuff going on up there as we laid on the cement floor. And my next-door corpse, the person I was lying next to, was Wilbur Bowker, who later became Dean of Law. But back then Wilbur was only 16 and had just arrived from Ponoka, so he was a small-town boy. He was even more scared than I! We lay there shivering and shivering.

"We were called upstairs, either singly or in small groups, into a mock operating theatre. Each of us was laid down on an operating table, blindfolded, and then the medical students took over, including a guy nicknamed Nasty Dunn. They all had stethoscopes and checked us—they didn't want us to have a heart attack. Then they took our pulse, examined us, opened our mouths, and next we heard someone clear his throat with a Crrrrrrr sound. Then something cold was dropped into our mouths. You can imagine what we thought it was, but we found out later it was only a peeled grape. "After that, we were operated on. At least that's what we thought. The Med students had sharp instruments—we could feel them, cold and hard, on our bare skin—and we thought they were scalpels."

(UAA 86–26–1)

crawling methodically on your hands and knees, plucking weeds by hand for nine hours a day. It was the lowest order of work and I earned $40 a month. The Chairman of the Greens Committee was George Steer, of the law firm Milner Steer, and he would come around with the head greens keeper and they would check our work. He was like a general coming to inspect the troops."

Hugh also had a stint watering the greens, from 9 P.M. until 6 A.M. Then he was promoted. "I became a greensman and, using a push mower, I kept the greens manicured. I earned $80 a month."

Campus Life in 1926

The campus in 1926 hummed with sports events, live theatre, debates, dances and dating, and late-night poker. There was no lack of school spirit, and competition for good grades was keen.

Hugh dove headfirst into life at the U of A, and so did all his classmates. They were an extraordinary group, and there wasn't one who entered into a career who didn't make a mark. Hugh Morrison and his classmates went on to become ambassadors to Czechoslovakia and to Sweden, senior newspaper editors and foreign correspondents, business entrepreneurs, professors, inventors, technology wizards, top lawyers, including Supreme Court justices, physicians, playwrights, best-selling authors, and publishers.

It was an unusually successful group. Why? Were they the elite of society and simply expected to perform as such?

"It was elitist in the best sense of the word," says Hugh. "The idea in those days was that not everyone would go to university. But if your sights were set on the professions or the arts—sciences didn't loom so large in those days—you headed to university. It didn't matter if you were from a farm or a small town, it only mattered that you had the ability."

Hugh hit the books, but like his classmates, there was hardly an extra-curricular activity that passed him by. "I was an early cut from Wallace Sterling's Golden Bears, but I joined the inter-faculty hockey team and quarterbacked for the Arts/Commerce/Law team—and I was the sports editor for *The Gateway*." Games were well attended, everyone had been drilled on the cheers during initiation, and an all-male cheerleading squad led the yells.

St. Joseph's College was the spot for handball (the priests were very competitive, according to Hugh). And it was easy to get a group together for late-night poker at St. Joe's in "Felp" Priestly's room. "His first two names were Francis and Ethelbert," says Hugh, "and we called him 'Felp.' He was little older than we, and a brilliant English student. I can remember telling my dad one night that I had to go over to St. Joe's to Felp's room to study. Instead we played poker all night and I recall that there was also a professor who joined us as the night wore on." Felp later made his name as one of Canada's most celebrated scholars and received an honorary degree from the U of A in 1973.

Live Theatre

HUGH SAYS that nothing, but *nothing,* animated students' lives in the 1920s like theatre.

"I was a pretty typical student," says Hugh. "We had all had read the great plays, we'd been to theatre many times, and it was the norm to have been involved in producing or in acting in plays in high school. We were not observers—we were in it—we were part of it. And it wasn't just for Arts students—it was for everyone. We gravitated towards some of the avant garde writers, maybe because we already knew the classics. We wanted plays that were challenging, or cutting-edge. And for almost all of us, we aimed to win the coveted Shield."

So most students were ready, from day one, to be involved in the Inter-Year Play Competition. From registration through to exams, each class—freshmen, sophomores, juniors and seniors—chose their plays, selected the directors and actors, and practiced. It would all be over in one night, when all four plays were performed and judged.

Hugh was president of the Literary Society and directed the class play that won the Shield in 1929. "There were students from just about every Faculty who participated in theatre productions," says Hugh. "There were students from Medicine, Engineering, Law, Science, Arts, Agriculture— and some were so good that they ended up in theatre instead of their intended profession. Walter Little, an Agriculture student whose father owned the Prince of Wales ranch, ended up in Hollywood. So did Law student Teddy Cohen."

Nasty Dunn

IN HIS JUNIOR YEAR, Hugh's father suddenly died. Frederic had caught a cold coming back from a trip north subbing for another judge, and the cold developed into pneumonia, often fatal in those days before antibiotics. Hugh's secure life and steady routine vanished. His mother and sisters moved to Vancouver to be with relatives, and after a summer as the caddy master at the Point Grey Golf Club, Hugh came back to Edmonton to the family home, where he was in charge of letting rooms to boarders. He signed up at Athabasca Hall for his meals.

"I was an outsider at Athabasca because I didn't live in residence," says Hugh. "I was assigned to a table and in those days, there were freshmen at one table, sophomores at another and so on. There was always a senior student in charge of a table, and at my table, the senior student was Nasty Dunn, my 'surgeon' during freshman initiation. Nasty Dunn ruled our dinner table. We called him Nasty because of his raw, frank language, which was influenced by his medical training. His language was—shall we say— anatomical.

"Now I will never forget this. One day the waiter came up to our table with a covered bowl of food for Nasty to serve to us. 'Well! What have we got today??' Nasty then removed the cover from the bowl with a dramatic flourish, looked at what was in the bowl and announced, 'Shit sauce with placenta stew!!' Many of the students at the table were from small towns and farms and had never encountered language like this—some of them became nauseous and had to leave the table. Nasty had a reputation for doing this at the beginning of each term. Later in life he became a well-known physician in Ottawa."

The Rocky Mountain Goat Club: The U of A's First "Fraternity"

FRATERNITIES had been banned from the U of A since the earliest days when students were told in 1909 to disband their secret societies, the Upsilon Upsilons and Pi Sigma Phi. Both President Tory and Provost MacEachran were "dead set against fraternities," according to Hugh.

Leading the charge to approve fraternities in the late 1920s was a student named Donald McDonald. "He had come from Berkeley, a university in California," says Hugh, "and he brought to the U of A the idea of fraternities, and also popularized the idea of a cheerleading squad to lead yells at sports games. Both ideas were adopted from the United States."

For the summer season of 1927, young university men from across Canada and the United States, including Donald McDonald, had jobs as chauffeurs at the Banff Springs Hotel. These young men formed a private social club—it had no written constitution and no secret ritual—and they called it the Rocky Mountain Goat Club. Hugh and his friend Eric Gibbs were invited to be members and given a small pin as the emblem of membership.

That fall, students at the U of A formed a committee, the Athenian Club, and lobbied for approval to form fraternity chapters. Fraternities were still banned, but the University allowed the Rocky Mountain Goat Club to function on campus since no secret oath or ritual was involved.

Then, in 1928, Donald McDonald transferred to the U of A. It so happened that this was the same year that Tory ended his long tenure as president, and it was Tory who had been the staunchest opponent of fraternities.

"In 1929," says Hugh, "the year after Dr. Tory left, the University ended the ban on fraternities and members of the Rocky Mountain Goat Club formed the nucleus of one of the first men's fraternities at the U of A, Delta Mu, later part of Phi Kappa Pi, the only Canadian national fraternity. 'Delta' and 'Mu' are two Greek letters signifying 'Donate Magnificente,' or 'give magnificently.' Undergraduate Herb Surplis conceived of the Latin meaning for Delta Mu, and also noted that these two Greek letters were also the initials of founding member Donald McDonald."

Rhodes Scholar

HUGH HAD the teaching and research stars of the day as his professors. "Dr. Alexander was a *stimulating* teacher," says Hugh, and students were transfixed by Broadus. "By the time I reached English 2 with Broadus, I knew that I wanted to be an English major."

Cecil Burgess, professor of Architecture, taught him medieval history in a one-on-one class. Geneva Misener, the first woman faculty member, taught an "after-hours" class at 5 o'clock each afternoon, open to all, an introduction to classical Greek. "I was a member and learned from her the basics, such as the Greek alphabet and fundamental conjugations. These lessons have stayed with me my whole life," says Hugh.

But it was in Hugh's first year of university that he encountered a professor who changed the direction of his life. Geoffrey Riddehough was hired to teach German, but for some reason ended up teaching Hugh's English 1 class.

Hugh was destined to be a lawyer, just like his father. But one day Professor Riddehough called Hugh into his office and told him how good he was at English. "Think about Honours English—it would take an extra year. When the time comes," said Riddehough, "you should apply for the Rhodes Scholarship." Hugh never said anything to his parents, but after his father died in Hugh's junior year, Hugh remembered Riddehough's encouragement. "That one thoughtful moment on the part of my first English teacher changed my life." Hugh aced Honours English and ultimately went to Oxford on a Rhodes scholarship.

In 1927, the U of A had a visit from the choir boys of Westminster Abbey and the St. George's choir from Windsor Chapel. It was the first time the full cathedral choir had crossed the Atlantic. The Dean of Windsor, the Very Reverend Albert Victor Baillie, accompanied the choir. After their performance at the U of A, the Dean asked President Tory to select two students to come to London for a year and live under his care at Windsor Castle. The Dean was a promoter of young artistic talent, and the two U of A students would join budding artists from around the Commonwealth for a year devoted to study and creativity. Henry Marshall Tory made his choice: Lou Hyndman, Sr. and Walter Little. Hugh watched as his older friend Walter set off for London.

"Walter was in *Shall We Join the Ladies*, the university play I directed in 1929," says Hugh. "He was my friend. When I went over to Oxford in 1930, Walter gave me a letter of introduction to the Dean of Windsor, and I spent my three years at Oxford as the Dean's occasional houseguest at Windsor Castle. Can you imagine it? At 22 I had my own butler, Dawson, whose job it was to awaken me at an appointed hour and to serve me morning tea." It was a far cry from Ma Brainerd's or the dining hall at Athabasca.

"Ryderizing"

"There were a number of us at Oxford who were from the United States or from Canada and other Commonwealth countries," Hugh

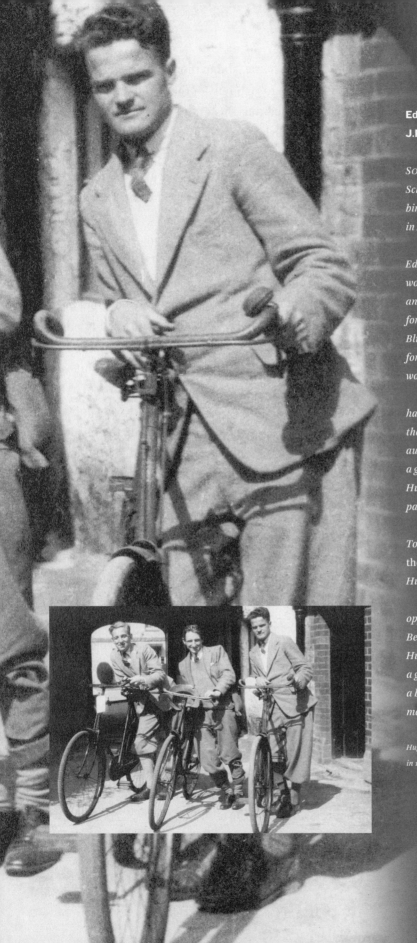

Edmund Blunden, C.S. Lewis, and J.R.R. Tolkien

SOON AFTER Hugh was selected as the Rhodes Scholar for 1930, he convocated—on his 22nd birthday, May 15, 1930. At Oxford, Hugh majored in English.

"One of my tutors was the famous poet, Edmund Blunden. He was inspiring, and a wonderful mentor who accompanied a friend and me on Saturday bicycle trips to country pubs for lunch. During one of my tutorials with him, Blunden came out with some words I have never forgotten: 'There is something beyond the stars worth watching and waiting for.'"

After eight written exams over five days, Hugh had an oral examination, in his final year. One of the examiners on his committee was C.S. Lewis, author of The Chronicles of Narnia. "Lewis was a great teacher and a dramatic lecturer," recalls Hugh. "His field was 16th century literature. He packed the house."

Another of Hugh's examiners was J.R.R. Tolkien. And how was the author of the Lord of the Rings trilogy as a teacher? "Dry as dust," says Hugh. "His subject was Old English philology."

The Rhodes Scholarship also gave Hugh the opportunity to meet Prime Minister Bennett. Bennett arrived at Oxford in 1931 for a tour, and Hugh spent a day showing him around. "He took a group of us to dinner, and we were all keen for a beer and a smoke. But we didn't dare. Bennett made it clear he partook in neither."

Hugh Morrison (right) and Edmund Blunden (centre) in Oxford in 1932. (Private Collection)

remembers. "We were far from home, and in those days it was much too expensive—and took too long—to go home for the holidays. There was a Lady Frances Ryder who decided that this group of young men needed some exposure to proper English culture and so we were placed with various families at the Christmas break and for other holidays. Let me begin by telling you that all of us knew we had to pack a tux for dinner. We did know that the upper crust of English society dressed formally for dinner.

"I arrived at the magnificent country home of Lady Heath-Caldwell for a week-long holiday, and was whisked upstairs by the servants, with instructions that tea would be served in a half-hour. I dressed quite smartly and came downstairs to meet my mud-spattered hostess (she had been out riding) and her niece Joyce. Lady Heath-Caldwell didn't mind at all sitting down for a very proper English tea in her muddy riding habit.

"It was a lovely, very civilized tea, and I learned that his Lordship was down with gout and confined to bed. So it would just be the three of us for dinner. When we parted, Lady Heath-Caldwell advised me very politely, but in no uncertain terms—to dress for dinner. I walked up the very long staircase, in a quandry. Surely a tux would be overdoing it given that my hostess had sat through tea in covered in mud. And there would only be three of us for dinner—my hostess, her niece and me. I had no idea what to wear. I opened my bedroom door, and to my everlasting relief, a servant who was to be my valet had not only unpacked my suitcases, but had also laid out my dinner clothes. The tux. I was saved.

"The three of us—Lady Heath Caldwell, Joyce and I—were seated at one end of a huge table in a vast dining room, and attended by a host of servants who served a five-course meal. I never lifted a finger. Glasses were constantly re-filled and empty plates immediately whisked away.

"After dinner came the port. This was the one item we handled by ourselves—the port decanter—no servants. Lady Heath-Caldwell passed the port to Joyce. Joyce passed the port to me. And I passed it back to Joyce. At that precise moment, her Ladyship's sharp intake of breath stopped all conversation. Joyce looked at me aghast. Joyce turned to her aunt, and said in a shocked tone, 'He reversed the port!' I was 18. I didn't know that port had to be, by tradition, passed around the table in one continuous direction, without being set down on the table.

"But the next day, I felt much better when Joyce and I were out in the woods for a walk and she asked me what 'necking' was. I guess there were a few things we Canadians knew that the English didn't."

Hired and Fired

WITH ARTS DEGREES from the U of A and Oxford's Merton College, Hugh began "real life" as a reporter on Fleet Street with Lord Beaverbrook's papers, the *Daily Express* and the *Evening Standard.* It was smack in the midst of the Depression. "After four months," Hugh says, "my tenure, along with that of several others, was abruptly terminated. Reason: 'economy.'" But two of his old U of A buddies gave Hugh a hand. Eric Gibbs (BA '30, LLB '32) and Matt Halton (BA '29, LLD HON '56) were by now also fledgling reporters, one in London and one in Toronto. As undergraduates, they had teamed up with Hugh in drama productions and as *Gateway* editors.

At the peak of his career in journalism, Eric Gibbs was the *Time and Life* editor for Europe. Matt Halton would become Canada's star reporter during World War II, serving as Washington bureau chief for the *Toronto Star.* Matt's son, David Halton, was a long-time reporter for the CBC.

But in 1934 Matt and Eric focused on advising the newly-fired Hugh Morrison about getting a job in journalism during the middle of the Depression. How did Hugh fare? He ended up back in Canada, at the *Toronto Star.* "I was a 25-year-old prairie kid," he says, "with a veneer of three years at Oxford and European junkets in between, plus four months finishing school on Fleet Street, where I never saw more than 100 words of my copy published. And I had never been to Toronto before. I crawled off the overnight day coach from New York, left my trunk in hock at the station, and arrived at the *Star's* office at 8 A.M. My friend Eric was there, and the editor sent us out for breakfast. Then I was to come back for orders."

The evening before, an 11-year-old Austrian girl had wowed the city of Toronto at the annual skating carnival at Maple Leaf Gardens. This youngster had upstaged the famous Sonja Henie, and the *Star* wanted her story. "I'd learned some French and German at university," says Hugh, "and while playing hockey in Europe with the Oxford team. So in a mixture of halting German and French, and in her halting English, I interviewed this young girl who had captured the city's heart, rushed back to write reams of copy, was too nervous to eat lunch, and then when the paper came out—guess what? There was my story, on the front page, cut way down, but all mine word for word. It took just one day on the *Star* to give me more actual thrill and experience than four laggard months on the famous Fleet Street row of English journalism."

Taking a Chance on the Fledgling CBC

HUGH WAS HOOKED. He remained in journalism and public relations for another twenty years, as assistant editor of the *Toronto Star Weekly*, and as a partner with a public relations company in New York City, on assignments that took him from Scandinavia to the Congo. But it was his biggest gamble in the job market that, in the end, gave him the most satisfaction. He took a chance on the infant Canadian Broadcasting Corporation, at a time when there was no money in the budget to hire him.

It was 1938. "The CBC had just started up in 1936," Hugh says, "and I wanted to be part of it. It was the Depression, I was newly married and I had a good job that paid $40 a month. When I was with the CBC's first chief, Gladstone Murray, talking about a job offer, the CBC comptroller came in and told him there was no money to hire me. But I knew what they were trying to create at CBC—coast to coast voice communication. I wanted to be part of it. They found $20 a month to pay me. When their next budget was approved, I was raised to $30 a week."

Hugh became the Supervisor of Talks and Public Affairs, originating and producing a series of Sunday-night radio talks called *We Have Been There*. "With the Second World War, before the USA came in," Hugh explains, "these talks brought to the microphone notable Canadian and Allied observers from the various theatres of war. More than 30,000 copies of the booklets containing these Sunday night talks were sold in paperback volumes to listeners in Canada and the United States at 25 cents a volume." Try to find one today—if you do, they are worth at least $25.00 a volume, 100 times their original price.

Yerex of TACA, The Man Called Intrepid, and Roald Dahl

IN 1943, Hugh met a remarkable New Zealander with a vivid name—Lowell Yerex. Yerex had turned his World War I flying experience into a career building the largest air freight line in Middle America and the

Caribbean. Hugh was offered a job with Yerex's airlines, TACA and British West Indian Airways. With the CBC's blessing, Hugh took a leave of absence to be Yerex's executive assistant.

The CBC wasn't the only one to give Hugh the "OK" to work with Yerex. The government of Canada gave him a release from selective service and granted him an exit permit, which was a necessary if you wanted to leave Canada. Why? It so happened that Yerex's air freight business was of strategic importance to the Allies, and part of Hugh's job was to manage "certain wartime confidential activities." In fact, Hugh became part of the network run by William Stevenson, code-named "The Man Called Intrepid" by Winston Churchill. Much of Hugh's work was based in New York City and Washington. "Part of my job," says Hugh, "was to pass messages and documents to another operative at the British embassy in Washington. At about six foot six, he was easy to spot. We never spoke much, but years later I read his famous children's books, including *Charlie and the Chocolate Factory*." The operative was Roald Dahl. Sign on to his website, and you will be in for "marvellous and mystic surprises."

Hugh returned to the CBC after the war with help from a future prime minister. "I had learned to speak Spanish," says Hugh, "and with Lester Pearson's help in his role as Ambassador to the UN, I returned to the CBC to take over the section concerned with broadcasts to Latin America, in Spanish, Portuguese, French and English. It was a great opportunity. But once it was organized and running, it became routine."

It was then that Hugh turned to community service. In 1952 he was approached to direct public relations for the Community Chest of Toronto and then for the United Community Fund of Toronto—precursors of the United Way. Hugh helped raise over $160 million over his 20-year fundraising career.

Pierre Trudeau

"IN THE 1980S," Hugh recalls, "I had a chance meeting with Pierre Trudeau. I was in Ottawa for an annual meeting of Rhodes Scholars hosted by the governor general, Roland Michener, U of A Rhodes Scholar in 1920. A mutual friend of ours—a Rhodes Scholar with me at Oxford—phoned from Vancouver to bum a ride to Ottawa for the Rhodes dinner Rollie was hosting. The fellow who needed a ride was Jim Sinclair, and as a thank-you for the ride, he invited me to lunch the day before the dinner. On our way to lunch, we kept driving and driving and I asked him where we were going. It turned out Jim's wife was babysitting their grandchildren at the family cottage on Harrington Lake."

As soon as Hugh arrived, he realized that the cottage was Prime Minister Trudeau's, and that it was Margaret Trudeau's mother who was doing the babysitting.

"Lunch arrived from 24 Sussex," says Hugh, "and then a helicopter landed, unexpectedly. Who should appear without notice but Pierre. He hoisted Justin on to his shoulders and invited me for a walk down to the lake. Actually, he *rolled* down the hill to the lake, as did Justin. When we got to the shore, I declined various challenges—swim in the lake? Take out the canoe? And then we talked about the upcoming Rhodes dinner. I told him about my friendship with Rollie Michener—both of us from small Alberta towns—Lacombe and Vegreville." Pierre shot back, jabbing Hugh in the ribs, "Two good French Canadian names and don't you forget it!"

A Ladies' Man Settles Down—Four Times

HUGH'S ADVENTURES were not restricted to work. He was married three times. And at age 86, as a widower, he made a cold call to his very first girlfriend to re-introduce himself.

"My first wife was Florentine St. Clair Sherman—a Rockette in New York City," says Hugh. "The headline in *The Edmonton Journal* was 'Ex Rhodes Scholar to Marry Gotham Dancer.'" His second wife, who predeceased Hugh, was Patricia LeMoine FitzGerald, daughter of a member of the Group of Seven.

Hugh's third wife was Marita La Fleche. "Imagine my surprise," he says, "when I saw a newspaper article about the closing of a famous Montréal coffee house, Le Bistro Lou Lou, frequented by the likes of Harry Belafonte, Genevieve Bujold, and Leonard Cohen—and in this article was a mention of my wife. It so happened that the poet Leonard Cohen had once scribbled on the wall by the outside tables, 'Marita, where are you? I'm almost thirty: Leonard Cohen.' This story was recounted in the newspaper article. Why in the world had Leonard Cohen been trying to reach my beloved wife?"

It turns out that in Leonard Cohen's younger days, he and Marita La Fleche had frequented that same Montréal coffee house. Leonard Cohen was taken with the older Marita, and pursued her. Marita would have none of it, and rebuffed Cohen with a pat on the head and the advice to "try again when you're 30." Cohen's scrawled message had been a very public, and well-publicized, attempt to find her.

After Marita died, Hugh, well into his 80s, took one of his biggest risks ever. He rekindled the friendship of an earlier love, Celie Getchell, whom he had met during his time at Oxford. "I never forgot her. I knew Celie was living in New Jersey, but we hadn't seen each other since 1932. I had also heard that her husband had died. So, after visiting friends in New Jersey in 1994, I called her 'out of the blue.' We ended up together in a very happy relationship."

Retirement?

After leaving the United Way at age 65, Hugh was a full-time Teaching Master in public relations at Humber College until 1978, teaching part-time after that. A contingent of his students attended the 2001 alumni ceremony in Edmonton when Hugh was presented with the U of A Alumni Honour Award.

At 91, Hugh returned to Oxford as the guest of honour of the current Oxford hockey team, which was about to play its 100th anniversary game against rival Cambridge. Hugh is one of the few surviving members of the ice hockey team of 1931–1932, which not only beat Cambridge, but, as Hugh likes to note, "went on to win the 1932 English and European championships." At the 2001 opening ceremonies at Oxford's new rink, before a crowd of 1,200, Hugh was presented with a special jersey bearing his name and the number 31, denoting the year he played on the team. The former *Gateway* sports editor capped off the event by writing an article about the game for *The New York Times*.

At 96, Hugh works with an assistant each day on his writing projects—from Shakespeare to Van Paassen, the *Toronto Star's* famous foreign correspondent. When friends head to Thornhill from Toronto for a visit, Hugh, who has just passed his annual driver's test, drives down to the subway terminal to pick them up. Back at Hugh's high-rise, the dining room and den are crammed with draft articles and book chapters to add to Hugh's publications—two books, numerous feature articles, short stories, and poems.

"I'm 96 years old. Along the way," Hugh says, "I've been fired twice and hired twice. I've been recruited for jobs and I've resigned. You haven't really lived until you've experienced all four—hired, fired, recruited and resigned—and taken the risks that mean a major change in your career and life. For me, it was my arts degrees—a broad humanities education that included literature—that I drew on whenever an unexpected curve came my way. Get a broad liberal arts education. Then go take some risks. You'll find you have a solid foundation to stand on."

THE STUDENTS' UNION IN THE 1920S

AFTER EACH ANNUAL SU ELECTION, President Tory would present the "St. George's Banner" to the incoming SU president. The large, colourful banner showed St. George slaying the dragon, and at the top were the words "*Un Dieu, Un Roi.*" The banner was the insignia of office for the new student president. The message was clear. No matter how independent the SU seemed to be, it was the University that held the reins.

On the other hand, U of A students had, from the University's beginning, a higher level of self-government than any other university in Canada. In the area of student discipline, for instance, the Student Court, the discipline committees, and the internal, student-run systems in the residences dealt with most behavioural problems without any involvement from the University committee that legally had the final say.

At the beginning of the decade, the Students' Union was $2,000 in debt. And students weren't showing up at the 11 A.M. Tuesday morning Union meetings in Convocation Hall to discuss and decide on Union business. To top if off, in the early 1920s, there were some fearsome battles when the sophomores tried to initiate the freshmen, many of whom were battle-hardened World War I veterans. In 1921, all of Garneau was awakened on a calm Sunday morning when fighting broke out between the two classes. In 1922, there was a repeat. As the yearbook proudly described it, "We were face to face on the field, ready to convince our opponents by force of arms, in this case fists, of the righteousness of our cause.... Although the victory nominally rested with the enemy, the casualty list showed it had been dearly bought."

In an aerial view of campus circa 1929, the Garneau community is in the foreground. From left to right are St. Stephen's College, the Medical Building (Dentistry/Pharmacy), the Power Plant, the Arts Building (with North and South Labs jutting out to the north and facing the quad), the quad, and the three original residences—Pembina, Athabasca, and Assiniboia.
(UAA 82–171–101)

Union president, H.R. "Tubby"
e was to be immediate change,
away.

Tubby Thornton cleared the
ld-style initiations were toned
npus; the SU constitution was
l students (the "Union") with
ncil. The regulation requiring
ed, although many continued
n graduate.

s rewritten again, this time at
shoff, later Canada's ambas-
at changed the form of govern-
ings at all of the entire student
uncil became the legislative
new discipline articles were
the two student disciplinary
e women.

END OF THE DECADE—TORY'S DEPARTURE

HENRY MARSHALL TORY announced his resignation in 1928 to become president of the National Research Council. The Council had tried to recruit him in 1923, but Tory had given in to the pressure of campus groups that he stay. The students, in fact, marched to his house chanting the University yell to show their support for Tory.

By 1928, it was a different story. Tory accepted the NRC's offer. He met with the minister of education, Perrin Baker, to hand in his resignation. "The pioneer in Dr. Tory was never dormant," Baker says. "Tory seemed to feel that there was one more thing he had to do." As Tory put it to his faculty members, "I am a pioneer. I get the wheels turning and then I move on. Now, I must move on."[39] One of the first things Tory did after leaving for the NRC was to hire away from the U of A two fine professors: the dean of Engineering, Dr. Boyle, one of the Ring House residents who had helped Sonet slip the 228 litres of wine past Tory, and Robert Newton, who would return to the U of A as dean of Agriculture in 1940.

Tory and Baker worked hand-in-hand to select the next president. Baker travelled to Chicago and across Canada. On his trip, he visited with Dr. Tory's brother, the lieutenant governor of Nova Scotia, to discuss the situation. Baker wanted someone with "a quality of moral earnestness." Baker interviewed Robert C. Wallace in Winnipeg, and the decision was made. Wallace, a professor of Geology at the University of Manitoba, had taught in secondary schools in that province, and had served as commissioner for the North. Wallace had a pronounced Scottish accent and a calm demeanour, and one student described him as "a man's man."

The U of A turned 21 years old at the end of the decade, with President Wallace at the helm. A new, "palatial" Tuck Shop opened; some students were questioning the value of initiation; and *The Gateway* no longer had a seat on the Students' Council, allowing it to criticize the Students' Union more freely. Ottewell became registrar and served in that position for nearly two decades. The regulation prohibiting overtown functions for men and women was abolished, meaning that students could now hold parties downtown. In 1929, women legally became "persons" eligible for appointment to the Canadian Senate. In the same year, the University decided to allow fraternities on campus. But bigger changes were in store for the U of A.

In 1929, the stock market crashed. A world-wide depression was around the corner.

"We went from the bright and optimistic Twenties to the lean and barren Thirties."

—Dorothy Niddrie Chalmers
(BSC 1936 (HEC))

Timeline

Enrolment and Finance, 1930–1939

- Fall student head count: 1,833 (1930); 1,995 (1939)
- Operating budget from the Province of Alberta: $576,388.00 (1930); $425,000.00 (1939)
- Full-load undergraduate Arts tuition: $85.00 (1930); $110.00 (1939)
- SU membership fee: $13.00 (1930); $14.50 (1939)

Key Dates, 1930–1935

- Fraternities make their first appearance (1930)
- Dentistry becomes a School under the Faculty of Medicine (1930)
- First graduate (research) scholarships, named in honour of Robert Tegler (1930)
- The University affiliates with Mount Royal College of Calgary (1931)
- The University abolishes freshman initiation (1933)
- Carnegie Corporation gives the University $30,000 to develop Drama and Fine Arts; Banff School of Fine Arts opens under the auspices of the Department of Extension (1933)
- The Ski Club formed (1934)
- Western Board of Music is established (1935)

1936–1939

- President Wallace leaves to head Queen's University (1936)
- Dr. Kerr, the first dean of Arts and Science, is appointed president (1936)
- Elizabeth Sterling Haynes travels over 16,000 miles in Alberta, teaching drama and adjudicating plays (1936)
- Ned Corbett leaves Extension to be director of the Canadian Association for Adult Education (1936)
- Grade 12 replaces Grade 11 as the University entrance requirement (1937)
- Last year all faculty members can have their photo taken together as a group (1937)
- The committee on graduate studies becomes a School (1938)
- School of Pharmacy is placed under the Faculty of Medicine (1938)
- Last Founders' Day tea hosted by former Premier Rutherford and his wife Mattie (1938)
- School of Education becomes the College of Education (1939)
- Between 1930 and 1939, the library adds 25,000 volumes to its collection

Selected Campus Buildings, 1930–1939

- No new buildings constructed on campus in the 1930s

Beyond Campus, 1930–1939

- The CPI drops 22% between 1929 and 1933
- First traffic light is installed at Jasper Avenue and 101 Street (1933)
- There are 300 theatre groups in Alberta (1933)
- Adolf Hitler becomes German chancellor (1933)
- CBC established (1936)
- The first jet engine is built (1937)
- Edmonton's Al Rashid mosque is the first mosque in Canada (1938)
- Nazi warplanes bomb Warsaw; on September 3, Britain and France declare war on Germany (1939)
- *Gone With The Wind* wins the Oscar for Best Picture (1939)

To help make ends meet during the Depression, the Christian Brothers (who administered St. Joseph's College) planted a huge vegetable garden. In this photo, taken at the corner of 114 Street and 87 Avenue, St. Stephen's is in the centre. The back of St Joseph's College and the cupola of Dentistry/ Pharmacy are to the left.

(UAA 69-95-293)

VIGNETTES FROM THE 1930s

THE 1930S OPENED with the stock market crash and ended as World War II began. The world economy was grinding to a halt.[1]

Dorothy Annie Niddrie Chalmers (BSC '36) remembers how "from a streetcar on the High Level Bridge, we could look down and see men panning gold in the river. They could make a dollar a day at that, and live on it—barely just!"

Marjorie Montgomery Bowker (BA '38, LLB '39, LLD HON '91) recalls one girlfriend who couldn't return for her second year because there had been a crop failure back home in southern Alberta.

Doug Burns (BA '51) remembers one student in the 1930s, Hugh Hamilton Beach, who could just barely make his tuition, and who had only enough money for room and board for one month. "The caretaker of the Arts Building made an agreement with Hugh that he could sleep in the Geology lab in the Arts Building," says Doug, "but Hugh had to be out by a certain hour." The caretaker would have been Harry Lister, Reg Lister's brother. Hugh Beach graduated from Medicine in 1934 and died in World War II.

Anne Wheeler (BSC '76, D LITT HON '90) remembers her dad, Ben, saying that to get a little cash as a medical student in the 1930s, he scoured ditches for bottles. Ben Wheeler (MD '35) was captured in the fall of Singapore during World War II and had in his care 1,000 British prisoners of war in a Japanese forced-labour camp in Taiwan.

Hector MacLeod (MSC '16), the student who led the U of A troops into battle in World War I and who by 1930 was a professor of Engineering, says that "unemployment was widespread and money scarce. Students could get little or no summer work and even after graduation they entered a society which was unable to make use of their services."

In 1933, faculty salaries were reduced by between 7 and 15 per cent. Over at St. Joseph's College, which faced a desperate financial situation, a huge garden was planted where the Education Car Park now stands in order to put food on the table.

President Robert Wallace—The U of A Turns 25

AT THE 1928 CONVOCATION and installation of Robert Wallace, R.B. Bennett, Leader of the Opposition in Parliament, gave the keynote address and received an honorary degree. The celebratory occasion, however, had a dark undertone. Bennett never forgot a political defeat and was known to bite back when angry. One famous commentator from the 1930s said of Bennett that "he has a talent for discovering things about people, an inclination to believe the unfavourable, and a genius for ultimate retribution."[2] Bennett had ample reason to be unhappy with the U of A: as Leader of the Opposition in the Alberta legislature in 1907, Bennett had seen Edmonton get the University and not Calgary; then, in 1915, the Faculty of Agriculture was sited at the U of A, and not in southern Alberta as he had envisioned. He conveyed his stance crisply in a warning that the University of Alberta would be torn down brick by brick and "cast...into the North Saskatchewan River."[3] At Wallace's 1928 installation, Bennett's anger was still simmering, and it would boil over once more later in the decade. But his target then would be Tory, not Wallace.

The students took a shine to President Wallace. Alumna Marjorie Montgomery Bowker remembers that "Dr. Wallace always delivered a lecture in Convocation Hall at the beginning of the year to first-year students—he called it *This Our University*. It was very impressive—inspiring—for new students, their first encounter with the University."

In *The Gateway*, one freshman described how Wallace's talk calmed an audience of nervous freshmen after their first few bewildering days on campus:

Monday Afternoon—Arrive alone—luggage at every side door—students rushing about already, but not a face I know. Lunch (in Athabasca)—we blunder through somehow. A short active figure and shiny domed head: "Gottcher red cahds, boys? Gettemasquickasya can." Then, pityingly, "In the Ahts Building, freshies." I follow the crowd to the Arts Building. I try to join in—raised eyebrows and mildly contemptuous half smiles...from the elite sophomores. I try again. An upperclassman tells me what to do, asks my name, tells me his. I get my number, but must wait to register til tomorrow. The first pep rally—suave men in green and gold blazers, Freshette executives, the coach. They sing the Alberta cheer song for us. Not such hot singers, but their singing of it makes that song a pledge.

Tuesday Morning—Standing in line again—in the hall at last. The faculty adviser—sympathetic and human. A short man with a large bald head, keen quizzical eyes and humorous mouth OK-ing registration forms—student union officials.

The evening lecture in Convocation Hall—a murmur of anticipation; the president enters. Young looking to be the chief executive of a university, he gives the impression of quiet power that shines through—an introduction of the president of the Students' Union, Ted Bishop—Mr. Cameron (the Librarian)—Dr. Sheldon (freshman adviser)—he seems as human as if he weren't a professor of Mathematics at all.

The final words of the president telling us what he hopes the University will mean to us long after we have left its halls. The quiet flow of a mellow Scot's voice beneath which the confusion of regulations and time-tables melts away, a voice that grips us and carries us on until we see a glimmering wholeness in the thing of which we have so recently become a part. A faint sigh—a relaxing of hushed, listening faces as he finishes.

The surreptitious fellow Freshie as we leave the hall—Whew! He almost had me cryin'.[4]

Robert Wallace was president the year the U of A turned 25. Students, however, were hardly aware of the big anniversary. It was the depth of the Depression and the event was marked quietly. At Convocation, old-timers Dr. Broadus and Dr. Will Alexander were given honorary degrees. There was a series of four public lectures, later published in a slim volume, and a modest booklet outlining the University's history from 1908–1933. The booklet described one scientific discovery after another. These breakthrough discoveries, all made at the U of A, were anchored in a "pioneering past" that had led to such "practical solutions." The discoveries related to insulin; the origins of wild oats; cheaper methods of mining; and new ways to analyze coal, waste gas and soil. Also in 1933, Dr. Broadus published *The Story of English Literature;* Elizabeth Sterling Haynes was criss-crossing the province coaching drama groups; and the Faculty of Extension took its lantern slide shows to 230,000 Albertans. The 1933 commemorative booklet set out, for the first time, the University's position on teaching and research: "The University encourages research primarily because it makes for better teaching." And in a definitive statement, the value of the founding faculty was reaffirmed: "The central Faculty of Arts and Science is necessary in any university. Without it, there is no university."

During Wallace's eight years as president during the Depression, enrolment grew and there was considerable institutional development. An affiliation with Mount Royal College was an economic blessing for students from Calgary, who could save on room, board, and travel by starting their studies at home. Wallace's experience as a schoolteacher helped shape teacher training in the province, and by the end of the decade there would be a College of Education. Soon thereafter, teacher training came under the control of the University instead of the provincial department of education—a first for Canada.

Even though enrolment hovered at the 2,000 mark when Wallace was president, he knew many students by name, and he epitomized the caring qualities that defined the U of A. Charlie Stelck (BSC '37, MSC '41, LLD HON '03, Order of Canada) came to the U of A as a freshman in 1934 on a Tegler Scholarship. When Charlie finished writing his first exam in Geology, he learned that his father had died. "It was President Wallace who drove me home," Charlie says.[5] In 1936 Wallace was recruited away from the U of A to be principal of Queen's University.

The Ritual Calling—1930

THERE'S ONLY ONE FACULTY on today's campus that displays its own emblem on its buildings—the Faculty of Engineering. The "Geer" emblem has elements of both the logo of the Faculty of Engineering and the logo of the Engineering Students' Society (ESS), which was formed in 1919. In 1923, the ESS designed an emblem that incorporated a beaver, an element borrowed from the logo of the Canadian Society of Civil Engineers (later the Engineering Institute of Canada).

Regardless of whose logo it truly is, today's Engineering emblem epitomizes the strong spirit that still exists among the Engineering students. Something unusual and significant happened on April 21, 1930 to cement that spirit. In 1922, an Engineering professor at the University of Toronto addressed a national meeting of engineers and "urged the development of a tribal spirit among engineers." The idea took off, and Rudyard Kipling, of Khyber Pass fame, was asked to write "an oath or a creed to which... young engineers could subscribe." In response, Kipling penned "The Ritual Calling of an Engineer" and also sent an earlier poem, written in 1907, entitled "The Sons of Martha."

The poem used a biblical reference to the Mary and Martha story and described how engineers, (the "Sons of Martha") were solemnly charged with taking care of everyone else (the "Sons of Mary"). It is, for instance, the Sons of Martha who move mountains and control floods, and they undertake amazing feats while the rest of the world is totally unaware that their safety and well-being are in the hands of the Sons of Martha—the engineers.

And the ritual? It involved a formal induction into a special group. The induction was referred to as the Iron Ring ceremony, and the group new members were joining was called a "Camp." The first such induction was held in Toronto, where Camp I was established.

Camp VI was established in Edmonton on April 21, 1930. "To date," according to former Engineering Dean George Ford, "eleven thousand five hundred candidates have been inducted into Camp VI."

A GLANCE AT THE CALENDAR, 1930-1939

THE CALENDAR settled in to a predictable pattern over the years, and there are few surprises in the editions of the 1930s. The academic schedule took on a more modern look, although the inclusion of Ash Wednesday underscored the continuing strong Christian character of the University. Charter Day was still celebrated to mark the passage of the 1906 *University Act*, and there was just one Convocation, always on or about May 15. For the entire decade, the academic schedule listed two meetings per year of the full Students' Union, that is, a meeting of *all* students—one meeting in October and another in April. But the business of the SU was, in fact, now handled by the Council.

The 1936–1937 Calendar had a new first page, printed in red ink: "Special attention is directed to the fact that registration in Engineering, Architecture, BSc in Nursing, Medicine and Dentistry is restricted, and prospective students in these courses should get their applications in well before September 1." If students had trouble paying their fees during the Depression, there was now an option to pay in instalments.

The names of all students were still included in the Calendar during the 1930s, with a notation of each student's program and year. By 1939, the entire timetable for every program and course was listed in the back of the Calendar. So, if you were in second year Civil and Electrical Engineering, you just looked up the appropriate page and your entire schedule for the year was laid out before you—Monday through Friday, from 8:35 A.M. to 4:25 P.M., and Saturday from 8:35 A.M. to 1:35 P.M. Everyone got an hour off for lunch. Until 1939, students not living in a campus residence or at home with their parents had to have their living quarters approved by the University.

Every course had a number, listed the required textbooks and gave the name of the instructor. Taking introductory Statistics? That was course #42 in the Math department and Ernest Sheldon was the instructor. "Yule and Kendall" was the textbook, and a student would find it over in the bookstore in the basement of the Arts Building. General Dairying was taught by H.R. Thornton—few of his students knew that he had been SU president in 1921. Ophthalmology was course #52 and Mark Levey, another former SU president, taught it. Contemporary Philosophy? That was #53 and it was taught by the chief disciplinarian, Provost John MacEachran.

The history of the University, as well as its academic development, has always been recounted in the Calendar, and it's clear that Tory's vision that the University be the academic control centre for the professions was realized as this decade opened. By 1930, the University administered the capstone examinations for ten professional groups, from architects to physicians.

The governing powers of the Board and Senate hadn't changed significantly, and the General Faculties Council, comprising the president (no vice-presidents yet), the deans, and all department heads, kept a check on inter-faculty relations and discussed larger questions of University policy, both educational and disciplinary. And it is a sure bet that in the 1930s, the General Faculty Council was spending a lot of time discussing discipline.

The Calendar Bans Liquor on Campus[6]

THE CALENDAR included a section on student discipline from the very beginning. In 1908, it was simply one sentence:

> All students are expected to submit themselves cheerfully to the Statutes, Rules, Regulations and Ordinances of the University, and no student will be permitted to continue in attendance at the University whose presence for any cause is deemed by the Senate prejudicial to the interests of the University.

By 1934, however, the discipline section was a full page and legalistic in tone, and codified two new, momentous rules: no more liquor on campus and no more rites of initiation.

Reg Lister tells the story of how it came to pass that no liquor was allowed. He knows the reasons well, for he was the person the University put in charge of enforcing the new regulation forbidding liquor in the residences. "For the first few years the residences were opened," says Reg, "liquor was no problem. But when the boys returned [from World War I] in 1919, liquor was flowing pretty freely. These were prohibition days when you could not buy liquor without a doctor's prescription and that was supposed to cost $2.00. I believe the doctors were allowed a certain number of prescriptions a month and the drug stores did the selling. The nearest drug store to the University was Steen's, at the end of the High Level Bridge.

"1919 was a year of good parties and lots of poker games. Many misde-meanours were overlooked or excused as a result of the war. Years went by and the returned men left; but they passed on something that the rest had to follow." What they had passed on was, of course, a tradition of drinking.

In 1929, shortly after Dr. Tory left as president, the University approved fraternities and, says Reg, "their parties were held in residence...wild parties. Some of the older students said that because liquor was prohib-ited, some students could not control themselves. So the University gave permission for students over 21 years of age to have liquor in their rooms.

"This," Reg intones, "was the start of many bad things. Non-residents and fraternity boys came to residence to do their drinking. Every Saturday night there would be big parties, and windows would be broken, bottles thrown all over the walks, garbage cans dumped down the stairs, and the buildings left in a mess for the weekend."

This went on for a few years and then the University laid down the law with this terse regulation: "The use of, bringing or having of liquor on University premises, including residences, is strictly prohibited."

When President Wallace asked Reg to be the enforcer, Reg knew it would be no easy task, but alumni remember him as fair and even-handed in enforcing liquor regulations. Reg knew when to overlook something and when to get tough. Reg recalls reporting 15 of his best friends right after the new regulation came into effect, and the students were fined or put out of residence. "However," Reg points out, "I never lost a friend nor were there any hard feelings. I warned them all that it had to be done and told the bad ones that they should never have come back into residence. One said that I would never catch him but that if I did I should turn him in. Well, I caught him and I turned him in. He was put out of residence. You have to play ball with the students—not sneak on them. But if you catch them fair and square, they will take their medicine. Everything was much better after this."

Forty years later, in 1976, when Athabasca Hall was gutted and reno-vated, eight bottles of whiskey were found, "concealed in the walls and the flooring."[7]

In this graphic from the 1934 Evergreen and Gold, *students make reference to the legal fees associated with the lawsuit Mr. Powlett and his son, Armand, filed against the University. Armand's experiences during initiation caused the popular annual event to end abruptly and permanently.*

(1933–34, Evergreen and Gold, *p.189)*

C. Armand Powlett—Initiation is Outlawed[8]

THE 1934 CALENDAR also prohibited hazing, and it was all because of one infamous incident. Everyone who remembers the incident refers to the student who was involved simply as "Powlett." Perhaps it's because a famous lawsuit bears the family name, twice: Powlett and Powlett v. University of Alberta.

Reg Lister remembers Mr. Powlett arriving at his room in Athabasca Hall in 1933. Mr. Powlett had dreaded initiation well before he arrived on campus, and his anxiety was evident after he got off the train from Calgary and made his way to campus. Reg Lister recalls it in detail in *My Forty-Five Years on the Campus.*

"His room was number 41, north basement," writes Reg. "I happened to be going by just as he arrived with his keys. There were two keys on the ring, one for his cupboard and one for his door, and he was very nervous and having trouble opening the door. I stopped to help him open the door and lift his trunk into his room. I had a little chat with him as I did with all the students. He seemed to be a nice boy but didn't know what University was all about. Other students had threatened him and promised him a bad time during initiations (and initiations were rough in those days), so the boy was all worked up before he ever got started."

Reg sought and received assurance from the students in control of the week-long initiation that Powlett "would take no harm," and Reg made sure he checked on Powlett each day.

Three days later, when Reg stopped in to see Mr. Powlett in his room, Powlett had a bad nosebleed, and when Provost MacEachran saw him the next morning at breakfast, MacEachran sent him to the infirmary. The infirmary physician sent Powlett to the University Hospital.

According to Reg, "This did it! Powlett thought he was being thrown out of University and it made him much worse than he had ever been." Court testimony tells of Powlett's three-day initiation: Powlett and others were "forced to leave their rooms in their night clothes," taken to Assiniboia, stripped, and then, according to court records, dragged "back and forth along the floor of the corridor. When the dragging was complete, the students were forced to take a cold shower." The next day, Powlett was taken to the gym and was asked The Key Question of initiation: "What is the highest form of life?" The answer was supposed to be "a sophomore." But Powlett refused to give the desired answer. Instead he answered with the name of his family's famous friend, someone whose photograph he kept in his room—R.B. Bennett. Bennett was now prime minister of Canada.

Powlett was singled out for special treatment after his refusal to answer The Key Question appropriately. "His hair was cut in a grotesque manner (for the second time that day) and the words 'R.B. Bennett'...were written on his forehead in India Ink. He was forbidden to wash these letters off without permission." There were more cold showers and more dragging along the corridor. Then "he was compelled to crawl naked through an archway formed by the legs of other students, and was repeatedly slapped as he crawled through their legs." He was taken before a mock sophomore court and ridiculed for his admiration of Bennett.

One of the sophomores noticed that Powlett's speech was becoming incoherent and took him back to his room. It was the next day that Reg Lister found Powlett with a nosebleed, and soon Powlett was in the psychopathic ward of University hospital. He was later transferred to a mental hospital, diagnosed as "definitely insane."

The Students' Union quickly abolished initiation. The Senate held an investigation and decided that Mr. Powlett was "a nervous, highly strung boy" who "was rather dreading initiation before he came to the University." Powlett's father then sued the University, the Board of Governors, and the Senate "for breach of contract and tortious negligence." Mr. Powlett was awarded damages of $50,000, and his father $6,800. Both the University and Mr. Powlett's father cross-appealed.

The result? In short, Mr. Powlett senior won his case, but the $50,000 damages for his son were reduced to $15,000. Armand spent a year in a mental hospital and was released. The Board of Governors paid the medical and legal fees.

U of A students placed a gravestone on campus with this inscription:

Initiation is dead.
Cost of Funeral...
One Hundred Thousand Dollars.

As a result of the Powlett case, Senate passed the following resolution that was published in the Calendar:

All interference on the part of any student with the personal liberty of another or any conduct on the part of any student subjecting another student to any indignity or personal violence is forbidden. No initiation ceremony involving personal violence, hazing or destruction of property may be held within the buildings or on the grounds of the University, such student activities being expressly forbidden under penalty of suspension or expulsion.

Freshman initiation was now a thing of the past.

THE EVERGREEN AND GOLD

THE UNIVERSITY YEARBOOK, published by the Students' Union, created some of its most sumptuous editions in the 1930s. Leather-bound, weighing in at three to four pounds, they chronicled every student activity and were full of engravings and photographs. Throughout the 1930s, the yearbooks harkened back to the pioneering days of their parents.

Many *Evergreen and Gold* editions are collectors' items today. The 1939 *Evergreen and Gold,* for instance, has a burgundy-coloured leather cover, and when you run your hand over it, it feels like a sculpture. The engraving on the front cover depicts a pioneer family travelling in an ox-drawn covered wagon, inching their way through tall prairie grass. In the far distance, set against huge cumulus clouds, is the pioneer family's eventual destination—majestic, art-deco skyscrapers.

In 1930, the yearbook's format was nine inches high and ten inches wide—perfect for publishing a sizeable photo of each student. Each page contained just three to five photos and for seniors, yearbook staff wrote a carefully crafted paragraph, called an epitaph, about each graduate. Ruth Bowen (BA '31), the researcher who later interviewed many early U of A grads and professors, and daughter of the lieutenant governor who refused to sign controversial bills passed by the Aberhart Government, was described as follows:

Ruth—the girl with the nut-brown curls and impudent freckles that belie those wide serious eyes; Ruth—the girl of many gifts and more achievements; the dreamer and the worker fused into one vibrant personality; Ruth—but this is too effusive for Ruth—she deals in sincerities, not effusions.

For Ruth, the girl of ideals and aspirations that she is, one can only wish the attainment of that purpose, which to those who know her, is so sure. Ruth is [a] member of the Alpha Upsilon fraternity.

By 1934, the yearbook format had changed to 12 inches high by nine inches wide—this made it easier to squeeze in more photos. By 1939 the graduands' photos were packed in, a dozen to a page, and there were no more epitaphs describing the students who convocated. Just the name, degree, and hometown. The reason was simple: the University budget was down during the Depression, but enrolment was up, from about 1,560 students in 1929–30 to some 2,327 students in 1939–40.[9]

THE CAMPUS IN THE 1930s—
CRAMPED QUARTERS

SIMPLY PUT, no new buildings were constructed in the 1930s. Coupled with the increased enrolment, this made space a big issue. Typically, students saw humour amidst the severity of the problem. Larry Alexander, son of Dr. Will Alexander (Doc Alik), used his position as editor-in-chief to take a jab at the problem in the December 5, 1939 edition *The Gateway:*

> 1929: Overcrowding in University residences—Geology class holds lab in Corridor of Arts Building
>
> 1931: Chemistry class holds lab in Covered Rink (the skating rink—freezing)
>
> 1932: Ventilation system in Arts Building enjoys prolonged rest—ten students suffocate in lecture
>
> 1934: [Engineering] Drawing rooms moved to University Farm Buildings
>
> 1937: Beds placed in corridors of Arts Building to accommodate overflow from residences...

To get a sense of how crowded the campus was in the mid-1930s, walk to the Arts Building, and turn left after you enter the front doors. The small, panelled room pictured on the historical marker was the Library reading room for some 2,400 students. The stacks were located in the basement. Rutherford Library, the first stand-alone library on campus, did not open until 1951.

THE BANFF CENTRE FOR THE FINE ARTS [10]

A SHORT HEADLINE in the October 28, 1932 *Gateway* heralded the birth of one of the finest arts-based institutions in the world, the Banff Centre. For decades, it functioned as a satellite campus of the U of A. The headline simply read: "Carnegie Endowments to Department of Extension."

Andrew Carnegie was an entrepreneur who amassed a fortune in the United States. His company was infamous for hiring its own police force at the turn of the century to put down one of the largest workers' strikes, but when Carnegie died, he made sure his considerable wealth was put to good public use. The Carnegie Trust funded libraries across North America. The U of A's Rutherford Library as well as the Calgary Carnegie Library (Alberta's first library), both received Carnegie grants.[11] And it was a $30,000 Carnegie grant to the Faculty of Extension that kick-started today's Banff Centre, which began life as a summer school to teach theatre arts under the guidance of Elizabeth Sterling Haynes and Ned Corbett.

Taking Theatre to the People of Alberta— Elizabeth Sterling Haynes and Ned Corbett

BY THE END OF 1932, with the Depression deepening, Elizabeth Sterling Haynes, as the sole instructor in dramatic arts in the department of Extension, had travelled to every out-of-the-way corner of the province. Elizabeth started a provincial drama league, and taught theatre groups in big cities and tiny farming towns. She was a whirling dervish, committed to guiding ordinary people who had a deep desire to write, produce, and act in plays. "She seemed to be everywhere," says prairie theatre expert Stuart Ross.[12] In one year alone, Elizabeth logged 16,000 miles criss-crossing the province.

Elizabeth worked with a man who was a consummate administrator with a missionary zeal for reaching out to rural Alberta. His name was Ned Corbett, the man after whom Corbett Hall is named. With a cigarette dangling from his mouth, and a dashing look in his eye, Ned was an ordained minister who switched vocations early on, making adult education his life's work. A superb storyteller, Ned had a facility for mimicking any local accent or mannerism and for "summing up in a flash a situation of character."[13] And like his predecessor Al Ottewell, Ned was only in the office when he had to be. His work, just like Elizabeth's, was out with the people of Alberta.

In 1932, Ned had appointed Haynes as instructor in dramatic arts in Extension, and let her "define her own duties."[14] Ned recognized the intensity of the demand for theatre instruction across the province and, as he explained it, Alberta's communities didn't just want amateur productions, they "wanted to do good drama." Sending Elizabeth out into the field was the first step.

Then there came a conflicting juncture of events. On the one hand, the demand in rural Alberta for theatre education reached a peak. But

Bretton Hall, first home of the Banff Summer School.
(UAA 78–80)

on the other hand, the Depression was at its depth. There was no money. Interest payable on government bonds was suspended in 1935, and the Social Credit party would soon be issuing the scrip that has since been termed "funny money."

So who decided to begin a theatre school in Banff in the midst of the Great Depression? Most scholars chalk it up to a collaboration between Ned and Elizabeth. And it was. But someone had to have the initial inspiration.

In *200 Remarkable Alberta Women*, Kay Sanderson says that the summer school in Banff was Elizabeth Sterling Haynes's idea. Sanderson quotes Elizabeth as simply saying, at the time, "Let's start a school of drama in Banff."[15] Maybe Elizabeth was worn out from all the travel around the province. Maybe she couldn't get to as many towns as often as she was asked. Maybe 300 theatre groups in Alberta were too much for one person to oversee personally. If so, perhaps Elizabeth resolved some of those problems by suggesting that the people come to the teacher, instead of the teacher travelling to so many students. Ned Corbett tells us that Elizabeth "discussed the problem with me on various occasions," and the two of them drew up a plan for a summer school that was rejected by the Alberta Drama League. Ned Corbett was persistent, and he was a skilful administrator. He took the idea back to the University, enlisting the help of President Wallace, who signed over $1,000 from a Carnegie grant to kick-start the Banff summer school.

Ned and Elizabeth expected about 25 students for that first summer session, but 130 enrolled, paying a fee of $1 each for registration. There were so many students that first summer that, as an emergency solution, the beds in the residences at the U of A were hurriedly dismantled and trucked down south for that inaugural 1933 summer school at the "campus in the clouds."

By 1937, U of A graduate Don Cameron (later a federal senator) had shifted the focus of the school and had put it on a more business-like footing. His vision and Elizabeth's were distinctly different, and Elizabeth left for New Brunswick to run a government-sponsored summer drama school for teachers. She stayed for the year, teaching in small towns and organizing a provincial theatre festival.

In 1938, Elizabeth came back west to the U of A. During the 1940s and into the 1950s, despite her declining health, she taught drama, established scholarships for budding actors, and adjudicated, directed, and acted in plays. Alumni who saw her in *The Madwoman of Chaillot* say they will never forget her performance. In 1955 she returned to Ontario because, one alumnus says, Elizabeth knew she would die shortly and she wanted to be at home. Elizabeth Sterling Haynes died in 1957.

In that same year—1957—the Banff School of Fine Arts celebrated its 25th year. Its course offerings included theatre, ballet, painting, music, handicrafts, interior decoration, oral French, and photography. Short story and radio writing were taught by famous playwrights Elsie Park Gowan (BA '30, LLD HON '82) and Gwen Pharis Ringwood (BA '34). A.Y. Jackson, Walter J. Phillips, Charles Comfort, A.C. Leighton, and Henry Glyde all taught painting. Some of the Banff Centre's courses were transferable to the U of A.

Today, the Banff Centre has an operating budget of some $40 million. Programs at the Centre embrace the arts, leadership development, and mountain culture, and the Centre is home to a world-class conference facility. The Centre hosts over 20,000 conference attendees annually and teaches more than 5,000 students each year. Visiting faculty have included

Margaret Atwood, Stephen Hawking, Ben Heppner, David Suzuki, and Veronica Tennant. President Wallace's $1,000 gamble on Elizabeth and her idea has paid off royally.

R.B. BENNETT STRIKES AT "THAT MAN TORY" [16]

IN 1935, former President Tory was ending his first term at the National Research Council (NRC), a federal institution he had helped to found. Tory had thrown himself into building the NRC, and it seemed that a second term for him was assured. But Tory's old nemesis, R.B. Bennett, was waiting to pounce. Shortly after Tory's appointment, Bennett was elected prime minister, which gave him the power of re-appointment over "that man Tory," as he was wont to refer to the former U of A president. Bennett had never forgotten the slight to his home city of Calgary when the provincial university went to Edmonton, and he associated Tory with the decision. Tory's dismissal was abrupt. Former U of A President Newton says it was the wife of Tory's successor who broke the news to Annie Tory, and Annie in turn was the one to tell her husband he was out of a job. Tory's biographer, Ned Corbett, called it "shabby treatment." But it didn't take Tory long to bounce back. He soon had a Plan B: establish Carleton University.

WILLIAM HARDY ALEXANDER— POLITICAL FIRESTORM [17]

IN THAT SAME YEAR, Will Alexander caused quite a stir when he became involved in provincial politics. The 1935 election was fought in the midst of dire economic circumstances, and there was a new party on the scene called the Co-operative Commonwealth Federation, or CCF. The CCF was a democratic socialist party, and William Hardy Alexander, Doc Alik, was assisting with a CCF campaign in Calgary. He was the first member of the faculty to become involved in politics. Not only was he helping with a campaign, but it was rumoured that he would run in West Edmonton as a CCF candidate. Doc Alik's political involvement quickly became a subject of discussion on the floor of the Legislature. The issue, said President Wallace, was difficult, and set the rights of citizenship against the best interests of a university that received its main financial support from the government. The Board debated the matter, and in January 1935 it passed a policy drafted by President Wallace that barred professors from "participating in partisan politics in the provincial field."

It was front-page news in the *Edmonton Bulletin*. The Students' Union called a meeting of all students. Board member Elmer Roper went public with his opposition to the policy. The Board backed down enough to let Dr. Alexander finish his work with the CCF campaign in Calgary, but Doc Alik backed out of plans to run for office himself.

GLIMPSES FROM THE GATEWAY, 1930–1939[18]

"Harry Lister's Welcome"—October 3, 1930

WHILE REG LISTER kept the residences running smoothly, his brother Harry reigned supreme in the Arts Building as head janitor. The students loved both Lister brothers. In 1930, *The Gateway* asked the University president and the SU president to publish a welcome message to new students in the first fall edition of the paper and afterwards decided they should have included a welcome from Harry. After all, every student had classes in Harry's building, and it was Harry they would meet every day, and not either of the two presidents. Harry Lister's message to the new students was tongue-in-cheek: "Tell them," he said, "tell them to wipe their big feet before they come into this building and not to let me catch them smoking in the halls. Tell them they can do as they darn well please in Athabasca and my brother won't say a word." If students needed Harry after hours, they just buzzed the front door bell of the Arts building. The door bell, little noticed nowadays, is still there to the right of the front door.

"Varsity Tuck Shop Ad—We Have The Best One In Canada Where You Can Get Anything A Student Needs—The Rainbow Room Is Free For Any Student Functions And Meetings" –October 3, 1930

IN 1930, Tuck Shop owner, Mr. McCoppin, put in a nickel-plated bar—the absolute latest in its day. The Tuck Shop, said *The Gateway*, had become an institution. Students described it as a home away from home.

"Initiation Festivities End With Grand Flourish Saturday"—October 3, 1930

"FULL OF THE CUSTOMARY ZIP and energy that always characterizes the sophomores; all the new students were duly collared as they emerged from Convocation Hall and were dragged across campus to the Chamber of Horrors in Athabasca." This would turn out to be one of the last initiations.

"History of the Gymnasium Project"—October 3, 1930

THE SU WAS GETTING READY for a big vote on whether or not students would finance their own gym and pool. It was a project that originated during the University's earliest days and in 1920, resident architect Cecil Burgess drew up plans for a combination SUB and gym. But the cost of the 1921 Medical Building prevented any other new construction at that time. By 1930, the SU and the administration decided that the only way a SUB and gym would be built was if the students financed it themselves, the same way they had financed the construction of the covered rink a few years earlier.

"Additional Improvements Made During Past Summer"—Banjo Sidewalks—University Farm Moved—October 3, 1930

WOODEN SIDEWALKS were everywhere on campus up until 1930. Students called these walkways "banjo sidewalks" because the boards made a "plank plank" sound when you walked on them. In 1930, the banjo sidewalks leading to Arts were replaced with concrete. The wooden sidewalks that connected the residences remained, but their rotting boards were replaced.

The old cinder road behind the residences was straightened and gravelled. The CKUA station got a "fresh coat of paint" and its power was increased by 50 watts. And later in October, the University farm, originally housed on the 100 acres purchased after Agriculture was made a faculty in 1915, was moved south. The University hospital, the Red Cross huts, and the new Normal School (today's Corbett Hall) had sprung up on the perimeter of the farm, and the animals and patients needed some space between them. Put bluntly, the farm smelled a little too ripe. In 1920, an additional 240 acres had been purchased as farmland, and in 1930 the legislature voted to move the farm and stables south.

"Engineers Stage Snappy Smoker—Incense Burnt At Shrine of Godless Altar of Nicotine—Interesting Film Enjoyed By All"— October 30, 1930

IN THE 1930 VERSION of today's Week of Welcome, the girls all attended a tea hosted by the Wauneita Society, but for many years it was the Engineering Students' Society that hosted the freshmen boys, always at a smoker. Sometimes they even handed out free cigarettes. In 1939, said *The Gateway*, "Varsity's Engineers held the first class smoker in the upper gym on the night of the 24th. The program was complete, from the smokes to the silent drama, the latter being a film showing the construction of Mazda bulbs loaned by the General Electric Company of Canada." Little wonder that students needed an incentive to attend.

"Noted Orators Here To Debate"—November 20, 1930

THIS HEADLINE heralded the legendary Imperial debate, where the best debaters from English universities challenged the young Dominion. The resolution in 1930? "Resolved that this house favours a dictatorship." Felp Priestly led the U of A to victory.

"Final Polishing Touches Put On Inter-Year Plays—Convocation Hall Now the Scene of Various Histrionic Activities—Mystery, Comedy and Suspense Fast In the Making—Dec 5 Is Night of Nights"— November 27, 1930

THE GATEWAY overflowed with theatre-related news in the 1930s.

"Ken 'Scoop' Conibear Wins Coveted Award—Is 1931 Rhodes Scholar—Rhodes Scholarship Is Fitting Climax To Brilliant Career— Was Self Taught For Major Part Of Early Education"— December 4, 1930

KEN CONIBEAR, the one whom other students "most looked up to," was off to Oxford for an Honours BA in English Language and Literature.[19]

The High Level streetcar in 1931. At the time, this was the highest streetcar crossing in the world. (COEA 10–332)

Raised in the remote north, Ken's family was one of the first, if not the first, white family to settle in Fort Smith outside of those involved with the church or the Hudson's Bay Company. Ken was a hunter and trapper, and was largely self-taught. He and his sister Mabel came south to Edmonton for the last two years of high school before enrolling at the U of A. There Ken was *Gateway* editor-in-chief, Students' Union president, a wrestler, football player, and boxer, and deeply into drama and debating.

Ken was a big bear of a man with a gentle heart and a knightly presence. He fought hard for any cause he deemed worthy. Students saw him as a gentleman and an unwavering champion for what was right.

When Ken came to Edmonton, there was only one thing his mother worried about. She had heard about the High Level Bridge and the trolley car that made its way across the top of the trestle with no railings. Mrs. Conibear's big strapping son could hunt, trap and navigate the icy reaches of the north, but Mrs. Conibear was afraid her son would topple from the trolley down into the river far below.

Ken survived the High Level Bridge, conquered Oxford, and went on to write novels about the northern wilderness. In 1936, he managed the European tour of Grey Owl, the wildly popular Aboriginal environmentalist who was later revealed to be the Englishman Archie Belaney. But in 1936, the attention of all Europe and Canada was riveted on Grey Owl and his compelling environmental message.

Ken eventually settled in Vancouver, in a home on Point Grey high above the water. From the beach far below, all the way up to his back door, there was what one newspaper called "a spectacular" series of steps and landings, with quiet spots to sit and enjoy a 180° view of Vancouver. Over the years, hundreds of strangers who walked along that beach meandered up the spectacular staircase and met Ken, for unlike other owners who had gated off public access from the beach to their magnificent properties, Ken had put up a sign that said: "Welcome, stranger. Rest a while."

A lake in Wood Buffalo National Park is named in Ken Conibear's honour. When he died in 2002, *The Globe and Mail* called him the Kipling of the North.

"The Sow's Ear," "The Pig's Eye," and "Casserole"[20]

THESE WERE POPULAR, regular columns in *The Gateway.* "Casserole," begun by Geoffrey Hewelcke, was packed with awful jokes; in later decades, when the column became too racy, it was dropped, and the students conducted a mock burial. "Casserole" was reborn in the 1960s with feature articles designed to spur student debate about such social and political issues as accessibility to higher education and the war in Vietnam.

"The Sow's Ear" and "The Pig's Eye" vied for top spot in the 1920s and 1930s as political commentaries and were originally written by undergraduates Herb Surplis and Felp Priestly, two student luminaries of the day. Herb became a well-known journalist on the *Calgary Herald* and Felp one of Canada's leading English scholars at the University of Toronto.

"Ad for Steen's Drug Store"—February 5, 1931

THE CLOSEST DRUGSTORE to the University was Steen's, located across the High Level Bridge "at the end of the car line." In 1930, they were selling "Valentines—good variety—from 5 cents to 35 cents."

"Last Week's Opera Scores Big Success—'Bohemian Girl' Plays Two Nights to Capacity Audiences"—February 5, 1931

OPERETTAS packed the house for at least three nights running. About 100 students were in the cast and crew.

"Canadian Forward Pass"—October 9, 1931

RUGBY? Football? Or rugby-football? *The Gateway* is a maze of terminology for one of the top front-page sports. Former *Gateway* sports editor Hugh Morrison sorts it out: "The Canadian football game, before 1931, "was generally called 'rugby,' although the term 'rugby' would be misunderstood today as English rugby, which is a wholly different game. No forward pass (by hand) is allowed in English rugby, and this rule had survived in the Canadian game. With the introduction of the forward pass, Canadian football adopted this American rule, which had long been allowed in the US game."

As *The Gateway* put it, "the most important change in the western Canada rugby rules for the current season, pertains to the forward pass play and are quoted here in their official form:

'General Definition'
A completed forward pass is one that having crossed the line of scrimmage before it has touched (a) the ground (b) an ineligible player or (c) any obstruction on or back of the goal line. The pass must not go out of bounds. If a pass goes out of bounds, even though touched by an opponent, the touch rule does not apply and the pass will be considered as incomplete and penalized as such."

Die hard sports fans will understand the significance of the new rule. The Canadian game would never be the same.[21]

"Walk-Rite Shoppe" Ad—October 23, 1931

"OF COURSE YOU'RE GOING to the SOPH RECEPTION and your new evening gown is here. Priced from $12.95. The latest in New York inspirations keyed to the modern tempo with a promise of fascinating, glamorous social evenings throughout your college year." University students were now a targeted market for local merchants.

"U of A Tennis Team Holds Intercollegiate Title—Alberta Retains Trophy—Alberta Co-eds Make Clean Sweep"—November 4, 1932

CONDITIONS WERE WINTRY, but the U of A retained the intercollegiate tennis title. "The Albertan co-eds were much too strong for their Saskatchewan sisters. Miss Dorothy Brown and Miss Priscilla Hammond...only lost one game each in of their matches."

"Matt Halton"—November 4, 1932

MATT HAD BEEN editor-in-chief of *The Gateway* in 1928–1929. His old student newspaper followed his career until Matt died in 1957.

In 1932, *The Gateway* reported that Matt was finishing at London University, where he studied on an IODE scholarship. He had just won honours in journalism. "What more could any man want?" asked *The Gateway*. "Matt has won a wife and a swell job. Married this fall to Jean Campbell, also a grad of Alberta, he is going to London as European correspondent for the *Toronto Star*. Who says *Gateway* work is not good training?"

In 1933, *The Gateway* reported to campus that Matt had to flee Nazi Germany because of his outspoken articles. By the time the war was in full swing, Matthew Halton was reporting from the battlefields to thousands of Canadians huddled around their radios. In 1956, a year before he died an untimely death, Matthew Henry Halton received an honorary degree from the U of A.

"Varsity Rink Prepares for 32–33 Session—$25,000 Venture Nears Completion"—November 4, 1932

STUDENTS HAD RAISED $5,000 towards a skating rink, and then received permission from the Board of Governors to borrow the remaining amount. The rink opened and the students paid off the debt by means of a $3.00 levy on all students. *The Gateway* thanked former SU president Mark Levey for having "crystallized the agitation" back in 1924, and devising a creative funding scheme that paved the way for the first student-run building.[22]

The Varsity Rink

"SOME PEOPLE SAID that the Rink was as important a structure as the Arts Building," Marjorie Bowker remembers. *"It was located near today's Jubilee Auditorium, and depending on the vagaries of the weather, we could have ice, snow, or slush. Three times a week—Tuesdays, Thursday evenings and Sunday afternoons—we could be seen, following a hard day of study, streaming out of our residences, skates thrown over our shoulders, heading for our beloved Rink. There we would be, swaying rhythmically to a favourite waltz or to* The Man on the Flying Trapeze. *At intermission, we would watch the caretaker shovel snow through the open door at the back of the old Covered Rink. Students from those days would surely sense that something was lost when the Rink was replaced by a modern facility."* [23] (UAA 69–97–693)

"All-Time High in Enrolment—Record Freshman Class"—
October 2, 1936

THE RESIDENCES WERE FILLED, and there was a long waiting list for out-of-town students.

"Broadus Remembered—He Loved the Land"—January 8, 1937[24]

DR. BROADUS, the first professor hired to teach English, died in December 1936 after a brief illness. The president and every dean wrote tributes in *The Gateway*.

The dean of Agriculture, Dr. Howes, had often judged amateur boxing matches with Dr. Broadus, and the two men were good friends. Howes quoted from Broadus's personal letters to the many agriculture students who had gone off to war in 1914. Dr. Howes also remembered Broadus's kind willingness in teaching public speaking and journalism to agriculture students, who later made Broadus their honorary class president. The dean of Law, John Weir, wrote how Broadus had given his "brilliant best" to the University. Weir described in no uncertain terms how Broadus consistently refused to accept from any one—including any student—a work or opinion that was not well presented. If an essay or thought was pompous and not meticulously argued, Broadus called the author to account.

But no tribute was more moving than that of Broadus's next door neighbour, Will Alexander. In 1911, as young professors, they had purchased adjoining properties. Alexander and Broadus then built their homes side by side in a wilderness near Keillor Road on Saskatchewan Drive:

> Those of you who admire Edmonton and the University as centers of urban civilization will in most cases never understand why Dr. Broadus and myself determined some 26 years ago to dwell far from the madding crowd—no matter; we retired to the head of White Mud Trail—what a beautiful place it was then!—and we proceeded to hew our homesteads out of the wilderness. There followed many interesting experiences—felling trees and reducing them to firewood with cross-cut saw and axe, driving fence posts and stretching wire on them, fighting grass fires till we came near exhaustion, chasing away the all too friendly horses and cows who came to pay us unso-

licited visits, and for diversion, long trips to pick the wild raspberries or the cranberry that grows on the high bush. Even in early November last, he came over one morning in his slacks—the favored garment of Belgravia—and while I constructed and slung on its hinges a little postern gate he sat on a carpenter's tress nearby and discoursed Socratically of things practical for suburban dwellers and things academic as became professors. Had I but known—but how could I know—it was to be the last of many rural sessions? What I want to record of him then, is that he loved the land and the fruits of the land, the home and the infinite simple but fascinating chores that make the home literally the work of our own hands.

"Governors Accept Dean Alexander's Resignation Wish— First Member of University Will Leave to Accept Latin Professorship at California"—November 3, 1937

WILL ALEXANDER, the first professor appointed at the University of Alberta and beloved by the students, was leaving for a professorship at the University of California at Berkeley, where, as a young man, he had received his Master's and PhD degrees. Doc Alik's life was recorded in *The Gateway:*

> Born in Ottawa—BA from the University of Toronto—two graduate degrees from Berkeley—taught in California high schools before taking his first professorial appointment at the University of Western Ontario—recruited to the University of Alberta by President Tory— recognized as one of the foremost authorities in classical work in Canada—regular contributor to classical journals in England and America—Fellow of the Royal Society of Canada—visiting professor at summer schools conducted by the University of California and Columbia University in New York—traveled extensively in both Greece and Italy—Honorary Doctor of Laws from the University of Alberta in 1933.

The news of Doc Alik's departure took up most of the front page. He was recognized "by the students of this University both as a staunch friend and as an inspiring lecturer and has been a prominent citizen in the educational life of this Province for 30 years."

Why did Will Alexander leave? Perhaps he sought and lost—to Dr. Kerr—the presidency of the University of Alberta. And maybe the death of his friend Edmund Kemper Broadus 11 months earlier sealed Doc Alik's decision to leave.

At one point in his career Will Alexander was a candidate for the CCF. He was the first professor to attempt to run for political office and both the president and Board of Governors objected. Years later, it would become a right of academic staff at the University to run for office. The former deputy prime minister of Canada, Anne McLellan, is without a doubt the most well-known example of a professor who sought and won political office, and who retained her professorship while so doing. Doc Alik was a trailblazer in standing up for the right of a professor to espouse her or his political views.

"From Every Corner of the University Comes the Cry—Next Year, We'll Build a Students' Union Building"—May 15, 1939

IT WAS A CRY that had been heard since the 1920s—we need a Students' Union Building. But in 1930, with the Depression staring students in the face, undergraduates voted down a proposal to charge students an annual fee to establish a building fund. By 1935, the Students' Union was again lobbying hard for a Union building, and a special fee was voted in. By 1940, $143,000 had been saved towards a Union building, and in 1950, students would finally move into their first SUB.

MEET ALUMNI FROM THE 1930s [25]

MEET SOME OF THE STUDENTS who read those *Gateway* headlines when the ink was fresh.

Dorothy Annie Niddrie Chalmers (BSC HEC '36) [26]

DOROTHY NIDDRIE CHALMERS has quite a history. Her father, John G. Niddrie, was in the first class at the U of A in 1908. An expert in Latin, he was one of only ten high school teachers chosen by the University in 1929 to assist with the newly-instituted practice of teacher training. Dorothy's great uncle was John W. Niddrie, the pioneer missionary. If you have ever travelled Highway 1A on the shortcut route from Edmonton to Banff via Cochrane, you have passed the tiny white chapel where John W. Niddrie served.

Four generations of Dorothy's family have attended the U of A. In 1990 her husband, John West Chalmers (Jack), was the oldest student at the U of A and the oldest graduate in attendance. Jack was getting his fifth degree. Dorothy and Jack raised six children, and all six have U of A degrees.

Dorothy looks back to the early 1930s in excerpts from a speech she gave in 1956: "When I was going to university, it was the period during which George V died, Edward VIII came and went, and George VI ascended to the throne. For a while we even had a Conservative government in Ottawa, under R.B. Bennett. Edmonton was a city of 75,000 people and there was a great rivalry, of a friendly nature, between our fair city and our sister city to the south. Edmonton was worrying about building another bridge over the Saskatchewan River—and finally did, in 1955—the Groat Bridge.

"It was in the middle Thirties that the Social Credit Party gained power in Alberta under Mr. Aberhart, and introduced one of the most important changes in our educational system—the 'school division' method of administration. You may think this has nothing to do with Household Economics, but it has, and I'll tell you why. It led to the centralization of our schools and a great increase in demand for Home Economics teachers. Previously, there had been very few openings for teachers in this field."

The Pope's Reprimand

"YOU KNOW WHERE the Library now stands? There was solid bush. There was no Engineering Building, no Biological Sciences Building, no gymnasium, no Students' Union Building, no Nurses' Residence—most of the nurses lived in St. Stephen's College—no infirmary, no cafeteria, except for a small one in the basement of St. Joseph's College—and wasn't it popular! There was no Household Economics building. There were no wings to the Medical Building, which was described as having a Queen Anne front and a Mary Anne rear. What is now Corbett Hall was then the Normal School, while the School of Education, as it was called, was located in a corner of St. Joe's College."

Dorothy's memories of St. Joseph's College and Corbett Hall hearken back to the late 1920s and well through the 1930s, when the University began its involvement in teacher education. In 1928, a School of Education was inaugurated at the University. In 1929 Corbett Hall opened as the provincial Normal School, offering teacher training courses. By 1939, the U of A's *School* of Education became the *College* of Education and finally, in 1942, a *Faculty*. In the mid-1940s, teacher education and training became the sole responsibility of the University, and the government-run Normal Schools were closed.

But back in the early 1930s, yes indeed, the School of Education held classes in St. Joe's. And Dorothy is abundantly correct that the cafeteria in St. Joe's—Little Tuck as it was called—was popular—a little too popular. After their education classes at St. Joseph's College, student teachers repaired to the Little Tuck afterwards. According to the *New Trail*, "Education students know how to have a good time, and word of these boisterous goings-on reached Rome. The Pope sent a firm letter warning that the 'cabaret' in the basement of St. Joseph's must cease."[27]

Streetcars and Trolleys

"WE HAD STREETCARS in those days—adult fare one nickel," says Dorothy. "The first trolley bus came to Edmonton in 1939. (Trolley buses did not ride on permanent tracks as did the streetcars.) Imagine riding the bus downtown just for the fun of it!" she says. "It was so quick, so quiet, so uncrowded. But at the beginning of the Thirties, there was no bus of any kind between Ninth Street and the University. What a long, cold walk that was in winter! Not until the latter part of the decade did Bus Number 1 weave its erratic way between Steen's Drug Store (which was located on the far end of the High Level Bridge) and the Tuck Shop by St. Steve's." And as students came over the High Level Bridge, Dorothy remembers that they could see the "caged crows that Zoology professor Dr. Rowan was teaching to migrate north instead of south. Because he succeeded, we (and all Zoology students) pored over his book called *The Riddle of Migration*."

The 1930s was a decade that Dorothy Chalmers describes as barren and lean. There were a lot of material things that students simply did not have. "Times were hard indeed," says Dorothy. "In those days, girls did not get married as young as they do today—certainly not if they really wanted a career. It was unheard of for the two to go together. Competition was too keen.

"But what *did* we have? Well, in what is now Windsor Park we had beautiful green country, where we could go for long walks, hikes, and picnics. What a place for a romance! We had Dr. Wallace as University President, and Miss Florence Dodd as dean of women. And of course we had Reg Lister. We had Saturday night house dances for the modest sum of 25 cents, where we danced to such dreamy tunes as 'Stay as Sweet as You Are,' 'Moonlight Madonna,' 'You Are My Lucky Star,' 'Tea for Two,' and 'Goodnight Sweetheart.' We also had sirloin steak for 15 cents a pound, butter at 25 cents, tea 50 cents and coffee 29 cents per pound. And a full-time housekeeper could be hired for $15 a month."

70th Anniversary—A Bond of Friendship

MOST OF DOROTHY'S CLASSMATES went into one of the few accepted professions for women in the 1930s, hospital dietetics. Dorothy chose teaching.

"I think that our class, 1936," she explains, "was typical of the times. We numbered twenty-two. A few, a definite minority, became teachers; the rest went into hospital dietetics. The girls who graduate today (in 1956) are fortunate in having such a wide choice of careers. But I would have still done the same as I did. I have no regrets on that score.

"Personally, I found teaching to be full of adventure, and many amusing incidents come to mind. For example, when I took my last position, right up to the last minute I wondered if I was really going to have a job at all. At midnight before school opening, they were still laying the floor in the classroom.

"And if the teacher had problems, so did the students. It was in that same classroom that a little girl made some white sauce in the top part of a double boiler. Nobody reminded her to put water in the bottom part, so she didn't. Result: no more double boiler. Another young lady in that school created excitement and amusement when the paper bag in which she was heating her buns burst into flame in the oven. It reminds me of the time my husband once oven-heated some buns in a polythene bag in which they were bought. He said they tasted fine! The melted plastic frosting gave them an 'interesting' flavour."

In 1956, long-serving Director of Household Economics, Mabel Patrick, retired. Dorothy spoke at Miss Patrick's retirement about life in the 1930s, and she read a poem written by her husband, "a man who knows more than a little about Household Economics." Dorothy's husband Jack, who passed away in 1999, was a professor at the U of A. Here is his poem about House Ec:

> Estrogens, extracts, halogens and hormones,
> Proteins, pastries, fish eyes and frog bones,
> Calories, colons, how to fold a sheet;
> Sucrose and levulose and things we shouldn't eat;
> Food facts and diets, salt-free and bland,
> Broccoli and carrots; fresh, frozen, canned.
> How to plan a kitchen or decorate a room;
> How to run a washer, where to buy a broom,
> When to make a Christmas cake, where to store a pan.
> Most important thing of all, how to catch a man!

In 2006 Dorothy celebrates the 70th anniversary of her graduation from the U of A, and in the same year, the University marks the 100th anniversary of the passage of the *University Act*. As Dorothy puts it, "Wherever we go across this Dominion, we find others with whom we have so much in common because we have been Household Economics students at the U of A. These people are our friends, even though we may not have met them personally. This bond of friendship is something that the University has given us in addition to our professional training. Because of it, the University—and Miss Patrick and her staff—will always have a warm place in our hearts."

Fraser P. Macdonald (BA '34, '35 BED)

IF YOU COULD HEAR Fraser Macdonald speak, many of you would know his voice instantly. Fraser was the originator of the popular CBC radio program *Ballet Club* in the 1940s and was its host well into the 1960s.

When you visit Fraser, his white cat Casper always comes to the door first, and when that door opens, you hear music. There is *always* music. Fraser has a storeroom filled with boxes of tape recordings—all carefully labelled—and in the living room there is a wall neatly stacked with video tapes. And it's hard to keep your eyes off his magnificent library of books. Hundreds of books. A closer look in the storeroom reveals dozens of 8-millimetre films of old movies like *The Birth of a Nation* and *The Sheik,* and videos of Fraser's travels around the world.

Fraser is a man who lives and breathes the arts. How did music enter his world? It's a story that weaves in and out of Edmonton's history, the early years of the CBC, and Fraser's friendship with Hugh Morrison, the alumnus who has already led us through student life in the 1920s.

"There are two people who changed my life," says Fraser. "Hugh Morrison and Deems Taylor. Neither one knew it at the time, but they opened the door to my career in music, opera and ballet. Let me tell you about it."

Garneau in the 1930s

FRASER MACDONALD was born in Toronto in 1912. He likes to note with a wry smile that he entered the world a mere twelve days before the *Titanic* sank, but his life was punctuated more than once by the best of luck.

Fraser was five years old when his family moved to Edmonton, and he grew up in Garneau, near Saskatchewan Drive, two houses down from Al Ottewell, then the director of extension, and a half block from Hugh Morrison.

"My parents moved into 8609–111 Street in late 1918 or early 1919," Fraser says. "In those days, the area between 109 Street and 110 Street, at least up to Whyte Avenue, had lots of trees—not big trees—you wouldn't call it a forest, just 'the woods'—mostly birch and poplar. But the blocks between 110 and 112 Street, having been pastures, had lots of houses. And there were none of the big apartment buildings that you see now. There *was* a three or four-storey apartment on the corner of 111 Street and 88 Avenue, but it was torn down many years later when the U of A began expanding its territory. So, back when I was growing up in the 1920s, you could sit on your back step and chat with your next door neighbour, and maybe look over a vacant lot across the lane."

Fraser and his friend Hugh Morrison were four years apart, and they went to Garneau Public School, a simple wood frame building down the street from the University on 84 Avenue between 111 Street and 112 Street. This wood-frame building began as an elementary school and became a high school in 1927. A new elementary school opened in 1923—a sturdy brick building that still stands today on 87 Avenue at 109 Street.

The high school students in the old wood-frame Garneau were a close-knit neighbourhood group, and when its first graduates "invaded Varsity" in 1929–1930, they all came well-versed in dramatic arts and dominated theatre at the U of A.[28] As the 1935 Garneau high school yearbook put it in a retrospective article, it was Garneauites like "Ringwood...Marg MacKenzie... Macdonald...and a dozen others that have worked on plays at the U of A— acting, directing and stage-managing." Fraser Macdonald—no doubt about it—loved the stage. And Fraser loved music.

In the 1920s, elementary school comprised grades one through eight, and high school embraced grades nine through twelve. You could enter the U of A after grade 11. After elementary school, Fraser parted ways with his elementary school friends.

"In 1926, after grade eight," says Fraser, "my friends went off to Strathcona High School, but *I* didn't because being fourteen, my mother let me stay out of school...to study piano playing with Mme. Le Saunier for a year. And by the next fall, 1927, the old Garneau School was reopened as a high school, so that's where I went."

After Fraser completed Grade 11—in the midst of the Depression— his mother urged him to decide on Normal School to prepare for life as a teacher.

"Back in my high school days," says Fraser, "I was naive enough that I had never thought about having to go out and earn a living, so my mother decided that school teaching was a job I might get, and I assumed she was right. In other words, I didn't decide it, she did."

And so Fraser attended Normal School, preparing for life as a school teacher, far from the world of music and theatre. But he was only at the Normal School for a couple of weeks when he suddenly learned he had won a three-year scholarship to the U of A. Better yet, the scholarship could be used right away or postponed until he finished grade 12. Fraser decided

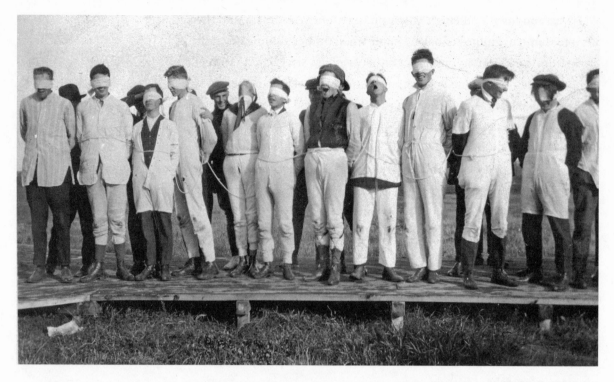

Blindfolded freshmen, dressed in pyjamas, on a boardwalk in the Quad. (UAA 85-64-003)

to get his grade 12, and a year later, after high school graduation, Fraser headed five blocks down the street to the U of A. A whole new world was opened to him, and part of that new world was theatre.

Fraser Loses Pyjamas, Keeps Dignity

THE FIRST HURDLE to overcome at University was initiation. "We were instructed to wear pajamas," says Fraser, "so my father lent me a pair. My memory hasn't retained just *how* mine came off, but my guess is that my father's pajamas didn't fit me—too big—and they somehow slid off during the initiation activities.

"When each freshman ended his initiation," says Fraser, "he immediately left by the back door of Athabasca Hall, and then re-entered the building by a different door—also at the back. And because I was stark naked I probably should have hurried as fast as I could to the other door; but I decided I must keep my dignity, so I didn't run. I walked. I didn't care if anyone saw me or not. If they did, at least they wouldn't chuckle at seeing me scampering to the other door!"

Fraser had both Will Alexander and Edmund Broadus as teachers. They were both good teachers, he says, but Broadus was "more fierce" than

Doc Alik. "After University," Fraser adds with a smile, "I considered writing a novel about my university experiences, but I never did it. I was going to call Dr. Broadus 'Wydips.' Get it?"

Fraser was best friends with Dr. Alexander's son Larry—Fraser and Larry were *Gateway* writers together. "I wrote for *The Gateway* under the name FPMac and it was mostly reviews and poetry," says Fraser. "Two of my *Gateway* columns were 'Sez Me' and 'Misc Misc.' I also acted in the Inter-Year Play Competition, and students from all across campus were involved in those plays—it was a great experience."

And then Fraser, the scholarship winner, hit a wall. He failed a course. "I didn't formally graduate until the following year," he remembers. But Fraser bounced right back and was off to graduate school at the U of A for teacher training in the days when a BEd was a graduate degree. Fraser finished his BA in 1934, formally graduated in 1935, and received his BEd soon after.

Tiny Towns, Opera, and War

THE DEPRESSION was at its worst when Fraser was starting out as a high school teacher.

"I had fallen in love with opera when I was a kid because it combined the two forms of entertainment that I already loved—music and theatre, including movies—actually, mainly movies," says Fraser. "I can remember when I was taken to my first opera. It was 'Cav and Pag'—*Cavalleria Rusticana* and *I Pagliacci*. I saw them performed in Edmonton in 1921 when I was nine years old and I saw them again in Edmonton in 2002 when I was 90." But there was no chance for Fraser to teach his dream subjects in high school.

"I first taught in the little town of Peers, 20 miles out of Edson, and boarded each month at a different home. This spread out boarding money among a number of farm families. By then I knew I would be teaching chemistry and so I took a course in it at U of A, and another in Greek.[29] I subbed in Edmonton, and then I taught in Joffre for two years and finally one year in Lacombe. The whole school system was changing at this time." Through it all, Fraser still dreamed about studying music.

World War II intervened. Fraser was exempt from active service because he was short-sighted, and instead he got a job with a construction firm. The firm that employed him in 1940 had an interesting history of its own: way back in 1911–1912, they had installed streetcar tracks and paved Portage Avenue—today's Kingsway. Edmonton was booming in 1912: Strathcona and Edmonton amalgamated that year, the population increased by 64%, and building permits were up 400%. When Portage Avenue was paved by Fraser's construction company, the plan was that a new neighbourhood would spring up, but it never happened. The boom went bust, and for the next two decades the two paved miles of Portage Avenue, near Blatchford Field (the future Municipal Airport), were used as a landing strip and as a quiet spot to learn to drive a car—until 1939, the year in which Canada had its first visit from reigning royalty, George VI and Queen Elizabeth, the Queen Mum who died in 2002 at the age of 102. Edmonton was the last stop on their Canadian visit, and a big turnout was expected. The question was where to seat everyone so they could see the King and Queen; the answer was Portage Avenue.

Bleachers were built on both sides of Portage, hiding the fact that it was a street in the middle of nowhere. 68,000 Edmontonians filled the bleachers on June 2, 1939 to watch the King and Queen ride up and then down Portage Avenue.

Fraser remembers the name-swapping that occurred right after the royal visit. "Portage Avenue had been paved prior to the outbreak of World War I," says Fraser, "but Kingsway Avenue, which criss-crossed it, hadn't; and all further work on it was dropped because of the war and an economic depression—and never got picked up when the war ended. And because Portage Avenue was such a long, paved road, the King and Queen were sent to go from one end to the other and back again. Hundreds of seats lined both sides of the avenue and were built for the occasion. And because the King and Queen had gone from one end to the other of Portage Avenue, it afterwards seemed like a bright idea to exchange the names of the two avenues, so that Portage Avenue is now called Kingsway, and Kingsway became Portage Avenue. Appropriate, don't you think?"

After another royal visit in 1951, Portage was renamed Princess Elizabeth Avenue.

A Friend Was Listening

IN 1940, while working at his new job in the construction firm, Fraser still dreamed about music, opera, and ballet, and devised a plan to study at the Toronto Conservatory of Music.

"I divided my weekly salary into three parts," he says. "If I remember correctly, my weekly salary was $20. So I gave my first $20 to my mother, the second pay cheque was my spending money for three weeks, and the third went into a savings account for my planned visit to Toronto.

"You see, I wanted to be a teacher in Edmonton rather than in the country or small towns—after all, my home was in Edmonton—so I hoped that the Edmonton School Board would be sufficiently impressed in my having taken courses at the Toronto Conservatory of Music that they would hire me as a teacher when I came back. Realistically, I should have known that wouldn't happen, but I pushed that bit of reality out of my mind."

Radio was king in the 1930s—no TV and no computers. Radio had everything. There were live broadcasts with news, music, sports, educational programs, and shows like "The Lone Ranger" and "The Green Hornet." Entire families huddled around the radio when a favourite program aired.

One of the most well-known radio commentators during the Depression was music critic Deems Taylor. Taylor was also a prolific, popular, and versatile composer of operas, choral works, incidental music, comic operas, and operettas—with intriguing titles like *The Breath of Scandal* and *Mistress of the Seas*. Taylor wrote music for the King of Jazz, Paul Whiteman, and received the first commission ever from the Metropolitan Opera in New York. In his heyday, Deems Taylor's operas were performed more often at the Met than any other contemporary works. And even though Deems Taylor died in 1966, you have probably heard his voice—without knowing it. Deems Taylor was the narrator in the 1940 classic Walt Disney movie *Fantasia,* re-released in 2000.[30]

"When I was teaching in Joffre," says Fraser, "I listened to Deems Taylor on the radio. Something he said in one of his intermission talks on the weekly broadcast of the New York Philharmonic Symphony Orchestra prompted me to write a long letter to him about the value of listening to music for its own sake."

Friend and fellow alumnus Hugh Morrison picks up the story: "I was a producer at CBC at the time," says Hugh, "and I was listening to this radio broadcast by *the* Deems Taylor, a big name on the radio, who broadcast his show from NBC in New York. On air, *live*," says Hugh, "Deems Taylor was talking about this insightful letter he had received from a man in a little Canadian town he had never heard of. The town, of course, was Joffre and the man was Fraser Macdonald." And so Hugh, who knew both the man *and* the town, enlightened his radio colleague Deems Taylor.

Fraser had his year at the Toronto Conservatory of Music, and on the side took ballet classes with dancer and choreographer Boris Volkoff. "And Hugh Morrison gave me the occasional 'appearance' in some of his talk shows," says Fraser. Soon after, Fraser was hired by the CBC on Hugh's recommendation.

Fraser wrote scripts for CBC music programs, and then went on to originate the popular radio program *Afternoon of a Balletomane*, later *Ballet Club,* which aired for some 20 years. At first, it was other announcers whose voice was heard speaking the words that Fraser wrote. "I don't remember for how long I chose the records for the program and wrote the script which was read by one of the announcers. Then I made a visit to New York to see some ballets that a European company were performing. When I came back, I stopped one of the CBC executives in the hall and explained that I wanted to give my own impressions and views of the ballets described in one particular *Ballet* program, and would it be all right if I read it myself, instead of the announcer. He said OK quite casually, so instead of just announcing that one program, I went ahead and became my own announcer for *Ballet Club*." That is how Fraser Macdonald's voice, like Deems Taylor's, became a regular in the homes of Canadian radiophiles, and Fraser finally lived out his dream.

Allan McTavish (BCOMM '36)

ALLAN IS A SCOT through and through. His father was a McTavish, his mother a MacKenzie, and his wife a MacDougall. Perhaps an inherent thrift is what helped him get through the Depression. "I took grade 12 instead of going to University after grade 11," says Allan, "because it was cheaper. The 1930s were the years of 'getting by.'" Allan became the first executive director of the Institute of Chartered Accountants of Alberta.

The McTavish Business College

"I WAS AIMING TO BE a chartered accountant from way back," says Allan, "and I'm glad I did because it opened up all kinds of doors for me. I was Executive Secretary of the Institute of Chartered Accountants and was active with the Canadian Institute of Accountants. This led to interesting travel around the world a couple of times, including some accounting experience in Malaysia." Accounting was a natural career choice for Allan, whose father had started a business school in 1905, the year Alberta became a province.

"It was the wild west when my father came to Alberta," says Allan. "1905 was a perfect time to start a business, and he named his school the Grand Trunk Business College because of the railroad that was supposed to come through Edmonton. At the time, 'Grand Trunk' was a name to be reckoned with."

It would be years before Edmonton was connected to the rest of the world by rail, but the fledgling school flourished and was renamed the McTavish Business College. "The thing was," Allan explains, "the people who worked in offices at that time had very little education. They had maybe grade eight, and if they were going to get any business training, they had to get it at a business college because there was no commercial high school. I've got pictures of my father's old school, and one corner was set up with a bank teller's cage. Most of the students had never even been in a bank, so they took turns in the cage cashing dummy cheques for one another. From there they went on to learn shorthand. Typing wasn't important in the early days, but eventually it became *the* important thing to know, and of course now it's called keyboarding. I hate the term!

"So I went through business class at my father's school and, among other things, learned shorthand. That was one of the best things that ever happened to me. Boys today sneer at shorthand and typing as something undignified—I sure got it all the time from my fellow students. But those skills helped me a lot. I took four years of university class notes, all in shorthand. And typing? One of my sons is now a lawyer and what does he do everyday? Types. He says the best thing he learned to do before becoming a lawyer was to learn to type properly."

Life on Campus

ALLAN WAS AT THE UNIVERSITY from 1932 to 1936 as a Commerce student, and graduated with honours in Economics. "I chose the U of A because my father couldn't afford anything else. And it was right here. We lived at 10164-119 Street, so to get to university, all I had to do was cross the river to get to class."

"We were young and healthy. We walked right over the frozen river in the winter. Climbing up the south bank was sometimes a task, but it was OK. But then again, taking the streetcar was no picnic either. The streetcar went across the very top of the High Level Bridge, and it was scary if you thought about what was between you and the river down below. But they switched the car around before it crossed the trestle so that the door didn't open out to the edge of the trestle. It opened towards the center of the bridge and that's where you got out, if you had to.

"There wasn't much to registration," he remembers. "You'd be asked, 'So what do you want to take? Commerce? It's over there.' And you sat down with somebody and you filled out your form and that was it. There wasn't much choice in your program, except for the language requirement. All the Commerce guys had to take a language other than English, and I took Spanish over at St. Joe's. It was easier. Then, after registration, there was a scramble to get your books—second-hand if possible—and figure out your timetable."

And, of course, there was initiation. Allan was in the last class to get that treatment. He was initiated the same year as fellow freshman Armand Powlett. "I was living at home," he says. "The ones who lived on campus took the brunt of initiation because they were right there on the scene. I really didn't think initiation was all that bad. It was really nothing much. The sophomores shaved some of my hair off—and I had hair back then, so it made a difference! And you were given four choices of some torture they might put you through. If you were ordered to do something by a sophomore, you just said, 'yes, sir!' and did it. My class was the last to go through freshman initiation. Freshman Armand Powlett had a nervous breakdown during initiation, sued the University, and initiation was banned."

Some Campus Personalities

"I ALSO REMEMBER Miss Dodd, the Warden of Pembina," recalls Allan. "We steered clear of her! And MacEachran? I thought of him as the chief campus policeman.

"The two presidents when I was a student were Wallace and Kerr. Wallace was a man's man. But Kerr was a stiff academic type, and his wife? She was the wife of the president, you understand. Now don't forget. She was the wife of the president. Now, if you hadn't got it straight the first time, she was the wife of the president. It was just awful."

Allan says he knew all his classmates. "It was easy," he says. "All the classes were in just two buildings, the Arts and Med, so we all saw each other when we were changing classes. You saw everybody at least once each day, and you got to know students from the other Faculties. And most of the exams were held in Con Hall. The Library was in the Arts Building too. It was the only place to study. There was no other place to sit around and do anything. No SUB, for instance. So everyone studied, went to class and took exams in just a few buildings."

Just how small was the campus when Allan was a student? In 1937, the year after Allan graduated, a photo was taken on the front steps of the Arts Building. In the photo were all the U of A's professors—the last time they would fit onto those front steps as one group. Today, there are as many professors in the Faculty of Business alone as there were in 1937 in the entire University.

Favourite Professors

"MY FIRST LECTURER was a guy called Francis Winspear," Allan says. "His first lecture consisted of this: 'Well, I'll be looking after you as far as bookkeeping and accounting are concerned. This is my name,' he told us. And he wrote it on the chalkboard—only he couldn't write it—he couldn't write worth a damn—and he wrote down the name of the text-book and told us to get it for the next class and that was the sum total of my first class at university. That was Winspear. The thing was, the guy was smart—he was awfully smart. He knew his stuff. And it was fascinating later on to watch how he made his fortune.

"The professor I remember most was George Elliott, head of Economics. He was a terrible lecturer, but he got the ideas across and I liked him.

Harold Poole was there for a while too," Allan remembers, "and he was matter of fact and up-to-date and you got the answers bang bang bang, right now. That was interesting and different and good."

And then there was Broadus. "There used to be guys like me who didn't have Broadus as a professor, but who would drift in to his class and take any empty seat we could find. We would just sit there and listen to him. Broadus had *such* a background. He was challenging and students loved it." Edmund Kemper Broadus died the year Allan graduated.

More Than Just Accounting

"ALL MY TRAINING was clickety click," says Allan "But it was the extra-curricular things that were more important than being a bookkeeper or accountant. I was a city boy and didn't live on campus," he says, "but I was president of the Economics Club. We would meet several times a year at someone's house and one of us would read a paper—you actually had to READ it—and then you would discuss it like crazy and you went on from there. Our professor, Mr. Elliott, let us ramble on and he would only comment when we were completely off base."

The 1936 yearbook recounts some of their topics: "Fascism, Communism, party politics, imperialistic wars, and the sins of high finance." Allan was also a member of the Commerce Club, where speakers included people like Ernest Manning, a future Alberta premier.

Allan belonged to the venerable Philosophical Society, one of the oldest clubs on campus, founded in 1912, when the first president was engineering student James Adam, who addressed the Society on the topic of "The Supermoralism of Nietzsche." By 1935–1936, the "Philosoph" Society heard papers from the crème de la crème of the professors on such subjects as "Men, Monkeys, and the Modern Mentality" (Professor Rowan); "Hellenism: The Relentless Mind" (Professor W.G. Hardy); and "The Social Aspects of Science" (Professor Hector MacLeod).

Allan was also a piano player. "When I was younger, I wanted to take a paper route for pocket money but my mother said I should take piano lessons instead. So the deal was my parents paid, and I got a small allowance, and I dutifully took music lessons and learned to play the piano. Playing piano? It was a godsend."

Allan's piano-playing is remembered not only by his University and Air Force buddies, but by a lot of "downtown" Edmonton Rotarians. Rotary always started with *O Canada* and ended with *God Save the King*; in between there were almost always a couple of old rousing sing-song numbers. Allan sighs when he laments that Rotarians don't sing like they used to.

Allan also learned to swim, earning money during his University days as a lifeguard. "And I taught myself to sail—the hard way," he says. "I worked at it year after year. Later on I was Commodore at the Edmonton Yacht Club at Seba Beach, but you know, my wife would never sail with me after we had this one rousing argument while she was crewing for me. 'That's it!' she said. And she meant it."

Dating in the 1930s—I Started to Think for Myself

"I MET MY WIFE Margaret when we were both in Victoria High School, but she was going out with a friend of mine. And in University, she was a Pi Phi and I didn't see much of her. But when we did start dating right after graduation, the big deal then was the supper dances at the Hotel Macdonald. None of the kids nowadays has a tux, but I *had* to have one back then. We looked very dignified when we went out. You dressed up formal and away you'd go. Elegant.

"At that time, it was prohibition," Allan recalls, with his eyes twinkling, "but everybody brought a bottle and put it under the table—at least we got away with it. We used to get pretty tight, and that wasn't good for us but we did it. There were also big parties in those days, but for less formal dates we did all kinds of things, like swimming and skating."

Dating was one thing, but when it came to marriage, problems arose. "When I was in university," Allan says, "I started to think for myself. And that got me in bad with my parents because I quit going to church. My parents were continuing Presbyterians—that means they didn't join the United Church when Presbyterians merged with the Methodists and Congregationalists. My mother liked my girlfriend Margaret but then found out our prospective bridesmaids were Roman Catholic, and that was a dreadful situation. My mother said, 'Cancel the wedding!' Roman Catholics were not to be spoken of. When I was a kid, two doors down were the kids I should have been playing with, but they were Roman Catholics. You have no idea how strict things were in those days. So I gave up church."

Allan McTavish was a skier and remembers the Outdoors/Ski Club's "suicide hill." The object of this steep, nosebleed run was simple: don't fall off. "If you fell off the toboggan," says Allan, "there was no place to go except into the dense woods."

(Private Collection)

Financial Woes During the Depression

"I TAUGHT ACCOUNTING at my father's college while I was in University," says Allan, and "I guess you'd call that a co-op program nowadays. It was interesting to be taking the subject at the same time you were teaching it, and it helped pay my way through school.

"Aside from the teaching job I had at my father's school, my parents paid for school. Looking back on it, my poor father must have really suffered to put his kid through university, because he didn't have any money. Running a business college during the Depression wasn't easy. Students would attend an eight-month course and stay for only three or four months—long enough to get a job. Then they'd leave. And my father would refund their tuition for the rest of the eight-month term. He had a tough time. But there were enough new students coming in all the time so we could survive. That was it. Survive. We got by."

Lunch? "I brought my lunch from home, and sometimes I ate in the cafeteria at the Normal School. It was good and cheap. As for Convocation, I definitely went. If you didn't, you were fined."

"After graduation with my BComm," Allan recalls, "I articled with Peat, Marwick, Mitchell, and Company at $25 a month, although I did get a few small raises."

The War and After

IN JUNE 1940, Dunkirk was evacuated and France was occupied by the Nazis. It was also a month of critical change for Allan. He had passed his exams and attained his CA designation. But then Allan's father had a stroke and Allan had to take over the Business College just as he was getting married to Margaret. Allan tried to join the Air Force but was refused because he was running a business and employing people. That was the situation until 1945 when Allan was told he could finally join the Air Force. "That turned out to be ridiculous," he says. "The war was all but over, but after waiting so long, I got the prize package: an Observer's Wing, a Commission, and a Discharge, all at once."

After the war, there were years of trying to build a business, and trying to keep active at the same time. "Somehow I got into the job of Executive Secretary with the Institute of CAs," says Allan. "It was an easy job—to start with—but soon the post-war flood of accountants and students from all over the world started to pour in. The profession expanded, rules kept changing—there was no end to it, so I finally had to give up, and get back to the Business College.

"One thing led to another, and I became a member of the Senate at the University. A nothing job in those days because Senate had been stripped of its powers following their denial of an honorary degree to Premier Aberhart. But after a few years I got bounced to where I really had to work—to the Board of Governors. A great experience, but one term was enough.

"By this time," says Allan, "it was time to close the Business College. That was painful for me, but it had to be done. My wife and I were then free to travel the world, and try anything that came along. We had a chance for a cheap trip around the world, and we took it. Then we heard about a job right up my alley in Malaysia and my wife and I spent the next six months in Kuala Lumpur. Delightful! But once home, I was glad to be back in Edmonton.

"Today, if I were to give a little advice to students, it would be this: Learn to do something. That's all. Be practical. And don't be too fussy about the first job you get, as long as you learn something while you are doing it. Watch other people and learn from them. And don't forget that life isn't all work."

Marjorie Montgomery Bowker

(BA '38, LLB '39, ORDER OF CANADA '90, LLD HON '91)[31]

IN 1934 Marjorie Montgomery of Wetaskiwin, Alberta registered in Arts and Law at the University of Alberta. Some people at the time might have said, "What? A girl of all people—studying law, coming from a small town of all places, and in the middle of the Depression, the worst of times."

Yet that's exactly what Marjorie did, and it was the first step in what would lead to a distinguished career in law. Marjorie was born on Prince Edward Island, and at an early age she came with her parents to Wetaskiwin, where she received all her schooling. Her father was a successful businessman, but it was her mother who encouraged her three children to think of university while they were still very young. Marjorie's mother had been a school teacher in Prince Edward Island and had attended Prince of Wales College in Charlottetown (now the University of PEI)—quite amazing in 1908. Marjorie's father was related to L.M. Montgomery, author of

David Ho Lem, the first Canadian of Chinese descent to graduate from the University of Alberta. (Private Collection)

Anne of Green Gables. "My dad probably would not have sent me to university on his own," says Marjorie, "had it not been for my mother's influence." Marjorie's older brother, James, graduated before her in Civil Engineering, and her younger sister, Dorothy, later in Commerce—both from the University of Alberta. One of Marjorie's great regrets is that her father did not live to see her graduate from Law in 1939; he had died a few months earlier.

"I have often been asked (being female) if I experienced prejudice in law school or in the practice of law," says Marjorie. "My answer is a clear NO. My law class was small—only 19—and predominantly male. The boys became my good friends. Years later I would refer to them as my 'brothers.' In the classroom and on exams, I was competitive, and was probably respected because of that. Outside of class, we laughed and joked, but rarely dated. It was only after I left law school and became a practicing lawyer that I was told I should have expected prejudice—but I didn't."

Marjorie Remembers David Ho Lem

"IN A SENSE we were an elitist group," Marjorie recalls. "Our poorer friends back home were denied the opportunity of higher education—either because the family couldn't afford the price, or they lacked an appreciation of the need or the value of a higher education. Both had to be present in parents—i.e. money and parental motivation."

The students who did register at the U of A came from "all over the province." Marjorie remembers students from places like Olds, Vermillion, Camrose, Carstairs, High River, and Wetaskiwin. "Many came from BC," says Marjorie, "since their University was not yet really established—places such as Trail, Vernon, Kimberley, Prince George, Kamloops.[32] Obviously, we were a diverse lot in terms of geographic roots. Many came from farms (our main industry at the time), and some had fathers who were doctors, accountants, newspaper editors, or merchants, as was my own father."

Marjorie remembers something else. "As I scanned through my *Evergreen and Gold* yearbooks," she says, "another factor became evident—and I hesitate to mention this—nearly all students were of Anglo-Saxon origin—rarely would one find anyone with a name of foreign origin—an indication of immigration policy prevailing then. I can't remember seeing a black student, though I remember a Chinese student from Calgary. In other words, we were a homogeneous student population, which we would consider now as a disadvantage in an educational venue."

The Chinese student from Calgary whom Marjorie remembers was David Ho Lem, the first Chinese Canadian to graduate from the U of A. David graduated in 1937 with a Commerce degree and excellent grades. Unable to get a job because of his ethnicity, David started his own company and was extremely successful. David's niece, Suzanne Mah, was the first Canadian woman of Chinese descent to graduate in Law from the U of A, and David's great nephew Patrick, who has studied at Faculté Saint-Jean and the Faculty of Business, is the third generation of the Mah/Ho Lem clan to attend the U of A.

Life on Campus in the 1930s

WHAT WAS A STUDENT'S DAY LIKE back in the 1930s? Marjorie has written about it, and these are some of her recollections.

"Classes dominated," Marjorie remembers. "I had Dr. Broadus for English—what a melodious voice and what a beautiful reader. In Law, my favourite teacher was Dean John Weir. And there were excellent overtown lawyers as lecturers at the University—notably George H. Steer, with whom I would later article as a student-at-law."

Rutherford Library hadn't been built yet, and "we studied in our rooms," says Marjorie. "Meals were in the residence halls and were quite formal. There was no Students' Union Building, and students relaxed and met with friends in residence, in classes (which were small), at dances, at the Tuck Shop, in student clubs, or at the skating rink."

Marjorie also participated in that new fad, skiing. "I was one of the few students at that time who had learned to cross-country ski," Marjorie remembers. "There were only about six of us in the Ski Club." In 2005–2006, the Ski Club had over 2,000 registered members.

Cultural activities did not take a back seat to sport in Marjorie's life. "There were so many student plays and operettas," Marjorie remembers. "Senior students directed short plays and skits throughout the year, but the most popular feature was the Inter-Year Play Competition, with seniors, juniors, sophomores and freshmen all competing for the coveted Shield. The climax of the year was the spring play; and, occasionally, university plays were entered in the Provincial Dramatic Festival."

"The U of A Cheer Song"—1935

IN 1935, the Students' Union decided it was
time the University had an official cheer song,
so the Union staged a contest, and the best three
songs were played at a formal dance. Students'
applause decided which song would win the $100
prize. Undergraduate Chet Lambertson (BA '36,
MA '39, PHD '41), a familiar face on campus as
a popular dance band leader, had the winning
entry. Chet had trouble rhyming all the lyrics, and
so his friend Bob (R.K.) Michaels helped with that.

Back in the 1930s, though, there was a set of
alternate lyrics, which began "Whip up a Beer for
Our Alberta...."

Professor Richard Eaton arranged the music in
the 1950s. The Cheer Song is the standard encore
after concerts performed by the Richard Eaton
Singers, an internationally acclaimed symphonic
chorus led today by Dr. Leonard Ratzlaff. The U
of A Mixed Chorus also performs the cheer song
under the baton of Dr. Bob de Frece, and the
Students' Council starts each of its meetings with
a rendition of the Cheer Song.[33]

(Department of Music Collection)

Marjorie reels off the names of some of the operettas produced in the 1930s: "*The Mikado, HMS Pinafore*, and *The Gondoliers*, all performed in Convocation Hall by students. Coming as I did from a smaller community, the operettas were my introduction to philharmonic music. It opened up a whole new world, and opera became a life-long interest.

"Rugby games in the fall—Canadian football—were great—lots of camaraderie. *Everyone* would attend. The playing field was located behind the three residences, and although there were bleachers along the side, most of us sat on the grass. Everyone cheered, although few of us knew the rules or how the score was kept. We cheered anyway! All the players—in those green and gold uniforms—they were heroes, and we would hope to catch a glimpse of them later on in the lecture halls."

Living in Pembina

MARJORIE LOOKS BACK on her first three years, when she lived in Pembina Hall. "There were about 130 women living there," she recalls, "and it was always full. It was a wonderful opportunity to make lasting friends. For years afterwards, I would associate different towns with friends from my Pembina days. From our rooms in Pembina Hall," muses Marjorie, "we girls would see President Wallace pass by our windows early each day, on a brisk walk, very dignified, cane in hand, for his morning stroll.

"Life was very pleasant in Pembina. We had our own girls' dining room—long tables with assigned places that changed every month. It was very formal, with Miss Dodd (dean of women) presiding and reciting the University Grace in Latin. The cost of room and board was $27.50 a month.

"If you were going out after 7 P.M., you had to sign a register," Marjorie recalls. "First 'out,' then 'where to,' and finally 'in.' I recall one occasion when there was a forecast about the end of the world and the fall of the High Level Bridge, one girl signed out as 'gone to see the Bridge fall.'

"The latest sign-in time was 11:30 P.M., and special permission was needed for later. Late leave (1 A.M.) was allowed twice a month. Saying 'nightie-night' to the boyfriend had to be done outside the front door. We could reserve space in the sitting room for early evening—but all men had to be out by 10 P.M.

"The formal dances were all held in the dining room of Athabasca Hall," Marjorie remembers, "and no girl went unescorted, except for the first dance of the year sponsored by the women's Wauneita Society. Tuxedos and evening gowns were the prescribed attire and it was surprising how many men owned a tux. The Junior Prom was *the* major social event, and the Midwinter was hosted by the seniors. There was also the Undergrad Dance, which was hosted each year by students from a particular Faculty. In 1938, it was Law's turn, and because I was on the Law Executive, it fell to me to organize that dance. Everyone pitched in to help. But most important of all were the regular Saturday Night Dances because they were just great fun, very informal, held in the basement gym in Athabasca Hall, admission 25 cents."

World War II—Differing Views and Devastating Losses

"THERE WERE REGULAR OPEN FORUMS in Convocation Hall, Intervarsity debates where you competed for the McGoun Cup (Alberta won against UBC in 1939) and finally, there were Provincial Debates, where university teams travelled to rural towns to debate with smaller local teams. An imperial debate was held here in 1935 when a team came from Britain. And, of course, since those were the days of radio, there were debates on CKUA. I participated in one—I think the topic was *Women's Place in the World.*

"On one occasion," remembers Marjorie, "Convocation Hall was filled to capacity to hear a debate on war and peace. The guest speaker was a Major General who had fought in World War I, and he was a strong supporter of the military. During the discussion, I rose to speak, opposing his views, and speaking for the cause of peace. It created quite a stir in the audience. The Major General would see his wish fulfilled," says Marjorie, "with the outbreak of war in 1939.

"Little did we realize in our rather carefree lives that the end of the decade would usher in the Second World War—the worst in all history. My law class graduated in May 1939, and war broke out less than four months later, in September 1939. I had many friends who enlisted and never returned, including James Constabarus, the Gold Medal winner in my law class. He was so poor—I remember that Jim would walk across the High Level Bridge to get to class because he couldn't afford the 5-cent trolley fare. And he was brilliant—Ronald Martland, later a justice of the Supreme Court of Canada, said he had never encountered a more brilliant mind than James's.

Students in the 1930s experienced the crushing loss of student friends whose lives ended before the opportunity to fulfill the talents for which they had been trained.

"And Dean Weir? I think he died of a broken heart, listening to the radio every day when the casualty lists were read. There were so many of his students who died.

"In my five years at the U of A," says Marjorie, "I experienced a growth in character and personal maturity that was quite apart from academic and professional benefits provided by the University. This came in part from the pervasive scholarly environment, which students could absorb, often without awareness.

"We came primarily for learning, but that is only part of what we took away. We gained so much from our close associates on campus— something they call 'the university spirit'—that comes from the laughter, jokes, songs, even pranks—adjusting and living in harmony with others, shaping our adolescent characters—even idle times in the Tuck Shop chatting about seeming trivialities, yet gaining a better understanding of the past and a philosophy for the future. Perhaps, the greatest lesson of all was that learning had only begun here, and must continue over a lifetime.

"And over the years, I have come more and more to realize the value of an Arts degree as a prelude to professional training. My university course was formally called 'Combined Arts and Law,' consisting of two years in Arts, followed by three years in Law. A variety of general Arts courses opens the mind to broader fields of learning, and lays the foundation for a continuing pursuit of general knowledge."

First Woman Family Court Judge[34]

MARJORIE GRADUATED in 1939, and in 1940 she married a young lawyer named Wilbur Bowker. Upon marriage, Marjorie's career as a practising lawyer came to an end temporarily—married women simply did not work in the 1930s. But the war changed all that. Women, including married women, began to enter the workforce in droves during World War II in various capacities. Marjorie Bowker took over her husband's law practice for three years while he was away on active duty in the Canadian army (1942–1945).

Over the years, Marjorie practised law, raised three children, held dozens of leadership positions in the Edmonton community, and was an unfailing support for her husband, who was dean of Law from 1947 to 1968. In 1966, Marjorie was appointed as the first woman Family Court judge in the province, at a time when there were no other women holding judicial positions in Alberta. She held that position, as well as that of Juvenile Court Judge, for 18 years. In 1995, she was honoured by the Canadian Judicial Council as one of seven pioneer judges in Canada. Two of the seven were Supreme Court justices, and Mrs. Bowker was the only honouree from the prairies. But many Canadians would remember Marjorie Bowker for something more. Following retirement, she wrote three best-selling books on public issues.

In 1988, as Canada was locked in debate about the Canada–US Free Trade Agreement, Marjorie Bowker read the document as "a quest for self-enlightenment," sat down at her typewriter and wrote a 58-page analysis in plain language every Canadian could understand. It was published as a book entitled *On Guard For Thee* and sold some 50,000 copies at a low cost that was achieved because she declined royalties. As *The New York Times* reported on its front page on November 8, 1988, "At street-corner bookstalls, in student unions and in other places across Canada...people are snapping up copies.... Mrs. Bowker's point-by-point analysis of the agreement has become a potent political force." This was her first best-seller. Marjorie went on to publish *The Meech Lake Accord: What it will Mean to You and Canada* in 1990 and then, in 1991, *Canada's Constitutional Crisis: Making Sense of it All.* Both were also national best-sellers.

Marjorie has some advice for students today. "Looking back after 60 years, I am amazed at the educational smorgasbord available when I went to the U of A. I am sure similar opportunities are available to students today, both academically and on the extra-curricular side. All I can only say is, Partake!"

MEMORIES OF TWO OF THE EVANS SISTERS

Sylvia (BA '33) and Anne (BSC HEC '37)

ONE SISTER became a high-ranking officer in the Air Force during World War II, one of only a handful of women at the top. A decade later, with the Cold War between Russia and the West in full swing, Ottawa called on her to return to the RCAF and work at their headquarters in Ottawa as the advisor for women personnel.

Her name is Sylvia Evans, a 1933 U of A Honours graduate in Modern Languages. Today, at age 90, she loads her van with skis, picks up a half dozen of her "Trekker" club buddies, and explores the near and far corners of the province. A member of the Alpine Club of Canada for over 55 years, her biggest worry in life right now is that her new van won't hold enough ski equipment.

Her younger sister, Anne Evans Crofton, also joined the RCAF and was part of an early convoy sent to England during World War II. She spent ten months underground as a "filter officer," converting data from radar stations in order to plot Allied planes as they fought their way across France. She and her confrères were constantly on the move to secret locations in England as part of the protection they were offered by the Royal Air Force.

Anne was a 1937 BSc graduate in Home Economics, with a 1960 after-degree in Education from the University of Victoria. At age 85, in the middle of packing up for a three-week trip to Kauai, she can recall in a snap what it was like to ski across the frozen river in the 1930s and sit in on Dr. Broadus' English 2 class.

An Edmonton Founding Family

SYLVIA AND ANNE were two of five children born to H.M.E. (Harry) Evans and Edith Isabel ("Isby") Jackson Evans, both university graduates. Harry came to Alberta in 1906, representing a group of investors interested in developing the coal reserves in the Pembina River area. In those early days, Harry would travel two days from Edmonton by horse to reach the Pembina-area town named after him, Evansburg. In 1918, when the city tottered towards bankruptcy, the local business community persuaded Harry Evans to serve as mayor. He was reluctant, but ran and won—voter turnout was an unprecedented 70%. Harry Evans left the city solvent by the end of his term the following year.[35]

Edith came west on a train trip and met Harry, who then went back east to get to know and then court her. Edith and Harry married in 1910, and they were both active in the Edmonton community, helping to build the new Christ Church, amongst other things. Together they ran a vibrant household in a spacious, rambling home on an acreage overlooking Groat ravine. There was a hockey rink behind the house, and a grass tennis court. Near the stable was a shed for the dairy cow, and chickens ran free in the yard.

In those early years, when there were no house numbers to identify individual homes, they named their Groat ravine perch Sylvancroft. Sylvia remembers one letter to her dad, mailed from England, that was simply addressed to "H.M.E. Evans, Sylvancroft, Stony Plain Road, Edmonton." "The postal service had tried and failed to deliver it within England," she remembers. "In the corner of the envelope, in pencil, someone had written, 'Try Canada.'"

Growing Up In Edmonton—The Paper Chase and Pick-up Hockey

WITH FIVE CHILDREN, Harry and Isabel's home was alive with the kinds of activities that were common in Edmonton's early years. "It's not easy to look back some 80 years and describe what life was like," says Sylvia. "I can tell you that there was a lot of family-based fun, and lots of outdoor activities where both parents and children could be involved."

The paper chase was a prime example.

"We'd have a paper chase in the Groat ravine and in the fields near Stony Plain Road and 124 Street, sometimes on foot and sometimes on horseback," remembers Sylvia. Two people would be the "hares," and the rest of us were the "hounds." The two hares would head out in advance, with a sack of tiny scraps of paper, and proceed to set a trail. False trails were cunningly set here and there. All of us hounds would follow the hares, and the idea was to catch the hares before they got back home. My dad had a baby carrier, so even the littlest ones, like my younger sister Anne, were out there having fun."

Anne remembers the Sunday hockey parties at the house. "Hockey was the only exercise a lot of people got in the winter in those days. Mother loved parties, but of all the family members, father was the most likely one to suggest a party, and a hockey get-together was a favourite. Father would be out on the big make-shift skating rink, totally involved in a game. He was usually dressed in riding britches, and he would look up from the ice and greet any of the arriving guests who came walking down our long driveway, like this: 'Get a stick!'

"Father would tell them 'Join my side!' Or he'd say, 'Join Isby's side!' Once in a while it would be local flying aces Punch Dickins or Cy Becker who would join us for hockey, and you know, they played a pretty good game.

"And so neighbours would join one of the competing teams as twenty or more people—children and parents alike—played pick-up hockey. We used children's hockey sticks, and the men were restricted to using one hand, so the game never got too rough. There was one woman who would tend goal in a huge fur coat, lying down across the net to block any shots. It was great fun to watch some of our house guests from England, who had never skated, heading towards the boards—which were low—and then, not knowing how to stop, they would plunge head-first into the snow banks piled high around the rink's perimeter. There was also a bonfire behind the rink, and sometimes Granny Jackson would serve up hot potato cakes at the 'tea party,'" adds Sylvia. "It was wonderful family fun." Anne remembers that "we would have to leave the rink lights off for at least 20 minutes before our young brother Vaux would come in from playing hockey."

Today, if you visit Sylvia, who lives in the family home atop Groat ravine—and if it's cold enough—you're bound to find a pick-up game of hockey in full swing in front of the main house, with the ice illuminated by a single, old-fashioned string of lights. There's lots of laughter, and no one's in skates, just shoes. But they're going at it as hard as if it were the Stanley Cup finals.

Radio, Rachmaninoff, and the First French Radio Station

SYLVIA LOVED THE THEATRE and music, and remembers vividly the groups that came through Edmonton to perform, including D'Oyly Carte, in the magnificent art deco Empire Theatre. "Those were the days when Little Theatre was becoming really popular, and I volunteered behind the scenes," she says. "We were one of the families who hosted receptions for the actors. My dad would take us to shows and concerts, and afterwards, we would go back stage—I think dad had met some of these people while in New York on business. I remember meeting violinist Yasha Haifetz and pianist Sergei Rachmaninoff—Rachmaninoff would hunch over the piano as he played, and he was magnificent. These were also the days when radio was on the rise, and I can remember during my university days reading French plays, live, on the first French radio station in Canada outside of Québec."

There were informal get-togethers at the house on the weekends, where someone always sat down to play the piano or violin, and there were charades and pantomimes. Sylvia's favourite pantomime involved several guests huddled under a green bedspread, heaving up and down, trying to simulate ocean waves. Sylvia's sister Anne can still see one guest dressed in a salmon-coloured evening dress, wriggling beneath a blanket or a bedspread in front of the guests, trying to get them to guess she was a lobster.

The Toboggan Hut

"Almost everyone had a piano in those days," says Syliva. "Records were new, and squeaky. We sang songs around the piano and there were camp songs and picnics in the summer. Dad gardened, and we all golfed—both my parents, my grandmother and all the kids—and my parents were involved with the development of the Edmonton Golf and Country Club."

Anne remembers that "badminton was played indoors in winter and outdoors in summer, and we had a tennis court near the stable—we also did a lot of riding. Skiing was new when I was young, and tobogganing was popular in the winter. There was a toboggan run on this side of the river with a warm-up hut down at the bottom. Inside there was a sign that said, 'Please don't make fun of our coffee—you may be old and weak yourself some day.'"

Home-Schooled

SYLVIA AND ANNE'S PARENTS had definite ideas about education. Along with other neighbourhood children, Sylvia, Anne and their three siblings were home-schooled in the mornings so that in the afternoons, no matter how bracing the winter weather, the entire brood could be bundled up to spend the afternoons outdoors in the snow or skating on the home-made rink just outside the front door. "The time outdoors instilled in me a life-long love of hiking, skiing and exploring which has kept me pretty fit all these years," says Sylvia.

One of the Evans children's teachers was a Russian émigré, Tatiana de Marbois, who had lived at the Russian Czar's winter palace, where her father was governor. Tatiana later fled Russia by train with her British-born husband Nick. To avoid having Nick questioned during the nightly bed checks on the train, Tatiana hid Nick under her bedcovers, pretending to be very pregnant.

Tatiana spoke three languages, Nick at least six, and both exuded adventure. Nick told thrilling stories about his naval days in World War I, and Tatiana taught the Evans children languages, sculpture, art and needlework, "and everything else," says Sylvia.[36] Other families organized dance lessons or cooking lessons at their homes. Sylvia, Anne, and their friends took dance lessons from Lotta Boucher, a woman who "did a mean dying swan number," according to Sylvia. All told, it was an on-the-ground way to learn geography, history, languages, and social graces.

The next governess was beloved Mrs. Hobbs, who founded Queensmead, one of Edmonton's earliest private schools. Sylvia would later run this school herself, operating it out of Sylvancroft with several other teachers. Sylvia introduced even her youngest pupils to languages, much earlier than was done in the pubic schools. She didn't believe in homework until students reached grade nine, and incorporated music and art into the daily routine. Former students now in their 70s still remember carefree days packed with creative learning.

Sylvia remembers a time when the school board examiner came to Queensmead to see just what was going on at this private school. Most of the children in the school were young, but in the upper grades there were two 13 year-old girls and Sylvia's 11 year-old brother Vaux.

"The examiner asked the girls, who were in grade nine, some questions about algebra, and Vaux would interrupt and ask if he could be allowed to answer the questions. Vaux, as the only 11 year-old at Queensmead, had been taking math with the two girls who were in grade nine and he was good at it. Then the examiner asked a question about some novel—you know, asking what they thought about this or that aspect of it—and the three pre-teens said what they thought, and then they, in turn, asked the examiner what he thought about another novel. Well, the examiner was stumped. He wasn't prepared to answer questions, just ask them. But the children, you see, thought this was all a conversation, and not an exam. They were genuinely curious about what this grown-up thought, and he couldn't answer their question!

"Being home-schooled was a wonderful way to learn, very unstructured," Sylvia says. "We would explore so many different subjects in a day, usually in connection with some object or book in the house, or some current event. It was a very natural way to 'be in school.' We were always asking questions and, in turn, being questioned right back by our teachers. So by the time I got to University, I really had no fears about classes and exams."

Sylvia and Anne at the U of A

ALL FIVE EVANS CHILDREN attended the U of A—Sylvia, Louise, Anne, Honor, and Vaux. They were all, in their own way, outstanding. "It wasn't unusual for whole families of children to go to the U of A," says Sylvia. "Not many Albertans could afford to go far afield to established universities like the University of Toronto, and having the U of A in Edmonton gave Albertans the opportunity to get a university education right here in their home province."

Every student in the Faculty of Arts and Science was required to take two of the following four languages: Latin, Greek, French and German. Before starting university, Sylvia lived with an aunt in England for two years, attending St. Margaret's Boarding School in Folkstone. She honed her French during a three-month stay in France, and in 1928 she took Latin, her first course at the U of A, as a part-time student.

Full-time studies for Sylvia started in 1929. "Registration was simple," she says. "You had the Calendar outlining the courses, you sat down with someone from the University to talk about what courses were required for your degree and what the options were, and then you decided for yourself. That was it. It wasn't complicated. But by the 1990s, when my nieces and nephews were going to University, they knew what they wanted to study, but they didn't know if they could get in to the department or faculty they wanted."

The 1933 yearbook epitaph for Sylvia said, "Her attitude towards higher education is unparalleled in history. With complete nonchalance, she passes triumphantly through the ordeal of examinations." However, in one of her first university examinations, in Math, Sylvia was sure she had failed, since she had only worked her way through five of the eight questions. But when Sylvia went to Convocation Hall to check the posted results, she saw that not only had she passed, she had won the Academic Women's Association scholarship. "I don't think *anyone* finished that exam, and the prof must have marked us on just four or five questions."

Anne entered the U of A in 1934 at the age of 16 and graduated at the top of her class three years later. As part of her pre-university schooling, she took French lessons at a local convent. In fact, all the Evans children took French lessons, way over in Strathcona, at the Ursuline convent—a long streetcar ride from Glenora. The convent boarded children from rural Alberta who attended Catholic school in Edmonton, "and the sisters were happy to teach us French," says Anne. "We went in the afternoon, when the other children were in school, so we never saw them. I can still remember the smell of wax on the floor, and the rows of little beds in the convent."

First Week on Campus

ANNE AND SYLVIA REMEMBER almost nothing about their first week on campus. Sylvia went through initiation, which was nothing taxing for the girls. "We just wore silly clothes," she says. "It was much rougher for the boys." Sylvia's friend from Banff, Priscilla Hammond, entered in the same year, and Sylvia showed Priscilla around a campus she already knew well. It was pretty easy to navigate, with just the three residences (Athabasca, Assiniboia, and Pembina), the Arts Building, the Medical Building, St. Stephen's College and St. Joseph's College and, of course, the Tuck Shop. Sylvia remembers that "all my classes were in the Arts building—it was the central point on campus."

Anne's only memory of her first week on campus was taking Economics 1 over at St. Joe's. "There was a classroom in the basement with a door at either end. There was one student who came in the east door, signed the attendance sheet, and walked out the west door. The prof. didn't notice a thing—he just went on and on with interminable sentences."

"I was the third sister to go to the U of A," Anne says. "Sylvia had taken History and 'moderns' and my sister Louise had majored in Literature. Sylvia signed me up for Greek and Philosophy, but I wanted to do something my sisters hadn't, but I didn't know what. My mother said it didn't matter what I took, but told me to make sure I could earn my own living, the world being what it was, with a deepening depression. So I took Home Economics."

It was a challenging BSc degree, just two courses short of the Honours chemistry degree, but looking back, Anne regrets she didn't take Medicine—it was an era when few women entered that profession.

Dr. Sonet and Dr. Broadus

"TORY PICKED THE BEST PROFESSORS," Sylvia says, and "almost all my professors were good, exciting. I liked them."

One of her favourites was Dr. Sonet. "He was quite a character and he had such enthusiasm." One of Sylvia's friends remembers Sonet's pre-class demonstration of hand-to-hand combat, a skill he had to learn while training for service in World War I. Sonet's dramatic display was conducted, of course, entirely in French. "Seventy years later and I've never forgotten it!"

"But," Sylvia recalls, not skipping a beat, "my Physics professor understood the subject so well he couldn't explain it to others. He didn't think it needed explaining. He meant well, but he just read from his notes. Pretty boring and hard to follow. If he explained it once, he expected everyone to know it. And if they didn't get it he couldn't see why."

For Anne there is no question that Dr. Sonet was her best professor. "He was a wonderful teacher. He called us his 'sunshine.' He'd come in to class, his academic gown flowing behind him and slightly off his shoulder, and he would mince dramatically around the classroom, bringing such life to his lectures. He might, for instance, start off by telling us about whatever play he had seen the night before. It was a great way to bring everyday reality to language learning. And he drilled us in grammar. To this day, I can still recite the grammar drills.

"There was one student who would come late to Sonet's class—let's just call him 'John' Dowdell. In those days, you simply didn't arrive late for class, or you were marked absent, and in every class, attendance was taken, usually by the professor. When John would come in," Anne recalls, "Sonet would say, 'Well! Better never than late!' and he would pretend not to recognize Mr. Dowdell. He would address him during the class as 'Miss Doodle' or 'Mr. Dawdle.'" Mr. Dowdell got the point, and so did the rest of us.

"My sister Louise had Broadus for English," says Anne. "I only went to one of his classes, but I will never forget it. Late one afternoon Louise and I skied across the river, and she took me to Dr. Broadus's 5 P.M. class. He was quite a performer, and on that day he read aloud to us from Thomas Hardy. It was spellbinding. But there was a moment when Dr. Broadus looked up from his book and he saw a student in the back of the room reading *The Gateway*. Dr. Broadus solemnly announced to the class, 'SOMEONE is reading *The Gateway*.' There was a pause, and Dr. Broadus's sonorous voice filled the room. 'It's not for myself that I mind, but it is an insult to Thomas Hardy.' The room was still, and silent. I doubt that anyone ever read *The Gateway* again in Broadus's class."

Paying For Tuition

SYLVIA AND ANNE LIVED AT HOME and, as was the case with nearly all students in the 1930s, their parents paid for their education. They walked or skied to school over the frozen North Saskatchewan in the winter ("down the Groat ravine and away we would go"), and the "longsuffering" dads in their Glenora neighbourhood took turns driving U of A students back and forth across the river. "Sometimes Judge Harvey and my dad would race each other across the High Level Bridge," remembers Anne. "And sometimes we took the streetcar to University," adds Sylvia, "but the streetcar was pretty slow going because you had to walk blocks to get to where the streetcar line started, and then change to go over the High Level Bridge, with a long wait for the connecting car."

Classes were held six days a week but, says Sylvia, "we had five months off in the summer, so it evened out." The long break allowed students from rural areas to seed and harvest a crop. Others could get a job that would pay for the next year of university. "But if you didn't need the money," cautions Sylvia, "you didn't take a job away from someone that did." That was the unwritten dictate of the Depression.

Social Life and Delta Gamma

SYLVIA AND ANNE HAD an active social and athletic life within their neighbourhood by the time they started university. On campus, Sylvia was in *Le Circle Français* run by Dr. Sonet, and helped start up the first badminton team. Anne later played on this team, in the year the U of A won the league championship.

Sylvia also served on the Social Directorate, but remembers nothing about it. Why? The main function of the Social Directorate was to greet the visiting sports teams, and in the early 1930s, with the Depression in full swing, inter-varsity sports were suspended—thus there was little for the Social Directorate to do but to have their photos taken for the yearbook.

Sylvia and her siblings knew how to hit the books, but they also knew how to have fun. Sylvia's friends remembered that during her university days, "in those amazing spare moments of hers, she would get up some unique party." While Sylvia was in the midst of her undergraduate years, the Depression deepened, and "you just made your own fun," she says. The annual profits from the family business dropped from some $44,000 to $1,500.[37] "We invited people to 'hard times parties,'" recalls Sylvia, "and used newspaper for a tablecloth. It was fun to compete to see who wore the most faded, frayed, patched clothes."

The Debate Club was one of the most popular and long-standing groups on campus, and Anne tells of one encounter between Students' Union president, Art Bierwagen, and the witty Mark McClung, Rhodes Scholar for 1936 and son of the famous Nellie McClung. "Art arrived at the debate," remembers Anne, "and announced, '*This* is a battle of wits, you know.' Mark instantly shot back with a one-liner: 'So brave of you to come unarmed.'"[38]

The Evans sisters belonged to Delta Gamma, one of the first women's fraternities on campus. Sylvia recalls how Delta Gamma got its start.

"A group of women who had been members of Delta Gamma in the United States sponsored us," says Sylvia. "We applied for a charter and a couple people came up from the States to see if we were suitable. We had to raise about $1,000 for the charter, and one of the ways we did that was to work at the gift service at Eaton's department store. We had a little office over there and we wrapped up the gift orders. Eaton's would give us a small percentage of the order in return."

Sylvia remembers one order vividly. "It was the Depression, but there was this one teacher in the country who had saved up from her meagre salary to buy presents for her entire class. She sent us the money with a note asking that we choose the presents for her class. It was quite a challenge because we had the feeling that these presents were probably the *only* presents each child would receive."

Earning $1,000 for the DG charter was no easy task. "There was one well-to-do woman," recalls Sylvia, "who ordered a double mattress through our service—a Christmas present for her husband—and she asked that it be gift-wrapped. It was our job to do this, and it was in the days before Scotch tape. Our wrapping paper consisted of thin tissue paper—red, green, or white—and we had stickers that you licked to hold all this tissue paper together. The mattress kept wriggling around but we finally managed to wrap it. I'm sure it wasn't a gift—I think this woman only asked for gift wrapping as a way to support our efforts to get a charter."

By 1934, when Anne began her studies at the U of A, Delta Gamma had bought a house. It was the centre of social activities, and home to some of the fraternity members. "We had nicknames for almost everyone," Anne remembers. "The nicknames were all bestowed with great affection—we dubbed one of our Physics profs 'Molecule Smith,' and then there was 'Bullneck Mark' and 'Porky Jones'—you get the idea. No one was exempt.

"We had the brightest but most scattered girl living at the house," says Anne. "Her stockings were always sort of wound around her legs, and one day when she couldn't find the belt to her coat, she used a scarf instead. She was brilliant, just brilliant, but she was also just like the proverbial absent-minded professor. Her name was Sheila, and we nicknamed her 'Goofy.' And Sheila had a puppy. One night Sheila's date came to the door. Sheila couldn't find her shoes, so there was a big search. Finally we found Sheila's shoes in the oven, where she had put them so her puppy wouldn't get at them. Off she went on her date.

"Sheila was a medical student. One day before heading off to class, she asked if any of us had seen her scapula. It turns out Sheila had borrowed this bone in order to study it, and she had to return it to the lab. We all searched the house. It turns out the puppy had found the scapula before we did."

As for dating, there were formal dances at the downtown hotels, or you'd go on a date skating or skiing. The Tuck Shop was the hot spot on campus for coffee, a meal, or a game of bridge. "People didn't shack up in those days," says Anne, "and it was rare for a girl to ask a boy out. We had what we called Secret Sorrows, where there would be this boy you liked, but you would never get to meet him unless *he* asked you out."

Graduation

SYLVIA AND ANNE BOTH GRADUATED at the top of their class. Anne was only 19 when she finished her last exam. Sylvia took a post-graduate course at Columbia University in New York City.

Both sisters had a variety of jobs after graduation—school teaching, retail in New York City, hospital dietetics, and helping to prepare 4,000 meals a day at the Toronto Eaton's. But it was World War II that dominated their postgraduate days. Anne recalls that when she and Sylvia belonged to the Alberta Women's Service Corps and took First Aid, they failed jaw bandaging. "The object was to bandage someone's jaw so tightly that they couldn't talk, but when we practiced on each other, whoever was bandaged up could still chatter away. Jaw bandaging was not our strength." But the Service Corps provided a natural bridge to wartime work for the Evans sisters.

Sylvia—"I Picked up a Job Application for Someone Else"

IN 1940, Sylvia walked into an Air Force recruiting station to pick up an application for one of her girlfriends, Jane Laidlaw. Sylvia ended up applying herself and served in Toronto, Calgary, Montréal, and Halifax during the war. On a special assignment in Ottawa from 1945–1946, she was the private secretary to Princess Alice, wife of the Earl of Athlone, the governor general. Later, during the 1950s Cold War, Ottawa called Sylvia back into service to provide advice as women were again enlisted into RCAF trades.

In the April 26, 1951 edition of *The Edmonton Journal*, the front page was packed with news about the conflict on Korea. Deeper in that edition, there was a report headlined "Edmonton Woman Selected to Direct RCAF Service." The woman was Squadron Leader Sylvia Evans, who had been invited by Ottawa to return to service as the advisor to women. In the article, Sylvia points out that there were women in the nursing and dietician professions who held higher ranks than hers in the forces. One of Sylvia's last acts during her World War II service was to write a report advocating that women have the same ranking system as men, and that the pay for

Squadron Leader Sylvia Evans is to the left. Anne Evans Crofton, to the right, was a "filter officer" with the Air Force. (Private Collection)

the various ranks be equal. The recommendations in her report were enacted by the time of her service during the Cold War in the 1950s.[39]

Anne: Convoy to War-Torn Europe

ANNE TOO SERVED in the Air Force. She remembers sitting across from the recruiter as he was reading a telegram about her new duties. "I was reading upside down," she says, "and could see words like 'dangerous' and 'underground.'"

Anne went through basic training. Soon after, she left for Halifax. "There were 24 girls on one of the first convoys that went to England," Anne remembers, "and on our first day out of Halifax, the Germans blew up one of our tankers. An American destroyer came to rescue us but mistakenly sheared off the bow of one of our convoy's troop ships. A friend on that ship was sent home to Edmonton and phoned my parents to say that I was all right, but my parents weren't allowed to know where I was heading."

Anne's ocean crossing lasted a harrowing ten days. "One of the girls in our group was Connie Duff, and it was on our first night out that the tanker was blown up. It was a harrowing experience. The people who had already experienced an ocean crossing were much more scared that those of us for whom it was a first-time crossing—but there was quite a panic—

for everyone. We had an immediate boat drill, with everyone on deck in their Mae West vests. And later, down on Deck Four, Connie Duff would chant, over and over in German, '*Hans und Fritz, Ich bin freundlich.*' 'Hans and Fritz, I am friendly.'

"The night after the tanker was blown up, we had finally settled down to sleep. There was a loud crash, and we thought we'd been torpedoed. But it was only a glass water bottle that had fallen to the floor. We were all scared. But Connie got out of bed, took off her regulation tin-rimmed glasses, put on her own glasses and said, 'I'll be dammed if I'll go to my death in government issue glasses."

There were, however, light moments. Anne remembers a priest who was with their convoy. "He would start a rumour," explains Anne, "and then check his watch to see how long it would take for the rumour to make the rounds of the ship and get back to him."

"When we reached Britain," says Anne, "we were met by cheering crowds, and what started out as a six-week training course ended up as ten months' service as a filter officer, tracking airplanes by radar. Our first posting as filter officers was in a condemned house. At night, we could hear water running down the inside of the walls, and rats splashing around in it.

"A lot of my time was spent camouflaged in various secret locations in England, plotting radar information and tracking Allied airplanes. On the radar screen we could see two planes approach each other in the air, and then you couldn't tell one plane from the other. After the dogfight, only one plane would emerge."

"After my time as a filter trainee was over," Anne remembers, "ten of us were sent for officer training in the Lake District. The training really should have occurred right at the start of our posting, but that was just not to be. So we had our training afterwards.

"One person who was part of this training was a woman named Eve Eaton. Eve was from Lille, France—her father was English and her mother was French. Eve's French, of course, was flawless, and her English excellent but accented, and she spoke in a very deliberate way. And Eve knew what it was like to have your country invaded.

"One night we were all going to walk to a movie. You need to know that during much of the war, all of England was under a blackout—no lights at all could be turned on because the Germans were bombing us. But one night, one of the girls thought we shouldn't go to a movie in the pitch black because we might be attacked on a dark street. Eve's response? In her accented and careful English, she simply said, 'I would kill him.' Eve, you see, had been trained as a commando."

Anne finished her officer training and returned to service in Canada for the rest of World War II.

By 2004, three generations of the Evans clan have worked or studied at the U of A—under the names of Evans, Spencer, Peers, and Cavalier. Collectively, they are a family with a rich history, attached to both this city and to the University.

Priscilla Hammond and Sammy Ives—They Never Saw Tomorrow[40]

SHE WAS A HIKER and a horsewoman, raised in homes all around the world, but with a family life based in Banff with her mother and four sisters. The yearbook said she could cause "a perfect furore on the dance floor," and when she was a senior, her classmates elected her to write the history of the Class of 1933. Her name was Priscilla Hammond (BA '33).

And him? He was a "wonderful guy," son of a future chief justice, a little younger than Priscilla, and terribly in love with her. His name was Sammy Ives.

There isn't a U of A graduate from the late 1920s and early 1930s who doesn't know what happened to Priscilla and Sammy. Their parents grew up together in Lethbridge, and so when Sammy and Priscilla both arrived at the U of A, there was an easy familiarity grounded in a long family friendship. By the time Priscilla was a senior at the U of A, Sammy was her boyfriend.

Sammy can't tell us about Priscilla's time at university, but alumni Hugh Morrison and Anne Evans Crofton can—they were her classmates.

"I was in love with Priscilla," says Hugh Morrison, "and so were a lot of other young men. I wrote a poem about her which was published in *The Gateway*, and another that I have kept for myself." Priscilla's yearbook described the effect she had on her male classmates: She "is one of those rare females who blush readily and unreservedly," and "there is traffic congestion in the halls when she passes."

"She was my friend," says Anne Evans Crofton, "and I remember how beautiful she was, sparky and fun, and with a delicate sense of humour.

*Top: Priscilla Hammond
being presented at Court. This
photograph still hangs today
in the Delta Gamma fraternity
house. (Private Collection)*

*Bottom: The Hammond sisters
spent many happy days at their
Banff home, and hosted large,
casual house parties, with
"a hundred pounds of turkey,"
transported from Edmonton
"on the mud boards of
our cars."*
*(Whyte Museum of the Canadian Rockies
6068)*

She was very smart, but also wonderfully naïve. One day she asked me how farmers went about planting stubble in their fields. She had a way of endearing herself to you."

What Anne knew, but most of Priscilla's other friends did not, was that Priscilla had a heart defect. Diagnosed when she was 12, Priscilla spent the next six months in bed. Despite a grim prognosis—her doctor said that if Priscilla was very careful, she might live to 30—when the time came for university, Priscilla chose to "just do everything," and went at undergraduate life full tilt, even though it put her at risk.

Priscilla joined the Delta Gamma women's fraternity, served as vice-president of the Literary Society, and was a stand-out in English. She was a deadly shot in badminton and tennis, and in 1931–1932, with Helen Mahaffy, won the intercollegiate doubles crown in tennis. During university breaks, Priscilla shuttled around the world with her family to homes on the Riviera, in London, in the Bahamas, and in California at Coronado. One of her summers was spent working with 1927 U of A graduate Rache Dickson in the publishing business in London. She was presented at Court. It was a full, exciting undergraduate life.

Priscilla's mother, Edith Burnett Hammond, was a warm hostess and opened the family homes in Banff and London to Priscilla's student friends. "I remember going to the flat in London one evening for a visit when I was just beginning studies on a Rhodes scholarship," says Hugh Morrison. "I stayed far too long visiting with Priscilla and Mrs. Hammond, and all of a sudden, it was close to curfew for me as a freshman at Oxford. I thought I was done for because there was no way you could get past the Porters' Lodge at the gates if you were late. But Mrs. Hammond had a chauffeur drive me the 60 miles back to university. You should have seen the look on the faces in the Porters' Lodge when I so royally arrived at the gates of Merton College, Oxford, moments before curfew at midnight."

At the family house parties in Banff, Sammy Ives was often a guest. In those days, house parties were a way for young people to get to know one another in a chaperoned environment. There was hiking, riding, and lots of golf and tennis. "We built a tennis court behind our house in Banff," says Priscilla's sister Tilda. "It wasn't even on our property." But no one minded back then. "Banff was a simpler place in those days." Anne Evans

Crofton remembers that they would transport "a hundred pounds of turkey down to the house parties on the mud boards of our cars."

In May 1933, graduation day came and went for Priscilla. She travelled back to Banff to be with her mother and sisters. On one perfectly gorgeous summer day, Priscilla and two of her sisters decided to saddle up their horses, ride to Mount Edith, and hike in the mountains for a look at the glacier lilies. There was a photo taken that day—three beautiful young women with wide grins mounted on their horses, all against a backdrop of the Rocky Mountains.

When they got home, Priscilla laughed at what a good sweat they had worked up on their hike, and joked that she must have lost a couple of pounds. She popped downstairs to weigh herself and dropped to the floor. She was dead. It was one week after graduation. She was just 21 years old.

Anne Crofton remembers that Sammy was travelling back from England on a "cattle boat"—a long trip. When he arrived back home, Sammy Ives heard the news. He was alone. He walked downstairs to the family basement and took his life.

The small, close-knit campus community was stunned by both deaths. Rache Dickson, in London, called Hugh Morrison in Oxford with the news. "I couldn't believe it," says Hugh. "Nobody could believe it."

Sammy left a note asking to be buried next to Priscilla. It wasn't possible; Priscilla had already been buried in the family plot. And so Sammy's father bought the gravesite closest to where Priscilla was, and that is where he buried his son. When the Judge died, he was buried next to his son Sammy, and when Mrs. Hammond died years later, she was buried next to her daughter Priscilla.

Today, in the old Banff cemetery on Buffalo Street, Priscilla's and Sammy's graves are a stone's throw from one another.

Priscilla was a quiet risk-taker who lived her life to the fullest. She graduated in 1933, and died one week later.
(Private Collection)

Priscilla and Mrs. Zaidee Mahood Stewart

MRS. STEWART WAS A POET. In the 1930s and 1940s, her work appeared in the *Alberta Poetry Yearbook*, published annually by the Canadian Authors' Association. Poets from across Canada sent in entries, but only some 50 poems were chosen for the *Yearbook*.

In the 1933–1934 yearbook, the following poem appeared, with an editorial note that owing to the special nature of the poem, the author did not want to be identified. In 1950, Zaidee Stewart put her name to the poem. It was published in a slim volume entitled *Banff Holiday*. The poem speaks in a universal way to the loss of a loved one.

A Memory of Priscilla Hammond

Perhaps each bird as sweetly sings,
Perhaps the stars are just as bright,
As when my darling spread her wings

For the long flight.
The river still flaunts past my door
Its million sparkles, diamond-wise,
As when she watched it from the shore
With happy eyes.

And it is well. No one would choose
To close the flowers, or shroud the sun,
Because their lot had been to lose
A best-loved one.

And yes, though nature seems to be
Impervious to grief or caring,
A different world it seems to me
Without her sharing.

And how did Mrs. Stewart come to know Priscilla so well? She was the "wonderful" Hammond family housekeeper, and was there when Priscilla died.[41]

END OF THE DECADE

IN 1939, King George and his Queen, Elizabeth, came to visit Canada. They knew the world would soon be at war, and they came to rally the troops.

The King and Queen were right. On September 1, Hitler invaded Poland. War was about to engulf the world again.

"And when we go, a little of our youth will stay behind, on the campus, forever."

—Patricia Scott Schlosser
Toast the University, 1949

Timeline

Overleaf: The mood on campus in the 1940s was exuberant despite the war in Europe and Asia. To kick off the fall sports season, each Faculty and School participated in the Varsity Parade. Here, the "Home Reccers" from the School of Household Economics lead the way, spoofing their nickname "House Eccers." (UAA 72-58-323)

Enrolment and Finance, 1940–1949

- Fall student head count: 1,943 (1940); 2,935 (1949)
- Operating budget from the Province of Alberta: $428,000.00 (1940); $1,300,000.00 (1949)
- Full-load undergraduate Arts tuition: $110.00 (1940); $130.00 (1949)
- SU membership fee: $14.50 (1940); $10.50 + $8 building fund (1949)

Key Dates, 1940–1949

- Cecil Burgess, first and only professor of Architecture, retires (1940)
- President Kerr resigns, and Robert Newton is named president (1941)
- The military controls the Covered Rink, student residences, and the Normal School (1941)
- Miss Florence Dodd, longest-serving dean of women, retires (1941)
- Faculty of Education is established (1942)
- First issue of *New Trail* (1942)
- Dr. John MacEachran, first provost, retires and is replaced by P.S. Warren (1944)
- School of Dentistry becomes a Faculty (1944)
- The University is given sole responsibility for teacher education (1945)
- Enrolment nearly doubles as veterans return (1945)
- Last publication by *The Gateway* of each student's final exam grades (1946)
- The Memorial War Organ in Convocation Hall is rededicated to those who died in World War II (1946)
- Registrar Albert Ottewell, a member of the first gradating class, dies (1946)
- Henry Marshall Tory dies (1947)
- Reg Lister, long-serving superintendent of residences, made an honorary member of Convocation upon his retirement (1949)

Selected Campus Buildings, 1940–1949

- The University cafeteria, known as "Hot Caf," opens on the site of today's Central Academic Building (1942)
- First Observatory (1943)
- Nurses' residence (1946)
- Ten-year campus building boom begins (1947)
- The first building (a "chalet") goes up on the Banff Campus (1949)

Beyond Campus, 1940–1949

- Dunkirk is evacuated and France is under Nazi occupation (1940)
- Japan bombs Pearl Harbour and the United States enters World War II (1941)
- Over 42,000 Canadians killed in World War II
- The Nobel Prize in Medicine is awarded for the discovery of penicillin (1945)
- The United Nations General Assembly holds its first session (1946)
- Leduc #1 comes in, ushering in Alberta's oil and gas industry (1947)
- First parking meters in Edmonton (1948)
- The transistor replaces vacuum tubes, introducing in the computer era (1948)
- The Communist People's Republic is declared under Mao Tse-tung (1949)

VIGNETTES FROM THE 1940s

President, Board Chair, and Chancellor

THE CAMPUS was still small, and life revolved around the Arts and Med Buildings, the Covered Rink, the Tuck Shop, and the three old residences—Athabasca, Assiniboia, and Pembina. It was easy to find your way around. The jitterbug was popular, and Frank Sinatra was on the airwaves.

In 1940, the president was Dr. W.A.R. (William) Kerr, who had a long association with the U of A. When Tory was away for months at a time running the Khaki University after World War I, it was Kerr who had taken up the reins as acting president. From 1914 to 1936, Dr. Kerr served as dean of Arts and Science, and in 1936 he was appointed as president, a position he held until 1941.

The chairman of the Board in 1940 was the long-serving Justice Horace Harvey who, later in that year, was summarily replaced by the Aberhart government, apparently in a move to wrest control over CKUA from the University; Justice Harvey's successor was Howard H. Parlee.

The Chancellor in 1940 was former Premier Rutherford, founder of the University. Within two years, the campus would mourn his passing.

Gwen Pharis Gets Married

GWEN PHARIS, one of the students inspired by drama teacher Elizabeth Sterling Haynes in the late 1920s, graduated in 1934 with a BA. Gwen devoted herself to theatre, eventually becoming one of Canada's most famous playwrights. In the mid-1930s, Gwen started working in the Faculty of Extension. She got married as World War II broke out, and that created a problem, for married women weren't supposed to work. So Gwen kept her marriage secret. And then one day, President Kerr found out that Gwen Pharis was really Gwen Ringwood. The president summoned Gwen to a private meeting in the Senate Chamber, the most formal of the University's meeting rooms. It was just the president and Gwen.

"I didn't tell them I was married," explains Gwen, "because you weren't supposed to work at the University if you were married. Finally, my husband Barney, he was interning, he got a little legacy, so we had enough money, and I felt awful about being such a hypocrite. So I told Donald [Cameron, head of Extension] that I was married and pretty soon I got a call from Dr.

Kerr. It was after the New Year and we'd been married in September, and I went into the Senate room and there was Dr. Kerr. I felt quite small and sat down at the other end [of the room]."

Gwen thought she was going to be fired, but she held her ground, and Dr. Kerr ultimately backed down. The reason was a simple one. "The war was on," says Gwen. "It was 1940...women were needed to fill the jobs left by the men who went to war." And that's how Gwen, and many other married women, finally got the chance to work outside the home.[1]

Barbed Wire Surrounds Athabasca Hall

IT WAS THE WAR in Europe that defined 1940. After the fall of France in 1940, military training on campus was compulsory; for male students that meant 110 hours of training during the academic year, capped by two weeks of summer boot camp at the Sarcee training grounds in Calgary.[2] To squeeze in the required training, the start of classes was moved back half an hour, from 8:30 A.M. to 8 A.M. From 4 P.M. to 6 P.M. each day, the men trained, usually in the Covered Rink, which was turned into a drill hall. Most male students didn't have enough time to change from civilian clothes into the uniforms required for their afternoon drills and parades, so uniforms were seen everywhere on campus throughout the day.

By 1942, the Athabasca, Assiniboia, and Pembina residences were taken over by various branches of the armed services and "transformed into a military camp." Reg Lister remembers that they "removed the beds, tore down the doors, and built a barbed wire fence around the residences, complete with police and armed guards at the gates."[3] Students were suddenly put out of their rooms and had to board in private homes in Edmonton. All the traditions of residence life—the dances, the camaraderie, the communal meals—ended. With no more women's residence, Miss Dodd, the dean of women and warden of Pembina, was, in effect, out of a job. Reg Lister stayed on to oversee a new kind of life in Athabasca, Assiniboia, and Pembina.

Unlike World War I, when the campus was drained of staff and students, most students and staff stayed put during World War II and did what the federal government encouraged: they served their country by staying at university. The government declared a dozen or so disciplines as essential to the war effort, selectively boosting enrolments. Law was not included in the list, and enrolment dropped to a low of nine students in 1944. Physically able students needed a 65% average to stay in university and avoid active service. By 1943, if they failed one course, they were not only out of university, but their names were reported to the Mobilization Board.

Students and staff put their shoulder into the war effort in every way. Many enlisted, and everyone was involved in fundraising for war-related or relief causes. Women students asked that wartime training be compulsory for them, just as it was for the men. Research on campus shifted gears to support the war effort. Classes in Medicine and Dentistry were accelerated to produce graduates faster. The Students' Union raised money for an ambulance, and the "Meds" and "Geers" held a penny race as a fundraiser. The competition between these long-time rival faculties involved laying a trail of pennies from the Tuck Shop to the Med and Arts Buildings, forming a giant "V" for "victory." In 1946, with the war over and demobilization complete, veterans poured back to university.

Joe-Boys

IN THE 1940S, Canadian naval trainees were boarded at St. Joseph's College, and its residents became known as Joe-Boys. Senator Nick Taylor ('49 BSC), remembers that the College itself was called "the Russina Hotel, an obvious twist on the fight between the Vatican and communist Russia in those days."[4]

Mr. Taylor lists the Joe-Boys of his day: Don Lougheed, later executive vice-president of Imperial Oil; Frank Quigley, later justice of the Alberta Supreme Court; Bill Dickie, later energy minister; Ken Moore, a future chief justice of Alberta; Marcel Lambert, who became speaker of the House of Commons; Bob Colborne, the future founder and owner of Pacific Western Transportation and Red Arrow bus lines; Gordon Leslie, later president of Trans-Alta Pipelines; Robert Kroetsch, winner of numerous poetry and writing awards; and Tom Walsh ('49 BA, '53 LLB, '89 LLD HON), a Calgary lawyer. If you needed a role model or mentor, this group would cover just about every skill set.

LOVE AND LOYALTY—THE NEW TRAIL

IN THE EARLY 1940S, a financial crisis engulfed the long-standing alumni magazine, *The Trail*, and prompted the Alumni Association to team up with the Faculty of Extension to produce the *New Trail* magazine, which is received today by thousands of U of A alumni. As the first edition's lead article put it in 1942, "Ours is not a rich University. Since the very beginning, its record is one long miracle of accomplishing much with little means. Many things have been done by individuals for love and loyalty."

It was the same story with both the Faculty of Extension and the Alumni Association—a long list of volunteers had kept both organizations going over the years. To breathe life into the *New Trail*, Dr. F.M. Salter of the English Department volunteered to be editor, Extension and Alumni Association officials took over the associate editorship positions, and the chancellor, Board chair, and president all signed on to the advisory board. *New Trail*, off to a shaky start in 1942, has now been a going concern for six decades.

When the war ended, a flood of veterans, funded by the Department of Veteran Affairs, enrolled at the U of A. The federal funding meant, for the first time, that the doors of the University were opened to students who otherwise could not have afforded the cost. And all those "returned men," as they were called, precipitated a crisis—for housing, for classroom, lab, and recreational space, and for a Library. Even bicycle parking was scarce.

A GLANCE AT THE CALENDAR

THE 1940 AND 1949 editions of the University Calendars are the bookends of this era. With a dull grey utilitarian look to them, and printed on tissue-thin paper, the Calendar increased in length by two-thirds between 1940 and 1949, and by the decade's end it brimmed with course and program descriptions. The 1940 Calendar describes the Board of Governors as the body responsible for the finances and management of the University, with the Senate in charge of academic matters. By 1949, the Calendar lists General Faculties Council as the academic governing body. It was a cause célèbre.

One of the Senate's responsibilities since 1908 had been the conferral of honorary degrees. By 1941, Senate rubber-stamped the recommendations of a committee guided by President Kerr, Board Chair Parlee, and Chancellor Rutherford.

Senate's approval, in fact, had become so automatic that the honorary degree recommendations were put forward for approval on the very day they were to be conferred at Convocation. And there was only one convocation ceremony in those days. Senate was expected to approve the recommendations at the morning meeting, with the honorary degrees conferred that afternoon. It had worked that way for years.

Enter Bible Bill

IN 1941, Premier William Aberhart was one of the Senate Committee's two nominees for an honorary degree. Known as "Bible Bill," Aberhart's twin religious pulpits had been the radio and the Calgary Prophetic Bible Institute. Remembered for his "Social Credit" economic theories, Aberhart led Albertans to expect $25 each in government-issued scrip—a huge sum in the depths of the Depression—if he were elected.

And elected he was. In 1935, Aberhart's Social Credit team trounced the long-reigning United Farmers of Alberta (UFA). Once in power, three of Aberhart's bills landed in the Supreme Court of Canada because the lieutenant governor, the Honourable J.C. Bowen, refused to sign them. One bill would have controlled the free press so that only information agreeable to the government could be published. The other two bills would have regulated credit and banks. In 1937, the Supreme Court upheld the lieutenant governor's right to refuse to sign the bills. Aberhart weathered the storm and stayed in office.[5]

Bowen's decision to refuse to sign these three bills had been made at a time when there was fierce debate about maintaining an expensive "royal court" in a democratic province deep in an economic depression. The Mundare and Pincher Creek Social Credit Leagues had in fact called for Bowen's resignation, a move supported by the Social Credit convention in January 1938—soon after the Supreme Court decision. In April, Bowen was told to move out of Government House by May 1. On May 1, Bowen told the government it needed an Order-in-Council to force him out. The government response was swift—Bowen's telephone service and other utilities were cut off. The required Order-in-Council was then sent to Bowen. In an ironic twist of legislative history, Bowen had to sign the order that forced him out of the place that had become his home, Government House.[6]

Was Aberhart's action taken on the basis that democratic Alberta, scarred by the Depression, should not have a lieutenant governor? Or was it taken as a "get even" measure against Bowen? Whatever the reasons, Government House was never again home to the lieutenant governor. The Order-in-Council Bowen signed went further than ending his telephone and utility service. The Executive Council's decision that Bowen had to sign stipulated that no further appropriations should be made "for the maintenance and upkeep of [Government House]." The minister of public works was directed to obtain "immediate vacant possession of the said house and premises, together with such furnishings, goods and chattels therein or thereon as are the property of the province." Bowen moved to the Hotel Macdonald and the furnishings of Government House were sold at public auction.

The following year, in 1938, six Alberta daily newspapers and 90 weeklies were given Pulitzer Prizes for their "struggle to preserve the freedom of the press." Aberhart was indeed a controversial nominee for an honorary degree.

The Honorary Degree Debacle—One Vote

IT WAS ALL A MATTER OF TIMING.

In 1941, the Senate had the opportunity to reflect on the Aberhart nomination. For the first time in the history of the U of A, there was a one-week lag between the Senate meeting and Convocation. Senate would be voting on the Aberhart nomination well before the actual ceremony.

On the day of the vote, it was Board Chair Howard Parlee who was, by chance, in the Chair of the Senate, substituting for the ailing Chancellor Rutherford. Chancellor Rutherford walked into the meeting as the Aberhart drama was unfolding. President William Kerr was also at the meeting. The first vote was taken. Premier Aberhart was denied an honorary degree by one vote. At the end of the day-long meeting, Mr. Parlee asked Senate to re-open the question of a degree for Aberhart. The re-vote produced the same result: a one-vote denial.[7]

It was a disaster.

President Kerr and Board Chair Parlee both resigned. Chancellor Rutherford's already fragile health deteriorated. It immediately became clear to the public that prior to the Senate's vote Premier Aberhart had already been invited to receive an honorary degree by the president and the Board chair. In fact, the premier had already written his convocation address.[8] But he would never deliver it, and the refusal stung.

In the next sitting of the legislature after the honorary degree debacle, the Senate was stripped of all its academic powers except, ironically, the power to award honorary degrees.

The General Faculty Council (GFC), established by President Tory as a "joint meeting of all the individual Faculty Councils," with all the professors present, had dealt with grass-roots academic matters for decades, but without formal legislative power. It was now given authority over aca-demic matters. The Board's powers were strengthened and a Deans' Council was established to deal with student discipline and to make recommendations to GFC. Also, one student was given a voting position on the new Senate. By 1972, students had voting parity on GFC.

The radical change to the Senate's powers was just one of many recommendations made by a "survey" committee whose members Aberhart had handpicked to review Alberta's post-secondary education system. The report made many far-reaching recommendations, including a proposal that teacher education be taken over by the University and that Normal Schools be closed.

The whole legislative world of the University was turned upside down in one swift stroke. It took a decade for the dramatic changes to settle in. The Senate, though sidelined as a legislative body, saw its responsibility as an advisory body evolve into a role envied by other Canadian universities. The U of A's Senate became the University's bridge to the public, playing a role unique in Canada.

President Robert Newton

ROBERT NEWTON was named to succeed Kerr. He took the helm at a difficult time for the University: its governance was in turmoil; its relationship with the provincial government was turbulent; and its policies had to be adapted to face a world at war. By most accounts, Robert Newton was a mild-mannered gentleman, but there had to be some steel in his spine and some savvy in his style to navigate the choppy waters of 1941. In his unpublished memoirs, Newton provides a clear picture of his style and personality through his summarized philosophy of administration:

1. People work best when contented and happy. Avoid upsetting them unnecessarily. If necessary, lead them a step at a time.

2. Make associates, rather than assistants, of your staff. Plan their work with, not for, them.

3. Recognize and cultivate diversity of talents in your staff. Allow for a normal share of defects in each.

4. It is sometimes better to pass over minor mistakes, or infractions of discipline, leaving correction to be made by example, or at a time when it can be done unobtrusively.

5. Strive to create a corporate sense of responsibility. This depends on each individual feeling he has a real job to do, and will be fostered by delegating...responsibility.[9]

Newton quickly established a good working relationship with the provincial government and with the premier. His administration prepared for world war, and for the involvement of the University. He was also instrumental in keeping the Banff School afloat and thriving in the 1940s. "The primary purpose of the School," he says in his memoirs, "was to help rural Alberta to become culturally self-sustaining...but there was a danger of undesirable screening on the basis of ability to pay. We did not want to operate a school for 'rich Americans.'"

The problem was that the Carnegie grant, which had kick-started the School in 1933, ran out a few years later. The U of A, which had covered the School's deficits for some five years, could no longer afford to do so. "By the time I became president in 1941," Newton says, "the Director of the Banff School, Don Cameron, had about reached the end of his tether in improvising accommodation and equipment. The old theatre in which the work had begun was finally condemned to be torn down in 1939. Then, rather than see the school collapse, the people of Banff supported their School Board in building an auditorium with 500 seats, and with classrooms in a lower floor which could be used by the School Board in winter as well as by the School of Fine Arts in the summer. The University equipped the stage...and built and equipped the first permanent residential chalet in 1947, at a cost of $60,000."

President Newton considered asking the government to fund Banff as a permanent third U of A campus, but that seemed an unlikely prospect with millions needed for the Edmonton campus and with a Calgary campus on the horizon. And so Newton went to work finding a private donor to help fund the Banff School for the Fine Arts.

Newton manoeuvred for two years to arrange a private meeting with Mrs. J.H. Woods, widow of the publisher of The *Calgary Herald*.[10] It was well known that Mrs. Woods wanted to establish a suitable memorial to honour her late husband. At a dinner party in the fall of 1945, President Newton finally got his chance to talk with her. "I was agreeably surprised," Newton says, "when Mrs. Woods seized eagerly on the Banff proposal.... We drove together to Banff soon afterwards, to look over possible sites.... None of the sites we inspected that afternoon, as we tramped through fresh snow, were entirely adequate, but early the next spring the National Parks authorities, whom both Don Cameron and I had visited in Ottawa, gave us a magnificent site on the slope of Tunnel Mountain." Mrs. Woods funded two more chalets—one to serve as an administration building and dining hall, and the other to serve as a residence.

The Banff School's expansion has never stopped. Today, the Banff Centre has some 18 buildings, including a theatre, teaching and conference facilities, an art gallery, residences and staff quarters, a state-of-the-art recreation centre, and eight tiny, exquisite cabins that serve as retreats for writers and artists.

Emma Read Newton

ROBERT NEWTON may have been the president during the war, but it is Emma Newton whom so many alumni remember. Mrs. Newton was awarded a degree in Arts from the U of A in 1931, and took classes in the 1940s when her husband was president. This was uncharted territory—the president's wife taking classes. In fact, no one took courses who was not registered for credit. And so the University passed a regulation that under certain circumstances, people could sit in on classes. Generations of students can thank Emma Read Newton for the ability to audit classes.

"Emma Read Newton really liked being the president's wife," says one alumnus. "We used to joke that when letters would come from Dr. Newton about this subject or that, it was really Emma who had drafted them, and so we would call these letters "Emmanations." Another alumnus says that he used to see a bobby-soxed Emma Read Newton walking down the hall when classes changed, and he thought she was just another student. "Little did I know! I didn't realize until long afterwards that Emma probably had a big impact on my education." The Newtons were a close team. Robert, in his memoirs, described Emma as his "staunch ally."

Emma was also a staunch ally of the arts and a force to be reckoned with. She was used to having input at high levels in the University. Emma had, for instance, been influential in lobbying for the fine arts during President Tory's term. Her piano renditions were featured when CKUA made its first broadcast, and she had an eye for art. The paintings she donated to the University hang in special places on campus, away from the sun and cherished by those who are fortunate enough to have them in their offices.

EVERGREEN AND GOLD

EACH YEARBOOK PUBLISHED in the 1940s is a time-travelling treasure. Open up any one of them, and you will be transported back to campus life during the war and the peace that followed.

The influx of veterans after World War II caused the *Evergreen and Gold* to scale back the number of its pages, but the quality of the volumes is sumptuous—leather-bound volumes, some as heavy as five pounds, all works of artisan engravers and printers. The 1940 edition featured shimmering foil inserts—green, gold, and red—depicting each of Alberta's major industries, and linking those industries to specific degree programs at the University.

All the old *Evergreen and Gold* editions had featured a section with formal, stiff-figured photos of senior administrators. But in 1941 the yearbook contained life-like artists' sketches of the senior administrators—people like Miss Dodd—the fearsome warden of Pembina who never let her female charges stray. At last, Miss Dodd leaps to life thanks to the artist's pen-and-ink rendering.

These ten wartime volumes of the *Evergreen and Gold* chronicled student life, but they also honoured the hundreds of students, staff, and alumni who served, or died, in the war. The numbers were overwhelming and their names were printed on page after page in the honour rolls.

In every edition there was a careful attention to the detail of everyday life: Reg Lister walking down Whyte Avenue with a loaf of bread under his arm; married student couples cradling a crying newborn before heading off to class; groups of students bundled up, posing in front of the perfect log cabin that was headquarters to the Outdoors Club; forlorn young men leaning out of a train window on their way down to Calgary's Sarcee Camp for summertime military training; young women off to the Prom, outfitted in yards and yards of organza and silk and accompanied by young men in starched shirts and tuxedos.

Saying Goodbye to the Great Ones—Rutherford, Tory, and Colleagues

IT WAS A DECADE when the *Evergreen and Gold* said goodbye to nine outstanding individuals who had shaped the U of A.

Former Premier Rutherford, now chancellor of the University, died in 1941. Students called him the "grand old man," the founder of the University, whose life was intertwined with the history of the province. He was the person who had shepherded the *University Bill* through the first Legislature; the one who bought River Lot 5 as the future home of the U of A; and he was the man who built his home next door to River Lot 5 so that he could watch his young creation grow.

But for students, he was remembered as the premier who picked them up in his red Packard on the way to school on a bitter winter day, or the chancellor who let students use his personal library. Generations of alumni remembered the hospitality of Chancellor Rutherford and his wife Mattie, who hosted them in their home on graduation day.

John Weir, the founding dean of Law, died in 1943. Dean Weir, it is said by one of his students, died of a broken heart from listening to the radio broadcasts that relentlessly recited the names of so many of his students who died in World War II. Here is how the *Evergreen and Gold*, in the "In Memorium" section, remembered Dean Weir:

> For the first time since its founding twenty-one years ago, the Law School opened without Dean Weir. His untimely death removed from the University a professor whose knowledge of his chosen field was a source of repeated wonder....
>
> He possessed to a high degree the art of teaching, so that always his students were led to make their own discoveries.... No more unassuming man lived. His life was his family, his professional associates—

and the law....His students and graduates mourn his death and treasure his memory.

The first director of Extension, Albert Ottewell, died in 1946. His death was followed in quick succession by the deaths of Donald Ewing Cameron (after whom Cameron Library is named); Jimmy Adam, designer of the first University Crest; and Henry Marshall Tory. Students dedicated the 1947 yearbook to Dr. Tory, and *The Gateway* reported on the memorial service held in Convocation Hall.*The Gateway* recalled the breadth of Dr. Tory's "lively interest" in the University and its people—he was the visionary president who planned a campus where others saw only scrubby brushland. He was also the caring, down-to-earth president who knitted socks for the soldiers overseas during World War I.[11]

A magnificent oil painting of Tory hangs in the restored Senate Chamber in the Arts Building. "It is good to have the portrait," said R.K. Gordon, one of the U of A's first professors, "... and the people who look at it will know that our first president was a man of no mean account. The University of Alberta is his best memorial."

Tory—founder or organizer of four universities: UBC, the U of A, the Khaki University, and Carleton College, later Carleton University—was mourned further afield. In an editorial titled "A Great Spirit," *The Evening Journal* in Ottawa, described Tory's ambitious fund-raising campaign for Carleton College, undertaken when Tory was 83 years old:[12]

The intent and not the deed
Is in our real power; and therefore,
Who dares greatly
Does greatly.

Edouard Sonet, Ernest Sheldon, and Reg Lister

IN A GOODBYE of another sort, *The Gateway* reported on March 14, 1947 that the beloved Dr. Sonet was leaving the U of A for Berkeley. Sonet's friend and colleague William Hardy Alexander had gone to Berkeley in the 1930s, and it was very possibly Doc Alik who paved the way for Sonet. Students remembered Sonet as enthusiastic, funny, dramatic, and vigorous in the classroom. "The University is to lose one of its most versatile and

At the war's end, the University prepared for a huge influx of veterans. As reported in New Trail *in 1946, "Four Nissen huts have now been erected as well as several re-struck army huts...[located approximately where the Central Academic Building now stands]. Cement has been poured for the foundation and basements of both extensions to the Medical Building. Every floor of the Arts Building has undergone changes, some of them very extensive, and the same statement might be made of all buildings on the campus. The facilities of the School of Dentistry are to be expanded so as to make sure that no veteran desiring to qualify as a dentist need be turned away. Just where the extra equipment is to be placed is a problem....."*

(UAA 76-35-138)

aggressive profs to the United States," lamented *The Gateway*. And in 1947, Ernest Sheldon, the earliest advisor to freshmen, retired, as did Provost P.S. Warren. The new provost was Dr. Harry Sparby, an education professor who had been principal of Grande Prairie High School for six years and a high school inspector in southern Alberta. A new generation of professors and administrators was taking over.

At the end of the decade, in 1949, Reg Lister, superintendent of residences and friend and mentor to students for five decades, retired. In that year he received many honours, but perhaps none were so heartfelt as being crowned King of the popular Mardi Gras dance by the students.

GLIMPSES FROM THE GATEWAY—1940-1949 [13]

"Maritime University Withdraws from CSA Body"—January 16, 1940

THIS WAS THE FIRST *GATEWAY* HEADLINE of the 1940s, and the headline that marked *The Gateway*'s 30th birthday. Mount Allison University grabbed the banner headline when it withdrew from the Canadian Students' Association. Canadian students attending the CSA national conference had voted against conscription, and then promoted a national war policy that was independent from Britain's. Students at the "Mount" saw this move as anti-British and anti-war. The next month, *The Gateway* reported on "mob action" as UBC students added their voice to the growing protest against the CSA.

"Aggressive Army Element Dominates Japan"—October 4, 1940

THIRD-YEAR LAW STUDENT Morris Schumiatcher had won a cross-Canada essay contest sponsored by the Japanese government. The title of his winning essay was "Why Canada and Japan Should Cultivate Friendship," and the prize was two months in Japan. Morris came back with a chilling report.

"The Japanese," he said, "like the Germans, believe they have a mission to perform. Theirs is a superior race and it is their sacred duty to guide the destinies of Asia. The conquest of Manchuria was the first step in this mission, and the Chinese war is the second." The present premier, Prince Konoye, intends "to institute a new order in the east, beginning with the economic and military treaty with the Fascists."

A Campus Building Spree in the 1940s

CONSTRUCTION ON CAMPUS *during the 1940s was entirely war-related and included a Drill Hall and a cafeteria, the beloved "Hot Caf." By 1968, the campus still had fascinating spots, where old buildings rested in the shadows of shiny new structures. In this photo, the long-gone North Lab abuts the long-demolished Hot Caf; Cameron Library is centre back. Behind North Lab is the Medical Building (today's Dentistry/Pharmacy).* (UAA 67–452)

THE POPULAR HOT CAF *was built when the RCAF took over Athabasca Hall and its dining hall. Simply put, there had to be another place on campus where people could gather to eat. Hot Caf was designed by I.F. Morrison and Cecil Burgess and built by the RCAF with help from Engineering students.* (UAA 69–97–283B)

In the same issue of *The Gateway*, it was reported that some 900 U of A students would be doing required military training—110 hours a month—during the academic year. An accompanying photo showed students learning to use gas masks. Within a year, U of A women would also be taking military training at their own request.

Wartime issues of *The Gateway* reported on students and alumni who were at the front. Matt Halton (BA '29), a *Toronto Star* and CBC reporter, was forced to flee Nazi Germany, and Eleanor Aiello (BA '39), the popular student elected to write the class history, was "teaching English at a girls' school in unoccupied France when last heard from."

"John Dallamore"—October 8, 1940

JOHN WAS A RECENT GRADUATE in Mining Engineering. Shortly after Convocation, he joined the RCAF and was stationed in Cairo, Egypt. John was the first alumnus to die in the war.

"Movement To Bring Back Sadie Hawkins To Campus Started—Council May Make It Official"—October 1940

NEWS OF THE WAR vied during the 1940s with headlines about student social activities. There were innumerable dances—the Wauneita formal, the Sophomore Splash, the Junior Prom, the Engineers Ball, the Med Ball, and house dances.

Sadie Hawkins Week was a favourite of the students, but frowned upon by the University, probably because the students held overtown dances during Sadie Hawkins Week, far from the watchful eyes of university officials. At the October 1940 overtown dance, admission for the men was "two cents per inch of a man's waistline." The women, of course, had to circle their waists with a measuring tape to determine the entry fee. It was a little too risqué for some administrators.

The girls produced a spoof issue of *The Gateway* printed on pink paper ("Gals Govern The Gateway!" was the headline), and, of course, during Sadie Hawkins Week, the girls got to ask the boys out.

The University pressed the students to end Sadie Hawkins Week, and the SU and the administration eventually reached a unique compromise. They agreed on a new name for the week, and all proceeds would go

Editions of The Gateway *in the 1940s were packed with advertisements for clothing, school supplies, and the ever-present cigarette.*

towards the war effort. The new name? "Waw Waw Weekend." It was a play on the name of the campus group called the Women's Auxiliary War Services. It was also a word taken from Longfellow's *Hiawatha*, in which "waw waw" meant "wild goose."

So how did Waw Waw Week work? As *The Gateway* put it, "It's going to be a woman's weekend with the men as the Waw Waws, which all adds up to a wild goose chase by the women, for the men." The men loved it. So did the women.

"Edmonton Lawyer Named Chairman of Governors—Chief Justice Harvey Replaced by H.H. Parlee in Shakeup; Three Board Members Out"—October 22, 1940

JUSTICE HARVEY had been Chairman of the Board since 1917. He learned from an Order-in-Council that he was no longer chairing the Board.

The Gateway saw a tie between this move and the Social Credit government's desire to take over CKUA. *The Gateway* noted that the first matter to be discussed by the reorganized Board would be "expansion and commercialization of the University radio station. The matter has been one of marked controversy and difference of opinion, and may have had no little bearing on the recent action of the Aberhart administration."

"Golden Bears Continue on Triumphal March"—October 25, 1940

BY THE 1940S there was a separate sports section in *The Gateway*. This particular sports report just about burst through the margins of the newsprint with rave reviews of a "thrill-packed" game. The Bears trounced the Maple Leaf Athletic Club 27–0.

The bleachers were filled at every game in the early 1940s, and everyone knew the cheers and yells by heart.

"Outdoor Rink is Completed"—December 6, 1940

THE COVERED RINK that students had fought so hard for was taken over by the government for military training, and throughout the war all hockey and recreational skating were moved to an outdoor rink, with only a small shack as the change-room.

"Scientific Research Vital to War Aid"—Function of Research Council to Canada's Industry Described by Dean in Philosophy Address"—January 10, 1941

TALKS GIVEN to the Philosophical Society never failed to capture the lead story in *The Gateway*. The banner headline in January 1941 introduced one of many articles about research and the war effort. In this article, Dean Robert Newton, who would within months be president of the U of A, described how the Research Council of Canada was born out of the First World War "to mobilize scientific resources and manpower." World War II was seen as cementing the role of a university as a research engine for the war effort. The 1947 *Evergreen and Gold* devoted an entire section to "Military and Research" on campus. In his memoirs, Newton said that there was such "excessive deflection of scientific research to wartime projects" that after the war there were concerted, special efforts "to nourish the spirit of enquiry after new knowledge, regardless of its apparent applicability to immediate problems. The advent of the atomic era made the importance of this so clear that government, and even industrial, laboratories now sponsor much of so-called pure science research."

"Mikado Opens Friday Night in Convocation Hall—Grand Array of Starry Talent Presents Gilbert and Sullivan Favorite In Annual Production"—January 24, 1941

THE MIKADO swept to front-page news for three successive editions, and in the following two editions, the banner headlines reported on the spring play. *The Mikado* was a sell-out, an extra show was mounted in Edmonton, and the operetta was taken to Calgary. Soon after, however, the operettas were suspended because of the war. This suspension, in fact, spelled the end of these popular productions, and the Philharmonic Society disbanded.

"Colour Night Ceremony For Awards—Executive, Literary, Gateway, Yearbook, Athletic Honours to be Presented Next Friday—First Occasion That Event Has Been Held"—March 14, 1941

THIS FIRST COLOUR NIGHT kicked off a long tradition of publicly acknowledging students who had excelled in extracurricular activities. Sponsored by the Students' Union, it cost students 50 cents to attend.

"Reminiscences of Freshman Week"—October 1, 1943

THE STUDENTS' UNION was now running Freshman Introduction Week, with a tea and a hike for the "freshettes" and a smoker for the "freshmen." There were dances, a pep rally where the cheerleaders taught the incoming students all the yells, and then a big Mixer in Convocation Hall where the freshmen wore their green and gold beanies and bibs. Everyone jitterbugged the evening away.

"U of A Engineers May Elect Queen To Reign At Their Annual Ball"— December 17, 1943

"PRACTICALLY EVERY Engineering faculty on the continent chooses some campus woman to reign over different events," announced *The Gateway*, "and the engineers at the U of A have decided it was high time they took a step in that direction."

Selection of the Engineering Queen became a huge event on campus for two decades, and the queen was crowned at the Engineers' Ball, where long dresses and tuxes were *de rigueur*.

For Arts and Science students, the big event was the Mardi Gras dance, where everyone dressed in fantastical costumes and a king was elected and crowned. Engineers and "Artsmen" had an intense and creative competition in which they kidnapped each others' king and queen candidates, stashing them away for a day at lake cottages or in local hotels.

"Varsity Show Proves Smash Hit...Pretty Girls, A Chorus Line, Lilting Melodies, Comedy Skits, Piano Teams And A 13-Piece Jazz Band"—March 22, 1945

THE VARSITY SHOW was the brain-child of Law student Joe Shoctor, who went on to found the Citadel Theatre. The hilarious rendition of "Stan, You Made the Pants too Long" was the talk of campus in 1945. In 1946 Joe's 400 Club Show raised money for World Student Relief. The big hit that year starred Joe as "Bubbles La Vergne." As alumna Dorothy Jones told *New Trail* in August 2004, those who saw Club 400 won't soon forget it. It was a classic.

"More Than a Thousand Freshmen Register—Crowds Jam Con Hall Registration Desks"—September 27, 1945

JUST AS IN 1918, war veterans were now sitting side-by-side with young high school students, and the campus was packed. Army huts were erected near today's CAB to serve as teaching and office space, and veterans were stacked into the Covered Rink in bunks until quick and cheap housing could be constructed.

"Spring Plays To Be Revived After Three Years"—February 22, 1946

IN THIS BANNER headline, students heralded the return of a phenomenally popular campus event. The play to be produced? It was *Stampede*, written by alumna Gwen Pharis, a 1934 graduate and, by 1946, a famous playwright. The choice of director, too, was front-page news. Sidney Risk, advisor to the Drama Society and director of dramatics for the department of Extension, would direct the play. With his five years' experience on the stage in England, and a track record of directing popular plays in Edmonton to his credit, *The Gateway* described Sidney Risk as "one of the most dynamic bundles of atomic energy ever to flash across our campus."

"Introducing...Miss Maimie Simpson"—October 8, 1946[14]

"DON'T LET THE YEAR go on too far before knowing what you are aiming for." This was the advice of the new advisor to women students, and a former Students' Union vice-president, Maimie Simpson (BA '22). Miss Simpson was later described in an *Evergreen and Gold* yearbook as the beloved confidante of "the girls." In 1951, the Board of Governors changed Maimie's title to dean of women.

Maimie graduated from the Camrose Normal School and immediately after started teaching at the U of A. During each summer of her post-secondary schooling, she worked in a rural school to finance her education. She was associated with the University for four decades and warmly remembered by the students. She always remarked that her experience in rural schools had shaped her life philosophy:

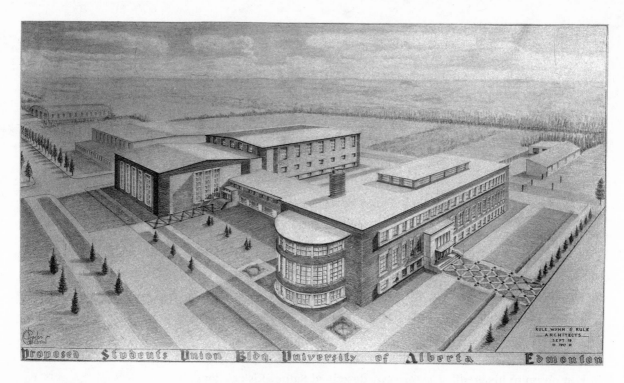

Proposed Students Union Bldg. University of Alberta Edmonton

"Architect's sketch of the proposed Students' Union Building was presented for approval by the student body. Members of the Students' Union Advisory Board, under Chairman Bill Pybus, 1947 president of the Students' Union, spent many hours' work before finally accepting plans proposed by the architectural firm of Rule, Wynn, Rule." (The Gateway, November 22, 1946). Clearly recognizable is module 1, today's University Hall. The second and third modules, an auditorium and a swimming pool, were never built. Later, a pool was built as part of the University's first Physical Education building.

(UAA 72–19–206)

I had learned how other people lived, something of their hopes and aspirations, of their disappointments and their joys, how they were able to accept the inevitable with courage. In those days they didn't call it a philosophy of living, but it was a philosophy of living, one from which a young teacher could learn much. Of one thing I am sure—my understanding of young women, and of young men, for that matter, had much greater depth because of my rural experiences. I am genuinely sorry for young teachers who, today, go straight from the Faculty of Education to a classroom in the city. They will never know what they have missed.

"Council Views Plans for New Union Building"—November 22, 1946

STUDENTS' COUNCIL examined the blueprints for their new union building. Three separate units were planned, and each could be built independently of the others. One unit would have offices, lounges, billiard tables, and a cafeteria, another a gym, and the third a "swimming tank" and an auditorium that could seat 1,600.

"First Mock Parliament to Convene Friday"—February 25, 1947

THE BIG ISSUES featured in the speech from the throne were price controls, housing, and old age pensions. Mock Parliaments became known as Model Parliaments, and many student participants would go on to careers in municipal, provincial, or federal politics.

"Final Examination Results"—June 6, 1947

IN TEN PAGES of tiny print, every student's exam results were published.

"Convocation Largest in University History—Med and Dent Numbers to Be Limited this Fall"—June 6, 1947

RECORD NUMBERS were graduating from the U of A, and labs were so crowded that quotas were introduced in Medicine and Dentistry.

"Alberta Welcomes Back Former Students to the Campus— Alumni Debate Tonight"—October 10, 1947

ALUMNA ELSIE PARK GOWAN, "well-known Edmonton dramatist," and Mayor Harry Ainlay would be taking the affirmative side on this question: RESOLVED that Edmonton is a better city than Calgary. Alumni J.V.H. Milvain and Harold Riley, both barristers, "will defend the southern city."

"From That Great Big Hole...The New Library"—October 17, 1947

THE UNIVERSITY was finally getting a new Library. As *The Gateway* put it: "Slowly, but, after twenty years of rumour, surely, it's coming. Clanking concrete mixers and gangs of workmen are now at work on the new library building which will house all the library facilities at present scattered throughout the University."

In 1947, there was no stand-alone Library. The Library at that time was located in room 110 in the Arts Building and had a seating capacity of 80. There were almost 5,000 students at the U of A at the time.

When the Library was finally completed in March 1951, it was named in honour of the first premier and founder of the University, Alexander Cameron Rutherford.

"Junior Pictorial Shopping News from Eatons"—December 16, 1947

THIS FULL-PAGE AD featured real students modelling ball gowns, hats, and clothes for class, skating, and watching football games. A red and black skating skirt, for example, sold for $5.95.

"Get ready for an important formal!" the advertisement boomed. A two-piece blue rayon moire taffeta ballet dress, perfect for a formal dance, cost $29.50.

One of the ads featured Reg Lister's daughter: "Mary Lou Lister is ready for the Christmas whirl in a bright green wool hooded dress with sequins, $29.50, and her shoes, La Gioconda suedes, at $13.95, have a festive bow of coloured mirrors!"

"$400,000 Offered to Building Fund"—January 9, 1948

"MONTHS OF student financial negotiation for the Students' Union building bore fruit with the offer of a $400,000 interest-free loan from officials of the provincial government for SUB." With $100,000 in a reserve fund, students were ready to start building the first of three planned modules of the SUB. The Board of Governors agreed take over maintenance of the building once it was constructed, and private donors (including Francis Winspear) who had funded the furnishings were made life members of the SU.

"Engineers' Queen?—Pat Scott"—January 20, 1948

"SHE'S KNOWN around the campus for her engaging smile and her charming personality." Pat was Canadian University Press editor for *The Gateway*, a member of the Ballet Club, and a yearbook editor. She'd soon be taking over the presidency of the Literary Society.

This was just one of a dozen articles leading up to the Engineers' Ball. The year 1948 marked the tenth anniversary of this popular formal dance, and attendance hovered at around 400.

"Campus Vets' Diaper Derby Sees 106 Mewling Moppetts"—February 17, 1948

WORLD WAR II VETERANS, married and back on campus, were busy having babies. And baby pictures dominated the front page of this *Gateway*,

The Edmonton Eskimos are Born!!

"Shelve Football on U of A Campus—Scrap Rugby for Year; University Athletic Board To Sell Equipment." So read the Gateway headline *on February 8, 1949. The first line of the accompanying article said it all: "Football is dead on the U of A campus." The reason was simple: There was no competition—the only available team was Saskatchewan, and only for two games.*

And so the University shut down football and sold their green and gold uniforms to the new Edmonton Eskimos, thus providing the Esks with their colours—green and gold—which they wear to this day. Rugby back Joe Shoctor (left), seen here in 1942, was instrumental in starting up the Edmonton Eskimos. (UAA 72-58-843)

which reported on a contest held in Hut A, in which three little ones were chosen to represent the U of A at a national "Diaper Derby" contest.

"Double Convocation for May Graduation"—March 12, 1948

THE LARGEST CLASS in the University's history, with about 900 graduates expected, meant that for the first time, there would be more than a single convocation ceremony at the McDougall Church.

"Board May Boost University Fees—Rising Costs said to be Reason"—February 15, 1949

FEES WERE TO BE RAISED this year an average of 15% "to meet increased costs of operation." President Newton said he would work to lobby the federal government to subsidize education. *The Gateway* editorial characterized the increase as "a sock in the teeth."

"Record Vote Elects Miller President"—March 11, 1949

THREE-QUARTERS of the student population turned out to elect the SU president—Law student and future chancellor, Tevie Miller.

MEET ALUMNI FROM THE 1940s [15]

Esther Miller (BA '27)

Staff Member in the Registrar's Office During World War II [16]

ALUMNA ESTHER MILLER joined the Registrar's Office in 1928. During her years on campus, she observed campus life closely and vividly remembers the working conditions during World War II.

"The War catapulted the whole University into a new, untried phase," explains Esther. "The staff in the Registrar's Office became restless—in a period of four months we had nine staff changes, until we began to suspect we were operating a training school for office workers. They joined the Air Force, they married the Navy, they went to work for the American Army which had 'taken over' Edmonton, at higher salaries than we could afford.

"The students felt compelled to join the forces and go to war, while the University and the Government set about to retain those students in the sciences and medical sciences, because trained and qualified personnel in

Esther Miller (right), the epitome of a staff member who faced impossible circumstances with competence, caring and ingenuity. In this 2006 photo, she celebrates her 100th birthday. (Private Collection)

these fields was desperately needed in all branches of military service. And so in order to meet this demand—and the impatience of youth—many courses were accelerated...and final examinations and Convocations were scheduled with shocking frequency."

Stay in school, the government said. The provincial and federal governments established a loan program to encourage students to stay in school. And units of the Army and the Navy moved into St. Joseph's College and St. Stephen's College, offering board to young men who took specialized training in engineering and the sciences.

"The climax was reached in 1945 when the war ended," says Esther. "It started quietly enough. We thought we were geared for the return of the servicemen to University....In the early spring, telegrams, army signals, airmail letters of every description began to pour in, and before midsummer we were inundated with mail....it was like a tidal wave. Mr. Ottewell (the registrar), returning from his vacation asked, 'Is the ship still afloat?' and we replied, 'a bit of the mast is just visible.'"

"Can You Hold a Pencil?"

"WE SPILLED OVER into the Law Library next door (in the Arts Building) where the bushels of mail had to be opened up and sorted each day. Wives waiting for the return of their husbands would phone to say they had heard we were needing help, and although they could not type, they would be pleased to do anything if we could use them. Our stock question came to be 'can you hold a pencil?' and they were hired for half days or whatever time they could spare."

Esther describes registration in September 1945 as staggering. The number of undergraduate students doubled, but the registration system hadn't changed in years.

"The registration period came; long lines formed to the right and left and down the middle....Each new student had to be registered separately," remembers Esther. "We petitioned for group registration and were assured that it would not work. Instead, each and every fee card was made out by one or two staff members and special fees, such as the $5.00 laboratory fee and the $10.00 graduation fee, were assessed individually as the registration indicated. We petitioned to have these fees absorbed into the general fee structure and not individually assessed, but to no avail.

"We found one veteran white and shaken, perspiration standing on his forehead, trying to get through the lines. He had been wounded and was just out of hospital. We all cut the red tape for him, but we wondered if there could be others suffering alone, unnoticed."

The "Educational Paul Bunyan" Dies in 1946

"THE TERM SETTLED DOWN," remembers Esther, "and we had just begun to relax a little when suddenly one morning we were informed that Mr. Ottewell had been rushed to hospital for an emergency operation. It shortly became evident that there was no cure and we were greatly saddened. He was able to return to the office and carried on briefly, but died within the year."

Albert Ottewell's death marked the end of an era. Albert was the grade eight dropout who won the gold medal in Classics when he graduated with the U of A's first class in 1912. After his passing in 1946, there were no others from our first graduating class left on staff at the University. Ottewell's death was front-page news.

On campus, everyone knew him as the registrar, and many remembered him as the first director of Extension, the first editor of *The Gateway*, a captain in the Khaki University, the first president of the Alumni Association, and as an outspoken, common-sense gentleman with a huge storehouse of jokes and songs.

In Edmonton, Ottewell was better known for his 19 consecutive years of service on the Edmonton Public School Board (eight as Chair), his presidency of the Canadian School Trustees Association, and for his service to the city archives, the health board, the Canadian Club and his church.

In the province, there were thousands of rural Albertans who, before 1920, were touched by Ottewell's brand of magic. "Everything about him," said one of his colleagues, "his voice, his laughter, his appetite, and his energy—was gargantuan." For rural Albertans, Ottewell was the living exponent of Extension's outreach:

> He thought nothing of spending most of the night with a group of farm people, say at Pincher Creek in southern Alberta, and then starting at daylight after consuming a couple cans of salmon, his favourite breakfast, to continue a similar meeting at Coronation, about 300 miles away. This was in the days when there were few if any highways.

Albert Ottewell—ex-miner, ex-farmer, and ex-lumberjack—wore out a half-dozen Model Ts making his rounds to homesteads around the province as director of Extension.

"Probably no one in Alberta," reported *The Edmonton Journal* on July 20, 1946, "devoted as much time and effort to the cause of education as did Albert Edward Ottewell."

There is nothing on campus named in Albert Ottewell's honour, but his legacy resides in today's outreach efforts of the Faculty of Extension and in the memories of the hundreds of pioneer families whose homesteads Albert visited in the days before radio, TV, or computers.

Everyone Co-operated and Every Minute Counted

ALBERT OTTEWELL was succeeded as registrar by G.B. Taylor, a man who watched postwar registration double in one year.

Esther Miller remembers that "as more space was required, it was necessary for the registrar's office to move several times. In 1928 it was situated in Arts 219. It then moved across the hall to Arts 212...then Arts 235 and

These women staffed the Registrar's Office during the years when registrations—and graduations—doubled. Even though resources never kept pace with burgeoning student numbers, each student was nonetheless always seen as an individual and attended to with great care and attention.

(Private Collection)

Arts 239....It was indeed a happy day when we moved to new quarters on the second floor of the new Administration Building.

"Perhaps the most appreciated assistance [from other departments] was the close co-operation in the printing of the Convocation programs and diplomas. There was never sufficient time between end of term and faculty meetings and the submission of the program material for printing. Even minutes counted."

Esther remembers asking the impossible of the printing department at the last possible moment before Convocation. "Could an n be changed to m, could an s be added, could a student's name be changed from Charles William Doe to William Charles Doe. We would phone in haste as further checking would reveal an omission or change, wait with bated breath as Mrs. Donnan, head of the printing department...rushed to see whether the printer had started the press on that page—no, they had not, the change could be made, and once more we all thanked the gods for Mrs. Donnan and her staff."

Students Just Needed Someone to Talk To

"To reflect on the students who wandered in and out of our lives, both in the Registrar's Office and later in the Student Awards Office, gives meaning to the reason for it all," says Esther.

"Under the old First Year or Freshman Committee, each student had been assigned an advisor in their first year. Later, Counselling Services was established [as a place] where students could go for advice. But there were a great number of students for whom I had the most personal concern and connection—they were the ones who had no real problems, but who just wanted someone with whom they could discuss their ideas and concerns. They would come and sit at your desk, ask for an application form, and when all business was finished, they would sit on, and you would know they just wished to chat a bit. So you would say, are you enjoying your courses? How is the work progressing? And they would burst into eager conversation—they liked this course, but that course was giving them difficulty. You probed a bit, but after all this was not your field, but you responded to the light in their eyes and chatted on and perhaps made a few suggestions. Finally the bell would ring and they would dash to the next lecture."

Esther Miller, who had been a student during the 1920s, retired in 1965 after 37 years in the Registrar's Office.

Douglass Carr (BA '42, BDIV '45)

The Second Green and Gold Generation Arrives

Reverend Douglas Carr's father was in the first U of A graduating class in 1912, and so attending the U of A was "a natural choice" for Douglas. His years on campus spanned the war, from 1939–1945. He entered the U of A in September 1939, just days after Hitler invaded Poland. Douglas's convocation in June 1945 occurred one month after Germany surrendered to the Allies. Two months after Douglas' convocation, on August 6 and 9, atomic bombs were dropped on Hiroshima and then Nagasaki. Japan surrendered a week later, on August 15, and World War II was over.

War News Took Three Days to Reach Canada

"WE ALL KNEW THE WAR NEWS," Douglas remembers, "but in those days there was no TV and the news took two or three days to reach us. All of us were encouraged to stay in school, finish our degrees, and then join the army. I had 26 classmates in 1939, but by the time of Convocation in 1945, the numbers dwindled to only six, because students graduated, entered the army, and there were no new ones to replace them at university.

"All through my undergraduate years," says Douglas, "two afternoons a week, all the male students headed to the Drill Hall west of St. Joe's for military training and parade practice. We all were required to join the Canadian Officers Training Corps, or COTC, and then once you graduated and joined the army, you went in with a rank, having already taken some training. You weren't just a raw recruit."

St. Stephen's College and "Raids"

"I DON'T REMEMBER registration at all," says Douglas, "and I was lucky in that my dad and the United Church paid most of my university expenses. My summer jobs clerking at a store and working in missions rounded out a slim budget. I remember my first week of classes as scary. I was young, I came from Lacombe, and the U of A was a big place.

"I was enrolled in a BA/Bachelor of Divinity course and boarded at St. Stephen's College. During that first freshman week, you'd be sound asleep and then suddenly you'd find yourself dumped out of bed on to the floor. Of course, when we became sophomores the next year, we did the same thing to the rookie freshmen. There were pep rallies where you were taught the University yells and, yes, I do know all the words to Chet Lambertson's University Cheer Song.

"There was one night during Sadie Hawkins' Week when there was an awful racket outside—it was the Medical and Engineering students from Athabasca Hall coming over to raid us. They came storming in and they would grab whoever was around and 'tub' him. They got hold of this one student, Roger, who was well-known singer on campus; everyone knew who he was. He was in full formal attire—tuxedo, good shoes—and the Meds and Geers dunked him in the tub. So we went for the fire hoses and doused them right back. Water was cascading down seven flights of St.

Steve's stairs. The housemother phoned the St. Steve's principal who walked in, took one long look around, shook his head, and with a big smile on his face, just walked away. Then the city police came to investigate and when they left, all the tires on their cars were flat."

And that wasn't the only raid.

"The nurses lived in one wing of St. Steve's," remembers Douglas, "and it was completely shut off from the rest of us. But there was a gym on the 5th floor, with a high partition to separate us from the nurses. One night we took a ladder to the gym and we all climbed the partition. All of us wore sneakers so no one would hear us as we dropped down to the nurses' side of the partition. Each of us was stationed at a different point, and at a pre-arranged signal, we rushed into all the nurses' rooms, all at once, and dumped them out of their beds. Our escape route was down the long cylindrical fire escapes that attached to the various floors of St. Steve's. These would funnel you down from any floor right to the ground outside.

"Now the nurses had a housemother and she was a strict battle-axe. She was furious with us and went to Principal Tuttle to demand that we be punished. He called us all in and suggested we send the housemother a bouquet of roses. We did. It worked. Nothing more was ever said.

"And, by the way, we all felt sorry for those nurses because they had a 10 P.M. curfew and once a month they would be allowed to stay out until midnight—a late pass. This made it tough when it came to dating. You'd be across the street from St. Steve's in the Tuck Shop, and if there was a nurse with you, she'd constantly be looking at her watch because if she was even a minute past the 10 P.M. curfew, she lost that one monthly late pass. The girls in Pembina also had a curfew and Miss Dodd, the dean of women, was known to be very strict. If you were dating a girl from Pembina, you had to knock on the front door of the residence hall. Miss Dodd would answer the door, seat you in the waiting area, and then she would go get your date."

Douglas also remembers the traditional rivalry played out between the students in the Faculties of Engineering and Arts. "There were Med students who stayed at St. Steve's at one point," he says, "and there was this one Med student who was always up to some kind of a prank. So one lunchtime, they were serving sliced beef, and out of his pocket, this Med

Sadie Hawkins Week

"SADIE HAWKINS WEEK was a big hit with students," says Doug Carr. It was based on the Al Capp comic strip where the girls would be the ones to ask the boys out on a date. Of course at St. Steve's, the boys all wanted to be asked out, and so we devised a strategy. We had a great housemother, very co-operative, and we hung big banners out the north windows, facing the Tuck Shop and the Med Building. On the banners were our names and phone numbers. It was a great way to attract the girls—we got a lot of dates. This went on all week and was really popular with all the students. On one of my dates, I was invited over to a women's fraternity and they dressed me up like Daisy Mae, right out of the famous comic strip. Who could ever forget THAT?!"

(The Gateway, *October 29, 1940*)

Sadie Hawkins

"And no two ways about that, either"

PROCLAMATION

Know all Dogpatch men what ain't married by these presents, and specially Li'l Abner Yokum:

Whereas there be inside our town limits a passel of gals what ain't married but craves something awful to be, and

Whereas these gals' pappies and mammies has been shouldering the burden of their board and keep for more years then is tolerable, and

Whereas there be in Dogpatch plenty of young men what could marry these gals but acts ornery and won't, and

Whereas we deems matrimony's joys and being sure of eating regular the birthright of our fair Dogpatch womanhood,

We hereby proclaims and decrees, by right of the power and majesty vested in us as Mayor of Dogpatch,

student pulled a piece of sliced 'something' and he threw it across the table. The people at the table took one look at it and knew exactly what it was. It had that distinct smell to it, you know—it was a chunk from a stiff lab. So we all got up en masse and walked over to the Tuck Shop and had lunch there."

The Roof of St. Stephen's

DOUGLAS SAYS that all the boys have fond memories of the St. Steve's roof. "You could climb to the roof ," he says, "and look down seven stories from this perch. In fact, you had a bird's-eye view of the tubular fire escapes and of the small, flat platforms that led from each floor out to the fire escape. On hot days, the nurses used to lie out on those platforms in their bathing suits and of course they were easy targets. So we would climb to the roof and sprinkle water on them. And if I look back now at the year-book photos, I can tell you that I knew nearly every one of them."

Hangouts in the 1940s

"THERE WAS NO STUDENTS' UNION BUILDING back then," says Douglas. "The Tuck Shop was the centre of activity. After two years of residence in St. Steve's, I batched it in a basement apartment with some friends on 83 Avenue, and on days when I didn't make my own lunch, I ate at the Tuck. There were no cinnamon buns in those days—just doughnuts—that's all that was available during the war. The Tuck was popular for dates because very few of us had cars. No parking problems on campus back then! You had to take a streetcar to go overtown to downtown Edmonton, and the nearest streetcar stop was at Steen's drugstore up by the High Level Bridge. It was a long walk in the cold. But the big dances were held at the Hotel Macdonald. There was no place on campus big enough, and we would all be dressed in formal attire, with the girls in long dresses. So we'd get three or four couples together, and share a cab.

"In my last two years," Douglas continues, "I lived off campus and only came here for morning divinity classes at St. Steve's. But I always saw the inter-year plays and the operettas—they were just excellent and played to packed houses. Living off campus disconnected me from a lot of what was happening with student activities, but in my first few years I was very involved with inter-faculty hockey and inter-faculty football. Inter-varsity sports were suspended for most of the war and it was the inter-faculty competitions that were popular.

"One of my friends kept after me to attend Colour Night at the Hotel Macdonald, which was the event where sports awards were announced, but I didn't have the money to go and I had no tux. He just kept after me, and I finally went. What my friend knew, but I didn't, was that I was being awarded a Big Block A for my involvement with sports. It was a memorable night."

Sliding to Dr. Hardy's Class

"IN MY FIRST FOUR YEARS, all my classes were in the Arts Building except for English. My English class was so big that it had to be scheduled in one of the amphitheatres in the Med building. When I lived at St. Steve's, if we were late for class, we would slide down the fire escape, which got us outside quickly, right on to the grass by the Arts quad.

"I had a happy time at the U of A—there isn't one bad experience that stands out. My favourite professor was Dr. Hardy in Classics. He made his subject live. Hardy had travelled extensively in Italy and Greece, and he knew his subject. He was organized and prepared. And we all knew that Dr. Hardy wrote popular novels set in ancient Middle East, Greece and Rome. One of my favourites," says Douglas, "was about Moses, and was titled *All the Trumpets Sounded*. Hardy was a kindly man and had a way of correcting students without any embarrassment. I had other good profs, like Dr. R.K. Gordon in English and Dr. P.S. Warren in Geology, but Dr. Hardy stands out."

Dr. Hardy liked to tell his students that they should come away from their university years with one thing: "the ability to think for yourselves, the urge to examine every question and every problem on its own merits, without being trammelled by prejudice." It was, Dr. Hardy said, "the habits of mind and thought" that would persist after graduation.[17]

Convocations and then Ministry in Richmond

"I WENT TO BOTH MY CONVOCATIONS," says Douglas, "the BA at the McDougall United Church in 1942 and the Bachelor of Divinity in 1945, held at St. Stephen's. For the BA, we were all seated at the front of the auditorium and called up to the stage one at a time to receive our parch-

Top: For decades, the two emergency slides at St. Stephen's were the source of great pranks and fond memories. There is no account of these slides being used for their original purpose— evacuation of patients in an emergency—but generations of students found other more ingenious uses for them. (UAA 72-58-294)

Bottom: A view of St. Stephen's College provides a rare image of the two slides used by students. (UAA 90-60-012)

ments. I can still remember being 'hooded' on stage in front of some 1,500 people. After my BDiv in 1945, my father, who was also a United Church Minister and president of the Alberta Conference, participated in my ordination. A few months later, he died very suddenly, and I took over his ministry in Richmond, near Vancouver. I've served since then all over the West—a rewarding life."

Eric McCuaig (BA '42, LLB '47)

HE WAS BORN in a grand, gracious home on Saskatchewan Drive and grew up right on the edge of campus. When it came time to choose a university, his father, Stanley McCuaig, favoured his own alma mater, Queen's. But there was a special maternal grandfather who had some very close connections to the University of Alberta. Eric McCuaig's grandfather was Alexander Cameron Rutherford, former premier, founder of the U of A, and then chancellor. That's how Eric McCuaig, in 1939, came to be registered at the University of Alberta. "It was a happy choice for me," says Eric. "My years at the U of A were very stimulating academically and lots of fun. All my memories are wonderful. But when my own children were ready for university, there was a little push from the McCuaig side of the family that at least one of my girls attend Queen's, and that is where my daughter Brenda went." And right now? "Two of my nieces are students here at the U of A, one in Law and one in Nursing." That makes four generations of Rutherford descendants who have attended the U of A since 1908 when Eric's uncle, Cecil Rutherford, joined the first entering class.

Born in Rutherford House

Eric was born in his grandparents' home, in the elegant mansion known today as Rutherford House. A provincial historic site, Rutherford House sits atop the escarpment at the edge of campus on Saskatchewan Drive, in the shadow of the Humanities Centre. It is one of few remaining buildings on campus that are etched lovingly in the memories of generations of students. Rutherford House was first home to the premier, then site of many Convocation parties hosted by Chancellor and Mrs. Rutherford, and later was the DU fraternity house before being designated as a provincial historic site. Every year for five decades, students planted a memorial tree on campus in Rutherford's honour, signifying the importance of Premier

Rutherford to the lives of the thousands enrolled at the U of A from the University's founding in 1906 to Rutherford's death in 1942.

Eric grew up during the Depression and entered the University in September 1939, just as World War II started. "Money was scarce during the depression years," says Eric, "and I remember my grandfather's large vegetable garden, where he would stake out plots for all the neighbourhood children so they could learn to grow vegetables. He would supply the carrot seeds, the seed potatoes, and would always be available to advise the novice gardeners about planting, weeding and harvesting."

Buying the Wallace's Cottage

"OUR NEIGHBOURHOOD LIFE was so rich with friends and experiences," remembers Eric. "I had at least a half-dozen friends near my own age and we grew up very close to one another, went to Garneau Elementary School together, and then most of us went to the high school that was housed in the north end of today's Corbett Hall. When I went into the Navy during the war, the commanding officer of my last ship was a boyhood friend from Garneau, a few years older than me, George Manning.

"Another stand-out memory I have of the Depression concerns President Wallace, who left the U of A in 1936 to be principal of Queen's. The Wallaces had a modest cottage on Lake Wabamum and Dr. Wallace wanted someone to buy it who would enjoy it as much as his family had. He said he just couldn't leave Alberta without settling this. One day he talked to my dad and asked if he was interested. They sat down and worked something out—I'm not sure what because at the time dad was being paid for his legal work in chickens and vegetables—no one had money. And then dad had to go back to his home in Ontario and when he got off the train, he slipped and was injured in a bad fall. The railway offered him a financial settlement, and dad used the money to buy the Wallaces' cottage. My brother lives out on that property now, though the house has been rebuilt."

Eric enrolled in the BA/LLB program, a combined course that would save a student one year of study. Every fraternity rushed him ("I think they knew who my grandfather was"), and he joined Phi Delta Theta. "I don't remember much about freshman orientation," he says, "but the fraternity initiated us—nothing too terrible. Merv Huston, who was later the dean of Pharmacy, was one of the alumni members, and we had him

Key to 1945 Map

1. Campus residences for faculty
   (the "Ring Houses")
2. Campus residence staff
   (Reg Lister's home)
3. Drafting Lab
4. Assiniboia Hall (Men's residence)
5. Plant Science
6. Horticulture
7. Athabasca Hall (Men's residence)
8. Pembina Hall (Women's residence;
   tennis courts to the west)
9. West Lab (Students' Union Building
   in 2006)
10. Stoker Lab
11. Provincial Gasoline Testing Lab
12. North Lab
13. Arts Building
14. South Lab
15. Cafeteria ("Hot Caf")
16. Works Department
17. Works Department
18. Machine Shop
19. Power Plant
20. Infirmary
21. Medical Building (Dentistry/Pharmacy
    Centre in 2006)
22. Athletic Field and Track
23. Drill Hall and Temporary Gymnasium
24. St. Joseph's College
25. Animal Houses
26. St. Stephen's College
27. Scout Hut
28. Varsity Rink
29. Observatory
30. University Hospital
31. Plant Barns
32. The Normal School (Corbett Hall in 2006)
33. Plant Barns

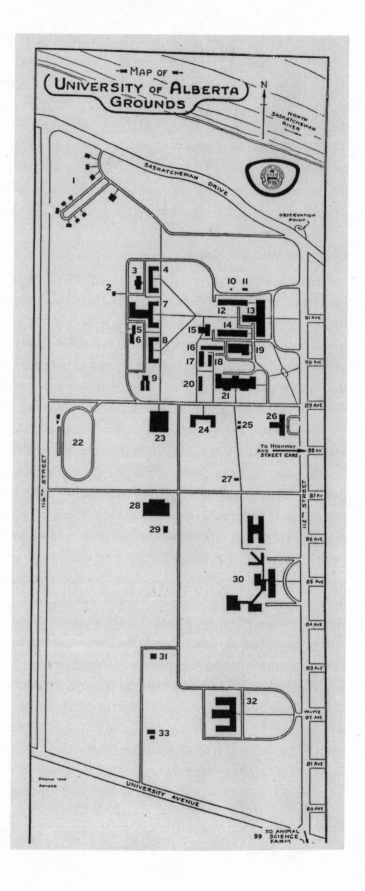

as a speaker every chance we could get. He was incredibly funny and the author of several best-selling humour books.

"I took an extra year to get prepared for university," says Eric. "There were two high school courses I did OK in but I didn't think 'OK' was good enough for university. My math teacher in high school was also the principal and as a consequence, he was away from class a lot. That meant we had assignments to complete during class instead of receiving regular instruction. So after graduation, I went to Old Scona high school and took math again, with a great teacher, and got over 90. It was a relief, and also a good lesson about teaching and learning."

Some Campus Memories

SATURDAY CLASSES were started after the war broke out as one way of lengthening the school week in order to accommodate trainees from the Navy and Air Force who were billeted in the residences. Everyone groaned over the 8 A.M. start time—and the elimination of the lunch hour. The Students' Union lobbied the city for streetcar service that would allow students to get to the Arts Building for the early 8 A.M. start.

In 1939, there were only about 2,300 students, and the campus was small. "All my classes were in the Arts building except for English," says Eric. "English was a big class and was held in an amphitheatre in the Medical Building. There were really only two buildings on campus, the Arts building and the Medical building—and the three residences; Pembina, Athabasca, and Assiniboia. St. Joe's and St. Steve's were also on campus and of course there was the Tuck Shop.

"We all joined the COTC and took training in the Drill Hall and in the Covered Rink—also known as the Varsity Rink. In May, after exams, we spent two weeks at Sarcee Camp in Calgary, learning how to handle a gun, and to march. It was basic training. They weren't very prepared for the deluge of students who came to train—I think we got a blanket and some rubber matting to sleep on. As for food, I remember raw onions, cheese, and pork and beans. It was rugged."

Weir, Cairns, Salter, and Bowker—Born to be Teachers

"IN ARTS, I would say my favourite professor was Dr. Salter in English," says Eric, "because he knew his subject so well—and he could really communicate with students. I remember his English 53 class, Shakespeare. We had to read 21 plays during the year, and the exam consisted solely of numerous quotations. You had to know what play they were from, who spoke the lines and what the context was. It was tough, and my grades were good but not great. I worked hard on the one essay assigned at the beginning of the year where we had the entire year to complete it. I worked really hard. Two of us got the highest grades on that essay—Peggy O'Connor and me.

"In Law," Eric remembers, "where I took some courses early on as part of the combined degree, I had John Weir and, later, Wilbur Bowker as teachers. They were outstanding. They knew their material and they could teach it—they were born to be teachers.

"I also had Laurence Cairns, a wonderful teacher who was in the first U of A graduating class. I often wondered how he made to it to the 8 A.M. classes from the west end, where he lived. The streetcar service, where you went across the top of the High Level Bridge from the other side of the river, was not scheduled to get you to an 8 A.M. class. Mr. Cairns probably had to leave the west end at 6:30 A.M. to get here for an 8 A.M. class. Cairns was not only a good teacher but a great pianist—he would always be the one to sit down at a party and play the popular songs."

Paying for School—The Mayfair, Parents, and the Navy

ERIC REMEMBERS how he paid for his university education. "I worked in the summers at the Burns meat packing plant and also at the Mayfair Golf Club, cutting the lawn. That money went for books and for part of tuition, which was about $150 then. My parents helped, and I lived at home. They fed me. There was no room and board charge.

"Then, in my second year, the Navy came through Edmonton on a recruiting trip and I went to see what it was about. I was selected for war service. But they told me stay in school until I was needed, and I had a great time in 1941–1942. I worked at my courses, but I was also in the chorus for *The Mikado*, the annual operetta. Several of my friends had leading roles but the chorus was just fine for me. We had four sell-out shows in Edmonton and then took the train to Calgary, where we had three sell-out shows."

Dean Bowker

DEAN BOWKER, the quintessential teacher, human being, and administrator, was remembered by generations of students for his wit, rapier memory, and ability to shape young lives. Wilbur Bowker was brilliant, precise, disciplined, and had a "warm friendliness" that made him a great teacher. Dean Bowker had a personal rapport with all his students, and enthralled Convocation audiences by reciting the full names of every graduand without reference to written notes. Who were some of his students? Let Chancellor Emeritus Louis Desrochers (LLB '52, LLD HON '78) describe the Class of 1952: "a future premier, a future attorney general and treasurer, a future justice of the Supreme Court, three future provincial judges of the Province of Alberta, a future personal advisor of the prime minister of Canada, and several leaders of the profession."

When Wilbur Bowker retired from the deanship, dozens of his students and colleagues contributed their written recollections in a Liber Amicorum—a book of friends. Here is one comment, from Justice Laycraft: "A principal function of a Dean of Law is to impart to his students a sense of the purpose and the philosophy of law, and of the high standards of ethics so necessary in an honourable profession. Every contact with [Dean Bowker's] students served this same purpose." (UAA 69–19–20–549)

The annual operettas were discontinued during the rest of the war, along with many other activities that had become standard and traditional at the university. For the first time, there was only one candidate for Students' Union president, an election by acclamation.

"I was almost finished with my BA in 1942 when the Navy came calling," Eric remembers. "I hadn't taken my exams and neither had many other students. The University decided that we would be graded on the work we had done to date, and so I received my BA degree in absentia and was off to Halifax as a Navy recruit.

"During the war I was moved from posting to posting—Halifax, Ottawa, Halifax again, and finally I was posted to Saint John's, Newfoundland, where I served for most of the war. When the Battle of the Atlantic was being fought, we made 21 crossings between Saint John's and Londonderry, Northern Ireland. After VE day, we sailed from Halifax to Victoria, and after all those years of war, it was like a cruise. War in Europe was over and the writing was on the wall for Japan. We reached Victoria right after VJ Day. I was discharged and went back to school to finish my law degree. There were only 11 of us in the law class and only three that I had started with in 1939."

Back from the War

IN 1947, the University was launching into a building program to accommodate the doubled student population. Wings were added to the Med Building, and temporary buildings popped up all around campus. Eric was one of the returning veterans.

He finished his law degree in 1947, was called to the bar in 1948, and then joined his father Stanley's law practice in Edmonton. Eric served as president of the Law Society of Alberta, as a Bencher, as a member of the University of Alberta Hospital Board, and as a University senator.

Mabel Pratt Robblee (JR EDUCATION DIP '45) and Stu Robblee (BSC AG '45)

IT'S A CLASSIC STORY of boy meets girl.

She was a "House Eccer" from Camrose, and he was an Aggie from Cayley. They graduated in 1945, just as World War II was ending. And how did they meet? In their day, when an upcoming University dance was announced, a boy would ask a girl to go. Fine so far. But in the 1940s, in the week before a University dance, the male students would trade dances with the other men who were going to the dance and they would keep a record of these trades on their dance card. Then, at the dance itself, the boy and the girls would go—as a couple—to the next name on the dance card, and trade dance partners for that particular dance. And that's how this Aggie and House Eccer met: at a traded dance.

The girl? Her name is Mabel Pratt Robblee. The boy? His name is John Stuart ("Stu") Robblee.

Why University?

STU: "Simple. My dad came from PEI and homesteaded in Saskatchewan. He wanted me to go to university—he thought farming was too hard a life. So after high school, I enrolled in the Agriculture Faculty and studied field crops and livestock."

MABEL: "I was motivated to go to university by two things—I wanted to improve my circumstances and make more money than the low entry salary I was earning for teaching.

"There were four career choices for women in the 1940s," Mabel explains, "household economics, teaching, nursing, or stenography. When I came to the University, there was only one woman in Dentistry and only one in Medicine. My choice was teaching. Up until 1937, teacher training was done in what were called Normal Schools. There was one in Calgary, one in Edmonton, and one in my hometown of Camrose. I went to Normal School in Edmonton in 1940–1941. We were all called 'Normalites.' I then taught in a one-room school up north for a year. In my second year, I taught the primary class, which comprised grades one, two and three, in a three-room school. Room and board cost me $30 a month and my annual salary was $740. When income tax started, the take-home pay was even less.

"Teachers were 'frozen' to their jobs," Mabel says. "There was no way out unless you went into the armed services or got more education. If you taught for two years and did a six-week summer school course at the University, you could get a permanent certificate to teach up to grade nine. And if you went to the University for four years, you received a certificate to teach up to grade 12.

Army Training for Women Students

MEN WERE REQUIRED to do military training while on campus, and so were the women. "Women had to complete 60 hours—at their own request—of army training, over one year," remembers Mabel Robblee. "In my first year, I had four labs, and afterwards, I'd tear down to the Drill Hall for the 4 P.M. start of training. Usually I was in loafers, but one day I wore shoes with a higher heel. It was an awful experience. Lucky for the boys that they had proper uniforms.

"We learned target shooting, and because we had to lie on our tummies, we wore slacks, but you would never wear them to class. In the fall, we marched outside, and when it got cold, we marched in the Drill Hall, which was formerly the Covered Rink."

"In my second year," says Mabel, "we were given four choices: stay in army training with possibility of promotion; work in the blood bank; knit for an hour; or serve coffee at the canteen for the boys on the 5:00 P.M. break. You see, the boys were marching twice a week from 4:00 P.M. to 6:00 P.M., with a break at 5:00 P.M., and we got 'credit' for serving doughnuts and coffee. Afterwards a girlfriend and I would go to the Tuck for a milkshake—I needed the sustenance after a ten-hour day before my long walk back to the boarding house."

Large photo (UAA 72-58-499)

Inset (UAA 72-58-578)

"I decided that more education was the key. So I rallied the money to go to university and enrolled in Home Ec, which I took in 1943–1944. And, by the way, I got my 'permanent to grade nine,' as we called it. In 1944, I decided to switch to Education. There were no student loans in those days and my brother helped me with tuition. Then, in 1945, the University took over all teacher training and the normal schools were closed. Alberta was the first province to have universities take over the training of teachers, and I became part of the first combined class in education/home economics. They designed a one-year program for us, and we all were assured jobs afterwards. After I graduated from the U of A with a junior diploma in 1944–1945, my monthly teaching salary doubled. And in 1941–1942 the tuition for my Ag program was $93 and the entire cost of my first year for everything—tuition, books, room and board—was $475."

Stu remembers long lines at registration, but "most of my courses were pre-set and so it wasn't a problem for me. All the freshmen had to wear green and gold wedge-shaped 'army hats' during Freshman Orientation Week and there were lots of get-togethers and sing-alongs. I can still sing the entire U of A Cheer Song. But it was meeting the president of the Ag Club that really meant a lot to me. His name was Bill Corns, and he later became a professor. He welcomed me so warmly. It was wonderful and I've never forgotten it."

Favourite Teachers

"WE WOULD BOTH SAY our favourite prof was Dr. Sandin in Chemistry," says Stu. He taught Organic Chemistry and we knew that he was doing cancer research—he wanted to find a cure. He was so nice, so knowledge-able, such a great human being." Mabel remembers Dr. Sandin's first admonition in class: "He said, 'Now class, we're bound to have a few fires, but we don't want too many of them. Then this student started her lab work," says Mabel, "and suddenly, from her lab bench, a plume of fire shot right up to the ceiling. Lucky for us the lab assistant was right there with a fire extinguisher.

"Dr. Sandin was so kind to the House Eccers. We had hours of labs and a lot of science in our programs, and we were in his class with pre-med students and science students. He seemed to understand the difference."[18]

Sandin (pronounced "San-DEEN") was also remembered by two fellow chemists, Walter Harris and Ray Lemieux. Dr. Harris described Dr. Sandin's teaching in glowing terms: "His popularity as a lecturer was legendary throughout the department, the University, and beyond. He cultivated close personal relationships and had a major impact on many students. For generations of students, he was an idol and the object of hero worship. He took pride in lecturing without notes. On some occasions, he would go through an act of fumbling for a piece of data. He was a dramatic show-man and entertainer." Dr. Lemieux is equally complimentary: "Benjamin (Reuben) Sandin, or 'Rube' as everybody called him, was a legend in his own time. He was a great teacher and a good person. I remember a comment he made after receiving a teaching award: 'A pat on the back is worth much more than a kick in the seat.' He had a lot of great sayings. He once said, 'When you interview students who want to come into honours chemistry, you should always look at their shoes. If there is a little manure on their shoes, accept them.' He was respected as a teacher throughout the world and, taking into account the circumstances and environment that then existed at the University, he made a truly remark-able contribution to the improvement of chemical knowledge. Thereby, he established a research atmosphere which is of vital importance to university teaching."

Mabel says that having been a teacher up north for two years, she had a lot of catching up to do. "In my bacteriology class, for instance," she says, "we were using microscopes, but many of us had never had the benefit of ever seeing a microscope in high school. We had to find and identify bacteria and most of us didn't know how to use the microscopes. The professor was pretty stern, but the lab assistant, Miss Tredger, was the one everyone turned to. She had a line-up of students needing help. She would adjust the microscope, find our little bug and then say, "Ahhhhhh, there you are." She inspired confidence. Our watchword when we were in trouble was, 'Get Miss Tredger!' Years later, Miss Tredger married Stu's brother and became my sister-in-law." Stu adds that the University even let Peg Tredger keep her job for a year after she got married.

"Dr. Moss taught us Botany," recalls Stu, "and was very strict. Never smiled. One day I was in a florist shop buying Mabel a corsage for her graduation, and I was about to graduate too. Dr. Moss, who happened to be there, came over to me, smiled, and wished me good luck. I pretty well almost fell on the floor! And Trigger Tracy, the English teacher who got his nickname because he was a COTC army training officer, once told me something that I later learned was so true. He gave us Aggies the task of writing an essay about any agricultural topic. I wrote about harvest—from the beginning of the process to the end, and described it in detail. At the end of the essay, my tone was 'whew! thank goodness all that hard work is over and done with.' I got a good mark, but what has stuck with me all these years is Trigger Tracy's comment. He said that at the end of my essay, he could sense a 'sigh of relief that the harvest was over instead of seeing harvest as an accomplishment.' After a career as a district agriculturist, I can tell you that the English professor was right."

"Dr. Salter also sticks in my mind as an excellent teacher," says Mabel. "He really put the fear of the Lord in us. He was one of the few professors who would still wear a black academic gown to class, which at that time made him seem severe. There was a long list of books to read and all the essays had to be neatly written out by hand—no typewriters in those days. For the first class, we had to write an essay and I worked so hard on it—I knew he was tough. I passed. But he said the class marks were so low he wasn't going to count that one. Too bad!"

Social Life During the War

"I MET MABEL at an overtown dance at one of the downtown hotels," remembers Stu. "The big dances were held at the Hotel Macdonald or at the Corona Hotel, the only two decent hotels at the time. It was the days of tuxedoes for the men and long dresses for the women. Most of us couldn't afford cab fare, and so we boarded the streetcar in all our finery and headed over the High Level Bridge to get downtown." Mabel explains that, "You were supposed to have an escort for every dance, and your escort would always send you a corsage to wear on your dress. But with so many men away at war, you sometimes went to a dance on your own. As for the long dresses we all wore, during the war you simply couldn't buy one. You couldn't even buy enough material to sew one. So we improvised by finding the longest skirts we could and adding a fancy top. Even by 1946, when Stu and I were married, you still couldn't buy enough material for a long dress. And the unwritten dress code for university classes was also pretty formal in those days. I wore a suit to most of my classes and Stu wore a white shirt and tie.

"Our first date was a house dance," recalls Stu. House dances used to be held in Athabasca, Assiniboia, and Pembina, the three student residences, but during the war, all the residences were turned over to the Army. And so in our day, house dances were usually just in the fraternities and sororities. Liquor was rationed during the war, and you couldn't afford to buy much anyway, so drinking wasn't a big part of the fraternity scene."

"On other dates," adds Mabel, "you might go to a show at the Varscona Theatre at Whyte Avenue and 109 Street for 25 cents, or lunch on Jasper Avenue. There was a good Chinese restaurant on Whyte Avenue. None of us had much money in those days and it always astonishes me when I see a dinner bill for $50. For those of us who went through the war, it's still a bit unbelievable. At our wedding reception in 1946, the turkey dinner cost a dollar a plate, and when we got married, we lived on $150 a month."

After Graduation

"AFTER MY BSC," says Stu, "I was going to get a Master's but I had met Mabel, and we both got jobs after graduation—and, by the way, we both went to our Convocations—everyone did. I know that today not all students do that. Our graduation ceremony was in Convocation Hall—very small. My first job was as a district agriculturist in Wainwright. Basically, this meant you were a teacher, helping farmers bring in a better crop or teaching better livestock management. I made a good salary—$150 a month. We started our married life on that and even managed to save money. The war taught you to watch your money."

Mabel remembers teaching for a year in Camrose, and then she and Stu were married. "After our second child was born, in Wainwright, I was approached to teach—there was a teacher shortage. This was the early 1950s. I found a widow to look after the children and tend the house. I drove to Irma for some classes, and some were in Wainwright. You could feel the resentment and disapproval from the other women in town. This was the early 1950s and the view then was that you should be home looking after your children. Then the minister's wife also got a housekeeper to look after her children and her home, and she started to teach. It was very interesting to watch people's reactions."

Today, these two grads have three children, five grandchildren, and one great-granddaughter. In 2006, they celebrated their 60th wedding anniversary. You might say that they're dance partners for life.

Pat Scott Schlosser (BSC HEC '50)

IN 1950, she was one of 70 Household Economic students to cross the stage at the McDougall United Church to receive her degree. After that, the McDougall Church was too small to hold all the U of A grads.

By 1990 this alumna was the wife of the Board Chairman. She thus watched thousands of U of A students convocate in Jubilee Auditorium, and was on hand afterwards to greet new graduates and their families. Was she ever bored watching so many students get their degrees and greeting grads and their families afterwards? Not once. "I knew what it took for each of these students to reach the convocation stage, and I loved watching each and every one of them receive their degrees," she says.

Her name is Patricia Scott Schlosser, and her friends describe her as the epitome of grace, intelligence, and warmth. It is those qualities that mark her long volunteer commitment to the U of A. In her senior year, Pat was awarded the silver "A" ring for her volunteer activities, and she carried forward that commitment to volunteering all her life, both in Edmonton and at the University. Pat has served as an alumni representative and, as wife and chief supporter of her husband John Schlosser, who chaired the Board of Governors from 1978 through 1990, Pat was on hand for nearly 100 convocation ceremonies, meeting students and their families in her warm and engaging way.

"Choosing the U of A was easy," says Pat. "Our family moved from Regina just as I was finishing high school and our new home was one block from the University—11045 Saskatchewan Drive. So the choice was a natural one, but getting in was an up-and-down experience. My high school in Regina waived the requirement that I take final exams and instead based my grades on the past year's grade 12 work. But at the last minute, the U of A said I had to take the grade 12 exams. I blush to confess that I had slacked off a little once I learned I didn't have to take grade 12 finals. It was quite a panic to prepare for them at the eleventh hour. But prepare I did. Then, at the very last minute, the U of A changed its mind. I was in without having to take the exams. We moved from Regina in the summer,"

The Wauneita Lounge

These women shine with the exuberance of the 1950s. They were all members of the Wauneita Society. "I don't remember where the Wauneita Lounge was when I began my studies," remembers Pat Scott Schlosser, "but I remember exactly where it was when I graduated in 1950—in the first Students' Union Building (today's University Hall) where the president's office is now. It was a huge space and had an unstaffed kitchen. SUB opened in 1950, the year I was married, and my wedding reception was in the Wauneita Lounge. Years later, when my husband John chaired the Board of Governors, the Board Office was right down the hall from where our wedding reception was held." (UAA 69-19-1538)

Pat recalls, "and I didn't know anyone in Edmonton. I was an only child and a bit of a loner. But it turned out that a member of the Delta Delta Delta (Tri Delt) women's fraternity lived right behind us and she took me under her wing."

The University and its surrounding neighbourhoods were relatively small-scale in 1947, when Pat went to her first class. She remembers Windsor Park as a field, with sheaves of wheat dotting it in the fall, and with just a few houses. And near where the Faculty Club now stands, there was a "ring" of houses where the president and senior professors lived. At the time, the Toonerville trolley was still running in the McKernan area.

First Week on Campus

"REGISTRATION? I hardly remember it," says Pat. "In Home Economics, your pattern of courses was pretty well laid out for you and there weren't any options until your last year. There actually was very little room for options—in our first two years, over half our required courses were in Chemistry, Biochemistry, Physiology and Bacteriology—all with three-hour labs—and so there wasn't much time for anything else. And because the pattern of our courses was pre-set, there were no line-ups for registration. You just went over to the Registrar's Office and paid your fees.

"All the women automatically became members of the Wauneita Society, a women's group that was important for all women students," Pat explains, "but especially for the residence girls from out of town.

"My best memory from my first week on campus was Frosh Week. There was an entire week devoted to it, and a theme—in our year we wore straw hats everywhere. There were box lunches, afternoon tea dances, and those straw hats were everywhere.

"Frosh Week was also a time when you could sign up for extracurricular activities. It was a wonderful week. Maybe because my mother was a reporter back in Saskatchewan, I signed up for *The Gateway*, where I was a reporter for two years."

Toes Soaked in Scotch

"I ALSO JOINED THE BALLET CLUB," Pat remembers, "which had just started up in 1947. I had taken some lessons, but had never been on pointe. We practiced all year, but our pointe shoes didn't arrive until just before the performance in Con Hall. So here was the sequence—we unpacked the shoes, went on stage, and performed on pointe. There was no time to work up to it. After the performance, our toes were so sore, and mine were absolutely purple. I was supposed to soak them at home in rubbing alcohol, but we didn't have any. So my dad poured some Scotch into a bucket and that's what I soaked my bruised feet in."

Pat was also involved in the Literary Society, first serving as the secretary and then as the president. "In those days," she says, "the Literary Society was the group that was the liaison to the Students' Council for all the arts groups—for instance the drama society and the public speaking group. One issue for the public speaking group was that they need a full-length mirror—I suppose that today you would need to videotape your presentations in order to practice, but in my day it was a full-length mirror they needed. And I got them their full length mirror." Pat continued her support of arts groups after graduation. In 1982, she spearheaded a fundraiser for all major arts groups in Edmonton, including the opera and symphony, editing a cookbook called *A Taste of the Arts*. "We raised a lot of money," she says, "and you won't find a copy in any second-hand bookstore. Everyone's copy is witness to heavy use, spattered with a little antipasto or cookie batter."

Classes and Campus Personalities—"She Knew Me by Name"

PAT WAS A HOUSE ECCER.

"That's what we called ourselves," she says. "And we took a lot of science. All my Chemistry classes were in the Med Building, in the big amphitheatre, and we were right in there with the pre-med students. All my other classes were in the South Lab. There was no variation to the routine—Science and 'Home Ec' courses. I loved my program, but I regret that in my last year, when I had only one option, I took another science. I regret it because I could have taken Classics, an option I would have loved."

Classes in 1947 were different—a mix of high school students and returning veterans. Pat recalls it distinctly. "There were all these bearded men in my classes, just back from the war. They were returned veterans. They were totally different from those of us who were just out of high school and doing goofy things after class. Two undergraduates I remember were Michael and Eileen O'Byrne. They had a baby, and in his 'spare' time Michael was the SU president. The Byrnes lived in the McKernan area, along with many other vets, at a time when there were few houses in that district—there was just a lake, flat prairie and then these shabby apartments that looked like motel units."

Favourite teacher? Pat has a quick response. "I think all of us in my class would say Miss Hazel McIntyre. She taught all the cooking labs and so she knew us all. She had a very gentle personality. And all of us would remember Maimie Simpson. She was the dean of women, and what a wonderful woman. She had a small suite in St. Stephen's College. Throughout the year she entertained every single freshette in her suite with tea. There would be six to eight of us at a time. We all wore gloves and a hat. Miss Simpson was so charming, not seriously proper. She was keenly interested in you and you just glowed when you came out of there. To top it off, you had also met a few new people. At Christmas, the House Eccers would always bake Dean Simpson a special cake, and I got to deliver it because I lived in town. She knew me by name. She knew all of us by name."

Formal Dances and Engineering Week

"IT WAS ALWAYS SKIRTS that were worn to class," remembers Pat. "There was no written dress code—it was just expected. Maybe we would wear pants for something like a wiener roast.

"If you needed to buy clothes, you usually had to go downtown. For instance, in the late 1940s there were lots of formal balls at the University, and let's say you needed a ball gown. The Bay, Walk-Rite or Johnstone Walker's were the three big stores downtown, and if you couldn't get it there, you just couldn't get it. Actually, a lot of us just sewed our own gowns. To shop downtown, you would slip on a pair of white gloves, short ones, and you would probably wear a hat. Johnstone Walker's was especially proper—there were all these lovely old ladies on their staff and you always watched your Ps and Qs.

"To get downtown, you took the trolley over the High Level Bridge— the top of the High Level Bridge, up above where cars go nowadays—and in my day they didn't reverse the car. It was a great ride, but not reversing the car meant that if there was a problem and the car had to stop, the door would open to the outside of the bridge and you would be perched right at the edge of the bridge. And remember—you were riding on the top of the bridge, not the enclosed part down below. Now let's say you have your dress for the ball, perhaps the Engineers' Ball, which was one of the biggest. You would have a printed invitation and inside the envelope would be a dance card. You would fill this out yourself, or boys would call you and ask for a dance. You always knew whom you would be dancing with, for each dance, as long your card was filled out in advance.

"Your boyfriend would pick you up, and he always arrived with a corsage. An elaborate corsage. To give you an idea, my graduation corsage had a dozen pink roses in it. That's how it was done in the late 1940s.

"There would be a group of us who piled into a car and off we would go. The back seat, by the way, closed with the kind of 'hook and eye' latch you see on a screen door. When we arrived at the dance, there was always a receiving line. The president might be there, or the dean of women—it depended on who was giving the dance. Then, if your dance card was full, you knew who your dance partner would be for each dance."

Pat was crowned as Engineers' Queen in 1948. She explains how it worked.

"These were the days when each branch in the Engineering Faculty picked a candidate for Queen. I was the candidate for the Civil Engineers. There were eight candidates in total, and, for a week before the dance, we would be escorted around campus by two Engineers. Their job was to make sure that the Arts students didn't kidnap us. If you were kidnapped, they took you off to a hotel and locked you up so you couldn't participate in anything during the week leading up to the ball. It was all great fun, including the pranks. A friend told me about one time when a group of guys got hold of a pig as part of a prank for the Engineers' Ball. It was 26° below—Fahrenheit. They greased the pig and had one of the girls at the Engineers' Ball open the window from the inside of the Ladies' Room. The guys let the pig in through the window. Of course, this was supposed to cause great havoc, with a greased pig running amok. But I hear that the pig was so cold, it just stood there in the middle of the floor and shivered. Someone picked it right up and stored it safely for the rest of the dance."

Convocation—"You Knew You were Cooked!"

CONVOCATION in the University's early days was held in Convocation Hall in the Arts Building, but this capstone event was switched to the McDougall United Church in 1931, when the number of graduands exceeded Con Hall's capacity. It wasn't until 1958, when the Jubilee Auditorium was built, that the convocation ceremony was again back on campus. Pat was in the last class to convocate at McDougall United Church.

After graduation, Pat did a year of dietetics at the University Hospital. "You needed this year of interning," she explains, "in order to be qualified for most professional positions. It was a fascinating and satisfying year because there were a lot of young men who had returned from the war as paraplegics, and we took care of them. Our budget was so restrictive, but despite that, we had to figure out the best diets for these men. And we spent time with them. We cheered them up. After that interning year, I thought I might work as the dietician at St. Steve's, but I took a job at the gas company, at the Blue Flame Kitchen. There were two of us there. The next year I was married to John Schlosser, a man I had met when I was in high school. We were both raised in Saskatchewan and we met 'at the lake.' By 1949, when I was 19, we were engaged."

"When I graduated in 1950," says Pat Scott Schlosser, "it was the Chancellor who conferred your degree, and this is what happened. You stood before the Chancellor and then kneeled. You placed the palms of your hands together, with your fingers pointing towards the Chancellor. He would look you straight in the eye, place his hands around yours and say, 'admito te.' The words mean, 'I admit you to the University.' You just knew you were properly cooked after that!! You had your degree. You were part of the University."

(UAA 69–19–402)

"We Are not a Collection of Buildings"

IN 1949, Pat gave the "'toast to the University'" at a Panhellenic event held at the Hotel Macdonald. She still has the three-page hand-written toast, written on the reverse side of stationery from her dad's company. It is worth sharing:[19]

Tonight, and with humility and a deep appreciation of the honour, I rise to propose the toast to the University.

The University—in its broadest sense—the established centres across the world dedicated to the pursuit of higher learning, the appreciation of culture, the delving into the humanities, the broadening of man's vision.

To come close to home—our University—the seat of learning now so well established after 42 years of planning, pioneering and development and progress. From modest beginnings it has steadily grown to the institution we know today—*our* Alma Mater—source of our fond affection, our sincere pride.

What is the University?

Not a collection of splendid buildings, well-equipped labs, competent professors and eager students. Not just the thrill of competitive sports, or the learning to live together in residence or fraternity house, the democracy of the Students' Union or the wonderful comradeship through three or four crowded years.

All these are university—but here is something more—that intangible "something" that is "Varsity"—the chatter in the Tuck—the "meet you under the clock in Arts"—the hum in Med 58 just before the lecture begins, the row on row of little brown tables in the Drill Hall.

These are the fleeting and formative years—all too fast-moving to enable us to get full benefit from the lectures and the library.

Winston Churchill, speaking before the Massachusetts Institute of Technology in recent years, laughingly stated that it had never been his privilege to attend a university, but that he had managed to get by. That impressive audience of top-flight scientific minds appreciated his joke—the transcending greatness of the man denying any implication of boastfulness. But we are not all Churchills—and he emphasized the privilege of attendance.

Privilege it is to become a part—a very small part for a very brief time—of a University. And when we go, a little of our youth will stay behind, on the campus, forever.

Hail, Alma Mater dear, out on the prairie wide,
Up where the foothills crouch 'neath giant snow-peaks cold.
Naught save this strain we hear that swells like ocean tide
All hail, Alberta, with thine Evergreen and Gold!

Hail, Alma Mater dear, we sons and daughters true,
Lift at thy shrine today our voice of song upraised.
Hark to our anthem clear! We pledge our faith anew;
All hail, Alberta, with thine Evergreen and Gold!

Will you rise to toast our University.

"I had three glorious years at the U of A," says Pat. "It was enriching, so memorable, and it changed my whole life."

W.A. Doug Burns (BA '51)

FROM HIS PERCH as Students' Union president and then as a University administrator, Doug Burns watched six presidents lead the University of Alberta from 1947 to 1988: Robert Newton, Andrew Stewart, Walter Johns, Max Wyman, Harry Gunning, and Myer Horowitz.

Doug was the first full-time president of a national Canadian student organization, and as an early student lobbyist at the federal level, he won support for the first-ever national scholarship program. Along the way, Doug organized some of the inaugural mega-events on campus, including Varsity Guest Weekend (VGW). He remembers the 1950s Snake Dance, when a chain of up to 8,000 students made its way across the High Level Bridge and down Jasper Avenue, tying up traffic for hours. There was one memorable year when cars were rocked back and forth after their drivers tried to move through the snake-dancing throng. Doug was also on the scene when the University president and the mayor finally found a way to transform the Snake Dance into a tamer civic reception at the Agricom, part of today's Edmonton Northlands Park.

Students swarming for the Snake Dance. In the 1950s, up to 8,000 students at a time took part in this orientation event.

(UAA 69–19–24)

Cleaning Chickens at Woodwards

DOUG ENTERED THE U OF A in 1947 when he was 18. His father had suffered a massive heart attack when Doug was in grade 12 and had two more heart attacks during Doug's first two years at University. The third one was fatal.

"I worked part-time at Woodward's after school and on Saturdays from grade 11 on to help out with family finances, and also worked as a student postman for two weeks at Christmas time because students with honours standing in high school did not write December exams and were out of school two weeks early. Once I was in University, I also got a job as a student deputy registrar, and I worked nights as a student librarian in the law library.

"The Woodward's job was great because it was flexible," Doug explains. "I could go to work at 6:00 A.M. and get in some time before heading to campus. I could also go back to Woodward's after class, and put in a few more hours. One of my jobs was to clean chickens. Believe me, when I got on the streetcar after work, people kept their distance. Maybe it was because I still had a few bits of chicken liver sticking to my shoes."

There was only one thing worse than chicken liver sticking to your shoes: registration.

Registration in the Late 1940s and Early 1950s

DOUG WAS HIRED as a part-time deputy registrar after answering an advertisement in *The Gateway*. He quickly came to learn all the ins and outs of registration. In the 1940s, there was no registration by telephone, and no Beartracks/Bearscat registration on the Web. Back then, you registered in person. "In-person registration" meant that you arrived at the Arts Building with hundreds of others at a precise time, lined up, and registered one at a time.

In the year Doug entered the U of A, 1947, there were almost 5,000 students on campus—a huge increase because of all the veterans returning from World War II. "Registration—if you can believe it—all took place in Convocation Hall in the Arts Building," remembers Doug. "Convocation Hall only holds 300 students."

"You arrived at Con Hall at the time you were told to be there," Doug explains, "and you waited your turn. Con Hall was all set up with desks and chairs. The registrar was there, actually physically there, and he explained all the basics about filling out the forms that were on the desk in front of you. They were really clear that you needed to write your surname first. Why? I found out later," says Doug, "that every single form was manually filed in a box, alphabetically.

"Everyone registered by their class, so the upperclassmen were registered first, then the juniors, then the sophomores, and then us—the freshmen—and you also registered alphabetically within each class. Freshmen with a surname that began with X, Y or Z were the last to register. After writing your name on the registration form, you filled in your required classes. Everyone had to take English, Physical Education and a language other than English, except for the Engineers. Once your requirements were written in, you'd see what room was left in your schedule for options.

"Now you need to know that at the back of Con Hall, by the entrance doors, there were what was called 'class cards,' and there were profs from every department waiting at the back by these class cards to give you more information about the various courses, both required and optional. If you had conflicts between your course selections, the student deputy registrars helped you. It was complicated by the fact that the Calendar listed the names of the professors who taught the various sections—and of course, some students wanted Professor X for a particular class because he had taught their mother, while some students wanted Professor Y whom they'd heard was a great teacher.

"There was one card for each space in each class," says Doug. When the cards were gone, there was no more space in the class.

"The required introductory English class might have four sections, or divisions, and so there would be, say, 100 cards for English 2, section 1, 100 cards for English 2, section 2, and so forth. You had to get up out of your seat and go claim a card to get a space in a particular section. The smart students knew to get up from their seats right away and get their options cards first. Why? Because you would always be able to get into the required courses. It was the options that were tough to get into. But I knew the ropes and registered in an hour. For others it took two hours or more.

"I should add that all new students would wear freshman regalia, like a beanie and a green and gold scarf. You addressed all the upperclassmen as 'Sir' or 'Ma'am,' and you did what they told you. There was a little intimidation, but it wasn't bad. Orientation lasted a week, and there was a big bonfire, a sing-song, and address by the SU president, and the 'must event' was the Snake Dance. If there was a discipline problem, it was the provost who was in charge—P.S. Warren and then Dr. Sparby in my time," recalls Doug. "Dr. Warren was rules-oriented, but fair. Dr. Sparby was nice, gentle. If you got a note from P.S. Warren, you were scared! If you got a note from Dr. Sparby, it was something warm in tone. They were just different in their approach."

It's been nearly 60 years since Doug paid his tuition, but he remembers the amount exactly. "Tuition was $118 for the year plus SU fees, an athletic fee and a health services fee. I think one of the extra fees was optional, and I am pretty sure that the vets were exempted from the extra fees." In addition to helping out his mother, Doug paid his own way through school.

Mixed Functions and Varsity Varieties

EIGHTEEN-YEAR-OLD DOUG learned the rules quickly. "Mixed functions ended at midnight," he says. "The dean of women, by the way, always made sure there was a chaperone at these events—usually a married vet and his wife. The guys didn't have a curfew but the girls did. The guys would take their girlfriends home to meet the curfew and then go back to the parties. Some of the girls would sneak out, though, and in the Nurses' Residence, well, that was interesting because it was just under construction and there were a lot of ladders around. So the girls would go in the front door, sign in with the supervisor, and then we'd use the ladders to get them out. Plus there were plywood doors because of the construction, and they were so easy to get through.

"On Tuesday nights, the Garneau Theatre had sneak previews, and this was a popular date night. Somebody would always get a party together afterwards. The girls were allowed so many sleepovers during the school year but they had to leave a phone number. It would be something like 'Mrs. Jones and a phone number.' That would do it. There were no such restrictions on the boys."

Doug was president of the Inter-Fraternity Council (IFC). "There was something in either the *University Act* or in the associated regulations which prohibited liquor within a mile of campus," he says. "My guess is that Dr. Tory had this written in very early on in the University's history. Fraternities were technically within the mile, and there was a lot of discussion about it. Chancellor McNally was a Baptist and wasn't predisposed to having liquor on campus. But the provost, the police commissioner and fraternity representatives met, and the long and the short of it was that the University turned a blind eye to this rule.

"There were lots of dances," says Doug, "but most students could only afford one of these formal events—and the women were always beautifully dressed up. The Tri-Service Ball was a big 'do' and all the guys were in uniform. Bar None was also big. Many of these dances were held at the Hotel Macdonald—they were very 'pro university' when it came to big functions. The *maitre d'* was Mr. Hudson—his daughter was a student and he was great to us. And the other big dance was Sadie Hawkins—very popular.

"Varsity Varieties was a snappy song-and-dance revue and also really popular. It grew out of the "Club" thing, which was a scripted variety event, and a fundraiser. There was a "Club" in each graduating year— "Club '51," "Club '52," and so on. Joe Shoctor started these "Clubs" around 1948. These were very professional shows, and Joe would start the planning

For decades, Varsity Varieties nailed down the attention of thousands of ticket-holders. "These are students on stage?!" So said many doubting Edmontonians, but every performance was sold out. Here, Anne Wheeler is at centre stage. She was the star performer in the 1950s, and made her mark later on as a film-maker. (UAA 70-122-68-740)

and the tryouts in the fall, but the production wouldn't debut until spring. Jeannie Lougheed was a singer and dancer in these—she was good! Anne Wheeler acted in some of the plays—the one everyone remembers is *The Princess and the Pea*. But once Joe Shoctor graduated, no one else would put in the time to make Varsity Varieties happen."

Classes and Favourite Professors

DOUG LIVED AT HOME in the west end throughout his university days. To this day, he can recite the bus schedule, including the colour-coding on the front of the buses that indicated each individual bus route. "The bus at 109 Street and 88 Avenue was so crowded, you'd be hanging on to the outside of it. And in January, we could walk across the river, and it was really safer to do that because there was so much frost on the tracks over the High Level Bridge, the approach to the Bridge was dangerous."

The University was overflowing with students in the postwar years. There was no Rutherford Library yet, and Doug remembers studying in the hallways in the Arts Building, where one small room served as the study hall portion of the Library. But he never studied in the basement. "The bookstore and post office were there, and it was noisy. You could use a classroom, but you had to leave it tidy." Doug also studied over in the Drill Hall—in the corner, sitting on the floor.

"In Law," says Doug in a snap, "my favourite professor was Wilbur Bowker. He insisted that people be ethical, and you couldn't parrot answers back to him. You were there to question. And a dean who taught students?? That was unheard of. Dean Bowker taught property and torts, and he made those subjects interesting.

"In Arts, Bob Follinsbee was a stand-out. You had to take a science course and he taught part of a combined Botany-Geology course. At the time, Dr. Follinsbee was getting a lot of press about his research on meteors, and his role in oil discoveries. He was very shy. You'd have to initiate a conversation with him, but when you did, you'd find out things you'd never learn in class."

The class Doug looked forward to most was George Hardy's in Classics. "You couldn't believe when class was over, it went so fast," says Doug. "And Dr. Hardy endeared himself to students because he told us that he wanted us to get good grades, and he would give us clues about what would be on the exams."

Varsity Guest Weekend (VGW)

DOUG WAS ELECTED SU president in 1953 in a hotly contested election. He had already served as IFC president and as the public relations officer (PRO) of the SU. "In the PRO job you could really get things done. Peter Lougheed was SU president in 1951 and he heard that UBC had a great event where people from the community were invited on to campus. Peter sent fellow student Ivan Head out to investigate, and we started what became Varsity Guest Weekend."

Former U of A President Walter Johns describes the VGW that Doug organized in 1957 as "the best ever."[20] People came from all over the province to see what was going on at a university their tax dollars supported, and VGW was a hugely successful way to open the doors of the ivory tower to the people who paid for it. More than 6,500 Albertans came to see exhibits,

Our Banner.

Given by Earl Grey, Governor-General of Canada in nineteen hundred and eleven to the University, "where its design might stimulate the students to the emulation of St. George, and to devote their lives to the redressing of human wrongs."

Dr. Tory presents it each year to the incoming President of the Students' Union as his insignia of office.

Hand-stitched in Wantage, England and presented to the University in 1911 by the governor general, the St. George's Banner was described in the 1941 Evergreen and Gold *as "the emblem of the authority of the Students' Union and each spring [it] is taken to Convocation Hall to symbolize the transfer of power from the outgoing to the incoming student administration." The Banner disappeared in the 1980s.*

(UAA 81-171-95)

tour campus, and hear the University symphony orchestra and mixed chorus. Varsity Varieties was a sell-out. Audience reaction? "Wow! These are students on the stage?!"

"We also started up two dinner programs," says Doug, "the Civic Dinner and the Parliamentary Dinner. For the civic function, we invited the mayor and aldermen, and for the parliamentary function, we invited the premier and MLAs. We had a male and a female student on deck to take each MLA around campus and talk to the government reps about their experiences as students at the U of A. The students were so enthusiastic about their professors and their classes—it definitely had an effect. And the university administration was very supportive. President Johns said that, really, the administration should have been organizing these functions themselves. And while we appreciated the administration's guidance, it was a student-sponsored event. We got to know the politicians in an informal

way and could always pick up the phone to make an appointment if there
was something we wanted to accomplish."

After Graduation

AFTER GRADUATING with his BA, Doug enrolled in an after-degree program
in the Faculty of Education. But soon he was elected SU president, and
then president of the National Federation of Canadian University Students.
He moved to Ottawa for a year, and that spelled the end of Doug's time in
Education.

When he came back to Edmonton, Doug enrolled in Law. "Two years
of law school," he says, "showed me I was not cut out to be a lawyer."

Then, came the military. "I had had summer employment as a call-out
officer from the reserve army since obtaining my BA," he says, "and so
when I was offered a continuous active service call-out in the regular army
as a Personnel Selection Officer after Law 2, I opted for full-time military
service and withdrew from University. Along the way through Arts, Law
and Education," Doug relates, "I became politicized. Through my involvement with the Students' Union and the Interfraternity Council (IFC), I
found I could get things done, and that's how I discovered I liked administration. I learned the essence of administration."

Doug's extracurricular life as an undergraduate gave him an invalu-
able set of relationships and an insider's knowledge of what made the
University tick. He knew the premier, the president, and the provost. He
put his experience as an Arts, Law, and Education student to work.

"It took me a while to figure out that what I wanted to do in life was
university administration," says Doug. "But I wasn't sure what the career
path was in terms of formal university education. Shortly after my military service ended, Vice-President Walter Johns phoned me to ask if I
would be secretary of the Undergraduate Admissions Committee. This
meant, for one thing, that I dealt with all admissions appeals," he recalls.
It was the beginning of a long association as an administrator with his
alma mater. Doug served for 23 years as an Administrative Professional
Officer until he retired in 1988. He was the University of Alberta representative on the Alberta Teachers' Association Teacher Qualification Committee
for 10 years—a committee that bridged the government and the University
in evaluating such matters as qualifications of teachers. Long before the

days of sophisticated computer applications, he initiated an in-house computerized transfer guide of post-secondary education courses, which was compiled and distributed by the Department of Advanced Education. It was revolutionary in its time. Doug also served as assistant registrar and as the University's ceremonies and protocol officer.

"If I had a piece of advice for students today," says Doug, "it would be that you need to feel fulfilled in what you are doing not only with your formal education, but also in the way you use your education as you go through your whole life. I still remember the president's advice to us at his farewell party: 'Have an impact in your life. Do one thing to make a difference.'"

END OF THE DECADE

ROBERT NEWTON'S PRESIDENCY began in the midst of world war and ended during peacetime, in 1950. But peacetime wasn't really so peaceful; the first atom bombs were dropped by the United States during Newton's term of office, and in 1949, Russia detonated its own bomb, setting off a new phase of the Cold War. President Newton's parting words to students in his last convocation address summarize the decade best:

Many of you graduands will live to see the year 2000. That is a solemn thought, because so much can happen in half a century nowadays, and you cannot escape either your share of responsibility for it, or the consequences. The first half of the twentieth century had been marked by great additions of material power in the hands of mankind, through control over the forces of nature. But these have not saved us from grievous calamities that made this half century a disappointing and disastrous period. War on a worldwide scale appeared for the first time. It happened twice, and the second time, it was total war. This period also saw the first appearance of the atrocious sin of genocide. It saw democracy in eclipse in many countries, and threatened in our own....It saw freedom obliterated over a large part of the earth.

In your half of the twentieth century, try cultivating the things of the spirit instead of power, and see if you will not have a happier life than we had. We have shown you how to build good roads, bridges, motor cars, and aeroplanes, but we have left you to discover how to use these to bind mankind together in peace and brotherhood. You must learn to speak the word that is "with power," the word that heals. Place the emphasis in education on thought and speech. Worship God and not the atom.[21]

"The Snake Dance...Bar None...1,300 at the Wauneita formal...Edmonton campus to be capped at 6,000...World University Services raises $4,000 for Hungarian students...Mixed Chorus, Merry Meds and Varsity Varieties pack them in... Sputnik is launched...first computer on campus.... best-ever Varsity Guest Weekend...Joe Clark and Lou Hyndman in Model Parliament...first Convocation in Calgary...50th birthday for the University of Alberta...Jubilee!"

—*WALTER JOHNS, president, University of Alberta at Edmonton and University of Alberta at Calgary, describing the 1950s in* History of the U of A, 1908–1969

Timeline

Enrolment and Finance, 1950–1959
- Fall student head count: 2,999 (1950); 7,663 (1959)
- Operating budget from the Province of Alberta: $1,400,000.00 (1950); $3,947,000.00 (1959)
- Full-load undergraduate Arts tuition: $130.00 (1950); $215.00 (1959)
- SU membership fee: $10.50 + building fund $10 (1950); $11.25 + building fund $10 (1959)

Key Dates, 1950–1959
- In 1950, President Robert Newton takes early retirement and Andrew Stewart is named president
- First-ever federal grant to Canadian universities; U of A gets $461,000 (1950)
- First-year Arts and Science offered in Calgary as a lead-up to a second Alberta university and an affiliated junior college in Lethbridge (1951)
- School of Graduate Studies is established (1952)
- Al Ryan, warden of Assiniboia, becomes provost (1953)
- After a polio outbreak, a School of Physiotherapy is organized in the old RCAF canteen (1954)
- School of Pharmacy becomes a Faculty (1955)
- School of Graduate Studies becomes a Faculty (1957)
- Dr. Walter Johns becomes the first vice-president (1957)
- L.Y. Cairns, member of the first graduating class, is named chancellor (1958)
- President Stewart leaves to become head of the Board of Broadcast Governors (1958)
- Vice-president Walter Johns is named president (1959)

Selected Campus Buildings, 1950–1959
- First Students' Union Building, today's University Hall (1950)
- Rutherford Library (1951)
- Engineering Building (1953—called Civil/Electrical in 2004)
- Biological Sciences Building, today's Earth Sciences Building (1954)
- Jubilee Auditorium (1957)
- Administration Building (1957)
- Chemistry/Physics complex construction begun (1958)
- Physical Education complex (1958)
- A decision is made to open a two-building campus in Calgary by 1960 (1958)

Beyond Campus, 1950–1959

- Over 32,000 Canadians die in the Korean War and its aftermath (1950–1957)
- The first male nurse graduates in Canada (1951)
- The first contraceptive pill is synthesized (1952)
- Polio reaches epidemic proportions; Jonas Salk develops a vaccine (1953)
- CFRN becomes Edmonton's first TV station (1954)
- The first McDonald's opens and Disneyland debuts in California (1955)
- Groat Bridge built; Westmount opens as Edmonton's first mall (1955)
- Nat King Cole is the first black entertainer on a show broadcast by NBC (1956)
- The USSR launches two Sputnik satellites, and the space race is on (1957)
- Men and women are allowed to drink together in Edmonton's hotel beer parlours (1958)

VIGNETTES FROM THE 1950S

Post-War Release

STUDENTS WHO ARRIVED on campus as 18-year-olds in 1950 lived their youth while World War II was being fought. They were ready to have some fun. Fraternities and clubs were in full swing, and there was one formal ball after another.

Tevie Miller (BA '49, LLB '50, LLD HON '91), who later became chancellor of the U of A, was the Students' Union president. As the decade unfolded, students crowned Reg Lister King of the popular Mardi Gras dance. But nearly all the other old-timers from the U of A's earliest days were gone.

The new wave of professors and administrators in 1950 were U of A grads from the 1920s and 1930s—Wilbur Bowker (BA '30, LLB '32), dean of Law; Alex Cairns (BA '38, DIP ED '40), assistant registrar; Marjorie Sherlock (BA '27 and IODE scholar), chief librarian; Don Cameron (BSC AG '30), director of extension; Al Ryan (BA '39) and Maimie Simpson (BA '22), respectively wardens of Assiniboia and Pembina. Al Ryan was later named provost, and Maimie Simpson was the first dean of women who bore that title with the approval of the Board of Governors.

These grads from the 1920s and 1930s were now part of a more matured U of A that offered a wide array of programs. The U of A now had, for instance, a department of Fine Arts, and the undergraduates in 1950 dedicated their yearbook to Canadian art, inserting plate after colour plate of Canadian paintings throughout the *Evergreen and Gold*. Famed painter Henry Glyde had joined the department of Fine Arts, and virtually every student saw three of Glyde's works each day. The magnificent mural in Rutherford South is his creation (Glyde painted his own image into this work). The painting that hangs in the Galleria between HUB and Rutherford is also by Glyde, as is the frieze carved above the 1950 Students' Union building (today's University Hall). In 2006, Glyde's oil paintings fetched $3,000–$4,000 on the art auction circuit.

The U of A celebrated its Jubilee in 1958. Colour photos appeared for the first time in the *Evergreen and Gold*, Xerox machines were about to make their entrance, everyone was in civilian clothes, and there weren't many around who remembered a campus where military uniforms were a common sight. The class system was abolished—no more classification as a freshman, sophomore, junior, or senior. Rock 'n roll reigned, with Elvis Presley topping the charts. And the U of A had two healthy, rapidly-growing educational offshoots. The campus at the Banff School of Fine Arts now had three chalets, including an administration building, and the Calgary campus was thriving.

The president from 1950–1959 was Andrew Stewart, a savvy former farmer whose academic background was in economics and business. The Board Chair was Charles Macleod. And the chancellor was the class wit and popular piano player from the entering class of 1908—Laurence Yeomans Cairns.

In the 1950s, the old-timers who built the U of A—like Reg Lister—were exiting the scene. Today, we know about them primarily from historical sources. But students from the 1950s are familiar names in 2006: Peter Lougheed, the former premier, was Students' Union president from 1951–1952; Joe Clark, former prime minister, was the *Gateway* editor-in-chief in 1959; and Senator Joyce Fairbairn was an *Evergreen and Gold* staffer for the 1958 Jubilee edition of the yearbook.

The 1950s was a carefree decade for students whose parents had survived World War II. There were many pranks, but no one could outdo John Appleyard in this department. John, a student from Peace River, was chosen as president of the freshman class by the Golden Key Society. John was also known to students through his regular letters to *The Gateway*. And then a sensational front-page story in *The Gateway* reported that John had been murdered. *The Gateway* headline was $3\frac{1}{2}$ inches high and was accompanied by a photograph of the Frosh president "lying in the snow near his home on the bank of Whitemud Creek."[1] The campus was stunned.

But there was a hitch. John Appleyard never really existed--he was the fictional creation of two undergraduate students, Ron Ghitter and Al Bryan.

A GLANCE AT THE CALENDAR—1950-1959

DURING THE 1950S, the size of the Calendar increased by 70%. The 1950 Calendar was still a dull utilitarian grey, but by 1959 the Calendar had a green and gold cover, and there was a modern look and feel to the paper and font. By 1959, photos accompanied the text, including a photo of the new Administration Building, looking utterly lonely and raw. The West Lab, an old wood-frame building, stood to the west. There was no grass,

University of Alberta

ANNOUNCES COURSES

FOR THE

1959 - 1960 SESSION

IN

EDMONTON
Regular Session
Arts and Science (Also
 Summer Session)
Agriculture
Commerce
Dentistry
Education (Also Summer
 Session)
Engineering
Graduate Studies
Household Economics
Law
Medicine
Nursing
Pharmacy
Physiotherapy

BANFF
Summer Session
Art
Ballet
Choral Technique
Drama
Radio Acting and
 Production
Leathercraft
Music
Oral French
Photography
Playwriting
Short Story Writing
Weaving

CALGARY
Regular Session
Arts and Science
 First Year Only
Commerce
 First Year Only
Education
 First Two Years
Engineering
 First Year Only
B.Ed. in Industrial Arts
 First Three Years
Nursing
 First Year and Three
 Clinical Years
First Year Courses
 preparatory to
 admission to:
  Dentistry
  Law
  Medicine

AND

THROUGHOUT THE PROVINCE
COMMUNITY LIFE CONFERENCES IN SUMMER
COMMUNITY ART CLASSES IN 27 CENTRES

AND

ADULT EDUCATION CLASSES ALL YEAR ROUND
THROUGH THE DEPARTMENT OF EXTENSION

For information on regular session apply to The Registrar
For information on other courses apply to
The Director, Department of Extension

University of Alberta, Edmonton

no landscaping at all—just plain dirt, freshly raked. The Administration Building was two years old.

The words "Edmonton and Calgary" appeared on the front of the 1959 Calendar, a testament to the rapid growth of our sister institution. The academic schedule for the entire decade embraced the U of A, the Calgary campus, and the Banff School of Fine Arts.

Every Calendar in the 1950s opened with a campus map, and if you compare the 1950 and the 1959 maps, you can see at a glance how the original 258 acres had been filled in with buildings during the post-war construction boom.

In the Calendar sections covering student discipline, there was one notable change. By 1959, it was against the rules to raid a residence. "The Board of Governors considers the raiding or unlawful entry of the residences as a very grave offence. Any such occurrence will be reported to and dealt with by the Board," the Calendar stated bluntly.[2]

An Edmonton lawyer occasionally tells the story behind this regulation, and there are several other upstanding citizens in Edmonton and Calgary who will remember the story, in part because a few of them spent the night in jail on account of it.

Bagpipes in the Night

IT WAS THE 1950S, and a group of exuberant students were celebrating the election of a Students' Union president. The group had just trooped through the Nurses' Residence in the middle of the night. The students were led by a bagpiper who ended up outside the Nurses' Residence, face down in the snow. He'd had a little too much to drink. The group then made their way over to Pembina Hall, at the time a women's residence. Maimie Simpson, who lived in an apartment on the top floor, recounts the rest of the story in her memoirs under the title "Bagpipes in the Night": "The results of the Students' Union elections had been announced and a celebration started that lasted until almost dawn. About 3:40 A.M. I was wakened by the sound of bagpipes. Then I heard muffled voices, and slightly above these voices I detected that of our House president, Vi King.

"Soon I was in the corridor outside my bedroom door. Our House Committee members were doing their best to turn 'the invaders' back, down the angled staircase to the north, and outside. We never were actually sure how they got inside!

"The piper was on the top step of the staircase having a marvellous time. We, too, would have enjoyed the bagpipes if the timing had been at a civilized hour, but the warden of a women's residence does not, as a rule, appreciate any kind of music at 3:40 A.M.

"There had been, as you may have guessed, a bit of over-celebrating, and I heard one student, with a 'thick tongue' say, as our House president tried to get the invaders off the floor and out the north door, 'Don't be so mean—Vi—don't be so mean, all I want to do is say 'good-night' to Miss Simpson.' Vi didn't feel Miss Simpson would appreciate 'good-night' at that particular moment!

"Finally, they were out on the front lawn where they gave a 'concert' for the girls. But, alas, before coming to 'visit' us they had made an uninvited call at the Nurses' Home, as a result of which the city police, unfortunately, had been called. The 'concert' was just ending when the police wagon arrived and the entertainers were taken to the police station where, during the night, I understand the 'concert' continued and those on duty were entertained by the piper and his friends.

"In the morning before the students were to be charged with unlawful entry, and for disturbing the peace, our provost arrived and was able to bring them back to the campus to be dealt with by the Students' Disciplinary Committee. Thus, no criminal record.

"At the University of Alberta there has always been an understanding that, where humanly possible, students should be dealt with by campus authorities. Our city police were most cooperative."[3]

As a result, the Board passed its "raiding regulation." Students continued with panty raids at both Pembina and the Nurses' Residence, but without the bagpipes to announce their arrival.

THE CLARE DRAKE ERA—1953–1989

THE CLARE DRAKE era at the University of Alberta began when Drake (BED '58, LLD HON '95), spent the 1953–1954 season as assistant captain and leading scorer of the Golden Bears hockey team, which went on to win the Canada West championship that season. He spent the following season coaching in Germany, and then on October 21, 1955, *The Gateway* reported on the appointment of Clare Drake as interim head coach of the Bears: "From star player to coach in two years! If Drake's almost meteoric rise in hockey serves to illustrate his ability, the Bears should do well by their new coach!"

The team won the Canada West title that year, and in 1958–1959, he returned as head coach and lecturer in Physical Education. The achievements that followed speak for themselves: six CIAU championships, 17 Canada West championships, two-time CIAU hockey coach of the year, four-time Canada West hockey coach of the year, two-time Edmonton Sports Man of the Year, three seasons as head coach of the Golden Bears football team, with a winning record on each occasion. In 1967, he became the only head coach ever to capture two major CIAU titles in one year— one in football and the other in hockey.

Clare Drake also found success in coaching various national hockey squads over the years. He was a co-coach of the 6th-place Canadian Olympic team at the 1980 Winter Games. He coached the Canadian Student

ARTS

Fae, facul, factus,
Fac faculty,
Arts in general
      Ph.D.
That's the way we yell it,
This is the way we spell it—
      A-R-T-S.
      Arts.

MEDS

The knife — the saw — the saw — the
   knife (slow)
Sit down—lie down—we want your life
   (faster)
We sing—you cry—we live—you die
   (very fast)
   MEDICALS.

DENTS

Good teeth, bad teeth,
What's the diff?
Pull 'em out, yank 'em out,
Biff, Biff, Biff!
Toothe Ache, Dentures, Blood, oh, Yea,
Strong arm Dentists, U. of A.

LAW

Treason, Graft or Fraudulence,
Bigamy, Theft or Negligence,
First offence, or Innocence
You get the clink
We get the chink.
LAAAWWW.

> **Varsity, Varsity, Rah, Rah, Rah,**
> **Varsity, Varsity, Al-ber-ta,**
> **Hi-Yi, Ki-Yi, Rah, Rah, Rah,**
> **Rip it out, tear it out, Alberta,**
> **Varsity, Varsity, Hip-Hoo-Ray,**
> **A-l-b-e-r-t-a.**

COMMERCE

Markets, Trade and Transportation,
Bonds, Accounts, Administration,
Money, Banking, Business, Law,
Commerce, Commerce, Rah, Rah, Rah!

WAUNEITA YELL

Ki-yi itiki, ki, yi, yip,
Wauneita, Wauneita, zip, zip, zip,
War-paint, Battle-axe, Peace-pipe, gore,
Wauneita, Wauneita, Evermore.

NURSES

N-U-R-S-E-S-
Call upon us in distress,
When you're well you don't want us,
But when you're sick—
Oh, what a fuss....

ENGINEERS

T-Squares! Compass! Transit! Chains!
Engines! Bridges! Dynamos! Drains!
Coal mines! Railways—Every Day!
ENGINEERS! ENGINEERS! U. of A.

PHARMACY

Lotions, Potions, fiat chart,
We know 'em all Secundum Art,
Watch the spell binders,
We are the pill grinders
Hydrolizing, carbolizing, olea
PHARMACY, PHARMACY, U. of A.

AGS.

Agriculture—Agriculture—Var-si-ty
Agrico, Biblico, Zip, Zap, Zee,
Triticum, Labrium, Bulbican, Bac
Incus, Humus, Igneous, Lac,
Varsity, Varsity, U. of A.
Aggies, Aggies, Hip Hur-ray.

IN 1908, a group of students decided that the new University of Alberta needed a "yell"—a way to cheer the University and its sports teams. The first "yell" was shouted out by students at the University's inaugural public event—the Convocation held in the fall of 1908 in the old IOOF Hall in Strathcona. The university yell was also shouted out, by the women of the Wauneita Club, at the first organized practice for a U of A athletic game, a rugby practice match on Saturday, October 22, 1910. By the 1920s, it was the "Rooters" who led the cheers at sports games, and each faculty had created its own yell.

(Evergreen and Gold, 1925–26, p.136)

On October 8, 1985, Clare Drake became the winningest intercollegiate hockey coach in North America, with a 7–6 overtime victory over the Red Deer College Kings. With his 556th victory, he passed the record set by the late John MacInnes of Michigan Tech. (Photo courtesy of Clare Drake.)

National Team to a silver medal at the World Student Games in 1972, to a gold medal in 1981, and to a bronze medal in 1987. And in 1984, he coached Team Canada to its first gold medal at the Spengler Cup.

The 1980s were particularly special for Drake, as he became a full professor at the University in 1982. Clare Drake was inducted into the Alberta Sports Hall of Fame on October 11, 1980. Then on January 21, 1983 in Saskatoon's Rutherford Rink, he won his 500th game as head coach—over the same team, in the same building, and on the same date as his first victory back in 1956.

After 28 seasons of coaching the Golden Bears, Clare Drake announced on July 11, 1989 that he was retiring. Thus ended a golden era. He left behind an untouchable record of 697–296–37 and a legacy of bringing out the very best in every player he coached. Following his departure from the U of A, Drake spent two seasons as an assistant coach with the NHL's Winnipeg Jets. Inducted into the Canadian Sports Hall of Fame in 1989, the "dean of university hockey" is recognized on the University's Sports Wall of Fame, a recognition wall located in the Van Vliet Centre, the building which also houses the rink renamed in his honour—the Clare Drake Arena.

THE EVERGREEN AND GOLD

At Last, New Buildings

AS THE 1950 STUDENT YEARBOOK ANNOUNCED, after some 25 years
with no new, permanent facilities, there were five buildings under construction or poised to open. These were the first major buildings to be constructed
since the Medical Building opened in 1921. The new buildings were set
cheek-to-jowl with the army-style Quonset huts that had hurriedly been
erected on campus in the 1940s as a temporary measure to help deal with
the burgeoning post-war enrolments. The war-time Drill Hall was moved
to make way for the new Students' Union Building, but there was still a
military presence on campus—COTC, the Navy, and the RCAF. Later in
the 1950s, the temporary buildings erected during the war were moved or
demolished, including the Quonset huts that stood where today's CAB is
located.

Buildings seemed to appear like mushrooms for most of the 1950s:
first there was Rutherford South, then the first SUB, followed in order of
construction by the small brick building that still houses St. Stephen's
College, the LDS Church, Pavillion Central (at Collège Saint-Jean), Earth
Sciences and Civil/Electrical Engineering (both in 1954), the Administration
Building, and the Sub-Atomic Research Centre. A Chemistry building (with
the top floor devoted to Physics) was under construction, a new heating
plant was built, and the "Med" got an addition. And just in case there
weren't enough new buildings to satisfy everyone, the province built the
Northern Alberta Jubilee Auditorium to celebrate its own Jubilee.

Students thought about taking out a loan to help construct a physical
education building, but the University and the province took on that task.
Students also hoped that "future classes would witness some proof of a
balanced campus in the construction of a fine arts building and perhaps
even a solution to the residence problem."

There was only one controversial issue for students concerning the
new buildings. The proposed sites of the Administration and Chemistry
Buildings meant that the wide open spaces that had defined the quad
since 1911 would come to an end. By 1959, the quad was penned in on
all sides.

The University of Alberta

Sixty-first Session

Calendar 1968-69

Edmonton, Alberta

The First SUB

DURING THE 1950S, one building was welcomed by students above all others. The first SUB, opened in 1950—with separate lounges for men and women. By 1954 the lounges were mixed, except for the Wauneita Lounge, which remained open only to women. The 1954 yearbook description savoured the presence of the new SUB, "the centre of student activities":

Upon approaching SUB you are first aware of the spacious well-kept lawns and flower beds which border the building and set it apart from the other campus buildings. The main floor consists of a large rotunda (the Mixed Lounge) lined with shelves housing various well-earned trophies and plaques. The Mixed Lounge plays host to meetings, forums, musical rehearsals, concerts and weekend dances. The West Lounge, formerly the Men's Lounge, is well-equipped with a TV set and lounge chairs. Upstairs is the unique and beautiful Wauneita Lounge, decorated in knotty pine with maroons and greens enhancing the atmosphere of the bravery and unity of the Indian tribe Wauneita, which encompasses all women students at university. Here new freshettes become loyal members of Wauneita, as they take their tribal vows in an inspiring ceremony. Over the stone fireplace [on the south wall] hangs a mural, depicting the ancient Cree legend, painted by Professor Glyde of the Fine Arts Department.[4]

The Glyde mural that hung above the stone fireplace is now on display in the Rutherford Galleria and is accompanied by a plaque that proclaims the title of the work, *When all the World was Burned.*

Close by the Wauneita Lounge (now home to the president's office) were offices for the yearbook, *The Gateway,* and the Photo Directorate. There was a Music Room, and at the east end, where today's Board of Governors' offices are located, there was a faculty lounge, precursor to today's Faculty Club. Downstairs on the main floor, the Students' Union had had a Council room and offices, all located where the University Secretariat is today. The SU's secretary-accountant was Mr. Walter Dinwoodie. On the ground floor were a games room outfitted with billiard and ping-pong tables and, where the vice-presidents finance and facilities are situated today, there was a cafeteria. Now there are about 20 staff in those two vice-presidential suites. But in 1959, that same space—known as the "caf"—served low-cost meals to some 5,200 students daily. Alumnus Doug Burns remembers that there was a House Committee for SUB, "and two students lived in the basement of what is University Hall. They were in charge."

The First Free-Standing Library

THE ENTIRE CAMPUS welcomed the opening of Rutherford Library, which in 1951 replaced the small library located in Rm 100 of the old Arts Building. The Rutherford replaced. This exquisite oak-panelled room could seat 80 people, with the book stacks conveniently located in the basement just below. In 1950, there were only 285 "reading room" spaces for the 6,000 students enrolled at the U of A. Clearly something had to give, and librarian Marjorie Sherlock made it happen.

Between 1948–1951, Marjorie Sherlock (BA '27) and President Newton conferred over plans for the first free-standing library building on campus. The president was determined to keep the building on budget, but Marjorie had a different goal. She was going to have the best Library in the country, including a spacious reading room, the latest in technology, marble staircases and floors, and brass railings for the staircases. President Newton drew the line at the brass railings, and he locked horns with Miss Sherlock over the fine finishing touches for the new Library. On November 23, 1956, *The Gateway* published a lavish, photo-filled, two-page spread about Rutherford Library, describing all those fine finishes, down to the country of origin for the lush hardwoods that graced the Library's interior. Marjorie Sherlock's brass railings and the rare hardwoods, stand as a testament to her determination to make Rutherford Library the absolute best.[5] To this day, a member of the custodial staff volunteers her time to polish the brass railings.

The Library's name honours the founder of the University, former Premier Alexander Cameron Rutherford. As chancellor of the University from 1927–1951, he would often invite students to study in his private library at his home on Saskatchewan Drive. It was indeed fitting that the first free-standing library on the campus was named for him.

For all the formality and pomp that accompanied the official opening of the new Library in 1951, there was an incident that upstaged it all. Former Chief Librarian Bruce Peel regales us with his version of one of the U of A's enduring stories of a student prank:

On November 25, 1948, the Honourable John Campbell Bowen, Lieutenant-Governor of Alberta, laid the cornerstone of the new library building. The ceremony had been preceded by 48 hours of anxiety for university officials, as the engraved stone disappeared from the site during the night. When the one-man campus security force failed to locate the missing stone, the President called upon the Faculty of Engineering to manufacture a facsimile out of wooden slabs covered with fast-drying cement. A telephone tip an hour before the ceremony led to the recovery of the cornerstone in the alley behind the Tuck Shop. Years later a solid citizen of Calgary gleefully narrated to the Librarian the inside story of the cornerstone caper.

The chief librarian never revealed the identity of that "solid citizen" of Calgary.[6]

Orientation Week and Model Parliament

THE 1958 *Evergreen and Gold* was a sumptuous volume. Its gold foil cover, deeply etched in contrasting evergreen, bore the bold-font title, *Golden Anniversary 1908–1958*.

The year started off with Frosh Frolics, a series of parties and events to welcome new students, and ended with Colour Night, where sports and involvement awards were given out. At the beginning of the year, the Students' Union organized a Civic Dinner, where they partnered with the administration in hosting various levels of government in order to make the case for support and funding. Big, campus-wide dances were popular— the Pembina Prance, Bar None, the Tri-Service Ball, the Wauneita formal, and the Miss Freshette dance. There were football nights where students cheered on the Eskimos, fashion shows in the Wauneita Lounge, Songfest, and the Med Show. The Engineers took a full week for their event—Queen Week. Treasure Van brought in products from all over the world, with the proceeds going to developing nations. Club 58 and Varsity Varieties entertained the whole campus with their comedy and punchy song-and-dance numbers. *Inherit the Wind* was produced on campus, and Studio Theatre, with its Quonset-hut home now gone, was looking for a permanent stage. Hockey, basketball, football, skiing, and tennis were popular.

Model Parliament was back. Participants included Peter Lougheed (BA '51), Lou Hyndman (BA '56, LLB '59), Joe Clark (BA '60), and Laurence Decore (BA '61). Preston Manning (BA '64) was here at the same time as Clark and Decore. There you have, collectively, from the Liberal and Conservative/Alliance parties, the students who would become mayor, premier, finance minister, prime minister, and leader of the Queen's Opposition. Imagine the debates.

GLIMPSES FROM THE GATEWAY—1950-1959

"6th Annual Mixed Chorus Recital"—January 24, 1950

THIS WAS THE BANNER HEADLINE that opened a decade of *Gateway*s. The Mixed Chorus had 130 members and performed for three nights running under the baton of Professor Richard Eaton. It was his third year with the Mixed Chorus.

"President Rescinds Ban—Council and President Reach Agreement; Declare Truce in Battle of the Press"—February 7, 1950

THE ENGINEERING EDITION of *The Gateway* had been banned by President Newton, who described the paper as lewd, vulgar, and "moronic rubbish."

The Gateway saw it differently. They said the "campus was dead" and students were apathetic. Why was there apathy? *The Gateway* reviewed all the functions that the University had cancelled over the past five years: The engineers' parade ("disturbed lectures"), the annual engineering ball, the engineering edition of *The Gateway*, Varsity Varieties ("not becoming the caliber of university students...").

"We are not children," said *The Gateway*. Administration, they said, had stepped in too fast, and didn't let the students deal with their own affairs. On February 14, the editor and engineers were cleared of charges in a unanimous decision by the Students' Union. *The Gateway* was deemed not obscene by the Student Enforcement Committee, but the editor was found to have demonstrated a lack of discretion regarding the material published. The SU said it would be inclined to reprimand the editor if the administration hadn't already done so.

"The Bookstore Man—Charlie Hosford—Retires. Started With A Single Shelf Of Textbooks In 1912"—October 2, 1952

CHARLIE SERVED AS HEAD of the bookstore for 40 years. His motto was "'we can procure any book published."

The bookstore was in the basement of the Arts Building. It was entirely inadequate for the thousands of students at the University in the 1950s. There were one-way doors, in and out, as an attempt to direct the flow of thousands. Lines were so long that some students set up bridge tables, inching the table forward as the lines progressed. It was an "annual free-for-all of jostling, cursing students scrimmaging for a direct line position in front the University Bookstore entrance."

"Students Demand Free Speech"—February 19, 1953

AT A GENERAL MEETING of the SU, students voted overwhelmingly in favour of asking the Board of Governors to reverse a decision that Dr. James Endicott be banned from speaking at the Political Science Club. Dr. Endicott ended up speaking in a private home on the subject of the ceasefire in the Korean War.

"History of The Gateway"—February 26, 1953

THIS WAS PART FIVE of a history of *The Gateway*. Back in 1928, the writer reported, *Gateway* editor Matt Halton had instituted a series of articles written by alumni living and working around the world. In contrast, the writer lamented, the *Gateway*s of the 1950s only had campus news.

"Burns Elected Union President as 2,100 Voters Swamp Polls"—March 12, 1953

DOUG BURNS, director of Varsity Guest Weekend and president of IFC and the COTC Mess, garnered 74% of the vote. A year later, he would be meeting with Prime Minister Louis St. Laurent to ask the federal government for $5.5 million for 2,500 bursaries. Asking the federal government to finance students was a "first" because education was, by law, a provincial responsibility.

"First PhD Awarded by University"—October 29, 1953

THE FIRST DOCTORATE went to Clayton Person from the department of Plant Science. Unlike spring Convocation in 1953, which was so big it had to be held off campus, the fall ceremony Clayton attended was small, and everyone fit into Convocation Hall.

"Parking Situation Worsens as More Students Drive Cars"—The Gateway, January 27, 1956

The number of cars on campus had quadrupled in the previous six years. "It is estimated," wrote The Gateway, *"that the average person spends just about as much time, or even more, driving the last two blocks to the U—then looking for a parking spot—than he does from his drive from his room thru the city to the campus." By 1958, with only one spot for every three cars, parking was rationed on campus.* (UAA 69-19-361)

"Football Killed—Manitoba Varsity Won't Participate"— November 30, 1954

THE FOOTBALL TEAM was disbanded for the second time in six years. There simply weren't enough teams in the league, and the gate receipts didn't cover the operating costs. And so university students bussed to Clarke Stadium to cheer on the new Edmonton Eskimos. Post-game pep rallies featured the ever-popular Snake Dance, big parades, and rousing pep rallies.

"Artsmen Strike Back With a Vengeance"—October 28, 1955

THE ENGINEERS KIDNAPPED four of the five candidates running for King of the Mardi Gras, the popular dance with fabulous costumes that was sponsored by Arts students. But perhaps the best engineering prank occurred in January 1957, when civil engineers bricked up the front doors of the Med Building during the night. "The reinforced concrete and brick structure bore the message *In Loving Memory.* Three janitors took all morning to break it down with sledge hammers and chisels," the *Gateway* reported.

"5,400 Visitors Pack Campus for 5th Annual Guest Weekend"— February 28, 1956

"CAPACITY CROWDS—parents and high school students from as far away as Taber, Barons, Grand Prairie and Rocky Mountain House flocked to the University from every direction." Varsity Varieties packed in 2,200 people, with 100 students in the production.

Jerry's Barber Shop—1950s

JERRY'S WAS LOCATED IN SUB and offered patrons "Three chairs to serve you—Haircuts styled for you, not merely sold to you—We specialize in brushcuts, boogy-cuts, Collegecuts and Ducktails."

"Former Gateway Editor Matthew Halton Dies"—December 4, 1956

A NATIVE OF PINCHER CREEK, Matt was editor-in-chief of *The Gateway* in 1928. *The Gateway* followed Matt's career for three decades. Matt Halton was Canada's most famous foreign correspondent and commentator during World War II. After graduation, he started his career in journalism at the *Lethbridge Herald*, and later worked for the *Toronto Star Weekly*. He covered the Spanish Civil War, saw war shaping up in Europe, and warned the world about Hitler. Matt joined the CBC in 1945 and was its European correspondent. He covered the summit conference in Geneva in 1955. In May, 1956, he was awarded an honorary degree and addressed Convocation. His son David also had a long career on CBC television as a reporter and commentator, and David's son also works at the CBC.

"CBC and TV Microwave"—March 15, 1957

EXPERT SPEAKER JAMES FINDLAY said that "television should arrive in Edmonton this fall. Perhaps it will reach Edmonton," he added, "in time to allow people to watch the Grey Cup."

"Bear Footballers Growl Again After Nine Years Absence From WCIAU Gridiron Wars"—September 26, 1958

FOOTBALL WAS BACK on the campus. Fifty male students turned out for practice on day one, and Steve Mendryk, the Edmonton Eskimos defensive halfback (and member of the Physical Education faculty) was the coach.

"Registration Exceeds all Previous Years—1,705 here and at Calgary Branch"—September 26, 1958

REGISTRAR ALEX CAIRNS (BA'38, DIP ED'40) reported that 1,705 new students registered at the U of A and down at Calgary.

"Removing a Slum"—September 26, 1958

THE HATED QUONSET HUTS were torn down, and although the department of Drama was temporarily out of a home, everyone was happy to see the "ten-year U of A headache" disappear.

"Jubilee Week Set to Roll October 26"—October 17, 1958

THE WEEK KICKED OFF with a religious service, and the surviving members of the first Convocation gathered for the special ceremony. One of the honorary degree recipients was Max Wershoff, who as an under-graduate student had headed a committee to reform the SU constitution. Max was now the permanent Canadian representative to the United Nations.

"Observatory Move Planned"—October 24, 1958

"HIDDEN AMONGST THE WEEDS behind Varsity Rink is the Observatory." The Observatory now had to be moved, because "the city had grown up around it," and there were too many lights from 113 Street and a nearby parkade for it to function.

"Golden Jubilee Edition—That We May Continue to Grow"— October 28, 1958

HALF THE FRONT PAGE was taken up with a photo of two massive con-struction cranes. The week-long program featured the inaugural Henry Marshall Tory lectures, and early U of A prof Barker Fairley came back to give a public lecture. Laurence Cairns (BA '12) was named as chancellor and remembered the early days of the University when dancing was banned and something called "Conversats" were the order of the day. During a Conversat, when the music began, Cairns told *The Gateway*, "the couples would promenade around the room arm-in-arm, and try desperately to think of something to say to one another. It was...an ordeal."

"Stewart Resigns"—November 14, 1958

ANDREW STEWART, who had won the hearts of students with his first kick-off at a football game, turned in his resignation to the premier and headed off to Ottawa to chair the new Board of Broadcasting Governors. Stewart had been at the U of A for 23 years.

"One Bias Clause Remains"—November 14, 1958

"ONLY ONE of the 12 frats and sororities on the U of A campus retains racial and religious discrimination clauses in its constitution—and even this fraternity, if it had its way, says it would have these clauses stricken from it." Constitutions of most fraternities were handed down by interna-tional or national groups, and they could not change the discriminatory clauses in them. Each fraternity and sorority detailed its membership practices for *The Gateway*.

Within a year, one sorority, Tri Delt, discontinued its chapter—not enough interest. Only 87 of 470 new women students joined sororities in 1959.

"Johns New President"—January 23, 1959

WALTER JOHNS, professor of Classics and the first vice-president at the U of A, was to assume duties as president on February 1. Walter Johns would lead the University through the turbulent 1960s.

"Clark named Editor"—February 3, 1959

JOE CLARK got the unanimous vote of the Students' Council to be *Gateway* editor. Joe had been with *The Gateway* for two terms, was managing editor for a year, and had left "surprisingly few knives in assorted backs."

"Residence Problems—'Living Out' Provides Expensive Expedient—Residence Plans Indefinite—Last Residence Erected in 1915"—February 27, 1959

IN 1959, only 10 per cent of the University's 4,600 students could be accommodated in U of A residences—Athabasca, Assiniboia, Pembina, the Nurses' Residence, and St. Stephen's. The first phase of Lister Hall was still a year away from completion.

MEET ALUMNI FROM THE 1950s[7]

Frank McMahon (BA UNIVERSITY OF OTTAWA '54)

FRANK MCMAHON was the first dean of the University's Faculté Saint-Jean, the only Francophone faculty west of Winnipeg. Following his BA, he earned three degrees from Saint Thomas in Rome, a Master's in Theology from the University of Ottawa, and a PhD from the University of Montréal. Frank was ordained as a Catholic priest in 1963, took a leave in 1971, and left the priesthood in 1973 ("too caught up by the rules," he says.) Frank and his wife Rosemary have raised four children, and nowadays Frank is home by 6 P.M. to cook dinner for his wife, daughter, and grandson Antoine.

Even though Frank McMahon's degrees don't include the designation "University of Alberta," he really *was* a student here. Frank completed his BA in the days when Faculté Saint-Jean was affiliated with the University of Ottawa, and not yet a part of the University of Alberta. He was a high school student at Collège Saint-Jean, and was later on campus in the Faculty of Education. Frank McMahon's story reflects the history of Faculté Saint-Jean and the development of language rights in Alberta.

The Story of Faculté Saint-Jean (Campus Saint-Jean)

FACULTÉ SAINT-JEAN, affectionately known as the "Fac," started life in Pincher Creek as a minor seminary run by Oblate missionary priests. It opened in 1908, the same year the University began classes at the old Duggan Street School in Strathcona. Why did a school that would eventually be a champion of French education spring up in Pincher Creek? It's a story every Francophone Albertan knows: "In the Northwest Territories, Francophones represented the majority of the non-indigenous population and by law, the Territories were bilingual," Frank explains. "But in 1892, as waves of English-speaking immigrants arrived from Ontario, a law was passed prohibiting schools from teaching in the French language." Establishing private schools was the only way the French language and culture could be preserved in Alberta, and a 100-year fight began for Francophone parents to be able to send their children to schools where French was the language of instruction. Schooling in French preserved more than language. It preserved a way of life.

Frank's colleague Ed Aunger quotes part of the 1892 law: "All schools shall be taught in the English language but it shall be permissible for the board of any district to cause a primary course to be taught in the French language."The exception for French language instruction, Aunger notes, "allowed a course in reading and comprehension at the primary level (that is, during the first two years of schooling). However, the prescribed text, a bilingual reader, was—perhaps by design—best suited for teaching English to the French-speaking population. When the course was offered, the allotted time generally varied between a half-hour and a full hour per day, strictly controlled by the local school inspector."[8] In short, there really wasn't any schooling in French. To deal with this problem, as Frank McMahon succinctly puts it, "French private schools sprang up."

« Le premier édifice de Saint-Jean, la "maison blanche" et le couvent des religieuses de la Charité de Notre-Dame d'Évron, » France Levasseur-Ouimet, Connaître l'histoire de Saint-Jean, c'est savoir qui nous sommes. *(PAA OB 5658)*

Juniorat Saint-Jean

IN SAINT-JEAN'S INFANCY down in Pincher Creek, there were just two teachers and three students.[9] "The school was termed a Junioriat," explains Frank, "a minor seminary for boys considering ministry or lay religious life." In 1910, the school moved to downtown Edmonton, and then, in 1911, to Saint-Jean's current location in Strathcona, with a three-storey red brick building, 29 students, and five professors. "For Francophone boys who didn't want to consider religious life, the Jesuits had a college, and the Sisters of the Assumption taught the girls," says Frank. Saint-Jean was bilingual until 1927, when Rome decided that Oblates in Alberta and Saskatchewan would be a French unit and so became officially French. Following that decision, Saint-Jean was still bilingual, but with a strong emphasis on living in French.

This is how historian Dr. France Levasseur-Ouimet has described the beginnings of Faculté Saint-Jean:

La paroisse Saint-Michel de Pincher Creek que le père Albert Lacombe, O.M.I. avait visitée en 1869, promet de devenir populeuse. Dans une letter date du 1er août 1908, le père Grandin, O.M.I. demande au

père Hétu, O.M.I. curé de Pincher Creek, d'accuellir dans son pres-
bytére le père Daridon, O.M.I. et les premiers élèves du Juniorat:
Perry, Mordon et Barney. Ce dernier est le seul qui va persévérer
jusqu'à la prêtrise. C'est le début de Saint-Jean.

Conformément à sa mission, dès sa foundation le Juniorat Saint-
Jean offre les cours classiques à partit des langues latine et grecque.
On ne negligee pas pour autant les mathématiques et les sciences.
On y enseigne aussi le français. Bien que sans affiliation officielle,
Saint-Jean suit déjà le cours de l'Université d'Ottawa.

Bien qu'ils parlent couramment le français, les premiers élèves
sont plutôt Anglophones. Ainsi les cours sont en anglais jusqu'en
1926 alors que les Canadiens-français deviennent plus nombreux.[10]

Collège Saint-Jean

IN 1928, Saint-Jean, without an official affiliation with the University of
Ottawa, nonetheless followed Ottawa's program and also began teaching
the Alberta high-school curriculum. Frank continues the story: "In 1943,
the Jesuits faced a financial impasse and could not continue operating
their private school for Francophone boys. Consequently, the Oblates
decided to take in boys who didn't necessarily want to be priests, and
thus became Collège Saint-Jean." All the while, Saint-Jean was extending
its relationship with the University of Ottawa, increasing enrolment
annually, and affiliating with the University of Ottawa in 1931. Saint-Jean
also expanded its physical facilities, including construction of the elegant
"Maison Blanche" which, sadly, burned to the ground in 1958. Academic
life at Saint-Jean was enriched with choral music, theatre productions,
and all manner of sport—especially hockey. The first student newspaper
was published in 1937, and in 1949, seventy members of the Saint-Jean
student choir travelled to Québec. The tour was a huge success and was
living proof that French culture was surviving in Alberta. As Levasseur-
Ouimet puts it, "Pendant un mois, ils parcourent le Québec pour offrir
des spectacles. Dans les journaux de l'époque, on dira d'eux qu'ils sont
les témoins de la survivance et de la culture françaises en Alberta. Ils
charment, soulèvent un vif enthousiasme et remportent un immense
succès."[11]

Faculté Saint-Jean

IN 1961, Collège Saint-Jean established a School of Education in affiliation with Laval University.[12] In 1963, the education program was delivered in affiliation with the University of Alberta, making Saint-Jean a junior college. In 1966, the Arts program at Saint-Jean was affiliated with the U of A, putting an end to the affiliation with Ottawa. By 1968—a banner year for Francophones in Alberta—the first two years of the U of A BA degree were offered at Saint-Jean, and Saint-Jean was also offering the only bilingual nursing program in the West. In 1970, Collège Saint-Jean transformed into Collège Universitaire Saint-Jean, offering U of A programs. The following year, Saint-Jean's role as a Francophone high school was taken over when École J-H Picard was established in co-operation with the Edmonton Catholic School Board. In 1977, Saint-Jean was awarded full Faculty status, and in 1978 the name "Faculté Saint-Jean" was approved by the Board of Governors.

These changes occurred as the province reviewed its *School Act*, and in 1968 made it legal to teach children in grades 3–12 in French for 50% of the day. In 1971, other "heritage" languages were allowed the same instructional leeway. By 1976, 80 per cent of the day's instruction could be in French, for all grades. In 1990, the Supreme Court of Canada ruled that Alberta must provide for schools "managed and controlled by the French-speaking minority," paving the way for a Francophone school board. [13]

Frank and the "Fac"

IT WAS AGAINST this background that Frank McMahon was born in 1937 in St. Paul de Métis. "Dad was originally from Ireland," says Frank, "where only the highly educated spoke French. My mother was a schoolteacher with roots in Québec. So for both these reasons my father asked to be transferred to a French-speaking town so that his seven children could learn French. My father, by the way, immigrated to Canada in 1911. He was bumped off the *Titanic* and took another ship, and he started out in Canada as a grain elevator agent in Hanna."

Frank and his six siblings all went to university or college, and he explains why. "My parents, especially my father, insisted we go to university. He thought this was the best way of getting ahead, and that anyone with a university education was part of the elite of society. My only brother and I became priests, one of my sisters a nun, three of the girls went to Normal School and then to university for degrees, and one sister went to agricultural college."

In 1950, when Frank was 13 years old, he came to Collège Saint-Jean as a grade 10 high school student. "My older brother left home when I was five years old, and from then on I was surrounded by five sisters," says Frank. "So I loved Collège Saint-Jean because I was around guys, and they were such a fun bunch. We played a lot of sports—everything was organized for you and I liked the structure.

"I boarded at Collège Saint-Jean. It offered the high school curriculum and a three-year Arts degree. Room, board and tuition were $35 a month, and my parents paid. But when I was 16, I got a job with the City Parks and Recreation Department. It was horrible. Basically, you weren't allowed to work. I'd arrive at 8 A.M., but no one worked until 8:45 A.M. Then we'd dig a few fence post holes, have coffee, and dig a little more. The next day, we'd fill the fence post holes we'd dug the day before. We were told that we had to leave work for other people. The worst was laying sod at Clarke Stadium—we planted and unplanted sod ten times. Boring!"

Two Views of History—French and English

"At Collège Saint-Jean, the profs were a small, closely knit, group. It was very different from the U of A. We learned Latin and a little Greek, and there was lots of philosophy and French literature. We put on French plays, like Molière's *Le Bourgeois Gentilhomme*. I had a good memory—I knew everyone's parts—and for every play we put on, there was a full house.

"My best teacher was a priest from Saskatchewan who had been a missionary in Peru, Professor Bugeault. He taught Math and French. He presented things in a dramatic way, and he had an ability to relate to students as a person. Professor Bugeault was also in charge of discipline. He assumed everyone was decent and we were on the honour system. We had to figure out the rules and regulations for ourselves, and he had a good sense of humour about it all. I had only one problem with my teachers. One of them turned out to be my brother. It was awful."

While Frank was attending college, he studied Canadian history through Alberta Education's social studies program in English but also through the University of Ottawa program. This meant Frank was taught both the English and French versions of Canadian history.

Frank warms to the topic. "Take the 1840 *Act of Union*. The English view was that Lord Durham was an emancipator, and that the Act was an enlightened, forward-looking piece of legislation. You have democracy and you are your own masters.

"But the French view of the *Act* was that the British sought assimilation through the *Act*, and wanted us to become English Protestants. The *Act of Union* was seen by Francophones as a retrograde, regressive, piece of legislation that meant, for one thing, we could not keep our language. These differing viewpoints were discussed very openly. There were two visions of the country and not everyone was expected to agree.

"Half the staff at Collège Saint-Jean were from Québec. The Catholic Church in Québec was very restrictive at that time, and its views were stern and severe. So there was no buy-in from the Québecers for the Anglophone point of view. On the other hand, the tenor in the West was democratic and open, so there was discussion of these issues. In addition, the Québecers distrusted the U of A campus, which was seen as anti-Catholic. There was very little interaction with St. Joseph's College. It was a language thing."

To Ottawa, Rome, and Back

AFTER HIGH SCHOOL at the Collège, Frank went to the University of Ottawa for his BA. Then it was off to Rome for three degrees. "Rome was top-level," he says, "very creative and intense. There were 23 different nationalities studying at St. Thomas, and their credentials were incredible—Oxford, the Sorbonne—they were all brilliant. The Director of our house would study all day in preparation for giving us a half-hour talk in the evening. Studying in Rome was liberating. The basic idea was that you could combine Catholicism with intellectual life and have no fear in confronting new ideas. In 1961, when I was at the seminary in Rome, I was asked to go to Cameroon to teach. I did that for a year, and loved it."

Frank returned to Ottawa in 1963 for a Master's in Theology, and then it was back to Edmonton. "I wanted to teach English, and registered at the U of A for the first year of Education so that I could teach in Alberta. But the department where I studied was a decade out of date. They were into behaviourism in psychology, the history of education, and very rules-

Mealtimes at Collège Saint-Jean

FRANK MCMAHON remembers the food at Collège Saint-Jean: "We had baked beans three times a week for breakfast, and they were very good. There was lots of bread and butter, and I paid extra for milk. Aside from breakfast, the only other good meal was lunch on Sundays, simply because it was cooked after 7 A.M. Mass. All the other meals were cooked before Mass, and that meant the food was kept warm for a good hour. By the time it was served, the food was mushy, greasy, and abysmal. I couldn't eat it. I was a chubby kid when I arrived, but quickly lost 15 pounds. Oh yes, there was a potato field on the campus and we'd all go out and dig potatoes for our dinner. After my parents moved to Edmonton in 1953, I lived at home. The food was a lot better!" (PAA OB 6183)

oriented, very puritanical. So to stir things up a bit, I did a paper on *Playboy* magazine, which at the time was on the cutting edge of a new value system. Students were certainly reading *Playboy* and it was a time of fundamental social change when you really needed to relate to your students. My only regret is that the nuns at the Collège, I am sure, found my stash of *Playboys*, without knowing these were my research tools! I also did a presentation for an education class on 13th-century universities and how enlightened they were—just to show the contrast with the stodgy University of Alberta. In my Education classes, I thought, 'I can take these profs on anytime!' I'm grateful for the English classes I was taking, because these were fun courses, with no inhibitions, and lots of good discussion. There were other disciplines that were very advanced, very special at the U of A— Chemistry under Harry Gunning and Ray Lemieux for one. Art McCalla, dean of Agriculture and Forestry and later dean of Graduate Studies, was highly respected at Collège Saint-Jean. He had integrity and he was a real intellectual."

While Frank was studying at the U of A, Ermineskin School at Hobbema was suddenly in need of a Principal. Ermineskin was a residential school run by Roman Catholic priests from Québec. "Their outlook was colonial and paternalistic," says Frank, "and having taught in Africa, where you worked within the native peoples' own culture, I didn't agree with the notion of rejecting aboriginal culture. That just doesn't work. In Africa, local culture and Christianity were integrated. Here, the approach was so destructive. But the word got back to Edmonton that what I was doing was against the gospel, and I was out. I assumed I was being sent back to Africa. I had been very happy there so that wasn't a problem for me."

But all the while, when Frank was in the Faculty of Education and at Hobbema, he was having breakfast, every day, with the man who was the Rector (in effect, the president) of Collège Saint-Jean. His name was Arthur Lacerte. Breakfast conversation focused on the dozens of initiatives that were brewing, some of them concerning the possibility of integrating Collège Saint-Jean with the University of Alberta. Frank was absorbing everything over bacon and eggs.

Rector and Dean of Saint-Jean

IN 1967, Father Lacerte left to take a leadership position in Manitoba, and the administration of Saint-Jean was divided in two, with Father Thibault heading the religious community and Frank as rector of Collège Saint-Jean.[14]

"Being Rector was like having a rope around my neck," Frank says. "I was only 30. I felt enslaved, but flattered. I liked structure, but I didn't like *creating* structures like schedules and timetables. The thought of being Rector was intimidating, but I wasn't capable of saying no, so I got the job. I certainly had some insecurities, but I was definitely not intimidated by the U of A. I was a PR type. And what was needed was not an administrator, but new ways of doing things. And I knew where all the key issues stood from all those breakfasts! It wasn't a time for structure, it was a time for vision and it was imperative to get people on board. There needed to be a vision for the faculty members at Collège Saint-Jean to be brought into. I needed a team, and it worked out well. It was rocky at times. There were many midnight meetings, followed by meetings at 9 A.M."

In the background was Louis Desrochers, a leading member of the Francophone community and chancellor of the University from 1970–1974. "I have a lot of respect for Louis Desrochers," says Frank. "I could count on him."

In his 13 years as head of "the Fac," Frank witnessed fundamental changes as Collège Saint-Jean transformed itself. When Frank took over as Rector in 1967, there were no contracts for the staff and, he adds, "no rules and regulations." Frank steered Collège Saint-Jean through its first "integration" agreement with the U of A in 1970, and led the Collège to full Faculty status in 1977–1978. He was dean in 1974 when the Oblates left Saint-Jean, oversaw the University's purchase of the Collège's land and buildings in 1977, and then guided a strategy that resulted in a 60 per cent increase in undergraduate enrolment.

Frank stepped down as dean in 1980. "By then," he says, "the institution had a sense of direction and everyone was pretty much on board." Frank went back to school. In 1986, he got his PhD from the University of Montréal.

"We are comfortable being part of the U of A," says Frank. "In our past, we were first a minor seminary, and that denominational identity was lost over time, as was the case for other institutions. Then we became an institution defined by cultural and linguistic factors. I strongly believe that these are enhanced by our commitment to scholarship as part of the University of Alberta."

Frank looks back to his undergraduate days at "the Fac." "There were nine of us who graduated in 1954 with our BA degrees," he remembers. "Now we are five. We've all stayed close to one another for the last 50 years, and will remain close friends for the next 50."

Joyce Mattson Cutts (BPE '54)

IN 2004, Joyce Cutts was inducted into the University of Alberta Sports Wall of Fame. During her university days, she played for the Pandas Basketball team (1950–1953) and the Pandas Volleyball team (1953–1954). Joyce also played intramural badminton, swimming and track and field.

Fasten your seat belts to hear what Joyce did *after* university.

Joyce was a member of Canada's senior women's slow pitch softball team that won the gold medal at the 2002 Michigan Senior Olympics, and was on the silver medal team the year after that in Richmond, Virginia. She won the Canadian Senior Doubles Championship three times in her age category. In 2002, 2003, and 2004, Joyce represented Canada in the Over 70 World Tennis Championship in both singles and doubles, and made it to the round of 16 in all three years. In 2003, she was the Ontario Singles Champion. She's also won many 10-km road races in Ontario and Québec in her age category.

There's more. Joyce was Québec's senior "C" badminton champion, and in 2000, 2001, 2003, and 2004 she was Niagara District's Senior Woman golf champion. In 2002, in her hometown of Welland, Ontario, she was the Master's Athlete of the year.

Why University?

JOYCE WAS BORN in Saskatchewan, raised on a farm, and then moved to Medicine Hat during World War II. "I was the first in my family of 11 children to go to university," says Joyce, "and my mom always encouraged us to go on to higher learning. In the 1950s it seemed as though all young women were nurses, teachers or stenographers. My two older sisters had chosen Nursing and I did not want that—I wanted to be a teacher. I was always a sports enthusiast, and when I found out that the first year of a Physical Education degree was being offered, I chose that route."

In her first year, Joyce roomed near campus with a couple who both taught at the University.

"I had a room in their basement," remembers Joyce, "and had a small stove where I could cook my own meals. I helped out around the house to help pay for my room, and also did chores like canning pears, which I had done a lot of on the farm. Things were going fine. Then one day early in the fall, I got a phone call from the wife, who was on her way home and wanted to get a start on dinner. She told me to turn the heat on under the vegetables, which were already on the stove. I did as she asked and went down to my room in the basement. Well, she didn't get home in time and the vegetables burnt to the bottom of the pans. Later that evening she came downstairs with the pots and a scouring pad for me to clean them. I did not say a word, but I was terribly hurt. I felt I had done nothing wrong.

"At the time, Mamie Simpson was the dean of women, and she invited everyone in first year for tea. I received an invitation, and when I arrived at her place, she asked me how things were going. I burst into tears and, between great sobs, told her the story. I asked her if I could get out of the arrangement and she said I could. I packed my things and went to live with a Home Ec student from Grand Prairie who knew my sister's best friend. The rent was $35 per month and I got help from my mom. I also worked part time in the equipment room at one of the students' dorms and handed out towels. So financially I just got by.

"If I had it to do over again, I would stay in residence that first year. It would have helped me to have studied with other students, and I don't think I would have been that homesick. Believe me, I felt very homesick that first year. Every time I got a letter from my mom I would burst into tears. I often went to Sunday dinners at the Women's Residence, and that was nice because I would sit with my Phys Ed classmates, Ev Hague, Billie Niblock and Pat Hardy. I'm still in touch with Billie."

First Impressions

"My first day of classes was a bit frightening," remembers Joyce. "We were given a list of books to buy and I didn't have enough money for all of them. Taking notes was hard too. We simply weren't used to that. My

While others at the U of A had held the title dean of women, Maimie Simpson was the first to carry that title on approval by the Board of Governors. Students found her warm and inspiring. She was their confidante, solved innumerable problems and taught thousands of freshmen how to behave in polite company.
(UAA 73–161)

Chemistry class was held in a large amphitheatre, and the professor never did learn any of our names. We had a lab once a week, and I was pretty much lost there too. My friends who lived at fraternity houses got help by having their friends' class notes from the previous year, or copies of the Zoology labs. I didn't have that advantage, and it was harder for me.

"Because I lived off campus, I really had to get up early. In Phys Ed we had classes six days a week. Every afternoon was a science lab or a Phys Ed activity—dancing, basketball, volleyball, badminton, and swimming, to name just a few. If you were on a team, there were also practices. So I was very busy. In the winter it was cold, but we weren't allowed to wear slacks in class. To keep warm, we wore knitted overstockings. Walking down to the Education Building, now Corbett Hall, was also a chore because we only had ten minutes to switch classes, or we would be late.

"I did go to church at Highlands United Church Sunday evenings, mostly because the minister, Reverend Frank Samis, and his wife Eunice, were from Medicine Hat and I'd been their babysitter. It eased the home-sickness. It's been over 50 years, but I still stay in touch with Eunice.

"I should add that being in Phys Ed gave me a great group of friends. We were all pretty close because we took so many classes together. And there was a hidden advantage—in the mixed dance classes we got to dance with the boys in our year. It was great! I still remember my favourite dancers—Don MacIntosh and Don Newton.

"We all knew where the Tuck Shop was. I know students who used to skip their labs and go there and learn how to play bridge. It was a great social hang out, and people also met at the Hot Caf, which was the university cafeteria located over where CAB is today.

"There weren't many buildings on campus—less than a dozen. There were the women's and men's residences (Athabasca, Assiniboia and Pembina), the Old Arts Building and the Med (today's Dentistry/Pharmacy Centre), the huge Drill Hall where we had exams, and the Education Building that's now Corbett. Rutherford Library had recently been built, and when I wasn't studying in my boarding house, that's where I did my homework. The Agriculture Building was built during my four years at the U of A. I remember that building vividly because the front doors were made of glass, and one student unknowingly walked right through them."

Campus Memories

"ONE OF MY BEST MEMORIES concerns the University Open House, where the outside world was invited to campus to see first-hand the different aspects of each Faculty. Pat Austin, our dance teacher, volunteered her mixed dance class to perform. Well, we practised the Mexican Hat Dance, the tango, and some others dances, and then performed them one evening in the big Drill Hall. I was so into the rhythm or whatever, that many people commented on my interpretation of the Mexican Hat Dance. And it just felt so good! In fact, there was this one professor—I didn't even take courses from him—who came up to me one day and mentioned my dancing. This professor would sometimes sit with Elaine Fildes in the Cafeteria. We all felt that he was sweet on her. Well, I had a bit of a crush on him too. The day I left the campus, I went to his office to say good bye. I was quite emotional. I think he somehow knew that some students developed feelings for their teachers. He was very nice in his farewell and wished me success in my teaching."

Joyce worked hard to finance her education. "For my first year," she remembers, "I had $225 saved from buying war saving stamps. My sister Irene and I worked in the Medicine Hat Greenhouses for five years (from the age of 12 to 17), and I saved every bit I could. To finance my second year, I worked in a lab at the Suffield Experimental Station doing things like washing test tubes, injecting mice, and typing up my professor's summer research. Suffield in those days was doing classified research, and I remember the labs were working on animals. I contributed some feral cats, which the lab paid $5 each for. Looking back on that, I'm not proud of the cat business. One got loose in the bus one morning on the way to work, and no wonder. It was probably scared half to death.

"The next summer I worked at a glass factory in Redcliff, Alberta and earned $200 a month. By at the end of the summer I had $800—just enough to pay tuition and get by for the year. I stayed with a dentist and his wife right near the High Level Bridge, and baby-sat so many nights a week. I always made my own lunch and then ate at the Cafeteria for supper with my boyfriend.

"For my last year at University, I got a teaching job at Elkwater, which was only 40 miles from the Hat. I taught during May and June, and really enjoyed the rural kids. I stayed with a family during the week and then went home to my parents' place in the Hat every weekend. I remember teaching the kids lots of track and field activities and playing baseball with them at recess and at noon. I did exactly what my rural teachers did with me when I was attending a one-room school back in Saskatchewan.

"Then in July I went up to Edmonton to direct a summer camp for under-privileged children sponsored by the Imperial Order of the Daughters of the Empire (IODE). The children were chosen by the school nurses. As a kid, I had attended United Church camps every summer and I organized similar activities for these kids. They loved it, and many did not want to go home after the two weeks. I really connected with the children. Most of them were newly-arrived immigrants who had never had the chance to attend a summer camp. Each child was given a small personal bag with their own toothpaste, soap, etc. and when I went around to see how they were settling into to their cabins, I found them all eating their toothpaste. These kids had never had flavoured toothpaste before. They were used to salt or baking soda.

"I also had some financial help from one of my Phys Ed Teachers, Miss Alberta Hastie. I helped her make up and then mark first-year health exams. I would stay late at Christmas and help her finish the marking, and then go home for Christmas. It meant extra money for me and that was impor-tant. Miss Hastie also told me that there was an essay contest on the subject of TB, and so I got the application for the competition, did lots of research, I won the prize that year—which also gave me some extra money."

Favourite Teachers—Skills for Your Whole Life

"I LIKED MY ZOOLOGY PROFESSOR," says Joyce. "He was well-known and funny in that he often had a nail instead of a button to keep his lab coat on. There was a rattlesnake in the lab, and he would come down to Medicine Hat in the summer to catch them—Medicine Hat was quite famous for its rattlesnakes.

"I liked all my Phys Ed Teachers and couldn't name just one favourite. I really enjoyed the dance classes that Pat Austin taught, and she was a very good volleyball coach as well. My volleyball skills stayed with me for a long time and later in life, I competed both in California and in Montréal.

"Elaine Fildes was also a very good teacher and great basketball coach. I was very impressed with her tennis skills, and that's one reason I continued playing tennis so much after leaving University. I've won three national doubles titles as a senior, I was the Ontario champion in singles two years ago, and Tennis Canada has asked me to play in international tournaments. But the best thing about playing tennis all those years is very personal—I met the love of my life, Robb Cutts, on the tennis court.

"I also thought highly of my Anatomy teacher, Herb McLachlin, and was very fond of him. I have remembered more of that course than most because it helps me to understand how the body works. So that's the kind of effect good teachers can have on a student—you learn skills that stay with you for life."

Convocation and Life Afterwards

"JUST GETTING THROUGH university was a big challenge for me. I often had dreams that I hadn't passed, but when I would wake up, I knew that I had in fact graduated. Convocation was very special. My mom couldn't afford to come to Edmonton to see me graduate, but I knew she was proud.

"I believe that each student should be responsible for their own education, at least to some degree. It certainly meant a lot to me knowing I had done this myself. I should add I did have some help. Our family lost a brother, Vernon Mattson, in the war. Mom received an extra amount of money from the government because Vernon died in the line of duty. Mom gave me that money, and I kept track of it. When I started teaching, I paid it back in order to help the next sister, Enid, and then Eunice Mattson get their education. They in turn helped the next one, and so on down the line. As the first in my family of 11 to go to university, it was important to me to see the others have the same opportunity.

"My time at U of A certainly changed me. I became aware that there was so much to learn that later in life I spent summers reading all sorts of things. Having taken so many science courses at university—Chemistry, Zoology, Physiology—I really liked teaching science at the grade 7 and 8 level. I organized science fairs during my last ten years of teaching. My students were good at it, and my principal sent our school's winner and me to London, Ontario to attend a national science fair. That was rewarding."

After leaving university, Joyce taught school—elementary, junior high and high school—in Alberta, Ontario and Québec. She coached the MacDonald College volleyball team in the early 1960s, and in 1974 she coached the boy's team from John Rennie High School to the Montréal City and District Championship. After her two children both had reached school age, she began a 20-year career teaching full-time, and coached every sport at the elementary and high school levels.

In 1972, Joyce was awarded a sabbatical on the basis of her excellent teaching in order to study at the University of London in England. Newly separated and with her teenagers Kathryn and Byron in tow, Joyce was off the other side of the world to be a full-time student once again. "That year was scary," she says. "I was over there on my own. I hadn't studied for 20-some years, but I had a good professor and by January I was doing really well." Joyce received a Graduate Diploma in the education of physically handicapped children.

Today, Joyce splits her time between her home in Welland, Ontario, and her winter getaway in Daytona, Florida, where she plays tennis with a local team four or five times a week. "On the side," she says, "I play golf and duplicate bridge to stay sharp." In 2004, she was in Philadelphia participating in the world tennis competition. Joyce ranks 31st in the world.

Joyce has some advice for students today. "Stay in residence at least the first year. You'll make friends easier and faster than if you lived off campus, and you'll also be able to share study times and get help with certain assignments. Participate in all kinds of physical activities, stay close to your family, and try to support yourself to some degree. Don't be afraid of taking small-paying jobs during the summer—they all help you in later life. And all through your life, make sure your mind is active. Stay informed and keep learning."

Joyce likes to note that she has been the same weight for 50 years and today, in her 70s, as a competitive tennis player on the international scene, she cautions as follows: "Take it easy on the alcohol, no smoking, and eat healthy food!"

Grant Fairley (BCOMM '56)

In 1954, this freshman from Calgary lived in Room 123, Athabasca Hall, at a time when Athabasca was a residence for male students. His lone window overlooked a parking lot. He wasn't sure what he wanted to do in his life. Today, this alumnus has a corner office in downtown Edmonton's Bell Tower, with a 260° view. How high up is the office? If you get too close to the window and look down, you might just break into a sweat. And what did he end up doing? This alumnus started off in insurance and then founded, with partner Dennis Erker, a company that became one of western Canada's largest independent life insurance and employee benefit brokerage firms.

His name is Grant Fairley, and he's a big bear of a man with definite opinions and a golden heart. But in 1954, as a senior at Western Canada High School in Calgary, he was a self-described "runt." Here's how Grant

An aerial shot of the University in the 1950s showing the expansive quad where Grant Fairley and his fellow residents of Athabasca Hall played football. By the end of the 1950s, the quad would be penned in on both sides, with the Administration Building to the south, and the V-wing and Avadh Bhatia Physics Laboratory to the north.

(University of Alberta Alumni Affairs)

Fairley made his way to the U of A, grew up, and then made it to the top of the heap in the business world.

"Both my parents were Scottish," says Grant, "and both families immigrated to Canada because of work opportunities. My mother's dad came over as a carpenter for the CNR, and my dad's father was a butcher. There was a shortage of butchers in Calgary, and so the geographical match was made. My dad was bright and streetwise," says Grant, "but he only finished grade 6 before following in his father's footsteps to become a butcher. And for me? There was no question about it. My dad made sure I went to University. He thought there were better options for me than the food trade, and he was determined that I would get the education he didn't have." Grant's friends will tell you that for all his success in the business world, Grant is still, at heart, the son of a butcher. If you're lucky enough to be a dinner guest at Grant's when he's serving prime rib, you're in for a real treat.

Face-Off with Polio

"IN 1943, when I was 8," remembers Grant, "a polio epidemic swept Alberta. I was one of the unlucky ones. My throat was paralysed. But I was also lucky in another sense, because no one before me had ever survived this kind of paralysis. And I did survive it. I even got through school, and I credit my grade 3 teacher, Mrs. Watts, for that," says Grant. "She would let me fall asleep in class, but I kept up with the work, and made it into grade 4.

"I was an aggressive kid and I loved hockey. But there was no more of that after the polio. Maybe it's one reason I'm such a hockey fan today.

"Polio stunted my growth," says Grant, "and I was a little guy for many years. I never grew—from age 8 until well into high school—I just never grew. I was a very sports-oriented kid, and the aftermath of polio was tough to live with. I'd be in a locker room with guys my own age, but I was a boy amongst men. I was only 4' 11" and 95 pounds. I was too little to play on the teams I loved, but I was the water boy and the bat boy, that kind of thing."

There is one person who changed Grant's life, and the two of them recently re-connected after a gap of 50 years. "There was this Phys Ed teacher and coach," says Grant. "His name was Johnny Mayell. He had served in World War II and was a retired airman. I was the water boy, but Johnny called me the 'assistant manager,' and told me that what I was doing was important. And he gave me a nickname. I was 'Sparky.' This one teacher and coach had a more profound impact on me than anyone else in my life. His message to me was, 'You're not just a little boy.' At a low point in my life, when I was insecure, this man made me feel that I mattered. I felt I was contributing, that I was a part of the team. And then finally, by the end of high school, I started to grow. I got taller, I put on weight, and I started to look, physically, like my chronological age. By the time I finished grade 12, I was on a provincial championship football team. But it's the lessons I learned from Johnny Mayell, and not the high school sports honours, that have stuck with me my whole life."

In 2003, Grant went back to his high school reunion. Hundreds of people attended, and there was a huge bulletin board where you could post the name of someone you wanted to find. Both their names were up there— Grant was looking for Johnny Mayell, and Johnny was trying to find Sparky.

University at Last

"IT'S FUNNY," says Grant. "I got good grades in high school, but all I can remember is the one subject that was so tough. English. I had to take a supplemental. Despite that, I got into the U of A, and *that's* where I wanted to go. The University of Calgary was in its infancy. In the year I graduated from high school—1954—Calgary was just offering, for the first time, Commerce courses.

"My grades were good at university, but I continued to worry about my English mark. I was afraid I'd get put on probation or, as we put it then, bounced out. For one year, I was on Students' Council as the Commerce rep. My friend Karl Reardon and I decided to run a fundraiser, so we planned a dance. We called it the Probation Bounce, and on the night of the dance, we dressed up as a cop and a convict. The dance was a big hit with students all across campus. Maybe we weren't the only ones worried about getting put on academic probation.

"Tuition for my three-year degree," Grant remembers, "was about $500 a year. My dad said, 'I'll pay it,' and I know he was proud to do that. I ended up as the one responsible for earning spending money. So I worked part-time at the Bay and in the summer, later I drove buses for Brewster Transport in Banff. There was a minimum salary, low-cost accommodation, and tips. The real money was in the poker games with the other bus drivers. I paid my own tuition in my second year from poker winnings.

"But after I started earning my own money—my own salary—I stopped playing poker. I couldn't bear to lose money that was so hard to earn! And I'll tell you this: if you ever have a second thought about gambling hard-earned dollars, don't do it."

Grant says that he had no great ambition as a freshman, and wasn't sure what he wanted to do. His dad had pushed him to go to University, and Grant wasn't going to disappoint his parents by failing. "I wouldn't want to face *those* consequences.

"All my classes at the U of A," Grant remembers, "were in one building—Arts. I don't remember much about Freshman Orientation Week except that we wore frosh caps—beanies—and the fraternity rush was on. It was stressful. I had friends from Calgary in Delta Upsilon (DU), and friends in Phi Delta Theta (Phi Delt). I had to choose, and I chose DU. That meant in my second year at the U of A, I would be moving to the frat house, and I would have a DU 'older brother,' Bill Winspear. But in my first year, in 1954, I lived in Athabasca Hall when it was a men's residence."

Athabasca Hall

ATHABASCA HALL, now home to the Department of Computing Science, was the first building on the University of Alberta campus. Flanking Athabasca Hall in 1954 were the two other residences—Assiniboia (for men) and Pembina (for women). Grant's room on the first floor of Athabasca Hall is, today, a mail room. "It was a small room with a single bed and a desk, and I did most of my studying there," Grant says. "I learned a lot of economics and accounting at that little desk. There were common wash-rooms down the hall and a lounge with a fireplace on the main floor. Don Anderson, a brilliant engineering student, organized crib games for his buddies in Athabasca," remembers Grant, "and there was lots of sports activity. There were enough male students in the residences to make up good teams, and we played football out in the fields behind Athabasca, or in the quad. We played against fraternities, and we played rough. It was great.

"The dining room was behind the lounge," says Grant, "and we had all our meals there. I ate every meal at the same table for the entire year. We had communal meals at set times, and these were in the dining hall that was attached to the back of Athabasca Hall, where part of today's Computing Science Department is. We always said the University Grace first, although I don't remember it. But I *do* remember the roast beef and gravy. And I will never forget Bruce Kimura.

"Bruce was the senior student in charge of our table, and he was always seated at the head of the table, with the rest of us seated along the sides. Bruce was responsible to Reg Lister for our behaviour in the dining hall, and Reg was responsible to the provost, Al Ryan. We were always well-behaved. Bruce was a really big guy, and he was older than most of us. No one got out of line when Bruce was around. And I mean Bruce was *really* in charge. The way it worked was that all the food was served on big platters, and each platter always went to Bruce first. Especially at dinner, there would be all these hungry guys checking out the platter of meat, but Bruce would just hold onto that platter, slowly examining it. Then he would look us all in the eye, one by one, and spear the biggest piece of meat. No one ever questioned Bruce's right to the biggest chop."

Sunday Dinner with the Tweddles

"THERE WAS ONLY ONE MEAL that was never served in Athabasca Hall— Sunday dinner. It was the cook's night off. One of my classmates sort of adopted me," Grant remembers, "and I had Sunday dinner at his house for three years. His name is John Tweddle, and we are friends to this day. John lived over where the High Street shopping centre is located, near the old Bruce's Confectionery, which has since been moved down to Fort Edmonton Park. John's mother, Eleanore Griffith Tweddle, was—like me—from Calgary, and she was a 1930 U of A grad from Home Economics. I guess Mrs. Tweddle knew what it was like to be away from home, and she sure fed me well. Even after 50 years, I remember her Sunday night dinners—roast beef, potatoes and lots of gravy."

Grant made lifelong friends at the U of A, many of them from his small commerce class of some 35 students. "About a third of that class turned out to be real leaders in the business world," says Grant. "John Tweddle became a partner in Price, Waterhouse, Coopers. And not only did he feed me Sunday dinners, he tutored me in accounting when we were students. I could learn quicker from people than I could from a book, and John was great with numbers.

"Dick Haskayne was another classmate. Dick was from Gleichen and his father, like mine, was a butcher. Dick became chairman of the Board of TransCanada Pipelines, and the University of Calgary's School of Business is named after him. Then there was Ross Walker," adds Grant. "He became chairman and CEO of KPMG Canada and then International Executive Partner of KPMG International. The 1956 commerce class was an incredibly competitive group. But there was a woman who outshone all these men. She was the Commerce Gold Medal winner in 1956—Elaine Penner."

One of Grant's friends in the Athabasca residence was Gordon Morrison, one of the first U of A grads to make an Olympic team. "Gordie was on the 1952 Olympic ski team, which competed in Oslo, Norway, and he was an incredible downhill and giant slalom skier. Gordie coached a nine-member university ski team in 1954 and took us to an inter-varsity meet in Banff. One of our downhill skiers was John Holland. We called him 'John, John, the Atom Bomb.' I'd done a little cross country skiing around Calgary, so Gordie got me on the team, and then there was this guy named Eddie Michaud from Québec. Eddie was going to be one of our ski jumpers. You know ski jumping, right? That's the event that takes place on a huge hill with a launch ramp—394 feet high. Well, there we were up at Mount Norquay where there were all these European competitors. Our team was ready for the jump but we couldn't find Eddie. We finally found him *under* the ski jump. Eddie said he was watching the action and 'picking out a jumping style.' But he looked pretty scared to us. I don't think Eddie had ever really jumped before. And you know, when it came his time to do it, he wasn't all that bad! As for me, I think I came in second to last. I ran into a tree. But it was our coach, Gordie Morrison, who anchored that team. Gordie was one of the finest people I ever knew. A leader and an outstanding athlete. Smart—got a PhD in Engineering and formed a firm with Max Berretti. He was killed in 1972 at Mount Chetwynd along with three other mining engineers from Australia, and the crew, in an airplane accident. A great loss."

Delta Upsilon

AFTER GRANT'S FIRST YEAR in Athabasca, he moved to the DU house—11153 Saskatchewan Drive. It was, in fact, the former home of Premier Alexander Cameron Rutherford. Today, the home is a carefully-restored

From 1940 (when Mrs. Rutherford died) to 1969, Premier Rutherford's mansion on Saskatchewan Drive was home to the Delta Upsilon fraternity. (UAA 69-19-607)

historic site, but back in 1955, the house was showing its age, and made a great fraternity hang-out.

"There was one private bedroom on the main floor," Grant recalls, "and a few bedrooms on the second floor. We studied in these rooms, and stored our clothes here. All DU residents, however, slept on the third floor, in 'the pit.' There were bunk beds, no windows, and two holes in the wall. Snow blew in during the winter. There was this one guy who would get so cold, we'd find him downstairs in the morning—sitting, all scrunched up, on top of the hot water radiator. He looked just like an owl.

"All our meals were at the DU house, and dinner was a sit-down affair. One of our housemothers was Mrs. Kieffer. She lived in the house and made all our meals except for Sunday dinner. The Tuck Shop was right down the street and there were students like Norm Macintosh who just about lived there, playing bridge. The Tuck Shop was great fun. You'd always meet neat people.

"We had a lot of fun with the constant inter-fraternity rivalry," says Grant. "One time a buddy and I saw a porcupine up in a tree by the Arts

Building. We decided to capture it and release it later on during a Phi Delt formal dinner. We got the porcupine into a garbage can, but the Phi Delt dance was a ways off and we didn't think a garbage can was a very humane place to keep the porcupine. So we blocked off the bar at the DU house—we had a beautiful wooden bar, very nice—and penned in the porcupine. Well, the porcupine ate right through the bar. We got into deep trouble. But we still carried through with our plan and released the porcupine in the Phi Delt House, in their shower. Believe me, they were pretty surprised. I have no idea how they got the porcupine out of the shower, and there was some talk afterwards about calling the Humane Society, but it never happened."

Favourite Professor, Favourite Dean

GRANT IS QUICK TO RECALL his favourite professor. It was J.D. Campbell in accounting. "He was loud and demonstrative, and would stomp around the room while teaching us accounting. I never forgot what he taught me. He kept my attention. The next year, I had a prof who was the opposite—quiet. Too quiet for me. He'd put you to sleep.

"Then there was the dean, Dr. Lindberg. He came from the USA and was only at the U of A for a year. His philosophy was that to maximize your career, you should be making five or six major job changes during your career. That was a very different approach back in the 1950s.

"Dean Lindberg would have private one-on-one meetings with each student. He'd look at your grades and give you a frank assessment. He certainly had *me* pegged! 'Grant,' he said, 'You're in the top half of your class, but you're just doing enough to get by. You have more intelligence than you're using.'"

Graduation and Life Afterwards

GRANT REMEMBERS his graduation present with a big grin. "When I graduated in 1956, my parents were so proud. My dad gave me a car—a 1950 Chev. He paid $800 for it. I was very grateful to my parents, in part because I'd had quite a superior attitude in my first year—I'd felt like such a Big Man on Campus when I was a freshman, and I know I communicated that attitude to my parents. Later in life, when I was speaking all over the USA on insurance matters, I flew them to Reno, where I was to give a speech. It was quite a moment to see them in the audience." No doubt, there was a touch of pride in them, too.

Right after graduation, Grant was lined up for a training program with Peat Marwick & Mitchell (now KPMG) to become a chartered accountant, but his brother-in-law steered him into the insurance business. "Looking back," Grant says, "I'd say it was a perfect match. I'm a people person and like to develop relationships, and that's what insurance marketing is all about. It was a struggle for a while, but by 1963 I was in the top 1 per cent in the world. In 1979, I was president of The Forum, an international organization with only the top couple hundred insurance agents as members. I was the only non-American to be president. In 1981, I became president of the Life Underwriters' Association of Canada, an Association of 18,000 members at the time.

"And you know the best lesson from my early days in business? It came from my university friend John Tweddle. I went to him early in my career to sell him an insurance policy. This is what he told me: 'Grant, you'll get my business when you deserve it.' That woke me up, and I worked hard. And eventually, I did get John's business."

Grant's career flourished. He founded his own company, which has evolved into today's FE Advisory Group, a multi-service financial advising firm with offices in Edmonton and Calgary, and affiliates throughout Canada and the United States. Grant remembers one of his first staff members, Joan Shergold.

"Early on, when my business first took off," says Grant, "there was a woman who worked with me named Joan Shergold. She would quietly say, 'Mr. Fairley, I have some things to go through with you.' And she would methodically run through files, records, commissions, RRSPs and the like. And I would think, boy, am I ever organized. And then Joan was killed in a car crash. I rapidly discovered just what a good manager Joan had been. She made me aware how important it is to know your strengths— and weaknesses—and to know and value the strengths of those around you. I later hired a woman named Cathy Vetsch and told her, 'Your job is to manage me.' She's now my partner in the company."

Today, Grant divides his time between homes in Scottsdale and Edmonton, and the phone never stops ringing at either place. Either it's his kids or grandchildren, or one of dozens of friends or business associates from around the world. Grant golfs, fishes, is fanatical about hockey, football, and fine wine, and has developed a love of the arts. Grant always finds time for community involvements. He's served on the University Hospital Board, and has chaired the NAIT Foundation Board. And when Grant is in Edmonton, he's at the office every day, mentoring the new partners and "opening doors" for them.

Grant has a little advice for today's students. "It's simple," Grant says. "Enjoy life."

Myer Horowitz (MED '59, LLD HON '90, ORDER OF CANADA)

TODAY, there is a theatre on campus named after him, but back in 1958, he lost out in the competition to be funded as a Kellogg fellow in the new graduate program in educational administration that was started in 1957. He came to the U of A anyway. Twenty years after receiving his MEd, Myer Horowitz was named president of the University of Alberta.

A Nine-Month Wonder

MYER DESCRIBES HIMSELF AS a "nine-month wonder."

"In 1949 I graduated from high school in Montréal," Myer explains, "which meant you graduated in grade 11. Two years later I went on to do teacher training for the required nine months—so I was one of those 'nine-month wonders,' out there teaching at age 19. My wife Barbara, on the other hand, who was also a teacher, had already finished her university degree. One of my biggest goals in life, ever, was to earn my BA, and I did that, over several years, at night. I finished in 1956, the year Barbara and I were married."

Soon after getting his BA, and shortly before they were married, Myer and Barbara were assigned to teach in the same school. Driving home one day, Barbara asked Myer what he thought about the notice that had been circulated in school that day. The notice touted Canada's first-ever graduate program in Educational Administration, to be offered at the U of A.

"I really hadn't looked at this notice," recalls Myer, "but when I did, my question was 'where's the University of Alberta?' Now I HAD taught geography, so I knew the U of A must be in one of the big urban centres, either in Calgary or Edmonton." Myer says that there's only one thing

that saves him a little face. A few years later, when his department chair recommended that Myer do a PhD at Stanford, Myer's first question was "where's Stanford?"

The new graduate program in "Ed Admin" was funded by the Kellogg Foundation, on the condition that the U of A share in the initial cost and eventually take over the program. It's been thought that Myer was one of the Kellogg Fellows, but that isn't so, on two counts. First, in typical graduate student fashion, Myer was more than just a student. Myer was, for instance, helping to support his family. "I didn't come in the first year the program was offered," he explains, "because we needed to save enough money to help my mother with the mortgage during the year I'd be at the U of A and not earning a salary.

"And I was never a Kellogg Fellow. I wasn't accepted." And so the big question was how to fund, personally, the year's study. Barbara got a leave of absence for a year from her teaching job," Myer says, "and the Edmonton Public School Board gave her a position for the year I would be working on my Master's.

"The Ed Admin department couldn't have been nicer," says Myer. "They told me they had some money to pay our travel expenses out to Edmonton, and then they decided that there should be a departmental newsletter, and I would be the paid editor. Those were only two ways they helped us financially. They really stretched the balloon for me."

The department chair was Dr. Art Reeves, a man whose entire family became close friends with the Horowitzes. "When I arrived in Edmonton," Myer remembers, "Art wanted to talk to me about why I hadn't been selected as a Kellogg Fellow. None of the other students knew I wasn't a Fellow, but the faculty and administrators did. I was the oddball.

"Art told me that, naturally, they had communicated with the employers of the Kellogg applicants, and in my case, they called the Protestant School Board of Greater Montréal. I knew the man they talked to—he was a very thoughtful, kind person. What this man told Art Reeves is this: 'There are no Jewish principals here yet, and so I have to tell you that I am not sure Myer would become an administrator under this board'—Art told me that perhaps they took that comment more seriously than they should have. I was very uncomfortable because he didn't have to tell me anything—they'd already been very kind. I may not have been a Kellogg Fellow, but I received absolutely superb treatment at the U of A."

The Horowitzes arrived in August and quickly found a place to live. "Barbara and I rented a white clapboard house where the Telus Centre now stands. The house where we lived was a so-called 'wedding cake' house. That's exactly what it looked like—a wedding cake. The owner had chopped it into suites, and our suite had once been the living room. This meant we were the only tenants in the house with a front entrance, and to top it off, we had a verandah. The cost? It was $65 a month with everything included. And I still remember the address—11107 88 Avenue."

There was a minor disagreement, however. Myer's wife, Barbara, thought the suite needed paint. And that sent Myer off on an interesting pathway.

A Double Life

"I WASN'T INTERESTED in painting the suite," says Myer, "and you have to know that in those days, classes at the University didn't start until the end of September. Barbara was teaching by the beginning of that month, and so I looked around campus for an 'office overload' job. I'd gone through a commercial program in high school and could type, and I had also been a junior accountant between high school and teachers' college."

Some unknown person on campus directed Myer to the personnel office. "In those days," Myer recalls, "the personnel office consisted of a man named

Murray Cook and a half-time secretary. I was ushered right in—no waiting. That was definitely a sign of the times. Mr. Cook asked me a few questions, and then came back in with the chief accountant, Murray Rousell, who fired some technical questions at me."

And that was it. Mr. Rousell asked Myer when he could start. Myer's response? "I'm not doing anything today." And so began Myer's working career as a part-time non-academic staff member.

"I worked full-time for three weeks until my classes started, full-time in the spring, and then part-time in July and August since my two classes were both in the same half day. "It was a very important part of my year," Myer says. "Every dollar was important to us, of course, but I didn't really have to take this job. It was something I really wanted to do. There were many developments over the years that were anchored in my work in the Bursar's Office."

One day a new machine appeared in the Bursar's Office. "It was a kind of duplicating machine," explains Myer. "Not the smelly alcohol kind, and not a Gestettner with the purple ink. This machine took a photograph of a printed page. I was allowed to use it to run off a copy of my thesis. This meant my typist didn't have to use carbon paper to make second and third copies. Naturally, I paid for the use of the materials."

It was revolutionary! Myer had to get permission from the dean of Graduate Studies to have his thesis duplicated on a Xerox machine. "I told Dean McCalla about my double life as a graduate student and non-academic staff member, and about my access to the Xerox machine. He had only one question for me about duplicating my thesis. "Will it fade?'" Myer couldn't say for sure. Dean McCalla agreed to give it a try and to work out any problems later on.

By the end of September 1958, classes had begun, and Myer was walking each day down to the Education Building. "All my classes were held there during the academic year. There was a small room in the basement of the Education Library, where the graduate students would study. The doctoral students had a desk and the MEd candidates had a chair at a table. Needless to say, you couldn't leave your books and papers there overnight. They all had to be hauled home. There was a cafeteria in the basement of the Education Building where you'd have your lunch at the same table as the professors and teaching assistants. What great interaction! But if I had more than an hour for lunch, I walked back to the suite on 88 Avenue for lunch. It was cheaper."

Soon it was time to pick a thesis topic.

"We all had to meet with the Department Chair to talk over our thesis topic," Myer remembers. "I decided that I wanted to explore what kinds of support were in place for the families of what in the 1950s were called severely retarded children. Myer had seen an article on the subject in the magazine section of the newspaper and he made a cold call to Winifred Stewart, who immediately became one of his lifelong friends.

Myer had not picked a mainstream topic. "When I met with Art Reeves, the Department Chair," says Myer, "I went in pretty gingerly. I told him I wanted to look at problems associated with severely retarded children. 'That's Ed Psych,' he told me. But I pressed on and said I wanted to examine what educational opportunities there were for these children, what parent groups existed, what the financing structure was. He asked if it would suit me if he were to be my supervisor—because the topic was offbeat. We picked Herbert Coutts and Gordon Mowat as my supervisory committee. What an incredible team. These professors were leaders in the profession. They gave me all the rope I wanted," says Myer.

Favourite Teacher

MYER SAYS HE HAD OUTSTANDING TEACHERS—Art Reeves, Harold Baker, John Andrews. Myer regrets that he never took a course taught by Gordon Mowat, who was vice-chairman of the Cameron Commission on Education and so on leave in the year when Myer took his Master's. "If I had to pick just one best teacher, it would be Harry Sparby. He was the guru in comparative educational administration in Canada, and he was an extra-super teacher who was well-organized and clear in his presentation. He knew when to keep quiet and let others speak. Sometimes he just waited and waited, which forced us to enter into a discussion. The first graduate course I ever taught was at McGill, and it was 'Sparby's course.' We would all talk about this in our little group as we progressed in our careers: 'I taught Sparby's course.' It was a mark of honour."

President Horowitz

For the future president who presided, with the chancellor, at some 60 convocations, Myer never had the chance to be hooded on stage with his Master's robes.

He took his oral examination in July 1959, finished his two summer courses on August 12 and left Edmonton on August 14 by car for Montréal. "I never did go to Convocation," Myer says. "Both Barbara and I had jobs to get back to. I am not even sure we discussed it as an option. I later received a copy of the program from the Registrar's Office, but I never saw the yearbook."

Ten years after attaining his MEd, Myer would come back to the U of A as the chair of Elementary Education. In 1972, he was named dean of Education. In 1975, he became vice-president academic, and from 1979 until 1989 he served as president of the University of Alberta. Today he is an adjunct professor at the University of Victoria and is involved with the Centre for Youth and Society. He has been a member or Chair of a number of councils and boards at Royal Roads University, and he chairs the academic council of University Canada West.

Myer has some advice for today's students. "You won't neglect your formal university studies, of course, but remember that there is much to learn while at the University from your interaction with others and from the numerous activities in which you can get involved."

Jack Dunn (BA '65 UNIVERSITY OF ALBERTA AT CALGARY, BED '66 AND MA '79, THE UNIVERSITY OF CALGARY)

JACK DUNN taught in 16 Calgary schools during his elementary teaching career, and in retirement he turned to writing history. With two books under his belt, Jack is working on a history of the North West Mounted Police.

Jack Dunn may have received his two undergraduate degrees in the 1960s, but it was the late 1950s when he began university in his hometown of Calgary. "It was 1958," Jack remembers, "and today's University of Calgary didn't have its own campus, or its own name." It was known by one and all simply as 'UAC,' short for The University of Alberta at Calgary." The UAC was a branch campus of the University of Alberta, and during Jack's days as a student, there was a relentless push for Calgary to be a separate and independent university.

The sign at the entrance to the Calgary campus. (UAA 69-12-309)

The U Of A Gives Birth to the University of Calgary

BACK IN 1909, Calgarians felt robbed. That's how *The Calgary Herald* put it.[15] First, the capital of the new province had gone to Edmonton, and right after that, Premier Rutherford had chosen his home riding of Strathcona as the site for the new provincial university. Calgarians knew their geography. Putting the university in Strathcona, across the river from Edmonton, was simply a shell game. It meant Edmonton had won again. From that moment forward, Calgarians were determined to have their own university. Until 1915, they privately financed Calgary College. But Calgary College folded when the legislature refused to give it the power to grant degrees. The government extended an olive branch to Calgary by giving it the only Normal School in the province, and so, for a while, Calgary had a lock on all teacher training in Alberta. But by 1930, Edmonton, too, had a Normal School, located in today's Corbett Hall.

The University of Calgary began life in 1945, when the government-run Normal Schools closed and the University of Alberta took over all teacher training in the province. The moment that decision was made, every teacher in the province's two Normal Schools instantly became U of A professors of Education. Just like that. The Edmonton Normal School became part of the University of Alberta's Faculty of Education. The Normal School in

The University of Alberta, Calgary Campus

FROM 1905–1945, the province was responsible for training teachers. The "Normal School" pictured here was established in Calgary, in 1905, for the purpose of educating schoolteachers. When the University of Alberta was given responsibility for teacher training in 1945, Calgary's Normal School served as the campus for the U of A's "southern branch" of its Faculty of Education— and within two decades, this "southern branch" would become The University of Calgary.

In his June 2005 speech to Convocation, University of Calgary President Harvey Weingarten noted that "the Calgary Normal School eventually became the founding faculty of the U of C" and that 2005 marked the "100th anniversary of teacher education in Calgary." In 2006, the University of Calgary celebrated its 40th year as an autonomous institution.

(UC 82.010–01.02–1)

Calgary became a southern branch of the U of A's Faculty of Education. The new teacher training program controlled by the U of A meant that the first year of Arts and Science would be offered at the Calgary branch.

The moment the U of A took on responsibility for the Calgary branch of the teacher education program, the SU sent an emissary down south to see if the Calgary students wanted to join forces with the U of A Students' Union.[16] The answer? Yes. Students in Calgary adopted most of the SU's structure and traditions, including an *Evergreen and Gold* yearbook and a version of *The Gateway* called *Cal Var,* short for Calgary Varsity. Calgary students established the Wauneita Society on their campus, and even adopted the banned Sadie Hawkins Week.

In the blink of an eye, Calgary had the beginnings of a university. Over the next 20 years, it would grow to be the world-class University of Calgary we know today.

As the 1950s ended, one of the longest-standing U of A traditions was coming to an end. For decades, U of A students from Edmonton went to the train station in September to greet their fellow undergraduates travelling up from Calgary to attend the University of Alberta. By 1959, the numbers were dwindling, and in 1962, there were only six students on the train.

By the time Jack Dunn was in university, Calgary's desire for a separate identity was evident in all its name changes. In the space of five years, the "University of Alberta Faculty of Education, Branch Campus" went through three official name changes: "University of Alberta in Calgary," and then "University of Alberta at Calgary," and finally "University of Alberta, Calgary." All the while, everyone just called it UAC. Hugh Morrison (BA '30) remembers another suggested name—the University of Southern Alberta. "Then," he says, "some wag shouted out the acronym—'USA—that's just great!'"

When the U of A turned 50 in 1958, a week-long celebration on the U of A campus ended with the first-ever Convocation held in Calgary, at the Southern Alberta Jubilee Auditorium. Immediately afterwards, the sod was turned for the UAC's first two buildings. By 1962, the University of Calgary was poised to become independent from the U of A, and in 1966 Calgary became a separate, distinct university.

Jack Dunn at UAC

"I WENT TO MOUNT ROYAL COLLEGE in 1957, my first year of university," says Jack, "because I just couldn't get through my high school French and Mount Royal, which was affiliated with a university in the United States, didn't require senior matriculation. In those days, getting senior 'matric' was tough and only 15 per cent of the student population got it. So I took Engineering at Mount Royal, and hated it.

"I wanted to go to UAC, and that meant learning French to get my senior matric. I worked at Safeway for a year to support myself, and I studied French. I got my matric, and in 1958 started at UAC. And that year of taking French? Twenty years later when I had to fulfill a language requirement for my Master's degree, all my French came back, just like that.

"In 1958, there was no Calgary campus at all. We were on the SAIT campus, where the old Normal School was, and there had been a military base there, so some of our classes were in these old army sheds, and we were surrounded by artillery and army jeeps. This would be at today's 14 Street and 16 Avenue, where the TransCanada now is, but back then it was the edge of the city, all fields.

"It was packed in 1958, but you knew everyone by sight. It was like a high school, a very cohesive group, and we were all together for a very long school year. There were no breaks like today's Reading Week, and classes went right up to December 23. I remember one class close to Christmas where the prof didn't show up. Someone in the UAC office phoned him at home, and he rushed in to our class in his pyjamas, with an overcoat on top. There must have been some Christmas party the night before—it was obvious he was hungover.

"Back in 1958 there were a lot of students at UAC getting their Junior E certificate, which meant you went to university for a year and then you could teach. They were paid the minimum wage and taught in all the small schools in rural Alberta. If you had a Junior E certificate, the monthly salary in those days was $250, about $3,000 a year. For the rest of us though, we finished our year at UAC on the SAIT campus and then we had to go up to Edmonton to the U of A to finish our degree."

"I Knew No One, I Met No One"

IT WAS A TOUGH YEAR for Jack. In the days before Lister Hall, Jack lived about 40 blocks south of campus in a basement suite. "A lot of students did this," he remembers, "and the rooms were pretty bare, with a single light bulb hanging down from the ceiling, that kind of thing. I had $5 a month to spend after paying my $60 room and board. I couldn't afford the bus. I walked everywhere."

Unlike the UAC campus, where the students all knew each other, the U of A campus was huge. "In Edmonton, I knew no one, I met no one," Jack says. "I had no money. I got fed up. I played a lot of bridge and I played hockey. One day I took all my hockey equipment, walked all the way downtown to sell it, and I ended up being offered only $2 for it. I wasn't going to haul it all the way back across the river to my room, so I took the $2. I bought four beers, 50 cents each, and then I was broke again."

Jack says that in 1958, there were five students who didn't pay their tuition on time. He was one of them, his roommate was another. Jack says he knew the other three. The University kept trying to find me, but I moved. Tuition fees were inexpensive—about $180, but I couldn't afford to pay my tuition on time, and neither could my roommate. My plan was to avoid paying my tuition until I got my income tax refund in the spring.

"My roommate couldn't even afford the bus fare up to Edmonton from Calgary. I was playing hockey in Calgary when I was at UAC and the team was going to Edmonton by bus. So I made my friend the 'stick boy' and he came along for free on the bus with the team. Today he's a multi-millionaire, but back then neither of us had any money.

"I was used to being frugal. My parents had been through the Depression and then the War, and my father always thought another depression was just around the corner. My mom had graduated as a nurse from the Calgary General in 1935 and was the only one in her class to get a job. And to stay in that job, she had to keep her marriage to dad a secret since married women couldn't work in those days.

"We were the kind of family where mom canned constantly. Once, it was 144 quarts of Saskatoons, and boy, did we get sick of Saskatoons. And if we took a car trip, we always packed our own food. So I was used to making my own way in the world and cutting corners. Bus fare home to

Calgary was inexpensive but still I hitchhiked home, even in winter when it was 30 and 40 below."

"But living on almost nothing in Edmonton? I got fed up," says Jack. "I dropped out a month before the school year finished. I went back to Calgary and worked for the city, in the transportation department, and then I helped build sewers with a crew of Italian immigrants. I was the only student, and they were great to me."

Jack earned enough to go back to school, and arrived on the new UAC campus.

Back at UAC

THE FIRST CAMPUS at Calgary was small and simple: Two utilitarian one-story buildings and a parking lot opened in 1960. Jack remembers that "students at UAC liked to joke that the parking lot was built before there was a Library."

The campus was near the old two-lane Banff highway, and Jack remembers it as "just prairie. A lot of grass and mud. We had no gym—we went over to the SAIT campus for Phys Ed. There was an outdoor hockey rink just beyond one of the two campus buildings."

Thirty-five years after his undergraduate days, two professors stand out in Jack's memory. "I had an eccentric professor named George Self. I wrote an essay—the history of Bulgaria—for one of his classes and hand-delivered it to his office. 'Want to see a fast way to mark a paper?' he asked me. He flipped through to the end of the paper, and read through my bibliography. Dr. Self said he could tell from the bibliography that I had done my work. He never read the essay. I got an A. And in my fourth year," recalls Jack, "I had to be evaluated on my student teaching. You would be taking a full course load and on top of that, a prof would sit in and observe your teaching at all three levels—elementary, junior high and senior high. The prof who was evaluating me would sit in the back of class with a sour look on his face, and believe me, every time I caught a glimpse of him, it was frightening. I thought from the look on his face that he was going to fail me. But at the end of the year, we heard that he had taken off with another professor's wife, and had taken all the evaluations and grades with him. The University gave everyone in the class a 'B'."

One day Jack found out that Calgary School Board representatives would be on campus, interviewing for positions. "I went down into the basement of one of the campus's two buildings, and applied for a teaching position in elementary. I was sure I would get it because elementary teachers made less money than junior or senior high teachers did, so everyone would apply for the higher paying jobs. I was hired in about 20 seconds."

Graduation and Life Afterwards

ONCE JACK RE-ENROLLED in university, he kept on taking courses, even after he started work as an elementary school teacher. He took courses at night and during the summer session. The payoff would come when he had his degree. "A degree meant about $1,000 more annually in your pay," says Jack, "a lot of money in those days.

"One day I got a letter from a Dr. Finn at UAC. It turned out I had fulfilled my BA degree requirements but didn't know it. I rushed down to the school board and got five months' back pay. On top of that, I had taken so many extra courses that I was also close to having my BEd. I got that the next year."

There was even more good news. Unexpected good news. It turns out that Jack had also taken so many courses that he had partially fulfilled his requirements for a Master's degree. In 1979, he completed his MA.

Today, Jack is immersed in researching the history of the NWMP. When last sighted, Jack was on his way into the stunning MacKimmie Library, on the 213-hectare campus of the University of Calgary, where the two small buildings he knew as an undergraduate are dwarfed by its 34 academic buildings. The University of Calgary has almost 29,000 students, 2,450 support staff and 2,360 full-time and part-time academic staff.

And Jack's words of wisdom for students today? "University education is only a small beginning. Make learning a lifelong pursuit."

Lorna Cammaert (BA '62)

FOR THREE DECADES, this woman was teacher, counsellor, and mentor to hundreds of people—especially women. After a 28-year, full-throttle career as a professor of Educational Psychology and associate vice-president at the University of Calgary, she's now an award-winning basket weaver and owner of a basketry supply business. On most Saturdays, you can find her

Lorna Cammaert, whose student ID is shown here, has been a trailblazer her entire life. As she wrote in one of her books, "You are not pre-programmed to an inevitable outcome." (Private Collection)

at the bustling Ganges Market on Salt Spring Island. Her name is Lorna Cammaert, and as Lorna strolls through Ganges's outdoor market, she often stops to listen to a young woman's problems about job or family, or else she is corralled by someone who wants her to take on a leadership role in a local organization.

Salt Spring is part of the Canadian Gulf Islands, located a short ferry ride away from Sidney, BC. The Gulf Islands are part of a chain that stretches south into the United States, where the islands are known as the San Juans. Ganges is the name of Salt Spring's one large village—there are no traffic lights, just one stop sign. The Saturday Ganges Market offers the finest in arts, crafts, and organic foods. During the summer, you might bump into Goldie Hawn or Luba, Barbara Streisand or local resident Robert Bateman. They're all at the Ganges market for the back-to-the land food, and to buy the products of world-class artisans who work in wood, glass, fibres, oils and clay. The Ganges Market is the 1960s, all grown up. The social, creative and environmental consciousness is palpable, and Lorna Cammaert is at the centre of Salt Spring's artisan community.

Lorna was an undergraduate at the University of Alberta in the late 1950s and early 1960s, first at the Calgary branch, then located on the SAIT campus (the "Tech"), and then at the University of Alberta in Edmonton. "I was the first one in my family, on either side, to go to University," Lorna says. "My dad had immigrated from Belgium to Canada after World War I, and he never had the chance to finish high school. My mom grew up in a small town in Saskatchewan, and had to work from an early age. They ended up with two kids, both with PhDs, my brother Ron and me."

But Lorna was almost side-tracked away from university in her last year of high school. "I had good grades," she remembers, "and I knew I wanted to go to university. I *felt* it. In fact, I wanted to go away to university—I thought going away was part of the experience. My parents didn't have much money but they were very supportive. So were my Math and Chemistry teachers, both men. But the women who were counsellors in my high school said I should take sewing at SAIT. They were well-meaning, I'm sure, and I did like to sew because it was part of my creative side. But I left that particular counselling session laughing to myself, and I went ahead and registered for university.

"Counselling in those days was so bad, I had actually decided by grade 9 that I could change that, I could do it better. So I planned to be a high school counsellor. To achieve that goal I needed to take Psychology, and so that's what I decided to take at university. Besides, I had met someone who had taken Psychology at Purdue, and that sealed it. I never wavered in my decision. Psychology was it."

The University of Alberta at Calgary (UAC)

LORNA ENROLLED in the three-year BA program at the University of Alberta and started out at UAC in 1959. "There was no campus at Calgary yet," she recalls, "and so we were on what is today the SAIT campus, which also includes the Alberta College of Art. Back then, SAIT was called the Provincial Institute of Technology and Art. The main building was the old Normal School, perched up high on a hill. It was a big red brick building with two high towers, similar in style to Corbett Hall on the U of A campus. The Library was up in one of the towers and we shared space with the art and tech students.

"There were only four profs who taught Arts courses—two in English and one each for Psychology and Philosophy. Our classes were small. There were only 8–10 in my first-year Psychology course, and many of us had been high school friends. We simply sat around a table—no desks. The Philosophy prof, Dr. Winspear, would have students over to his house. It was small-scale and personal.

Aerial view of the first Calgary campus. (UC 82.009–01–07–1)

"I was part of the Wauneita Society, a group to which only the women belonged. We were initiated at some point early on—there were camp-fires and I remember some of the women students with feathers in their hair. There was a 'Wauneita Lounge' just for the women, and the Society organized sports and sponsored a welcoming tea. It was very formal and you had to wear white gloves. There was also a general initiation for all the 'frosh,' as we were called. You had to be respectful to the older students, and you wore a green and gold beanie. I still have that beanie, and a photo of a group of us in the beanies in front of the SAIT campus.

"There was a ton of freedom that first year," remembers Lorna. "Freedom to think and explore. Freedom not to go to class. And there was one class I chose not to attend to because I wasn't learning anything from the prof. When the class time came around, I went to the Library instead, and read history. I passed.

"Nowadays on the University of Calgary campus, there is a traditional event each spring called Bermuda Shorts Day. Basically, it's party time, and a lot of students *really* let loose. When I was associate vice-president in charge of students in the 1980s and 1990s, I had to deal with the more extreme situations associated with Bermuda Shorts Day. It was an ironic twist, because a group of us in 1960 started Bermuda Shorts Day, on April 1. It was a warm spring. Students shed their winter clothes, switched to shorts for the day, and played games outside.

"Colour Night in Calgary was at the Palliser Hotel, and that's where all the awards were given out, both for involvement in sports and other organizations. All the girls were dressed up in long gowns. We all wore gloves. It was the days of dance cards and corsages, and you always went with a date. I had a fine time in that first year."

When Lorna finished that first year at UAC, there were plans to move the budding branch campus in Calgary to its own physical site near the old Banff Highway, where two modest buildings and a parking lot had been built. "But they were only offering two Psychology courses. I wasn't interested in either one," Lorna remembers, "and I wanted to go away to university. I'd had a scholarship in my first year and worked at the YWCA as a cashier at the swimming pool during the summers in high school—good pay for a girl. So I had some money of my own. I think my parents helped a little, but they couldn't afford much. Tuition was about $300. I had enough to go up to Edmonton to the U of A, and that's what I did.

"My family had a car by 1960," says Lorna "My mom and I drove up to a small apartment I had found in one of the Garneau houses. It was on the third floor of the house, and it was very tiny. There were two beds, a hot plate, and a little place to sit. When I met my roommate, I realized she was the great-niece of Henry Marshall Tory—Helen Tory. Helen was a Home Ec student, but she didn't know how to cook meat. I taught her to make porcupines on our little hot plate—they were meatballs and rice, made so that the rice would stick out—hence the name. Helen and I made most of our own food, and we were very creative with the hot plate, but the hot plate was under a gable and you couldn't stand up straight and cook at the same time. For water, we had to go down a flight to the bathroom. Two flights down, on the main floor, we had one shelf in the fridge that was ours. We climbed a lot of stairs to make a meal."

Coming to the U of A in 1960

"THE U OF A? It was really big!" That's how Lorna remembers the Edmonton campus in 1960. There were 12,783 students and some 33 buildings. Compared to the young Calgary campus, which was still in rented quarters, the U of A was a huge change. "All my classes were bigger," says Lorna. "It was exciting. I was *really* away! I liked it.

"Registration was in the gym at the U of A, and you went from table to table to table, signing up for courses. There were all these rules and regulations about what you had to take. I figured out how to take the classes I really wanted, and I snuck it by them. I took what I wanted to take. Most of my classes were in the Old Arts Building or in Corbett Hall, which we called the Education Building at the time. I studied in the little library in the Old Arts Building and sometimes ate in the cafeteria in University Hall, the first SUB. Upstairs, there was a Wauneita Lounge for the women students, and I remember the fashion shows that were put on each fall.

"I loved the U of A, but I hated Edmonton. In my second year I moved to the upstairs of a house on Saskatchewan Drive, opposite a brewery. There were four of us, each with a bedroom, and there was a common kitchen. It was a long, long walk to campus, and there was so much snow that year, piles of it, and it was so cold. We had to get all bundled up in pants and parkas for the walk—and then we changed into skirts for class.

"I travelled back and forth between Edmonton and Calgary a lot, by train. I had a pass—good for one trip. But if the conductor knew you were a student, he gave you back the pass. I went to Calgary every time the weather report said there might be a chinook.

"Each year I could take more and more of the classes I wanted. My GPA got better and better. I didn't work during the school year and I was very studious. I took out a student loan, and in those days, if your grades were good enough, they forgave your loan. In my second year, I had a woman prof! It was nice to have a role model. All the other professors were male.

"I didn't have a favourite professor," says Lorna, "but I had a favourite assignment. I liked my Psychology prof. He had worked in a mental institution in Saskatchewan, so he was experienced. And he was a parapsychologist. For one assignment, we had to search out someone who believed in telling fortunes, and interview them. We all knew that the gypsies were in town, but they were in a seedy part of Edmonton, and I

was the sweet and shy type, so that was out for me. Instead, I went to the
Blue Willow restaurant on Jasper Avenue. They had a tea leaf reader.

"It was a big thing to go downtown in those days. No one had a car,
and life was centred on the campus. Your world was defined by where you
could walk. So going downtown was an adventure, and to see a tea leaf
reader? I've never forgotten it."

Lorna belonged to a fraternity in high school, but, she says, "I didn't
like the fraternity scene in Edmonton. The girls went around in gaggles
and didn't do anything independently. The Pembinites also went around
in a gaggle and for both these groups, norms were imposed. You had to
dress and act a certain way, and date certain guys. That wasn't for me."

"The dance I remember the best," says Lorna, "was Bar None. It was the
last dance before exams and it was big—held in the gym. As for dating, a
movie at the Garneau was a popular thing to do, and you might have pizza
afterwards—it was one of the newest foods. I dated some of the fraternity

boys who lived behind the house where I was renting. There were lots of long conversations on the one phone in that rental house we four girls shared.

"There were also parties at the frat houses and in students' homes. There was a fair bit of drinking, but I wasn't a drinker. I was a Baptist at the time, and Baptists didn't drink. I went to the Baptist church in Strathcona, I sang in the choir there, and there were a lot of gatherings for young people. I led a quiet life and was studious. I had been very involved in extracurricular activities in high school and at UAC, and wanted a break, I did work for *The Gateway*.

"My classes were all full-year classes," says Lorna, "and they were just starting to talk about half-year classes when I graduated. Finals were big essay exams, which lasted three to four hours each. Normally there would be five topics, and you picked three. It was common to have, say, three three-hour exams in one day, and then a break for a few days before your next exam. A lot of students were very anxious during these long breaks. I sewed—it was relaxing, and it fed the creative side of me. The Garneau movie theatre brought in special movies during these exam breaks, and a lot of students went to the Garneau during the week to deal with the stress of the long exam period."

Convocation and Life Afterwards

LORNA'S CONVOCATION was held in the brand new Jubilee Auditorium. "My mom and younger brother came up for it," she remembers, "but my dad was a labourer and couldn't take the time off. It was a very special day because I was the first one in the family ever to graduate from university.

"Convocation was very ceremonial. You knelt in front of the chancellor. We were all worried about how we would get up from the kneeler because we were in long robes. The chancellor dubbed you on each shoulder and said something in Latin to signify that you had graduated. The auditorium was filled with people even though there were relatively few graduates compared to today."

By the end of her undergraduate days, Lorna discovered that there was no quick route to becoming a high school counsellor. "First you had to get an education degree and teach. Then, when you had enough seniority, you could become a counsellor. That would take too long. I still had the same vision," says Lorna, "but I decided I would go to grad school to be a psychologist. To do that, I had to save money, so I worked at the YM/YWCA in St. Catherine's—the year Kennedy died—and I worked in Victoria for a year after that. Then I decided to head to a US university with a psychology program approved by the American Psychological Association. Of the universities I applied to, the University of Oregon wrote me the nicest letter, and that's where I went. I got my MA in 1966. I loved it. I loved the learning. I did my internship in Illinois, learned the two languages I needed, and finished my PhD in two years—just at the time the bottom dropped out of the market. I ended up coming full circle and took a job as an assistant professor and counsellor at the University of Calgary. It gave me great satisfaction to be teaching students who were going to be high school counsellors."

Lorna has a long list of accomplishments amassed during her 28 years as a professor and administrator. "Psychology is in everything I've ever done," she says.

Lorna served as president of both the Confederation of Alberta Faculty Associations and of Calgary's Faculty Association at a time when key contractual changes were made. Active in the Canadian Association of University Teachers, she is one of 13 recipients of the Sarah Shorten Award, which recognizes outstanding achievements in promoting the advancement of women in Canadian universities and colleges. Lorna is a founder of two national organizations, including Senior Women Academic Administrators of Canada, and a life-long advocate for equity. During her ten years as associate vice-president (student affairs) at the University of Calgary, she travelled the world in her role as chief advisor on international affairs, and served as the equivalent of dean of students. She started or organized the Canadian Sex Research Forum, the Contemporary Women Program, and a mentoring program for academic women at the University of Calgary.

If you google Lorna, the first pages record her involvements on Salt Spring Island, as a basketry artisan and as president, past-president, or board chair of a number of island organizations, including the Gulf Islands Community Arts Council and SWOVA (Salt Spring Women Opposed to Violence and Abuse). During the tourist season, she welcomes visitors from around world to her basketry studio on Mount Erskine Road.

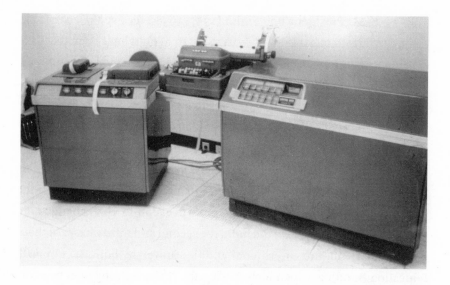

According to Dr. Keith Smillie, Professor Emeritus of Computer Engineering, "The LGP–30, the University of Alberta's first computer, was delivered in October 1957, was the size of a desk, weighed 800 pounds and cost $40,000. It was replaced by an IBM 1620 in May 1961 but was kept for teaching purposes for another two years." (UAA 91–118)

Lorna says she has always advised students to "follow your heart and dreams." But for a woman like Lorna, who made her own choices in an era when independence and individuality for women went against type, here is her defining statement. It's from a book Lorna co-authored, titled *A Woman's Choice: A Guide to Decision-Making*: "You are not pre-programmed to an inevitable outcome."

END OF THE DECADE

First Computer and a New Gym

IN 1957, the first computer arrived on campus—an LPG–30. In the same year, the student yearbook, the *Evergreen and Gold*, was produced by a new technology—lithography. Liquor was still banned, and students were searching for personal self-expression. For some students, the 1960s launched an era that went way beyond self-government through the Students' Union. A movement was afoot to put students at the starting-gate of governance. Students wanted a significant say on the Board of Governors and General Faculties Council.

In 1958, the University celebrated its Golden Jubilee. The chancellor was Laurence "Eucalyptus" Cairns, the "tall drink of water" from the 1912 graduating class, who could play every popular song on the piano in any key, who as a young law student was gassed in World War I but survived. Cairns returned to serve his community, and the University, with unparalleled verve and commitment.

In 1958, SU President Bob Smith (1957–1958), received a letter from University President Andrew Stewart. No letter could have been received with more joy by four decades of student presidents. The gym that students had fought for, and established a building fund for beginning in the 1920s, was to become a reality, thanks to a generous contribution from the government of Alberta. Students had planned for an indoor skating rink, a gym, and a building of their own for more than 30 years. In 1950, they opened the first of three phases of the original Students' Union. The next two phases of the original SUB were to include a gym, a skating rink, and a swimming pool. The government's decision in 1958 changed all that, and the students never did build the second and third phases of their building. Instead, the government and the University built the Physical Education Building, which included a gym. The swimming pool became part of the Phys Ed Building, and the third phase of the original SUB, a large auditorium, wasn't built until 1967, when the new Students' Union Building opened. The new SUB included the auditorium, later named for President Emeritus Myer Horowitz.[17]

President Walter Johns

IN 1959, Walter Johns took the helm as the University ended its Golden Jubilee. The SU president in 1958–1959 was Lou Hyndman, who later served the province in many capacities, including minister of education and provincial treasurer. While he was SU president, Lou oversaw the great debate about turning the spectacular and spacious Wauneita Lounge into a mixed lounge where male students would be welcomed. It was the beginning of the end for the Wauneitas. The opening of the lounge to both sexes marked the onset of feminism. Soon women would be part of the mainstream of university life, both in terms of their numbers and their impact.

The new University president in 1959 probably didn't know it, but ten years later his words would ring true as a harbinger of the '60s: "It had been an interesting ten years throughout the 1950s," he said. "The women had worn plaid skirts and knee socks in the early part of the decade but were changing to tight-fitting leotards by the end....The men wore their hair short and neatly combed and beards were rare, with [one] notable exception."[18] President Johns named the bearded student—P.J. Clooney—but the lonely Clooney would soon be joined by many others who let their hair grow long.

Walter Johns was an incomparable scholar in the Classics and a gentleman. He served as the University's first-ever vice-president during the 1950s, when male students wore shirts and ties to class, and women had a defined, circumscribed place in society. But Walter Johns was about to be president during the turbulent 1960s, when girls wore miniskirts and ran for SU president, and boys had long hair and beards.

Quaecumque Vera

THE END OF THIS DECADE witnessed a pinnacle in the development of post-secondary education in the province. An ad in the 1959 *Evergreen and Gold* stated, that the "University of Alberta announces courses for the 1959–60 Sessions in: Edmonton, Banff and Calgary." In Edmonton, there were 13 Faculties or Schools listed, as well as summer school. For Banff, the summer session included programs in 12 subjects, including art, drama, and music. And down in Calgary, the branch campus was hard to hold back.[19] They were offering first- to third-year courses in nine disciplines. Within two years, they would have their own campus—just two buildings— and Calgary was on the path to independence. Up in Edmonton, in fact, a decision had been made that growth should be capped at 6,000 students, and the U of A had approved several junior colleges. In addition to Calgary, there were now Camrose Junior College, Mount Royal College, and Lethbridge Junior College. Students began their programs at these locations and finished at the U of A.[20]

Mary Hendrickson, in the 1958 Class History, vowed that students were "firmly resolved to be independent in thought and action, refusing to become 'assembly-line ingredients in our cake-mix society.'" But, she added, "We realize that the privilege of a university education carries with it the obligation of continuing the search for 'whatsoever things are true.' May we fulfill our trust."

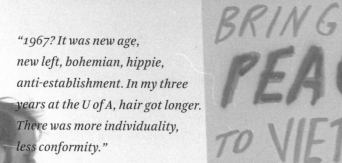

"1967? It was new age, new left, bohemian, hippie, anti-establishment. In my three years at the U of A, hair got longer. There was more individuality, less conformity."

—MYRA DAVIES (BA '69)

Timeline

Hundreds of students in the 1960s protested—against apartheid, the tenure system, high rents, tuition increases, and the war in Vietnam. One of the anti-Vietnam placards read: "Children should grow up, not blow up." This photograph, taken by J. McLaren, was published in the 1966 Evergreen and Gold.

(UAA 69-19-488)

Enrolment and Finance, 1960–1969

- Fall student head count: 8,964 (1960); 24,793 (1969)
- Operating budget from the Province of Alberta: $6,000,000.00 (1960); $43,486,000.00 (1969)
- Full-load undergraduate Arts tuition: $215.00 (1960); $400.00 (1969)
- SU membership fee: $11.25 + building fund $10 (1960); $27.50 (1969)

Key Dates, 1960–1969

- Walter Johns serves as president (1959–1969) as enrolment soars from 5,000 to 17,500
- Reg Lister retires and then dies (1960)
- The Faculty of Arts and Sciences splits into two Faculties (1963)
- President Johns' proposal to the board for a fundraising campaign is resoundingly defeated (1963)
- First broadcast of a course at the U of A in Calgary (1963)
- General Faculties Council (GFC) meets for five hours and approves 93 pages of course changes
- Calgary, Lethbridge and Banff Centre are separated from the U of A (1966)
- School of Library Science is established (1968)
- Max Wyman succeeds Walter Johns; he is the first president appointed by the board of governors and not by government (1969)

Selected Campus Buildings, 1960–1969

- The campus comprises 133 acres with 12 major teaching buildings (1960)
- Varsity Rink is torn down (1960)
- Bhattia Physics Lab (1960)
- Students begin planning for a new SUB (1961)
- The Edmonton Normal School is renamed Corbett Hall in honour of Ned Corbett, long-time director of Extension (1963)
- The sod is turned for the Faculty Club (1964)
- The Tory Building opens (1966)
- The second SUB opens (1967)
- Hot Caf demolished to make way for the Central Academic Building (1969)

Beyond Campus, 1960–1969

- Oral contraceptives usher in the sexual revolution (1960)
- Construction begins on the Berlin Wall (1961–1962)
- The Northern Alberta Institute of Technology opens (1962)
- Grant MacEwan Community College opens (1962)
- Rachel Carson publishes *Silent Spring*, warning against the use of pesticides (1962)
- US President Kennedy assassinated (November 22, 1963)
- The Beatles top the charts (1964)
- Miniskirts and bell bottom pants (1965)
- First space walk (1965)
- Cultural revolution in China (1966)
- Star Trek debuts (1966)
- First human heart transplant (1967)
- Pierre Elliott Trudeau sworn in as prime minister (1968)
- Martin Luther King and Robert Kennedy are assassinated (1968)
- American Neil Armstrong walks on the moon (1969)
- Britain sends troops to Northern Ireland (1969)
- Thousands protest the war in Vietnam (1969)
- Woodstock rock festival features three days of peace, love, and music (1969)

VIGNETTES FROM THE 1960s

President Walter Johns, 1959–1969

WALTER JOHNS was a professor of Classics and an accomplished scholar and administrator who guided the University through a surge in enrolment and the expansion of the post-secondary system in Alberta. Dr. Johns was president of the University of Alberta at Calgary when that institution, along with the Banff Centre, achieved independence from the U of A. In that same year—1966—the University of Lethbridge became a degree-granting university. Dr. Johns was part of the planning for this system of universities and colleges within the province.

Walter Johns headed the U of A during an era when students were actively protesting and advocating for a voice in academic planning and policy-making. He was president in 1969 when the *Universities Act* was amended to allow for a student representative on the Board of Governors. In his retirement, Walter Johns wrote a comprehensive institutional history of the University of Alberta.

Dr. Johns is remembered as a kind and compassionate person. Once he phoned Chief Librarian Bruce Peel at home to discuss an urgent business matter. The Peels didn't hear the phone ring, but their daughter, a toddler, did. She was too young to understand that she was supposed to get her father to the phone, and President Johns patiently stayed on the line for a good ten minutes before the Peels realized that their child was on the phone—with the University President.[1]

In 1969, Dr. Max Wyman succeeded Walter Johns as president. Wyman was the first president appointed by the Board of Governors rather than by the government.

The Boomers Arrive

THE 1960S was an era of stark juxtapositions. On the one hand, there was extensive social change, embracing everything from "free love" and the organic food movement to a deep realization that society's attitudes and laws were inherently wrong in relation to Natives, Francophones, and the economically disadvantaged. Every accepted norm came under scrutiny—from how one dressed to what one smoked. Women's lib was in the news. Issues like the right to abortion, the naturalness of women's participation in campus politics, and their full involvement in all disciplines were subjects of persistent debates in Students' Council and conversations in coffee houses.

On the other hand, there was a great deal of fun to be had on campus. The antics of Freshman Introduction Week, the bawdy, sometimes sexist, Med show, and the Broadway-like productions of the Jubilaires all suffused the 1960s.

In the 1960s, a relentless flow of baby boomers filled the campus. This wasn't just a spike in enrolment similar to the quick booms that occurred after both world wars. All those babies born after World War II just kept rolling onto the U of A campus. In 1960, there were about 9,000 registered students. By 1969, over 20,000 students attended classes. The Administration was warning that "quotas were coming," and that enrolment had to be limited to forestall a decline in educational standards. Earlier, there had been a plan to limit the size of the student body to 6,000 students.

Athabasca Hall in the 1960s

IN THE MIDST of social upheaval during the 1960s, one daily event on campus remained constant—meal-time in Athabasca Hall. By the 1960s, the oldest building on campus had shed its multiple identities and served only as a residence—the purpose for which it was originally designed.

Larry McKill was a resident in Athabasca in 1961–1962. He recalls in a snap that a single room with seven-day board was $75 per month, tuition was $250 for both terms, and the SU fees were $35. Larry says that all students stood when a bell rang, and the proctor said grace. Over 40 years later, Larry can still reel off the Latin grace: *Fac Deus noster, ut hoc cibo refecti, quaecumque vera*. As he puts it, "One doesn't forget after all the repetitions!"

"We sat at large tables," he remembers, "five to each side and one at either end. In my day, the one at the head served the meat, the next two the potatoes and vegetables. The one at the far end served tea one night, coffee the next, from silver service. Since one server from the kitchen was responsible for three to four tables, there was always pressure to get seconds, when available. There were no seconds until all the food was served up and mainly eaten, and so the slow eaters, like me, were placed

Reg Lister at the time of his retirement. (UAA 78-108-197)

at the end that received the first plate. The race then began—about six minutes for dinner, less for lunch.

"Many times I think of the dining room experience, which was rather old-fashioned even for its day. We had to have ties and jackets on every evening except Saturday and Sunday. Sunday at noon was Sunday 'dinner,' and we dressed up. For all meals, one had to be in the ante-room (now the Heritage Lounge) exactly on time—6 P.M.—and we all had to be seated together. Latecomers had to ask permission of the head resident, at the time, as I recall, Jim Horsman from Red Deer, later the minister of advanced education. And, by the way, only people elected to the house committee got to stay in residence for more than one year unless space became available during the year. I moved to Ontario for my third year, and meals were served cafeteria style and no dress code was in place. It was quite a contrast.

"I should add that breakfast was served between 7 and 9 A.M., first-come, first served, for all three residences; you filled in a table and then another was started. In the ante-room to the dining hall there were numerous couches and chairs along each side wall, and this is where we waited at noon (12 sharp, bagged lunches for those with classes at noon) and at dinner time (6 sharp, late-comers could be refused entry depending on the head resident) for the doors to open. Only in the morning and on Sunday noon dinners did men and women students eat together.

"It was the sexist custom of the day for many men to sit in the ante-room and rate the women as they came over from Pembina to eat breakfast: the ratings were savage and often audible. One morning, to all the men's surprise, a large contingent of women occupied all the seats and began a very audible rating of the guys as they slinked their way to the dining room."[2]

1960—Reg Lister Retires

REG LISTER RETIRED in 1960 after 45 years on campus. Mentor and role model to thousands of residence students, he described for *The Gateway* in 1960 what the campus was like in 1908. "The campus was just a field when I came," he said, "a field. Period. Mud. Where the University Hospital is we walked there behind the sloughs. By St. Joseph's College, there were wagon trails...nothing else on the campus. It was all bush."[3]

By 1960, when Reg retired, the first residences to be built in almost 50 years were under construction, and the complex would soon bear Reg Lister's name.

Before Lister Hall opened, hundreds of U of A students were living in freezing cold rooms or attic garrets with a hot plate to cook on, and for many, one bare bulb was the only source of light. By the mid-1960s, the University set basic standards for landlords who wanted to list their basement or attic suites on a central university register. There had to be adequate study facilities, adequate light, furnishings, bedding, ventilation, water, and bathroom facilities. The University also decreed that all off-campus housing "should be rented exclusively either to men or women," and that "students shall not entertain students of the opposite sex in their living quarters." By 1970, the University was declaring that in the residences "men would be expected to have women out of their rooms at a reasonable hour'."[4]

Mrs. J. Grant Sparling, Isobel Munroe, and Major Hooper

SOON AFTER REG LISTER RETIRED, "Major" Hooper—he had been a Major during the war—was appointed the male student advisor, with responsibility for student groups, fraternities, and clubs. Reg's long-time colleague, Maimie Simpson, was about to retire as dean of women. Miss Simpson's successor was Mrs. J. Grant Sparling, who was to be "guide, counselor and confidante to two thousand co-eds on campus."[5] Isobel Munroe (BA '35), a social worker and day-care advocate, succeeded Sparling in 1968. Sparling, Munroe, and Hooper dealt with students during the turbulent 1960s when students questioned all societal norms, and social and sexual values were upended. White gloves and receiving lines would soon disappear, as would chaperones at dances. By the end of the 1970s, there would be no more dean of women or provost / "male student advisor," but rather a dean of students.

Two towers of the Lister residences were constructed in 1962 (Kelsey and Henday), and the third tower (MacKenzie) opened in 1968. The new residences were the cause of one of the first protests on campus. In 1964, 500 students presented a petition to President Walter Johns, objecting to a 20% fee increase planned for the residence complex.[6]

Top: The brand new Lister Hall, when there were still only two towers and young saplings outside. (UAA 82–54–2)

Bottom: By 1968, a birth control information booth was set up in SUB, and pamphlets on birth control were handed out at registration. The booth in SUB was run by the new Student Committee on the Status of Women. "We're trying to get people to realize it is not unrespectable to talk about birth control," said committee member Lynn Hanley.[7]

(UAA 69–109–67–507)

The new residences that would become known collectively as Lister Hall were originally planned as men's residences. There was to be an additional residence for women. But given the housing crunch, and given the numbers of men and women students, it just wouldn't work. And so the University had to consider having both male and female students in one complex. By 1968, when MacKenzie Hall, the third tower, was completed, it would be occupied by equal numbers of men and women.[8]

The Wauneita Society

IN 1960, if you were a female freshman, you were automatically inducted as a member of the Wauneita Society, a group that provided leadership training and social companionship on a campus that was predominantly male. "The ceremony began as the girls filed into Wauneita Lounge, singing the Wauneita song. Two representatives of the frosh class were led before Wauneita President Gail Lewis [who was clad in a blanket with an Indian motif] who told all the girls present to answer 'yes' if they wished to become members of the Wauneita tribe."[9]

By 1969, the Wauneita Society quietly died out as women students were integrated more fully into university life. The Wauneita Lounge in SUB had already been opened to both sexes, and in 1968 the first woman SU President was elected in her own right. Faculties like Medicine and Law were opening up to women in large numbers. The 1969 *Evergreen and Gold* included a photo of Beverley McLachlin, the Law student who won the Horace Harvey Gold Medal, and who went on to be chief justice of the Supreme Court of Canada. But before the Wauneita Society made its quiet exit, it was, like the newly-minted Student Committee on the Status of Women, passing out birth control pamphlets during registration.

The Graduate Students' Association

IN 1962, the Students' Union asked the University to approve a compulsory $30 SU fee for graduate students. Their reasoning was that graduate students were also using SUB and other SU facilities, and they belonged to SU clubs. A Graduate Students' Association had been formed in 1959, but participation was voluntary, and only about one-third of all graduate students belonged to the new group.[10] Initially, the University only approved a $5 fee, but in 1968 the amount was raised to $15. Graduate Students' Association President Peter Boothroyd walked out of a University meeting in protest. In 1972, the GSA incorporated as a separate association.

Students Flex Their Muscle[11]

IN 1965, as the *University Act* was under review, students were demanding "25% control of the Board of Governors." President Walter Johns declined to comment. In 1968, 3,500 students marched to the Legislature to protest a hike in tuition fees. In 1969, the Students' Council advocated the abolition of the tenure system "as a method of evaluating academic staff." Students wanted a new means of evaluating teaching ability, and they wanted students to have parity on hiring committees. In 1970, students were talking about a pass-fail system to replace marks and grades. In 1972, students gained voting parity with professors on General Faculties Council, the academic governing body.

On the national scene, there was a cross-country student protest when the United States announced it would test the atomic bomb in the Aleutian Islands. The protest ended with BC students blocking the biggest border crossing between Canada and the US. It was a protest authorities applauded. Mitchell Sharp, the federal external affairs minister, wished the demonstrators success in halting the test.

At Simon Fraser University, eight professors in the department of Political Science, Sociology, and Anthropology (PSA) were either refused tenure or

In March 1968, Students' Union
President Al Anderson (in
black glasses and tie) led 3,000
students over the High Level
Bridge to protest increased
tuition fees. Accompanied by
SU President-elect Marilyn
Pilkington and Treasurer Phil
Ponting, Anderson met with
the education minister and
Premier Manning. During
the meeting, they presented
a petition signed by 6,500
students requesting an increase
to the government's operating
grant to the University.
(UAA 69–109–67–575)

given only one-year contract renewals. One of the dismissed faculty had "just received a $7,000 Canada Council grant to continue research on the attitudes of the working class in Vancouver." Hundreds of students and faculty went on strike at SFU for 41 days, and "hundreds more tried to get into the first afternoon of the teach-in on democracy and the University. The teach-in was scheduled to run for the duration of the PSA strike." SFU's administration then moved to dismiss the eight faculty members. At the U of A, both the SU and the Department of Political Science condemned SFU's actions.

Across Canada, there were sit-ins and takeovers of university buildings to protest policies on hiring, tenure, and inequity, and to advocate for representation on governing bodies. But the biggest national story centred on the Canadian Union of Students (CUS).[12] In a nutshell, the CUS had become involved in activist politics, issuing statements on foreign policy and engaging in deep debate about unequal class structure. At the U of A, there was constant tension between those in support of the CUS and those who opposed it. In 1966, SU President Al Anderson led the campaign for the SU to withdraw from the CUS. Anderson's effort were continued by Marilyn Pilkington, the relatively conservative SU president for 1968–69. However, in the following year, 1969–70, the SU president was the relatively left-leaning David Leadbeater, who supported membership in the CUS. As *The Gateway* put it in 1969, the University's Diamond Jubilee year, "at the University of Alberta, a particularly radical council...faces a particularly conservative campus and a particular blend of unconscious isolationism."

In 1969, the University of Toronto withdrew from the CUS, crippling the organization financially. At the U of A, 7,000 students voted by a margin of three to one to leave the CUS. In 1981, the Canadian Federation of Students was founded to lobby against cutbacks in funding.

In the United States, social and economic change in the universities was led by the Students for a Democratic Society (SDS), and a free-speech movement flourished at Berkeley. At New York University, students "sat in," taking over the president's office, and at universities across the US, each April heralded the "rites of Spring," when students would protest, and the US National Guard would respond with tear gas. At Big Ten universities like the University of Wisconsin, the armed National Guard was regularly posted outside university buildings. At Wisconsin, protesters had bombed a lab that was engaged in war-related research, killing a graduate student who was working in the lab late that night. At Kent State in Ohio, student protesters had been killed while protesting the war in Vietnam. Canadian students also knew, from regular headlines in their student newspapers, about the Chicago Eight—protestors associated with groups like the Students for a Democratic Society who were charged with conspiracy under the 1968 amendment to the *Civil Rights Act* when they crossed state lines to protest at the Democratic National Convention held that year in Chicago. It was a *cause célèbre* that made people think deeply about civil rights, especially the right to free speech.

THE CAMPUS IN THE 1960s

BY THE END OF 1960, said *Gateway* writer Bill Samis, the University would have a ten-storey, $3 million Education Building, as well as "a new library, new residences, possibly a new Fine Arts Building and an enlarged Students' Union Building [today's University Hall]. It will also have few if any of the temporary structures erected during World War II. The present Education Building, which is Corbett Hall, is planned to accommodate 350. There are presently 1,499 Education undergraduates."[13]

The old Varsity Rink, erected in 1927, and the Drill Hall, erected during World War II, were demolished—but not the vibrant memories of students who skated there three times a week, or who drilled there

daily in anticipation of going off to war. The Physical Education Building, which supplanted the Rink, had been the brainchild of the Students' Union. A gymnasium was originally to be attached to the south side of the SUB. But physical education had emerged as a discipline, not simply a form of recreation, and so the University took hold of the idea. And so, in November 1960, the Physical Education complex, including the new Varsity Arena (now the Clare Drake Arena), opened to the west of the SUB building.

The original SUB, with its student lounges, cafeteria, barber shop, bridge tables, SU offices, third-floor faculty lounge, and women-only Wauneita Lounge, had opened in 1950 when there were about 6,000 students. By 1961, SUB was far too small for a student population of 12,783. On the students' wish list for a new SUB were a larger cafeteria, conference and meeting rooms, and additional office space for the Students' Union administration, the SU publications, and student clubs. Students wanted at least one large lounge and a number of smaller ones, possibly an art gallery, and maybe a university chapel. A "SUB expansion referendum" was held, and in 1962 over 2,500 students voted "yes." But the administration nixed the SUB expansion plan in part because the administration wanted a bookstore in the new SUB, and they had their own plans for expansion of the Physical Education Building. The location of the new SUB was changed to just west of the Administration Building, where the old West Lab stood.[14] The new SUB opened in 1967.

"Big Building Boom Blossoms"[15]

IN SEPTEMBER 1962, work on the Education Building was ahead of schedule, and construction (at a cost of $6 million) began to the west of the Jubilee Auditorium on two 11-storey Y-shaped residences intended to house 1,200 students. A related food services building was also being built. Construction also began that summer on a $2.5 million library (the Cameron Library) and a $1 million addition to the Nuclear Research Centre.

All in all, between 1960 and 1969, 23 major buildings were constructed, including the Lister Complex, Tory, Bio Sci, Cameron Library, SUB, Chemical/ Materials Engineering, Chem Centre West, Tory, Van Vliet West, V Wing, Clinical Sciences, and Education South. In the 1970s, construction slowed to a mere dozen major buildings, including CAB, Chem Centre East, Education North, HUB, Humanities, Law, Mechanical Engineering, Medical Sciences, Rutherford North, and Van Vliet East. The Tuck Shop was torn down to make way for the Fine Arts Building.

A GLANCE AT THE 1960 CALENDAR

THE 1960 CALENDAR succinctly captured the growth of the campus: "In Edmonton, the University possesses 857 acres (campus, 133 acres; farm, 724 acres). The campus, located about two miles from the business centre, borders the wooded southern bank of the North Saskatchewan River. It contains some twelve major teaching and research buildings, in addition to student residences, service buildings and two affiliated colleges. Adjoining are the Alberta Research Council, the Provincial Laboratory of Public Health, two teaching hospitals and the Northern Alberta Jubilee Auditorium.

"At Calgary, the new campus extends to about 230 acres, and is situated on the Banff Highway, at the western limits of the city. The two buildings in Calgary are designed to house Arts, Education, Science and Engineering.

"The Banff School of Fine Arts, which is administered by the University, is located in the mountains. A few courses for university credit may be taken there in the summer months."

THE GATEWAY, Friday, November 15, 1968   C-7

THIS UNIVERSITY BELONGS TO THE STUDENT!

DIG IT

EVERGREEN AND GOLD—1969

THE *EVERGREEN AND GOLD* published in 1969 celebrated the University's 60th anniversary, its Diamond Jubilee. As reported in the *E&G*, it had been a year of intense student protest, captured in a popular poster titled "THIS UNIVERSITY BELONGS TO THE STUDENT." During 1968–1969, students gained a seat on the Board of Governors and were fighting for parity with professors on General Faculties Council (GFC). GFC, which until 1969 had held confidential meetings, succumbed to pressure and opened its doors to the public and press. Student representation on the Senate increased from two seats to seven. American social activist Dick Gregory drew a sell-out crowd in SUB, and there were teach-ins to raise social and political awareness. Students were involved in raising money for the World University Service and SHARE. When the University razed homes in North Garneau to expand the campus, students protested, and the yearbook recorded the story.

Campaigning for Student Rights

Students for a Democratic University spearheaded a push for student power and student rights, embracing a host of issues—from adding students to tenure committees to ensuring students' access to their university files. And a group of students, led by the ever-present Jon Bordo, made an unannounced visit to the dean of Arts.[16] Bordo and the Student Defense Committee (SDC) planned to rally 800 students to drop in on Dean of Arts D.E. Smith to protest tenure and hiring decisions concerning two Sociology professors. Only 30 students participated in the rally, but during their visit to Dean Smith's office, they discovered that "secret" files were kept on students and staff. This set off another wave of protest, and the SDC presented a list of demands to the administration. There was also a "drop-in" on the new president, Max Wyman, who invited the students in to the University Hall Council Chamber for a two-hour discussion.

(UAA 69–19–68–831–001)

The 1969 *E & G* also documented the Med show, which played to a packed house, and the House Ec fashion show, which made the local newspapers. The Orchesis modern dance group was hot, the U of A symphony was in full swing, folk music was popular (Gordon Lightfoot, Buffy St. Marie and Glenn Yarbrough performed on campus that year), and the honorary degree recipients in the Diamond Jubilee year were Pierre Trudeau, UN Secretary General U. Thant, and William Schneider, president of the National Research Council, a federal granting agency that had been advocated decades earlier by Henry Marshall Tory.

Also in 1969, the Wauneita Society held one of its last formals before making a quiet, permanent exit.

The 1969 *Evergreen and Gold* has something else of interest: one of the last photos ever taken of the St. George's banner. Hand-stitched in England and presented to the Students' Union in 1911 by the governor general, the banner symbolized the authority of the SU. The banner was last seen in 1981 when it was rescued from the garbage bin outside SUB, where it had been tossed during construction of the Bearpit, the SU's storage facility. The banner has since disappeared.

GLIMPSES FROM THE GATEWAY—1960-1969

"Assiniboia Won't Make Golden Anniversary—End in Sight"— January 22, 1960

ASSINIBOIA, the University's second building, was to be demolished to make way for a new Education Building. There was a protest, and the Education Building was re-sited.

"Fall Convocation Held at Calgary Auditorium—Over 450 Degrees Conferred"—November 1, 1960

"THIS CONVOCATION OFFICIALLY OPENED the Alberta branch of the University here," proclaimed *The Gateway*. Dr. Malcolm Taylor was installed as principal. Taylor predicted a spiralling rise in campus enrolment, staff, and facilities. He was right.

"15,000 tour U of A Campus on Varsity Guest Weekend"— February 28, 1961

MORE THAN 4,000 PEOPLE attended Varsity Varieties, the song-and-dance show conceived by Joe Shoctor. During "VGW" there were river chuckwagon races, a big dance, displays in all the major campus buildings, and an all-day nursery in the Students' Union Building. The University Symphony and the Mixed Chorus held concerts. There were endless coffee and hot chocolate parties, and teas, and the Ballet Club hosted lunch. Studio Theatre performed *The Merchant of Venice* for the second time that year. The campus vibrated with activity.

"Library Smoking Rooms Will Give Way to Books. The Rutherford Smoking Room Will Be Sacrificed for Stack Space for at least One Winter Session"—December 1, 1961

"THIS WAS CONFIRMED MONDAY in an interview with Bruce Peel, chief librarian at Rutherford," *The Gateway* reported. 'I strongly believe that students should have a place for relaxation and smoking in a library," said Mr. Peel, "but this is a necessary and temporary measure. The only other alternative is to stop ordering books."

"Miss Freshette 1962 Named Tonight"—October 12, 1962

THE FRONT PAGE of *The Gateway* had a photo of five women in short shorts and high heels arrayed in a kick line. "Miss Freshette 1962 will be named at the annual Block A dance in Phys Ed Gym," said *The Gateway*. It was still an era of beauty queens.

"Bears Best Birds Beaten"—October 19, 1962

THE GOLDEN BEARS beat the UBC Thunderbirds 30–0 before 2,000 fans.

"Remembering Walter A. Dinwoodie"—January 9, 1963

IN A SPECIAL memorial issue, *The Gateway* remembered this "friend of the students" who had worked with the SU for 15 years. Walter Dinwoodie "contributed to the growth of a strong and independent student government....He was always able to find time to discuss the many problems in university life with students involved in extracurricular activities. He kept

Top: During the 1950s and most of the 1960s, Varsity women were crowned as "queens." Two of the most popular events were the crowning of Miss Freshette (a first-year student) and, as pictured here in 1965, the crowning of the Engineering Queen. By the late 1960s, there were continuous protests that beauty contests objectified women. (UAA 69–19–308)

Bottom: Kick-lines were a popular part of student political campaigns in the 1950s and 1960s. (UAA 69–66–852)

**"Picturesque Garneau Faces
Massive Hatchet Job"**

"SOMETIME IN THE DIM PAST," *wrote* The
Gateway *on October 13, 1967, "an idiotic planning
board let the lands which are now Windsor
Park slip through the grasp of the University."
The University was now poised to expand into
Garneau. "Even now," said* The Gateway,
*"bulldozers and scrapers are busy levelling the
block north of the Tuck Shop, turning what was
once a quiet residential street into a temporary
parking lot." The fraternity house that was the
original Garneau mansion, all the houses along
90th Avenue, and all the houses in North Garneau
were, according to* The Gateway, *scheduled for
destruction.*

    The Gateway *was a strong supporter of the
Garneau neighbourhood. The original Garneau
home, with the property acquired in 1874, was
on the lane at the rear of 11108-90 Avenue. An
old maple tree planted by Laurent Garneau still
stands.* The Gateway *subtitle had this to say
about the Garneau community: "They Belong."*
(University of Alberta Alumni Association)

the machinery of student government operative. He was the man who helped ideas become realities. He found a way of making budgets matter less than problems; he made the Students' Union the smoothly functioning apparatus it has become. He died suddenly at age 57....Walter Dinwoodie was never too busy to see a student; a constant stream of students entered his office every day. Extracurricular activities will suffer for his passing."

"Universal Accessibility"—September 22, 1965

THE CANADIAN UNIVERSITY STUDENTS CONGRESS was planning a "national Day of Awareness [in the] fall as part of a long term plan to achieve universal accessibility to higher education." At the top of the CUS accessibility agenda was elimination of tuition fees. The Canadian Union of Students represented some 138,000 university students attending 45 member institutions.

"I Have Seen Registration"—September 22, 1964

JON WHYTE, a graduate student, wrote this poem about registration: "I have seen the best minds of my generation raving, stark, hysterical, mad through the rigours of registration, who fought the IBM machines and ended up perforated, who stood in line for hours just to find that their choice of class had already been filled...." By 1968, *The Gateway* was running a composite photo of students and cattle lining up for registration.

"Finian's Rainbow—a Jubilaires' Production"—February 16, 1968

THE JUBILAIRES, comprised of students who were not in the BFA program, sold out three February performances of *Finian's Rainbow* at the Jubilee Auditorium.

"University Women's Club Defends Home of Alberta's First Premier—Board of Governors Decides to Tear Down Rutherford House"—November 27, 1969

MANY PROTESTED THE PROPOSAL to tear down Rutherford House, but no group was more persistent that the University Women's Club (UWC). The first phase of the Humanities Complex involved destruction of the mansion Rutherford had built in 1911. The UWC said that the House "represents much of the beginning of a province, a city, a university, and that to destroy the house is to destroy part of our provincial heritage." In reply, a representative of the University's planning group said, "I'm sure these ladies are well-intentioned, but they are thoroughly misinformed. The committee has gone into great depths on the question and are convinced it is in the best interests of everyone involved that the building be torn down to make room for the Humanities Complex."

In response, the UWC raised $17,000 to save the building. The University finally reversed its course, and the building, which had been the DU fraternity house for 20 years, was saved from the wrecker's ball. It was restored by the provincial government, and today it is an oasis in the midst of a bustling campus, where tea is served each afternoon. Rutherford's library is perfectly intact on the first floor, and it does not take much imagination to remember back to a time when Rutherford would invite university students to come to the house to read through his vast collection of Canadiana and to study in his private library.

"Sexuality and Society—Topic of Discussion in Jubilee Auditorium"—September 18, 1969

A FILM CALLED *Human Reproduction* was the on the cards for the evening, after which there would be a panel discussion. The panellists included Dr. Vant, Sister St. Francis Cabrini, Reverend Dan MacMillan, and Dr. Jean Nelson. *The Gateway* promised that "there will be questions from the floor." Dr. Vant's lectures had been a big draw on campus since 1945. They were first held just for women, and then given for the men in separate sessions. Dr. Vant spelled it all out, from descriptions of various birth control methods to advice on when (and when not) to have sex.

"Cabaret Night—Dinwoodie, 8:00 pm to 1:00 am"—"SUB Comes of Age"—September 19, 1969

IN 1969, the drinking age was 21, and the new SUB threw its first party. Drinks were "fifty cents each; bottled beer three for a dollar. Lots of food available. Dine, drink, dance—bring proof of age." And as *The Gateway* reported, "Whether they called it Cabaret Night or a 'social function', Thursday was SUB's first wet bust-out for students. Upwards of 600 chuggers and sippers danced to the Winnipeg Carpetbaggers or Polka Kings or something—take your pick. Whoever it was, we hope they were 21 or there's gonna be trouble." In 1971, the drinking age in Alberta was lowered to 18.

Excerpts from the "Casserole" Column

The Gateway revived the popular "Casserole" column from the 1920s. The new Casserole covered social and political issues and many controversial topics of the day. Here are some highlights.

"Vietnam War Protest" and "LSD"—October 15 and November 24, 1967

Under the headline "The Military Reacts...to the hippie menace" came this special report to the Canadian University Press from Washington: "Teams of US Army infiltrators dressed like hippies were spread through the crowd of demonstrators during the antiwar demonstration at the Pentagon October 21."

"Lennon and Ono"—September 16, 1969

"John Lennon and Yoko Ono were in Toronto this summer staging a week-long bed-in for peace. During the week, Lennon phoned Berkeley, where the massacre of People's Park has taken place, and said words to the effect of: 'You guys are doing really good things, but remember, be non-violent: you've got to change their heads.'"

"Kahn-Tineta Horn Verbally Scalps Whites—"We're your Landlords and the Rent is Due"—September 19, 1969

The caption to Horn's photo read, "A pox on your cities. Why don't you all go back to where you came from?"

"This University Doesn't Serve the People"—September 19, 1969

"The sons and daughters of the people will protest when their teachers tell them that labour struggles are subversive," wrote the Students for a Democratic University. "They will protest when they are taught that the government is right to interfere with the workers' struggles. They will protest when they are told that wage increases cause inflation. They will

By the late 1960s, there were continuous protests that beauty contests objectified women. In this 1969 photograph taken at an SU election rally by Steve Makris, a woman holds a sign that reads: "Women are beautiful, radical women are more beautiful, liberated women are the most beautiful of all."

(UAA 69–19/proof sheet 68–821)

insist that the University be a place where the sons and daughters of the people learn about the peoples' struggles."

"Pollution"—October 2, 1970

IN THE FIRST WAVE of awareness about pollution, Casserole ran a four-page spread on water pollution and a three-page spread on air pollution.

"College Saint-Jean Now Belongs to the U of A"—December 3, 1970

"THE UNIVERSITY OF ALBERTA and Collège Saint-Jean d' Edmonton today signed an agreement under which the Collège becomes an integral part of the University. They were first affiliated in 1963. With the new agreement it is hoped to preserve the French culture in Alberta, and to make some students fluently bilingual in French."

"Introduction to Encounter"—October 3, 1969

THE SUB-HEADLINE EXPLAINED what the new-age term "encounter' meant: "For those who seek relief from superficiality and alienation, a one-evening program introducing several methods of increasing inter-personal awareness and growth. Casual clothes recommended. Bring a pillow to sit on. Five dollars adults; three dollars students."

One local institute running encounter events was Cold Mountain. They advertised a two-day session on "Body Awareness and a Sense of Being: A Weekend With the Well-Known Doctor Edward Maupin of Esalen Institute, Big Sur, California. To awaken a sense of self more primary than ideas, definitions and fantasies. Fifty dollars." Another ad promoted a "Residential Workshop. An intensive 'live-in' workshop using a variety of methods to promote self-growth and change...."

"Women Invade Masculine World—Medicine and Law become Co-Ed"—October 9, 1969

"TWENTY-FOUR GIRLS are enrolled in first-year Med, twenty in Law. Judy Gabert, first-year Medicine, wanted to be a doctor all her life: 'I want to see the attitude that women must be crazy to want to get into medicine changed.' Judy feels that girls are accepted by the male students, but there is a small amount of opposition from the older male doctors, who, Judy says, dislike girls being trained as doctors and then getting married and wasting their careers. The Law student, Laura, has not noticed discrimination in her classes. 'The guys tease us, but it's all in fun.'" The article goes on to say, "She doesn't want to be thought of as a feminist invading the ranks of male society. She thinks it's perfectly natural for women to be in the professions."

"Abortion is Women's Goal"—September 29, 1969

"THE UNCONDITIONAL RIGHT to abortion should be the prime goal of the women's liberation movement" was the bottom line for a speaker from the Young Socialists in Canada. Some of Young Socialists' other goals were free daycare centres, pregnancy leave without loss of pay, an end to discriminatory hiring practices, and universal free distribution of birth control information and devices. Also, "housewives should receive a wage from the government because their work is 'socially necessary labour and should be paid for as such.'"

First Jubilaire Production—September 29, 1969

THE FALL SHOW was *Stop the World, I Want to Get Off!* Tickets for the sellout production were $2.

"Installation of a President: 1969"—October 7, 1969

MAX WYMAN was being installed in the midst of protests and social change. The caption beneath his photo was a Wyman quote. It read, "In dissension there is strength."

"Council Socks Queen's"—October 9, 1969

"A LONG-TABLED MOTION by Academic Vice-President Liz Law withdrawing Council's financial support for 'any contests or other activity which relegates women to object status' passed in a 10–6 vote."

"Miss Law, speaking in support of the motion, said women should not be considered sexual objects and that a beauty contest is, in effect, a public auction."

"[Computerized] Circulation System for Library—October 10, 1969

BEFORE 1969, students had to fill out and sign a separate form for each book they took out of the library. A computerized circulation system was about to revolutionize the process. "U of A students will no longer be suffering from writers' cramp after taking books out of the library," said *The Gateway*. "The present McBee system will be replaced Wednesday by a new IBM system. All you have to do is pick up your new card and you present your new card with the books—no writing is involved." In the October 9 edition, there was a notice from Chief Librarian Bruce Peel: "Library cards are now being distributed in the Cameron Library. Important!! The new punched cards are a must in the computerized circulation system going operational next week in the libraries."

"Non-Academic Staff Want Seats"—October 16, 1969

SUPPORT STAFF wanted permanent seats on the Senate, GFC, and the Board. At this point, the only seat they had on a central body was a non-voting seat on the Senate.

"Student Health Says They Won't Prescribe the Pill to Unmarried Women"—October 17, 1969

BY 1970, the Pill was available at the Student Health Centre.

"Pot Harmless"—October 20, 1969

"EVEN THOUGH he wants the spread of marijuana halted, 'at all costs,'" reported *The Gateway*, "a high-ranking RCMP official said that marijuana has no known pathological effects and actually produces much less violence than alcohol."

In the same edition was one of the first ads for pantyhose. The brand name was "Whisper" and they cost $1.79 a pair. Stockings would soon be passé.

"Bisons Power Sweep Leads Way to Unblemished Record"—November 4, 1969

YES, despite all the upheaval on campus, sport was, as always, big news in *The Gateway*.

"The herd trampled the Golden Bears 38–2 before a crowd of 3,300 at Varsity Stadium," said *The Gateway*. The Bisons finished the season 6–0, but in the accompanying photo, a student named Don Hickey, #73, was shown running towards a major score. Don Hickey later became vice-president of facilities and operations at the University. The following fall, the Golden Bears defeated Royal Military College 74–0 "before some 7,500 spirited onlookers."

"Pipes Break in New BioSci Complex—Construction Features Could Endanger the Students Working in Laboratories"— December 4, 1969

THE TROUBLE with the pipes in the new building gave reporters at *The Gateway* an opportunity to have a field day with other concerns about the building: "Everyone hated the new BioSci building—certain features potentially dangerous—drainpipes which carry acids are made out of glass—one of the pipes in the main floor elevators burst, spilling water all over the floor—labs on the first floor had only one door, which could be a fire hazard— the doors close automatically and could lock a person in very easily—fire extinguishers installed only on the first floor—no showers available near the labs—heat in the labs is up to 90 degrees—experiments have been spoiled—labs on the first floor are located directly above the boilers—no heat in the lavatories—the design of the building has been described as resembling that of a monastery—there are few windows, and the color scheme is depressing—every time they drop something upstairs we get flakes of cement coming off the ceiling in the staff room—there's no place for students to hang up coats in the labs—no place to eat lunch, no place to study, drain pipes under the sinks leak constantly, and there are cockroaches."

Architectural historian Kathryn Ivany provides the background. "The Biological Sciences Building was the last building on campus for which Public Works supervised the construction. It was built by several different contractors working at once, and has interlocking floors and departments." Popular legend has it that when all was said and done, floors, doors and walls did not line up. It is also said, in an unsubstantiated report, that in recompense for the disastrous construction débacles, the University received 26,000 floor tiles from one of the builders.

"Nursing Education"—December 12, 1969

IN A TWO-PAGE SPREAD, *The Gateway* explored whether or not nurses were cheap labour. The vice-president of the Alberta Association of Students advocated fundamental changes in how nurses were educated. She wanted "an effective student voice, both for education and living arrangements, a student bill of rights, [and] abolition of Nursing residences so that [nursing students could] live in the community with other students."

MEET ALUMNI FROM THE 1960s [17]

Fran van Dusen Olson (DIPNU '63)

A Pioneer Background

FRAN OLSON is known today as the trailblazer who founded Edmonton's Festival of Trees, and as the first woman to chair the University Hospital Foundation.

But back in 1960, she was just 18-year-old Fran. Dressed in the blue-striped uniform and black stockings that identified her as a probationary nursing student, she was beginning the first of three years of study for a diploma in Nursing.

There's a fearless, "let's-make-it-happen" quality to Fran Olson. No matter what the apparent obstacles, she buckles down and gets the job done. Not much can stop her when her mind is made up.

"My grandmother pioneered in Saskatchewan, travelling from Québec by red river cart and then living in a sod house. My dad was born in Saskatchewan in 1915, ten years after Alberta and Saskatchewan became provinces, and he settled in Alberta." Fran remembers being raised in Jasper Place, which at that time was a separate town from Edmonton. "It was a simpler time," Fran says. "For instance, when we took the bus in to Edmonton, there was usually a lot of mud. We wore gum boots to walk to the bus stop and carried our shoes with us. We left our gum boots at the bus stop, and they were always there when we came back." Fran also remembers that as a little girl, her mother could put her on the bus all alone to visit her grandmother. "The first bus driver made sure I changed buses at the right spot," she says, "and the second bus driver knew exactly where to drop me off."

Fran Olson as a Nursing student. Fran would later chair the University Hospital Foundation and found the Festival of Trees. Fran's future husband, Al, was an engineering student at the time this photo was taken. (Private Collection)

For Fran and her three sisters, there was no question whatsoever about going to university—it was expected. Her father's view was that "for *this* generation, you simply had to have an education."

It just so happened that Fran's aunt was president of the Alberta Association of Registered Nurses. "She was a great role model," says Fran, "and so nursing was a natural choice. Back then, nursing and teaching were standard occupations for women—girls were told that these professions were 'something to fall back on if anything ever happened to your husband.' That sounded funny to me since, at age 12, I had never thought about getting married."

Entering the three-year diploma program instead of the longer degree program was also an easy choice. "But by the time I finished high school at Ross Sheppard," explains Fran, "I had found the love of my life, and Al was going to be finished with his engineering degree in 1963. I chose the diploma program in nursing because I would finish in three years, at the same time as Al. I also liked the 'hands on' aspect of the diploma program, where you were right out on the wards from day one."

Living on Prem 50 Weeks a Year

"I LOVED NURSING," says Fran. "I had a marvellous time, and in 2003 our entire class gathered for a 40th reunion. We share a tremendous camaraderie." The camaraderie comes not only from living together in the Nurses' Residence, but also from supporting one another through long school days and a gruelling shift schedule.

"In addition to our university classes," Fran explains, "we had to work one shift—either 7 A.M. to 3:30 P.M., 3 P.M. to 11 P.M., or 11 P.M. to 7 A.M. If you had the night shift right after one of those long afternoon pathology or biology labs—too bad! You did both. Even tougher was the night shift followed by a morning class. Each one of us had long, long days, and we worked six days a week, the entire year, except for the two weeks in the summer when we had vacation.

"And we were all skinny little things, all of us. Probably because the hospital food was so awful. Even the smell of it turned my stomach. So we all ate in residence, where there was no cafeteria. We lived on cereal, noodle soup, and Prem. Lots of Prem. It was a kind of canned ham.

"By the end of our first year," Fran says, "most of us had night shift at the Mewburn Pavilion, where we were left in charge of an entire floor. I was 19 years old and in charge of all these old guys. It was a little frightening, but it was expected of me, and I did it. Now? I'd be horrified with a teenager in charge of a hospital floor if my 90-year-old father was there. But we had good training from British women in their 40s. We thought of them, at the time, as the old British taskmasters. They taught us well."

Tossing the Dreaded Shoes off the High Level Bridge

YOU COULD ALWAYS TELL in what year of the diploma program a nursing student was by looking at the uniform she wore. Fran remembers a great deal of ceremony and tradition associated with uniforms. "For the first year," she says, "we wore black shoes and stockings—which we hated—and a blue-striped dress. Over the dress was a starched bib and apron, topped with an awful starched collar held in place with a collar pin. Our necks were raw."

After six months, probation was over and, in a formal ceremony, students were given a traditional nurse's cap. In the second year, the blue dress was replaced with a pink one.

"The best thing about second year," says Fran, "is that the dreadful black stockings and shoes were replaced with white. We did a Snake Dance all the way down to the High Level Bridge and tossed the hated black shoes and stockings into the river."

High-jinks with Fran

WITH 12-HOUR DAYS, including Saturdays, and a strict 10:30 P.M. curfew, was there ever any fun?

"We had a housemother, the wife of a retired minister," recalls Fran, "and a night supervisor named Mrs. McNeil, who vigilantly checked us in. We did get three late passes a month—one for 11:30, one for midnight, and one for 2 A.M. Mrs. McNeil would sit by the back door and clock us in, one by one. If you came in after 10:30 P.M. and didn't have a pass, you lost all your late privileges. This made it hard to date because the guys didn't have any restrictions. And my boyfriend Al was a member of the Phi Delta Theta fraternity and they had these *amazing* parties." So who would risk losing their late passes? No one. Instead, they manoeuvred creatively around the curfew.

"Now Mrs. McNeil was a large woman and she didn't move very quickly," says Fran. "So this is what we would do.

"If you were late and had no pass, your classmates would go to the end of the building and open the locked door, setting off the fire alarm. Mrs. McNeil would heft herself out of her chair and slowly make her way down to the other end of the building to investigate. Whoever was late could then sneak in through the tunnel that connected our residence with the hospital, or come in through the back door. The alarm always stopped before Mrs. McNeil ever got to the other side of the building, and by the time she was back at her post, whoever was late was safely upstairs. The other method for avoiding Mrs. McNeil was to tie sheets together and lower someone down to the ground from our third-floor rooms."

Panty Raids

IN THE *EVERGREEN AND GOLD* yearbooks, there are photos of panties adorning campus trees. Fran explains how a 1960s panty raid worked.

"We had a lot of fun in the 1960s, and some Faculty group was always up to something. Take the engineers. They always found a nursing student who would let them into our residence for a panty raid. None of us had much money, and we all hand-washed our personal laundry. The wooden dryer racks in the bathrooms were always crowded with freshly-washed panties and bras. The engineers would pick a day, come early in the morning, and then set off the alarm. We would all be sound asleep in bed. Then these guys would storm into our bathrooms and snatch our undies. The next day all our lingerie would be hanging outside in the trees."

Life After Nursing

"AL AND I MARRIED in 1963, right after our graduation from Nursing and Engineering. I always thought I would go back and get my degree. I wish I had. Especially after I had children, it would have given me so much more opportunity. With the diploma, you were limited to general duty nursing on rotating shifts—nearly impossible if you had a young family. A degree would have opened the doors to teaching, administration, public health or research."

For Fran, who had three young children, shift work was out of the question. But she discovered that she had developed an underlying set of skills as a diploma nurse, a set of skills with a universal applicability. "I knew from my diploma experience that I loved the 'people side' of nursing. Our whole class was a compassionate group. We focused on developing a caring bedside manner and we listened carefully to people's medical problems.

"I wanted to use my people skills, and so I enrolled in Grant MacEwan's media and communications program. Then I worked in my husband's construction company doing marketing. They needed someone who could listen to what clients were saying and 'translate' the engineering side of a proposal into language that a client could understand. It was a lot like listening to patients' problems and then explaining to them, in a way they could understand, what was going to happen as they went through the health care system. As our construction business grew, we set up a more formal marketing department, and I moved into the human resources area—another people-related area."

Fran also put her experience in nursing to work when she chaired the University Hospital Foundation. "I had worked with health care professionals before," she says, "but I also had learned a lot about how you could really connect with the Edmonton community. I wanted to change the Foundation's basic approach to fundraising so that Edmontonians would open their hearts and their pocketbooks to help the Foundation achieve objectives we all understood and shared." One of Fran's fellow Board members credits her with "turning the Foundation around and modernizing its fundraising capability." Fran also founded Edmonton's Festival of Trees, an extraordinary event powered entirely by volunteers. The Festival of Trees has raised over $7 million in 19 years.

Fran has some advice for today's students. "Nursing is one of the essential links in the health care chain of survival. Whatever path you choose, remember that caring and compassion for others is the key."

Myra Davies (BA '69)

MYRA'S YEARS at the U of A were smack dab in the middle of the 1960s. There wasn't much happening around her that she didn't get into—the new left, the new age, the new Students' Union Building. She was on the committee that produced the first teacher evaluation guide and ran the first and only art gallery in SUB. Myra moved from a circle of fraternity friends to the subculture of bohemians, radicals, and artists who appeared on the campus scene in the 1960s, to union organizing. In what she calls her "Red Emma period," she and Percy Wickman organized the first certified bargaining unit on campus in SUB. She entered the Faculty of Law from whence she transferred to McGill. "I *loved* university," she says. "I came alive."

"I grew up in Edmonton's West End, in Laurier Heights," Myra says. "My mother wanted me to go to university. Our deal was that if I didn't get in, I could go to the College of Art in Calgary, but I wasn't ready to leave home yet. I can't think of anyone who went off immediately to school somewhere else. When I started at the U of A, I was young, naïve and more interested in boys and skiing than academic pursuits. The only people I knew on campus were frat boys I'd dated while in high school."

Social Life and First Impressions of Campus

"I LOVED the Fraternity spring formals. These were elegant affairs held in good hotels downtown. We wore long gowns in pastel colours. For the Sigma Alpha Mu formal, I bought a long black dress, though my mother said I was too young for black. It was very Jackie Kennedy. Sigma Alpha Mu was the Jewish fraternity and the Alums there reputedly didn't care for members dating non-Jewish girls, but my date and I thought I could pass for Jewish. When I ran into my childhood dentist at the dance, I knew that ruse wasn't successful. The frat scene was not always as benign as this.

"The Catholic fraternity's spring formal was preceded the previous weekend by 'The Pig Party,' where boys went down to 97th Street and picked up the ugliest women they could find and brought them to their frat house for a party. The 'brother' who brought the 'ugliest girl' won. The trophy, a gold pig on a wooden base, was awarded at the formal. We women, in our pastel gowns, sat through this in silence. There was no sense of solidarity. Even among the belles of these balls, it was survival of the fittest. One had to be entrancing without 'giving anything away.' If you had sex, from then on the boys would describe you with this line: 'she goes.' This kept me virginal.

"There were also the DUs—the Delta Upsilons. They lived in Rutherford House on Saskatchewan Drive and these boys knew how to drink hard and party."

Myra graduated from high school in 1966. "That summer," she remembers, "I gave up frat boys and turned my attention to Jeff Dvorkin, a history student who'd already spent a year in France. Jeff came from my end of town and our little brothers had a rock band together. Jeff went on to become head of CBC Radio News and later of Public Radio in the States. His arty political friends pegged me as a frat type and some of the women were quite rude, but I persevered. By September, I had 'gone arty,' as one of my frat acquaintances put it."

Myra's mother had taken her to the University's Open House the year before Myra started her BA, but as was the case for many students, the Open House didn't seem to orient Myra very well.

"On my first exploratory walk around campus I got lost and ended up near Saskatchewan Drive by the Ring Houses. I didn't know where I was. I was disoriented, exhausted, and in tears. Peter Amerongen came along and rescued me. Peter was a DU frat boy whose father was Speaker in the House. "Later on," Myra says, "Peter dropped out, grew out a bushy beard, and moved into the Pembina River farm co-op started by a professor at the U of A. The one time I was out there for a party, they roasted a pig in a pit outside.

"Registration was confusing and time-consuming. It was held in Convocation Hall in the Arts Building, girls wore skirts and nylons, and many boys were in jackets and ties. You stood in a long line to register for each course. The Prof sat at a little table at the front of the line. If the course was full when you got to him, too bad.

"The Arts Building—with its Beaux Arts architecture and bronze busts of great men in the lobby—reflected the ideal of Liberal Arts. Up on the third floor, in the Art Department, there were big plaster casts of Greek marbles, though by then they were no longer used for drawing classes. The lounge, to the right as you came through the front doors of the building, was old-fashioned with a fireplace and built-in oak cabinets, like an English gentlemen's club. The classroom on the opposite side of the foyer was where Henry Kreisel lectured. I used to sneak in sometimes. He was so popular you couldn't always get a seat."

The Original SUB

MYRA SAYS that the original SUB was a great hangout. "There was a huge ballroom on the second floor and a big cafeteria in the basement," she remembers. "As you came up the stairs from the front door," Myra says, "the Wauneita Lounge was to your left. Every woman student was automatically a member of the Wauneita Society. We lost the women's lounge in the move to the new SU building. Wauneita, and the Office of Dean of Women, seemed to be irrelevant and elitist vestiges of the past. We should have transformed them, but nobody thought of it. We weren't conscious of ourselves as women in a political sense. The Women's Movement came later."

Tea with the Dean of Women, Mrs. J. Grant Sparling—
Convention in the Midst of Change

"THE DEAN OF WOMEN, Mrs. Sparling, invited all 'co-eds' to tea in her lovely old-fashioned apartment in Pembina Hall in groups of 10 or 12. Gloves and skirts were *de rigeur*. I wore white kid gloves with a pink Italian knit suit and a bow in my Annette Funicello hair. By contrast, my new boyfriend, Jeff, wore black turtlenecks, smoked Gauloises cigarettes, played twelve-string guitar and sang Parisian ballads at Giuseppe's. No pink Italian knits welcome there.

"While I was in first year," Myra remembers, "a friend got pregnant. We were so ignorant that we went to the main library and looked under "A" for Abortion to try to find out what it entailed. We found descriptions of the horrors of back street abortions in the slums of nineteenth century London, but nothing that explained the process, which was still a criminal code offence. Discreetly, we let word out that we were looking for a doctor. It had to be a proper doctor. The year before another friend had died from a botched job by medical students. My mother was scared stiff that we'd end up in jail as I booked a motel room near the Royal Alex and collected the things that would be needed. Thank God the pill came out soon after that, although to get it you had to pretend to be married."

Two Different Worlds—The 1950s and the 1960s

IN 1966 the Tuck Shop still served its famous cinnamon buns. "A hot dinner cost almost nothing," remembers Myra. "Good, cheap, and served on thick crockery dishes. The front part of 'Tuck' was a canteen-style shop that sold personal items and candy—the only place on campus where these items were available. One passed through the shop to the restaurant with its long lunch counter and booths with mirrors above them. The floor was battleship linoleum and the air was hazy with steam and cigarette smoke. There was a big room for parties in the basement. Everyone—from frat boys to old Profs who ate there because they weren't married—went to Tuck, but the dominant group was a loose sub-culture of intellectuals, artists and activists.

"The first time I went to the Tuck Shop was on a sunny afternoon in late August, 1966. I was with Jeff. I was still working on securing his affections—a new boyfriend being central to my change of style and social circle. We sat in a booth with Jon Whyte and John Thompson—two heavy-duty English department philosopher poets. Jon showed me his ID card. It began with 59. That meant he had first registered in 1959, and *that* in turn meant he was old. I didn't understand a word they said but they didn't treat me like the bubblehead I was, which was a relief. I concluded even intellectuals were susceptible to feminine charm. I also realized I was intellectually retarded. There was work to be done if I was ever to hold my own intellectually with them. I was very keen to get started.

"Jeff's circle included Carol Harmon and Anne Green—Drama students interested in the strange plays of Wilfred Watson, an English prof, Chris Rideout, who was doing a Master's on T.S. Elliott, and Barry Record, a black playwright from the Caribbean. Barry had a beautiful blond girlfriend, Terry Turner. One afternoon in the Tuck Shop, Terry asked me, 'Where are you politically?' 'I have no idea,' I replied. 'Let's find out,' she said. I answered her questions as best I could and she pronounced me 'a moderate.'

"Evenings, the bohemian scene into which I was insinuating myself often congregated at Giuseppe's Pizza Parlor on 109th Street—a basement with a black ceiling and pseudo Picassos on the walls—to listen to bongo-playing poets and folksingers with guitars. During the day, it was coffee at Hot Caf, more classes. Hot Caf stood where CAB is today. Built during World War II, the building was utilitarian and had a spare, military look. It was one large space inside with long windows of little panes of glass. You could sit in Hot Caf as long as you liked, and look out those big windows, and they had the same cinnamon buns as the Tuck Shop.

"We all had one foot in the 1950s and one foot in the 1960s," says Myra. "Outside of the arty scene, women were still going into Nursing, Home Economics or Education and many admitted they were on campus to get their 'MRS.' In other words, they were looking for a husband.

"My mother wanted me to rush a sorority and though not interested, I did it—but I wasn't chosen. During 'rush,' you went to tea in Garneau sorority houses with slipcovers on the furniture and long drapes. It was very 1940s. For Frosh week, some boys still wore green and gold freshman beanies. There was hazing, and not only at the fraternities. Engineers dyed the first year students blue—it was done in a big vat outside their building.

"I have to thank the many foreign students I met at the University for broadening my world. Prem Saigel, from India, was in the English

Leonard Cohen, one of many poets, musicians, and artists to visit the U of A in the 1960s.
(UAA 69–16-66–506)

Department and had two brothers. One was in Chemistry and the other was in jail in India for political activity. It was said that a couple of small African men, who lived at the International House, had been with the Mau-Mau in Kenya. I have no idea if this was true but it endowed them with major cachet. These people and others like them brought the outside world into Edmonton.

"Leonard Cohen visited the English Dept that fall. He was at all the arty parties singing 'Susanne.' So many women talked of 'having been with Leonard' that one had to wonder. One rarely saw concert pianist Marek Jablonksi during the day, but he cut romantic figure at night dashing about in his long black cape. He was back from Warsaw after winning the big Chopin competition. The first woman to wear a mini-skirt on campus was English student cum poet, Patricia Hughes. She wore the mini with black tights, a black top, and black eye make-up on her very white face. Mary Van Stolk, who was said to be an ex-model who'd been on the cover of *Vogue*, personified the 'Ban the Bomb' movement. Later, she founded the environmental movement at the U of A with a campaign called STOP (Save Tomorrow, Oppose Pollution). As a first year student, most of these characters intimidated the hell out of me, so I didn't often actually speak with them. But I watched and listened and was fascinated.

"On the other side of the cultural divide," says Myra, "a traditional 'Varsity' vibe ruled over at the old Students' Union Building—today's University Hall. That winter, Al Anderson was elected president of Students' Union. He was conservative, with slicked-backed hair and Elvis Costello-style glasses. The student musical theatre society, Jubilaires, and the Glee Club, were leftovers from the 1950s whose days were numbered, though we didn't know that yet. The Jubilaires put on a terrific production of the musical comedy, *Once Upon a Mattress*, starring Anne Wheeler, at the Jubilee Auditorium. Anne was hilarious. Later, she became a filmmaker."

The New Left

"WHEN I WAS IN SECOND YEAR, the New Left emerged in a group called Students for a Democratic University, led by two grad students from the great beyond—Mort Newman and Jon Bordo. During my first visit to the Tuck Shop in August 1966, Jeff had pointed out Jon Bordo, identifying him then, erroneously, as 'a Trot'—in other words, a Trotskyist or Trotskyite—

depending if you were for or against. Mort Newman and Jon Bordo spoke out all over the place, in complex Marxist language that wasn't easy to follow. Mort was tall and lanky and came from New York. Bordo, small and wiry, was from Montréal. They both had shaggy hair and wore army jackets. Jon Whyte affectionately described Bordo as 'a wharf rat.' I thought he looked like Bob Dylan. In any case, Bordo and Newman were the U of A's versions of Abbie Hoffman and Jerry Rubin. Witty, charismatic and sexy, they connected us to the transnational student movement.

"Mort used to hang outside the executive offices in the new Students' Union Building just to make SU President Marilyn Pilkington nervous. He called it 'hulking.' Wherever these guys went, suits got nervous. *The Edmonton Journal* referred to them as 'outside agitators.' The *Journal's* view was that the University should keep them out. The University, as represented by President Johns, did not succumb to this kind of pressure.

"One day, as I was headed into the new Students' Union Building, Mort burst through the double doors followed by a boisterous crowd. 'Hey,' he called out happily. 'Come on with us—we're going over to occupy the President's office.'" It was as if this action was a lark and, in a sense, it was. The presidents of that era, Dr. Johns and later Dr. Max Wyman, knew many of these boys by name and had the wisdom to take a laid-back attitude to student demonstrations. By and large, so did the Edmonton police. With the exception of *The Edmonton Journal*—which was acidic, provocative, and not always factually correct—the authorities responded to protests with civility and some willingness to negotiate. Soon various boards began taking on student representatives. Ultra leftists pegged such reformism as co-option, and it was. But it was better than the violent confrontations going on in the States."

The New SUB

"IN SEPTEMBER 1966, the new SUB opened. It had the best of everything. The main floor was a transit hall with an information desk and the gas flame fireplace. The Art Gallery and the music listening room were below the theatre, and the meditation room and offices for campus Chaplains were at the other end. The second floor had the Theatre and a theatre lobby called 'The Blue Room.' Then there was a big cafeteria, and the Dinwoodie ballroom along with the Students' Union executive offices, *The Gateway*

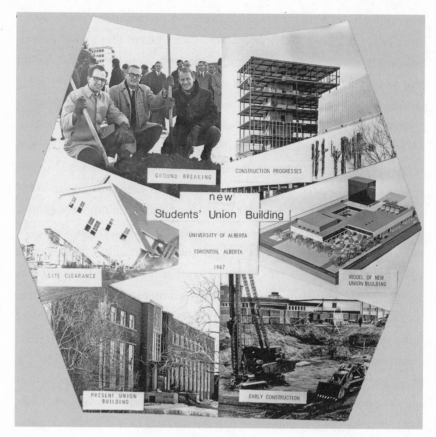

and the radio station. The tower housed a ceramics studio, hotel rooms and Room At The Top. The basement contained a bowling alley, curling rinks, a Bank of Montréal, and the lower level of the bookstore. The building was furnished with designer furniture from Europe. Bertie Richards, the architect, was especially happy with the Art Gallery and the new Students' Union permanent art collection. One per cent of building cost had been spent on works of art. I immediately began developing a program for the Gallery—for instance, getting National Gallery accreditation to host their travelling shows. Bertie came by often to see how the Gallery program was coming. I made the Gallery into a centre for new art forms—not just stuff on the wall, though we had that—but action art, new media, and cross-disciplinary projects. Margaret Atwood read poetry there many times, but our specialty was the 'happenings'—big multi-disciplinary and participatory art events—for which we took over the theatre and other parts of the building. A show of photos from the cultural revolution in China led to an occupation of the Gallery by Maoists. We faked a power cut and evacuated the building to get them out of there. A report of this in the *People's Canada Daily News* described me as 'a running dog lacky of American Imperialism.' On the other hand—not apropos this show—Jon Bordo told me when the revolution came, I'd be minister of culture.

"Of all guest speakers who came to the Students' Union," says Myra, "the Black Panthers were the most memorable. Some New Leftist group arranged this and persuaded the Students' Union to provide funding. I remember those four Panthers—all in black leather jackets and military berets with dark glasses—striding four abreast down the main hall of the Students' Union Building. In Dinwoodie, they stood together on a high platform as Fred Hampton spoke. A few months later, he was murdered in his bed by government forces. He'd been our guest so we all felt personally connected to his death and by extension to the whole race war in the States. Later, there were two other speakers I remember because I taped them on black and white video tape—Rene Lévesque in Dinwoodie, and Abbie Hoffman in the Kinsmen Field House.

"In the winter of 1968, Marilyn Pilkington was elected president of the Students' Union. She was conservative and wore good wools and pearls. As the date of a demonstration against fee hikes approached, there were calls for Marilyn to get out there and lead the march. She finally did it, but she was extremely uncomfortable about it. I understand Marilyn later became dean of Osgoode Law School. David Leadbeater, vice-president on Marilyn's council, was all for protests. He organized a big teach-in on American Influence in Canada and brought in Mel Watson to speak in SUB Theatre.

"After Marilyn," says Myra, "David Leadbeater was president of the Students' Union from 1969–1970. Still in the Young Liberals then, he was being groomed by Trudeau and agonizing over whether he was already too left wing for the Grits. He joined the NDP and we started going together. 'You have the look of a radical,' he told me admiringly, but I didn't think of myself as 'a radical.' That tag required more command of Marxist theory than I could muster then."

"Women Don't Belong in Graduate School"

BEFORE MYRA CAN SPEAK a word about her favourite professors, she remembers, instantly and vividly, a professor who shut her out. "I was in my qualifying year for Grad Studies. At this time the BA was a usually a three-year degree and you only did a fourth year to go on to Grad Studies. This professor from a small prairie town was living a Dr. Chips fantasy. He had a phoney English accent and loved to wear his academic gown with a hat in the style of Henry VIII. I queried him about a grade. I'd expected better. He said he'd thought about that at the time, but since he didn't approve of women in graduate school, he'd gone with a lesser grade. He told me this flat out. Supposedly the Sixties were the era of liberation and self-empowerment. But at the time this happened, it was 1970, and *that's* how empowered I was. Mortified, I said nothing about this to anyone. A few days later, passing the law building, I stopped in and asked about their program. I was ushered into the dean's office and interviewed on the spot. I had great grades, and I was in. I gave up the idea of graduate studies in the humanities and went into Law."

Best Professors, Classes, and Convocation

"J.B. TAYLOR taught the 100-level survey course in Art History. He looked like a bank manager in his bow tie and grey suit, but he was inspiring. George Rothrock in the History department made the French Revolution come alive. Henry Kreisel's English classes were wonderful. Sheila Watson encouraged women to be artists or writers. I took Ted Kemp's Aesthetics course—he was in the department of Philosophy. Kemp was a great educator with heart. Brother Donatus taught a history seminar—great. Richard Frucht's lectures in Cultural Anthropology opened my eyes to colonialism and what we now call 'globalization.'

"By second year, I'd decided to concentrate on Art History, although the Art department was studio-oriented. That year, a new department head from England hired a pack of young artists from England and the States. There were no MFA programs in Canada at this time and therefore there were no qualified Canadian candidates, or so he said. Some people felt this smacked of colonialism. The new instructors were young and full of themselves but they exposed us to trends in New York and London: Op Art, Pop Art, Conceptual Art, Techno Art—and so on. Older faculty, artists such as Norman Yates, David Cantine and Robert Sinclair, were our connection to Canadian art. Last to arrive, but not least, was an art historian, Dr. Jetska Sybesma, from Holland. She was the first scholar I ever met. I mean to say, she was the first to present her subject in the context of rigorous scholarship. Jetska was all about disciplined methodology. Great teacher for the serious student. If I'd had more courses from her, I might have gone on in academe."

Myra is quick to say that she didn't go to her Convocation. "It was irrelevant. My mum was upset. She wanted a grad picture. *Gateway* photographer Forrest Bard, known as the Woodland Poet, took one for me but she wasn't pleased with it because it had arty filters. When I graduated from Law, I had a conventional grad picture done for her, but I didn't bother with my Law convocation either."

Life After Graduation

AFTER MYRA GRADUATED and spent time as director of the SUB Art Gallery, she hosted and produced a weekly CKUA radio program about visual arts and did the qualifying year to prepare for graduate studies. Then she went to law school, beginning at the U of A and finishing at McGill.

"I meant to article, but it never happened. After a decade as a performing arts producer, I became an artist. I've made films and videos and created and directed non-conventional theatre. I've toured Europe several times and released three CDs as a spoken word and performance artist. My content usually relates to the dialectic between canon culture and women's sense of self.[18] Summers, I'm on the faculty at the Banff Centre as senior advisor to artists in residence.

"For my generation, most of our parents hadn't gone to university themselves. They were products of the Depression and the War. Some had been refugees, even concentration camp survivors. The parental class could be annoyingly conservative, but they did support universal access and they expected the University to do more than train us for jobs. When a friend of mine asked her father 'what am I getting out of all this?' His answer was, 'You're getting an education.' Tuition was low—$400 a year for Arts and $500 for Law. The University was supposed to make us into whole people who could build Alberta's future, not only in an economic sense, but also in the terms of culture, community and quality of life. In theory, we were all equally entitled to educational opportunity. This wasn't always realized, but it was an ideal on which there was public consensus."

Looking back, Myra believes she should have been more demanding and assertive. "I should have set my sights higher," she says. "I was halfway between a child and an adult when I went to university, and it was a whirl. I thought I was a lot smarter than I was, and I let the system carry me along. But I *did* get an education! I loved my time at the U of A."

Myra has some advice for today's students. "Get a humanities degree first," Myra urges. "The undergraduate years are the 'banquet days.' It's not always truth and justice they're dishing out there—one has to search that out for oneself—but it is a marvellous smorgasbord. Don't miss that."

Carl Urion (BED '70, PHD '78)

CARL WAS BORN just south of the Flathead Reservation in Montana. He was one of eight children and was among the very first Vietnam-era veterans to attend the University of Alberta on the American GI Bill. He taught at the University of Alberta from 1971 until his early retirement in 1997. Carl was instrumental in establishing the School of Native Studies and in 2004 was one of three Alberta Métis awarded the national Aboriginal Achievement Award. "That embarrassed me," he says, "because the award was meant to recognize achievement in Aboriginal higher education, but I have not been successful in making much of a difference in the way this university relates to Aboriginal people and Aboriginal issues." Others would disagree.

The area of Montana where Carl was born was once, like Alberta, controlled by the Hudson's Bay Company. There is a long history of formal higher education for women in his family. "My grandmother went to Drake University in the 1890s," he says. "As for the men, my great-aunt Helen said the feeling was 'why waste education on the men?' The men worked in the woods, in ranching, hunting, and in hauling freight in carts, while the women owned the real property and controlled the finances. It was the women who went to school. There are many women in my family who have gone to university, and a number have higher degrees, but I was the first man in the Montana branch of the family to get a PhD."

Carl adds that his family was bemused by the feminist movement of the 1960s. "In our tradition, men and women are equal, but we are from a tradition of strong women and my sisters reinforce that idea with my daughters. Maybe because of their areas of responsibility, women have focused more than men on formal education. In getting degrees, one of my nephews and I ran counter to the pattern in the family."

Carl went to high school in Wyoming, in a school district that was wealthy enough to afford to hire exceptional teachers. "It was a great education— good basic education and great programs in athletics and arts, especially music and drama—a very enriched program. I got a scholarship to go to university but didn't take it because I thought that at some point you would have to pay back the scholarship money to the donor, and I wasn't sure I could afford to do that. Can you believe it?!

"After high school, I was all over the map. I liked speaking Spanish so arranged to go to New Mexico to study languages. Instead, I worked in Wyoming for a while, then tried a small church college in Portland. That was a disaster. I worked and took classes where I could. By 1960, I was in San Francisco. This was during a transition from the post-war Beat period to the early days of the flower counterculture, before drugs turned the scene ugly. San Francisco was a great place to be at that time, and the campus life at San Francisco State College (now University) was vibrant.

"And then John F. Kennedy was shot. Students were unravelled. That event and the war redefined a lot of young people. For me, I was newly married and was trying to hold down a full-time job while going to school full-time. I didn't take school seriously at all and didn't even write my finals that winter. I somehow passed three of my courses anyhow. Then, because I was about to be drafted, I joined the US Navy, and went on active duty from 1964 to 1967. By the time I had completed my Navy hitch I knew that I didn't want to raise my kids in California. My wife was from Edmonton so we decided that was the place to go. I got an early discharge to attend Alberta College, but in fact enrolled at the U of A. I was admitted on probation because of my failed courses back at San Francisco State and got no net credit for all my previous work. So at age 27, with a wife and three kids, there I was at the U of A, enrolled as a first-year education student. I loved science, especially biology and organic chemistry, so thought for a while I might go into science or medicine. But my best experiences in a community had been on Crow Reservation in Southern Montana and I wanted to raise my kids in a community like that, so I decided that my goal was to get a degree and teach school in just that kind of place."

First Impressions of the U of A—"Belonging"

"I HAD MISGIVINGS about coming to the U of A," says Carl, "because I was admitted on probation. Grades had never meant much to me. Until I came to the U of A I seemed to be either top in the class or at the very bottom, and I could never predict which it would be. In my first year at the U of A I worked *very* hard, enjoyed the classes, and got great grades. In that first term I went from being on probation to getting called upstairs to be congratulated by Associate Dean Wilfrid Pilkington for getting a scholarship.

"I enjoyed registration. It was in-person registration in those days, and there were long lines, but I got all the courses I wanted. My two brothers-in-law lived near campus and they showed me the ropes."

The Tuck Shop was by far the best hang-out for Carl. "I loved that place. I loved the atmosphere. There were other spots on campus to hang out, like the basements of Cameron and Rutherford, but there was nothing like the Tuck Shop. As for studying, when I could, I studied outside. And I lived off campus in Queen Alexandra and walked a mile to and from University each day.

"My tuition was $300. I worked at the John Scott Library on weekends, when it was tiny and opened only for a few hours on Saturdays and Sundays. I also worked for Canadian Freightways as a rate assessor, because I'd been trained in transportation management in the US. As a grad student I waited tables downtown, at Primo's Mexican Restaurant.

"One of my earliest and most vivid memories of the U of A was attending a lecture-recital by a music professor, Manus Sasonkin. It was riveting. In that one session I could see that he was an articulate composer, a real teacher, and an engaging musician. I knew that I was lucky to be at a school that offered me the chance to hear people like Dr. Sasonkin."

Carl talks passionately about feeling affiliated with people and places. What does it means to affiliate? It means to connect and to attach to, to hold dear. *To belong.* How does one do that when one feels new to a situation or setting? For Carl, it was a dilemma for a while. In the US, his family would be identified as "part Indian," with ties to both Indian and white communities in Montana. Almost all his European ancestors had been in the charter settlements—Plymouth Rock, Virginia, and New Amsterdam—by the mid-1600s. Later, his family had been part of a network of Métis communities in Michigan, Wisconsin, and Montana. In Alberta, those ethnic lines meant something quite different.

When Carl came to the U of A, he expected to be part of an academic community. He also took it for granted that at the U of A he would meet scholars from the aboriginal communities in Alberta. First, it was a surprise to find so little sense of affiliation in the campus community, especially within the Faculties of Arts and Education. The place seemed impersonal to him—a higher education factory. Other urban universities in other cities provided better space where people could develop a sense of belonging, but the U of A seemed impersonal.

"In San Francisco, we had *created* communities where we could meet," says Carl. "At the U of A, some Faculties seemed like communities— Agriculture and Engineering were two—but in the Faculties of Arts and Education, the predominant sense was one of alienation. Compare that to the University of Toronto. They have a college system, where a large university is formed out of distinct smaller communities. The college is a community of people with faces and feelings where the real education happens. That community fosters better scholarship. There was no equivalent at the U of A."

The greatest surprise, however, was the apparent exclusion of Native people from Alberta's universities.

"Native People Can't Write Like This"

"DURING MY FIRST MONTH on campus," says Carl, "an outraged professor told me in front of a large class that I had plagiarized my paper because, he said, 'I *know* you are Native, and Native people can't write like this.' I told the professor, in front of the class, that I'd had a lot better academic preparation than most Alberta high school students and that I wouldn't be coming back to his class. I was probably as old as the professor and had been around the block a few times so I was sure enough of myself to speak back without anger. I didn't go back to his class except to write the exams. I got a 9 in the course, in the days when we were on a nine-point system. But how many 18-year-olds, from any background, could stand up to that kind of comment from a professor in the first month of class?

"Situations like that don't define the university experience for most of us, but racism is clearly an aspect for a majority of Native people who have been on campus any length of time. Some of us have been physically assaulted in racially motivated incidents and that's hard to forget. Between 1982 and 1987 I was director of the Office of Native Affairs, then Native Student Services. One day in 1987, someone in the Comptroller's Office simply removed my signing authority, and the signing authority of all the Native people in the office, explaining in a memo to Dean of Students Peter Miller that she was doing it to protect us, because Native people are well known to be subject to nepotism. I never have been able to figure out what kind of sense that made nor why it seemed unremarkable to so many who knew about it."

Hiding Ethnicity

"THERE WERE TWO OF US I know of who were Native, who were in University when I started at the U of A in 1967. I know of one Native woman who actually hid her ethnicity in the 1950s. By 1969, there were three or four Natives a year who were here studying. The fall of 1970 was a banner year because several Dene and Métis students from the NWT came to campus.

"It's strange that coming to university would have this effect, but being here really convinced me of the value of Aboriginal tradition. Other peoples' perception of us made us re-examine ourselves. Facing racism was part of that experience. Seeing the way Native people were characterized in scholarly discussion was an invitation for a re-examination of preconceptions. Some of us hadn't known we had been 'marginalized.' Those kinds of terms had not been on our radar. But some of our profs were quick to tell us that our schooling had been less than good, and that it had been oppressive. What a new perspective to us. Until I came to university I would never have said that Native scholars were trying to bridge two cultures. We were just who we were, and all of us unique. I still can't think in terms of bridging cultures."

At the time Carl was at the U of A, he was what was termed a "mature student." At 27, he had experienced a lot in life. And most of the professors he associated with were about his own age. "I was invited to their parties. I saw some interesting things. The wife of one of my profs was talking to a junior academic, a guy she must have thought was way too blustery, and at one point she obviously had had enough. She quietly reached down, took off her shoe, and pounded him on his head three times—blam, blam, blam. I felt a bit out of place in all this, but I also made a lot of friends."

Favourite Professors

"THERE'S A PROF who has been a model for me of uncompromising honesty and unflinching common-sense criticism of social theory. I disagreed with a whole lot of what he said and he listened, and restated his case. When I got to know him better I saw that he was genuine. His compassion and respect for other people, and his commitment to his subject, were real. My interest was in language and linguistics, but I followed Tony Fisher into research in anthropology and education. I ended up working with him as a graduate student and teaching with him as a colleague.

"In my first year," Carl remembers, "I had Ray Grant for a course about Anglo-Saxon English. I loved this subject, and Dr. Grant was demanding, very demanding. Every lecture was a thing of beauty, a well crafted exposition. And I was the only undergraduate in the class. I did well. I think I had the highest grade.

"The next year I had Joan Crowther as a professor. She taught Middle English and she was superb, just superb. She too was demanding, and a great communicator. There were only six of us in her class, and imagine me! I was the only undergraduate in *that* course, too! There were all these scholarly types in Dr. Crowther's class—experts in translation and all manner of esoteric subjects—I could never compete with them. So I shut up.

"One day Dr. Crowther came to me and asked that I stay after the lecture. She asked why I was not contributing during class. I was honest, and I told her I simply could not figure out what the other students were saying. She answered: 'Neither can I. That's why I want you to talk.'

"Joan Crowther was very supportive of me. I wrote one particular paper for her class where she gave me very detailed critical comments. But she also said, 'Publish this!' That's an incredible boost for an undergraduate student.

"I also admired Ruth Gruhn as a professor. She taught my first anthropology course and I decided to switch majors because of the way she defined the discipline. She cared enough about students to be superbly prepared, and she had a wealth of information. She showed real respect for students in the way she challenged people, and expected a lot."

Carl Urion

"YOU ASK ME what was a big challenge in University," says Carl. *"One challenge was communicating. There were so few Aboriginal people. There's been a spin with respect to 'counting' how many Aboriginals were here in the earlier years—in the 1950s and 1960s, there were a few Aboriginals here, in the mid-1970s, there were about 20 of us, and about 100 in the early 1980s. We have different perceptions of the terms understood between our two cultures as to how we inhabit this place. How do you foster communication between those cultures in a university setting? That was a big question in the 1970s."*

At a 1979 Native students powwow, George Saddleback of Hobbema gave Carl Urion a Cree name—White Cloud. (Private Collection)

Carl got great grades in his BEd program, and secured a scholarship to enrol in a Master's program in anthropological linguistics. "After the first year I did a Masters by-pass and headed right to a PhD. It took me seven years, but I did it while working full-time. I started teaching in Educational Foundations as a sessional in 1971, and then became an assistant professor in 1975."

Mentor Michael Asch and the Founding of the School of Native Studies

"ANOTHER MENTOR as a professor was Michael Asch, a professor in the department of Anthropology. His interests were broad—ranging from Aboriginal land use to music—and he's passionate about many of the same things I am. His work is simply brilliant. He is an interlocutor, a person who *engages* with you in talk."

Carl, Michael, and Tony, along with Ann Fanning, Peter Winters, and Tom Pocklington, comprised the moving force within the academic staff for the establishment of a School of Natives Studies. "It was meant to be a door—open both ways—between Aboriginal communities and the many disciplines that treat, or draw from, Aboriginal societies and cultures.

"The original idea [was] to bring all eight Alberta aboriginal cultures together to ask this rhetorical question: what does the composite Native community have to offer the University? We knew what we had to offer. The question was whether the University wanted to listen. Since Harry Gunning went on record supporting the Alberta Indian Education Centre's proposal in 1970, the university has been dealing in one way or another with how to benefit from sharing scholarly space with Aboriginal people here. We knew of significant areas of science, medicine, pharmacology, the humanities, and the arts where indigenous knowledge has been central to inquiry, but no place here that reintegrated that knowledge coherently. The original idea for the School of Native Studies was to organize research and scholarship around the indigenous conceptions of 'land' and 'language.' So, for example, in the land studies unit you could have land use and occupancy studies, information systems such as GIS systems, and scientific studies of lands and resources brought together in a single applied unit in which all those areas, where indigenous knowledge about land is already used, could be integrated. That didn't happen in the School. Instead, for better or worse, they've used what I think of as the Native Studies model first implemented at Dartmouth, where the disciplines, and especially the social sciences, define an interdisciplinary focus in terms of the object of study."

Convocation and Life After Graduation

"WITH THREE KIDS during my undergraduate years," says Carl, "money was an issue for me. I didn't think I could afford to attend Convocation and there was a fee you had to pay to get your parchment released if you didn't attend, so I walked over to the Jubilee Auditorium that day and slipped into the Convocation ceremony during the last ten minutes—into the balcony—and then got in line in the lobby to pick up my diploma as though I'd attended legitimately. I guess I still might owe the University that parchment release fee.

"For my PhD, there was no question but that I would attend, because my mom wanted to be there since it was the first PhD in the immediate family. At Convocation, to my horror, I heard an official announce that I was the first Aboriginal to get a PhD from the University of Alberta. It was a shocker because though it was well intended it wasn't true. Dr. Joe Couture, a Cree Elder, scholar and counsellor, had earned his PhD in counselling psychology six years before I did."

After his PhD, Carl says, "I just couldn't leave the U of A." Carl spent his entire academic career here, retiring early in 1997. "I was having terrible problems with my balance, and my doctor phoned one day in February 1997 with test results. She said I had to quit teaching right then. That moment. I was not to walk into another class. There was one month left in the term, but I had to quit that day. She made it very clear that my long-term health was at stake, and that it was too stressful to try to maintain my balance while teaching a class. It was very difficult for me not to meet with my last class of students. I went through a period of grieving about not seeing them through, and not even saying good-bye in person. My colleagues in Anthropology got together, took my outlines, and finished the courses for me as a team, and the students got a better deal in the bargain. And to be honest, the grief turned rapidly to a sense of freedom.

"My pride," he says, "is in my students. They stay in touch, and are all over Canada and the United States, and in several other countries. Some of them still think I am something, and I think the same of all of them. I ended up with five children and to me, having students is something like having kids—there is a bond between us that will never dissolve."

Brian James Silzer (BSC '69, BED '71, MED '78)

BRIAN WAS THE FIRST ONE in his family ever to attend university. After his BSc and BEd, he went on to a long career as registrar at the University of Alberta, and in 2001, he was scooped by our western rival to take on the Registrar's position at UBC.

But back in 1965, as a first-year medical student, Brian's shining moment was not so shining. He keeled over during his first medical rounds, and he knew instantly he had chosen the wrong field. It was a rocky start to a successful career.

Hooked on the U of A by Grade 9

IT HAS BEEN SAID that Brian Silzer is so true to the U of A that he "bleeds green and gold." But he was raised in *southern* Alberta. So why did he choose the U of A?

"My parents," Brian says, "were set on my becoming a doctor. So it was clear I was going to university. I was raised in Lethbridge and Taber, so the University of Calgary was the natural choice. But in grade 9, I got an honours award—an 'H' pin—and there was no way I was going to miss school assembly to receive the award. It so happened that the U of A Mixed Chorus was at my junior high school that particular day, under conductor Richard Eaton. The Mixed Chorus was snappy, fun and smart. I knew the U of A must be a special place, and the seed was planted. To me, going to the U of A was like going to Harvard.

"I have to admit I was also a big Edmonton Eskimos fan, a rarity in Lethbridge. As a kid, I used to bet all these dumb adults that Edmonton and not Calgary would win a game, and I made a lot of money. So when I turned 18, going to university in Edmonton meant I could go to the Eskimo games."

Top: Brian Silzer (middle) started out as a student contemplating the mysteries of university life on the steps of the Administration Building. After his graduation, the Administration Building continued to be the centre of his life when he became the U of A's long-time registrar. In this photo he is taking part in St. Steve's freshman initiative.
(Private Collection)

Bottom: A trip to rural Alberta by Richard Eaton's Mixed Chorus inspired Brian Silzer to attend the U of A.
(UAA 78-51-69-875)

Life in Saint Stephen's Residence

"SOME OF MY FRIENDS told me I just had to live at St. Stephen's, the old 'castle,' so I got a letter from the United Church minister and got in. There was a little group of us going up to Edmonton in 1965 for school, and I drove up with the Hammans. First we got my friend Bill moved in to Lister Hall—which was brand new, shiny, perfect—and then we drove over to St. Steve's. What a downer. St. Steve's was built at the turn of the century, and there'd been some hard living in there—it showed a lot of wear and tear. I thought, 'big mistake.'

"But I made great friends at St. Steve's—Mike Boorman, Reg Norby, Bob Steadward, Phil Ponting. We were always up to something. One time I was studying really hard and some guy came into my room. I told him to buzz off, and the next thing I knew there was a blazing fire in my waste-paper basket. That Stevite had dropped a match into it on his way out.

"Then someone knocked on my door, and you have to know that the keyholes of the St. Steve's doors were quite big—they were opened with over-sized skeleton keys. I went to the door and just as I got there, a flame shot through the keyhole towards me. What the guys had done was to light a match on their side of the keyhole, and then give it a shot of hairspray. It worked like a mini flame-thrower."

Then there was the time Brian and some of his friends climbed way up a narrow ladder, through one of the St. Steve's turrets, to the roof. They were about to conduct a physics experiment.

"We wanted to see what would happen if we dropped a bowling ball [from the roof]," Brian says. That would be a five-storey drop.

"It was a stupid thing to do, but we thought the bowling ball would just shatter on the sidewalk. Well, we dropped it and it bounced back up—almost five storeys, right back up towards us. We watched in fright and fascination as it formed a graceful arc over 88 Avenue, bounded over a line-up of cars, and then rocketed down a couple of storeys, finally landing on the lawn in front of the Tuck Shop. It made a huge hole. And for years there was a big divot on the concrete front steps of St. Steve's where the bowling ball first landed."

There was a "den mother'" at St. Steve's named Doc Johnson. The residents of St. Steve's remember him with great affection. "He put a lot of us to bed after we'd had a little too much to drink," remembers Brian, "and he knew where to draw the line if things went too far."

One day Doc Johnson asked the boys to decorate St. Steve's in anticipation of a special Christmas dinner for a group of United Church ministers. "'We didn't have any budget for this," says Brian, "and so we used what we had. Condoms. We blew them up and they looked just like balloons. We painted them red and green, silver and gold, and hung them from the ceiling. They looked great. But as the evening wore on, the paint must have penetrated the outer layer of the condoms, and they started to lose air. By the end of the evening, they looked just like what they really were, condoms."

And that wasn't all. After exams, the pranks really got going.

"There were two groups at St. Steve's," Brian explains. "There were the theologs, who were studying divinity, and the rest of us. We were the heathens. The theologs were pretty serious and so we heathens had our work cut out for us. There was one antisocial theolog who just wouldn't come out of his room and so we decided we had to fix this. We took something—I won't tell you what it was but it was a good size and really gross—and we took it down the hall to the 'T' junction of the building. From this vantage point, we could see this guy's outside window across the way. And his window was open.

"So we set our 'missile' on fire. We swung it several times in the 'T' junction, where there was lots of room, so we could get up some good speed. Then we released our flaming missile and it shot right through this guy's outside window and into his room. Of course, we had the fire hose ready. We stuck it out the hallway window, took perfect aim towards this guy's open window, and doused the flames. Our goal was achieved at last. The guy came out of his room."

Brian says that all the pranks built character and helped form fast friendships. "There's nothing like residence life to bond you to the university. Years later when I was travelling around the world to talk to alumni groups, all I had to do was show a slide of, say, HUB International, where the alumni had lived as students, and their faces would soften, they would smile, and I knew I had the audience's attention."

Clearly though, in 1965, residence wasn't the place to learn your manners.

Mrs. Sparling

"I LEARNED MY MANNERS from the dean of women, Mrs. Sparling," remembers Brian Silzer. "She had a suite in Pembina Hall. It was very high brow. She would serve tea to small groups of students, and we learned how to behave in a social setting. There was also the Wauneita formal each year, and you didn't go unless a girl invited you. It was very proper and it taught us how to get along in polite company." (UAA 69-19-351)

"I took this girl out on a date to the Beachcomber restaurant," recalls Brian. "It was a Polynesian place, and dimly lit inside. After we sat down, I started sawing away with my knife at what I thought was an appetizer. It was a hand towel. My date set me straight."

On the Wrong Academic Track From Day One

BRIAN ENTERED A BSC PROGRAM. "That program was the entrée into the Faculty of Medicine," he says. "*Everyone* in science was in pre-med. I achieved the grades to enter Medicine, but I was there for all the wrong reasons. It was my parents who wanted me to be a doctor, but I knew that the other med students were oriented differently from me in some fundamental way. Medicine wasn't for me, but I stuck it out for a year.

"My friend Mike Boorman's dad was a physician in Rimbey, and one morning Dr. Boorman took us on rounds. Some of the patients were in pretty sad shape. And Mike and I were a little rough around the edges after a late evening. Halfway through the rounds, it all got to me and I keeled over in a dead faint. When I came to, here were all these sick patients gathered around me, so concerned, and saying 'Doctor Brian, are you OK?' Here I was supposed to be taking care of them, and they were taking care of me.

"Then I bombed Histology. It was awful. I was positive, absolutely positive, that I had no future options. I have remembered that feeling of being alone and in a corner during my whole career as registrar. There are *always* options.

"I talked to my mom and my girlfriend Cecile. I finished up with an honours BSc before going on for a BEd."

Brian and Cecile married in 1968. "It was a struggle financially," Brian says. "I had a construction job in the summer. I should have been grateful to have it—we needed the money—but all I was really doing was moving dirt from one pile to another. I quit.

"I walked over to the Canada Manpower Centre in SUB in my construction clothes. I had no shirt on. I was wearing jeans and work boots and had on a hard hat."

The only job available was as a clerk in the Registrar's Office. Brian was interviewed by the very proper and British-educated assistant registrar,

Sandy Darling. "I had a choice of footwear for the interview—my work boots or a pair of sandals—that's all I owned. I wore the sandals. After all, it was the era of hippies, and sandals were in. Cecile rounded up a white shirt for me. When the interview was over, Mr. Darling told me 'You're not much, but you have to appreciate the others that have applied.' I guess I was the best of the bunch that day. I got the job.

"I worked in the back room, analyzing data. My big innovation was drawing pictures of classrooms. Profs would call in for classroom space and the women who assigned classrooms had never actually been in them. So I went to each classroom and drew a schematic, showing the whole set-up, from the seating configuration to the electrical outlets. We quickly had big binders filled with these drawings and the 'booking sheets.' It was a hit. We couldn't afford more than one copy of the binders, so we moved four timetabling clerks to one shared space, and set up a lazy Susan in the middle of their desks. They could whirl it around and all have access to the binders, and away we went. Whatever the state of the technology, it's all about a better mousetrap and better service," says Brian.

"Then came my first performance appraisal. I was told my sandals were not acceptable dress for the office. I was devastated, but it was character-building. I asked if they would wait until I got my first pay cheque so I could afford shoes."

Life After Graduation

BRIAN WAS IN THE REGISTRAR'S OFFICE for 27 years, with an additional short stint as director of the Board of Governors' Office at the U of A. From 1984–2002, he served as the University's registrar. One of Brian's innovations was telephone registration, which made its debut in 1985. In 2001, he and his staff paved the way for web-based registration before he left for UBC.

This is what spurred him to change the registration from the in-person system to registration by telephone. "Registration in the 1960s and '70s was grim," says Brian. "It took at least one full day and students had to walk around to every single department which offered the courses they wanted to take and get a computer card—a punched card—for each course. Part Five of registration was the last step and was held in what is now the Clare

Top: In 1960, the U of A campus was marked by many wide open spaces. (UAA 69-12-105)

Bottom: By 1967, the campus was jam-packed, with the new SUB, CAB, and Lister Hall all crowding onto the original 258 acres. (UAA 74-94-55)

Drake arena. One day an elderly lady came in and I asked her for all her punched cards. She didn't have any. It was news to her that she had to trek to several departments to collect these.

"She was physically frail but she was emotionally strong. It was clear she was not going to traipse all around getting these cards. So I did it for her. She was so grateful. I thought, there has to be a better way to register students." By 1985, the U of A had telephone registration—a first for Canadian universities.

"But you know what?" Brian marvels. "For all its convenience, I had students come in to the office to say they missed the long lines, where they had a chance to meet other students."

Next on Brian's agenda is a web-based, self-admission process for UBC. "Students can create their own profile as early on as they want," Brain explains. "Once they think they have what it takes to be admitted, they just press the 'Admit Me' button. If they are missing a requirement, they find out immediately. If they meet the admission criteria, they're in." It's clear Brian is still on the trail of a better mousetrap and better service to students. His advice to today's students is this—always go that one step further.

END OF THE DECADE

In 1968–69, the University of Alberta turned 60. The baby boomers who arrived during this decade, from the moderates to the radicals, called out for change. The boomers of the 1970s were on the receiving end of that call and were on this campus as deep social and political change took effect.

"1977? 'Peace and love, man'—
it was that era—the era of
'anything goes.' People were
living together, and that was
revolutionary. Students started
wearing jeans to class." HUB
was the student hangout.

—Sibéal McCourt Bincoletto
(BA '77)

Timeline

Enrolment and Finance, 1970–1979

- Fall student head count: 22,239 (1970); 21,702 (1979)
- Operating budget from the Province of Alberta: $50,098,000.00 (1970); $122,703,000.00 (1979)
- Full-load uUndergraduate Arts tuition: $400.00 (1970); $550.00 (1979)
- SU membership fee: $27.50 (1970); $35.50 (1979)

Key Dates, 1970–1979

- Collège Saint-Jean becomes part of the U of A (1970)
- A freeze on hiring is announced in light of a $3.5 million budget deficit (1970–1971)
- Spring and summer session introduced with six-week intensive courses (1971/1972)
- Students win parity with professors on GFC (1972)
- First advanced registration introduced—just for Law and Medicine—no more line-ups (1973)
- Harry Gunning succeeds Max Wyman as president (1974)
- Students prepare for a 25% tuition increase after the provincial government announces an 11% ceiling on funding to universities
- Collège Universitaire Saint-Jean becomes Faculté Saint-Jean (1978)
- First United Way Campaign on campus (1978)
- Alex Cairns, registrar since 1956, retires (1978)
- Myer Horowitz succeeds Harry Gunning as president (1979)

Selected Campus Buildings, 1970–1979

- Athabasca and Pembina Halls are condemned and then renovated (1970s)
- The Fine Arts Building opens near the site of the now-demolished Tuck Shop (1973)
- Former Premier Rutherford's home is restored and opened to the public (1974)
- Board of Governors agrees to buy HUB from the SU for $1 (1976)
- The Power Plant opens as the GSA's social centre (1978)

Beyond The Campus, 1970–1979

- Alberta's Tories win 49 of 75 seats, beginning an era of Tory governments under Premiers Peter Lougheed, Don Getty, and Ralph Klein (1971)
- Cable TV comes to Edmonton (1971)
- Video games and electronic calculators go on the market (1972)
- First women recruited by the RCMP (1973)
- Dr. Henry Morgentaler begins legal battles over performing abortions (1973)

- Trudeau's federal government quadruples oil export taxes (1973)
- First Heritage Days Festival (1976)
- First test-tube baby is born (1978)
- LRT begins service (1978)
- Disco is 'in' and *Saturday Night Fever* is a hit movie (1978)

VIGNETTES FROM THE 1970s

THERE WERE TWO university presidents during the 1970s: Max Wyman (1969–1974) and Harry Gunning (1974–1979).

President Max Wyman[1]

MAX WYMAN, a professor of Mathematics, was the first president with a U of A degree and the first Albertan to head the U of A. He steered the University through dramatic physical growth and deep social change.

Max Wyman was a former president of the faculty association who became the vice-president academic before assuming the presidency. That resulted in an interesting switch in roles: one month he was advocating at the bargaining table for the faculty, and the next he was part of the administration, sitting opposite his replacement as the faculty association president.

Max Wyman had an innate understanding of collegial governance and the value of playing out seemingly opposing roles in an environment of civil advocacy. As the University's leader from 1969–1974, Dr. Wyman demonstrated time after time an instinctive understanding of the desire on the part of faculty and students to participate in academic decision-making. He was at ease in manoeuvring the University through a massive change in its governance. During his time as president, faculty members settled in as a significant component of General Faculties Council (GFC), and students were given parity with the professors.

As a mathematician, Dr. Wyman's love of statistics played out at the racetrack, where he enjoyed playing the odds—a passion he shared with President Henry Marshall Tory. There is an unsubstantiated story that the University's budget deficits came under some measure of control during his presidency because of his masterful ways with numbers at the track.

President Harry Gunning[2]

DR. HARRY GUNNING, chair of the department of Chemistry, served as president from 1974–1979. As a post-doctoral fellow, Dr. Gunning was part of Dr. E.W.R. Steacie's research group at the NRC. He continued his career as a senior professor of Physical Chemistry in Chicago, where he spent time on the side as a jazz disc jockey—one of his many non-science pursuits. In the late 1950s, when Steacie was Chair of the NRC, one of his goals was to see that Canada's universities focused on basic research in the sciences and trained doctoral and postdoctoral students here in Canada so that the best minds were not lost to other countries. Steacie was instrumental in recruiting Gunning to the U of A, where Gunning built an internationally-known Chemistry department.

It is said that at a time when departments were not allowed to use their facilities budget for operating purposes—and *vice versa*—Dr. Gunning was the only department chair to find a quiet way around the rules. Interchanging both funds was one way he was able to purchase the equipment needed to build the department. In the same way, he was able, in other years, to recruit more staff than would normally be allowed.

Towards the end of his term as president, Dr. Gunning joined the students when they marched over the High Level Bridge to protest high tuition fees and inadequate funding for the University. His family was the last to live in the President's House on Saskatchewan Drive. By the end of Dr. Gunning's presidency, enrolment hovered around the 22,000 mark, and there was an increasing number of quotas in the faculties.

Two Views from the Top[3]

TWO PRESIDENTS, representing the administration and the students, sum up the baby boom era at its mid-point.

Max Wyman, after five months in office in 1969, said that "the University is growing old and growing big, and these are two events which tend to make it resist change. We must find a way of reforming it. I don't know how. It has been suggested that we could do it by getting greater student participation in General Faculties Council. One difficulty here is that the student members would change every year, but I'm quite prepared to support the move; I'm prepared to try the method. If it turns out to not be the right way to reform, we'll just have to find one."

Tim Christian, SU president in 1970 and later dean of Law at the U of A, described the philosophical underpinning of his presidential platform: "The role of university in society should be to function as a critical servant to the community. Students and faculty in the university should be engaged in examining and evaluating the assumptions upon which our society operates. We must question whether the predominant values are valid and ask if the institutions of society are just. We must raise crit-

Top right: SU President Tim Christian at an anti-Vietnam rally in 1970. (UAA 78–51–69–900)

Top left: University President Max Wyman in his office in 1966. (UAA 69–16–51)

Bottom: The System.

(The Gateway, *March 26, 1969*)

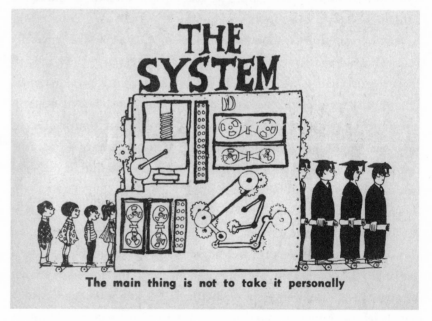

THE SYSTEM

The main thing is not to take it personally

ical questions when those in power advocate 'law and order.' When you find injustice, expose it, work for its removal—this sort of dissent should be recognized as one of the university's most valuable contributions to society." Tim also addressed the issue of the hiring and firing of professors, making reference to the headline-making tenure case involving Professor Ted Kemp. Dr. Kemp was considered an excellent teacher by students, but did not have a strong publication record in an era defined by the dictum "publish or perish." As Tim Christian saw it, "We must change the criteria for emphasis from the 'publishing syndrome' to the importance of good teaching."

Wyman supported students on the question of parity, and found a compromise on the issues surrounding tenure for Ted Kemp.

BUB SLUG—AN EDMONTON HERO DEBUTS IN THE GATEWAY [4]

BACK IN THE 1970S, young local artists Gerry Rasmussen and Gary Delainey enrolled in the Fine Arts program at the University of Alberta. The two became acquainted and, during their second year of study, they began collaborating in cartoon "jam-sessions" where one person would begin a story and pass it on for the other person to continue. During one of these sessions, the character of Bub Slug was born. It wasn't long before Delainey and Rasmussen were ready to submit their strip based on this character to *The Gateway*.

The comic debuted in early 1976, and for the next two years frequently graced the pages of the paper, developing a following in the University community. This was still many years before a comics section appeared regularly in *The Gateway*. Once writer Delainey and artist Rasmussen graduated, however, "Bub Slug" disappeared from print.

But sometimes an idea is too good to let go of, and so Delainey and Rasmussen reworked and pitched the concept to *The Edmonton Journal*. The newspaper took the bait, and in May 1985 *Bub Slug* began appearing as a full-page strip on the back page of the Saturday colour comics.

In a 1986 *Gateway* interview, Gerry Rasmussen revealed the motivation for the full-page format: "The four-frame strip has been done to death. It came about initially because of lack of space, where you wanted a strip that could run every day, that was an offshoot of your Sunday comics." In contrast, *Bub Slug* was longer, non-syndicated, and ran only once a week.

Bub Slug, the cartoon created for The Gateway *by Gerry Rasmussen and Gary Delainey, was a favourite among students. Here Bub Slug pays tribute to President Myer Horowitz.*

(Courtesy of Gerry Rasmussen and Gary Delainey)

They had been given a unique opportunity by *The Journal*: "The more I think about it, the more I have to hand it to them."

Set in a specific place—Edmonton—the lead characters of Bub Slug usually appeared in familiar settings and were frequently joined by local celebrities, including then University president, Myer Horowitz. This familiarity ensured that satire would always be a big part of the storylines. "We found out that what we really wanted to do...was to mercilessly lampoon things," explained Rasmussen in 1986. Indeed, the strip's distinctly local flavour set it apart from other strips at the time, or from any era, for that matter. Bub, after all, was a High Level Bridge waterfall maintenance man— it doesn't get more uniquely Edmonton than that.

For four and-a-half-years, *Bub Slug* ran in *The Edmonton Journal* comics. But in November of 1989, Delainey and Rasmussen were informed that the newspaper would no longer be running the strip. *The Journal*, in the midst of drastic internal changes, no longer wanted to be associated with *Bub Slug*, and cited declining reader interest as part of the reason for their decision. The last comic was to run on December 30th, featuring a reflective New Year's toast by Bub, which ended with Bub receiving bad news via telegram as his guests rang in the New Year. However, the strip never appeared, as it was deemed contrary to *Journal* policy at the time—*The Journal* did not allow farewells and frowned upon self-referential themes. Upset by this decision, and wanting to say farewell to their loyal readers, Delainey and Rasmussen contacted *The Gateway*, who agreed to run the final strip in the paper's January 4, 1990 edition. It was an appropriate homecoming for the hard-hatted Edmonton hero.

It wasn't long before United Feature Syndicate became interested in the strips Delainey and Rasmussen had sent out. The Syndicate was especially intrigued by Betty, Bub's wife—a strong female character that was lacking in strips at the time. In 1991, the strip *Betty* went into syndication and soon appeared in *The Edmonton Sun* and now, in over 100 newspapers worldwide. Both Delainey and Rasmussen still live in Edmonton and remain loyal to the Slugs' hometown in the new strip, sprinkling in references to the Edmonton Oilers, Whyte Avenue, and of course, West Edmonton Mall.

THE CAMPUS IN THE 1970s

THE 1970S was an era of parkades—seven parkades were planned—a record. In 1969, the tennis courts to the west of SUB were demolished to make way for Stadium Parkade, the first of these multi-level parking structures. The Windsor Parkade was built in 1971.

The University's long-range plan assumed that rapid transit would arrive on campus by 1980. "By then there will be little of the kind of parking we have now," said the vice-president responsible for facilities and planning. The thinking behind the plan was that students would be able to park at the university farm and commute to campus. Between 1970 and 1979, most of the roads that criss-crossed the centre of campus disappeared, and there was, for instance, no more parking right in front of the Old Arts Building or beside the Power Plant.

Several big-ticket buildings were constructed in the 1970s: Van Vliet East in 1970; CAB and the Law Centre in 1971; Mechanical Engineering, the Humanities Centre, HUB, and Medical Sciences in 1972; Chemistry East, Fine Arts, Education North, and Rutherford North in 1973. Out at the Devonian Botanic Garden, the Headquarters Building opened in 1978.

Athabasca, Assiniboia, and Pembina narrowly missed the wrecker's ball, and were either restored or renovated. The Tuck Shop, the Garneau Mansion, the West Lab, the Drill Hall, and Varsity Rink were demolished. Rutherford House was saved—just barely.

St. Stephen's College closed as a residence in 1975 because it no longer met fire regulations. It was in grave danger of demolition until 1977, when the provincial government designated it a historic resource and Alberta Community Development (today's Cultural Facilities & Historical Resources Department) moved in.

On November 2, 1976, six two-ton pre-cast concrete blocks on the southwest corner of Clinical Sciences began flapping in a 90 km/h wind. The blocks swung out as much as six feet from the building. The first three floors on the ground below were evacuated. The blocks were temporarily secured by cables. It was expected to cost at least $1.5 million to permanently fix the problem.

In 1978, renovations to Convocation Hall were completed, and the first concerts were held there on February 1 and 2. Later that year, a new organ was installed, with the dedication ceremony on October 1, 1978. That same

Top: The Chemical-Mineral Engineering Building, under construction in 1968–1969, overwhelms Ring House 7. Most of the Ring Houses were demolished in 1970 to make way for the Windsor Car Park. Note the broken scaffolding at centre top. (UAA 74-37)

Left: HUB Mall under construction.
(University of Alberta Alumni Affairs)

fall, the Power Plant opened as the Graduate Students' Association's (GSA) social centre. It contained meeting rooms, a restaurant-lounge, a bar, games rooms, and GSA offices.

In 1979, the first phase of the centralized energy management system that controlled heating, ventilation, and air conditioning was completed.

A GLANCE AT THE 1979 CALENDAR

ON THE COVER of the 1979 Calendar is a watercolour entitled "General View Looking North Showing Scheme of Buildings Proposed in 1912, Revised January 1915." The cover depicted a portion of the original plan for the campus developed by Percy Nobbs and Frank Darling, the Montréal architects who oversaw the early construction on campus in concert with university architect Cecil Burgess. Here's what the 1979 Calendar had to say about the campus at the end of the "baby boom" era:

> Of [the original] plan, Athabasca, Assiniboia and Pembina Halls... the present day Arts Building and the Power Plant...were all built between 1911 and 1915.
>
> The pace of construction slowed considerably with the start of the First World War and it wasn't until the end of the Second World

War that building activity picked up again. However, with the large influx of students resulting from the end of the Second World War and the need for rapid expansion of all facilities, the plan had to be abandoned.

In fact, the only decade during which the original plan was followed was the 1920s, when the Medical Building was constructed. During the 1930s, there wasn't a dime in the budget for construction. The flood of students after World War II forced the University to slap up buildings—many temporary—and the original, elegant, integrated campus plan was set aside. The influx of baby boomers of the 1960s and 1970s resulted in a period of relentless construction—35 major buildings in 20 years.

EVERGREEN AND GOLD BITES THE DUST

BETWEEN 1969 AND 1972, the *Evergreen and Gold* struggled to maintain its existence. Two headlines in the October *Gateway* issues said it all. One proclaimed, "Evergreen and Go," and the other, "It's Nevermore for *Evergreen and Gold*." The yearbook was about to incur a deficit of $44,000, and there were already five faculties that published their own yearbooks. Only a student petition could save the *E & G*. Underpinning concerns about cost was the fact that students thought the SU had taken their yearbook money and spent it on daycare centres, SUB expansion, and politically-oriented educational programs about topics like abolishing tenure.

In 1969, 92% of students voting in a referendum said they wanted a yearbook, but the percentage later dropped to 65.1%, edged out by the 65.3% who wanted to legalize marijuana. Even when the percentage in support of keeping the yearbook was 92%, Students' Council said the priorities would be political/social education (for instance, the hiring of a "women's worker") and services.

The 1971 yearbook was the last of the large-format yearbooks. It was, according to Frans Slater, treasurer of the SU, going to be "the last edition of the *Evergreen and Gold* because of the student body's general apathy towards its publication. Council feels that the yearbook has become an impracticality for a university of this size." After publication of the 1972 yearbook—a small-scale, xeroxed version of the grand old yearbooks of 1920–1971—the *Evergreen and Gold* disappeared, resurrected only once, in the University's 75th year, by undergraduate student Michael Ford.[5]

GLIMPSES FROM THE GATEWAY—1970-1979

"Boston Pizza Refuses to Serve Students With Long Hair"— January 13, 1970

AT ABOUT THE SAME TIME the local Boston Pizza was refusing to serve male students with long hair, the dean of women told one female under-graduate that her hair was too long and her skirt too short. That undergraduate went on the chair the Department of Sociology.

"Varsity Guest Weekend"—February 5, 6, 7, and 8, 1970

THE JUBILAIRES' production of the Broadway hit *Auntie Mame* packed SUB Theatre for four nights running.

"Frats Stereotyped Image is False?"—September 24, 1970

"HOW DARE YOU generalize so emphatically about organizations and individuals which you seem to view only at surface value," wrote one under-grad. "I, for one, have joined a fraternity which I consider to be a counter example to your hypothesis. Sigma Alpha Mu is as diverse an organization as you'll find anywhere. Long hair–short hair, right-wing–left-wing, indif-ferent, cool–not so cool, are some of the variations in appearance and attitude which mark our fraternity." The letter was signed by Henry Goldberg, Science II. "We benefit from each other's friendship," he said. "It's a unique and beneficial experience."

Doug Cuthand—October 1, 1970

THE *GATEWAY* now had an Aboriginal-section editor.

"Tuck Shop"—November 6, 1970

THE TUCK SHOP, home away from home for generations of students, was demolished.

"Course Guide Exists: SU to Publish One This Year"— December 1, 1970

AS THE FRONT PAGE proclaimed, "The Students' Union will again publish a course guide evaluating some courses taught during the 1970–71 academic year." The three aims of the course guide were to allow students to make a more informed choice of courses; to provide instructors with some feedback measure of their teaching effectiveness; and to foster an interest in maintaining a high level of university teaching. Students in Arts, Education, or Science were paid one dollar for each class they evaluated.

"Student Parity Recommended by GFC"—February 9, 1971

GATEWAY STAFFER Judy Samoil reported that "students at the University of Alberta Wednesday received parity with faculty on General Faculties' Council, the major decision-making body of the University. The special meeting, which was televised to over 700 students in the Students' Union theatre, resulted in a vote of 42–33 in support of recommendations by an *ad hoc* committee on student representation." President Max Wyman opened the meeting by saying that "a basic principle of the majority of the report said students are a constituent part of the university and not just clients of it, and that no constituent group should be large enough in GFC to carry a vote without substantial support from members of other constituent groups."

"Worth Commission Report"—February 18, 1971

"BY 1980," according to the Worth Commission, "large Alberta cities (with a population approaching 500,000) should have a multiversity, at least one university, two urban colleges and a technical college. The multiversities should be capable of handling 25,000–30,000 students and a major share of graduate level education, professional education and research. The Commission also recommends that by 1980, an 'open university' should be established in Alberta."

"SUB Staff Unionizes"—September 9, 1971

"STUDENTS at the University of Alberta, so long imagined to be above the struggles that beset the rest of society, have suddenly found them-

The Poundmaker

IN THE SPRING OF 1971, the Students' Union refused to name as editor-in-chief the person who had been elected to that position by the Gateway staff. Instead, the SU named its own head editor. The entire Gateway staff in effect seceded from the paper and formed a rival newspaper called the Poundmaker. Taking its name from a 19th-century Cree Chief, the Poundmaker covered the sessionals' fight for equality, sexism on campus, and a broad range of political issues, including a long-standing boycott of Kraft, which was taking over small-scale, family-owned cheese producers. There were articles on growing old, on being poor, on welfare, and daycare. The Poundmaker advocated a union of graduate students and for Native rights. The Canadian Union Press (CUP) supported the Poundmaker, which meant the rival paper, and not The Gateway, had access to advertising revenues and the CUP press service. The Poundmaker staff eventually made their point about control of the paper, and to this day Gateway staff elect their own editor-in-chief. In 2002, a vote by referendum decided that The Gateway should be autonomous in relation to the SU. (UAA 71–372)

selves in the unhappy position of employer, and in the midst of their own labour dispute. On behalf of the 20,000 students that he represents, Don MacKenzie, president of the SU, has decided to appeal to the Supreme Court of Alberta the certification that has given the Students' Union employees in SUB the right to form a union and engage in collective bargaining with the employers—in this case, the students." In the end, SUB workers were certified by the Alberta Board of Industrial Relations.

"Clowns Present Circus for Frosh"—September 9, 1971

"WITH CLOWNS, circus, candy floss and carnival, the FIW [Freshman Introduction Week] committee is trying to show freshman students the university as it really is. The committee has arranged a week of social events, through which they intend to see that the incoming student does not get the idea that the university is books and study and nothing more."

"SUB Art Gallery Is Too Expensive, Council Claims"— November 23, 1971

SU TREASURER, Frans Slater, wanted to trim the expensive SU-owned Art Gallery. Gallery Director Myra Davies defended the Gallery: "Other students and I have been developing this gallery for four years. Since then we've developed it to exceptional status recognized by the National Gallery." Davies said that "the Gallery's activities include the video library, a flea market, which is presented every second Friday, the biannual print rental, the various exhibits, musical facilities, reading areas, special events concerts, and availability of periodicals not readily accessible elsewhere." In the end, the Gallery was abolished. At the time it was established, 1% of the SU budget had been earmarked for the purchase of art.

"SU Working Hard...Reading Week Hoped For"—November 25, 1971

"THE STUDENTS' UNION will submit a proposal for a second-term Reading Week to the General Faculties Executive Committee Monday, December 6," said The Gateway. "The week-long break in classes would be held the last two days of February and the first three days of March for the purpose of 'work, study, and general relaxation period.'" In an SU referendum, 91.5% of students favoured the establishment of a Reading Week. Student

Counselling was worried about the dropout rate in March, and everyone thought the long winters led to mental and physical fatigue. Reading Week, however one used it, was for a "general release of tension."

"Native Studies Program Rejected"—December 9, 1971

A PROPOSAL for a Native Studies Program was put forward by the Graduate Students' Association. "Max Wyman said it was very presumptuous of any university group to try to tell Native people what to do. He said that he has been in discussions regarding the proposed Alberta Indian Education Centre, and it is clear that the solution for the Indian people is for them to set up their own school."

"Drugstore Man called Sexist"—November 20, 1975

A PLAYBOY promotional tour would soon be bringing Miss December to Varsity Drugs in HUB for a one-hour autograph session. The Gateway reported that the store booked the tour in light of the good sales of Playboy on campus. Protests aimed at the store's then-owner labelled him "everything from a fascist to a sexist," he claimed. The tour stop went ahead as planned.

"Proposal to Trim 'Fat'"—November 23, 1976

A PROPOSAL CALLING FOR a reorganization of the University's power structure was circulated among academic staff. The plan called for the transformation of General Faculties Council into an advisory body without decision-making authority and a shift of student representation to the departmental level.

"Dent Students Refuse Comment on Exam Boycott"— January 4, 1977

"ALL 41 FOURTH-YEAR dentistry students refused to write mid-term examinations this Christmas and all are now tight-lipped about their reasons for doing so," reported The Gateway. The matter was in the hands of the academic standing committee.

"GOD HAVE MERCY! General Election Shifts to Top Gear at Wednesday's Zoo Rally"—February 10, 1977

IT WAS BOUND TO GET WILD. SUB Theatre, normally used for the Students' Union annual election forum, was booked, so an estimated crowd of 500 jammed into Tory Lecture Theatre 1–11 to hear speeches from candidates informing voters about their slates. The crowd greeted the mask-wearing Conceptual Reality Alternative Party (CRAP) slate candidate Rene Le Lark with a thunderous ovation, and then demanded more speaking time after his allotted five minutes. Two speakers later, *The Gateway* reporters felt the rally "was fast becoming a free-for-all and the hecklers were taking over." Later, a member of the CRAP slate delivered a speech in Lithuanian, with bursts of English, bringing the crowd to its feet in support.

"Theatre of the absurd came to a Students' Union election rally," mused *The Gateway*. "But as people walked out the door they were talking about the election—and about the candidates. It was, some said, the best election forum of the 1970s." Jay Spark was elected president.

"Nutrition First at Incredible Edibles"—November 1, 1977

RETIRING Students' Union Food Services director, Wally McLean, was about to open his own restaurant in HUB, and as *The Gateway* learned, it would be "chiefly concerned with providing nutritious food which is efficiently served and as economical as any of the existing fast-food outlets on campus."

"5,000 Protest to Gov't"—March 16, 1978

OVER 5,000 STUDENTS AND STAFF gathered on March 15 to show their opposition to the perceived insufficient government funding for universities. "The March, organized by the U of A Committee to Oppose Tuition Increases and Cutbacks (COTIAC) and comparable committees in Calgary and Lethbridge, stretched longer than the entire length of the High Level Bridge," said *The Gateway*. Upon arrival at the Legislature, speeches were made by Premier Peter Lougheed, Federation of Alberta Students Executive Officer Brian Mason, and University President Harry Gunning, among

Eugene Brody, who had cerebral palsy, spent 23 years earning his BA and BSc degrees. Many students remember helping the determined Eugene up the steps of the Arts Building. Eugene was active in extracurricular activities and an advocate for student parking on campus. There is a Students' Union award in his memory. (UAA 70-122-680719)

others. NDP leader Grant Notley asked of the crowd, "Who says student power is a thing of the past?"

"NASA Finally Certified; Exclusion Problem Overcome"— September 29, 1978

THE NON-ACADEMIC STAFF ASSOCIATION of the University was certified as a bargaining agent, and steps were taken to begin negotiations on behalf of staff who had been without contracts since June 9.

"Disabled Students: Coping With Adversity"—January 26, 1979

IN THIS *GATEWAY* FEATURE, the work of the Disabled Students' Advisory Committee was spotlighted. The committee, composed entirely of disabled students, was created in November 1977 to act as a source of information and advice for students with disabilities. While the University had made progress in making its buildings more accessible, there was room for improvement, particularly in the areas of registration, washrooms, and housing.

"Stuck on 108 Street with the Car Park Blues Again"— October 23, 1979

THE *GATEWAY* reported that of the 3,000 students who had applied for parking spaces that year, 900 were refused, leaving many to seek other parking options. And for those who did get permits, it still wasn't always easy to find a place to park. Why did those lots fill up so quickly every morning? *The Gateway* found part of the explanation: "The reason assigned lots are filled is that the system works on a delicate balance. That is, 6,000 permits are sold for roughly 5,200 spaces."

"No Solution For Study Space"—October 30, 1979

NOT ONLY WAS IT HARD to find a parking space on campus, finding a place to study was just as difficult. A discussion of this matter at a General Faculties Council meeting lasted for only fifteen minutes before a motion passed calling for a committee to study the problem further. In the meantime, money from the president's contingency fund was used to keep the second-floor study area in Rutherford South open until 2:00 A.M.

nightly from Sunday through Thursday, and until midnight on Fridays and Saturdays.

MEET ALUMNI FROM THE 1970s[6]

Franco Pasutto (BSC PHARM '72, PHD '78)

MEET FRANCO PASUTTO, dean of Pharmacy and Pharmaceutical Sciences—a man who is passionate about honour, truth, loyalty, hard work, and standing up for one's personal beliefs.

Valvasone

FRANCO WAS BORN in Valvasone, a small town in a region of northern Italy—an hour-and-a-half from Venice along the borders with Austria and Slovenia. "Today, Valvasone is a jewel of a town," says Franco. "But during World War II, it was bombed twice, by both the Allies and the Germans, and occupied by the Gestapo. I've been back since, many times, and have heard stories of atrocity and poverty from my relatives.

"When Mussolini first came to power, my father briefly supported him, and then joined the resistance. He was captured by the Germans, and spent three years in a concentration camp. When the war was over, my dad walked all the way back to Valvasone and found it in shambles. My parents married soon after dad came back from the concentration camp, and I was born a year later, in 1947. This is how poor my parents were: in the dead of night, my father went to the village latrine, and dismantled it for the wood. From that wood, he made a bed and a chest of drawers. My crib was one of those drawers. Later in life, whenever my brother or I would whine and complain about anything, mom would remind us that the family's first bedroom suite was made from wood from the town latrine. My brother Gianni (who was born in Tofield) and I would buckle down and get on with whatever we were supposed to be doing. Embedded in that story was an enduring lesson in understanding how fortunate we were to be in Canada, and in knowing the value of hard work in making your life."

Franco's father came to Canada in 1950, leaving his wife and young son in Valvasone. Romeo followed the CNR in search of work, settled in Forestburg, and by 1954, he had saved enough money to book passage for Iolanda and young Franco to join him. "I remember the long boat trip," says Franco, "and finally we landed at Pier 21 in Halifax. Then came the endless train ride to Edmonton and along the way, I saw cars—I had never seen a car." Franco was six years old.

"The train station in Edmonton, back in 1954, was small and dimly lit," he remembers. "But to me, at that time? The lights were so bright—I had never seen so many lights, and I was immediately drawn to this little confectionary, just a few steps away from the train track, where there was a comic book stand. I had never seen comics. You could twirl the stand around, and see row after row of comic books. Then I looked up and saw a man. 'Are you Franco?' I said 'Yes.' The man said, 'I'm your father.'" They hadn't seen each other since Franco was three years old.

The Path to University

"WE LIVED IN FORESTBURG, in a two-room shack," Franco says. "How my parents managed it I'll never know, but one Christmas, there was a red wagon under the tree. I couldn't believe it. I raced this wagon all over, and then it disappeared. I discovered that my father had the wagon outside, and he was methodically banging a series of holes around its perimeter. I watched in silence. My father could make any tool. He could fix or build anything. But this...this red wagon was my Christmas present. I watched as my dad inserted dowels into the holes he had made, and then he built up the sides of the wagon with wooden slats. I knew better than to ask a question. I'd get smacked! When dad was done, we walked several miles together to a coal seam. We loaded the wagon, hauled the coal back, and used it to heat the house. So there went my wagon, but the house was warm. I learned early on just how consummate a survivor my father was."

In a few years, it was off to Edmonton, where Romeo worked in construction and Iolanda tended the home front. When the boys were older, Iolanda, too, went to work. "For years," remembers Franco, "my mother got up at 4 A.M. and went to the airport to make sandwiches for all the outbound flights. Both my parents worked hard. In our family, it was a disgrace to be a loafer and the will to work was instilled in us early, as was the value of a dollar. My father would walk all the way downtown from Calder just to save a nickel in bus fare. And yet he would never let me get a paper route to earn money. Why? All my spare time was to be spent studying. My parents wanted my brother and me to get as much education as possible. My father said there was no way I would end up doing what he was doing. You need to understand that my parents were self-taught," adds Franco, "and they never had the opportunity for much formal schooling. To them, education was key. So my path was clear. Junior high, high school, university."

Junior high for Franco was St. Edmund's. "I had a voracious appetite for knowledge and got great grades," says Franco. "The highest grade was an 'H,' for Honours, and next down was an 'A.' And an 'A' wasn't good enough for me or for my father. My father would look at my report card and say 'What is this "A?" Why isn't this an "H?"'"

"In grade 7, my teacher made a written comment on my report card that puzzled me: 'Francis has a gift rarely seen in modern youngsters—humility.' I had to look this word up—humility—and when I did, I realized that what my teacher meant was that I was *respectful*. And it was true. I was very respectful of my teachers. To this day, even though I'm the dean of the Faculty, I can't call several of my former professors by their first names."

Franco also had a strong sense of right and wrong.

"One day in high school I asked if religion was a required course for graduation and was told yes. I couldn't figure this out because the kids down the street at Queen Elizabeth didn't have to take it. So I called the school board and found out what the teacher said wasn't true. So I got a few of my friends together. We put money in a pot and decided to see who could get the lowest grade on every religion test. We knew the grade wouldn't keep us from graduating. The one with the lowest grade got all the money, and the lowest grade, consistently, was mine. I figured that you had to know the correct answer in order to figure out the *worst* answer and believe me, I had the worst answers. I never broke 5%."

My Name is Franco

"THEN THERE WAS THE QUESTION of my name. My name is Franco. Most of my teachers in elementary and junior high, however, insisted on calling me Francis. I didn't mind if people anglicized my name to Frank, but not Francis. I ended up in the principal's office over this, and I was strapped for asking that I be called by my proper name. I held out my hands, and I got strapped hard. When the principal was finished, I was expected to put my hands down and give in. Instead, I looked him straight in the eye and turned my palms up, in effect asking for more. I was expelled, and it wasn't the first time, but I always managed to hide these expulsions from my parents. I thought my father in particular would be furious with me. To make matters worse, I was forging my father's signature on the forms I had to take back to school when each expulsion period was over.

"One day my father came home early from work, and found me at home when I was supposed to be at school. So I had to tell him the story. He quietly took me by the hand and walked me to school. My father was an imposing man physically, with a big barrel chest—he was the best labourer in Edmonton—everyone wanted him on their work site—and he was strong. He simply told the principal, 'My son's name is Franco.' And that is when my teachers stopped calling me Francis."

High school for Franco was O'Leary. "The male students were all downstairs," Franco explains, "and the girls were upstairs. For the boys, our teachers were all male. In terms of social growth, this was catastrophic for a kid's development.

"In high school I was very athletic and competitive, but my dad wouldn't let me play sports—all my spare time was supposed to be spent studying. But I played football on the sly. I was also a member of the school wrestling team and one day I broke my leg. I only made it home because some guy on a motorcycle saw me hobbling home with this dangling, broken leg, and gave me a ride. I was white with pain but made light of it. The next day I went to the hospital, by myself, and was told I had a double fracture. I was put in a cast from toe to thigh, and as a consequence couldn't walk. I had no money to rent crutches, so there I sat outside the University Hospital until a Red Cross nurse took pity on me, giving me $2 for crutches so I could get home on the bus. When my dad found out I had broken my leg playing sports—which he forbade—he didn't talk to me for six months.

"But my grades were great."

University at 17—Unleashed

FRANCO REGISTERED at the U of A in 1965. "All I remember about registration is having to collect all those little computer cards for each course you wanted to take. For Chemistry, I had to line up forever. When I finally got to the front of the line, the course I wanted was full, and what I wanted was Organic Chemistry. But I was tenacious, and when I finally got into Organic Chemistry and saw all those structures, it was like they were talking to me. For other people, organic chemistry was like learning another language, but for me, it was simple.

"In a social sense, during my first year, a whole world opened up to me. I could do what I wanted—sports, fraternities, partying, power drinking, you name it. My total focus in junior high and high school had been on education and now, here I was at 17, and I can tell you that I'm damn lucky I survived first year. I was unleashed in every sense. University was a doorway I would never have encountered in Italy."

Franco rushed three fraternities. One was Phi Delta Theta. "The minute I walked up the stairs of the fraternity house, I knew it was a mistake," he says. "They were very conservative. Then I met the 'Zetes.' Later I learned they had a reputation as the crassest boors of all time, but I didn't know it back then. The guys all had short hair, but they weren't judgmental. However, the first thing they said to me was, 'You're a Wop.' Usually I answered this kind of comment with a punch in the mouth, but I decided to let it pass

The Tuck Shop, where the staff knew you by name.

(UAA 69–19–66–55)

for the moment. The Zetes accepted me—most of them came from working class families like mine. There are still ten of us who get together and go for a beer."

Franco's fraternity house was located where the Timms Centre stands today. Just across the way was the Tuck Shop. "The Tuck Shop," Franco remembers, "was very 1950s small-town Alberta. There was a really nice old lady who knew us all by name and she would do things like give us an extra muffin. The Tuck Shop was open late and had these cool booths, each with its own jukebox—just one nickel and you could play the latest songs. We would sit there and try to pick up girls.

"There was also the Hot Caf over where CAB is now. It was small and very crowded, with lots of tables. I never ate there. I always ate at home and saved my money for dating and for beer."

MLS?

IN HIS FIRST YEAR, Franco went into Medical Laboratory Science. "My heart was in archaeology," he says, "but there was no archaeology program at the U of A. I thought about medicine, which I loved, but I knew it would kill me if I wasn't able to heal a patient, especially if I had a child under my care. So that was out. I also loved science and chemistry, so I looked through the Calendar and discovered Med Lab Science (MLS). It combined the three disciplines I loved—medicine, science and chemistry—so I enrolled.

"It wasn't long before the MLS director phoned me, asking if I was sure I wanted this program. I knew it wasn't a casual phone call, so I probed a bit and was told I was the first male, ever, in the program. I thought, 'Babe heaven!' The first time I went into the MLS common room, which ironically happened to be the same space now occupied by the Faculty of Pharmacy, there were all these girls sitting around in various states of undress. They tried to eject me from the room. I told them 'Hey! I'm one of you guys!'

"Our class took a field trip, touring a lab in the old University Hospital, where there were rows and rows of women hunched over equipment. Suddenly I knew this wasn't for me. I asked the director—the man giving us the tour—about the opportunity for advancement in this field and he replied, 'You're looking at him.'" The following year, in 1966, Franco transferred to Pharmacy, and he's been there ever since.

"I had very few friends in Pharmacy," Franco says. "My hair was long enough to tuck behind my ears, my clothes were different, the profs didn't seem to approve of me, or my appearance, and the students all formed cliques and study groups. That wasn't for me. And so I studied by myself in the V Wing or at the public library. My social life, except for the fraternity I joined, was entirely off campus."

Second Year—Patent Leather Shoes

"ON MY FIRST DAY in Pharmacy, Dean Huston called me in and said, 'Tomorrow I want to see you back here with your hair cut and your beard shaved.' I was polite, but this was my reply: 'Dean, you can discipline me on academic matters but you can't discipline me when it comes to my hair and my beard.' And that was that. We later became friends, and when Dean Huston, a best-selling author, published his popular humour book on golf, I asked him to autograph my copy. He looked me in the eye and wrote, 'To another free spirit.'"

In his second year, Franco got a summer job in Fort McMurray. "I worked for four months in a kitchen serving thousands of meals to oil sands workers. I worked 12-hour shifts Monday through Friday, and then earned time-and-a-half and double-time on the weekends. Room and board were free,

and every night there was a different movie, also free. I saved what I earned. It was the first time in my life I ever had money.

"I transformed from a caterpillar to a butterfly. Gone were the glasses. I could now afford contacts. And remember when Henry Singer opened his new store, Henry III? It was stocked with those Beatles-era tailored shirts and the colours were vivid. I had a royal blue suit with matching vest, and a burgundy-coloured one too. My patent leather shoes were from Italy—$154. Believe me, I stood out. I wasn't a babe magnet—nothing like my two sons are—but when discos became popular, women would come over just to see who I was. They thought I was from Europe. Henry Singer, who became a good friend, would see me on the street and shout, 'Franco!' He'd tell me about a new line of suits he'd just gotten in, and I'd have the cash to buy them."

Paying for Tuition—Creative Banking

FRANCO NEVER TOLD HIS FATHER how expensive university was and devised a way to pay for his education himself.

"After two summers up north earning good money, I got used to a certain lifestyle. When I was no longer able to go north, I persuaded my mother to co-sign a loan. I borrowed $5,000 even though I really only needed $3,000. My mother was a saint. She knew when to talk to my father about family matters—and how to do it—and when not to say anything. She said nothing to my father about the loan. I used that other $2,000 to make the loan payments until the summer rolled around and I was making money again. And that's how I helped pay for my BSc."

Franco and R.T. Coutts

IN FRANCO'S FOURTH YEAR as an undergraduate in Pharmacy, he decided that life as a pharmacist wasn't for him, and he set his sights on a PhD program. His grades were good, but he decided they had to be better. "I was going through the motions in my first three years, and by that time I was hanging out a lot at the Corona Hotel, now demolished, but a great bar at the time. Then I took a class with Dr. Ron Coutts in spectrophotometry—that's a method for analyzing drug compounds. I loved it. Dr. Coutts was never pompous and he knew his stuff. He was well-prepared for every class and you just knew he would never try to buffalo you. 'R.T.' was passionate, and he could take the driest material and make it magic. He changed the course of my academic life. In my last year, when we were still using the nine-point grading system, I got straight 9s."

Franco got his PhD in 1978 and soon after was hired as an assistant professor. But first, he had one final incredible hurrah as an undergraduate student. Franco—no BSc yet—got to teach a course.

"I was two courses short for my BSc," he remembers, "and so I went to summer school. Dr. Coutts was going on sabbatical that summer, and they needed someone to teach the spectrophotometry course. Dr. Coutts thought I could do it, and I thought I could do it too. So 'R.T.' went to the dean—Dean Huston—to get permission. Dean Huston said, "You mean you want that guy with the beard and long hair to teach your spectrophotometry course?' Well, I taught the 'spec' course while I was finishing my BSc, and I failed the only two graduate students who were taking it. They both appealed, and the professor who chaired the appeals committee didn't particularly like me, but he supported the grades I had given. Later on, I taught his class too, and we developed a very respectful relationship."

Convocation and Life Afterwards

"I DIDN'T GO to either my BSc Convocation in 1972 or my PhD Convocation in 1978," says Franco. "I regret it. My parents would have been so proud. But years later, when I was an associate professor, I brought my parents over to my lab one Sunday. At the time I had three grants, two of which were from the Medical Research Council, about a dozen graduate students, and other personnel in a big lab. My dad didn't stop talking about this with my mother for months. In particular, he couldn't get over the fact that I had an *office*."

After Franco tells this story, he pauses and rotates his hands, so that both palms are up. The palms of his hands are calloused, very calloused. "These are not the hands of a typical professor," he says. "I *love* to work with my hands." Franco can make anything, fix anything. Just like his father.

In 1980, when Franco was a post-doctoral student, the dean of the Faculty died suddenly, and they needed someone to take over a senior course. Franco did it for no pay. "It was hard work," he says, "but I wanted to do it." It led to his first job as an assistant professor in 1981, and nine years later he was made a full professor. Along the way, he served as one of two academic staff representatives on the Board of Governors, on General Faculties Council and its Executive, and on the Association of Academic Staff. In 1999 Franco became dean of the Faculty.

Franco was awarded the University's highest honour as an outstanding teacher in 1989. "If I was good at teaching," he says, "it was because of people who taught me. At the University of Alberta, it was R.T. Coutts's teaching that changed my life. In junior high school, it was Mr. McQuarrie, my Grade 7 Science teacher. He always tried to get the best out of you, and years later, I tracked him down and told him how profoundly his teaching had affected me. Mr. McQuarrie and Dr. Coutts were both passionate about their teaching, and that is what every professor should bring to the classroom.

"I loved university," says Franco. "It opened up a vibrant new world and I'm grateful for the educational opportunities my parents never had." Franco may be at the top of his profession, but he defines success in personal terms and talks about his wife, Marianne, his two sons, and his new daughter-in-law. "Success," he says, "is raising kids you're proud of."

Franco's advice for students today comes from watching his parents make their way from Valvasone to Forestburg to Edmonton: "The harder you work," says Franco, "the luckier you get."

Anthony Lindsay Austin Fields (MD '74)

THE MAN WITH THE LONG NAME is just "Tony" to his friends. His career as a chemical technologist for Stelco took a turn in 1969 during his career there, and Tony is now vice-president, of Medical Affairs and Community Oncology, for the Alberta Cancer Board. In that capacity, he makes sure that the gold standard in cancer care, readily available in urban centres, is also available in rural Alberta. Tony is also a professor in the department of Oncology and Medicine at the University of Alberta and is a practising or consulting physician in four hospitals in Edmonton. Tony's patients, and the family members of those patients, know him as a caring, compassionate, committed physician. If you or a loved one has cancer, you want this man at your side.

Tony says his colleagues like to joke that he was born on a pirate ship. He has certainly cut a swashbuckling path through life. "I graduated from high school when I was 17 and spent my gap year teaching mathematics to girls aged 10–16 at the Lodge School in Barbados," says Tony. "Then I spent three or four years in England studying natural sciences at Cambridge. I worked for a fourth year while in England with one of the two geniuses I have known in my life, on a project involving the measurement of X-ray absorption in metals. I returned home in 1966 with no formed ambition, just a vague notion that I might want to be a diplomat. But I soon found out that, without friends in high places, I would only be a third-level underling. That wasn't for me. I *was* interested in a research project run in Barbados by McGill University—let's just say it involved development of a massive gun that could send a projectile three-quarters around the world. The pirate side of me was interested in the project, but I decided—in retrospect, wisely decided—not to get involved. Instead, I taught chemistry at Queen's College in Barbados, where my mom and three aunts had been teachers, and then mathematics again at the Lodge School, where my mom and three aunts had been teachers."

When Tony returned home from Cambridge in 1966, landing in Bridgetown's deepwater harbour by ship, there was an old friend who

had tagged along with his parents to greet him. "My friend said there were these girls I just had to meet, but I was just seeing my parents for the first time in years," recalls Tony, "so how could I get away? But with my parents' 'Okay' we were gone within half an hour to meet these girls. They were four CUSO volunteers from Canada, who had only been in Barbados for three weeks, and they were staying with a friend who was so close to our family that we called her 'aunt.' This is how I met my wife of 37 years, Pat Stewart. She was one of those girls my good friend wanted me to meet. Pat was from Winterburn, Alberta, and we quickly knew that our life paths would be intertwined."

Ten months later, in 1967, when Tony was 23, he and Pat married. Tony and Pat decided that their best prospects would be in Canada.

A Reluctant Doctor

"COMING TO EDMONTON meant a sure teaching job for Pat," says Tony, "so we'd have at least one salary coming in. I now had to decide what do to with my life. I didn't have the credentials to teach in Canada, and decided to take a job at Stelco as a chemical technologist, analyzing steel. I had learned chemistry as a kid from an uncle who was a dynamic teacher, but I knew this would not be my career. I had been raised on the assumption that if you had an education, the world would be at your feet, and I decided it was time for further training. But in what? That was the question. I had absolutely no idea what I wanted to do.

"Pat sent me to the University of Alberta vocational counselling department, which at the time was located on the top floor of the SUB tower. The counselling was free! They gave me many tests, including one test with 400 true/false and multiple-choice questions that made no sense to me. For instance, this was one question: 'The only thing in the newspaper worth reading is the comics.' I learned later that if you answered 'true,' it indicated that you would be more successful than others. A few days after taking the test, I had an interview with a Mr. Fisher. This was a life-altering experience for me. Mr. Fisher quickly got to the bottom line. He told me the aptitude test showed a 95% confidence rating that my career choices were to be three occupations, and an interesting mix it was: a psychologist, an Air Force officer as a distant third, or a doctor. I immediately said that I didn't want to be a doctor, and I had some experience upon which to base this statement. Two of my uncles were doctors and I accompanied one of them on his house visits and also spent time in his office—not involved with patients of course, but I had a chance to absorb and observe. My conclusion was that I had no interest at all in pursuing a medical career.

"But Mr. Fisher was quietly persistent. He asked me what I thought of really *being* a doctor. I told him I didn't have that kind of mind. I also didn't think I was good at memorization. 'You have no worries on that score,' he told me. I pushed back and said there was nothing he could say to persuade me to be a doctor. He pushed *me* back. I finally told him it would just take too long—six years. He asked me why that bothered me. The answer to me—back then—was perfectly obvious. I was 25 years old. Far too old to think about spending *six more years in school*. Mr. Fisher then asked me if I knew how old Albert Schweitzer was when he became a doctor. Answer? 35 years old. That hard fact countered my ultimate hurdle—my age."

The moment after Tony recalled this interchange with Mr. Fisher—some 26 years later—his pager beeped and he excused himself. It was a call from the Cross Cancer Institute, and Tony had a patient who needed his immediate attention. "It's the most complex case I've ever had," Tony said. Perhaps there was no better measure of the value of those extra years of schooling than Tony's ability to help patients in extreme need.

"Pat encouraged me throughout the months when I thought about truly becoming a physician," Tony recalls. "I thought back to my first-aid training at Stelco and my satisfaction in dealing with people who were injured. I thought back to my uncles who were physicians. I thought about a career, not a job. I decided to give it a try.

"Dr. Walter MacKenzie was the dean of Medicine back then," remembers Tony, "and Odette Hagen was the assistant dean of admissions. Odette was English, and she was elegant. We met to talk about my new-found ambition. She told me this: 'I prefer to tell you now, and I am terribly sorry, but you don't stand a chance'." Why? The agreement with the government was that the medical school was basically for Albertans. There were very few spots for non-Albertans and the competition was impossible.

"As Odette walked me to the door, we continued to chat. She asked if I was married, and I told her my story. 'Your wife is Albertan?' That's what she asked me. I was almost out the door. Her casual question was a turning point in my life. It may be hard to believe now, but back then if an Albertan man married a non-Albertan woman, the woman was considered an Albertan, and therefore in a privileged position in terms of getting a job. But the reverse? It just wasn't so. I was a non-Albertan male—a husband who had accompanied his Albertan wife to Canada. I didn't fit the mould. Odette held out a ray of hope. 'Let me speak to the admissions committee about whether or not you can be considered an Albertan.' If so, I would have a chance to be accepted by the medical school. And lo and behold, the answer was yes and I was accepted," says Tony.

"But I had no training in Biology and had to do one year as a special student before starting medical school."

1969—Special Student

IN 1969, at age 26, Tony began a new life. He needed to shore up his academic record by taking some basic science courses before embarking on a medical degree. As a Special Student, he was required to take five courses. Tony would also have been a Mature Student, a category of student fairly new to a university where the norm was first-year students who were 18-year-old high school graduates. Tony was also from another country, and was what the university called, in the 1960s and 1970s, a Foreign Student.

"That year as a Special Student," says Tony, "was like a job. I went to class. I went home at night. I did not take part in any university activities. I went to the Library between classes. This was dramatically different from my studies at Cambridge, where I participated in many activities. Here at the U of A, I was different from my peers. I was six or seven years older, while most other students had just graduated from high school. They were from Alberta. I was from another country and had been to another university. I had worked and was married. They were single and had no significant work experience. I was different."

Favourite Professors—Vic Lewin and John Kuspira

THE FIRST HURDLE was registration. "I had to take five courses," Tony remembers. "The line-ups for registration were long. I took Biology, Zoology, Genetics, Psychology and Anthropology. On the day I registered, *everyone* wanted into get into John Kuspira's Genetics class. In fact, students would alter their schedules in order to get into his classes. I was so lucky—I went directly to Dr. Kuspira before registration, explained my situation, and asked if I could be in his section. He gave me a book to read titled *The Cell*. Reading that book gave me a basic understanding of biology. That was what was missing in my science background, and John Kuspira understood that. On the actual day of registration, I was very lucky to get in to his section. He just happened to walk by, and told the registration staff to enrol me.

"My favourite professor from that year," says Tony, "was Vic Lewin. He taught Zoology 320, the class many students remember as the cat dissection course. Vic Lewin made learning so entertaining. When he explained how birds could fly, his analogy had to do with airplanes—short-range planes and long-range bombers and the differences between them. John Kuspira captured my attention in the same way that Vic Lewin captured my attention, but he had a different style. Dr. Kuspira was brilliant, and he reduced things to the essentials. He made us understand the principles that underlay everything. His genetic exams were fascinating. The questions couldn't be answered by simply remembering facts. His questions required that you work things out, that you understand and explain underlying concepts."

"I Cured Two Mice!"

THE FOLLOWING YEAR, Tony began his medical studies. "I loved med school!" he says. "I took Biochemistry in my first year and found the study of living molecules fascinating. A couple of the classes and labs dealt with cancer. One of the studies involved injecting mice with cancer cells. I cured two of those mice, I was thrilled to pieces! I asked the professor, Dr. Allan Patterson, if I could take the mice home. He was very kind in his response, but the rules would not allow it. Nonetheless, a whole new vista had opened up for me—cancer research.

"As Dr. Patterson's course wound down, I remembered his kindness to me and asked if I could work with him at the MacEachran cancer research lab for the summer. The summer before med school, I had gone back to my chemical tech job at Stelco, and planned to do that all during med school, but now I wanted more exposure to cancer research. As it turned out, however, the pay was only $250 a month and I couldn't afford to take the job. But Dr. Patterson managed to get me a research scholarship, and that is how I began a career studying cancer.

"I made a friend for life during med school—Laszlo Torok-Both. We were interns together, but we had met as lab partners in Vic Lewin's Biology 320 class. Laszlo and I did the frog dissection together, then the dogfish dissection, then the cat dissection. We worked hard to carefully dissect this cat. We worked on it endlessly to understand how the anatomy and the systems worked. We were obsessed. One day, we took the cat home to Laszlo's apartment in a garbage bag. We spread it out and studied the muscles, the bones. We studied every aspect of this cat's anatomy.

"Lazlo had this crusty old landlady. One day she walked right into the apartment unannounced. It happened to be the day we had the cat spread out on the dining room table. She took one look at us and said, "You Goddamn medical students, if you're not smoking dope, you're cutting up cats."

The Med Show

"I WAS IN IT!" says Tony. "It was bawdy and it was fun. There were line-ups of people to buy tickets and I have warm memories of all the shows. In 1973, I had a bit part impersonating Associate Dean George Goldsand. George and his wife Judy were out in the audience, and Judy kept looking over at her husband to make sure he was really sitting next to her, and not up there on the stage. I had him down to a T. During a previous this show, we had probably the largest model of a penis that ever graced a stage. We were doing a take-off on the Helen of Troy/Trojan Horse story and we had men being fired out of this fake penis one by one. It brought down the house.

"In our final year, we did a take-off on Jesus Christ Superstar. Our own superstar was Walter Yakimets, a highly-respected surgeon who was our honorary class president. We called him Wally Why in the show. In our skit we had the real Wally hidden away on stage, buried under a pile of fake boulders. At the end of the skit, we had him emerge quickly from under this pile of boulders and announce: 'It doesn't take me long to get my rocks off!' Ten years later, I was on stage as honorary class president doing my own cameo appearance."

Convocation and Life After

TONY DIDN'T ATTEND his Convocation at Cambridge—there were no family members able to attend. But he crossed the stage in 1974 when he got his medical degree, with his wife Pat and his family in the audience. In his graduation year, he was the recipient of the Moshier Memorial Gold Medal—named after the U of A alumnus who was one of the first to enlist in World War I. In 1974, Tony also received the John Scott Honour Award, the Conn Memorial Medal, and was the first recipient of the Walter MacKenzie Prize.

After Tony's first year of med school, his tuition was paid by a scholarship and he set his sights on being a family doctor. "I didn't give any thought to being a specialist," he says. "It was that timing issue again. I was a late starter in the medical field and to be a specialist meant years of additional training. But when I had my first experience on the wards, as a third-year medical student, a transformation occurred, and I knew that my heart was in internal medicine. Even before I rotated through other specialties, I was sure of this. So my plans were changing again, and I talked to a trusted mentor, Allan Gilbert. He encouraged me to go to either Toronto or Montréal for further study as a specialist, and I did my first rotation in oncology at St. Michael's in Toronto. I studied with an oncologist named Jim Goldie, who later became world-famous for his theory of drug resistance of cancer cells, a concept that changed the direction of chemotherapy research globally. There were only two of us at St. Michael's who took to oncology. I did that rotation a second time on a voluntary basis because Jim made it seem so interesting. Also, I felt closer to those patients than to any other group. I was on my way to becoming a specialist in oncology."

"So there I was in 1978, the chemist who never thought he would be a doctor, the family physician-in-training who was sure he would never take the time to be a specialist, and now the internal medicine and oncology specialist and chief resident who was sure he would never do a sub-specialty. Then Jim Goldie left for British Columbia and the chief of Medicine at St. Michael's sat down with me and said that if I would go into the subspecialty of medical oncology, he would give me a job. I loved St. Michael's and would have given my life for that place. To be offered a position there was the pinnacle of a medical career. So, off I went to be a medical oncologist and to engage in two more years of study! I often remember Mr. Fisher, the career counsellor who gave me that aptitude test in 1969 and helped me to see that I could start medical school at the ripe old age of 25. Back then, four years of university seemed like such a long time. By the time I finally finished with sub-specialty training, I had spent 11 years in further study of medicine. I always wanted to go back and tell Mr. Fisher that he had done me the biggest favour of my life. I wanted to tell him that I turned out OK. Then one day, I saw his obituary in the newspaper. I have always regretted that I had never gone to thank him. I never would have thought, at any point in my life, that I would move on from medical school to a specialty, to a sub-specialty and to administration, then to studying large populations—and now to trying to change how cancer is dealt with across Canada."

"A Trend-Setter in Cancer Care"

Dr. Jean-Michel Turc, head of the Alberta Cancer Board, describes Tony Fields as "a trend-setter in cancer care." He continues to enumerate Tony's achievements: "Tony spent two years as president of the National Cancer Institute of Canada and 12 as director of the Cross Cancer Institute," says Dr. Turc, "and now he is leading the way in Alberta to achieve the dream of a cancer-free province. Tony is very much part of our team.

"In Alberta, we many of the resources and attributes needed to advance the agenda of cancer control worldwide. We have the responsibility to lead the way and to invite other provinces to embrace our dream." That is the vision Tony is attempting to build in his capacity as vice-president for Medical Affairs and Community Oncology. Tony also continues to practise as a physician at the Cross Cancer Institute. He is hands-on and remains close to his patients while at the same time, he has the 50-thousand-foot view of cancer care in Alberta and Canada. Tony is a star on all counts."

In 2003, Tony Fields was inducted into the Alumni Wall of Fame at the University of Alberta. That honour was merely the latest in a series of accolades he has received. Tony was Professor of the Year in the Faculty of Medicine in 1982–1983 and again in 1983–1984. In 1994, he was awarded an honorary doctorate from Athabasca University. In 1997, he received a Black Achievement Award. He has served in executive capacities on ten major cancer boards and has authored many research papers. "He is regarded as a motivational authority in cancer control, inspiring a generation of medical students and residents with his energy, enthusiasm and dedication. To his patients, Tony is best-known and admired for his endless supply of compassion and caring." That was just part of his citation when Tony was inducted into the Alumni Wall of Fame.

Tony has some advice for today's students: "Look beyond your immediate vision. Look way down the road into the future, and make a difference—to your community, to society, and to the world."

Sibéal McCourt Bincoletto (BA '77, MA '06)

Sibéal is a woman with abundant determination and a huge ability to make change work to her advantage. She has made many gutsy decisions over the years, both in her personal and career lives. Twenty years ago, she hit the glass ceiling at work. After being diagnosed with cancer, she was given a 50–50 chance to live. She beat the cancer and then began a four-year wait for a hip replacement. In 2000, along with three other managers, she lost her job as a result of restructuring and then, two years ago, turned down her dream job to "re-find" herself. Today, Sibéal's on top of the world.

Granddaughter of a Freedom Fighter

SIBÉAL'S GOT GRIT. She's endlessly resilient. She's fearless in fighting for what's right. And it's all in the genes.

Sibéal's grandfather was Gearoid O'Sullivan, who during Ireland's struggle for independence was a leader of the Irish Volunteers and later of the Irish Republican Army. Both O'Sullivan and his cousin, Michael Collins, were key figures in the 1916 Easter Uprising, and both are depicted in the film *Michael Collins,* which stars Liam Neeson in the title role and Julia Roberts as Sibéal's great aunt, Kitty Kiernan.

Sibéal's maternal grandmother was Maude Kiernan. The Kiernan family businesses and hotel were burned to the ground by the British three times between 1910 and 1920, and three times they rebuilt. How? Sibéal's grandmother would run into the burning buildings to retrieve the financial records, so that the family had the tools to bounce back.

Then again, it could be that Dublin-born Sibéal inherits her defining characteristics from her mother, Ann O'Sullivan McCourt. "My mother was convent-raised, in Ireland," says Sibéal, "and right after she and dad were married, they moved to the West Coast of Africa. Mom had never been out of Ireland. She and dad moved 23 times in the first 12 years of their marriage, following dad's dreams and medical career." Perhaps it was moving all over the world as a child that gave Sibéal a special ability to adapt. "We lived in Africa, twice—in Tanganyika (Tanzania) and The Gambia—in England, Ireland and all over Canada. I never got to make close friends as I was growing up, but I learned to be resilient early on, and I could be comfortable living anywhere."

However it was that Sibéal came by her distinct combination of personal qualities, she is a force to be reckoned with. Sibéal has a quiet way of inspiring others to be confident in their own abilities. She can deftly coach small business owners to hammer out their first-ever business plan. She can manage a 500-seat theatre. She can plan a six-course gourmet meal for

300 people, or a three-day conference for 1,000. She can sew costumes or install drywall. Sibéal is creative, organized, full of energy, highly skilled, and has no tolerance for phonies. Sibéal says that if she's learned anything over the years, it's this: "If someone says or does something you don't agree with, speak up. Stand up for yourself."

A 'Lippy' Girl from Small-town Saskatchewan

"I ALWAYS HAD AN ATTITUDE," Sibéal says. "When I was 20 years old, they called it 'lippy.' Now that I'm in my 40s, people listen to me. Somehow, having an opinion is now valid—it's accepted and welcomed. I guess it's the age spread.

"There have been several distinct turning points my life, and one of them was moving to Edmonton when I was in Grade 12. We lived in a small Saskatchewan town when I was a teenager in the 1960s. There was no dance, no fine arts, no theatre, and I was a very creative kid. Brimming with it. I had no outlet for all this creativity that I felt so strongly. I was sure life was over. When we moved to Edmonton, I decided that whatever I did from then on, I would do for myself. No one was going to do it for me."

A year later Sibéal headed to the U of A. "I was fortunate that there was an excellent university right here at home. It made going to university financially feasible, and it was expected that I would go. My grandfather O'Sullivan was a lawyer in Ireland, my father went to university at age 16 and is a doctor. To top it off, my mother told me to get an education so I never had to be dependent on a man."

Registration in the 1970s—Developing Survival Tactics

SIBÉAL SAYS THAT REGISTRATION in the 1970s took at least two days. "There was no telephone registration and no registration on the Web," she remembers. "First came Part I, where you went to pick up your registration package. It was called 'In Person' registration. I think we picked up our packages at the ice arena. The Butterdome was just being built and when it was completed, that's where you stood in an excruciatingly long line to get your package.

"Then you made up your own timetable by circling in the Calendar the courses you wanted to take, and you picked your days and times. The Calendar no longer listed who was teaching each course—that was a problem

Registration—The Perfect Way to Socialize

"THERE WAS A LOT OF SOCIALIZING in the line-ups and we all swapped stories about classes and profs. Great fun! So when you found out what course a favourite prof was teaching, you could switch lines and have a chance at getting the prof you wanted. And if the class you wanted was full? By my second year, I learned to be tenacious," says Sibéal McCourt Bincoletto. I would just stay there at the front of the line, talking my way into the course. Of course I was holding up the line, so they invariably let me into the class. (UAA 74-51-71-025)

for students. Later on, I learned ways to find out who was teaching a particular section.

"With your registration package in hand, you went from building to building, to all the departments where you wanted to take courses. And each time there was a long line. You would wait and wait and when you got to the front, there was one person compiling the class list. Sometimes you'd get all the way to the front of the line only to find out that the course was full. So you'd have to join another line for another course or section. I let myself be bullied by this process the first year, but by my second year, I was wiser. There were ways to find out who was teaching a particular course or section, and you often could learn this from other students in the line-ups.

"My brother Peter was two years behind me at the U of A. There was no way I was going to let him be intimidated by the registration process, so I went with him to registration in his first year to make sure he got into all the courses he wanted. Peter is now a professor of Genetics at the University of Toronto. He just turned down a $1-million signing bonus from a private company—he likes being a professor. I guess he's now quite accustomed to handling the challenges of academe without the guiding hand of his older sister."

Sibéal says that registration as an MA student in 2001 was a snap. "I simply picked up a package and the rest was done on the telephone."

Four Faculties in Four Years—"I Had the Time of My Life"

"My dad was a doctor and he wanted me to go into Medicine. But I did whatever my parents *didn't* want me to do. The 1970s was the anti-estab-lishment era. The phrase back then was, 'Anything goes.' My time at the U of A was very liberating. I took all these courses, all over the map, and the University didn't bat an eye. There was no pressure to be highly competi-tive or to over-accomplish. It was the era of free love, and in terms of choosing your university courses, there was also tremendous freedom. It was easy to explore many different academic areas. I decided that I was doing whatever the bloody hell I wanted to do, and was in three faculties in four years. I took Political Science, then Home Economics, and then Drama. Political Science was fascinating then because we had huge debates about Trudeau's invocation of the *War Measures Act*.

"Looking back, I wish I'd had some counselling at university to help me decide what I was good at, what I wanted to do. After I graduated, I went from theatre administration to arts administration, to the hospitality industry, to tourism, and finally to small business development. After 20 years of moving around like this, in 1999, I enrolled in a Master's program in Small Business Management in Human Ecology. Now I'm in Special Event Management.

"I had the time of my life at the U of A. It opened up my whole frame of reference. You would turn a corner on campus and meet someone brilliant, or someone from another country. The professors were interesting eggheads and it was a very open community. I had a different type of education. It was a worldly education. It was a life experience. I was exposed to things like people living together. Back then, living together was revolutionary. The 1970s was also a time when, as a woman, you could speak out, have an opinion, and it was OK to have an opinion. It was great.

"Even though I was living at home, I earned my own money. I had a job at Woodwards from the time I was in Grade 12. Woodward's was great to university students. They encouraged their permanent staff to take their vacations in the summer so there would be jobs for us. And the jobs paid way above the minimum wage. I did everything at Woodward's—from the drapery department to selling fabrics."

"I remember tuition being raised from about $400 to about $600. Thousands of us crossed the High Level Bridge and marched on the legislature. The politicians didn't care, and some things never change. I'm appalled at the level of tuition now for undergraduates."

Campus Memories

"TODAY YOU SEE ALL THOSE 1970S CLOTHES coming back in style—the fringe, the chokers, the elephant pants. 'Peace and love, man'—it was that era. Students were *just* starting to wear jeans to class. Individualism was OK, and there was no pressure to follow the crowd, as there was in high school. I wore a long skirt to class, a jacket, and always a hat. A big hat. My favourite was a black fedora."

Sibéal remembers lots of construction on campus in the 1970s. "Fine Arts was new, and so was the Tory Building," she recalls. "Studio Theatre was in Corbett Hall and the Drama Department ran an outdoor theatre in the courtyard. It was called the Alberta Barter Theatre. I got very involved in that.

"Home Economics was in a little brick building across from today's Timms Centre, and one of my favourite spots was on the 6th floor of the Humanities Centre. It was a secret spot. There were big bubble chairs—they were intense colours, bright yellow and orange—and most days I brought my lunch and ate there. The Tuck Shop had just been demolished and HUB and CAB were the popular spots. The only place to eat on campus was in HUB and, back then, HUB was filled with private merchants—no franchised food outlets. I'd save my money, and once a week I would buy lunch at this fabulous store in the north end of HUB called Incredible Edibles. Their food was really innovative and it was the first time most of us had ever eaten quiche. They served it by the slice with a huge salad. I also loved CAB. On a two-hour break, I would sit there and watch people and listen in on conversations. Strangers would come right up to your table and start a conversation. Meeting people that way was commonplace.

"The Vietnam War was on and students had been killed by the US National Guard at Kent State. There were a lot of draft dodgers here at the U of A. Some were bitter and belligerent. They opened my eyes to how politics can influence your life in very real ways. Canadian students were blasé about the war. It didn't touch us. It was easy to be judgmental and condescending until you met these students who were draft dodgers.

"I have one other interesting memory. I joined a protest one day in the quad between Athabasca and CAB. The University was going to cut down an old tree. A lot of students gathered around the tree, but they cut it down anyway. When you look at the campus today and see how many trees have been taken down, it's interesting to think back to the concern there was for this one old tree."

Favourite Teachers—"Death Holds no Fear"

"I FELT SO COOL, so grown up when I went to university. I thought, '*I'm in university*.' I was such a snot. But I really *was* in university, and I had some great teachers. Ann Lambert in Home Economics was inspiring. I admire her. I absolutely adore her. She communicated enthusiasm, and she was young, a few years older than me. She taught with such passion, and she brought costume history alive. Dr. Lambert was a driving force in transforming Home Economics to Human Ecology. She was on my MA committee, and whenever I thought I'd never finish my thesis, she would tell me that I *must* complete my degree for the women of the world, because I have something important to say.

"John Orrell in English was another excellent teacher. I had the best time. He would read Shakespeare aloud and then we would go at it and take it apart. John Orrell took Shakespeare off the page and brought it right into the classroom. He made it live.

"Henry Kreisel was my drama teacher," remembers Sibéal. "He was so philosophical about life, and about whatever play we were studying. I can still hear him saying 'Death holds no fear for me because I've had my life and experienced so much. If I was a young person, I would be terrified.' I couldn't understand why at Dr. Kreisel's age he wouldn't be afraid of death. It took me a long time to understand what he was saying. His teaching has stayed with me for years."

What Sibéal didn't know was that Henry Kreisel had fled his native Vienna at age 26 when the Nazis annexed Austria. Thinking he was safe in England, Kreisel was arrested as an enemy alien, as were all German and Austrian nationals. Kreisel was interned in a camp in Canada. He set that experience down on paper, in a language that was very new to him—

English. His memoirs of life in an internment camp set young Henry on a pathway to undergraduate studies at the University of Toronto. Kreisel never stopped. After graduate studies at the U of A and the University of London, Henry Kreisel made Edmonton his home, and the U of A the focal point of his career. A prolific writer and popular teacher, Dr. Kreisel served as head of the department of English and as vice-president (academic) during the 1960s and 1970s. Students loved him.

Graduation and Afterwards—A Body in the River

"I DIDN'T GO to Convocation," says Sibéal. "It was an anti-establishment thing not to attend. But now, 26 years later? When I got my MA, I *marched* right across that stage."

After earning her BA, Sibéal enrolled in a graduate program in theatre administration, and that is where she encountered Tim Davison. Sibéal recounts the story.

"Tim was an administrator in Drama, and he came to Edmonton from Stratford. I learned so much from him. He *was* the course. He gave me one of the biggest opportunities of my life.

"One summer, the Wild Horse Theatre, which was located in a national park in Fort Steele, BC, called the U of A Drama department for help. It was a gorgeous 500-seat theatre, beautifully appointed to evoke the Klondike era. The problem was that their general manager had disappeared. Weeks later, they found his body in the river. Tim went to help out and he asked me to come too. When we arrived, we went straight to the manager's office. The contents of all the file cabinets had been flung to the other side of the room. We spent four days sorting through the mess. There was no budget, the proper papers for the actors had not been sent to Equity, and opening night was two weeks away. What an opportunity. What a challenge. Twenty actors were depending on us. We opened on time, and I ran the theatre by myself for the summer. I was 21 years old.

"I was also very involved with Summer Fest, the precursor to all Edmonton's current festivals. I was running this huge arts centre with 17 tenants. One day, the director came in and said there was no money to pay me that month. I left.

"Everyone said I was crazy, but I took a job as a desk clerk at a big hotel in Edmonton. Why? I decided I wanted to be able to work anywhere in the world, and the best way to enable that was by getting involved in the hospitality industry. If I'd had some career counselling, I might have made a different decision. The hospitality industry taught me about corporate life and made me a professional. I received superb training, including international training, and I learned proper etiquette for almost any situation."

Learning about Corporate Life

"THE CORPORATE WORLD made me grow up, and part of the growing up was learning about sexual discrimination. I had the skills and abilities to advance, but there was a glass ceiling for women. You could only go so far. It was tough to know you could do a particular job and then see a painfully incompetent man get it instead. I got angrier and angrier. During this time, I met William Bincoletto. We married, and soon after, I was headhunted by another big hotel chain. There was no chance for advancement here in Edmonton, so I resigned. I was yelled at by my boss for doing this, and was told that if I left for a competitor, things would be made difficult for William, who worked for the same company as me. So we just upped and left for Calgary.

"It took me a long time to find my way. I was diagnosed with cancer and given a 50–50 chance to live. But I beat it, with the help of my father, who was head of Alberta Health Care at the time. In the meantime, the Olympics were awarded to Calgary, and I ended up as the reservations manager for the Westin. They were very good to me in Calgary."

Just as Sibéal and William's lives were settling down in Calgary, William's employer moved him to Edmonton. A distance marriage wasn't for Sibéal, and she moved back to Edmonton.

"As luck would have it, I landed a job in tourism assessing grant applications," she says, "and found it used all my skills and experience. I had run a theatre, done a lot of marketing and knew the hospitality industry in Alberta's two major cities. The only problem was that my boss was a psycho babe. One day she came in to my office and said, 'Hmm, I can't decide if I'll fire you today. It depends on my mood.' But I loved my work, especially with the Northern Alberta Mayors' Caucus. Edmonton's mayor at the time was Jan Reimer. She told me I was one bright woman, and this gave me some protection from the psycho babe boss.

"My husband was working at the Alberta Liquor Control Board (ALCB), dealing with specialty wines. Suddenly, the ALCB privatized. William and many others were out of a job. At the same time, I too had been through some pretty mixed experiences. The worst was having one company I worked for restructure and walk three of us, three managers, to the door without any notice. This caused me to have a Scarlett O'Hara moment. Remember when Scarlett O'Hara is so down and out? Tara is a disaster, Twelve Oaks has been burned to the ground, everyone is starving? Scarlett says 'As God is my witness, I'll never starve again and neither will my folks'—or words to that effect. My sentiments exactly! I was determined we would see these disasters as temporary detours, and would navigate past them. That we did—my husband started his own company, and it's grown so rapidly, he's had to hire staff. As for me, I vowed I would bounce back with a vengeance. I thought that meant getting the same kind of high-powered, corporate job, just in another sector."

Turning Down the Job of a Lifetime

A YEAR AFTER being "walked to the door," Sibéal was offered her dream job, in government. Not only did *they* come after *her*, but the job meant great money, and prestige. She turned it down. Everyone told her she was crazy to give up the offer of a secure, high-paying job. Instead, she took a "song and a prayer" contract in an area where she thought all her skills could be applied. Today, as a consultant in event planning, she is the happiest she has ever been, and in her best-ever financial shape. This is how Sibéal puts it: "It's great when money and happiness coincide, but my choice in life is to be happy, even if it means a lesser income. My BA has taken me from the arts to the hospitality industry, then to tourism, and finally to business management. Now, I'm the last person laughing. I'm having such fun. To top it off, now that I have my MA in business development, I have my choice of jobs.

"I've learned that if you are willing to take a chance to make your life better, or if you need to bounce back from some crushing experience, you can do it. Realistically assess your skills and experiences, and then take a chance on a new direction in life." For Sibéal, that's meant some risky life moments and some great rewards. "When the chips are down," she advises, "way down, the proverbial 'other door' only opens if you march right over and open it up."

Brian Pisesky (BSC '79, DDS '82)

1 QUIK 4x4—that's the license plate on one of Brian Pisesky's two 4x4s. His other 4x4—the one he drives each day—is a black Cayenne S Porsche. Very cool. License plate? 2 Quik 4x4. Brian does nothing by half-measures. It's full throttle all the way.

Brian is an extraordinary dentist. Here are two of his patients' stories.

Patient #1: "I knocked out a front tooth while on the golf course. (Don't ask me how). I had to give a speech the next day and there was no way I could pull that off with a missing front tooth. I knew Brian was at a wedding, but I called him anyway. He said, 'Meet me at the office in an hour,' and I did. In between the wedding and the reception, Brian fixed me up with a new tooth. Then he went back for the party."

Patient #2: "Brian's my dentist because he's got this fierce pride about his work. I had an appointment so he could check one of my crowns. Brian asked me how the crown was. 'It's good,' I said. "Brian shot right back at me: 'Good?? Just good?? What's wrong with it?'"

The Sharpest Blades in Town

"MY MOTHER WAS BORN IN UKRAINE in 1929," says Brian, "and my dad was raised in a poor part of Edmonton, on the north side, one of a family of ten. My parents made sure all three of their kids went to university. There was no question about it. Dad graduated from the Faculty of Medicine in 1955 and practised as a vascular surgeon. I grew up hearing Dad tell us, 'Good is not good enough.' That phrase has stuck with me my whole life. The other thing that has stuck with me is the memory of my dad getting up in the middle of the night to make house calls.

"All three of us kids ended up in health professions—my older sister is a pharmacy grad from the U of A, and my older brother, a U of A medical grad, is an orthopaedic surgeon. As for me, I chose dentistry, and this is why.

"Dad used to take me hunting with his medical colleagues. It was my dad's doctor friends who persuaded me to go into dentistry. They said I'd have more control over my practice. This is the example they gave me to

Brian Pisesky attended Camrose Lutheran College in the mid-1970s. Today, it is the Augustana Faculty. For Brian, a Roman Catholic and a city boy, "it was an outstanding experience." (CS 5456–02–041–B)

illustrate what they meant by 'control': if you're a surgeon in a hospital and pick up a scalpel blade to perform an operation, it will be a hospital administrator who's ordered the blade. The administrator will have gotten a good buy on the blades, but won't have been committed to hunting down the *best* blades, the *sharpest* blades. But if you're a dentist with your own practice, you can order your own blades.

"That did it for me," Brian says. "I'm picky. So was my dad—his surgeries were on small blood vessels. My mom is picky too—she makes the best Ukrainian food in town."

Augustana University College—A City Boy in Rural Alberta

NOT ONLY was a university education always expected of the Pisesky children, but they all knew that if they *didn't* go to university, they would have to pay room and board if they decided to live at home after Grade 12. "It's the same rule now for my own kids," says Brian.

When the time came, however, Brian didn't end up at the U of A. He started university in rural Alberta, at Camrose Lutheran College, later renamed Augustana University College. In 2004, Augustana University College merged with the U of A. But Brian was at Augustana when it was a small rural college, out there all on its own. Here's how a city boy ended up at Augustana.

The Gold Foil Club

IN THE 1977 DENTISTRY YEARBOOK, there's a group photo with an intriguing caption: "The Gold Foil Club." The Club's creator, Brian Pisesky, explains its mystic origins: "Gold foils were tricky fillings, extremely difficult," he says, "and you had to do two of them in order to graduate. So we made a mockery of the gold foils to minimize the stress involved. We dressed up like riverboat gamblers, met in the Power Plant—my grad student roommate got us in—and, of course, what we drank was beer—liquid gold."

(Private Collection)

"I was a good basketball player, and captain of my team," explains Brian. "Augustana recruited me while I was in high school at Saint Francis Xavier. So there I was, a Roman Catholic city kid at a rural Lutheran college. The students were primarily from farming communities, and all from good Lutheran families. The kids were so naïve. They had few city life-skills. And a lot of them had never had any alcohol, so they would just down ten beers all at once.

"Augustana was an outstanding experience for me. Registration was a piece of cake and very personal; classes were small; most of the profs were good; and the school was well-run. I took all my hard-core, pre-dent courses at Augustana, and I made a ton of friends. We're still a close group. And our basketball team? We travelled all over the province."

Life as a Dentistry Student

"I TRANSFERRED to the U of A in 1977," remembers Brian, "and lucky for me that I had some friends who'd already been there for one year. They gave me tips on registration, which was a zoo at the U of A. I was still in pre-dent, so I had course options, and you had to walk from department to department as you filled out your timetable, course by course. It took all day. The key was to register in the smaller classes first—small classes always filled up quickly. But by the time I was in the dentistry program, you were just handed a timetable. There were no options in this program. It was very regimented for all 50 us in the class.

"My pre-dent classes were held in the Tory Turtle, and they were big, with maybe 250 students each. There was no chance to get to know the profs. But when I started dentistry, it was different. George Thorn was my favourite prof. He had a great attitude, a great personality. We asked him to be honorary president of our class.

"But the teacher who most influenced my life was a man I did a hospital rotation with, Murray Mickleborough. He was highly skilled and committed, with a sense of humour and a zest for life. I always wanted to be like him.

"Dentistry students were segregated from the rest of the university," says Brian. "Our days went from 8 A.M. to 5 P.M., with three-hour labs afterwards. Most of the time we were in the Dentistry/Pharmacy Centre, with only one class in another building.

"In the second year of dentistry, you had to learn how to give injections. We'd get together an hour before class—at 7 A.M.—and practice on each other. Your classmates were your guinea pigs and we would hit each other with injections for an hour and then go to class, frozen until noon. Today, as a practicing dentist, I pay more money for the sharpest needles. What I learned the hard way from these 7 A.M. practice sessions is that there are different levels of sharpness. So you can bet that I'm cutting edge with the needles I use on my patients.

"Pulling teeth? It's all in the wrist action. You rock the tooth back and forth. There's a lot of blood but it clots fast. You learn it on patients. You never know when you have a first-time yanker."

Tuition

"I lived at home until my last two years of university," says Brian. "Then I moved on to campus—10028–87 Avenue. I had a friend who had a PhD in Biochemistry and he had been on the list for something like ten years to get this house. He needed a roommate. I was the chosen one. Our rent was $246 a month, utilities included. Our deck overlooked one of the fraternity houses and during rush week there would be all these naked men in the street. Guess what? I decided not to join a fraternity.

"My parents paid for tuition and for my books. Tuition for most students was about $300–$400, but for dentistry it was about $1,000, and you had to buy a dental kit on top of that for another $6,000.

"I worked construction in the summer and originally was slated to work on a cement crew. But I lucked out and was first assigned as a swamper, which meant riding on a truck and dropping off barricades in advance of the construction trucks. It was the cushiest job. I cleared $6,000–$8,000 each summer, and the overtime was incredible. Sometimes I wonder why I became a dentist...."

The Dent Show

"When I started in my first year of dentistry," says Brian, "there was a welcoming stag, a boring skit night and a TGIF twice a year. The class really wasn't a close group. There were 50 of us in the 'Class of 1982,' including five girls. There were also 70 girls in the dental hygiene class and they never socialized with those of us in dentistry. I took one look at that situation and thought, 'I'm going to change it.'

"So I went to the Med Show and could see instantly why it was so popular. I was on the Dental Undergrad Society and we rented a hall and put on a show. It was just for people in the Faculty because there were a lot of in-jokes you would only understand if you were in dentistry. Lots of students were involved—the girls were involved, the few Asian students did a ridiculous skit about boat people. Nothing was sacred," says Brian, "and the first Dent Nite was a rip-roaring success. I also made sure we had TGIFs once a month. I wasn't too popular with the Mormon profs, but it kept the morale up among the students."

If it sounds as though Brian was having a little too much fun, you also need to know that he stopped playing basketball once he entered Dentistry in order to concentrate on his studies. "The drop-out rate in dentistry was high," says Brian, "and our group decided that we wanted everyone to graduate. We nearly made it—47 out of 50 finished up. Maybe the camaraderie had something to do with it.

"Our class was special. We were a bunch of misfits and had lots of fun. We had this one party where a medical student had so much to drink he passed out. Let's call him 'John.' We warned John about his drinking, but to no avail. So there he was, sprawled on the sofa. Someone took a felt pen and drew a trim little moustache on him. Then one of the girls came by and added sideburns and a goatee. John was still out like a light. Someone took off John's shirt and drew on his chest. Finally John's roomies took him home and the next morning he woke up, saying over and over, 'What time is it? What time is it?' It turned out he had a meeting with the dean of Medicine that morning. John went into the bathroom, saw what his face looked like and tried to scrub it clean. The ink wouldn't come off. Turns out it was indelible ink. Apparently John's meeting with the dean must have gone well because he's a practicing physician today."

Hangin' Out

THE CLASS OF '82 studied hard and they partied hard. "HUB and the Tory Building were brand new when I arrived on campus," Brian remembers, "and Java Jive in HUB was a hangout. Absolutely the best coffee. We had an hour for lunch and would grab a *Gateway* as soon as it came out so we could read *Bub Slug*.

"Room at the Top was popular, and on Friday nights the in spot was the Power Plant. My PhD roommate was able to get us into the Power Plant, which at the time was reserved only for graduate students and their guests. Then, of course, there was the Library. It was the stock phrase of the day: 'I'm going to the Library.' But *this* library wasn't for studying. The Library was the Library Lounge on 87 Avenue at 111 Street. Today, it's a restaurant called 'Scholar's.'

"There were also socials with the nurses," says Brian, "who were still all housed in the Nurses' Residence opposite the hospital, and the Education students also invited us for socials.

"University-wide events? There was Bear Country, the university athletic dance held at the Kinsmen, and of course the Beer Gardens at Freshman Orientation. During the year there was Aggie Week with Bar None, and Engineering Week—both very chauvinistic. In Engineering there were maybe 1% of the class who were women and they had the Lady Godiva ride, with a naked woman riding around campus on a white horse."

Convocation and Life After

DID HE ATTEND? "Yeah! Why wouldn't you? It's a proud moment for your parents and your grandmother."

In 1979, Brian organized a ski trip for his class. He called it the Magical Mystery Tour. Twenty years later, members of the Class of '82 still go on Brian's ski adventures. "It was simple," he says. "I planned the trips down to the tiniest detail. Everyone paid me in full, in advance. They got on the bus at the appointed place and hour, and didn't know where they were going. Every trip had a theme—Miami Vice, Star Trek, Jungle Safari, PJ Party, that kind of thing."

Those undergraduate ski trips continue to this day, and it's mostly the Friday night TGIF group—about 30 to 40 people—who still gather for the trips. The only difference is that the travellers are now in their 40s, not their 20s, and the buses to Jasper and Banff have been replaced by flights to famous, far-off Meccas of skiing."

Meet Me in Geneva

"ONE OF THE BEST TRIPS," says Brian, "was dubbed 'Tragically Sick.' We were flying somewhere for this trip and everyone showed up for the plane in casts, head immobilisers, and the like. Another year we went to the Olympics—but just like when we were students, no one knew where we were going until they got on the plane.

"Five years ago, I told everyone to meet me in Geneva, at a particular hotel, on a certain day, at a specific hour. They were all there waiting for me, but they had no idea where they were going. We headed off for a ten-day ski trip to Austria."

When Brian gave up competitive undergraduate basketball to focus on his dentistry studies, many of his high-school friends, who had become members of the Delta Upsilon fraternity, made him an honorary sports member. "We played football and basketball against other fraternities and faculties," he says. "A lot of us have played together now for over twenty years in the men's city basketball league. For five years in a row, we moved

The Tory Building stands in the centre of this 1971 aerial, with HUB, then still under construction, to the right. At the corner of 112 Street and 87 Avenue, across from the Home Economics Building, are the last two Garneau community homes on this street.

(UAA 74051–175)

up in the standings—from fifth place to first. We're in a different division now—we've been in the city majors for ten years."

The Cayenne S Porche that Brian drives shuttles him from basketball practice with his award-winning team to an office with the sharpest blades money can buy. The Porsche zooms him over to his mom's house for the best perogies in town. And then it's home to his wife and kids— "my family is the *absolute* best," he says. Brian's always after the best, always going full throttle in that 2 Quik 4x4. His advice to students? Go full speed ahead.

END OF THE DECADE

IN 1979, Myer Horowitz was named president. He would serve the University for ten years and would lead the U of A through to its 75th anniversary.

"I can do anything I want—be anything I want—that's how I thought about my life as I started at the U of A."

— ANGELA MENELEY SEKULIC
(BSC OT '90)

Timeline

Overleaf:

Angela Meneley Sekulic

(Private Collection)

Enrolment and Finance, 1980–1989

- Fall student head count: 21,831 (1980); 29,602 (1989)
- Operating budget from the Province of Alberta: $135,333,000.00 (1980); $233,831,000.00 (1989)
- Full-load undergraduate Arts tuition: $550.00 (1980); $1,068.60 (1989)
- SU membership fee: $35.50 (1980); $46.50 (1989)

Key Dates, 1980–1989

- President's Advisory Committee on sexual harassment formed (1982)
- 75th Anniversary (1983)
- Prince Charles receives an Honorary Degree (1983)
- World University Games are held with 6,000 participants from 87 countries (1983)
- School of Native Studies established (1984)
- CJSR, previously heard only on campus, goes public (1984)
- Two students launch a petition to impeach SU President Floyd Hodgkins (1984)
- A student street dance in Garneau turns into a riot (1987)
- Paul Davenport succeeds Myer Horowitz as president (1989)

Selected Campus Buildings, 1980–1989

- Assiniboia Hall renovated (1980)
- North Garneau housing plan halved in response to community concerns (1981)
- The Tennis Centre, Universiade Pavilion (Butterdome), and new student housing in Garneau are a legacy of the World University Games (1983)
- Walter MacKenzie Centre, Phase 1, opens (1984)
- Business Building opens (1984)
- Major renovations begin for both the Arts Building and HUB (1986)

Beyond Campus, 1980–1989

- Terry Fox begins marathon run across Canada to raise money for a cancer cure (1980)
- Repatriation of the Canadian constitution (1982)
- West Edmonton Mall opens on Sundays in defiance of *The Lord's Day Act* (1982)
- First CDs (1983)
- A hole in the ozone layer is discovered (1985)
- Peter Lougheed retires and is succeeded by Don Getty (1985)
- A tornado in Edmonton kills 27 people (1987)

- Canada signs a free trade pact with the United States (1988)
- The Berlin Wall falls and communism in Eastern Europe collapses (1989)
- Deborah Grey is elected as the first Reform MP (1989)
- China cracks down on dissident students, killing hundreds in Tiananmen Square (1989)

VIGNETTES FROM THE 1980s

President Myer Horowitz, 1979–1989[1]

DR. HOROWITZ was the first president to have risen through the full ranks of the University, from department chair to dean to vice-president and on to president. He knew the institution inside out and is fondly remembered by hundreds of staff and students as the president with a personal touch—no one who received a handwritten note from him has forgotten it. Excellent collegial relationships with all four constituent groups—undergraduate and graduate students, and academic and non-academic staff—were at an all-time high, despite a difficult financial situation for the University.

During the Horowitz presidency, there was an economic recession in the province. Across campus, the widely-held view was that government funding was entirely inadequate given the large numbers of students applying to university. Entrance requirements tightened up, tuition rose, and department budgets were cut almost every year. Part of the University's property to the south of campus (the "farm") was sold to the government to create an "endowment fund for the future" in order to provide kick-start money for innovative projects—what President Horowitz called essential extras. Horowitz and Board Chair Eric Geddes visited every major bank and insurance company, and other commercial entities, in order to raise funds.

Myer Horowitz launched the first university-wide teaching awards and established the portfolio of vice-president (research) in 1981, with Gordin Kaplan, a renowned biochemist and accomplished musician, as the first incumbent. Myer Horowitz remains deeply involved in post-secondary education. Most would say that no president was more beloved than Horowitz, and most would say that no one understood the university community better than he did. When Dr. Horowitz's second term ended in 1989, Paul Davenport from McGill University was named president—with a mandate to cut 21% from the university's budget.

Burton Smith, First Dean of Students[2]

IN THE MID-1970S, the University abandoned the notion that there should be separate deans for men and women. Instead, a single dean of students was appointed to oversee student life and activities and to be an advocate for students. The first dean of students was Dr. Burton Smith, a History professor beloved by his students for his common sense, and humane and academically rigorous approach to work, study and life. Dr. Smith assumed office in February 1977 and stepped down at the end of December 1981. He was called back for a second stint between January 1997 and June of that year. Burton Smith was followed by Dr. Peter Miller from the Faculty of Education, Dr. Jim Newton from the Faculty of Business, and Dr. Bill Connor from the Faculty of Arts, each of whom shaped the multiplicity of services available today to students—from counselling, emergency bursaries, and student advocacy to career and placement services.

Computing on Campus[3]

COMPUTERS made their first real appearance on campus during the 1980s. The PLATO computer system was installed on campus in 1980, and was used as an instructional aid through the rest of the decade. The first lab of 12 PC microcomputers was built in 1983, and the campus MicroStore opened in 1984. One of the more popular clubs on campus was the Computing Society, which provided members with an account and password that enabled them to access the University's main computer system.

The libraries were also greatly affected by new technologies. In the late 1970s, it was announced that the library would be modernizing its system of cataloguing books. Following the lead of the Library of Congress, it was decided that the old card catalogue would no longer be updated. The new cataloguing process began in 1980 and, at first, only books acquired after 1974 were listed in the new microfiche system. Because of this, students may have had to look in up to three places to do a complete search—the old card catalogue, the post-1974 microfiche catalogue, and another fiche containing the very newest acquisitions. Soon, the entire catalogue was available via microfilm machines and, later, on computer terminals. The GATE—a major new version of the online library catalogue—was launched in 1993, and was only recently replaced by a powerful web-based interface.

In addition to the changes in cataloguing, the total computerization of library circulation also required each volume to be bar-coded. A program to replace the old IBM punch card system began on December 8, 1987. Each volume in every library would eventually be given a unique barcode

that identified it to the library computer system. The computerized catalogue improved staff efficiency when checking in and charging out material
and made it easier than ever to track individual items.

A SPECIAL EVERGREEN AND GOLD— THE UNIVERSITY TURNS 75[4]

THE *EVERGREEN AND GOLD* had been discontinued by the SU in 1972,
but in 1980 a student ran for president on a platform anchored by a
promise to re-institute the yearbook. He lost the election, but one of his
close friends, Michael Ford, a BComm student who later entered Law,
decided to take matters into his own hands as the University's 75th anniversary approached. Michael formed the Evergreen and Gold Historical
Society with four of his friends. His advisory board of 21 included Chancellor
Peter Savaryn, Dean of Law Frank Jones, former SU President Doug Burns,
and Wilbur Bowker, a Law student in the 1920s who had later served as
dean for some 20 years. The special anniversary issue of the *Evergreen
and Gold* is one of the few extant records of the University's 75th year. Its
192 pages are crammed with photos and chronicles of student life, sports,
and government, and of special events like the conferring of honorary
degrees on Mother Teresa and Prince Charles, who had come to Edmonton
with his new wife, Princess Diana, to open the World University Games
being hosted in 1983 by the University of Alberta.

As was customary with previous editions of the *Evergreen and Gold*,
the 75th anniversary issue contained a message from President Myer
Horowitz. "I suspect," he wrote,

> that I shall look back to 1983–84 with mixed feelings. On the posi-
> tive side, the year began with Universiade '83—the World University
> Games—and with the visit of the Prince and Princess of Wales. We
> embarked on a new PhD program in Business. Our research activi-
> ties continued to grow in volume and to excel in quality. We joined
> with other agencies forming joint research and development compa-
> nies....These are only some examples of our happy moments.
>
> Unfortunately, this was also the year when, due to dramatic increases
> in enrolment and inadequate government funding, we have had to
> think of imposing even more severe quotas than we had previously.

For the first time we are incurring a deficit of several million dollars. Consequently, in spite of the need for additional staff due to the increase of about 5,000 students over three years and 2,000 more students than we had a year ago, we are obliged to delete more than 30 academic and 70 non-academic positions. This development is tragic and I fear that the progress of our university will be affected negatively for many years.[5]

WISEST [6]

WISEST is a nationally-known U of A program initiated by Dr. Gordin Kaplan and closely linked with U of A chemist Dr. Margaret-Ann Armour. WISEST seeks to promote the participation of women in the sciences by organizing conferences, summer research programs, and workshops.

While attending a seminar on microprocessors in early 1982, Kaplan, who was then the University of Alberta's vice-president (research), noted that there was only one woman among the 150 people present. This triggered the creation of a new group at the University of Alberta to promote participation of women in non-traditional careers—Women in Scholarship, Engineering, Science and Technology (WISEST).

The primary job of this group, said Kaplan, is to try to understand why women are under-represented in the hard sciences and engineering, and then to do something about it. Science and engineering were the focus of the first efforts of WISEST as these were, and remain, the areas where women are most under-represented.

The first step the newly formed WISEST took was the collection of data on the numbers of women in decision-making roles. The research revealed that, in December of 1981, only 19 per cent of academic staff at the University of Alberta was female. The numbers were even lower in the fields traditionally considered male: in the Faculty of Science only 5 per cent were female, and in the Faculty of Engineering only 2 per cent were female.

With the support of Dr. Kaplan and a volunteer committee, the group set about developing programs that would encourage women into these fields. These innovative strategies have made WISEST a leader among Canadian universities aiming to increase recruitment of young women.

At the core of WISEST's initiatives is a six-week summer program for young women and men entering Grade 12. Students join a research team and work on a research project in a non-traditional area. WISEST has "graduated" hundreds of enthusiastic students, and the program is widely recognized around the world.

THE MONTRÉAL MASSACRE[7]

IN 1989, 14 women, mostly engineering students, were murdered at École Polytechnique in Montréal. Sarah Kelly (BA '02) reports on the Montréal Massacre.

On December 6, 1989, no woman at the University of Montreal's École Polytechnique was safe from Marc Lepine, a twenty-five-year-old student who had recently been rejected from the institution's School of Engineering.

Lepine, born Gamil Gharbi, had been for years not only openly hostile to the feminist movement, but also to women themselves. He grew up in an abusive household where his father, an alcoholic, frequently physically abused his mother. Lepine's father believed that "women are servants to men."[8] His parents divorced when he was thirteen years old.

Lepine had applied to join the Canadian Armed Forces, but was thought unfit for military service. Lepine was, according to newspaper accounts, "obsessed by war."[9]

In November 1989 Lepine purchased a "Mini 14" hunting rifle, and on December 6, entered the halls of the École Polytechnique's engineering facility. Brandishing his gun in one class, he said, "I want the women," and immediately ordered the men to leave the classroom.[10] He proceeded to open fire on the women, all the while screaming "I hate feminists" over the sound of the gun. Afterwards he left the classroom, shooting wildly in the hallways of the building. Genevieve Caudin, who was wounded in the shooting, said "We heard everybody yelling in the corridor and the gunshots, but we thought it was a joke. Then he [the gunman] came in and said it was for real."[11] Student Robert Leclerc said at the outset of the shooting, "We thought it was a joke. We really thought it was some kind of joke. We were just trying to figure out what was happening." Robert later "found his sweetheart, crumpled up, lying on a stretcher. She looked like she had stared death in the face."[12] Student Michael Guy remembered being "holed up in a corner on the second floor with three

friends. We were joined by a woman who was bleeding profusely. I saw another woman take a hit in the head."[13] One of the first police officers on the scene discovered that one of the shooting victims was his daughter, Maryse Leclair.[14]

That day, Lepine killed thirteen engineering students and one University employee, all women, before turning the gun on himself. He left behind a three-page letter detailing his hatred of feminism.

On the same day as the massacre, the government of Québec declared three days of mourning, and the moment is commemorated to this day: a white ribbon worn on December 6 signals protest of male violence against women. The echo of this massacre was felt throughout Canada and around the world, but nowhere more so than on university campuses in Canada, where candlelight vigils drawing considerable crowds are held on the anniversary of the shootings.[15]

The events of December 6 prompted a vast change in the realities of Canadian politics and moved violence against women to the top of the priority list. Jack Layton, then a Toronto City Councillor, and now the leader of the federal New Democratic Party, founded the White Ribbon movement. The aim of the campaign is to eliminate gender violence through education and awareness. Suzanne Edward, whose daughter Anne-Marie was among those killed by Lepine, created the Victims' Foundation Against Violence. Universities across the country took steps to increase the number of female students in the sciences and in engineering and to make women feel welcome in these disciplines. By 2004, Statistics Canada reported that women's enrolment in such programs hovered at about 21%.

And yet, among young women who are currently in science and engineering programs at the University of Alberta, Marc Lepine's actions are virtually unknown. "When it happened we were so young—we don't have any memory of it happening," said one third-year engineering student.[16] Memories have faded, and many students wonder why bouquets of white roses, arrayed in groups of fourteen, appear in silent memorial on the U of A campus every December 6.

However, it is not entirely detrimental that observance of December 6 is not what it used to be—nor is it wholly arbitrary. After the tenth anniversary of the murders, families of the victims began specifically requesting that their loved ones' names be kept away from the annual vigils and ceremonies, lest they be remembered more as symbols than as human beings. These women have not died in vain; rather, they have prompted a nation-wide examination of the problem of violence against women. They have raised awareness; now, their families say, it is time to let them rest in peace.

As *The Edmonton Journal* wrote in its lead editorial on December 8, 1989, "with determined confidence, not anger, Canadian men and women should work harder in the decade ahead to achieve full sexual equality for children who will one day study engineering together in equal numbers."[17]

ENGINEERING WEEK—A TIME TO CHANGE [18]

AT THIS UNIVERSITY and all around the country, Engineering Week activities had long been associated with stunts, controversy, heavy drinking, and extreme notions of faculty pride. Student groups everywhere found themselves in hot water from time to time, but one particular incident on January 10, 1990 captured the attention of the campus and the country to such an extent that no Engineering Week would ever be the same. The Montréal Massacre was still very fresh in everyone's mind and the press associated the two events. Scott Davies (BA '04) reports on Engineering Week: "One Engineering Week tradition was Skit Night, an evening of raunchy performances and competitions between engineering departments. On this evening, a skit satirizing the classic TV show *Gilligan's*

Island was being performed by a group of students for the audience of 650. At one point, the castaways were being held hostage by head hunters, when men with machine guns arrived to rescue the castaways. It was at this point that people in the audience began debasing one of the female students involved in the skit, directing the imminent violence of the scene toward her, as they chanted 'Shoot the bitch.'"

Reports and stories of Skit Night grabbed hold of the campus consciousness, and made their way through the media across the country. Reflecting on a night filled with wild kick lines, crude jokes and chants, female dancers, and other skits laced with potentially troubling sexual and violent themes, it seemed to most people that things had gone way too far. The young woman targeted during Skit Night had already been humiliated as a result of a recent article published in *The Bridge*, the engineering students' newspaper, and had raised concerns in the local media about the sexism she encountered as a female engineering student. The violence directed against her on Skit Night appeared intentional and vengeful.

President Paul Davenport immediately expressed his concern, and told the campus he intended to follow up on the incident. Perhaps even more deeply disappointed was Engineering dean, Fred Otto, who had just been told days earlier by students that they were trying to improve the image of Engineering Week.

Two days after Skit Night, Otto set up a task force designed to study the extracurricular activities of engineering students. It was headed by Gary Faulkner, the chair of Mechanical Engineering. At that time, Dean Otto also banned publication of *The Bridge* until the findings of the task force became available. Among other objectives, it was hoped that the task force would serve to identify the realm of acceptable behaviour, thereby allowing a more closely monitored Engineering Week to continue in the future without the fear of similar actions reoccurring. Otto made it clear that he was acting on behalf of students, faculty, and professional engineers, who were all concerned about the negative image now associated with the U of A version of Engineering Week.

Days later, as the negative reaction continued to grow, Fred Otto took further action, filing a formal complaint about the behaviour of certain students and student groups during Skit Night. The Engineering Students' Society (ESS) also began taking steps to address the controversy. "Our first reaction is to say, well, why are you picking on us?" said ESS president Troy Roberts in *The Gateway*. "But in reality, we have to look at what we're doing, and it's time for us to change."[19] The ESS initiatives included formulating a new editorial policy for *The Bridge*, which would prohibit sexist content. Other initiatives involved the banning of the Lady Godiva Ride and the replacement of Skit Night performances with pre-screened videotaped productions.

At the same time, 12 students formed a group to discuss ways of showing the public that they were treated fairly in their experience as female engineering students—the general perception of Engineering at the U of A had become so controversial that there was great concern about the faculty's ability to attract students in the future. These 12 students, and the others—female and male—who joined them in their cause, were among those who found themselves doing whatever they could to repair the U of A's damaged reputation.

The campus community, the citizens of Edmonton, and people across Canada were especially shocked by what happened to the female student at Skit Night in light of the timing of the incident. It was only five weeks earlier that 13 female student engineers and a female staff member in engineering had been murdered at École Polytechnique in Montréal. Whether or not those involved in the Skit Night incident were intentionally echoing the violence of the massacre, it was clear that the underlying sexism needed to be acknowledged and dealt with.

At this time, the University administration, under the leadership of President Davenport and Vice-President Peter Meekison, established the President's Commission for Equality and Respect on Campus to examine the issue of sexism at the U of A. The plan to establish the Commission actually dated back to December, when a ruling was handed down regarding the controversial contents of *The Bridge*. In a November issue, Mayor Jan Reimer had been the subject of sexist commentary, and for it, the paper was fined $500 by the dean of student services, and it was recommended that a commission be established to examine the extra-curricular activities of students. Included in the commission were Peter Smy (chair of Electrical Engineering), Aruna D'Souza (SU VP External), Jim Vargo (associate dean of Rehabilitation Medicine), Anne McLellan (professor of Law), and Dianne Kieren (associate president academic).

In 1991, Engineering Week began to resemble today's event much more closely. Kick lines had both male and female students and were now referred to as "dance troupes." The Engineering Queen competition began naming an Engineering Ambassador instead of a Queen. And Skit Night was no more, replaced by pre-recorded, pre-screened movies. Festivities were toned down and less visible than in past years. A new concern for portraying a positive image began to shape the activities of engineering students, and by the turn of the century, it was clear that there were more reasons for student engineers to be proud of their faculty than there had been for a long, long time.

THE CAMPUS IN THE 1980s[20]

DESPITE A GROWTH in enrolment from about 28,800 to 29,600, this was not an era of substantial construction. Assiniboia was condemned in 1978, renovated, and re-opened in 1983. It now houses a number of administrative offices. Car parks remained at the core of the physical plan, and in 1983 the Education Car Park was constructed, followed by a major reconstruction of Windsor Car Park in 1988. South Field Car Park was built in 1989. The old Ring Houses, home to many early U of A profs, were demolished to make way for the Windsor Car Park. Only four original Ring Houses remain.

A GLANCE AT THE CALENDAR—1980-1989

ONE SET OF RULES printed in the Calendar is called the Code of Student Behaviour. The Code sets out the University's expectations and rules regarding a broad range of unacceptable academic and non-academic behaviours, including plagiarism, vandalism, and the like. The Code is drafted and debated by a committee comprising students, administrators, and staff. In 1980, the Code was one-and-one-half pages long. By 1989, the Code had tripled in length, and by the turn of the century the Code would consume 21 pages of 8-font print, reflecting an increasingly complex and litigious atmosphere. Between 1980–1989, there were several key lawsuits involving student discipline matters.

One such case involved a graduate student referred to as "Mr. B." Mr. B. arrived at his English class one evening two hours late, apparently drunk. His profane comments and bizarre actions disrupted the class, and he refused to leave. The class was dismissed. The incident reached the dean, who was concerned for the safety of other students, and Mr. B. was in essence expelled. Mr. B. appealed to the courts and won. For some time thereafter, he continued to disrupt classes, and the University again proceeded internally to expel him. The matter suddenly ended when Mr. B. was arrested on the legislature grounds with a gun, looking for the premier.

By the end of the 1980s the Code included a detailed section on "Exclusion from Class for Disruptive Behaviour," as well as a section on "Suspension and Expulsion of Students in Situations of Danger."

GLIMPSES FROM THE GATEWAY—1980-1989

"Punk Rock Banned"—March 25, 1980

THE STUDENTS' UNION made a decision not to hire any more groups or individuals to play punk music in SUB Theatre, RATT, or Dinwoodie Lounge. The ban on punk music resulted from incidents at recent concerts, the most serious being the previous week, when a police paddy wagon was called in after a fight broke out in Dinwoodie.

"U of A Enters Encyclopaedia Biz"—November 12, 1980

IT WAS ANNOUNCED that the New Canadian Publishing Company would be writing a Canadian encyclopaedia on campus over the next five years. "The Board of Governors Friday approved an agreement allowing the encyclopaedia staff to use university resources such as computers, libraries and building space," *The Gateway* reported. "In exchange, the university will get a share of the profits made by Hurtig publishers as well as an annual negotiable sum of money." The encyclopaedia was sponsored by the Government of Alberta as a 75th anniversary project.

"Strong Support for Centre"—January 29, 1981

"U OF A WOMEN now have a place of their own," declared *The Gateway*. The campus Women's Centre—the first of its kind in Alberta—was established by Students' Council the previous week, and about 40 women attended its first organizational meeting on January 28. The Centre was instituted in part as a reaction to the activities surrounding Engineering Week.

"Asbestos Dangers in Residence"—March 10, 1981

THE UNIVERSITY'S asbestos removal program was just beginning, and plans were revealed to strip and refinish ceilings in the Michener Park and Lister Hall towers. The ceilings had been found to contain a high concentration of chrysotile asbestos.

"Gateway Seized"—November 24, 1981

DURING PHIL SOPER'S PRESIDENCY, about 12,000 copies of *The Gateway* were seized by city police and fire officials, and then returned four days later. Allegedly, the Thursday edition was seized because it contained a story about an arson incident that had occurred in SUB the day before. Officials said the story may have been detrimental to the arson investigation, and could possibly have spawned copy-cat fires. The Students' Union was considering court action at the time this article appeared in *The Gateway*, and the matter of the impending lawsuit was eventually settled in late 1984 under Robert Greenhill's' presidency.

"Student Loan Demands On The Rise"—September 15, 1983

THE ALBERTA STUDENT FINANCE BOARD expected to receive a total of 38,000 student loan applications by year's end—an increase of about 24%. As well, the percentage of students applying for loans was up to at least 50% from the usual 30–35%.

"Saint-Jean Cooks"—September 20, 1983

COMMUNAL KITCHEN FACILITIES had just been installed in Faculté Saint-Jean's 73-year-old residence after students voted to close down the residence cafeteria. Students were doing their part to keep the kitchens clean and had encountered no problems with the new equipment and responsibilities.

"Copicards a Big Hit"—September 18, 1984

FOR THE SECOND consecutive year, colour-coded Copicards were available to students and staff, allowing users to perform coin-free photocopying on campus at the reduced rate of 6¢ per copy (in certain locations).

"GFC Approves Research Guidelines"—March 5, 1985

NEW ETHICAL GUIDELINES were approved to guide all human research done at the U of A, including the need for ethics committee approval, informed consent and confidentiality for participants, and increased responsibilities for the investigators.

"Registration Just A Call Away By March"—February 4, 1986

"REGISTRATION BLUES may become a mood of the past when the sophisticated computerized 'telephone registration' system opens at the U of A in March," suggested *The Gateway*. The new system was built around the not-yet-universal touch-tone telephone, and users would first need to pick up a registration package consisting of the U of A Calendar, Registration Procedures Booklet, Program Planning Booklet, and permission-to-register letter. Students would use the worksheets to plan their schedule and their telephone session, and then phone the system to begin the process. Of course, everyone would still need to line up in the Butterdome to receive their timetables, ID cards, and library validations for many years to come.

"Horowitz Can't Accept Cuts"—November 20, 1986

PRESIDENT MYER HOROWITZ was opposed to the looming funding cutbacks which could be imposed by the provincial government and felt that cutbacks could destroy the University. "The general quality of the institution would decrease dramatically and quickly," he said in a *Gateway* interview. "Society depends on a high quality university." Horowitz went on to state that he was opposed to increasing tuition and using private money to cover the potential shortfall in operating dollars.

"Women's Studies Degree Established at U of A"—March 10, 1987

THIS ARTICLE APPEARED in "Everyday Rebellion: *The Gateway* Women's Equality Supplement" and noted the University's intention to institute an interdisciplinary undergraduate degree program in Women's Studies in the Faculty of Arts. Already, persistent demand for balanced perspectives could be seen in the high enrolment in courses such as "Sociology of Sex Roles," "Feminist Theology," "Women and Politics," and "Sex and Status in Comparative Perspective." The concept of Women's Studies emerged in Canada during the 1980s and was already established at several other universities.

"Surgical Super Glue"—September 29, 1987

THE WALTER C. MACKENZIE Health Sciences Centre was chosen as the first facility in North America to clinically test the Tisseel Two-Component Fibrin Sealant, which could stop bleeding instantly by sealing tissue like "super glue."

"Fitness-Crazed U of A Students"—October 1, 1987

THE TREND TOWARDS physical activity for fun and fitness made a significant impact on Campus Recreation at the University. Participation in programs was on the rise, with over 8,600 individuals registered at the time this article appeared.

"Alumni Fork Over $4 million"—December 6, 1988

PROJECT LEADERSHIP, a program designed to raise money from University alumni, reached the $4 million mark in pledges. At a celebration of the program's success, President Horowitz told those in attendance that about 170,000 letters had been sent out and 200,000 phone calls made along the way.

"Students Free of WCT"—March 7, 1989

THE GENERAL FACULTIES COUNCIL EXECUTIVE passed a motion to discontinue the much-maligned Writing Competence Test requirement for both incoming and current U of A students. The joint committee between the University and Alberta Education recommended, instead, that a writing centre be established for students and professors, and that curriculum changes be made to better emphasize composition skills at the high school level.

"U of A Turns Trash to Cash"—February 7, 1989

THE UNIVERSITY'S paper recycling program was worth $150,000 per year in combined savings and the value of used paper sold. Universities in other Canadian and American cities were inquiring for information

The Butterdome

PRESIDENT EMERITUS *Myer Horowitz recalls how the colour of the Butterdome was chosen from a tiny swatch: "The year the Butterdome was built, I was attending a Christmas party and met one of the architects who worked on the Butterdome. I told him that many people were remarking on the colour and then I asked him who chose it. He answered, 'You—and other members of the Board Building Committee.' He was absolutely right. I went back to my office and checked the three to five inch binder on the 'proposed' building that is now called the Butterdome. The binder had been prepared by the architects for those of us on the Board Building Committee. On one of the pages was the swatch! In a sense, 'we' didn't choose it because it was proposed by the architects. We sure did approve it, however!" (*es 1821-2-003)

about the U of A recycling program, believed by some to be top among Canadian universities.

"Female Full-Time Prof a Faculty First"—October 3, 1989

THE FACULTY OF ENGINEERING hired its first full-time female professor for the Department of Civil Engineering, Faye Hicks. At the time, female students comprised less than 10 per cent of the engineering faculty, with most graduates opting for industry work rather than completion of a doctorate, regardless of gender.

"Campus Smoking Rules Frequently Ignored"—October 26, 1989

"MORE THAN A YEAR after the introduction of the University of Alberta's tough smoking policy, many people on campus continue to defy the rules," reported *The Gateway*. Enforcement depended upon complaints from others, and most violations were never reported. Some violations were also occurring because of poor signage and incorrectly placed ashtrays. It was felt that peer pressure and education about the risks of smoking would eventually enforce the policy most effectively.

"Dairy Board Declares Butterdome Historic"—December 14, 1989

APPEARING IN *THE GETAWAY*, this joke-issue article reported that the Canadian Dairy Council had declared the Universiade Pavilion a national historic site. Following the dedication ceremony, a wine and bread reception showed off the building's new Butter Museum. "The ceiling is a little high," a butter spokesperson was quoted. "I understand athletes once used this area, but obviously this is a more appropriate function for such a magnificent building."

MEET ALUMNI FROM THE 1980s[21]

Carolyn Karasiuk (BSC ENGG '83)

CAROLYN IS A GLOBE-TROTTING ENGINEER. She worked in Croatia while that country was at war. "Not a good place to be, you know, in the middle of a refinery when a bomb drops." And then there was South Africa ("almost car-jacked"), Italy ("fabulous hiking"), England ("great roast beef and Yorkshire pudding dinners in London"), and Dallas ("I played hockey on a men's team"). Today, she works at Esso in Edmonton and plays left defence on the Thorhild Panteras hockey team, who were the Northern Alberta Female Hockey League division champions in 2002. In 2004, Carolyn was a member of the Women's National Kayak Polo Team, and from 2003 to 2006, a member of Team Canada in Canoe Polo.

An expert in process control and system analysis, this U of A grad set aside her amazing career in 2000 to go back to school "just for fun and to recharge my batteries." She studied play analysis, film studies, and drama at the U of A and took acting classes at Grant MacEwan and television production at NAIT. In addition, she also took three engineering courses and honed her hockey skills in PAC 114 with Panda's coach Howie Draper.

Carolyn is legendary for one memorable vignette from her undergraduate days as a member of General Faculties Council, the University's academic governing body. At one of her first meetings, she positioned herself in the front row of the formal Council Chamber, as close as she could get to the president, who was chairing the meeting. As question period opened, Carolyn's hand shot up.

"Yes, Ms. Karasiuk?" University President Myer Horowitz could hardly call on anyone else. Carolyn's hand was almost in his face.

"Dr. Horowitz, it's like this. There's a whole group of us who run computer programs in the labs as homework assignments and these programs take a long time to debug. Sometimes we just have to stay in the lab all night. The problem is that the labs close at 11 P.M. And I hate to say it, but a few of us have found a way to…umm…open the doors after they've been locked at 11 P.M."

Students breaking into labs? The Council Chamber was silent. Carolyn continued. "It's actually pretty easy to get in after hours," she said. "Mind you, we have to hide out when the custodial staff come but that's the only way we can get the time to run our programs. And so my question for question period is: Can the computer labs be opened later than 11 P.M.?"

It was an exquisitely earnest appeal. All eyes were now on Dr. Horowitz. Sources say that the president had a hard time not splitting his sides. But his tone was even and serious as he asked the vice-president for facilities to look into the matter and report back to the Council.

*Top: "By the time I was 18,"
says Carolyn, "I was ready to
see the world. But first I came
to the U of A for an engineering degree. After my degree, I
DID see the world, and the year
1999 saw me in South Africa."*
(Private Collection)

*Bottom: Carolyn Karasiuk
teaching her nieces and
nephews to kayak. In 2005
Carolyn's World Master's
teams in both canoe polo and
ice hockey won gold medals.*
(Private Collection)

The following day, 24-hour computer labs made their debut on campus. Carolyn's frank approach worked. As Carolyn puts it, "I wanted to change things."

From Small-Town British Columbia to the U of A

"I WAS RAISED IN SMALL, or ridiculously small, towns in BC," says Carolyn, "so by the time I was 18, I was ready to see the world. There was also a part of me that didn't want to go to UBC simply because all my friends were going there. I wanted to be different. I thought about going into music, but my dad and brother are chemical engineers—so it must be in the genes. And, in those days, the U of A's program was one year shorter than UBC's, a huge plus since I did not really like school. Focus, get done with it, and then travel. My family was astonished that, at the end of my studies at the U of A, I announced that I would be heading to Waterloo for a Master's. It took a few years of experience elsewhere to make me realize how great my years were at the U of A. You felt that your profs were looking out for you. The atmosphere was informal and relaxing. That's my choice of atmosphere, for study, work, or life."

Registration

"I REMEMBER almost nothing about registration. In Engineering, the pattern of classes was set. For instance, there was just one Thermodynamics course at a certain time—that's when you took it. There was no choice involved, and the faculty just cut you a schedule. You could choose your Arts options, though, and I remember vividly having to drop out of English, which I really wanted to take, because I knew after the first few days that I could never handle all the reading in addition to my engineering classes. So I took music appreciation, which I enjoyed—but you had to listen to hours of tapes and couldn't take them from the library. I couldn't manage that, given my engineering schedule and the relatively restrictive library hours. So I smuggled a tape recorder into the library and taped all the music. That way I could listen to it late at night.

"The biggest registration event for engineers was getting your photo taken—you were around lots of students from different faculties and I think we went to the ice rink for this since the Butterdome wasn't built yet. This is when you got your student ID number. I still can recite it in my sleep and you need that ID number 20 years later to do anything at the University."

First Weeks of Classes—"Driven by Fear"

"ALL OF US IN ENGINEERING," says Carolyn, "remember being gathered together as a group and told, 'Look to your right. Look to your left. One of you will not be here at the end of the year.' This was inconceivable to me. I had spent so much energy deciding this is what I want to do—Engineering. I could not imagine failing. In that first year, I was driven by fear.

"By some fluke, I ended up in a single room in HUB, even though I was sure I had applied to Lister for a shared room. I can still rattle off my address—02A 8911 HUB Mall. I thought, 'what am I doing living on my own, living in a *mall?*' But being on my own made it easy to escape from drinking and parties, and I studied a lot. One night before exams, I went over to Lister to track down Blair, a guy who was really smart in our core engineering subjects. I needed his help understanding some concepts. I found him—he and Randy had had a lot to drink. But he sat down and helped me conquer the subject. How he got through the exam the next day with a hangover is beyond me. He said it was one of his better exams because he studied for it. And there was this other guy, Rob from Civil, who would come find me and ask me to coach him through Chemistry. We all helped one another, right from day one.

"In that first week," Carolyn remembers, "I can tell you that in every classroom I walked into, I looked for another female student and sat next to her. The women were the misfits, the minority. I met one of my best friends, Kelly-Ann, by sitting down next to her in Chemistry. In our first year, everyone was essentially in one big group, but by the second year, we all had chosen a specialization and mine was Chemical. There were about 40 guys and 6 girls. It was a struggle with some of the guys, but most were nice.

"Tuition was no big deal. It went up about $70 each year—from about $690 to $912. From the time I was 18, I had great summer jobs in the pulp mill where my dad worked. My union wages paid for my entire year and I lived at the high end in terms of budget. I was lucky.

"I also got a part-time job grading math papers. I was good in math. I loved it. I didn't need the money and why I did the marking is beyond me. There was one time when I came back from a conference and had my academic work to catch up on, and 200 math papers to mark. I found an empty classroom, put one exam paper on each desk, and then walked up and down the aisles, marking question one on each exam, then question two on each exam, and so on. It was assembly-line marking. I got it done but it wasn't fun. I was so busy going to class and studying—I don't know what got into me but I started serving on some committees. My friend Kelly-Ann and I decided or got talked into serving on GFC. There was this one student on GFC, Chanchal Battacharya, and he spoke at every single meeting. I thought, I can do this. So I wrote out a question for question period to try to improve things for engineering and computing students. I was probably pretty naïve in what I said at the time, but longer lab hours were crucial for students in engineering and computing and I wanted to see a change for students."

Engineering Week

"THEN SOMEHOW I ended up on the Engineering undergraduate student/ staff committee. One of the undergraduates had to play a key role on the committee and I was tagged to do this. It so happened that in this particular year, the engineers mistakenly published a raunchy article in the annual 'Godiva' engineering week tabloid. It contained violence against girls, and it made headlines in *The Edmonton Journal* and *Edmonton Sun*. The campus was in an uproar over it and so was the faculty. The police considered laying obscenity charges. When a complaint was filed with the Alberta Human Rights Commission, the dean decided that our little student/staff committee should handle this and listen to the complaints. It was quite an experience for a second-year student. Faculty, staff and students from across campus came to talk to us. These were the days when there was always a stripper at Skit Night and a Lady Godiva ride. As for the engineering magazine, I recall that its publication was eventually cancelled.

"We really tried to out do one another during engineering week. I was on the team that wrote one of the skits for Chemical. It was based on the movie *Rocky Horror Picture Show*, but it was about the 'MTS Horror Computer System' and we relied on gimmicks like sound effects. It was dumb and amazing—there were no swear words. But the Minerals were always very clever and came in first. 'MTS,' by the way, stands for Michigan Terminal System, and it was the reigning system of the day.

"Everyone from across campus came to see the ice sculptures that had been constructed in the quad. Some years they were crude. Other years they were marked by a fairly high degree of political satire. In the same year the infamous article was published, the MechE's created their 'artistic interpretation of the east-west energy war' as *The Edmonton Sun* put it. It was a rather graphic depiction of Prime Minister Trudeau 'kneeling over a prostrate Peter Lougheed with a massive *oil well.*' The caption said 'Pierre wants every drop.' It reinforced the bad reputation of engineers.

"One year when we lost the tug-of-war and I was being pulled into the water pond in a very cold January, a couple flashbulbs went off. The next day there were pictures of me in *The Edmonton Journal* and the front page of *The Edmonton Sun*. A reporter called and wanted me to be a Sunshine Girl. I thought, 'how tacky.' But then I thought, how different to have a woman engineer as a Sunshine Girl. So I decided to say yes, and wore to the shoot a pair of the white paper coveralls we use in plants to protect us from chemical spills. I think they were expecting a bathing suit. And oh yes! These were the years when we had engineering princesses. They were almost always women from other faculties. Each department had its own princess. One year my friend Laura, who started in Engineering but switched to Business, borrowed my Grade 12 grad dress when she was selected as a princess. I think the idea of selecting princesses disappeared years ago, but I believe they still have boat races. I was good at that. In elementary school we used to have apple juice races. That's the same idea in a boat race. The first person on the team drinks a pint of beer—no spilling allowed— and there is a judge to watch over you. Only when you have completely drained the glass can the next person on the team down his pint. Then the next person. And so on. First team to finish all their beers wins. That's a boat race."

Undergraduate Life—"Sports Kept Me Sane"

"EVERY MORNING, it was up early, run to EE, the V wing and Chemical Engineering, and then have lunch at home. One day I walked in my Physics class and saw my friends Hank and Warren, sound asleep and snoring. So I ran back to HUB, grabbed my camera, returned to class, snapped a picture and sat down. I missed maybe 15 minutes of class but the photo was worth it.

"It was great when my younger brother started at the U of A in my fourth year—except when his hockey equipment would be spread out all over my apartment. Sometimes I would meet the engineering guys in HUB and study. When I studied on my own, it was in the law library, a nice change of pace. I loved the law library. But most of the students studied on the 5th floor of the 'Chem Engg' building. All during the day and often 'til 11 or 12 at night.

"There was also sports. I played hockey and there were several faculty-based teams, including inner tube water polo. Some kind of sport was part of the routine. I still play hockey and have now started to kayak. All that activity kept me sane.

"My favourite professor was Dave Lynch," says Carolyn. "There were other really good ones, but he stood out. It was his first year of teaching and he was hard on us. But you knew if you did well, you had really earned your grade. When we were there still working at 11 P.M., so was he. He was finishing his PhD. You could go talk to him whenever.

"Every year as an undergraduate I made sure I travelled. I was on the look-out for opportunities. In my second year I went to a conference that only the third and fourth years went to—the World Chemical Engineering conference in Montréal. Other years I saw Saskatoon and Vancouver."

Math 31 and CNS ID

"THERE ARE TWO CHALLENGES that stand out from my undergraduate years," Carolyn says. "Just getting through first year was a victory. All the guys said to me, 'You come from *BC*?? No Math 31?? Good luck.' So I worked like a dog. I was keen. I was scared. I got old exams and read them all. I worked hard. And you know what? In the second year, half the guys who had gotten me so scared weren't around anymore. Academically, it was probably my best year.

"The second challenge involved an awful thing that happened to me. Something unfair. And thank goodness for Dean Adams. What happened was that I got to one point where I was really overloaded. I had a paper for one class all drafted in handwriting and to help me out, a student I knew said he would type it up for me. I gave him my computer ID and he typed my paper—but he also printed off something like 100 of his resumes on my account. I was called into the department chair's office and was told I could be expelled. Here I was this keener—an honour student. I thought I was being resourceful and it turned into a nightmare. The upshot was that students were no longer allowed to use another person's computer ID.

"As for convocation, I never went. I thought, 'I have my degree, that's it.' And my engineering ring? I felt the rings were made for the guys, so I got my dad to file mine down so it would fit better."

Check Out Drama

"LOOKING BACK I am struck by how much the U of A has to offer. I regret that engineering students can't take physical activity or skill courses for credit. And it's too bad that the curriculum is so structured that Arts options are hard to fit into your program. I had a wonderful year in 2000–2001 taking the Arts courses I wasn't able to accommodate while in the engineering faculty.

"Do you realize what's going on over there in the department of Drama and in the fine arts? In my year off, I would go to the free concerts at noon and I was bowled over by the quality of the performances. It's just one example of the smorgasbord that's out there. My advice to students is simple—take advantage of everything the U of A has to offer."

Around the World and Back

"I'VE FLOATED IN THE DEAD SEA. I've visited the Italian *Cinque Terres*— five tiny towns carved into the sides of hills that overlook the Mediterranean Sea and are stunning. I've looked out over the Cape of Good Hope wondering how many ships didn't make it. I've rock-climbed in Dijon and stood at 3,800 metres looking across at Mont Blanc. I've had offices with stunning views—like Big Ben or long, beautiful beaches along the Adriatic. And to think that all these memories are mine because I chose Engineering. Who would have ever guessed?

"Oh, yes. One tip from someone who's been around the world and back. Try and reduce the amount of paper and number of books you get attached to. They're painful to move."

"Expect the unexpected." As immigrants from mainland China, that is Caroline and Charles's advice to students today. In this 1973 photo, Charles and Caroline stand in front of an ice sculpture at Lister Hall with son Winston. Sister Alby was born three months later. (Private Collection)

Charles Pei (M.AG. '75) and Caroline (B.ED. '82)

TWO GENERATIONS of the Pei family have studied and worked at the U of A. "For over 40 years," says Winston (BA '93, MA '02), "someone in my family has worked in the General Services Building. We think of it as ours." The Peis' lives were shaped by smart decisions and good timing. Born in mainland China, these alumni started life half a world away from the University of Alberta. For Charles, it was much more than distance that threatened to keep him from seeing where his life would take him. And once his journey brought him and his wife to Edmonton, Caroline made a personal decision that created a legacy for Alberta's education system.

Here is the story of Charles and Caroline Pei, as told by Scott Davies (BA '04).

Charles—A Fighter Pilot Gets Cancer

CHARLES HAD HIS SIGHTS SET on campus life years before attending classes. "Back home in China, university was highly regarded by the people. To me as a boy it seemed a place to have fun, relax, and learn. The campus of the University of Kwangsi in China was peaceful and stable. When I was walking to school, I would follow a trail that passed by one of the walls around the university campus that used to be a huge private garden. When I looked over the wall, I could see students relaxing, singing and swimming in a pond, a beautiful patch of water. I thought, 'Wow, that's life!' I had a really great first impression of university life there.

"I walked that trail to get to my elementary school. My high school was a boarding school, and we all stayed there 24 hours a day. During the early stage of World War II, the Chinese air force had been wiped out by the Japanese, so the idea was to prepare the kids for future recruitment as air force pilots. Young pilots were needed then. The famous Flying Tigers of American volunteers was helping out as well as the Russians during those years when the Chinese were rebuilding our air force. In that air force preparatory school, we were separated from our families, and we grew up closer to each other than brothers in the school. I spent six years there, starting at age 12. We had access to the best education a government can offer in wartime—the teachers there were excellent, as they could have worked in their own field and felt personally involved in the war effort. Many of my fellow students went on to positions of enormous prestige and power."

After graduation, Charles entered the Air Force Officers Academy in Hanchow, China, and later moved to Taiwan with the school. While he was a young pilot, flying P-51 Mustang and P-47 Thunderbolt fighters, something odd happened. "I developed a cough," says Charles. "I had never smoked, never drank, and so it didn't make sense. One day when I coughed, there was blood, so I went to the hospital. They told me I had lung cancer, and I had to immediately undergo surgery to remove my right lung. There I was, only age 28. The main thing on my mind was that I didn't want my sister-in-law to be told that there might be no hope for me, because she was a widow with all the attendant problems of keeping her family going. After the surgery I was discharged from active service. I couldn't be a pilot anymore, and wasn't sure how long I had to live, so what could I possibly do? I decided to go back to university. My thinking was, while waiting to see if I was going to live or die, I'd better keep busy. If I could finish university and have ten productive years of life, it would be worth it. So I started from scratch at Taiwan University."

Coming to Canada

CHARLES KNEW that economic viability was the sole concern of the rural people in China, and decided to focus his studies on agricultural economics. While working towards his degree at Taiwan University, he had a summer internship at the Sino-American Joint Commission on Rural Reconstruction. That experience caught his attention. "Why not go out and learn something in the field?" The Chinese were not keen on the exact approach of the Americans to rural reconstruction, but he could see the difference between the research methodologies of North America and China. He knew he wanted to go to graduate school, but not in the United States. Instead, he based his decision to come to Canada on an academic journal article that inspired him. The scholar who wrote the article was working at the University of Guelph in Ontario, and so Charles applied to Guelph.

But he also applied to the University of Alberta. "I got the brochure from the University of Alberta," he remembers, "and it had a lovely picture on the cover of the Jubilee Auditorium and the Lister complex. As a big classical music fan, I was very excited by the fact that the concert hall was right there on campus." But scholarship money was slow coming from the University of Alberta, and so Charles arrived on the Guelph campus in 1966, making it to Canada just in time to celebrate the country's centennial the following year. "I remember my first day in Guelph. I was standing on a street corner, and someone came up to me and asked me for directions. Imagine how I felt! I had just arrived, and I really didn't know where I was, so I just had to say sorry! And I immediately felt right at home here." In Guelph, Charles worked toward his MAg, graduating in 1968. Wanting to go further in his studies, he planned to go to that "other" university, the one with the concert hall on campus. Before he could move to the University of Alberta, however, there was some very important personal business to take care of.

Caroline—A Languages Major Switches to Computing Science

CAROLINE SHUEH, whom Charles had known back in Taiwan, was in New York studying computing science, a field she thought to be the way of the future. "I enjoyed the New York culture," says Caroline, in the fluent English she learned as a languages major in Taiwan. "New York was very wel-coming, not unlike Edmonton in that way, but New York was sometimes scary for an immigrant." When living in Guelph, Charles would frequently take the bus to travel down to visit Caroline. "There was an interesting cultural difference," remembers Charles. "When I took Caroline out, I paid for our dates. Canadians did things like that, but for Americans, everything was 'dutch,' where couples split the costs."

On one occasion, when heading back to Canada after a visit, Charles experienced another slice of Americana. "I was on a bus headed for Ontario, and at the border, the Americans on the bus were grilled as to why they were leaving the country during the Vietnam War. 'Are you deserting?' they would ask them, right on the spot. It was frightening."

Starting Out in Edmonton

IN 1968, knowing that he would soon head to Edmonton and that he wouldn't be able to visit Caroline so easily, Charles got himself a little "insurance" and proposed to Caroline on his last New York visit. Charles and Caroline were married in June 1969 at the Strathcona Baptist Church in Edmonton.

Caroline found Edmonton to be "so big and so old," with a long history to be seen in the buildings and neighbourhoods. Another interesting feature in Edmonton: "It was hard to get used to the library system here simply because it was so easy to get books out of the library. Back in China, you just couldn't get books that easily."

In spite of her computing science training, Caroline found that getting a job as a programmer was not easy. "Everything was far behind here in relation to what was happening in New York, and my computing science experience was not recognized by the University. But Dr. Scott, the depart-ment chair, said I could work as a secretary in order to get established. I had been making a professional salary in New York, and it was hard to make a living at $300 a month. I was raising the children, Winston and Alby, and Charles was a grad student with only student loans and scholarship money. Between us we had maybe $500–600 a month."

In 1977, Caroline took her children Alby and Winston to the bandshell at the legislature grounds where they could be sworn in as Canadian citizens. That same year, Caroline began taking some Computing Science courses at the University of Alberta. "I would put the kids to bed, and then it was study time, which I enjoyed. I did well in the courses, except that I had a problem with math. I understood math, but I didn't know basic math terms in English, expressions like 'common denominator.' Back home in China, I had worked in the American Bank for two years, but we conversed mostly in Chinese. So in one class, I got a grade of four on the old nine-point stanine system. I was good at the math, but I struggled with the English. To justify the mark, I was told by my professor that I had progressed the most of all the students—from a zero to a four!"

Caroline and the Mandarin Language Program

IN 1978, with both children now in the school system, Caroline made a transforming shift in her educational path. "I wanted to get experience here in the English education program, since it was so different from back home. I figured that if I understood the educational system here, it would help me in raising the kids and putting them through school. So I switched into the BEd program." It was not clear at the time, but learning to be a teacher set in motion the beginnings of Caroline Pei's legacy to our school system—the Mandarin bilingual program in Edmonton public schools.

"French immersion was being pushed at the time Winston was starting school," recalls Caroline, "and Dr. Chen from Computing Science had a son who 'survived' French immersion. Before that, we weren't sure if a child whose first language was Mandarin or Cantonese, and whose second language was English, could also learn French in school. It worked for Dr. Chen's child, so I switched Winston into the French immersion program in the middle of Grade One. I knew some simple French from when I was a languages major back in Taiwan, and so I thought I could help him. Within a couple of weeks, though, he surpassed my knowledge of French! We were impressed with how quickly he picked up the language.

"I had been teaching Mandarin-language Saturday school for a couple of years, and I had found that the kids were forgetting what they learned from one week to the next. Seeing how quickly Winston picked up French when he was learning the language right there in the classroom, we became interested in doing a bilingual Chinese program. The Ukrainian program was actually the first of that kind, which started in 1971. Alberta was the only province where a language other than English or French could be used as an instructional tool, so we were in the right place and at an opportune moment.

"We knew more than half of the school board members at the time, like Jim Wiebe and Don Massey, and we talked with them regularly about the interest of parents of Chinese descent in a bilingual program. This moved things along. We also talked to the superintendent of the Public School Board, Dave King, and he said he could help, too. The school board had a very positive attitude about the idea, and they facilitated curriculum planning. Everything passed through the bureaucratic red tape very quickly. The first step was leasing the Strathearn and Glengarry schools, and we ran private bilingual kindergartens in 1981. I was the very first teacher. At the time, a special permit was needed from the minister of education to teach kindergarten. I was working on my Education degree, but I did not yet have formal experience teaching."

Caroline finished her BEd in 1982, and in 1983, the Mandarin bilingual program was approved for delivery in the public system. "We had to convince the community that Mandarin was the way to go," says Caroline. "Most immigrants to Edmonton from China spoke Cantonese, but we knew Mandarin was the language of the future because the majority of Chinese back home speak Mandarin. It is the official language in China.

"This university was ahead of others in terms of second- and third-language acquisition," says Caroline, "and the Edmonton Public School Board was supportive in the integration and translation of the curriculum into Mandarin. People like Professor Doug Parker and Professors Brian Evans and Bruce Bain were very helpful to us." Even the banks were cooperative: in the early stages of the program, the federal funding they were counting on was late, and Charles remembers having to go to the bank to borrow money for the project and, surprisingly, having no trouble getting it. "Caroline and I personally paid for many program needs, including the salary of a teacher's assistant!"

Caroline's legacy lives on today, with her first two grandsons in the bilingual program, learning both English and Mandarin.

Back at the U of A with Charles— "My Wedding was a Departmental Issue!"

CHARLES PEI remembers some of his favourite professors from his U of A days, when he was working on his Ph.D. program here. (He withdrew for personal reasons after completing the candidacy, but later finished with his second MA in Agriculture.) "I was most impressed with Dr. Travis Manning, our department head, a gentleman always striving for academic excellence and management success. Dr. Allan Warrack was a young, down-to-earth fellow who wore jeans and casual clothing. Caroline even mistook him for a student. Dr. Bill Phillips, who taught statistics and resource economics, was another favourite. Dr. Steve Hunka from Educational Psychology was a really smart guy. I took his courses on Theories of Testing and Measurement and was very impressed by him. Dr. Ho Hen Baldwin from the Department of Economics taught us quantitative methodology and was very good in his area. You could never stump him with a tough question!"

As with most alumni, Charles also remembers some not-so-good experiences. "In those days, the attitudes of some professors toward grad students were sometimes negative. Some of the profs acted as though they had done their time and it was their turn to be hard on the students. Of course, this wasn't right. For myself, I made mistakes too within the student body. One day, I was working on an complicated test measurement problem on the blackboard with very complicated math formulas all over the place, and a master's student came upon me and asked what I was working on. I was wrapped up in the problem, and I just said 'nothing' without even thinking about it. That student was insulted and probably felt like I had brushed him off, and it was not my intention at all. I have always regretted this because I think we should all treat each others' curiosity with respect.

"Another scary experience happened in my statistics class. It was my very first exam on campus. I remember that I was very relaxed the night before. It wasn't like Arts courses where you had to cram in all kinds of facts—you either knew how to do it, or you didn't. I listened to one of my records and then went to bed. But in the morning, my alarm didn't go off! So when I got up and realized I had slept late, I rushed to the exam room, and I had to try and explain why I was late. I must have turned off the alarm accidentally when I was checking it the night before. The professor sent me off somewhere to write it. Fortunately I made it—otherwise I could have failed even before I got started."

Charles remembers being friends with the staff, which consisted of several young professors who had graduated in the United States. "Since we were new in Edmonton and knew few people, my wedding was like a departmental issue. So many people from the Agricultural Economics Department were there at the wedding and in the pictures!"

"I had no window in my office, and I was the only grad student there. I got my glasses at about that time. Perhaps it was from having no window and inadequate lighting. I spent most of my time there, but you never felt like you were the only person with a particular problem. Everyone was ready to help out."

The Augustana Connection—The Peis are Adopted

CHARLES MET HIS BEST FRIEND, Will Pattison, in his early days at the University of Alberta. Will, now a farmer near Camrose, Alberta and occasional instructor at Augustana University, was also doing grad work at the U of A, and his wife was in Nursing. "That first Christmas here, I was all alone, and so Will invited me to join them at his campus Christian retreat in Banff. I could not go but mentioned my concern at getting married soon when none of our parents could be on hand to perform their roles as required. Will and Marian had just married. He suggested his father-in-law, Mr. Swanson, might be the person to ask. As it turned out he willingly stepped in for my wedding, and right there I had adopted my own Canadian family. Will's parents own a farm at Rocky Mountain House and he invited us there for Christmas dinner when both us had our newborn babies. When we got there, we realized we were among four generations of family members they were entertaining. There, with the Pattison families, we were celebrating our second Christmas together. They fit all of us in one space, with the tables of all sizes and shapes all joined together, snaking through

The extended Pei family,
linking Canada and China.
(Private Collection)

the house all the way to the door. Everyone in the Swanson and Pattison families basically adopted us, and our kids grew up with their kids, just like cousins. It would have been miserable with no family of our own out here, but the Swansons and the Pattisons completely welcomed us into their family."

A Little Advice from Charles and Caroline

WHEN ASKED TO PROVIDE some advice to today's newest U of A students, Charles has a lot to say. "This is a huge campus, so you're going to be quite confused. You have to face people you don't know, and maybe some people whom you may have previously avoided in your life. Here, they are all part of your life and your campus. You have to be yourself and you have to take time to get to know as many people as possible. This is the time and place to develop relationships and make friends you will have for the rest of your life.

"Be prepared to get into classes you don't like, and be prepared for some professors who will seem to be impossible. Be patient: you must survive it, and indeed thrive in order to advance. Don't worry too much, or you will get yourself into real trouble! Whatever required courses you don't like, remember that they are required for a reason. You may not realize it until you need the knowledge."

As for Caroline, she simply says to "always expect the unexpected."

Angela Meneley Sekulic (BSC OCCUPATIONAL THERAPY '90) and Peter Sekulic (BA '84)

PETER AND ANGELA met while they were students at the U of A. Peter was living at home, the epitome of a nose-to-the-grindstone student. Angela was up from Calgary, away from parental constraints for the first time, living in residence, and was having the time of her life.

Peter Sekulic (BA '84)

FROM 1993 TO 1997, Peter served as an MLA for Edmonton Manning. Today, he is the managing partner of Strategic Relations Inc (SRI). SRI specializes in corporate business development, specifically managing procurement initiatives for large corporations. Peter is also the president of the Lovinac Corporation, a policy consulting group, and president of SRI Business Solutions Inc., which assists organizations with knowledge management and the implementation of enterprise solutions. But in 1980, he just about didn't make it into university.

Why University?—"Bettering my Life"

PETER IS VERY CLEAR about why he went to university. "I'm the child of immigrant parents," he says. "I was born in the town of Lovinac, Croatia. My parents arrived in Canada in 1967 with two kids, two hundred dollars, and two suitcases. My dad went to work for Len Perry Construction. Years later, I met the son of the owner. This is what he told me: 'Your dad is a legend in our company. He could build anything. I remember how he could carry these huge concrete sidewalk blocks, one in each hand. No one else could do that.' Today," Peter says, "my parents are retired and live a very comfortable life. My parents are an inspiration to all those who know them, but most of all to me.

"The immigrant community I knew worked hard. It was a given back then, when I was growing up, that bettering my own life through education meant my parents had succeeded."

Peter Sekulic (left) on his way to Canada with his father Mat and brother Mike. Mrs. Kata Sekulic took the photo. "My parents came to Canada with two kids, two hundred dollars, and two suitcases," says Peter. "Bettering my own life through education meant my parents had succeeded." (Private Collection)

Frank Spinelli—"Your Word was Your Bond"

"WHEN I GREW UP, I was around people like Frank Spinelli, an icon in the Italian community and one of the 100 Edmontonians of the Century. For Mr. Spinelli and my dad, their handshake meant their word, and their word was a contract. In fact, better than a contract. When Frank Spinelli and my father shook hands on something, the future of that issue was certain.

"Once when my father was buying grapes from Mr. Spinelli, my dad didn't have enough cash on him. So he was about to leave the store to go to the bank, but Mr. Spinelli told dad to take the grapes and pay the bill the next time he was in the store. In fact, Mr. Spinelli told my dad that *he* would have to remember to pay because Mr. Spinelli would neither write it down nor bother to remember. I was 11 years old when I watched this happen. I learned early on that your word was your bond and that the community was your safety check. People trusted one another. Today, I run my business on handshakes, unless a contract is absolutely required for process."

An Intellectual Sherpa

PETER WAS AMONG THE FIRST in Edmonton's Croatian community to attend university. His parents, he says, who did not have the opportunity to finish grade school, knew little about university. They could really only define success at university in terms of being a doctor or lawyer, and no one in Peter's community had much experience with university. So Peter was largely on his own. He had to figure out what university was all about, and how to *do* it.

"I am truly blessed; I have had incredibly good friends throughout my life," Peter says, "and in high school that included George Chow. Without him, I would never have gone to university."

George holds engineering and law degrees from the U of A, and is a successful businessman in Calgary. Back in high school George, like Peter, was the child of immigrants—but with a difference. George's father, before reaching Canada, had spent time in England to earn an MA in Social Work. George was well aware of the value of an education, and he mentored Peter as Peter went through high school with grades in the 60% range. "I wasn't a natural for university," Peter says. "George, however, was. His grades were in the over-80% range. As for me, I had to go back and retake two courses in summer school. But you know? I did extraordinarily well the second time. George had reinforced for me the importance of studying. Nonetheless, I had a tough time with the formal mode of study, and when I got a dismal grade in Chemistry, I negotiated with my teacher. 'If you give me a good grade,' I told her, 'I promise never to take Chemistry again.' Those few per cent have made a world of difference to my life."

On a Golden Bears soccer scholarship for his first year, Peter enrolled in the three-year General Arts program, with a major in Economics. "I studied really hard. George and I came from the working class district of north Edmonton together, and we drove to campus each day in a green Ford Torino—the Starsky and Hutch car—and after classes we would get together in the Mechanical Engineering building to study. George understood how to study. For me, that was new. After a study session, we'd go to Mei Yee Lim's for Chinese food. I think of George very respectfully as my intellectual sherpa, dragging me up the mountain."

The First Week

"MY FIRST DAY on campus was just like my first day, years later, in politics. In 1980, when I was a first-year student at the U of A, I had never been to the campus. In 1993, when I was a new MLA, I had never been to the legislature. Your whole life, you face environments that are brand new to you. Approach each with your values in check and charge forward.

"The first week of university was process-driven. There were so many requirements—lots of activity just to get going. There were line-ups for everything, especially for the bookstore. And you needed so many textbooks. As for tuition, my parents would have sold the house to keep me in university, but they didn't need to," says Peter. "I did it without loans. Tuition was $500–600 a term. I had great summer jobs and was paid, then, what students make now. For a while I was a Psychiatric Aid in Alberta Hospital at $9 an hour. I cleared $20,000 one summer working in Sherrit Gordon's carpenter's shop."

HUB, the '80s Hangout

"I WAS COMPLETELY IMMERSED in my studies," Peter remembers. "I had five classes every day. I arrived on campus early, and stayed late. If I wasn't studying with George in the Mechanical Engineering building, I was in the library, and when it closed around 9 P.M., I had dinner in HUB. It was the great hangout. Java Jive had recently opened, and coffee shops were a new thing. And there weren't so many commercial places. I remember the French fries at Nancy's place in HUB—Nancy and her husband lived on the north side, so we had that in common. Their place was next to the Laundromat. Hey, did I mention those fries? They were great. Nancy would ladle tons of gravy on top."

Knuckling Down and Favourite Profs

PETER GAVE UP competitive soccer in his second year in order to concentrate on his studies. He remained active in his community and was on

"two or three" Croatian soccer teams. Peter's academic nose was to the grindstone. "I never slept in," he says, "and I was very focused on my health. I would come home late at night after studying and run for miles through the fields of northern Edmonton, all the way to Namao. I did go to parties, but even if I came home at 3 A.M., I would run. The best runs were in the winter when there was a full moon very late at night. It was a great way to relieve stress and stay fit—in retrospect, it sounds strange, but it was so peaceful and relaxing at that time.

"I had a few profs who taught differently," Peter says. "Their approach began with these questions: Did you require knowledge? Did you want to learn? These profs would then test your need for knowledge, and certainly not through multiple choice exams. They expected interaction in the classroom. Classes were smaller then, and if your professor expected more from you, the whole class was thus elevated. You had a responsibility to come prepared. Charles Nunn in Economics and Ivan Ivankovich in Business were two professors who taught this way. They were teachers I responded to."

Convocation and Life Afterwards

"I DIDN'T ACHIEVE to my own standards," says Peter, "so I didn't attend Convocation. It was not the success I wanted my parents to celebrate. After graduation, I applied for a job in Career Development and Employment. It was good fortune and good timing," he says. "I got the job and assisted with the development of the first Summer Temporary Employment Program (STEP), a program that created countless jobs for students. But after a few years, I started to worry about a glass ceiling in terms of salary. I was becoming a 'type A' in terms of career, just as I had become a 'type A' as a student. So I applied to a graduate program at the U of A, and Mike Percy, who became dean of Business later on, was assigned as my advisor."

Peter didn't finish his MA, and he explains why. "I couldn't find the context for the theory I was being taught. I did not think the marketplace worked quite as predictably as my courses suggested. I was an intuitive problem solver—this was not an asset in economics. It was one of the most stressful times of my life—trying to learn, unable to connect the theory to reality, believing 'business' to be much more than the sum of the theoretical marketplace parts, and yet not knowing enough to effectively challenge my professors."

There was one exam that clinched Peter's decision to end his Master's studies. "I was taking Econometrics, which applies mathematics and statistics to test and quantify economic theories and the solutions to economic problems. Students worked their tails off in this course, and there were very smart students in this class. I knew it was over for me, I was finished. So I went out the night before the exam, had a few drinks, and was very relaxed as I went into the exam. Heck, I was probably hungover. So I wasn't like a dog with a bone, which was my usual manner. Instead of trying to nail each question, I just wrote as much as I knew about each of the problem statements. When the grades were announced, the instructor said the class average was 8%. There were a lot of foreign students in tears—they were on temporary visas, and failure always presented a risk of early return to their home countries. Well, I scored about 16% on the exam. It was the second highest mark in the class. That pinned it for me. I knew all the other students understood the material better than I did. This exam went against everything I believed in. I still enjoy math and economics, though, and, ironically, in my consulting business, I write complex analyses founded in these disciplines for key players in industry and government. When I understand the context clearly, I am better able to achieve success.

"I learned an essential life lesson from this. It's important to think independently and differently, but then you need to validate your ideas. Once you have the confidence to challenge someone else's thinking, then work at gaining the respect of the person you are challenging. That's the key. In university or in the workplace, it's got to be a constructive kind of challenge; you have to be advancing something and adding value. My experience in graduate school taught me this, and I'm now much better at defining and achieving my goals."

"We Take Democracy for Granted"

"I CAME TO KNOW my graduate advisor, Mike Percy, on a personal level," Peter says. "He fuelled my drive to succeed as well as my interest in politics. It was fate and good fortune from my point of view, and I came to understand policy-making, the process of government, and the administration of government. I didn't agree with what was going on politically in the province, especially in relation to the impact on the public sector. It was 1990 and I was 28 years old. I decided to run for public office and also decided that if I was elected, I would only serve for one term. I wasn't after a government pension. I wanted to commit to having an impact on public policy and to representing the constituents in the area where I grew up.

"I knew it would be intense, but I'd always worked hard, and now that I was married I had Angela to help me. I was 30 when I was elected—the first Croatian-Canadian to serve as an MLA and one of the youngest. I never missed a single day of legislative work in three years. But I am proudest of a booklet I wrote for my constituents, explaining in a sentence or two every bill I voted on, documenting how I voted, and why I voted the way I did. It was my way of living out my commitment to be part of responsible, accountable government."

Of the 178 bills Peter voted on, there is one that stands out for him—Bill 31 from the 1996 sitting of the legislature. Its title was *Business Financial Assistance Limitation Statutes Amendment Act.*

"I had drafted similar legislation as a private member's bill," he explains, "but negotiated and collaboratively worked with the government which tabled their own bill and expedited its passage into an Act. At the time, government had lost over $2 billion by backing various private ventures. On one venture alone, the government lost $500 million, and I opposed the spending of public funds for the purpose of investing in private interests—ultimately supporting private gain. I voted for Bill 31 because some of the elements which I felt were important to redress this issue were in the government legislation. Bill 31 essentially restricted the government from gambling on private ventures from that point forward."

Reflecting on his time as an MLA, Peter maintains that it helped to be an immigrant. Peter had watched Croatia, his country of birth, forced into war—for freedom, autonomy, and democratic rule. In Canada, Peter says, "I believe we have become complacent and take democracy for granted. Democracy is a work in progress—it still requires us to work, to participate. Get involved. Engage in debate with your friends and neighbours. Vote. Okay can be good, and good can be better—only if we work at it, only if we participate. Nonetheless, I remain optimistic about Canada and Canadians, and I take great pride in being Canadian."

Brennan

PETER AND ANGELA were married in 1990, and their first child, Brennan, was born during Peter's campaign for public office. Brennan has a godfather who shadows his development very carefully. Brennan excels in school. He knows how to study, and he questions everything. At age 11, Brennan has a keen interest in architecture. If you show him a floor plan, he'll fold a piece of paper to approximate your design, placing it carefully *just so*. It's his way of helping you to understand how the lower storey of a house would nestle gently into a hillside location.

Guess who Brennan's godfather is? George Chow, Peter's buddy from undergraduate days at the U of A, the intellectual sherpa who dragged

Peter up the mountain. And Peter is godfather to George's son Christopher. "The friendship," says Peter, "has only grown over time, as has the mentoring."

Brennan—and his siblings Olivia and Jared—are nose-to-the-grindstone kids when it comes to school, but these three children are also impish souls who greet dinner guests at the door with their latest creations in visual art. There is another influence in the lives of these special children.

Meet their mother, Angela. She was a star student in high school with great grades, a dancer, and a self-professed high school "drama queen." Up from Calgary as a first-year student at the U of A in 1985, Angela was having the time of her life.

Angela Meneley Sekulic (BSC OCCUPATIONAL THERAPY '90)

ANGELA'S FATHER is about to be inducted in the Canadian Petroleum Hall of Fame. Angela's five siblings are coming from across Canada for the event. And so in between her career as an occupational therapist, being a Mom, and helping husband Peter with his businesses, Angela is preparing for 11 people to descend upon her household for the family celebration. She's used to big family gatherings and comes from a line of risk-takers, survivors, and achievers.

"My dad was one of six children," Angela says. "His mother was a schoolteacher and raised them single-handedly during the Depression. Five of the six kids went on to post-secondary education, and the sixth became a helicopter pilot.

"My mom was born in Ireland, one of nine siblings. She studied nursing in England, and then got the travel bug. Off to Canada she went, in the company of a girlfriend. Mom arrived in Edmonton, worked for a while at the Misericordia Hospital, and then she heard of an opportunity to work for an oil company as a nurse in Norman Wells, NWT, which is where she met my father. My mother is adventurous and courageous. She's had multiple sclerosis for more than half her life, and I admire the devotion she and my father have for one another."

In this family of achievers, university wasn't an option. "The only question was *where* you would be going to university," says Angela. "My father left his hometown of Maple Creek, Saskatchewan to go the University of

Saskatchewan in Saskatoon. He strongly believed that it would be good for us as well to attend a university away from home."

The High School Drama Queen Heads North to Edmonton

"I THOUGHT ABOUT taking an extra year to finish high school so I could participate in next year's musical. This notion was firmly squashed by my father. I had to buckle down to finish my coursework and to apply to university—the early admission deadline was quickly approaching.

"I remember perusing university calendars with my girlfriends in the career counsellor's office, pondering where we would go to university. Whichever one, we were pretty sure we wanted to go together. My friend Joanne suggested the U of A because she had a sister who went to Med school there and still lived in Edmonton. Although I wasn't completely sold on a career in Rehabilitation Medicine, my sister had just graduated from Physiotherapy at the University of Manitoba and it sounded like it suited me. The U of A had a reputable Rehab faculty. It was the only early admission application I submitted, and I was quite excited to hear I was accepted despite still having to complete three of the five matriculation courses—and being a frightening two credits away from the required 100. After many late nights cramming to finish coursework, preparing for Diploma exams—and the kindness of my Drama teacher who gave me five credits in 'Special Projects' for the drama productions I had performed in the previous three years—I made it. It was a squeaker."

Heading "Up North" to Edmonton to Residence Life

"I WAS 17 when I came to Edmonton. I believed university would be a breeze. My girlfriends and I were all pretty confident, in that egocentric way so typical of 17-year-old girls. I honestly felt that 'I had graced Edmonton with my presence.' We were particularly excited about going to West Edmonton Mall—Phase 3 had just opened and there was an Abercrombie and Fitch store located there. They didn't have one in Calgary, and we were one up on the friends we left behind.

"I'm almost embarrassed to admit that I was a typical Calgarian and believed that winter in Edmonton started in September. I had packed my parka, but it was such a beautiful fall I had to go home at Thanksgiving to get my shorts.

Snow statues were part of the
fun at Lister Hall in the 1980s.
(Private Collection)

"My brothers and sisters were full of tips on how to cope in residence. They told me what to take—a kettle to boil water for coffee, hot chocolate, packaged soup—and what to be prepared for—small rooms, communal showers. My father drove me up the Sunday before registration week and much to our surprise we ran into my British Columbia cousin, Susan, who had just completed a one-year exchange in Sweden. Her room was across the hall from mine, and I think it gave my dad some peace of mind. I lived in Lister Hall, in the Kelsey Tower, which was co-ed in the sense that different wings of each tower were all male or all female. It was a great group of people and a lot of fun.

"There was a lot of socializing in residence, especially around the TV in the common room. I have to admit that I was never much of a hockey fan, but playing on the rivalry between Edmonton and Calgary was too hard to resist. It was so much more fun to watch when you could cheer for the Flames when everyone else was cheering for the Oilers. The Flames ended up going to the Stanley Cup final that season—sadly losing in a sweep to Montréal. It was many years before I switched to cheering for the Oilers."

Registration in 1985 and Frosh 15

"REGISTRATION STARTED OFF in the Butterdome," Angela remembers, "then you went from department to department to register for the courses outlined in the Calendar for General Arts or Science. It was very time-consuming not only because of line-ups but because we didn't know where any of the buildings were. We had no conception of how large the campus was. To complicate it further, I registered for my math and science courses first so I missed out on getting into the required full-term English 200 class. It was very stressful to say the least. A very humbling and tiring experience— my first indication that university was going to be anything but a breeze.

"My sister had warned me about the 'Frosh 15,' the fifteen pounds that you gain living in residence for the first year. I was skeptical of her certainty— 'how can she be so sure?' Well, sadly she was right—inevitable really considering the lack of healthy food choices at the time. Not to say that there weren't tasty choices; there were the infamous CAB cinnamon buns (has anyone ever done a calorie count on those?!), and the Mini-Mart in Lister offered the best turkey club sandwiches on huge Kaiser rolls. Although tasty, these staples of my diet wreaked havoc with my blood sugar levels, compelling me to have a nap most afternoons and thus leading to...the Frosh 15, and poor study habits.

"It was a vicious cycle: sleep all afternoon, stay up late watching TV, drag yourself out of bed for 8 A.M. classes, skip breakfast, gorge at lunch, fall asleep, and so on. On top of that, I didn't know how to study or where to go for help if I didn't understand something. First term was pretty much a write-off. It was a shock—how could university be so hard when high school was so easy? My father's directive was terse: 'Smarten-up, Missy!'

"There was this one Croatian guy at Lister who was also from Calgary. He lived and breathed soccer and had sought out the Croatian team in Edmonton to play on when he had first arrived. He was insistent that I meet his soccer coach, Pete. The way he described Peter made him sound so responsible and organized. I remember thinking, 'He sounds like he's *40.*' But my friend kept at it, so a girlfriend and I went to a soccer game to 'check him out.'"

Peter passed the test. Their first date? "February 1st, 1986," says Angela. "The Garneau Theatre showed first-run films, and on our first date, Peter took me to see *The Colour Purple,* with Whoopi Goldberg. Then we went to Victor's. It was a place for 'older' people, not an 18-year-old like me. But Peter *was* older—23—and smart. He knew I was a dancer, and Victor's had a dance floor. It was a great first date."

Peter—Saviour and Slave Driver

ANGELA REMEMBERS her tuition exactly—under $500 per term, with books adding another $300. "Dad didn't want us to work during the school year," says Angela, "but in the summer after my first year I worked in accounts receivable at Petro Canada. I made great money—$7.50 an hour. I bought all my own furniture and put away a couple months' rent. So before the start of my second year, I moved to a bachelor suite in the Colonial Arms, across from the legislature. Rent was $315 a month including utilities. It was a little easier to eat less—no extra cash—and focus on my studies—no TV.

"Peter was very determined to pull up my marks. He had graduated in 1984 in Honours Economics and was working at Alberta Career Development and Employment. He was a slave driver. He was focused on health. He made me a deal—if I quit smoking, he would quit putting sugar in his coffee. I had terrible insomnia when I was quitting, but I did it. Peter would bring me Italian sandwiches, olives and red wine at the end of a night of study. My GPA shot up to 7.8, and I got into OT. I learned that hard work led to success and that you couldn't just sail through and expect good grades. It was the biggest way in which my university experience changed me."

The OT Cohort and a Favourite Professor

"THERE WERE 44 in our class that started in that September of 1987," Angela explains. "We were in the basic program, which took three additional years to complete. The dean was Martha Piper and the associate dean was Jim Vargo. Their idea of how students would learn best was to keep us together as a cohort. In our first term we had nine courses. We were fortunate not to have to pay for the courses over and above the standard five-per-term—I know that changed shortly after I graduated. Our heavy course load taught us to work together to ease the pressure. We had many group projects together, and also projects with the Physio students—this fostered teamwork.

"The cohort experience was my most memorable time at university. We had a great class, and became like a family. In fact, to raise money for our grad, we all got together in our third year and took turns selling our homemade muffins and coffee in Corbett Hall where, at the time, you could only buy food from vending machines—it really wasn't difficult to compete with the coffee that came out of those old vending machines. Housing and Food Services (HFS) weren't as pleased with our success and told us we had to shut down. Our class spokesperson John, always diplomatic, pleaded our case. In the end, HFS allowed *only* our group to engage in private enterprise until the end of April 1989. Our dinner-dance grad party at the Four Seasons in July 1990 was well-funded and fabulous.

"Corbett Hall was shared by Rehab Med, Faculty of Extension and the Studio Theatre," says Angela. "With the ever-increasing class sizes in the Rehab programs, the Faculty was outgrowing the space allotted to it. A portable classroom was added to the south of the building—everyone referred to it as 'The Rehab Trailer.' In September 1989, renovations in Corbett began, with plans for the entire building to be devoted to the

Rehab Faculty. During the time that it took to complete the renovations, the entire faculty was moved over to the Nurses' Residence.

"But because Corbett Hall was where we had done most of our schooling, someone in our class—probably John—decided to take a picture of all of us on the roof. Bill set up his camera on the east lawn and the whole lot of us climbed the rickety ladder in the Studio Theatre that went to the roof. I was scared to death to go up this ladder, but it was so important to all of us that we be together in the photo. So I went up the ladder with Bill and John encouraging me.

"During all this I had a favourite professor—Donna Ford. She taught Anatomy and had great ways of conveying information. I loved her classes and ended up tutoring other students. It was a far cry from my unmotivated days of first year."

Mrs. Sekulic's Sandwiches

"IN MY FIRST YEAR OF OT, Peter entered graduate school. To save money, he'd park in my free parking spot at my apartment building and we'd walk over the High Level Bridge together. We studied in Rutherford

Angela's class was one of the first to go through the Occupational Therapy program as a cohort—a bonding experience. Every student made it to the roof of Corbett for their class picture, climbing "the rickety ladder in the Studio Theatre that went to the roof."
(Private Collection)

North, and HUB was our hangout. Back then, there were a lot of privately owned stores and restaurants in HUB. My favourite places to eat were a vegetarian place that made the best soup and also a spot called the Pink Pantry, run by Norm and Nancy. However, money was tight and eating out was an indulgence, so thankfully Peter's mom would make sandwiches for him to bring. Some days she made so many for us that on our walk to university over the bridge each day, we'd give half of them to the homeless guys living in the bushes under the bridge."

Occupational Therapist

ANGELA'S CONVOCATION was in 1990. She didn't go—she heard it would drone on and be boring. At Convocation, graduates from the Faculty of Rehabilitation Medicine are given a pin—a miniature replica of a starfish. The starfish story is said to be emblematic of all rehabilitation medicine professionals:

> A man was walking down a white-sand beach when, in the distance, he saw a woman dancing along the shoreline. As the man approached, he saw that the beach was littered with starfish and the woman, in truth, wasn't dancing. What she was really doing was throwing starfish back into the ocean one at a time. The man said to her: "You can never save all these starfish. There are too many. You should just stop." The woman replied: "Ah, but see this one starfish I am holding?" She tossed it into the ocean. "I saved that one," she said.

Angela, however, has a different take on how occupational therapists approach their work.

"As Occupational Therapists," she says, "we were never taught to do anything 'one at a time.' We were always encouraged to find unique and efficient ways to carry out our jobs. If I was the woman on the beach, I would have either searched for a bucket or found some other way to throw more than one starfish back in at a time!"

END OF THE DECADE

In 1989, Paul Davenport became president of the University at a time when the provincial government tightened the budget belt and handed the administration a directive to cut 21 per cent from the university budget.

A 21 per cent cut was unprecedented at this university, where we had experienced great difficulty in sustaining 2–5 per cent cuts during the previous decades. A 21 per cent cut would reshape the University. Paul Davenport's five years as president would leave an indelible mark on the University.

"Going back to university, testing myself, learning—it changed me."

—Cecile Silzer
(bed '71, mlis '91)

Timeline

Enrolment and Finance, 1990–1999

- Fall student head count: 29,128 (1990); 30,740 (1999)
- Operating budget from the Province of Alberta: $242,269,000.00 (1990); $256,309,000.00 (1999–includes Conditional Grant)
- Full-load undergraduate Arts tuition: $1,228.80 (1990); 3,550.80 (1999)
- SU membership fee: $48.00 (1990); $45.68 + $52.84 (dedicated) (1999)

Key U of A Dates, 1990–1999

- Province cuts 21% cut from from the University budget by the Province (1990–1994)
- The LRT crosses the river to the University (1992)
- Undergraduate Dean Mortensen disappears from campus (1992)
- The Board declares a state of financial exigency (1994)
- U of A presented with an official coat of arms by the governor general (1994)
- Rod Fraser succeeds Paul Davenport as president (1995)
- The campus is on edge as all computerized systems face the "Y2K" challenge (1999)

Selected Campus Buildings, 1990–1999

- Book and Record Depository (BARD) opened in the old IKEA building on 50th Street (1993)
- Timms Centre for the Arts opens with support from a private donation (1994)
- Athabasca Annex torn down (1998)

Beyond The Campus, 1990–1999

- Nelson Mandela is freed after 27 years in prison for protesting against apartheid (1990)
- The World Wide Web is developed (1990)
- The Soviet Union dissolves (1991)
- Iraq invades Kuwait and US-led coalition invades Iraq (1991)
- The LRT has its first test run on the new bridge crossing the North Saskatchewan River (1992)
- Ralph Klein elected as the new leader of the PCs and then as premier (1992/93)
- Jean Chrétien's Liberals win 178 Seats, Bloc Québecois 54, and Reform 52 (1993)
- Harry Shoal is sworn in as Alberta's first Sikh MLA (1994)

- Québec votes narrowly to stay in Canada (1995)
- Diana, former Princess of Wales, is killed (1997)
- Britain returns Hong Kong to China (1997)
- Adult stem cells discovered (1999)
- Nunavut becomes a Territory (1999)

VIGNETTES FROM THE 1990s

President Paul Davenport, 1989–1994[1]

PAUL DAVENPORT succeeded Myer Horowitz in 1989. Davenport was a graduate of Stanford University and the University of Toronto and had been a president at McGill. He was the first modern president appointed from beyond the confines of the U of A. Davenport had a tough path to follow when he was handed a mandate to cut 21% from the budget. That he did, and a large number of faculties and departments merged as a cost-cutting measure: Dentistry, which was nearly eliminated as a discipline, ultimately joined the Faculty of Medicine; the School of Library Science merged with the Faculty of Education; the Faculty of Home Economics became part of the Faculty of Agriculture and Forestry; and the Faculty of Extension was placed on a cost-recovery footing. Several in-house functions were out-sourced. Many academic departments were merged. Residence rates and tuition increased, there was a salary rollback, and many academic and non-academic vacancies went unfilled.

President Davenport's budgeting strategy was to "make choices" by targeting specific areas for cuts as opposed to effecting across-the-board cuts. One of the defining documents published during his presidency was titled *Maintaining Excellence and Accessibility in an Environment of Budgetary Restraint*. Davenport signalled his strategies in his inaugural address. His message was that there would be deep cuts and extraordinarily tough choices to be made, but that, notwithstanding, the University of Alberta's reputation would soar not just provincially, but also on the national and international stage.

Davenport was the first president to be part of the newly formed Group of Ten ("Les Dix Amis"), comprising the ten largest full-service universities in Canada—a close equivalent to the Big Ten in the United States. He was also the first president to travel regularly and extensively in Asia and Europe.

Davenport's promise to the community was that he would maintain accessibility but, as he said in his installation address, it would be "access to quality higher education that we can all be proud of." With President Davenport's encouragement, the Faculty of Graduate Studies and Research, under the leadership of Dean Fu-Shiang Chia, created a program of graduate student recruitment scholarships as one way of strengthening the University's research capacity.

During his term as president, Davenport created a key administrative position: vice-president external relations. In the midst of deep cuts, this vice-presidential portfolio was responsible for external relations and the University's major fundraising activities.

Dr. Davenport left the University in 1994 after the Board of Governors launched a search process at the end of his first term instead of the pre-scribed review process. The unexplained about-face concerning the norm of presidential review for a second term threw the campus into turmoil. In support of Davenport, students and faculty papered their windows with signs that simply had the letter "P" written on them—Davenport's first initial. Paul Davenport went on to serve three terms as president of the University of Western Ontario, and a term as chair of the Association of Universities and Colleges of Canada. He holds honorary degrees from the University of Alberta (1994), the University of Toronto (2000), and the International University of Moscow (2002). He is a Chevalier de la Légion d'Honneur (France, 2001) and was named an Officer of the Order of Canada in 2002.

From July 1, 1994 to December 31, 1994, Dr. John McDonald, a professor of Physics who had served as dean of Science and was vice-president (academic) under Paul Davenport, served as acting president.

President Roderick Fraser, 1995–2005[2]

IN JANUARY 1995, Roderick Fraser returned to his *alma mater* and began two terms as the University's 11th president. On the day his presidency was announced, Dr. Fraser predicted that during the next decade there would be a sorting out of universities and that only a few would rise to the very top. "President Rod," as the students called him, set out to make the University of Alberta "indisputably recognized" in teaching, research, and community service. In fact, he said this so often that the in-joke was that President Rod would make the University *intergalactically* recognized in these three areas.

As soon as he took office in 1995, President Fraser initiated an aggres-sive early retirement and faculty renewal program. With many professors taking advantage of early retirement incentives, 1,174 new professors were hired during Fraser's tenure, leading the way in Canada in recruiting academic talent. A surge in research funding was one result—from $94 million to nearly $400 million by 2003–2004. Fraser also played an integral role in Edmonton and the U of A being chosen as the site of the $120 million NRC National Institute of Nanotechnology, and also in urging the government of Alberta to create a science and engineering research endowment, now known as the Alberta Ingenuity Fund. During his tenure, the number of U of A spin-off companies increased from 19 to 84. Enrolment increased from 29,000 students to over 35,000, with student scholarship dollars soaring from $13 million to almost $57 million. The number of graduate scholarships doubled—to some 2,550—and their value increased from $5.3 million to $18.8 million. Aboriginal enrolment increased tenfold. This was an era of competition and big numbers across Canada, and the U of A was in the lead pack.

Under President Fraser's leadership, 16 new buildings were constructed and another eight begun, with a total dollar value of over $502 million. One of the buildings constructed during the Fraser years was International House, one of only 15 International Houses in the world and the first in Canada. In North America, the only other International Houses are located at universities in Chicago, New York, Philadelphia, Washington, and California (Berkeley). Dr. Fraser raised the global profile of the University through a variety of international efforts—especially in China, Japan, Mexico and Central Europe. He signed 240 international agreements in 46 countries during his ten-and-a-half years in office.

Rod Fraser doubled the value of the University's endowments from $220 to $530 million. He raised more than $420 million in philanthropic dollars and built the U of A's assets to $2 billion. He initiated the annual Human Rights lectureship, honoured the service of non-academic staff at his annual summer picnic, and travelled the province to meet parents, alumni, and business and community leaders. As his presidency came to an end, he was appointed an Officer of the Order of Canada.

Computing on Campus[3]

THE ROLE of computers blossomed during the 1990s. On February 1, 1990, the University was officially connected to the Internet, and University

Computing Systems (UCS) established its first Unix-based services the following year. In 1992, UCS was reorganized and became Computing and Network Services (CNS), as it is known today. The General Purpose Unix (GPU) logon server was established in 1993, and a 50-km fibre optic network was completed in 1994. At the end of that year, the Michigan Terminal System (MTS) was decommissioned after 23 years of service.

In the fall of 1995, CNS began using today's automated SIMON Computing Account Management System for creating and managing all campus computing IDs. Each ID enables a user to log on to the University's computing system to access the Internet, library resources, lab software, and more.

The Students' Union, University of Alberta v. University of Alberta (1988), 62 Alta. L.R. (2d) 52 (Alta. Q.B.), (1990) 67 D.L.R. (4th) 593 (Alta. C.A.)[4]

THAT IS THE OFFICIAL CITATION for a court case involving a legal action taken by the SU against the University. Between 1988 and 1991, tuition and associated fees increased to a point where both student associations felt compelled to challenge the University's actions in court. Legal expert Dave Hannah explains the action taken by the Students' Union: "In response to a serious budgetary problem, the Board of Governors imposed a combined Library and Computing Services fee (LCS fee), in addition to a 10% increase in tuition fees. The Board had received the prior approval of the Alberta Minister of Education for the increase in tuition fees, but had not sought nor received similar approval for the LCS fee. The *Universities Act* stated that the Board required the minister's approval for 'fees for instruction,' but not for 'any other fees the Board considers necessary.' The SU applied to the court for a declaration that the LCS fee constituted a 'fee for instruction,' and thus required the approval of the minister of education. The SU's application was dismissed at the Court of Queen's Bench, and the SU appealed the decision to the Alberta Court of Appeal.

"The issue was whether or not the LCS fee was a 'fee for instruction' as defined by the *Act*. The court's response was 'no.' The fee remained."

The Graduate Students' Association (GSA) Takes the University to Court[5]

THREE YEARS LATER, the GSA took the University to court over two new fees approved by the Board in the face of a $2M deficit. One fee, the continuous registration fee, was charged to students who took time off before completing their thesis or program. The second fee was called a post-program fee, and was charged when students had finished course work, but were still being supervised. The trial court declared both to be fees for instruction and ordered the monies to be repaid or credited to graduate students. The University appealed. The appeal court declared that the continuous registration fee was *not* a fee for instruction and that fee remained. The post-program fee was another matter. It was declared a fee for instruction, and because it should have had, by law, prior approval by the minister, it was declared null and void.

THE CAMPUS IN THE 1990s[6]

THE EXTENSION CENTRE was built in 1992 as a partnership among the University, the provincial government, and the private sector. It was planned to house the Faculty of Extension at a time when Extension's traditional home, Corbett Hall, was being renovated for the Faculty of Rehabilitation Medicine.

There was great excitement, but also a tinge of sadness, when the Timms Centre for the Arts opened in 1995. Originally planned as a museums and collections centre under President Horowitz, it quickly changed course under the Davenport administration and became, instead, the new home of Studio Theatre.

In the fall of 1999, a staggering amount of money was being poured into University of Alberta architecture and infrastructure—a whistling $100 million to be exact. Areas slotted for renovation and expansion included Faculté Saint-Jean, the Stollery Centre, Cameron Library, and Materials Management. The University had just signed an agreement with TELUS, the company that replaced Alberta Government Telephones (AGT) when telephone service was privatized, to erect a building called the Telus Centre on the corner of 87 Avenue and 111 Street. The engineers were central to the expansion, with the construction of the Engineering Teaching and

Learning Centre (ETLC), and the Electrical and Computing Engineering Research Facility—two expensive and meticulously planned buildings.

A GLANCE AT THE CALENDAR

ONE STORY about the Calendar in this decade trumps all others. In 1996–1997, the Calendar went online. Anything a student needed to know about registration, course offerings, regulations, scholarships, and bursaries was just a click away.

GLIMPSES FROM THE GATEWAY—1990-1999

"Fight for Books"—March 1, 1990

OVER 300 PEOPLE showed their support for the "Save the Library" campaign at an outdoor rally on the steps of the Administration building. Speakers at the professor-organized rally described the frustration of having important resource materials cut because of poor funding, and pondered the consequences of not being able to preserve the existing collection.

"Cold Buster will be Back"—January 9, 1992

The Canadian Cold Buster, a snack bar developed by U of A physiologist Larry Wang to protect people from hypothermia, would soon reappear on store shelves after being recalled. An animal rights advocacy group allegedly poisoned 87 bars in Edmonton and Calgary, claiming that the process of testing of the bar involved freezing, starving, and injecting rats.

"Finally it's here"—Gateway, September 3, 1992

FROM 1913–1949 a streetcar made a precarious crossing over the High Level Bridge on a route that, for many, involved a long walk between streetcars, or long waits to change cars. Finally, in 1992, a new bridge connected the LRT to campus, whisking students across the river from points north.

The new LRT Bridge under construction, 1989.

(CS 1000–B–02)

"Food Fair, Relaxation Space Coming to SUB?"— September 29, 1992

PLANS TO RENOVATE the 25-year-old Students' Union Building into the "living room" of campus included the creation of a food court, a relaxation area, retail units, and a meditation room on the main floor, and a student services area in the basement.

"Bombs Away—U of A Year Kicks Off With(out) A Bang"— September 9, 1993

ON SEPTEMBER 7, Campus Security and the *Edmonton Sun* were tipped off by an anonymous male caller that four explosive devices had been planted in the Universiade Pavilion. Five thousand students who had been attempting to register were evacuated from the building for nearly three hours while police swept the building, with a bomb truck waiting outside. No devices were detected. The caller was apparently protesting recent cutbacks to "poor and young people."

"Sexual Assault Centre Here—Newest University Service Finally Slated to Open"—September 14, 1993

SPURRED BY A 1991 POLL stating that 41% of the University population had had an "unwanted sexual experience," the Sexual Assault Centre opened its doors in September 1993 as a place "for members of the University community to anonymously deal with the problem of sexual assault." Director Sandra Beggs solicited volunteers in hopes that the Centre would be fully operational by November.

"U Of A Student Arrested At Clayoquot"—September 21, 1993

MICHAEL PASSOFF, a PhD candidate in Forest Science, was arrested after taking part in a demonstration on Vancouver Island at the log sites on Clayoquot Sound. "I didn't go out there with the intent of being arrested," he said. He had spent a month at Clayoquot during the summer studying the ecology of the temperate forests as well as the political situation in the area. Passoff claimed that the decision to clear-cut nearly two-thirds of Clayoquot Sound was politically motivated, and that he "had to take a stand." He was charged with criminal contempt of court for blocking a road and preventing logging trucks from entering the area. There were fifty people arrested in all, and Passoff told *The Gateway* that only ten of them had legal representation.

"One In Ten"—A weekly column beginning September 23, 1993

COMPUTING SCIENCE student Curtis Hanson began a column called "One in Ten"—an exploration of campus experience as a gay student. "I'd like to educate you, the average person," he wrote, "about what gays and lesbians are *really* like." He stressed that his column was not inviting a discussion of morality, but rather attempting to foster an open environment for the discussion of sexuality. This column was the first of its kind in *The Gateway*.

"Non-Stop Studying"—October 14, 1993

FOR THE FIRST TIME, the Students' Union Building remained open for 24 hours a day during midterm week (October 24–29). Food court tenants remained open on a rotating basis so that students would always be able to get something to eat or drink; and there was sympathy for smokers, too: "Students who can't make it through the arduous hours of studying without a cigarette will be able to smoke in Dinwoodie Lounge on the second floor." SUB's 24-hour study space became a tradition on campus during midterms and finals over the course of both semesters.

"SUBtitles Open For Business"—September 8, 1994

AS AN ALTERNATIVE to the university bookstore, and in response to sometimes prohibitively expensive textbooks, the Students' Union opened the doors of a consignment-based used bookstore in the Students' Union Building in September 1994. Not only textbooks were on sale, however: this was also a push on the part of the SU to get more students wearing University of Alberta crested clothing. "At HUB," said Vice-President Finance and Administration Gurmeet Ahluwalia, "you'll see more Georgetown or UNLV stuff on students than U of A stuff. By making these items more affordable, more people will have them."

"Ballroom Blitzkrieg Ends WOW"—September 13, 1994

FOUR AMBULANCES were called to the Convention Centre on the night of September 11 in a bizarre end to a bizarre Week of Welcome. Thirteen casualties occurred, from such diverse afflictions as alcohol poisoning and broken feet during WoW's concluding dance. In an effort to dial down the furor surrounding the evening's events, Students' Union representatives protested that this was "comparable to last year."

"Smoking Sites Wafting Away"—November 29, 1994

THE UNIVERSITY announced its intent to prohibit smoking from all University-owned indoor property, beginning January 1, 1996. Areas owned by the Students' Union, certain portions of Lister Hall, and HUB Mall would be exempt from these regulations. Penalties would range from a $500 fine to expulsion, *The Gateway* reported.

"Pay-Less Day"—December 1, 1994

As PART of an initiative on the parts of the Academic Staff Association: University of Alberta (AAS:UA), and the Non-Academic Staff Association (NASA), staff at the University of Alberta planned to undergo one day per semester of work without pay for a period of three years. "It is important to realize that University professors are still striving to provide excellent and competitive education despite severe cutbacks," said Jon C. Stott, professor of English.

From the "Three Lines Free" Section

UNTIL THE TURN of the millennium, *The Gateway* provided a certain amount of space in every issue for a feature they called "Three Lines Free," in which any student could take up three lines of column space to make statements, send notes to their friends, or write extremely short anonymous love letters free of charge. Used as a meeting point for students within the newspaper, but more often as a subject of fun—owing to the fact that the vast majority of them made no sense to the average reader—the TLF section of *The Gateway* was extremely popular while it lasted. Here are some random samplings from 1994–1995:

> *Angelical Green Elephant, Welcome to the Elephant gang. By the way, you're the yummiest member in my eyes, Hope you're ready to riff! Love the Pastor's Wife*
>
> *Maz the Charmer: How about Star Trek and Brandy in bed again? Pleasecall—Z. The Pool Shark*
>
> *Markie silly. Thought the whole thing was silly confusion and backed off. Don't make me guiltier for it. You had said it yourself. And so now that it is done let us be happy done with it.*

"U of A Joins CASA"—January 31, 1995

ESCHEWING THE POLITICS of organizations like the Canadian Federation of Students, the University of Alberta Students' Union cast its lot with a far more conservative group, the Canadian Alliance of Student Associations (CASA), which was founded in 1995. CASA's mandate differed from that of CFS in that it favoured negotiation with federal government officials rather than protest, and organized a number of meetings with members of parliament and cabinet ministers over the course of a given year in order to effect positive changes to the lot of post-secondary students throughout Canada. The University of Alberta was one of CASA's twenty founding schools, including such post-secondary institutions as the University of British Columbia and McGill University.

"Ivory Tower Tech—Virtual Office Hours Become Reality"— October 5, 1995

"WALDEN POND" may not sound much like groundbreaking technology, but that's exactly what it was: interactive web pages had arrived at the U of A, and heralded a new reality in university coursework. Wes Cooper, professor of Philosophy and co-founder of Walden Pond, was enthusiastic about the project: "If 10 per cent of university professors use this technology, it will be a huge success."

"Eggcellent Protest—STORM Serves Klein a Breakfast of Dissent"— November 30, 1995

THE STUDENT ORGANIZED RESISTANCE MOVEMENT (STORM) wanted to make sure that Premier Ralph Klein got protein with his protest. The idea for the protest was sparked when Klein said on October 20 that "students' failure to throw food at government figures indicates apathy and acceptance of cutbacks." STORM's goal was to get the names of 1,000 students written on an equal number of eggs, to be presented—not thrown— to Premier Klein at the annual tree-lighting ceremony at the Legislature on December 10. "Klein was asking for a protest," said Andrea Steinward, a representative of STORM. At the time of going to press, over 150 signatures had been collected.

"Klein Won't Convocate"—April 2, 1996

ENDING A CONTROVERSY that had raged for the better part of the school year, Alberta Premier Ralph Klein declined the University's offer of an honorary degree, stating that although he was "deeply honoured" by the gesture, he preferred not to excite dissent on the University of Alberta campus. The decision was greeted with a general sigh of relief from the campus community. "The Senate all along should have had a rule against nominating sitting politicians," said Association of Academic Staff: University of Alberta (AAS:UA) president Rick Szostak. Klein's decision did not quiet debate on how to improve learning in Alberta, however. Both sides took the opportunity to get digs in. "Protests and disruption bring no embarrassment to me," Klein said, referring to the numerous protests of which he had been the target since taking office, "only dishonour to their own universities."

Fall 1997–Fall 1998: Space Moose

ADAM THRASHER entered the Faculty of Engineering in 1989. His cartoon strip *Space Moose* left no subject unscathed, from fraternities to Christianity and obesity, from sexual proclivities to racism. The strip entitled "Clobberin' Time" began in September 1997, with Space Moose donning war paint prior to a "Take Back the Night" march, held annually on Jasper Avenue as a protest against male violence. One particular strip was a graphic depiction of Space Moose opening fire at the women marching in the Take Back the Night rally—and hitting his target. Thrasher was disciplined by the University and appealed. In the November 5, 1998 issue of *The Gateway*, the front-page headline published the result: *Space Moose Beats The Rap.*

"Dewey's Kicks The Bucket"—January 16, 1997

IN JANUARY 1997, the Students' Union finally decided to cut its losses and close Dewey's, the much-loved hangout and bar in HUB Mall. The bar, which opened as Friday's in 1975, had been losing money for years, despite initiatives to breathe new life into it, and its closure coincided with the SU taking over the Power Plant Bar and Grill from the Graduate Students' Association later in the semester. Technically, the SU asserted, Dewey's was not closing but rather *moving* into a back room lounge space in the Power Plant, which would be considered a graduate students' lounge. The HUB incarnation of Dewey's officially closed its doors on February 7, attracting record numbers of customers; the bar was also eulogized at great length in *The Gateway* by former managing editor Chris "Fish" Griwkowsky.

"CFS Calls for End to Tuition Fees—Document Outlines Group's Plans for Barrier-Free Education Across Canada"—October 9, 1997

THE CANADIAN FEDERATION OF STUDENTS released a document advocating a three-step journey to breaking down barriers to post-secondary education: first, the elimination of tuition fees; second, a national system of grants complementing the current loan system and eventually usurping it entirely; and third, a post-secondary education agreement upholding national principles in the mould of the *Canada Health Act*. CFS national chairperson Brad Lavigne asserted that education's mandate should resemble that of health care in Canada, and that students were willing to make the commitment to going down this path. "Half of every business lunch is subsidized by tax dollars," he said. "Where do we find the money? It is within our means."

In a later issue, a headline appeared stating "Hoops Doesn't Buy CCS Pipe Dream," representatives from the Canadian Alliance of Student Associations (CASA), of which the University of Alberta Students' Union was a member, did not agree with the CFS vision. "The members of CASA believe that there is a contribution that individuals should make for their own education," CASA National Director Richard "Hoops" Harrison said. "We haven't come out against the possibility of free tuition in, maybe, a hundred years, if the Canadian economy can support it."

"Keeping Councillors No Easy Task—Keeping Quorum a Challenge as Student Councillors Are Leaving SU Meetings Early"—January 20, 1998

"WE WORRY from hour to hour whether or not we'll have enough people to make a decision," fretted Students' Union President Stephen Curran. Attendance at Students' Council meetings in the 1997–1998 term hit record lows, as a healthy number of voting councillors would show up for roll call, but filter out over the course of a meeting, leaving the Students' Union with something of a bare-bones Parliament. This crisis prompted Students' Council to take matters into their own hands, ultimately establishing the regulation that a member of Council could miss three consecutive meetings, or five aggregate meetings, before he or she was expelled from the body.

"Degrees Granted Overseas—U of A Planning to Hold Convocation Ceremonies in Hong Kong Next Week"—March 19, 1998

WITH TUITION on the rise and ever-dwindling support from the provincial government, the U of A's first-ever overseas Convocation excited no end of controversy. The convocation ceremony honoured 105 alumni from the faculties of Arts, Science, and Business alongside ten current U of A students. Many students were outraged by the decision and wondered at the cost, but Business graduate Catherine Kwan pointed out that it was an advantage for many international students, who are often pressed by financial need to return to their native countries and summer incomes before Convocation ceremonies take place.

"Vriend Ruling Expected To Benefit Gay Students"—April 7, 1998

THE GROUNDBREAKING Delwin Vriend ruling, prohibiting sexual orientation as grounds for discrimination under the *Alberta Human Rights, Citizenship and Multiculturalism Act*, was cause for celebration among gay and lesbian students across Alberta. After having been terminated from a position at King's College in Edmonton in 1991, Delwin Vriend took his case to court, and, seven long years later, came his reward. OUTReach co-chair Tamara Leigh heralded the decision as removing one more obstacle for gay and lesbian graduates entering the workforce, but Vriend himself was frustrated with the Alberta government. When he addressed a gathering of 500 celebrants the day the ruling was announced, Vriend stated that the provincial government had, "for seven years, whined and screamed and kicked and yelled all the way to the Supreme Court of Canada, because they want to discriminate against their own citizens."

"Student Stabbed on 114 Street—Violence Erupts in Midst of University Campus"—September 3, 1998

ON SEPTEMBER 1, Johnny Singh Jaswal, 19, stabbed a man at the intersection of 87 Avenue and 114 Street, about ten feet off of University property. The stabbing was apparently the culmination of a long-standing dispute. The man's injuries were not life-threatening, and he was in stable condition at the University of Alberta Hospital the following day. Jaswal turned himself in at police headquarters, and was charged with one count of aggravated assault and one count of possession of an offensive weapon.

"Yearbook May Be Resurrected"—September 17, 1998

THE *EVERGREEN AND GOLD* was making a comeback—or so hoped Students' Union Vice-President Student Life Abbas Sabur. The story was short and the dream was short-lived: "I'm not convinced that it's financially responsible," Sabur said. The Student Life Board was put in charge of assessing the feasibility of the project.

"A Mark Of Tragedy—Those Who Knew and Loved Him Remember Departed Bear Mark Goodkey"—March 25, 1999

MARCH 25, 1999 marked the third anniversary of the death of Mark Goodkey, University of Alberta Business student and defenceman for the Golden Bears hockey team. The fatal blow was struck when a puck hit him in the back of the head during a recreational hockey game in Stettler, Alberta. "I think that, in a lot of ways, he epitomized what the student athlete is all about: he took a great deal of pride in wearing a Golden Bears hockey jersey, and he took a great deal of pride in what he was able to achieve academically," said Rob Daum, head coach for the Bears hockey team. Mark McQuitty, a bartender at RATT and a legend unto himself, kept a shrine to Goodkey's memory behind the bar at RATT, which included one of Goodkey's hockey jerseys. "Everybody respected him," McQuitty said. "He was one of those people everyone wanted to talk to."

"International Student Tuition Fee Hike Defeated"— September 28, 1999

AFTER A LONG and passionate debate at the September 27 meeting of the General Faculties Council, a motion to double international students' tuition was defeated, with 60 opposed and 47 in favour. In the Students' Union Executive offices, a triumphant sign reading "60–47" hung on office doors. "We like to keep score," said SU President Michael Chalk, who attributed the victory at GFC to the efforts of Vice-President Academic T. J. Adhihetty. *The Gateway* writes, "Eschewing the traditional means of speaking from a sitting position, Adhihetty stood, and without notes, addressed all in the crowded Council Chambers, speaking passionately for ten minutes, urging GFC members not to raise international student fees as doing so would be 'a detriment to the University of Alberta.'" University Hall expressed a wish to work with students on alternative solutions. "We are looking forward to a fresh perspective," Chalk said.

"Development of University Property Raises Community Ire"— January 20, 2000

THE GARNEAU Community League was up in arms. "[The University] could put up a 20-storey condominium beside your house," said Susan McLeod, League president. The fury was over Section 50 of the *Universities Act*, which shut external bodies out of negotiations for development of University property that would potentially affect residential areas nearby. In an era of unprecedented expansion and development for the University of Alberta, this issue was particularly germane. University representatives insisted that they were meeting with concerned communities and doing whatever they could to meet their needs.

MEET ALUMNI FROM THE 1990s[7]

IN 1908, when the U of A first opened its doors, there were seven women in a class of 45 students. By 1999, there were some 23,000 women enrolled at the U of A, compared to some 18,000 men.

Meet four women and one man who graduated from the U of A. in the 1990s.

Winston Pei (BA [ENGLISH] '93, MA [ENGLISH] '02)

HERE IS THE STORY of Winston Pei, as told by Sarah Kelly (BA '02).

A Natural for University

WINSTON'S DECISION to go to university was shaped by his parents' experience. "Both my parents have degrees from the University of Taiwan and also from the University of Alberta," he explains. "There was no question about life after high school—university. And there was really no question but that university would be the U of A." Not only did Winston follow in his parents' footsteps in attending their Canadian alma mater, but he also works in the same building where both his parents worked and studied in the 1960s and 70s—the General Services Building (GSB). "Someone from my family," he states with a grin, "has worked in GSB for almost 40 years."

Campus Everyman

HOW DOES SOMEONE who meant to register in Civil Engineering end up writing a literary analysis of Nick Bantock's *Griffin & Sabine* for a Master's thesis in English? For Winston Pei, it was probably the same way that he wound up being a production editor, a campus ambassador, a Board of Governors student representative, a member of Senate and General Faculties Council, and just about everything in between during his years at the University of Alberta.

Winston himself says it best: "I was raised green and gold."

"What I was really interested in was architecture," Winston recalled, who graduated from the Harry Ainlay High School International Baccalaureate Program in 1988. "But the U of A didn't have a program in architecture, so I decided on Civil Engineering instead." What made him change his mind? "I honestly don't know," he said. "I just got to that point in the application form, and then everything goes blank, and suddenly I'm an English major."

Winston took his time with his two degrees at the U of A: starting in 1988, he finished his BA in English and Sociology in 1994, and moved on to a Master's program in English, which he ultimately completed in 2002.

Beginnings at the U of A

WHEN HE SAYS, "It dictated my whole career," what could Winston be talking about? Why, the orientation program at the University of Alberta, of course. "I was a SORSEy from Day One," Winston explained, referring to Students' Orientation Services, and giving the service full credit for giving him his toehold on campus.

The Powers That Be, however, didn't think much of his extracurricular activities. "My first-year English prof. told me not to bother applying for Honours," Winston remembered. "She told me to stop frittering my time and talent away on Students' Union stuff."

But it's easy to see all the ways in which the University of Alberta bene-fited from his frittering.

Gateway Memories

WHEN WINSTON was at the U of A, the offices of *The Gateway* were on the second floor of SUB, "a stone's throw from the SU offices," as he put it. Some of his fondest memories are from the two years he spent as *The Gateway*'s production editor.

"This was back before computers, really," he explained. "It was all waxers and rollers, and a huge phototypesetter that had these disks with pictures of each letter of the alphabet. Each letter of a headline was done one at a time, and press nights were *all night*."

He did confess, though, that the all-nighters were punctuated by fairly frequent trips to RATT.

His sister Alby recalled that she took some heat for those all-night press nights. "At five-thirty in the morning Winston was fast asleep, and *I* had to wake up when the phone rang letting him know that the paper had gone to press OK."

Winston soon found a solution to this problem, though: "The SU had a shelf with pillows and blankets, so I just slept there," he explained. Later, he rented a couch from a friend who lived near campus—"just the couch," he said. "I kept a toothbrush and contact lens solution in my backpack, and just went home every so often to wash my clothes." He had friends at Lister Hall, at HUB Mall, and at the Phi Delta Theta house, so staying on campus was no problem.

Winston describes a collegial if tense relationship between *The Gateway* and the SU executive. His friendly relationship with both organi-zations was put to the test on one occasion, though. "The SU budget was in deficit, and the Financial Affairs Board had worked forever to balance it *just so* for the following year, and suddenly *The Gateway* springs this proposal for a $150,000 computer purchase that just completely unbal-anced it," he said. "The people at *The Gateway* decided that I was chummy enough to go and present the proposal at Students' Council."

It was a daunting task, he recalled, but in the end, the vice-president (finance and administration) changed his vote, and all was well.

But this friendliness threw him a curve ball at the end. "People at *The Gateway* thought I was too nice to the people over at the SU," Winston said. Which he suspects was the reason why he was denied the position of editor-in-chief—which was then an appointment made by a panel of *Gateway* editors and volunteers—for two years running.

Just Say No

FOLLOWING HIS YEARS as production editor, Winston had an adventure of a very different sort. Usually, the SU election held in February and March of each year consumes campus's attention, but in 1992, Winston remembers, it was a different proposition altogether. "The races for vice-president finance, vice-president student services, and Board of Governors representative each only had one candidate," he explained, and interest in the election was low.

So Winston decided to take matters into his own hands.

"My friend Chris and I decided to mount a sort of 'fill in your name' campaign for the Board of Governors and VP Finance races, just to spice things up a little," Winston said. "It wasn't official, and we weren't registered—we just wanted to give the students some choice." And so the campaign name, *Just Say No*, was born.

It was an *ad hoc* operation, and it soon got them into trouble. As Winston supposed, on a campus where a boot can be elected president, anything is possible.

"We got the attention of the Chief Returning Officer and were hauled in front of the DIE Board," he said. The appropriately abbreviated DIE Board, standing for Discipline, Interpretation, and Enforcement, is the SU's judicial tribunal, and bane of any SU candidate's existence."

But then the Chief Returning Officer did a curious thing. "He told us to start coming to forums!" Winston remembered. "He said, if you're going to run, then run. It was the craziest thing." Did they start going to forums? Absolutely.

The election each year holds a number of forums, and *Just Say No* went to every one, even the one at Faculté Saint-Jean where, as Winston put it, "I was finally able to put my French to some use."

"At the forums, people would stand up and say 'Why should I vote for you?' And then Chris or I would reply, 'Well, we don't think you should, but you *should* make a choice instead of just acclaiming someone.'"

But then fate twisted again: the single candidate for the Board of Governors representative position dropped out of the race.

How did Winston respond to this? Well, when there was a by-election not too long afterwards, he ran a legitimate campaign, and he won. Suddenly he was the Board of Governors student representative for 1992–1993.

Winston has some great memories from that year, including the "travelling BoG meetings" held throughout Alberta in places like Lloydminster and Calgary. "On the Board at that time," says Winston, "were some key people in the Conservative Party and it was the year Ralph Klein faced down Nancy Betkowski for the leadership. As we travelled around Alberta holding Board meetings, I got to hear the most fascinating conversations about the leadership race. And more importantly, he recalled, "I got to stay in *great* hotels."

Winston's father, while acknowledging that being on the Board of Governors provided unique exposure for a student, had just one thing to say when he found out: "When will you be able to do any *studying?*"

Now, as a former member of the Board of Governors, Winston is entitled to don robes at any Convocation he pleases, and sit on the stage at the Jubilee Auditorium as students receive their degrees. "There were a couple of times when I was asked to be a procession marshal," he said. "One of my favourite things is being able to congratulate new graduates."

From Undergraduate to MA (English) and Beyond

THE SIXTH YEAR of Winston's BA program was taken up by a full roster of English courses, and 1994 was a red letter year indeed. "I was admitted to grad school, and I started in September, and then got married in October," he said. His wife, Jacqueline, has a PhD in Educational Psychology, and they have three children.

But the hard times weren't over yet.

"I was a terrible grad student," Winston confessed. "I had no work habits to speak of from being undergrad—I just pulled all-nighters all the time. Grad school was a kick in the teeth."

He remembers 1998 as his worst year at university. Soon after Jacqueline gave birth to their first child, Winston's advisor, Professor Edward ("Ted") Bishop, was in a near-fatal motorcycle accident. "There he was, hanging between life and death, and he was a *great* advisor, and had given me all these chances and ideas, and all I could think about was my thesis, and that it wasn't done yet."

Ted Bishop, to the great relief of all of his colleagues and students, Winston included, made a full recovery, and went on to write a memoir about the accident and its aftermath, for which he was awarded the U of A's own Mactaggart Writing Award in 2002.

Winston had some recovering of his own to do that year, and when he decided to resume his graduate work in 2000, he modified it to a project-based program. "It was my last chance," he admitted. "Jacquie was pregnant with Sydney [their third child], and things were pretty busy. If I didn't finish then, I never would."

In the end he completed his Master's in 2002, with thesis he had started earlier forming the basis for his final project. "But because Ted was my advisor," he related, "I ended up with a thesis-length final project anyway!"

What Came Next

TWO DEGREES LATER, Winston is still at the U of A—although now it's only two days a week, as opposed to going home once a week for laundry. He does software implementation and communications work for Advancement Services, but that's not the end of his involvement. He also does design work for the Juvenilia Press, a publisher dedicated to publishing juvenilia. He also works with NeWest Press, which has strong ties to the University's Department of English. Winston and his wife Jacqueline are also part-owners of Café Dabar, an internet café on Whyte Avenue. "We've set as our goal to provide a more civilized place to surf," says Winston. "We had such fond memories of 'doing coffee' on Whyte Ave as undergrads, we just found ourselves back there again."

A Little Advice from Winston

AS A FORMER Campus Ambassador, Winston has much wisdom to impart to current University of Alberta students. "Take in as much of this campus as you can," he entreats. "Don't let your program or your involvement stop you from doing *everything* else. It's beyond belief what's here for the taking."

Alby Pei and her cousin Karen Pattison Belich. (Private Collection)

Albertina Pei (BSC '96 (COMPUTING SCI), CERTIFICATE IN PHYSICS, '98, MSC '02 (ASTROPHYSICS) THE UNIVERSITY OF CALGARY, '02)

HERE IS THE STORY of Albertina ("Alby") Pei, as told by Sarah Kelly (BA '02).

It's rare that a woman gets to follow in her mother's footsteps as closely as Albertina ("Alby") Pei got to follow in those of her mother, Caroline; and it is even rarer that the daughter doesn't even know she's doing it.

"I liked Physics, that's all I knew," Alby relates. "But where are the jobs in Physics? So I started in Computing Science, and I had no idea then that my mom had done the same thing." Alby's mother Caroline had studied computing science in China, but after immigrating to Edmonton she earned a BEd—it was only the BEd that daughter Alby knew about.

Alby went to Harry Ainlay High School and graduated from the International Baccalaureate program in 1991. "University was a natural progression, and I didn't really give it any thought," she says. "You went to junior high, then high school, then university. That's the way it was."

A little less straightforward was what Alby wanted to achieve at university: she didn't know what she wanted to be when she grew up. "The U of

The Pei family at Winston's wedding. (Private Collection)

A was close, so I could stay at home, and I *knew* from my parents what a good school it was, so I decided to go there."

Alby remembers that back before *BearTracks*, or before you could register by phone, registration days at the University of Alberta were daunting indeed. "You basically had to spend the whole day at the Butterdome, shuffling through lines and getting your packages, and there were thousands of people there," she says. "But you got a lot of free stuff, too, so it was OK."

Better still was the lucky fact that her older brother Winston had gone through it all before her, and had some handy tips. "The best trick Winston ever taught me was about the lines at the Butterdome," she recalls. "You don't have to wait in the big line! Things were arranged alphabetically by last name, and all these students would spend hours and hours behind people whose last names started with *Z*, not knowing that when your time came, you could skirt the line. What a timesaver."

There were misunderstandings during those first days, too. "I remember people coming up to me and speaking Cantonese, thinking I was part of a Chinese student group," she says. "I wasn't a foreign student, and I didn't know what they were saying."

Alby remembers cheap food at the Power Plant and spending a lot of time in CAB in her first year. She loved her courses, so there weren't a lot of extracurricular activities initially, but thanks to her brother Winston, she recognized the rivalry between Arts and Science students almost immediately. "I guess I thought Science had more concreteness about it," she recalls. But after a barbeque for Student Orientation Services (SorSe), she changed her tune.

"My brother Winston was reading a syllabus from one of his Arts courses—it sounded like prison, the most terrible thing I'd ever heard, but he *liked* it. I'm definitely the numbers person in the family—he can have that stuff."

Part of the reason Alby had so much fun in Science was her professors. Were they good instructors? Sure, but it was their enthusiasm and ability get points across in an entertaining way that was important. "Math professors are the strangest lot," Alby relates. "One would use nuclear weapons and pencils in examples of linear algebra problems." She also remembers a Polish professor with a huge beard who always wore interesting suspenders. "He was *so* excited about Calculus. Another one," she remembers, "was just like Mr. Rogers. Every time he came back to his office from lunch he would take his jacket off and hang it up, and change into a Mr. Rogers sweater and Hush Puppies."

Campus Memories

IT WASN'T ALL going to lectures and cramming for exams for Alby; she found time for some fun as well.

"I was a volunteer with the Observatory on the roof of the Physics Building and president, for two years, of the Undergraduate Association of Computing Science. The early 1990s was a time of great change for computing, and I watched considerable evolution in how the University of Alberta treated computers, and the people who worked with them. We saw a lot of changes—from the time-sharing MTS [Michigan Time Sharing] system on AJ 510 terminals—to what we now take for granted in Windows boxes and server-oriented computer systems. The AJ 510 computers were horrible one-piece monitor-and-keyboard units with these monochromatic green screens—no mouse or hard drive," Alby explains. And that wasn't all. "They operated on a 'time-credit' system. If you ran out of 'time-credits' on the weekend when you were working on an assignment, you couldn't log off, because you wouldn't be able to log on again until you saw the System Administrator on Monday!"

Alby also saw a great evolution in the programming contests at the University of Alberta. "In my day, the programming contest was this little annual event at the U of A, but by the end of my studies I saw students going to the highest levels of international programming contests."

For fun, Alby and her friends went to Dewey's in HUB Mall. But for studying, the rest of campus was open to them—if they were willing to brave it. Alby rattled off V-Wing, Agriculture/Forestry, and CAB as frequent study hideaways, but it wasn't always easy. "In CAB," she remembers, "the air conditioning went off at a certain hour. The servers would start to overheat and all the computers would start crashing. When you're in Computing Science and the computers are necessary to your homework, that's a problem."

So what did Alby and her friends do about this dilemma? They walked through a star-canopied Quad from the overheated CAB to the sub-zero Assiniboia Hall, where it was equally uncomfortable, but at the very least, the computers worked. "Assiniboia Hall *did* have air conditioning, and how," she says. "We could do our homework all right, but we *froze*. Now, no one questions the need for a well-maintained and ventilated room for the servers. It's been an interesting transition since I started university."

Bob Beck

"IN COMPUTING SCIENCE," Alby says, "Bob Beck was a god. He was the systems administrator for the department of Computing Science, and because he knew where to find an axe, he started the most enduring tradition in Computing Science history. It was called the Terminal Bash," Alby remembers. "Every year we'd set aside an old AJ 510—those were such frustrating terminals—and we got out our frustration with an axe." The Terminal Bash took place in the General Services Building, where the department of Computing Science was then located, and later, in the Biological Sciences Building cafeteria.

It may have been tradition, but participants in the Terminal Bash didn't have the law on their side—not University law, anyway. "Campus 5-0—or the students' liquor police—would come by and you'd be hiding this *axe* behind your back," Alby remembers. And did libations lubricate these clandestine evenings? "Yes," Alby says, and will say no more.

Alby's Augustana Cousins

"WE HAD NO FAMILY at all here in Canada," say Alby. "My parents left China in the aftermath of war. We were separated from our relatives. We were alone here in Canada. You know how everyone has these memories of their grandmother in the rocking chair on the porch, the turkey in the oven, the Christmas tree perfectly decorated? We would have none of these memories if it weren't for the Pattison and Swanson families from Augustana Faculty in Camrose. Will Pattison was my dad's best friend, and since my parents did not have any family in Edmonton or Canada, Uncle Will had his in-laws stood up for my parents at their wedding in 1969.

"We grew up with their kids," Alby recalls. "My brother Winston is six months older than Marilea, the eldest, and I am six months younger than Steven. Karen and John arrived over the next ten years. We grew up visiting them out on the farm, playing in the trees around their house. They enfolded us. We were part of their family, and they were part of ours."

Almost all members of the Pei, Pattison, and Swanson families are University of Alberta alumni. "Uncle Will, who taught at Augustana College for many years, graduated from the U of A, as did his wife Marion. Three of their children, Marilea, Steven and Karen, are also graduates," says Alby. "Little John" is the only one still in university, at Augustana Faculty, and is currently serving as their Students' Union president.

"I have these wonderful memories of my Grandpa Swanson's drift-wood furniture and art," Alby relates, "and the big rope swing hanging from the big tree in the back yard of their house. And Grandma Swanson's lefse, and the smell of something good in the oven. Our cousins are these blonde, blue-eyed Scandinavians. When people ask us if we are cousins by marriage, we just look at them and say 'No.' Of course, no one can understand it. But we do. It comes from the heart and not from the genes. They *are* my family in every sense that is important."

Life After Graduation

AFTER CONVOCATING with a computing science degree, Alby followed up with specialized study in Physics followed by a Master's in Astrophysics. Alby is currently working as the program administrator in Northern Alberta for the SCIberMENTOR email mentoring program, an initiative between the Universities of Alberta and Calgary and the Alberta Women's Science Network, and sponsored by EnCana, NSERC, and Alberta Innovation and Science. The program targets grade-school-aged girls. "We provide email mentoring to girls across Alberta," Alby explains. "Girls are connected with women who have a connection with Alberta and who are studying or working in the fields of science, health science or engineering."

The goal of the program is to encourage girls to stay in math and science through their junior high school years, and to present it as a possibility in post-secondary education. "We want girls to have all their doors open when they get to university," Alby says. "We want them to know that there are more careers than doctor, lawyer, nurse, or teacher; we want them to know all about the amazing opportunities available to them."

As much as she loves the SCIberMENTOR program, other horizons beckon for Alby. She has recently taken a position in public programming at the Telus World of Science. "Bringing science and math to more people, everywhere!" she enthuses. "That's what I love. Fuelling my own curiosity and love for science by igniting it in others."

Alby has some advice for today's students. "I find it interesting," Alby muses, "that looking back, no matter what I tried to do when I set out, I seem to have followed in my mother's footsteps, from studying Computing Science to educating young children. Always be curious," she says, "and explore what interests you. You never know where you'll end up, but it's *always* a great adventure. I never regretted anywhere I ended up, no matter how unexpectedly I got there."

Cecile Keller Silzer (BED '71, MLIS '91)

SHE WATCHED the University of Alberta boom in the late 1960s and then, twenty years later, she experienced the budget cuts of the 1990s, both in the school system and at the U of A. Her name is Cecile Keller Silzer.

"I was raised in Brooks," says Cecile, "a southern Alberta town of about 2,500. My mother was a teacher and my dad managed a car dealership,

but most of my friends were farm kids and I spent a lot of time with them at their homes and on their farms. Looking back to the 1960s, I sometimes wish I had had the flower child experience, but that was really a city thing. Brooks is typical of rural Alberta, and it was a carefree upbringing. No stress, no drugs, no intense pressures.

"My mom had done her training in the days when you studied to be a teacher at Normal School, and she had that whole experience of being out on the prairies, in the middle of nowhere, on her own, teaching. I knew I wanted to be a teacher, and I loved books. So after high school graduation, I went to the closest university—the University of Calgary. In those days, you could take two years of university and then teach in the schools, finishing your degree afterwards. That's what I did, finishing up, course by course, at night."

So how did Cecile end up at the U of A? "Simple," she says. "A man."

The man turned out to be someone later described as having "green and gold blood," long-time U of A registrar, Brian Silzer. Cecile remembers how they met. "One day a friend came to me and said one of the local lifeguards wanted to meet me. His name was Brian. He was new to Brooks, but even so he seemed to have a lot of girlfriends. I thought it was sweet that he asked a mutual friend to introduce us."

Brian is quick to note that after he met Cecile, all those girlfriends vanished. Cecile and Brian married in 1968, and both graduated from the

U of A. And even though Brian is now registrar at UBC, the Silzers keep up their house in Edmonton, where their two children, both U of A grads, are living.

Cecile taught Grades 1–5 in Edmonton for 20 years and then made a decision that changed her whole outlook on life. She switched roles, and went back to school. The teacher was once again the student. "I did it for two reasons," Cecile says. "'First, teaching elementary school is a bit insular. You don't really interact with other teachers except at the annual teachers' convention. After 20 years, that wasn't enough for me. And by 1989, when I went back for a graduate degree, there were more behavioural problems in the schools, and less support for teachers from parents. That was the trigger for me.

"I wanted a break, and I wanted career options. That's why I chose the Library Science degree—I had the world of teaching already open to me, and with the Master's in Library Science (MLIS), I would also be qualified for library-related positions.

"Most of my courses were purely Library Science, but I took two graduate courses in Education as well, and I was amazed at how many teachers were going back to university for graduate degrees. The Education Building was filled at 6 P.M. with schoolteachers who had finished a day's work and who would go at it until 9 P.M. every night with classes and seminars."

What was it like going back to class after 20 years? Telephone registration was the first hurdle. "In the late 1960s," explains Cecile, "registration involved long line-ups and took most of the day. Twenty years later, you registered by telephone. Now this may sound simple, but it's only simple if you know how to do it. I went to my husband Brian, who had brought telephone registration to the U of A, and asked him to do the telephone registration thing and register me. He said no! He told me that to get the full benefit of being a student, I needed to have the 'experience' of telephone registration. So I did it. And that wasn't the only hurdle. I had used computers in the schools, but suddenly had to learn an entirely new system to do my papers. I was the oldest student in the MLIS program, and the others were so fresh, so young, so used to doing papers and taking exams. I had been out of that mode for so long. It was tough."

Life as an MLIS Student

"AS A GRAD STUDENT in MLIS," says Cecile, "I was at the University all day. Once in a while we'd get a break and go over to HUB, but classes and seminars went for most of the day, and we'd just grab something for lunch. My education courses were in the evenings, so there were some very long days. It bonded us as a class, and it was a small class—just 30 students. And there is no doubt as to my favourite teacher. Anna Altmann, without a doubt. She had high expectations, but was always there to support you. She was a literature specialist, and her lectures were always stimulating, exciting. I've never forgotten her classes.

"When I finished up and went back to teaching, I didn't see many of my classmates because, as a schoolteacher, there is little flexibility in the day to go out for lunch or a coffee. But when we run into one another, even after all these years, we always have a hug and instantly pick up the thread from our last conversation. A group from my class still meets regularly as a book club to talk about young adult literature."

Cecile's class is bonded for another reason. Their Convocation in 1991 was the cause of an intense, but quickly-resolved, controversy.

Between 1990 and 1994, the University cut some 21% from its operating budget. There were layoffs, tuition and residence fee increases, larger classes, and higher grades required for university entrance. It was also the year the University decided to stop publishing the names of graduands in the convocation program. There was an instant outcry, and the names were reinstated in 1992.

"Can you imagine it?" asks Cecile. We had all worked so hard. Then to get to Convocation and find your name isn't in the program. It was an awful feeling. And to top if off, it was the Registrar's Office that had made this budget cut. Ouch."

It took Cecile two years of intense work to complete her MLIS. One of her friends remembers seeing Cecile come late to a small party of old friends. "She joined us at about 10:30 P.M. and was unusually quiet. I found out she had been in classes since 8 A.M." Cecile is clear that returning to school was the right decision. "Going back to university, testing myself, learning—it changed me," she says. "I emerged much more self-assured, much more confident about expressing my views. I'm glad I did it."

Teacher Librarian

CECILE RE-ENTERED the school system with her MLIS, but "the budget cuts in the schools had a tremendous impact on the teacher-librarians," she notes. "By the time I left the system in 2001, I had one of the last full-time teacher-librarian positions in Edmonton. But I feel great about the influence I had, especially the home-reading program we started in one of my schools. Every single student participated, and if a student didn't have the parental support at home to help with reading, we arranged for that to happen right there at the school, with U of A Golden Key students, 30 of them, volunteering their time to help kids read an extra five hours each school term."

Cecile retired from the school system in 2001 and moved to Vancouver when Brian was named registrar at UBC. "As soon as I finish getting us settled into our new life, I know I have lots of options for volunteering. It may be organizing student tours at the art gallery or working in the museum bookshop." But there is one option Cecile talks about with a flash in her eyes: "I might just walk into one of the local schools and say 'give me a student who can't read.' I'll teach him."

Heather Taylor (BA NATIVE STUDIES, '97)

HEATHER TAYLOR had a rough beginning at the U of A, but today she is at the top of her game professionally. She's also enrolled in the MBA program at Royal Roads University. Here is the story of the only alumna ever to serve as an undergraduate student on the Board of Governors, General Faculties Council, and the Senate.

"Not going to university wasn't an option for me," says Heather. "It's not that it was an expectation on the part of my family—no one in my family had actually attended university except for my grandfather, who studied law and then became a judge. It's just that I was young and idealistic. I wanted to be a paediatrician or lawyer, and I needed a university education to accomplish that."

Heather's father is with the RCMP, and her mother is an insurance broker. The Taylors moved often as they raised their two children, Heather and Collin. "I started elementary school in Whitehorse," says Heather, "and finished in Ponoka, near the Hobbema reservation, which is also

where I went to junior high. High school was in Edson. When I finished high school, my counsellors said the choices were U of A, NAIT, Red Deer College, maybe Augustana, Lethbridge, or Calgary if we were pushing it. I wanted to take the petroleum land management program at the University of Calgary, but didn't get in.

"I was determined to enjoy Grade 12 as opposed to studying for departmentals, so I aimed for the absolute lowest mark I needed to get in to the U of A—65 % at the time. I phoned the Registrar's Office to confirm that if I got a 64.5%, they would round it up to 65% and they said yes. I don't believe in marks. Education is all about how you end up as a person. And I wanted to have a life, both in high school and in university."

First Year—Awful

"I REGISTERED IN 1992, in the days of telephone registration. It was frustrating because so many courses were filled up so quickly and lots were cancelled. Once you had your timetable filled out, you went to the Butterdome on an appointed day and hour and stood in long lines to get your ID card, then your student loan, and then came the bookstore—more long lines. I was very keen and tried to do all this all at once. You could literally stand in lines for a week.

"My most vivid memory of my first week is the size of the classes. They were bigger than the towns I grew up in. The University's population, in fact, was far greater than all of the Yukon. It was overwhelming. It's so easy to get lost at university. I didn't know a soul and it was hard to meet people. My brother chose to go to Augustana and many of his high school friends went there too. It was a good choice for him.

"I lived in three different places in the first four months. I was all set to live in residence, but ended up in an apartment with a high school friend. Let's just say it was a psycho situation.

"I paid for my education mostly with student loans and what I earned from working at my summer jobs in the Yukon managing swimming pools and my part-time job at Sunterra Market. My parents helped too, but I was $22,000 in debt when I graduated. I have most of it paid off, but it's hard to tell precisely because I've just borrowed money to do an MBA at Royal Roads in Victoria. University was expensive for me because I couldn't live at home—that wasn't an option because while I was in university, my parents lived up north."

Heather had an awful first year. "I'd never lived away from home before," she remembers. "I had jaw surgery and missed three weeks of school. That first Christmas my dad was not able to come south—it was too cold in the Yukon, where he was posted, for him to get out. And I hadn't learned to study. Plus I had the prof from hell for Political Science 101, and Political Science was going to be my major. One of the remarks on my first exam was something like this: 'Did you even study for this?' After that, I dropped Political Science as my major.

"RATT was my hanging-out spot," says Heather. "There were days when I thought a double Caesar was an adequate meal. I studied in SUB and Rutherford North and sometimes in Chemistry—I can still remember the smell of the Chemistry Building."

Heather looks back to her first final exams. "I had Microbiology and Calculus exams on a Monday and Tuesday, and I was keen to do well in

Math so I paid the fee to take extra Math at the Academic Support Centre. My strategy was to study all weekend for Monday's Micro exam, and then cram for Tuesday's Calculus exam. On Monday morning I was in HUB and double-checked the exam schedule. I suddenly realized it was *Calculus* I had on Monday, and not Micro. I went to the gym for the Math exam and cried for the first 15 minutes. Later, I realized I could have talked to the prof and deferred the exam, but I was too new to know this. It was devastating. When I got the letter requiring me to withdraw, I was in the tiny town of Ross River in the middle of nowhere. I wrote what I thought was a compelling letter to the dean and, thankfully, got back in."

Choosing Native Studies

"IN MY SECOND YEAR," says Heather, "I was faced with repeating the dreaded science options—because of the failure in Math—and chose Computing and Entomology. They really had nothing to do with what I wanted to study, but I took them.

"One day when I was in SUB I saw a display about the School of Native Studies and picked up a brochure. There was a really good employment rate for graduates in this program and I had spent part of my youth in the Yukon and near Hobbema. And then I realized that in Native Studies I only needed 9 credits of science instead of 12. Bonus!

"In Native Studies, you're a somebody and not a number. Everyone was very supportive, and everyone knew you by name. Great people, and I was treated well, even as a non-aboriginal.

"When I was there, the budget for the entire School was $350,000. This, in my view, is ridiculous. Native Studies doesn't bring in the big research dollars like engineering and science, but it's there for a purpose. And cuts to a unit like Native Studies have a profound effect on students. If you cut a faculty member, you're cutting two or three senior courses, and that dilutes the experience.

"I was ridiculed by my family for choosing Native Studies, but now they have all had to eat crow. I have done better financially than anyone in my family.

"I made another choice in my second year. I was studying in the law library and saw a poster advertising fraternity rush. I decided on the spot to go. Joining the Thetas was my saving grace. That's how I became involved in so many extracurricular things in my last two years—all because of the Thetas. It's that simple."

Favourite Profs

IN HER THIRD YEAR, Heather settled down academically. "I was taking eight classes a year, and in my fourth year I did 12 classes. I was taking senior level Native Studies courses, with just 10–12 people in a class. My schedule was such that on Monday, Wednesdays and Fridays, I was in class all morning, then in aerobics, and then it was downtown to Sunterra for work, then back for night class. I didn't have classes on Tuesdays and Thursdays, so I could work. I cleared so many required courses in those two years that by the last year, when I needed ten classes, eight of the courses I took were options. I did a double minor in Philosophy and Political Science.

"I had two professors who stand out," says Heather. "Dr. David Stewart in Political Science, who taught *Government and Policy of Alberta,* was one. This was a senior level course with 15 people. I was the only student in it not avidly aligned with a particular party, but I was running for a Students' Union executive position. It was a really interesting mix of students and Dr. Stewart brought in high-profile speakers actively involved in government, like Lou Hyndman, Pam Barrett and Jim Dinning. These people brought a real-life perspective to what we were learning in class. It was stimulating and we learned about the politics of the province—how Peter Lougheed ran his government, and how the province became so conservative. My other favourite professor was Pat McCormack. I took many of her senior courses. She made me see the stereotypical images of Indians portrayed in our culture, and she brought her research right into the classroom. She had good ideas, I liked her, and she made us think about graduate studies.

"None of my friends knew this," says Heather, "but the last class I needed to graduate was Philosophy 101. I needed the course—because it was a prerequisite—but not the credit. I failed. This happened in April, and Convocation was in June.

"I cried. Then I phoned Native Studies. They told me that the rewrite wasn't until August and the Convocation list would be approved in May. This timing, of course, meant that I wouldn't graduate. But the teacher, who was a post-doctoral fellow, let me rewrite the exam in early May. I've never forgotten that.

Kim Skibstead

HEATHER REFLECTS on her favourite volunteer activity. "I volunteered with Students with Disabilities Office, and got to work with amazing people like Mary Hyndman and Ann Kelly. At the time the Office was over in Athabasca Hall and I spent a lot of time there. I read text onto tapes and also was a scribe, taking notes in classes for students who weren't able to do that on their own. One of the students I had the privilege of helping was a young woman named Kim Skibstead. She had been blind since the age of 21, and decided to go into Speech Pathology—one of the first blind students to do so. She is an amazing person, and has given me a lot of good advice about life. Kim was always so together—every hair in place, perfect makeup, matching earrings, great outfits. I don't know how she did it, but obviously she had an ability to remember all those kinds of daily things we as sighted people take for granted. If you can believe it, one day when I escorted her to the washroom in Athabasca, I turned on the light for her. She heard the flick of the switch and laughed, reminding me that she didn't need the light.

"In 1997, when I was very involved with the SU, the Disabilities Office called me back in because a student needed a scribe for her last exam. It was Kim. I was thrilled. Kim now works in Calgary at the Children's Hospital. What a role model."

The Governance Queen

HEATHER IS THE ONLY STUDENT, in one undergraduate career, to have served on the Students' Union Executive, the Board of Governors, Senate, and both General Faculties Council and its Executive—both of the latter in elected positions, she notes.

"I'd been on GFC and GFC Executive in 1994 and one of my goals was to get a permanent seat on GFC for a student from Native Studies. I had to educate so many people to get this done—everyone thought we were a part of the Faculty of Arts, but Native Studies is a separate unit, and its distinctiveness was not widely understood. I'm very passionate about

Native Studies and wanted the students to have what was rightfully theirs—their own seat on GFC."

In 1997 Heather was elected as vice-president external of the Students' Union, serving with Sheamus Murphy, Stu McDonnough, Garth Bishop, and Steve Curran. "It was my best year," says Heather. "I met so many people and had so many opportunities. I'm friends to this day with the executive members I served with and am proud to say that when Garth Bishop got married, I was invited, believe it or not, to his stag. I'm still in touch with Hoops Harrison, who was vice-president external in 1996–1997.

"Actually, I had been very anti-Students' Union. Through the Thetas, I met people like Vlad Gomez and Shane O'Brien, and worked on their campaigns. I got hooked. That same year, I was on the selection committee to choose a new director for the School of Native Studies, served on the Board of Governors for two months, and was the undergraduate representative on the committee that decided to split the portfolio of university vice-president external and research into two separate portfolios."

Real Life Skills

"I ALSO PARTICIPATED in the Alberta Economic Growth Summit, chaired by Mike Percy. This group was charting the course for Alberta for the next ten years. I was part of the social/economic sector chaired by Bette Hewes. Other sectors focussed on areas such as agriculture and business. We went all over Alberta for meetings. There were, for instance, public housing meetings in Calgary, and meetings with Gary McPherson's group about Albertans with disabilities. It was an incredible set of experiences for an undergraduate student.

"I served on Senate in 1997, and I had great conversations with so many members of Senate. At the time I was taking a course from Professor Jim Butler called *Protected Areas Planning*. One day he asked me to get up in front of the class and talk about the Summit. It was a way of taking what I was learning outside of class right into the classroom.

"I learned real-life skills through extracurricular activities—interpersonal skills, how to run a meeting, facilitating group dialogue. These are skills that employers look for. They're skills that stand you in good stead your entire life."

Heather has a glint in her eye when she talks about CASA and what that organization accomplished in 1997–1998. "Hoops Harrison was president of CASA that year, and CASA had a direct influence on the federal government. It was the year of the post-secondary education budget. We lobbied Ottawa hard. On one trip we spent an hour with Paul Martin at the time he was finance minister. I remember watching the budget come down on the TV up in RATT. It was the year the Millennium Scholarship program was launched (I'm an assessor for that program now), and the year the government committed to contributing $400 annually to a prospective student's RESP. There were changes to the student loan system that year as well."

Convocation and Life Afterwards

DID HEATHER GO to her convocation? "Yes! Mom and dad flew down from the Yukon and my grandmother came from Saskatchewan. I was the first in three generations to graduate from university. Plus I was on Senate and so got to be on stage. I cried when the Convocation band played 'Pomp and Circumstance.' The elders were there to greet us on stage, and that was very special.

"I had taken advantage of so many opportunities while in university," says Heather. "I was burnt out by the time I graduated, and I wanted a mindless job. So I went to Dawson City that first summer and was a waitress and bartender. I had to dress in this can-can outfit, with fishnet stockings and a feather in my hair. I wanted to wear a sign that said 'I have a university degree and this job is my own choice right now.'

"Then I saw an ad in a newspaper for a natural resource planner in Old Crow. I applied and was the successful candidate. I was paid $42,000 and had no experience. Holy crap! And I didn't pay rent. I had three weeks holidays and we also got a week in the fall and again in the spring to pursue our traditional activities. It was a great experience. There are 250 people in Old Crow on a good day. It's an air-access community only, and by choice, it's a dry community. I lived in a log house with a wood stove for heat. I will never take central heating for granted again. But it was a break from the real world.

"In 2000, I was ready for something new and saw an ad in the newspaper for a job in Calgary doing the north of 60 work for an oil and gas exploration company called Devon Canada Corporation. I opened and shut the paper and then opened it again. This is what I wanted to try.

"There were 150 applicants. They narrowed it to 12. I flew down to Whitehorse for a one-hour meeting. Then on a Monday they flew me to Calgary. You have to understand that this is not a minor event because the airfare from Old Crow to Calgary is about $2,500. I interviewed on Tuesday and returned to Old Crow on Wednesday, the same day that I had organized a visit to Old Crow for Premier Pat Duncan—and she was staying with me. There's no hotel in Old Crow. On Friday I got an email asking when I could start. I had beaten out a cabinet minister for this job. I was on top of the world, but also felt badly about leaving Old Crow, especially since some of the people there are against oil and gas exploration. It was very hard. I cried. I had great relationships with the people there. I still go back to visit."

As the Community and Northern Affairs Advisor for the Devon Canada Corporation, earning $75,000, she was the face of a company that was the largest independent natural gas producer in North America. By 2006, she had moved on to TransCanada as their specialist in community relations. "I'm paid for what I know and who I know," she says. "I love working in the north."

Heather has some advice for today's students. "Get involved! There's more to learning than going to class. Your education should make you a better person. That's what you should want, and that's what an employer will want."

Marcie Brulotte Miranda (BA '99)

SHE DECIDED on a career as a Foreign Service Officer when she was 16, and pursued it for some seven years with single-minded purpose and a unique brand of personal courage. Along the way, she was Volunteer #1 at the U of A. One of her mentors calls her "Intrepid." This alumna shows no fear of the untried or the unknown. Fasten your seatbelts. Here comes Marcie Brulotte Miranda (BA '99).

"I'm a thirteenth-generation Canadian and a third-generation Franco-Albertan," she says proudly. On her father's side, Marcie's lineage stretches back to the French who came to Canada in Champlain's era, and there are towns in Alberta and Québec named for her forbears. On her mother's side, her great-great-grandfather George Gillies farmed in Clover Bar and brought the first Silver Ghost Rolls Royce to Canada. Marcie is the third generation in her family to attend the U of A, with some 17 Brulottes and Gillies having attended the U of A in six faculties.

"I grew up on stories about the U of A," says Marcie. "Both my parents went to the U of A in the 1970s. My dad, Gil Brulotte, was president of the Engineering Students' Society, and both he and my mom, Eileen Gillies, lived in Lister Hall. Mom was in Kelsey—it was an all-girls' residence back then, with no mixed floors. Dad was in Henday."

Not only were there no mixed floors in the 1970s, but there was also no liquor allowed in the residences. Then came one night when Marcie's father was in charge of the beverages for a communal dinner at Lister. It's one of the stories Marcie grew up on.

"The drinking age in Alberta was 21," says Marcie, "and that set the stage. Dad and one of his friends discovered that if you mixed Tahiti punch with 7-Up—and then capped it—the resulting mixture would have the appearance of champagne when you opened it. Lots of fizz. So dad and his friends took a load of empty Baby Duck champagne bottles and filled them with their Tahiti/7-Up mixture. Then these mystery bottles were placed on the dinner tables at Lister and uncorked, to the cheers of the students. But the administrators came within a hair's breadth of evicting my dad from residence. So you can see, from hearing stories like these, why I had an early familiarity and fondness for the U of A."

Culture Shock

"WHEN I WAS SIX," says Marcie, "my 18-year-old cousin went on a student exchange to France. I got to talk to her on the phone and when we hung up, I turned to my parents and said, 'I'm doing *that* when I'm old enough.'"

Marcie spent Grade 11 in France. "I loved it, plain and simple. One embarrassing, but illuminating thing happened to me there. It made me decide I wanted a career in protocol where I could represent Canada abroad. I made an awful cultural gaffe at a public dinner," remembers Marcie, "and I was totally unaware of it. I was at a dinner with representatives of the exchange organization, school representatives and other exchange students. My high school vice-principal was sitting next to me. My hands were politely folded and on my lap. The vice-principal said to me, '*Tu te joues?*' It means, 'Are you playing with yourself?' I was mortified. My host family hadn't clued me in that this was the wrong thing to do. In France, at the dinner table, your hands are always *above* the table. I just didn't know."

Marcie's Grade 11 year in France lacked one thing. "I was already fluent in French. I wanted the experience of total language and culture shock. So after grade 12 here in Edmonton, I made a deal with my parents that if they would let me do another exchange, I would come back and go to the U of A for a year."

Marcie selected Ecuador as her host country. She didn't speak a word of Spanish. "On the plane down, I learned '*de nada*,' which means 'It's nothing.' That's all I knew when I landed in Quito. I was supposed to go to a public high school for my second year of Grade 12, and plunge right in. It would be the complete language barrier I wanted. But the teachers were on strike and they put the six of us—six exchange students—into a private language school. We were divided into two little groups and had individual instruction for three months. I was fluent by the time the strike was over."

After Ecuador came the other part of the bargain with her parents—a year at the U of A. There was no problem being admitted, but there was a big problem fitting the courses Marcie wanted to take into an existing degree program. With Marcie still in Ecuador, her mother worked with the Registrar's Office on course and program selection. Marcie wanted a major in Political Science and a minor in Spanish—not possible in those days when you weren't allowed to take a language other than French at Faculté Saint-Jean. "That's now changed at 'the Fac,' as we all affectionately call Faculté Saint-Jean," says Marcie.

Marcie's program changed so many times—before she even set foot at the U of A—that the Registrar's Office said "no more changes or we'll start charging you!" Marcie settled into a French–Spanish double major, with advanced standing. She finished up her required courses well before graduation. By the time Convocation rolled around, Marcie had enough credits for minors in Anthropology and Political Science. Somewhere in between, she learned German.

How did she learn so many languages? "It's my dad who's Francophone, so it was really up to my mom to set the tone at home about speaking

French. And my mother saw to it that our home was bilingual. She made sure that French was a living language for us. There were enough family members around who spoke French, and my mother made sure we heard it every day. That made it easier to pick up other languages."

Marcie accomplished her schooling while facing a silent barrier every hour of the day. She's dyslexic. "In terms of language acquisition, my oral is good. My written is bad." Dyslexia was extremely frustrating, but she made sure it wasn't a controlling factor. "In the days when we had a 9-point grading system, I knew I'd never be a 9 student," Marcie says, "so I decided I'd be a good 6–7 student, and be a well-rounded one. In fact, I'd rather be a 6–7 student and learn something outside the classroom than a 9 student with no life."

Campus Memories

"I VOLUNTEERED at Week of Welcome before I even had my first class. I moved on from there. I tutored, taught swimming, aerobics and first aid, worked with student orientation, was a campus ambassador, and worked at the Information Desk in SUB. I was also part of the Safewalk program with Campus Security, and a dispatcher too. I was president of my fraternity, Alpha Gamma Delta. I consciously didn't become involved with the SU governance. I felt I could make a bigger impact at General Faculties Council (GFC).

"GFC is big," says Marcie. "All the deans and vice-presidents are members and there are about 100 faculty, students and staff. I learned *Robert's Rules of Order* and have taken that into every corner of my life, from church organization to fraternity meetings. And while on GFC, I learned how to negotiate. With all those competing interests, you can't always get what you want. You have to pick what battles to fight and what to let lie. I enjoyed it. I especially loved being on the GFC Executive because I felt I contributed to making the University a better place."

Some GFC executive members remember Marcie's last year of university, when she worked in the President's Office. It was a time when the president, Rod Fraser, was developing an international student policy. Before Marcie started working for "President Rod," she was crisply outspoken about certain components of the proposed policy. And after she started working for the president, his policy came up once again for debate

Her Honour Lois Hole

*"WHEN I FINANCED my studies, it was a sure bet
I would attend Convocation," remembers Marcie
Brulotte. "It was Lois Hole's last year
of Chancellor, just before she became
lieutenant governor. When I crossed the stage at
the Jubilee Auditorium, she gave me a big hug and
a kiss on the cheek. Out there in the audience,
my mom's jaw dropped. Mind you, I wasn't the
only student the Chancellor hugged that day,
but I was the first grad she knew who crossed the
stage that day. Remember, my name starts with
a B, beginning of the alphabet. By the time the
Chancellor got to the Zs, a lot of students had been
hugged." (CS 1998–9701–K–54)*

at a GFC executive meeting. Would Marcie back down now that she was a direct employee of the University's CEO? Not a chance. Marcie's hand was the first one up. She laid out her concerns in no uncertain terms. President Rod sat back and listened. Soon after, Rod Fraser put Marcie in charge of bringing to the U of A the Model Parliament of the Organization of American States (OAS). The year was 2000 and it was the first time the Model Parliament was held outside of Washington, DC. "And it's never gone back there since," says Marcie. "Washington and the American schools had had a lock on this event for years, and they weren't happy we took it away."

Lang, Lejnieks, and Lois Hole

MARCIE IS QUICK to name her favourite professors. "Drs. Lang and Lejnieks," she says. "They're both incredible gentlemen, unique in their own ways. Dr. Lejnieks was an immigrant from Latvia who settled in the USA and decided to come to Canada. He taught me political science and rescued a group of us when we needed a prof to organize a course around the OAS Model Assembly in 1999. The year we hosted the Assembly, there was a class of 30, and we were involved in every aspect of the Assembly. Newscasts were done daily by students in the NAIT journalism program, there were Internet radio broadcasts, and formal resolutions were put to the Assembly. There were 500 participants at the Shaw Conference Centre. It was awesome! Dr. Lejnieks was right by our side the whole time.

"My first class in Honours French was with Dr. Lang, a Texan who lost his drawl, went to France to teach, had a career as a wine trader, came to the U of A, and is now the dean of Arts at the University of Ottawa. I was scared in Honours French because the students were all older. He encouraged me. He taught me to use a dictionary. He pushed me gently to run for GFC. 'You have enough brains!' he told me, 'but I sure wouldn't do it myself!' Well, he and I ended up on GFC together, and we sat side by side at these huge meetings in the Council Chamber.

"When I financed my studies, it was a sure bet I would attend Convocation. It was Lois Hole's last year of Chancellor, just before she became lieutenant governor. When I crossed the stage at the Jubilee Auditorium, she gave me a big hug and a kiss on the cheek. Out there in the audience, my mom's jaw dropped. Mind you, I wasn't the only student the Chancellor

Since her interview, Marcie has given birth to two children, daughter Audrey and son Sebastian. Marcie's advice for students today is from Mark Twain: "Don't let your academics get in the way of your education."

(Private Collection)

hugged that day, but I was the first grad she knew who crossed the stage that day. Remember, my name starts with a B, beginning of the alphabet. By the time the Chancellor got to the Zs, a lot of students had been hugged."

The Foreign Service

MARCIE IS NOW on her second posting with the Canadian Foreign Service. She speaks four languages, has learned a little Tagalog from her posting in the Philippines, and is ready to learn Malay, the language of Malaysia, her current posting. And she gets plenty of practice in protocol at home. Her husband is the son of a senior-level diplomat.

"My husband Gus and I have a home in Ottawa, but two-thirds of my career in the Foreign Service will be lived outside of Canada. With an average posting of two years, we expect to be in 15 countries over the next 30 years. The only thing that's really hard about a career in the Foreign Service is that I miss the joy of watching my friends raise their children and having my daughter, Audrey, be there playing with them. We are not part of their daily lives, and I miss it. I've decided that I'll be the eccentric, crazy old aunt who sends unusual gifts from around the world. And now, with a baby of my own, she'll have lots of cousins in Canada.

"When the Foreign Service part of our lives is done, we plan to retire in Edmonton," says Marcie.

"There's something about this city. If it continues to grow, but maintains the things that make Edmonton so special—the connectedness, the community feel—this will be the place for us."

END OF THE DECADE

AS THE TURN OF THE CENTURY approached, there was only one thing on everyone's mind: would computers work at 12:01 A.M. on January 1, 2000? The problem was called Y2K—short for 'the year 2000'—and there was a world-wide scramble to ensure that computer systems were Y2K-compliant.

Computing Science Professor Jonathan Schaeffer explains why the world was so concerned: "In the beginning of the computer age," Dr. Schaeffer says, "there was not a lot of memory on computers. Today, we talk about computers with gigabytes (billions of bytes) of memory, but in the not-so-distance past, even a few kilobytes (thousands of bytes) was considered a lot! In those days, a mere 25 years ago, when people wrote programs, they took shortcuts to overcome the memory limitations."

By 1996, the Timms Centre for the Arts and the Extension Centre had been constructed (not visible in this photo) but, as can be seen in the western quadrant of this aerial, the Engineering Teaching and Learning Complex had yet to make an appearance. The 83-year-old Athabasca Annex, still standing in 1996, would be replaced in 1998 by a new building for the department of Computing Science.

(CS 1996-1515-H-49)

One shortcut involved representing dates in a computer. "Rather than store a year as the 4 characters '1967'," Dr. Schaeffer explains, "since 'all' years begin with '19,' they took the shortcut of saving only the last two digits of the year.

"Dates are used in many ways—including sorting," he says. "Thus, a date such as '97' (meaning 1997) is 'bigger' than '92' (1992). Everything works. But—when we hit the year 2000, the assumption that years began with '19' was now false. The year 2000 would be represented as '00.' Now if you sort dates, then '97' is bigger than '00'—when in reality, of course, 2000 is bigger than 1997. That is the basic idea. Programs written many, many years ago used this space-saving trick—and those programs are still in use today. And they all would do wrong things once we hit 2000."

Exactly what might go wrong? The heating system. Grading and admission systems. Personnel records. Almost every operating system in the University was not Y2K-compliant. A task force worked feverishly to ensure the campus would be in full working order as the millennium approached. There was even a plan to have university-run, back-up heating systems in place should the City of Edmonton computers go down.

On New Year's Eve 1999, everyone held their breath as the clock ticked over. January 1 arrived with all systems up and running, and the University of Alberta entered the new millennium with grades secured, and paycheques in the mail.

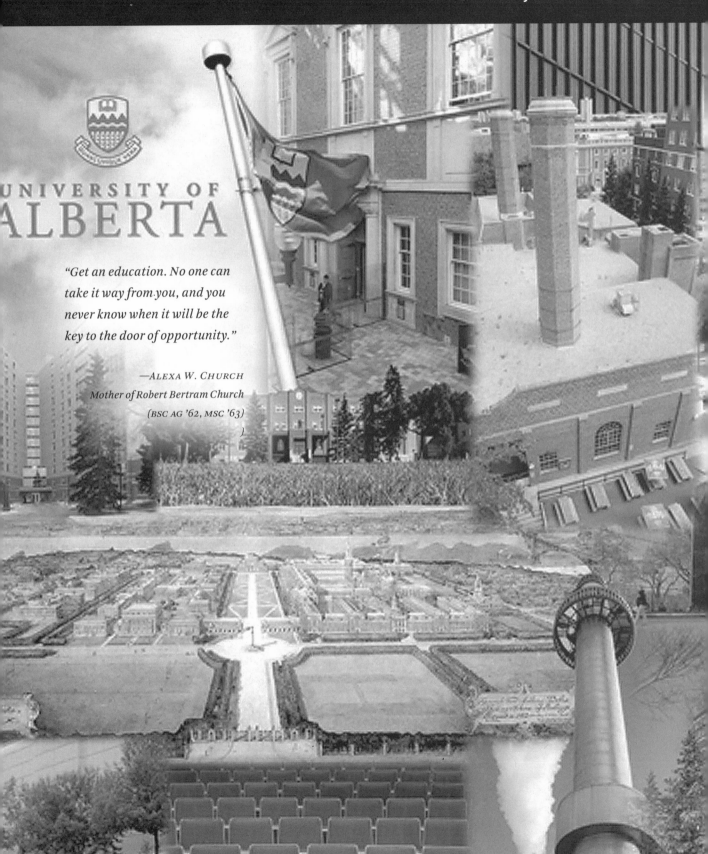

UNIVERSITY OF
ALBERTA

"Get an education. No one can take it way from you, and you never know when it will be the key to the door of opportunity."

—Alexa W. Church
Mother of Robert Bertram Church
(BSC AG '62, MSC '63)
)

Timeline

Overleaf: A collage of images chronicling the University's development and history from 1908 to 2006.

(Concept and photo selection by Darlene Stewart with images provided by Terry Nonay, Rose Litzenberger, U of A Archives, and U of A Creative Services).

Enrolment and Finance, 2000–2004

- Fall student head count: 30,990 (2000); 34,617 (2004)
- Operating budget and Access Grant from Province of Alberta: $259,822,000.00 (2000); $325,000,000.00 (2004)
- Full-load undergraduate Arts tuition: $3,770.40 (2000); $4,537.20 (2004)
- SU fees: $46.78 (Membership) + $55.18 (Dedicated) (2000); $57.22 (Membership) + $65.88 (Dedicated) (2004)

Key Dates, 2000–2004

- Revolutionary treatment of Type-1 diabetes—the Edmonton Protocol (2000)
- Pandas Hockey team begins a 110-game unbeaten streak (2001)
- University budget to be cut 4.4% over four years (2002)
- Web-based registration (Bear Tracks) launched (2002)
- First public wireless computer networks on campus (2002)
- 6.9% overall tuition increase approved and differential tuition fees to be introduced in Law, Medicine and Dentistry, and Business (2003)
- Letter grades and four-point GPA system introduced (2003)
- Merger of U of A and Augustana University College (2004)

Selected Campus Buildings, 2000–2006

- Telus Centre (2000)
- New residence and Academic & Cultural Centre At FSJ (2001)
- Computing Science Centre, joined with Athabasca Hall, is opened; Department of Computing Science occupies both oldest and newest University buildings (2001)
- Foote Field (2001)
- U of A Swine Research and Technology Centre (SRTC) (2002)
- Three major engineering buildings are completed, including the Engineering Teaching and Learning Centre (ETLC) (2002–2004)
- SUB renovations are completed (2002)
- Mary Schäffer Hall and U of A Conference Centre open (2003)
- Saville Sports Centre (2004)
- International House (2004)
- Five major buildings are planned for 2005–2006, including the Alberta Heart Institute, and the Centennial Centre for Interdisciplinary Science (CCIS)
- National Institute for Nanotechnology (NINT) (2006)

Beyond Campus, 2000–2006

- 57% of undergraduates in Canada are women (2001)
- Hijacked airplanes crash into the Pentagon and World Trade Center (2001)
- Canada wins gold in both Women's and Men's Hockey at the Olympics (2002)
- The first known case of West Nile virus in Canada (2002)
- Enron, the world's largest energy-trading company, collapses (2002)
- After one cow in Northern Alberta is confirmed to have BSE (Mad Cow Disease), the US bans imports of Canadian beef (2003)
- Global SARS alert (2003)
- Massive march in Edmonton to denounce the war on Iraq (2003)
- Giant tsunami in South Asia (2004)
- Government of Alberta indicates that Bill 1 will boost the University's finances and provide tuition relief (2004)
- War in Israel and Lebanon (2006)

Robert Bertram (Bob) Church and his mother Alexa. Alexa's advice remains as sound now as it ever was: "Get an education. No one can take it way from you, and you never know when it will be the key to the door of opportunity."

(Private Collection)

GET AN EDUCATION[1]

BOB CHURCH was inducted into the Alumni Wall of Fame in 2002. He is one of a handful of alumni to receive the Distinguished Alumni Award, the Alumni Association's highest honour. The Association described him as "a scientist, entrepreneur, and gifted communicator whose research helped to provide the foundation for many molecular biology techniques commonly used today. He has gone on to play an important role in influencing public policy for the support of science and technology." On the evening of the induction ceremony, Dr. Church's 94-year-old mother Alexa was in the audience. In his speech, Bob Church quoted his mother as telling him and his siblings as they were growing up to "get an education."

"The original quote," Dr. Church says, "was from my grandfather, who had little education. He came to the banks of the Bow River in 1890 and homesteaded at Balzac in 1900 on the farm I grew up on. The quote was the guide my mother and father brought all of us up under. There were five of us and we all have university degrees. Gordon has a BSc from the U of A, Beverly a BSc Nu from the U of A, Stan has an LLD—also from the U of A—and Mabel a BEd from the U of C. All of us are involved in farming and ranching today.

"My mother, Alexa W. Church, was born in 1907 on a farm east of Airdrie, homesteaded by A.D. and G. Black in 1904. Mother graduated from Normal School—now the University of Calgary's Faculty of Education— in the class of 1926. She is still active and living alone at her farmhouse at Balzac at 96 years of age. The night I was inducted into the Alumni Wall of Fame, I wanted to pay tribute to my mother and her generation for their foresight, from which I benefited so much. That is why I quoted her."

Get an education. Alexa Church's words have been a touchstone for three generations of Albertans, and will be for generations to come.

MEET STUDENTS FROM THE CENTENARY CLASS[2]

ON MAY 9, 2006, the University of Alberta marked 100 years since its founding. Known as Founder's Day, or Charter Day, this date marks the birth of the University of Alberta as an incorporated legal entity. On September 23, 2008, the University will celebrate another birthday—100 years will have passed since the first classes were held at the Duggan Street School (now Queen Alexandra) in today's Old Strathcona.

Meet eight students who will graduate as the University celebrates its 100-year history. The undergraduates you are about to meet are all enrolled in one of the University's original degree programs, offered under the auspices of the Faculty of Arts and Science in 1908.

Junaid Jahangir
(CLASS OF 2007, CANDIDATE FOR PHD IN ECONOMICS)

JUNAID WILL GRADUATE in 2007, 101 years since the University's founding. He is one of about 2,200 international students enrolled at the

University of Alberta. International students are a small but special group at the U of A. These students bring with them different life experiences, languages, cultures, and viewpoints, and they help everyone on campus see beyond Canada's borders. With a total enrolment of nearly 35,000 graduate and undergraduate students, international students represent just 6% of the student population, but they help create a diversity that enriches campus life.

Junaid was born in Pakistan and raised in Dubai, on the Persian Gulf. The Web describes Dubai as embracing "everything from rugged mountains and awe-inspiring sand dunes to sandy beaches and lush green parks, from dusty villages to luxurious residential districts and from ancient houses with windtowers to ultra-modern shopping malls....[It's] both a dynamic international business centre and a laid-back tourist escape; a city where the sophistication of the 21st century walks hand in hand with the simplicity of a bygone era. [It's] a cosmopolitan society with an international lifestyle, yet with a culture deeply rooted in the Islamic traditions of Arabia."[3]

Junaid's eyes sparkle as he relates, in flowing English with a slight British accent, what it was like to come to Edmonton from the warmth of the Persian Gulf. "Snow? I never saw snow in my life. One day I pulled back the curtain in my room in the HUB mall residence and there it was falling. Tiny pieces of snow, falling from the sky. I thought 'Jingle bells. Jingle bells.'"

Choosing the U of A and First Impressions

"FOR ME AND MY HIGH SCHOOL FRIENDS," explains Junaid, "university was simply the thing to do—it was the norm. I did my undergraduate degree in my home country of Pakistan, where a three-year undergraduate degree is the standard. When it came time to think about graduate school, I applied all over the place, but only to the best—in England, the USA and Canada. I knew the American universities would never accept a three-year degree, but I applied anyway. I was accepted by universities in England but they offered no financial support, so they were out. In Canada, I applied equally to the best universities in the east and the west and I chose the U of A in large part because there were normal Teaching Assistant (TA) duties and nothing more. The other university I considered required that you teach a course. But I knew that, at first, I would need to focus on my studies, in a very concentrated way, before teaching others. So having just TA duties—instead of total responsibility for a class—was a big factor for me.

"I knew Canada from the movies," Junaid says, "and I thought that Edmonton would be at the North Pole—frozen, and with layers of snow. I was warned never to touch metal or else my hand would freeze to the metal and never come off." Junaid arrived in Canada in August 2000, with a winter jacket on, and expecting the worst in weather. "But," he says, "it was sunny!"

When Junaid first touched down in Canada—in Calgary—he thought he had lost his luggage. "I was frantic. Then I saw this lady in a white cowboy hat, and she took me all over the airport looking for my bags. By the time we found them, I had missed my flight to Edmonton and I got worried all over again—this time because I thought I would have to pay for a second airfare. The woman in the white cowboy hat assured me that I would not have to re-pay for the flight, and she put me on to the next plane to Edmonton."

Junaid was all alone for his first few days in Edmonton. No one met him at the airport. "There was a sea of white faces. I knew no one. I was ready to take a cab when someone told me the shuttle was cheaper. I had pre-booked a room in HUB but as a failsafe, I also booked into Lister Hall for the first two days. I was in a small, dark room. It was so lonely and I was homesick. I missed my family, especially my grandmother. So I called home on a Telus card. Sometimes I wish I had never called home that first night because it made me so sad. I felt utter despair. I cried all night."

To make things worse, Junaid hadn't eaten for two days.

"I am Muslim and there wasn't much I could eat on the plane or in Lister. I walked across the street to the Mac store and the owner said, 'Have a muffin.' I had no idea what a muffin was. The man held up a muffin and said to me: *this is a muffin*. That muffin was my first real food in Canada." Soon after, Junaid met a taxi driver who took him around to places like Debaji's market and Parkallen Restaurant, and Junaid finally found places where he could buy food he was able to eat.

"I worked like a dog in my first few weeks," says Junaid. "I had come too far to fail. I had expectations for myself and so did my family and friends. I had to succeed. That very first week, I was waiting to meet the teacher I had come to study with, Professor Chantale LaCasse. Professor LaCasse is a specialist in microeconomics, and my dissertation topic involves electricity and market deregulation. As soon as I met her, I knew I had made the right choice. She was thorough, precise, and crystal clear. I learned how to split hairs with her. I questioned constantly, relentlessly. One day, she called me in and told me it was time that I started answering some of those questions myself. This was something of a shock, and she and I talked about that. This conversation transformed me. It made me a better person. It made me learn how to be a teacher myself."

Junaid soon found his first friendship group—the staff in the Department of Economics. "I had emailed back and forth with the staff in my Department," explains Junaid, "but of course I had never met or seen them." The first day I went to the Tory Building, I saw this woman at the water fountain, and I greeted her very formally, as would be proper in my country, by calling her 'Ma'am.' She looked up at me from the water fountain with a big smile and said, 'You don't need to call me Ma'am. Just call me Louise.' She pronounced her name a couple times so that I would get it right. Gradually, I got her name right. She was very patient. Louise is one smart lady!"

Louise Edwards, the Administrative Professional Officer in Economics, immediately put Junaid at ease, as did the main office staff—Charlene Hill, Margaret Howell, and Leslie Wayne. Junaid remembers Leslie as a "tall, fine woman with long hair and a wonderful smile. When I first walked in to her office, she looked up and immediately said, 'You must be Junaid!' It was a wonderful feeling—someone knew me, someone was expecting me. I found I could ask her anything and I peppered her with questions—where could I buy furniture? Where should I shop? I would grill her and she answered all my questions. It is very sad to me that Leslie has since passed away, but when I convocate in 2007, I want to have Louise, Charlene, and Margaret at the ceremony."

Junaid found another friendship group through his love for literature. "I enjoy the kind of fiction where the author constructs a totally different world—*Alice in Wonderland*, *Harry Potter* and *Lord of the Rings* are favourites, and I love Shakespeare. I found out that students in the English Department put on Shakespearian plays, and so I went to the audition.

They were casting men in female roles and *vice versa*. So in the next production, I might just be playing Maria, the servant girl, in *Twelfth Night*," Junaid says. "I love these plays, and the English students are always doing something a shade naughty with them, like the role reversal in *Twelfth Night*. Great fun."

The U of A also opened another door for Junaid. "I did my first-ever volunteering last year, and I found out how much fun that can be, and how rewarding it is. I met so many people. Then I started looking for a part-time job and discovered the Graduate Students' Association (GSA), where I could have both things rolled into one—a part-time job and that sense of contributing as a volunteer. Volunteer *and* get a pay cheque! That's the GSA. I'm their vice-president (finance and administration). Alexis, Tanya, Peter, Ashim—these are my fellow executive members. Whatever worries I may have, no matter who may be mean to me in any one day, I can always go to my friends at the GSA for advice and help. Whatever worries I have, they disappear. My GSA colleagues are my sounding board. When I am down, they cheer me up. These people are my family in Canada."

What the Future Holds

"MY HOMELAND of Pakistan is a time bomb," he says. "And there, I am a fish out of water. I am too liberal for the place I come from. There, you must conform. But, here, in Canada, you can be your own person. I hope to become a Canadian citizen. I might go into the private sector, like my teacher and mentor Professor LaCasse. Or I might teach. I would like to be a wise teacher like Gandalf in *The Hobbit* and *The Lord of the Rings*, or Dumbledore in the *Harry Potter* series. I like teaching and I think that if you can inspire students—like the professor in the movie *Dead Poet's Society*—that is very special indeed."

Becky Porcina (CLASS OF 2008, CANDIDATE FOR BSC)

BECKY PORCINA is part of the "Pisesky clan." Her grandfather is a 1955 graduate in Medicine, and her mother, Cheryl Pisesky Porcina, graduated from Pharmacy in 1977. Uncle Brian holds a BSc and a DDS degree ('79 and '82), and Uncle Wayne graduated from Medicine in 1976.

Becky's brother and three cousins are also students at the U of A—Kate is in engineering, Chris is in Science, and Cassandra in Dentistry. As

Becky puts it, "I didn't have to buy any textbooks!" And her brother Rob, a third-year Genetics student, helped Becky pick her courses and professors. "We're close," she says. "He's always there for me."

For Becky, "University was always something I knew I would do. I wanted to further my education, but I wanted to be close to home. I grew up hearing about the University of Alberta from my family, so the U of A was a natural choice. The U of A is a hard university to get into—I knew it was good."

A year ago, Becky was leaning towards an Arts degree, but, by summer, she had decided on science. "The arts come pretty naturally to me," she explains. "I love music, and I love to dance, especially ballet—I could never stop dancing. I live at home, and study in the dining room where the piano is. For a break, I play my favourite pieces. Fashion intrigues me, and in high school I organized two fashion shows—a huge amount of work. I'm crazy about shoes and work four hours a week in a shoe store to feed the habit. I love interior decorating. So I've always been the 'artsy' type. But I also love science, and like to see immediate results. I'm good with numbers and I like learning things in sequence. I felt that science would open doors for me."

Registration and Tuition

"REGISTRATION only took me half an hour," Becky says, "and this is how it worked. In my acceptance letter, it was suggested that I take certain courses, and I was given a password. I signed on to the Web and used a program called BearScat to register. Bear Scat is a computer program written by a U of A student, Stephen Kirkham, and it makes the University's registration program—Bear Tracks—easier to use.

"The first course I wanted was Chemistry 101. Bear Scat showed me every section of Chem 101, the prof., the time, and the place. You just pick the section you want, click 'open' and that's it. You're registered. Then I moved on to select a Biology class—and if I picked a section that conflicted with any class I already registered in, that class would appear in red on my schedule, telling me I had double-booked myself, and the computer also won't let you register in the wrong lab. Changes are very easy to make, and I made a lot of changes.

"One great feature of on-line registration is that a campus map pops up as you register for each course, showing exactly where that section is taught, so you can judge whether or not you can make it from class to class on time. There's only 10 minutes to get from one course to another, and I'm usually late for English because the Humanities Centre is pretty far from the science and engineering buildings where most of my classes are.

"My tuition is about $5,000, and my parents always put aside money for it, so I'm lucky that I don't have any student loans. And when I graduated from high school, my nana gave me money for books. My Nana also provides me with my favourite study food—perogies. I keep a stash in a basket in the freezer. They are the lightest, most delicious perogies you could imagne."

First Impressions and Favourite Professor

"I'M A DANCER," says Becky, "and spent many a day in SUB as a young girl, participating in dance competitions. In a way, I grew up in SUB. I'm very comfortable there and now that I'm in university, SUB is one of my hangouts. I also found I knew someone in every one of my science courses," says Becky. "All my junior high friends are here at the U of A, as well as the majority of my high school friends. I didn't go to orientation because I was familiar with the campus and knew that many of my friends would be here. And everyone is very friendly. The first week of classes, you can just ask anybody how to get to a certain building—so many people are new, and everyone is helpful.

"I have a lot of friends in engineering. After Chemistry class, there's a group of us who hang out in Cameron Library—we call it 'Cam'—and we eat and study together. I also have a study group for Math every Tuesday night. This gets us ready for our Wednesday math labs. And there's one guy I study with—our brains work very differently and it makes us good study partners.

"I was a little nervous at first. Except for English, where there are 30 in my class, my courses are all big, with enrolments of 200–400. You know you are pretty insignificant! But actually, even in the big classes, there is lots of interaction. The profs all put their notes on-line, so you can read those the night before class. For my Chemistry class, there are quizzes on-line and problem sets with the answers. Even some of our tests are on-line. I submit my Psychology assignments on-line, too—it's really the only way you could do it with 400 students in one class.

"All my professors are very good, but, yes, I have a favourite prof—Arthur Mar. He's my Chemistry teacher, and he is the sweetest person—and what makes him such a good prof is that he really, really wants us to learn. It comes across in class every day, and I think it makes us all relax.

"As for guys, I meet them through my friends," says Becky. "That way you don't meet any sleazeballs. I like dating university guys because they understand you have to have time to study. Tuesday night movies in SUB are great—it's like an indoor drive-in, with a huge projection screen and lots of soft seating." Becky has some tips for guys today—be a gentleman and open the door, and no swearing. "Those are my two rules for any guy I date."

What the Future Holds

"I'M NOT SURE yet what I want to do after my BSc," says Becky. Maybe something in the medical field. I want the time to learn and to think about what I want to do. It's that simple. But whatever I end up doing, I'm going to have fun doing it!"

Becky thinks that with so much course material on-line, many students rely on their textbooks and the on-line class notes, and skip lectures. Her advice to new students is simple: "Make sure you go to all your classes."

Cassie Tesche (CLASS OF 2008, CANDIDATE FOR BSC ENGG)

ON SEPTEMBER 10, 2004, Cassie crossed the stage at the Myer Horowitz Theatre in the Students' Union building to pick up a cheque. In the presence of Her Honour Lieutenant Governor Lois Hole, and with the chancellor, president, board chair, and provost presiding, Cassie received a $10,000 Dean's Citation entrance award from Engineering Dean David Lynch. From a first-year undergraduate enrolment of some 3,226, Cassie was just one of six entering students to receive this award. "It was exciting—and this means that along with other scholarships, I won't be in debt, at least for my first year. I'm so grateful to my high school Chemistry teacher for encouraging me to apply for this award."

Cassie was raised in Grimshaw, a community of some 2,700, and so the Edmonton campus of the U of A was something of a shock. "Walking down Main Street in Grimshaw you always see people you know," Cassie says. "Here, walking from class to class, you recognize one face among hundreds. My smallest class has an enrolment of 75, and my biggest is about 400. Lucky for me that in the summer of 2003, I spent six weeks on campus as part of a research team in the WISEST program—that's Women in Scholarship, Engineering, Science and Technology. Four of us from that program are now in Lister Residence together, so I've got a set of friends right off the bat." Cassie is one of about 625 women enrolled in the Faculty of Engineering, which began life at the U of A as a discipline called Applied Science sheltered within the founding Faculty of Arts and Science.

Cassie says that going to university was "drilled into my brain." There was no parental pressure; university was "just the place to go" after high school. "I checked the U of A report card on the Web because I wanted a university close to my family, but I wanted one that was right up there at the top with the big universities in central Canada. The U of A was it. Once I got here, I found the unexpected. There was a brand new building—the NREF (Natural Resources Engineering Facility)—and wow, what a bonus." The $65-million, nine-storey structure opened on October 1, 2003 and houses over 100 research labs for civil and environmental engineers.

First Impressions and Favourite Professor

"YOU BET," Cassie says, "I have a favourite professor after just one month—Alfred Dorey. He's energetic and fun. That matters a lot when you have so much material to cover. He tells us stories that relate directly to what we are studying. He has this book about buildings that failed, and each week he tells us one of these stories. These stories bring to life the lessons we are learning in the classroom.

"Thinking back on everything that has happened in this first month, I'd first say that registration on the Web was a snap—there were only four timetable patterns to choose from and only one optional course to fit in. The orientation here was incredible, especially the gathering of hundreds of students in Hawrelak Park. The energy of so many people yelling out their Faculty cheers was exciting, amazing—I've never experienced anything like it. If a group of engineering students shouts out their Faculty cheer, the Science students shout theirs right back, and then we yell ours back even louder":

> We are, we are, we are the engineers!
> We can, we can, demolish 40 beers!
> Drink rum, drink rum, and come along with us,
> For we don't give a damn for any damn man
> who don't give a damn for us!

Then Cassie rolls her eyes and laughs. "There is *so much homework*. It's very different from high school." Cassie's 1,700-page introductory physics textbook weighs in at about 35 pounds. That's just one required text she sometimes has to tote around in her backpack. "Think how much time there is in the term to catch up! Someone told me," she says, "that you won't get through your first year of engineering all on your own. So we study co-operatively. Sometimes you help someone else, and sometimes you're the one that needs help."

Cassie lives in the Lister Residence Complex named after the beloved first Superintendent of Residences, Reg Lister. "I like living in Lister. I'm in a single room in MacKenzie Hall, where two wings are for the girls and one wing is for the boys. I study in my room, and have a bowl of cereal here before heading to class or labs. Lunch and dinner are on my meal card, although I have now learned where the local Safeway is. There's usually something in the Lister buffet you'll like and if not, there's always pizza. Pizza will definitely get me through the year. Oh yes—there is one big change from living at home. At home I had my own bathroom, and now I share those facilities with 15 other girls."

What the Future Holds

CASSIE HAS A VERY FOCUSSED look in her eye when she explains that "math and numbers are my strong point." That would have to be so because in order to have been awarded that Dean's Citation, a student needs a minimum 95% average just to apply. But the first month hasn't been all study. "My cousin Greg," says Cassie, "is treasurer of the Agriculture Club. I went to one of their dances and it was great fun. So I went down to Red

Deer with the Ag Club to Billy Bob's. We played pool and we two-stepped the night away. My cousin Shelagh is also at the U of A, in Science, and my sister Melissa graduates soon with a BSc in Animal Biology. She took her last two courses at the Bamfield Marine Station on the west coast, a teaching and research facility run by the U of A in co-operation with four other universities. Melissa will be with me here next year when she starts her two-year after-degree BEd."

Cassie says that her sister has a passion for teaching. "Melissa wants to teach high school science. She's passionate about it. I want to feel that same kind of passion about whatever it is I choose to do in my studies and career. I think Engineering is for me, but I need some time to decide."

Cassie has a couple of tips for new students. "If you are in residence, get to know the people on your floor. They're the ones you'll be living with. And don't get behind in your studies. Keep at it. When I got behind after just two weeks, I called a friend. She said, 'Don't worry. The beginning of the semester is the best time to fall behind. Think how much time there is left in the term to catch up!' That's the attitude you need. There are a lot of people here to help you."

Karlynn Grenier

(CANDIDATE FOR HONOURS BA IN CANADIAN STUDIES, CAMPUS SAINT-JEAN)

WHEN KARLYNN GRENIER graduates in 2008, she will celebrate a double centennial. Not only will the University of Alberta turn 100 in that year, but so will Faculté Saint-Jean. And even though Faculté Saint-Jean's name has now been changed to Campus Saint-Jean, the students still refer to it fondly as "the Fac."

Karlynn grew up as part of the Francophone community of Edmonton, and she has her sights set on giving back to that community after she graduates. "Going to university has an element of personal satisfaction for me," she says, "and then there's another end result—the kind of job after graduation that will give me a lifelong satisfaction in the work I end up doing. Going to university can give me that. I don't know what my job title will be, but whatever I do, I'll be working, in French, within the Francophone community, and helping to ensure the survival of that community. Our identity is at the core of us all. We don't want to melt into the majority culture." Karlynn's statement sounds a bit like Canada wanting to maintain its identity in the face of living next door to the United States.

Karlynn is part of a strong, tightly-knit Francophone community in Alberta that was once the majority and then, with waves of immigration from Ontario from the 1880s on, became a minority. In 1892 the government of the North-West Territories passed a law that children would be schooled only in English. The restrictive language statute continued when the Territories gave birth to Alberta in 1905. The Francophone community has been fighting ever since, generation by generation, for the right to educate their children in French. No Francophone has forgotten this part of Alberta's history.

In 1908, the restrictive language law spurred the Francophone community to organize a French-language school in Pincher Creek, since this was the only way they could educate their children in their native tongue. The school moved to Edmonton in 1911, and was situated in the heart of Edmonton's Francophone community on today's 84 Avenue, Rue Marie Gaboury.

The tiny school that started life in Pincher Creek with three students now has an enrolment of 669 students from 17 countries and a teaching staff of 85. Campus Saint-Jean comprises some 15 acres with three teaching and research buildings, a conference centre, student residence, soccer fields, and a tennis/basketball court. Behind the main building is a very special spot: a grotto with a shrine to the Virgin Mary that is often visited by the public, especially the Polish community.

Lavallée

KARLYNN IS A GRADUATE OF École Maurice-Lavallée high school, the Francophone secondary school located two blocks from Campus Saint-Jean. Karlynn is careful to point out that Maurice Lavallée is a Francophone high school, and not an immersion high school. "For many immersion students who come to the Fac," she says, "French is a language to be spoken, while for Francophones, the French language is the essence of our identity. Our language was taken from us back in days of the Territorial government, and it has been a continuous fight for survival of our language, community and culture ever since. Our language is entwined with community and culture. We have a sense of urgency about its preservation."

Karlynn, like all those in Edmonton's Francophone community, grew up with Faculté Saint-Jean as a kind of community hall. "I spent my youth visiting the Fac, building snow sculptures or playing sports in the expansive fields behind the campus. Faculté Saint-Jean is part of a continuum of elements in the Francophone community that include Maurice-Lavallée and La Cité Francophone, a small mall near the Fac where there are all sorts of stores, services and community organizations that are run by and for Francophones. We all grew up in this environment. All these things are in one neighbourhood. The people at the Fac know the people at La Cité and so on. We all know each other by name. And so when it came time for university, I really didn't choose the University of Alberta. I chose the Fac. It was a natural extension of the way I grew up."

The Campus Saint-Jean fields where Karlynn played as a child embrace several acres behind the Fac's old residence—now the beautifully renovated Centre Saint-Jean—and have a sweeping view that takes in all of the campus as well as the downtown skyline. "From our location east of Old Strathcona," notes Karlynn, "we can watch Main, which is what we call the main campus. We don't call it the main campus, just Main. We have somewhat of a feeling of separateness. We call that feeling *méfiance*. In a way, we feel like the little brother campus."

First Impressions, Tuition, and Favourite Professor

"THERE ARE TWO DAYS of orientation for first-year students," explains Karlynn. For those of us at the Fac, day one is over at Main and then we are all at the Fac for day two." This is what day one at Main was like for Karlynn.

"I started to learn English when I was in Grade 4," explains Karlynn, "and there was a short period of time when me and my friends thought it was very cool to speak just in English and haul out all these interesting idiomatic expressions. But by the end of junior high we got the message— we are in the minority, and if the Francophone culture was to survive in Anglophone Alberta, we had to speak French. By junior high school, we all disciplined one another to speak only in French. I guess one of the defining moments for me was when I was part of a soccer team and we were all chattering away in French on the soccer field. The other team was of course Anglophone, and someone said to us, 'Why are you speaking in French? Aren't you Canadians?'

"So when we all got to the U of A for orientation—and *all* my Lavallée high school friends who went to university went to the Fac at the U of A—it was overwhelming. Just overwhelming. Everything was in English! There were so many people! You have to know that in my high school, there were only 53 of us in grades 7–12. We're so small. And here we are at the U of A Main, with all these people, and everyone speaking in English. I thought, 'Oh my God.' I couldn't get over it. It was culture shock. All the Fac students stuck together. We said to each other, 'OK, let's stick together.'"

And stick together they did. That first day was an other-worldly experience. "The orientation tour guide," explains Karlynn," was showing us all around campus and explaining where our classes would be. Of course, none of our classes would be on this campus. Our classes would almost all be at the Fac. But we all learned our cheers, and that pulled us all together. Our cheer was in French and here it is:

Ouais, ouais on est d'la Fac! Ouais, ouais, on est d'la Fac! On est qui?

Qui? Qui? Qui? Qui qui qui qui qui qui qui? On est d'la Fac!

"As for tuition," says Karlynn, "it's $5,200 for the year and I am financing this with the help of scholarships (Rutherford, Fellowship for Studies in French, and others) and plan to work during the four-month break to cover next 2005's tuition, which will include a 5.7% hike. One of the courses is required—English 101. It's the only course taught in English at the Fac. This is very hard for those of us for whom English is not our first language. We sort of wonder why at the Main no one has to take a course in French literature, but we have to take one in English. What's up with that? Believe me, English 101 is not easy when your whole life experience has been based in the French experience.

"So. Let me tell you about my favourite professor. His name is Charles Bellerose. He taught me my basic Canadian Studies course. He is from Québec, where Francophones are in the majority. So for him coming to Alberta, it was somewhat of a shock because he had his first experience with Francophones being in the minority. He constantly questioned everything we had grown up with. 'Why did we do *this*,' he would ask. We'd say 'To survive.' Then he would ask, 'Why did we do *that*?' 'To survive,' we'd say. He made me re-think everything. And I could watch the whole class learning along with him. The Francophones learned to re-think their given environment. The Anglophones learned to re-think the history they had been taught. He is intense and vocal. He criticizes things in a way that is very positive. He shared himself with the class and we learned from him what it was like to come from a Francophone community that was the majority to a Francophone community that was a minority. He made us think about the way we are."

Daily Life at the Fac

KARLYNN LIVES in north Edmonton, a good 35-minute drive from the Faculté Saint-Jean campus. Many of her fellow students drive from afar to attend the Fac. They come from Legal and Spruce Grove and even Falher. "I live at home," says Karlynn, "and I am at the 'Fac' by 8 A.M. I study and go to class here. There are few distractions—we have two foosball tables, and ping-pong, and not much else. Students hang out at the newly renovated Salon des Etudiants. There are lots of tables and chairs and sofas. Students move the sofas around so they can sleep or study or whatever—it's like a living room, and there is always French music playing.

"But the food is awful. It's supplied by the company that services the U of A. No one can afford the sandwiches and the hot food is awful. I hear that at Saint Joseph's College there's a chef who prepares homemade meals daily and even packs specially-made lunches in brown paper bags with a student's name written on them—that's food with love! We'd like some of that here. Remember—we are small, and there is no Subway at the Fac, or other outside supplier, so we are captive to what the University offers us.

"You're such a number at the U of A," says Karlynn. "But at the Fac you will find a place where everyone knows your name. We all know our profs and they know us. You actually know the name of the dean and he knows you. We think our dean is a great guy. It's a part of daily life for us to talk to Dean Arnal in the hallway. *C'est normale.* This is a way of life at the Fac. And if you want to know one interesting fact about our campus, it centres on the 'daridon.' This is a little house-like building on campus where I heard that the nuns used to study. Now it's a locale for offices with profs. There's an underground tunnel attached to this house. We all wonder where it leads. To the priests' dorms? We just don't know."

What the Future Holds

"I THINK I WILL GET a Master's degree after graduation," says Karlynn. "Right now I want to assess what the University has to offer and go from there. My parents are very supportive—although they would like to know now what it is I want to do after graduation—but I need some time to decide."

Karlynn has some straightforward advice to students coming to the Fac. "Be aware that there are cultural differences here," she says. "There needs to be an awareness on both sides about what it means to be born and bred as an Anglophone or as a Francophone in Alberta. We have this history. You must be aware of it. And once you are here, you must know that you are not a number. You are part of a community."

Saleem al-Nuaimi (CLASS OF 2008, CANDIDATE FOR BSC)

EDMONTON-BORN and raised, Saleem has definite ideas about where he's headed. "Going to university," he says, "is the cornerstone of life with respect to character change and maturation as a person. In high school you screw around and live in relatively isolated conditions. I heard someone say that at university, the world is writ small. University is a microcosm of the world. Right out of high school is the time of life to take advantage of that."

Saleem is a Dean's Citation award winner, which means he attained a minimum 95% average in high school. "I sweated out every exam in high school to attain this average, and even at that, you are only part of the applicant pool, so I'm grateful to have been selected.

"I wanted to be close to home, but I also wanted the best," says Saleem. "The U of A is recognized around the globe, especially in Chemistry, which is my father's discipline—and my older brother is currently in Chemical Engineering. I think that at the U of A, you are getting what you paid for. Anyone can learn, but to take what you learn and to transform that knowledge—to analyze and synthesize it—you need great teachers who are world-class researchers. My high school history teacher told us that during the late 1800s and early 1900s, students at Oxford and Harvard were told to head to Germany for a *real* education. That's the kind of education I want, and that's why I chose the U of A.

"And in grade 11, I was part of the WISEST program—Women in Scholarship, Engineering, Science and Technology—and yes, men are part of the group too. Dr. Margaret-Ann Armour, who basically runs the group, is awesome. She makes you understand how great science is on a world scale, away from the stereotyped basement labs.

"I love biology—you learn how and why things work. Once you learn about the environment around you, you can then tie that knowledge to beliefs and systems, and you can see the social applications. Religion and philosophy are more subjective, and you need to learn and think about these subjects because they open your eyes, but these are disciplines I think I can learn on the side. I am a very religious person, and so these subjects are very important to me. I also find the interrelation between science and the arts fascinating. Take English. I used to think it was boring until my high school English teacher, Mrs. Pawluk, got us into Shakespeare and Greek tragedy. This gets you into the philosophical realm, and you can delve deeply into this. With the sciences, you have limits."

First Impressions and Favourite Professor

"SO MANY PEOPLE! That was my first impression. My smallest class is Statistics—100 people. My other classes all have around 450 students. And everywhere, especially when you are standing in all the line-ups, you run into people you knew from elementary school. Everyone ends up at the U of A.

"My other first impression, after just a month on campus, concerns the Chemistry 161 labs. These are organic chemistry labs and they are super hard—everyone fears them. They are full of crazy guys—pre-Med students. All my first year professors have been great, but I have one professor for organic chemistry who is awesome—Ed Blackburn. He cracks jokes and lightens up the lectures. His outlines are simple and understandable. He takes a boring subject and turns it into something you can understand from an every-day point of view. We have a really thick textbook, and he basically tells us that, if you bought the textbook, use it for your workout. It's the *lectures* we learn from. Dr. Blackburn eases up a little on the week-ends and tells us to hit the Ship—which just means to relax. He's great."

Saleem has a strong track record as a volunteer. "I love to volunteer," he says. "St. John Ambulance, Life for Relief and Development—where we adopted a city in Iraq to rebuild—Capital Care—where we visit older folks who are sick—these are very rewarding involvements. I am also active with the University's Muslim Students' Association. I like to chill in the Meditation Room and talk about philosophy and religion. There are also other religious groups who share the Meditation Room, and it is very rewarding to talk to some of these guys in order to express and discuss our various beliefs and values. The other serious hangout is in Mechanical Engineering, but it's hard to find."

What the Future Holds

"YOU ADOPT A PLAN, then you change the plan." That sums up Saleem's view of his next four years. "There are so many opportunities here. You have to work hard to take advantage of everything that's offered. The key thing is that there is this one ultimate truth in your life, this one goal, but there are many pathways to this goal. You can't be narrow-minded or afraid of changing your pathway to attain this goal.

"By the time I graduate, I hope to be more open-minded. I like the challenge of good and respectful dialogue, especially when it comes to talking about religion and politics. You talk and argue back and forth, and find loopholes in each other's positions. That changes both people engaged in the dialogue. As for what I might do after my BSc, I might try politics."

Saleem maintains that in high school, most kids hang out with their friends. "But in university," he says, "the name of the game is to get involved."

William Davis (CLASS OF 2008, CANDIDATE FOR BA)

WILLIAM IS A NATIVE Edmontonian and a Dean's Citation winner for whom not going to university "was never an option." He says that "in high school you learn how to learn. But in university, they teach you."

William's father came from a farm background and went to university, but his classes all had enrolments of 200 and over. It was too much. "For me, though," says William, "university was always expected."

William also has two older brothers in the post-secondary system. One is at Concordia studying for the ministry, and the other is at the U of A in a combined Bachelor of Music/Bachelor of Education program. So the way has been paved.

William lives at home and studies there, side-by-side with his girl-friend, who is in Honours English. "HUB is too noisy and the Library is too quiet. Home's just right," he says. When it's time for class, William commutes by LRT from Clareview to campus. "The U of A is only a train ride away," says William, "and someone told me that it doesn't matter where you do your undergraduate work. But what I liked about the U of A were all the breakthroughs in science and technology I read about in the news." What William was reading about were discoveries like the islet transplant breakthrough led by James Shapiro, which opens the way for a cure for diabetes. At the same time, Linda Pilarski's work in nanobi-ology—a way to attack cancer cells—was making news. And BioMS was posting promising results with its drug to slow the progress of multiple sclerosis.

So why the Faculty of Arts when William is so interested in science and technology?

"I took sciences in high school," he says, "and felt that I conquered these subjects. But I didn't *like* them. I found them boring and tedious, and there was no future in them for me. I didn't want to spend my life in a white lab coat. With science, there's that sense that you will be stuck your whole life in the one specific job you got the degree for. And an Arts degree? Some people say you won't get a job. But look at the world around you. It's not made up entirely of science-heavy jobs. An Arts degree will give me flexibility.

"Besides, when I go for a long walk, it's not science I think about. I like the deeper thinking that comes with the study of subjects like religion and philosophy."

William is keeping his options open by taking the prerequisite course needed to enter the Faculty of Business. His Philosophy and Religion courses—the ones he likes best—are rounded out with Economics, English, Mathematics, and Statistics.

First Impressions and Best Hangout

"MY GIRLFRIEND is a year older than me," explains William, "and so I was on campus in my senior year of high school. What stands out for me is lunch in HUB and what a sea of people there are, all with huge back-packs, and all looking ahead, so intently. If you're not fast enough to get out of their way, you'll be run over. It's such a contrast to high school, where the halls are often empty. And most of my classes are big—200–300 in Mathematics, Philosophy and Economics, but only 30 in English."

"Then there's the bookstore. The line-ups are one-and-a-half hours long. There are just so many people. That's my enduring first impression. I also saw people in these line-ups that I knew from earlier school days but whom I hadn't seen for years. It seems as though everyone from your past goes to the U of A.

"I joined the jazz band," says William. "I'm the third trumpet. And believe it or not, this is a class! For credit! It's actually a class offered jointly by the U of A and Grant MacEwan Community College. There are classes plus two rehearsals a week and it is very intense. This was a big next step for me. I was in a high school band. This is very different."

William is quick to name his favourite hangout—"I like the couches in SUB."

What the Future Holds

"I HOPE I'LL BE SMARTER by the time I graduate in 2008. I like philosophy and religion because they make you think deeply and speak articulately. You *explain* concepts, you don't just memorize them.

"Maybe I'll go into Law or maybe I'll end up at the United Nations. Maybe graduate school. You can never get enough education."

William has a little advice for new students. "When you are in high school and looking ahead towards university, it's scary," says William. "The profs are scary, the classes are scary. But when you get here, it's exciting. It's your choice. You'll like it better than high school."

Andrea Martinson

(CLASS OF 2008, CANDIDATE FOR BSC, AUGUSTANA FACULTY)

ANDREA'S CLASS will go down in history for two reasons. Not only is she part of the 100th graduating class of the University of Alberta, she is in the first entering class of one of the U of A's newest faculties—Augustana Faculty, which has a history as long as that of the University of Alberta itself.

Norwegian agricultural settlers from Minnesota arrived in Alberta near Camrose in 1894 and, at the same time, in Norway, a Reverend Anderson planned to move some of his parishioners to the area today known as Camrose. Soon after, the first Lutheran congregation in the Camrose area was organized, attracting more settlers. Camrose soon emerged "as the major Norwegian community and cultural centre in north-central Alberta."[4]

As for Augustana Faculty, it began life in 1910 as a college organized by the Alberta Norwegian Lutheran College Association. Throughout its history, it has been known for the quality of its teaching, for its focus on the development of the whole person, and for extending beyond the intellect to the "heart and its affections."[5] Augustana University College began an affiliation with the University of Alberta in 1959, offered second-year transfer programs by 1969, became a degree-granting University College in 1985 by an Act of the provincial legislature, and in 2004 merged with the University of Alberta to become Augustana Faculty.

Coming to Augustana is quite special. First, you are out in the country. The wind blows stronger out here, and everyone smiles at you and says "Hi." Parking is easy. There are no classes at lunch hour on Tuesdays and Thursdays, and on other days, there is still time set aside just to stop and eat at the noon hour. That means almost everyone gathers at the cafeteria for lunch—homemade macaroni and cheese, sausages, salads and fruit, bread and butter. If you can't make it to the cafeteria, there'll be a brown-bagged lunch waiting for you.

Augustana University College

ANDREA DIDN'T CHOOSE the U of A—she chose Augustana University College. At the time Andrea was deciding where to go to university, Augustana was an independent post-secondary institution, separate from the U of A.

"I was born and raised in New Norway, a town of about 250 located about 20 minutes from Camrose," explains Andrea. "My graduating class numbered just 26, and 17 of us were together from kindergarten through to Grade 12. Eight of us went on to Augustana. And at Augustana, well, you come here and you know people, or at least you recognize them. Lots of us are from small towns in the area, but there also lots of students from other parts of the province. It makes for a very friendly community with a home-town feel to it.

"I was on the U of A campus just once, and also checked out U of C. They blew me away. I couldn't imagine going to either one. They're so big.

My mother says that when she was at the U of A, students had to *run* to get to their next class in the allotted ten minutes. Here, everything is close at hand. That's what I want."

What does the merger with the U of A mean to Augustana students? "We don't talk about it much. It still seems like Augustana to us. But we hope this merger will mean more modern space for us, and we look forward to the capital improvements." In fact, with the merger, $12 million dollars have been committed by the provincial government for new buildings—including a new student centre—and upgrading for many parts of the Augustana campus.

Andrea is the third in her family to go to Augustana, and so she has role models in her older brother and sister. "I decided to go to university because I want a decent-paying job," says Andrea, "and I know a decent-paying job means a university education. It's that simple. And I decided on Augustana because I wanted to play basketball, and this was my best shot, and I wanted to be close to home but yet have independence. So my parents, who are both U of A education grads, bought a house in Camrose, and a group us rent the house from them. So I am close to home, but yet have my own place. It's perfect."

Andrea says she knew from the time she was in high school that she wanted to focus on biology. "But I am torn," she says. "I love English. So I will see what it is I end up doing."

Registration and Orientation

THE AUGUSTANA CAMPUS wasn't new to Andrea. "I had been here for tours while in high school so I knew where everything was. Registration was easy because I had decided what I wanted to take by the time I was in Grade 12. There was lots of help available, but I knew what I wanted. Once I arrived here, the lines for registration were long but they moved fast and everything was well-organized.

"There was a 'First Class Bash' for new students and then, in the residences, a scavenger hunt and a talent show." About 450 of Augustana's 1,000 students live in residences connected to campus by an old wooden bridge known as Ole's Crossing, which, unfortunately, has been slated for demolition.

"My tuition is exactly $5,650, not including books," says Andrea. I have a couple scholarships, and one of them was totally unexpected—$3,500 from the U of A. So I don't have to work during the year and don't know how I would fit that in, in any event. I hope to do some research-related work during the summer to earn money for school." At the end of Andrea's first year, she was named as one of ten Rutherford Scholars, sharing the second highest average of all Rutherford scholars.

First Impressions and Favourite Professor

"I EXPECTED AUGUSTANA to be bigger than it was, but except for one class, everything is small, like in high school—my biggest class is about 60–70 and my smallest is about 20–25. I like the small class size. And it is one reason I chose Augustana.

"And yes, I have a favourite prof after just a few months. His name is Arzu Sardarli, and he's my calculus prof. His PhD is from Azerbaijan, and he's been a teacher for about 20 years. He's Iranian, and he's very funny. He was a little hard to understand at first. But his sense of humour and jokes and stories won us all over. He explains concepts clearly, and his pace is just right—no one ever falls behind. He reviews material, and makes sure everyone is up to speed. If anyone gets behind, his door is always open."

A Typical Day

ANDREA IS ON THE BASKETBALL TEAM, and coupled with her science studies, that accounts for almost every moment in her week. "I'm up early," she says. "Seven A.M. and I am off to class. I pack a lunch and won't be home 'til late. I have labs two or three times a week and each lab is three hours. I hang out at the Faith and Life Centre, which has lots of sofas and light. I have regular basketball practice, and games every Friday night and Saturday. We are on the road every week for a game, and with a three-hour Friday lab, a Friday night game is tough. We travel all over the province by bus, and it was only last weekend that I had a chance to sleep in. Sundays are homework days. My biggest lesson in all this? Time management!"

Fun is pretty simple at Augustana. "We rollerblade and hike all the near-by trails. Sports are big here, especially hockey and basketball, and we have a lot of biathletes. There's no Students' Union Building on our campus, and so [that's] not a place to hang out. I like to go to the big open area in the Faith and Life Centre—lots of room to spread out. I hope the merger with the U of A will mean more modern buildings, and more space for students."

What the Future Holds

"I MIGHT GO TO VET SCHOOL," says Andrea, "or go into chiropractic medicine like my brother. We'll see. I also love the arts. I need time to decide." And Andrea has some advice for new students. "I am not in residence," she says, "and so my advice would be to talk to as many people as possible. Don't be shy!"

FOR STUDENTS OF THE 21st CENTURY— TWO SPECIAL MESSAGES[6]

DICK TAYLOR AND JULIET MCMASTER are two seasoned alumni who are famous in their respective fields of Physics and English. Together, they represent the Arts and the Sciences—the founding Faculty of the University of Alberta. Dick Taylor was a student here in the 1940s and Juliet McMaster in the 1950s and 1960s. Here are their stories, and their advice to the students of the 21st century.

Richard (Dick) E. Taylor

(BSC '50, MSC, '52, PHD STANFORD '62, DOCTORATE (HONORARIS CAUSA), UNIVERSITÉ DE PARIS-SUD, NOBEL PRIZE '90, LLD (HON) '91)

DICK WAS BORN in Medicine Hat, Alberta in 1929, just as the stock market crashed and the Great Depression followed. As a kid, Dick was interested in explosives, and blew three fingers off his left hand during an experiment. He heard live symphonic music for the first time just as World War II was ending—courtesy of German prisoners of war who were interned in a POW camp in the Hat.

"My father was the son of a Northern Irish carpenter and his Scottish wife who homesteaded on the Canadian prairies," says Dick. "My mother was an American, the daughter of Norwegian immigrants to the northern

United States who moved to a farm in Alberta shortly after the First World War. Higher education was highly prized in the society of a small prairie town like Medicine Hat, and I was expected to continue on to university."

By his own admission, Dick was not a great student in his early years, but he loved to read and was good at math. Holding his breath over entrance requirements, he made it in to the U of A (with the help of "talented and dedicated teachers," he says). While at the U of A, he became increasingly interested in particle physics. Dick went on to earn two degrees from the U of A, a BSc and an MSc, and then a PhD from Stanford University in California, where he later worked on the construction of SLAC—the Stanford Linear Accelerator Center. In 1990, Dick Taylor was awarded the Nobel Prize in physics.

Dick Taylor's Message

"When my classmates and I graduated in 1950," he says, "we looked forward to the last half of the 20th century. You and your classmates will experience the first half of the 21st century. Those years should be years of exploration, discovery and choices. They are likely to transform you in ways that you can only guess now. Yogi Berra, the famous baseball catcher, is well known for his many deep philosophical observations. He's the one who said, 'It ain't over till it's over,' and 'It's a case of déja vu all over again.' Yogi Berra's advice to young people was, 'When you come to a fork in the road, take it!' Believe me, you are going to encounter many forks in the road over the next few years.

"You might think that people with extraordinary accomplishments start out as extraordinary students, but in general that is not the case. Some were pretty good students, others were unusually active in extra-curricular activities (including all-night poker games in Athabasca Hall in the days when it was a residence), but most of them were quite ordinary students who did not stand out in the crowd during their time here. I had been gone from the U of A for 38 years when I came back here with a Nobel Prize, and there were still a few professors around here who remembered me. They were surprised that I won the Nobel Prize. I mean *really surprised*!

"So you should be prepared to find yourself on a list of famous alumni like Roland Michener, former governor general of Canada, speaker of the House and ambassador to India; Clarence Campbell, lawyer at the Nuremberg Trials in Germany after World War II and later president of the National Hockey League; Supreme Court Chief Justice Beverley McLachlin; and former Prime Minister Joe Clark. I think that they would say the real prize in life is all about happiness and the satisfaction that comes when you have used your talents (and maybe some good luck) to achieve a reasonable fraction of your full potential.

"Incidentally, while luck *is* an important factor in success, many people have noticed that luck is sometimes correlated with dedication and hard work. There is a famous story about a lawyer who was asked if luck had played much of a role in his life. He replied, "Yes, indeed! I've been very lucky several times; usually about 4 o'clock in the morning in the law library.

"I want to tell you a bit about your University. It's rather young as these places go, but then so is Alberta itself. Not everyone was in favour of establishing a university here in 1906—one prominent Albertan said, 'We don't need any college here at all; if we did, it would be to turn out horse doctors.' By the 1960s Alberta was doing well and for quite a few years the provincial government spent a good deal of extra money on higher education. The U of A became one of the forefront research universities in Canada. In a research university, professors are expected to advance the state of knowledge in their particular fields as well as to instruct their students. The reputations of professors depend mostly on how successfully they carry out their research, but it is often the case that the best researchers are excellent teachers. The University takes a lot of pride in the accomplishments of the faculty and you should try and become familiar with at least some of the research that's going on around here. The U of A now ranks right up there in the list of Canadian universities excelling in research. And the U of A has the highest number of award-winning teachers at any university in Canada.

"But remember that universities are institutions of higher learning, and the learning is where you come in. Your learning should range well beyond what is taught in classes. Find out what others already know—you will be surprised at how soon you can reach the finite frontiers of knowledge in some particular topic. It is true. Really. You can start contributing to new knowledge in just about any field.

"But that also means that you have to keep on learning at high speed to keep pace with the rapid advance of new technologies. Never stop learning. The education you receive here at the U of A should give you the desire and the ability to catch up and keep up with the sciences and the arts over the next 50 years.

"Concentrate on something—one of the sciences, a technology, one of the arts, law, business, politics or public service. Pick something you enjoy, get good at it, and make a difference.

"Good luck! Especially late at night at the library!"

Juliet McMaster came to the U of A with two Oxford degrees, but still the department chair asked whether she was a serious student. Today, Prof. Emerita McMaster's accolades and accomplishments include being a fellow of the Royal Society of Canada, the University's first holder of a Guggenheim Fellowship, winner of the Molson Prize in Humanities and Social Sciences, founder and General Editor of the Juvenilia Press, and internationally acclaimed author. (Private Collection)

JULIET MCMASTER

(BA AND MA, ST. ANNE'S COLLEGE, OXFORD, '59 AND '62, MA AND PHD, UNIVERSITY OF ALBERTA '62, AND '65, FRSC '80, MOLSON PRIZE 1994, FIRST UNIVERSITY CUP WINNER 1996)

JULIET MCMASTER, world-renowned specialist in the British novel, wants students of the 21st century to have it *all*. That's the "jam" of your life—the icing on the cake. She wants you to open your minds.

Juliet was born and went to school in Kenya and took her first degree at Oxford University. In 1961, she came to the U of A as a graduate teaching assistant. Four years later, she crossed the convocation stage as the first person ever awarded a PhD degree in the Faculty of Arts. Just as she crossed the stage, the dean said, "Just a minute!" Juliet thought they had found her out, and that her degree was down the drain. Instead, the dean announced to one and all that Juliet, newly minted PhD, had also won the award as Alberta Woman Athlete of the Year for her prowess in competitive fencing.

Juliet was a first, but the road to her PhD was far from smooth.

Even though Juliet is quick to say that during her career she experienced little in the way of sex discrimination, there was one notable exception.

"When I came to Canada," she has written, "I was rather proud of my Oxford degree, and thought I'd be perfectly qualified to get into a program leading to a PhD. But the head of the English Department in those days was a bachelor of the old school, who thought scorn not only of PhDs (he didn't have one, you see) but also of women. 'Are you a serious student?' he asked me, I remember. He told me that PhDs were not worth having and that he had no intention of instituting one in his department. So I gave up, and betook myself a job in the City Library. And there I might have stayed but for another turn of fate to my advantage: that old-school bachelor retired, and Henry Kreisel took over as Head of English."

Dr Kreisel invited Juliet back to the English Department to the new PhD program. Juliet got her PhD in 1965, and became an Assistant Professor in the same year, and it's been a quick climb to the top of academe ever since.

Juliet McMaster is a fellow of the Royal Society of Canada, the University's first holder of a Guggenheim Fellowship, and winner of the Molson Prize in Humanities and Social Sciences. She is the author of *Jane Austen the Novelist* and of books on Thackeray, Trollope, and Dickens, and (most recently) of *Reading the Body in the Eighteenth-Century Novel*; she is co-editor of *The Cambridge Companion to Jane Austen*, and is also the founder and general editor of the Juvenilia Press, which publishes the childhood writings of famous authors.

Juliet loves the novel. As she once told *The Edmonton Journal*, "The novel is about people, and the way they think and act and feel. You could say that all literature is about people, but it's the novel that most gets inside the mind, that delivers the texture of life."[7]

In 1996, the U of A chose Juliet as the first recipient of its most prestigious award, the University Cup, awarded for excellence in both teaching and research.

Juliet McMaster's Message

"'WHAT'S THAT THING you profs do, besides teaching?' a student once asked me. 'Err—do you mean research?' I hazarded. 'Yeah, that. Why don't you teach *us* how to do that too?'

"The assumption that research is some deep secret knowledge that we profs are doing our darnedest to keep out of the reach of our students is part of the occasional Us–Them opposition that's more or less inevitable in a situation where one group has more knowledge and power than the other. But believe me, students, we're actually doing all we can to communicate that knowledge and share that power! And you'll be the ones who will go on to create new knowledge and share it more widely.

"Learning and teaching and research are part of a continuum that we're all doing together. You learn best from good teaching, and I never learn a text so well as when I have to teach it. And research—well, that we can do together too.

"I have devoted some time to inducting students into that nirvana of research, besides offering the regular coursework in the great authors I've had the chance to teach—Chaucer and Shakespeare and Keats and Jane Austen and the Brontës and Dickens and the others. I founded a small press, the Juvenilia Press, devoted to creating scholarly editions of early writings of big-name authors (you'd be surprised how much you can learn about an author by studying what she or he wrote as a kid!); and a major aspect of the enterprise is for students to learn editing skills by working hands-on with an experienced scholar in the production of a little book. This is one example of the teamwork on campus that is going on all the time among students and professors in many faculties of the University. We really are letting you into the secrets of our trade!

"'Never leave learning till the life to come!' said Browning, wise chap. (Well, actually he said 'Never leave *growing*,' but it's the same thing, really!) And the more learning you can do while you're in university and while learning is your full-time business, the more will stay with you, and the more you can build on it. I've made teaching my full-time business, but that's also to say I've been learning all along too. Since my retirement I've been re-tooling as an art historian.

"Alice in Wonderland was offered a job in which she'd get jam every other day. 'Every other day' meant that she could never get jam *today.*

I had a dragon of an aunt, who asked me, when I was looking for a job before going up to Oxford, what I wanted to do. I told her I hoped for a job that would awaken my interest, use and extend my talents, give me new skills and new insights, and yes, pay quite well too. "The trouble with *you*, young woman,' she said severely, 'is that you want jam tomorrow *and* jam today!' I had to admit that she was right. But I can also boast that in my long and concurrent careers as student and as professor, I've managed to get a considerable and continuing allowance of jam.

"I was a Professor of English for the last 35 years of the twentieth century. But before that I was a student here too. For my years of formal education I moved around considerably: school years in Kenya, first degree at Oxford, a graduate year in a women's college in Massachusetts, and then an MA and PhD at the University of Alberta.

"And here I've stayed, physically speaking. But the mind is its own place, and intellectually the world is my oyster. I have thoughts that wander through eternity. (There I go, quoting again. You can tell I'm an English prof.) My point is that your years as a student are your best chance to open your mind and to train it in ways that will last you a lifetime. Now is your time to concentrate on the *idea* itself, rather than its practical application. And the idea is liberating, where the application, as an end in itself, is simply that: an end.

"In my long time at the U of A, I remember good old days, and bad old days, and I like to sort them out. In the bad old days when I arrived, a woman student could expect to get a lower mark than a male student with the same set of answers (I remember one professor who was notorious for this); women professors in the higher ranks were a rarity; there was no such thing as student assessments, and profs could be pretty brutal in their comments on papers, pretty tyrannical in the application of petty rules.

"But in the *good* old days students understood more fully the privilege of being here to pursue an idea for its own sake, and there was less insistence that the university provide a vocational training with an assured job at the end of it. In the good old days, too, students mostly did their university studies full-time during the session, and waited till summer for the work that paid the bills. Some bills, I know, can't be paid with only a summer job. (Another good thing about the old days was that the fees were more affordable.) But a university education isn't meant to be fitted into the gaps between working hours. It's pretty hard for your thoughts to wander through eternity in those circumstances. If at all possible, try to make your university time *full*-time.

"But whatever the circumstances, *make the most* of your university years, whether in pursuing a discipline with passion, or disputing ideas with your peers, or working in the lab, or performing drama or music, or doing student government, or just hurling frisbees in the grassy quadrangles (I never said you shouldn't have any fun!). These are your salad days, and they deserve to be memorable."

THE NEXT 100 YEARS

IN 1906, the University of Alberta existed only as a piece of legislation. In 1907, on the day Premier Rutherford's government purchased the future U of A campus, there were a barn and two crumbling outbuildings on an old farm. The University had no presence, identity, or reputation. A year later, in 1908, when President Tory opened the University's doors to 37 students, there were only four professors, one support staff member, and a librarian. The University operated from four small rented rooms in an elementary school.

On November 5, 2004, Dr. Indira Samarasekera was named the 12th president of the University of Alberta. An engineer with a passion for the arts, she will guide the University of Alberta as it moves into the 21st century. As the 2006 and 2008 centennials are celebrated, the University of Alberta is a multi-campus educational powerhouse with 119 teaching and research buildings, 35,000 students, nearly 4,900 non-academic staff, some 3,200 academic staff including sessional instructors—and a reputation around the world for excellence.

But despite all the growth, the University of Alberta is still just a community of people who live, work, teach, and learn together. We are the heirs to many: Frederick Haultain and Alexander Cameron Rutherford, founders of the University; Henry Marshall Tory; who is in a class by himself; our first students and alumni—Albert Ottewell, Jimmy Adam, Ethel Anderson, Agnes Wilson, Laurence Cairns, and Decima Robinson; and our first staff and faculty—Reg Lister, Doc Alik and Dr. Broadus, and Elizabeth Sterling Haynes.

These founders epitomized the University of Alberta's values of cooperation, achievement, excellence, daring, openness, and trustful, caring relationships. Rutherford, Tory, and the first professors and students shaped our past. Today, in turn, thousands of students, staff, alumni, and friends are shaping the present, adjusting the vector that will send the University of Alberta into the future.

That's the next story....

APPENDIX I

Presents of the University of Alberta, the Constituent Associations and the Alumni Association: 1908–2006

* = interim
** = resigned

Presidents of the University of Alberta

1908–1928
Henry Marshall Tory

1928–1936
Robert C. Wallace

1936–1941
William A.R. Kerr

1941–1950
Robert Newton

1950–1959
Andrew Stewart

1959–1969
Walter H. Johns

1969–1974
Max Wyman

1974–1979
Harry Gunning

1979–1989
Myer Horowitz

1989–1994
Paul T. Davenport

1994–1995
W. John McDonald (Acting)

1995–2005
Roderick D. Fraser

2005–
Indira Samarasekera

Chancellors of the University of Alberta

1908–1926
Charles Allan Stuart

1926–1927
Nicolas Dubois Dominic Beck

1927–1942
Alexander Cameron Rutherford

1942–1946
Frank Ford

1946–1952
George Fred McNally

1952–1958
Earle Parkhill Scarlett

1958–1964
Laurence Yeomans Cairns

1964–1970
Francis Philip Galbraith

1970–1974
Louis Armand Desrochers

1974–1978
Ronald Norman Dalby

1978–1982
Jean Beatrice Forest

1982–1986
Peter Savaryn

1986–1990
Tevie Harold Miller

1990–1994
Sandy Auld Mactaggart

1994–1998
Louis Davies Hyndman

1998–2000
Lois Elsa Hole

2000–2004
John Thomas Ferguson

2004–
Eric P. Newell

Presidents of the Students' Union

1908–1909
F. Stacey McCall

1909–1910
Joseph W. Doze

1910–1911
A.J. Law

1911–1912
Albert E. Ottewell

1912–1913
W. Davidson

1913–1914
H.G. (Paddy) Nolan

1914–1915
R.C. Jackson

1915–1916
Arthur E. White

1916–1917
Robert K. Colter** /
Katherine I. McCrimmon

1917–1918
J.H. Ogilvie

1918–1919
P.F. Morecombe

1919–1920
C. Reilly

1920–1921
A.D. McGillivary

1921–1922
H.R. Thornton

1922–1923
Robert L. Lamb

1923–1924
John A. McAllister

1924–1925
Mark R. Levey (Marshall)

1925–1926
Percy G. Davies

1926–1927
Ernest B. Wilson

1927–1928
D.J. Wesley Oke

1928–1929
Anna Wilson

1929–1930
Donald Cameron

1930–1931
A.D. Harding

1931–1932
M.E. Manning

1932–1933
Arthur Wilson

1933–1934
Hugh Arnold

1934–1935
Arthur Bierwagen

1935–1936
Edward E. Bishop

1936–1937
Bill Scott

1937–1938
Arch McEwan

1938–1939
John A. Maxwell

1939–1940
J.P. Dewis

1940–1941
Jack Neilson

1941–1942
Ron Macbeth

1942–1943
Lloyd Grisdale

1943–1944
Gerry Amerongen

1944–1945
Alf Harper

1945–1946
Ron Helmer

1946–1947
Willard (Bill) Pybus

1947–1948
George Hartling

1948–1949
Bernard J. Bowlen

1949–1950
Tevie H. Miller

1950–1951
Michael O'Byrne

1951–1952
E. Peter Lougheed

1952–1953
Edward Stack

1953–1954
W.A. Doug Burns

1954–1955
Robert J. Edgar

1955–1956
John D. Bracco
1956–1957
John N. Chappel
1957–1958
Robert F. Smith
1958–1959
Louis D. Hyndman
1959–1960
John V. Decore
1960–1961
Alex F. McCalla
1961–1962
Peter S. Hyndman
1962–1963
David E. Jenkins
1963–1964
A. Wesley Cragg
1964–1965
Francis M. Saville
1965–1966
Richard T. Price
1966–1967
Branny Schepanovich
1967–1968
Al W. Anderson
1968–1969
Marilyn Pilkington
1969–1970
David T. Leadbeater
1970–1971
Timothy J. Christian
1971–1972
Donald G. McKenzie
1972–1973
Gerald A. Riskin
1973–1974
George W. Mantor
1974–1975
Joseph G. McGhie
1975–1976
Graeme Leadbeater
1976–1977
Leonard J. Zoeteman
1977–1978
E.J. (Jay) Spark

1978–1979
Cheryl A. Hume
1979–1980
Dean L. Olmstead
1980–1981
Nolan D. Astley
1981–1982
Philip D.K. Soper
1982–1983
Robert G. Greenhill
1983–1984
Robert G. Greenhill
1984–1985
Floyd W. Hodgins
1985–1986
Mike A. Nickel
1986–1987
David S.R. Oginski
1987–1988
Timothy I. Boston
1988–1989
Paul LaGrange
1989–1990
David Tupper
1990–1991
Suresh Mustapha
1991–1992
Marc Dumouchel
1992–1993
Randy P. Boissonnault
1993–1994
Terence Filewych
1994–1995
Suzanne Scott
1995–1996
Garett Poston
1996–1997
Garett Poston
1997–1998
Stephen Curran
1998–1999
Sheamus Murphy
1999–2000
Michael Chalk
2000–2001
Leslie Church

2001–2002
Chris Samuel
2002–2003
Mike Hudema
2003–2004
Mathew D. Brechtel
2004–2005
Jordan Blatz
2005–2006
Graham Lettner
2006–
Samantha Power

**Presidents of the Graduate
Students' Association**
1959–1960
Gordon D. Williams
1960–1961
Earl R. Milton
1961–1962
Ronald Brown
1962–1963
Norman Anderson
1963–1964
Norman Anderson
1964–1965
W.T. Painter
1965–1966
Dave Grudon
1966–1967
Peter Boothroyd
1967–1968
John Towler
1968–1969
Richard Watson
1969–1970
Richard Watson** /
Robert B. Newell
1970–1971
Orman Granger
1971–1972
John Hoddinott
1972–1973
Mohammed Adam
1973–1974
Peter Flynn

1974–1975
Susan Therrin
1975–1976
Jack Girton
1976–1977
John Cherwonogrodzky
1977–1978
Jim Talbot
1978–1979
Barry Mills
1979–1980
George McCourt** /
Myron Oleskiw
1980–1981
Paul Fisher
1981–1982
Patricia Whiteley** /
Niall Shanks
1982–1983
Bob Ascah
1983–1984
Richard Jehn
1984–1985
Gary Genosko
1985–1986
Kevin Giles
1986–1987
Annette Richardson
1987–1988
Florence Glanfield
1988–1989
Dwayne Barber
1989–1990
Ken Ross
1990–1991
Stephen Downs
1991–1992
Stephen Downs
1992–1993
Steven Karp
1993–1994
Frank Coughlan
1994–1995
Kimberley Krushell
1995–1996
Jay Krushell

1996–1997
Gordon Squirell

1997–1998
Peter Cahill

1998–1999
Kimberly Speers

1999–2000
Laura Bonnett

2000–2001
Shannon McEwen

2001–2002
Brad Wuetherick

2002–2003
Lee Skallerup

2003–2004
Lee Skallerup

2004–2005
Alexis Pepin

2005–2006
Toks Bakinson

2006–
Christine Delling

Presidents of the Alumni Association

1915–1916
Albert E. Ottewell

1916–1917
William R. Howson

1917–1918
Albert E. Ottewell

1918–1919
Charles Carswell

1919–1920
William R. Howson

1920–1922
W. Dixon Craig

1922–1923
J.D.O. Mothersill

1923–1924
D.J. Teviotdale

1924–1926
John T. Jones

1926–1927
Stella E. Russell (Ruttan)

1927–1928
Albert E. Ottewell

1928–1929
Alan B. Harvey

1929–1930
W. Fulton Gillespie

1930–1931
Laurence Y. Cairns

1931–1932
George D. Misener

1932–1933
Henry A. Dyde

1933–1934
J.R. Drysdale

1934–1935
Roy C. Jackson

1935–1936
Henry J. Wilson

1936–1938
Francis S. McCall

1938–1940
Robert H. Dobson

1940–1944
G. Brown Sanford

1944–1946
Hugh J. MacDonald

1946–1949
William H. Swift

1949–1950
Barclay W. Pitfield

1950–1953
C. Angus McGugan

1953–1954
William H. Swift

1954–1955
J.C. Kenneth Madsen

1955–1957
F. Rodney Pike

1957–1958
John W. Chalmers

1958–1959
Tevie H. Miller

1959–1960
Bruce A. Burgess

1960–1961
(Samuel) Robert Rogers

1961–1962
Haughton G. Thomson

1962–1963
Donald R. Stanley

1963–1964
A. Venor Calhoun

1964–1965
Donald R. Stanley

1965–1966
John E. Bradley

1966–1967
George Ross

1967–1968
Bruce C. Whittaker

1968–1969
Douglas C. Ritchie

1969–1970
C. Les Usher

1970–1971
Norman A. Lawrence

1971–1972
Constantine A. Kosowan

1972–1973
Arthur J. Anderson

1973–1974
Cyril J. McAndrews

1974–1975
Garth Fryett Q.C.

1975–1976
Wilson G. Sterling

1976–1977
Bernard S. Adler

1977–1978
Arthur M. Arbeau

1978–1979
Robert J. Edgar

1979–1980
F. Morris Flewwelling

1980–1981
W. Dave Usher

1981–1982
Jean E. Mucha

1982–1983
Frank Kozar

1983–1984
Edward R. Wachowich

1984–1985
Robert J. Heyworth

1985–1986
Burt P. Krull

1986–1987
Ken H. Christensen

1987–1988
Barbara Kozoriz

1988–1989
Reginald S. MacDonald

1989–1990
Marilou Neufeld

1990–1991
Marilyn Shortt

1991–1992
Christina A. Andrews

1992–1993
Grant H. Smith

1993–1994
Bryun W. Sigfstead

1994–1995
W. James Beckett

1995–1996
Lloyd E. Malin Q.C.

1996–1997
Maury G. Van Vliet

1997–1998
Peter J. Graham

1998–1999
Ralph B. Young

1999–2000
Lucille R. Walter

2000–2002
D. Bruce Bentley

2002–2004
Gordon E.W. Barr Q.C.

2004–2006
Dick Wilson

2006–
Heike Juergens

Presidents of Academic Staff Associations

Chairmen of the Faculty Relations Council

1938–1939
Ardrey W. Downs

1939–1940
George A. Elliott

1940–1941
William G. Hardy

1941–1942
Osman J. Walker

1942–1943
John Macdonald

1943–1944
Donald E. Cameron

1944–1945
Edward H. Boomer

1945–1946
Maxwell M. Cantor

1946–1947
Ralph F. Shaner

1947–1948
Karl A. Clark

1948–1949
Alexander J. Cook

1949–1950
John W. Gilles

1950–1951
Leroy A. Thorssen

*Presidents of the Association
of Teaching Staff of the
University of Alberta*

1951–1952
A.A. Ryan

1952–1953
Jules Tuba

1953–1954
Harold S. Baker

1954–1955
Herbert B. Collier

1955–1956
William G. Corns

1956–1957
Harold C. Melsness

1957–1958
Donald B. Robinson

1958–1959
Andrew T. Elder

*Presidents of the Association
of Academic Staff of the
University of Alberta*

1959–1960
Stewart R. Sinclair

1960–1961
Henry Kreisel

1961–1962
Donald B. Scott

1962–1963
Gordon L. Mowat

1963–1964
Grant R. Davy

1964–1965
E.K. Penikett

1965–1966
Ian Sowton

1966–1967
Edwin E. Daniel

1967–1968
Willard Allen

1968–1969
George O. Mackie** /
Donald G. Fisher

1969–1970
Warren E. Smith

1970–1971
Warren E. Smith

1971–1972
Burke M. Barker

1972–1973
Lloyd Stephens-Newsham

1973–1974
Peter Freeman

1974–1975
Grant R. Davy

1975–1976
Naomi Hersom** /
Ronald D. Bercov

1976–1977
E. Larry Eberlein

1977–1978
Ross Macnab

1978–1979
Ronald Coutts

1979–1980
Larry Milligan

1980–1981
Vembu G. Gourishankar

1981–1982
Vembu G. Gourishankar

1982–1983
Gordon Fearn

1983–1984
R. Peter Heron

1984–1985
Donald M. Richards

1985–1986
Ian Alexander Campbell

1986–1987
Jack Goldberg

1987–1988
B. J. Busch

1988–1989
John Bertie

1989–1990
James Robb

1990–1991
Frederick Van de Pitte

1991–1992
James Marino

1992–1993
C. Roderick Wilson

1993–1994
C. Roderick Wilson

1994–1995
E. Ann McDougall

1995–1996
Richard Szostak

1996–1997
William Reuben Kaufman

1997–1998
Paul Woodard

1998–1999
Wayne Renke

1999–2000
Maziar Shirvani

2000–2001
Jeanette Buckingham

2001–2002
Donald Carmichael

2002–2003
John Hoddinott

2003–2004
Gordon Swaters

2004–2005
Tom Keating

2005–2006
Kathryn Arbuckle

2006–
David C. Johnson

**Presidents of Support Staff
Associations**

*Chairmen of Branch 22 of the
Civil Service Association of
Alberta*

1947–1948
W.G. Stanton

1948–1952
Harry Gerrard

1952–1954
R.M. Scott

1954–1956
J.V. Williams

1956–1960
Les H. Rowe

1960–1961
Neil Burtch

1961–1963
C. Saunter

1963–1964
Les H. Rowe

1964–1965
Les H. Rowe** /
William Munawich

1965–1966
Les H. Rowe

1966–1967
Neil Burtch** /
William F. Noble

1967–1968
Geoffrey Panter** /
William F. Noble

1968–1969
Philip Arnold

Presidents of the Non-Academic Staff Association

1969–1970

Robert M. Scott

1970–1972

Martin Van Kessel

1972–1975

Geoffrey W. Williams

1975–1976

Dave Tomlinson

1976–1977

Horace Easy

1977–1978

Dave Tomlinson

1978–1981

Brendon O'Neill

1981–1984

Mildred Richardson

1984–1985

Brendon O'Neill

1985–1986

Kevan Warner

1986–1989

Brendon O'Neill

1989–1994

Anita Moore

1994–2002

Art Clarke

2002–

Joy Correia

– 112 –

FIRST TERM.

ENGLISH II

WEDNESDAY, JANUARY 25TH, 1911. MORNING, 9.30 TO 12.30.

1 Defoe:
   (a) Describe the type of fiction to which Defoe's novels belong, mention a few illustrations of the type before Defoe, and give the substance of the selection from Defoe included in the required reading.
   (b) Indicate Defoe's significant qualities as a novelist, and name three of his novels and three other works not in novel form.

2. Richardson:
   (a) Describe Richardson's personality, name his novels, and indicate the significance of his work in the history of English fiction.
   (b) Summarize and give your opinion of the required reading from Richardson. (Make your comments as specific as possible and try to support your opinions and expressions of preference by illustrations drawn from your reading.)

3. (a) Describe briefly the personality of each of the following authors, indicating as far as possible the contrast and differences of type afforded: Pope, Addison, Swift, Steele, Goldsmith, Johnson.
   (b) Point out any similarities of style, subject matter or point of view in the works of these authors which would warrant classifying them as a "typical eighteenth century group."

4. Pope.—Name the poem from which each of the following quotations is taken, state briefly the general nature of the poem, and explain *fully* every reference in each quotation.
   (a) "To love an altar built
       Of twelve vast French romances neatly gilt."

(b) "Yet ne'er one sprig of laurel graced these ribalds,
From slashing Bentley down to piddling Tibbalds."
(c) "All partial evil, universal good:
And spite of pride, in erring reason's spite,
One truth is clear, whatever is is right."
(d) "Those rules of old discovered, not devised
Are nature still but nature methodized."

"A needless Alexandrine ends the song."

"And praise the easy vigour of a line
Where Denham's strength and Waller's sweetness
join."

"The power of music all our hearts allow,
And what Timotheus was is Dryden now."

5. "Sir Roger at the Theatre": "The Chinese goes to
see a Play" . . . . .
(a) Name the author of each of the foregoing essays
and describe briefly the nature of the series in
which each appeared.
(b) Point out in a general way the likenesses and differences between the two essays.

6. Trace in a brief general outline the development of
the drama between the Restoration and the
appearance of Sheridan's *Rivals*.

7. Name the author and describe each of the following
briefly but with sufficient detail to show that you
have read it:
(a) The Deserted Village;
(b) The Speech on the Nabob of Arcot's Debts;
(c) London;
(d) The Vision of Mirza.

NOTES

Prologue

1. The main sources for information in this section are Ted Byfield, ed., *Alberta in the 20th Century: A Journalistic History of the Province in Thirteen Volumes,* vol. 2; Desmond Morton, *A Short History of Canada* (Toronto: McClelland and Stewart, 2001); and Don Gilmour, *Canada: A People's History, vol. 2* (Toronto: McClelland and Stewart, 2002). The advertisement quoted in the first paragraph is a composite from advertisements that appear in *People's History*, p. 12 and *Alberta in the 20th Century*, pp. 134–35. The title of this section is taken from Pat Brewster, *They Came West* (Banff: Crag and Canyon, 1979).

2. *Calgary Herald*, April 8, 1907, front page. "Between 7 o'clock in the morning and 4 o'clock in the afternoon, five trains arrived from the east conveying in all 1360 immigrants from Great Britain and Continental Europe....500 British, 400 Galicians, Austrians and Russians, 130 Poles, 210 Scandinavians and 30 Italians constituted the complete list." CPR Vice-President Whyte gave his name to Old Strathcona's Whyte Avenue.

3. *Calgary Herald,* April 10, 1907, front page.

4. Ruth Bowen, 6–3 (cited hereafter as Bowen), interviewing Perrin Baker, the minister of education in the United Farmers of Alberta government in 1921. In the 1960s and 1970s, Ruth Bowen (BA '31) interviewed many "old timers," including some of the first professors and members of the first graduating class. She was a researcher for former President Walter Johns, who wrote *A History of the University of Alberta, 1908–1969* (Edmonton: University of Alberta Press, 1981). Dr. Johns called Ms. Bowen's interviews "gems," but most of her research did not make it into his book. Her transcripts are faded and in rough draft. Some are straightforward interview transcripts and some are her own creative work, in the form of draft short stories, with quotes from interviews woven throughout. Ms. Bowen, as far as I can tell, never polished this work as she did with so many of the columns she wrote for *The Edmonton Journal*. When I found it hard to distinguish between Ms. Bowen's voice and the words of her interview subject, I made the best guess as to who was speaking, making editorial changes to quotations so that they made sense. Many quotations from the Bowen interviews are gently edited by, for instance, changing tense and eliminating ellipses.

Ms. Bowen's research is stored in the University of Alberta Archives as UAA 79–112 MG in a succession of numbered file folders. In subsequent references to her work, citations have two numbers. The first is the file number and the second is the page number within the actual file folder. In some instances, an entire file is cited and, if so, that will be indicated.

5. Bowen, 1–1. Winnifred Hyssop of Lethbridge was the first woman to register.

6. This quotation relates to the Calgary-to-Edmonton ox cart trip taken by Phillip Ottewell and is described in "The Androssen Unifarm," *Cherished Memories* (Calgary: D.W. Friesen and Sons, 1972), p. 157. *Cherished Memories*, pp. 566–83, includes short histories of the Ottewell family. The "Slat seats" quote is Agnes Wilson in Bowen, 15–2.

7. Agnes Wilson lived her married life in the United States, where she raised her two children. She returned to Edmonton following the death of her husband.

8. Bowen, 11–11, interviewing former Provost MacEachran. Information concerning the eulogy is from Reverend Douglas Carr, son of A.L. Carr, given orally to the author, 2003.

9. "Normal School" is a term defined in Byfield, *Alberta in the 20th Century*, p. 293. The source of this curious term for a teachers' college was the *École Normale Supérieure*, established in Paris in 1794 to be a model (or norm) for other teacher training schools.

10. The class photo is in Johns, *History*, p. 114*ff*. Other information about Mr. Ottewell comes from the City of Edmonton Archives file on the Ottewell family (which includes *Cherished Memories*) and from articles and obituaries in the *Edmonton Bulletin* and *The Edmonton Journal*. The quotation about the Riel rebellion comes from the Edmonton archives files, a history of R.P. Ottewell, p. 2, prepared for Fort Edmonton Park, where the original Ottewell log cabin stands. There is information about Mr. Ottewell and his role in Extension in David and Peggy Leighton, *Artists, Builders and Dreamers: 50 Years at the Banff School* (Toronto: McClelland and Stewart, 1982), chapter 1. University Calendars, *Gateways*, and convocation programs were also consulted. Also see *New Trail*, October, 1946, for J.M. MacEachran's eulogy for A.E. Ottewell.

11. Bowen, 15–1. Agnes Kathleen Wilson tells the story of immigrants, the railroad, and the Edmonton–Strathcona rivalry,

as do many professional authors, including Tony Cashman, *The Best Edmonton Stories* (Edmonton: Hurtig, 1976), "Edmonton Gets on the Railroad." The railroad story is also in Dennis Person and Carin Routledge, *Edmonton: Portrait of a City* (Toronto: McClelland and Stewart, 1981). Also see Byfield, *Alberta in the 20th Century*, pp. 144 *ff*.

12. Orally from Hugh Morrison, 2000. Hugh's father, Judge Frederick Augustus Morrison, was the equivalent of mayor in Vegreville, the first person to hold this position.

13. Person and Routledge, *Portrait*, p. 28. Dr. Cecil Burgess remembers taking the ferry when he was a new professor at the U of A in 1913. Also in Bowen, 15-1.

14. Bowen, 15-1. Speech by Agnes Wilson to the University Women's Club.

15. Bowen, file 1, pp. 1–2, Agnes Wilson's speech to the University Women's Club. Also see Ken Tingley, ed., *The Best of the Strathcona Plaindealer 1977–1998* (Edmonton: Pioneer Press, 1999); "South Edmonton Was Cheated," by Charles Denney, *Strathcona Plaindealer*, Winter, 1991, pp. 29 *ff*. Denny's short account keeps you on the edge of your seat.

In Jac Macdonald's *Historic Edmonton: An Architectural and Pictorial Guide* (Edmonton: Lone Pine Publishing and *The Edmonton Journal*, 1987), the point is made that within a month of the show-down, despite the satellite office approved for Strathcona, it was Edmonton that really won, as tenders were put out for a new Land Titles Building, the edifice that still stands at 106 Street and 101 Avenue, p. 28. The term "Twin Cities" was used in the Tingley, *Best of Strathcona Plaindealer*, although Edmonton and Strathcona were still truly towns, not cities.

16. Byfield, *Alberta in the 20th Century*, pp. 16–17, and *Gilmour, People's History*, pp. 21–22.

17. Byfield, *Alberta in the 20th Century*, p. 115, and Person and Routledge, *Portrait*, p. 60.

18. This story is told in many books, including Byfield, *Alberta in the 20th Century*, and Cashman, *The Best Edmonton Stories*, "Edmonton Gets on the Railroad." A recent account, written by Christopher Spencer, grandson of early Edmonton mayor H.M.E. Evans, appeared in *The Edmonton Journal*, October 20, 2002, section D. You can still walk the old railroad bed where the spur line came over the Low Level Bridge through Mill Woods and on to Strathcona.

19. Albert Ottewell, "University Had Modest Beginnings," *The Gateway* (October 4, 1940), p. 11.

Chapter I

1. This title is taken from a draft story written by Ruth Bowen, file 3. Most quotes from provincial newspapers in this chapter are from Ms. Bowen's research and are indicated by a UAA reference.

2. Haultain had a long career in the Territorial Government, but it was not until the Executive Council was established, with broader powers than its predecessor committees, that Haultain was recognized as a "premier." See p.183 in Wilbur Bowker, *A Legal History of Alberta, 1670–1905*, compiled posthumously in 2001 by Marjorie Bowker, and with notes and an introduction by her. This clear and well-organized manuscript is unpublished and available in the University of Alberta Archives as UAA 2001-165.

3. Byfield, *Alberta in the 20th Century*, p. 29.

4. *The Gateway*, May 15, 1925.

5. Bowker, *Legal History*, p. 189. D.R. Babcock, in *Alexander Cameron Rutherford: A Gentleman of Strathcona* (Calgary: University of Calgary Press, 1989), also makes reference to the use of the territorial ordinances as the basis for legislation passed in the first sessions of the provincial legislature, p. 33. Other sources for this period were Morton, *Short History*, especially pp. 166–67. Haultain's government, in 1903–1904, established 270 new school districts, E.A. Corbett, *Henry Marshall Tory: A Biography* (Edmonton: University of Alberta Press, 1992), p. 59.

6. Johns, *History*, p. 3.

7. Bennett and his friend Max Aitken, later Lord Beaverbrook, were the architects of three corporate mergers, resulting in Calgary Power, Calgary Cement, and Federal Grain (later the Alberta Wheat Pool), Byfield, *Alberta in the 20th Century*, p. 415. Bennett was a brilliant lawyer and a teetotalling bachelor with a severe personality. A reporter once complained to Bennett that it was impossible to get personal interest stories from him. Bennett snapped back, "That's because there are none." Byfield, *Alberta in the 20th Century*, p. 220. Also see pp. 46–50. Bennett became leader of the federal Conservative party in 1927 and was prime minister from 1930–1935.

8. This section follows closely on Byfield, *Alberta in the 20th Century*, section 1, chapter 3.

9. John Duffy, *Fights of Our Lives: Elections, Leadership and the Making of Canada* (Toronto: Harper Collins, 2002), p. 76.

10. Duffy, *Fights of our Lives*, pp. 30–75, and Byfield, *Alberta in the 20th Century*, pp. 52–69.

11. Edmund Aunger, "Legislating Language Use in Alberta: A Century of Incidental Provisions for a Fundamental Matter," *Alberta Law Review*, 42 (2004): 464–97. While English was to be the language of instruction, there was a small door opened for instruction in French, but so many controls were placed on French-language instruction that English was effectively the language of instruction.

12. Morton, *Short History*, p. 167.

13. Quoted in Byfield, *Alberta in the 20th Century*, p. 61.

14. Byfield, *Alberta in the 20th Century*, p. 65.

15. J.G. MacGregor, *A History of Alberta* (Edmonton: Hurtig, 1981), p. 191.

16. This and later references to Marion are from Byfield, *Alberta in the 20th Century*, pp. 29, 61, and 65–69. Marion was Marion Mackintosh Castellain, daughter of the lieutenant governor of the Northwest Territories. At the time Alberta and Saskatchewan became provinces, Haultain was close to penniless. All his savings had gone to support Marion and her child.

17. Quoted in Byfield, *Alberta in the 20th Century*, section 1, chapter 4, p. 75.

18. See Byfield, *Alberta in the 20th Century*, section 1, chapter 4, p. 75. Banff was named as our first national park in 1887; it was called the Rocky Mountain National Park at the time. Its claim for capital status was that it would be easily defensible in time of war. Tony Cashman notes that many other cities and towns also vied to be named as capital. Vegreville boasted its climate, noting that it had more ozone in its air than any other Alberta town. See "The Capital City," in Cashman, *The Best Edmonton Stories*.

19. Quoted in Byfield, *Alberta in the 20th Century*, section 1, chapter 4, p. 76. The first newspaper quoted is the *Albertan,* and the second is the Calgary *Eye Opener*.

20. Quoted in *Bowen* 1-1.

21. Byfield, *Alberta in the 20th Century*, section 1, chapter 4, "Oliver's Awesome Gerrymander that Buried Calgary as Capital," tells the story in more detail. Frank Oliver received an honorary degree from the U of A in 1931.

22. Corbett, *Tory* , p. 93. Tory's diary continues: "On returning home from British Columbia in the spring of 1906 I had stopped in Calgary and had met a group of people interested in the subject, and I had suggested to them that, now that the question of the Capital had been settled, if they could only forget about the Capital and ask for the university, they would stand a good chance of getting it, but they seemed so sure that they could still get the Capital that they refused to offer any compromise."

23. Quoted in Byfield, *Alberta in the 20th Century*, section 1, chapter 4, p. 78.

24. Quoted in Byfield, *Alberta in the 20th Century*, section 1, chapter 4, p. 85.

25. Quoted in Bowen, 3-4.

26. The nickname appears in Bowen, file 1. She quotes this in her Calgary *Eye Opener* reports, p. 1, from an open letter to the premier, written in Nov 25, 1906, written by editor Bob Edwards of the Calgary *Eye Opener*. Known better as "Eye Opener Bob," Mr. Edwards was a Conservative, but nonetheless a backer of the Liberal Rutherford. Witty, hard-drinking, and crusty, Edwards likely knew Rutherford when "Eye Opener Bob" lived in Strathcona.

27. Babcock, *Rutherford*, p. 4.

28. Babcock, *Rutherford*, p. 88. Babcock notes that GWG workers were unionized from the beginning and were some of the first employees in North America to work an eight-hour day.

29. Main sources for these sections are Babcock, *Rutherford*; Byfield, *Alberta in the 20th Century,* pp. 294–95; Bowen, file 1, especially her reports from local newspapers; and Corbett, *Tory.*

30. The quote and the complete letter are in Johns, *History,* p. 7.

31. Johns, *History*, pp. 6–7. For more information about River Lot 5, see chapter 4 of this book.

32. *Calgary Herald*, March 27, 1906, as quoted in Bowen, 1-8. The story about Rutherford telling Calgarians that the University would be built south of the North Saskatchewan River was told to me in 2004 by University Senator Rod Ponech.

33. Quoted in Bowen, 1-19.

34. Ruth Bowen tells this story in rapid-fire fashion, stringing together quotes from the newspapers of the day, from the Statutes of Alberta for 1910, and from the journal of the Legislative Assembly of the Province of Alberta, file 1, pp. 20-25. The quotes are all from the *Calgary Herald.*

35. The president, actually titled principal, was Reverend G.W. Kerby, a Methodist minister. Bowen, 1-24.

36. Bowen, file 1, pp. 1-25. A charter was granted, however, for a technical and art institute, today's SAIT and Alberta College of Art.

37. Babcock, *Rutherford*, p. 60.

38. See Patricia Roome and David Hall in Bradford J. Rennie, ed. *Alberta Premiers of the Twentieth Century.* Regina: Canadian

Plains Research Center, University of Regina, 2004, pp. 13, 27 for accounts of the commission.

Chapter 2

1. Henry Marshall Tory wrote to his wife Annie in 1905, saying, "This country fascinates me. There is wine in the air; a feeling of excitement...." Quoted in Corbett, *Tory,* p. 59.

2. Quoted in Bowen, 1-11. The emphasis on the word "province" is mine. In the context of Tory's fuller remarks on this topic, I think it is a correct emphasis.

3. Bowen, 8-4, quoting Cecil Burgess.

4. John Macdonald, *The History Of The University Of Alberta 1908–1958* (Edmonton: University of Alberta Press, 1958), pp. 12–13. Dr. Macdonald was a former dean of Arts and Science.

5. Mrs. Sheldon is quoted in Dr. William Hardy Alexander's *The University of Alberta: A Retrospect 1908-1929* (Edmonton: University of Alberta Press, 1929), p. 28. Also see Mrs. Sheldon's interview with Bowen, file 13.

6. E.B. Swindlehurst, *Alberta's Schools of Agriculture: A Brief History,* p. 11.

7. Bowen, 15-9, quoting Agnes Wilson.

8. R.K. Gordon, "University Beginnings in Alberta," *Queen's Quarterly,* LVIII (1952), p. 490 (cited hereafter as "University Beginnings in Alberta"). I removed one ellipses in this quote and added the phrase "back then."

9. Bowen, file 3, which includes a resumé of Tory, presumably written by Tory himself. McGill University College later grew to be the University of British Columbia. Tory had an incredibly broad reach across all of Canada when it came to organizing post-secondary education. See Corbett, *Tory,* pp. 51–64.

10. This is the Honourable Perrin Baker, minister of education from 1921–1935, recalling Tory in Bowen, 6-3. There are recollections of Tory in nearly every Bowen file.

11. Professor Burgess in Bowen, 8-3. President Newton is the person who remembers Tory humming hymns, in his memoir *I Passed This Way* (University of Alberta Archives, Edmonton, UAA 71–87), pp. 280.

12. Professor MacLeod in Bowen 12-30 ("vision"); Professor MacEachran in Bowen, 11-8 ("steel"); Professor Gordon, "University Beginnings," p. 490 ("chief inspirer of hopes and dreams").

13. Johns, *History,* 105.

14. Bowen, 10-7, quoting R.K. Gordon.

15. The quotes from Dean Bulyea are in Bowen 7-6 and 7-5.

16. Gordon, "University Beginnings in Alberta," p. 490, and Dr. Sonet in Bowen, 14-9, 10.

17. Bowen, 13-10, quoting Helen Sheldon.

18. Gordon, "University Beginnings in Alberta," p. 491.

19. Bowen, 15-1, quoting Agnes Wilson.

20. Bowen, 15-9, quoting Agnes Wilson. Beatrice Ockley had a Bachelor's degree.

21. Bowen, 12, no page numbers.

22. Human Ecology Exhibit, "Rites of Passage," University of Alberta, 2002. Curated by Professor Anne Lambert, with assistance from students and staff in Human Ecology and from University Archives. Also see "University Beginnings in Alberta," p. 495 on Tory's knitting skills.

23. Bowen, 13-5, quoting Mrs. Sheldon, and Corbett, *Tory,* p. 102.

24. Bowen, 10-6, quoting R.K. Gordon, and Corbett, *Tory,* p. 6.

25. Bowen, 12-4.

26. Bowen, 12-10, quoting Mrs. MacLeod, née Helen Montgomery.

27. Orally from Hugh Morrison, who was told the story by his neighbour R.K. Gordon. Professor Burgess, in Bowen, file 8, recounts marvellous stories of the first professors going to the mountains to camp, pan for gold, fish, and hunt.

28. Newton, *I Passed This Way,* pp. 284–85.

29. Newton, *I Passed This Way,* p. 285.

30. Bowen, 6-3, quoting Rae Chittick.

31. Ottewell in the October 4, 1940 *Gateway.*

32. Bowen, 8-3, quoting Cecil Burgess.

33. Newton, *I Passed This Way*, pp. 280–81, 283–84. This is a composite quote. On occasion I have changed Newton's pronoun references to "Tory."

34. Bowen, 11-4, quoting Provost John MacEachran.

35. Cecil Burgess in Bowen, 8-3, and Bowen herself, describing Burgess's reaction to the memory, Bowen, 8-3.

36. Bowen, 12-3. I changed the word "one" to the word "you."

37. Newton, *I Passed This Way,* p. 284.

38. Bowen, 6-1, quoting Perrin Baker. The date of the comment was May 20, 1936, and it was made by Tory at his retirement from the NRC.

39. Bowen, 10-7, 8, quoting R.K. Gordon. Two excellent articles about Tory are reprinted in *Sons of Martha: University of Alberta Faculty of Engineering 1913-1988* (Edmonton: Faculty of Engineering, University of Alberta, 1988), chapter 9.

40. Quoted in Corbett, *Tory,* p. 59.

41. Bowen, 15-4, quoting Agnes Wilson. It has always been a mystery why L.H. Alexander left after one year. The mystery is now solved.

42. Bowen, 5-11, quoting Ethel Anderson.

43. Sources include *Sons of Martha,* pp. 3–5; John Macdonald, *The History of the University of Alberta*; and William Hardy Alexander, *The University of Alberta: A Retrospect 1908–1929* (Edmonton: University of Alberta Press, 1929).

44. Muir's mother, Henrietta Muir Edwards, was one of the "Famous Five" and the first to sign a petition to the Supreme Court of Canada asking if the word "person" in section 24 of the *BNA Act* (Senate appointments) included female persons. The Privy Council of England eventually decided the question, and their decision meant women were qualified "persons" for appointment to the Senate. Thanks are made to Mrs. Marjorie Bowker for this footnote.

45. *Sons of Martha,* p. 4. The information about Muir's career at McGill is also drawn from *Sons of Martha.*

46. Bowen, 5-4, quoting Agnes Wilson.

47. From Will Alexander's memorial to Muir Edwards, as quoted in *Sons of Martha,* p. 5.

48. Evelyn moved to Ontario shortly after Muir's death.

49. I first learned of Will Alexander's nickname from Hugh Morrison. The nickname is sometimes spelled "Dok Alik" and has appeared in the yearbook as "Dokalik."

50. Bowen, 11-2, quoting John MacEachran. The student who remembers Drs. Alexander and Broadus as "inspiring" teachers is Hugh Morrison (BA '30), orally to the author, 2002.

51. Esther Miller in Johns, *History,* p. 147.

52. Bowen, 5-7, quoting Ethel Anderson.

53. E.K. Broadus, "Little Brown House," *Saturday and Sunday* (Toronto: Macmillan, 1935).

54. Bowen, 5-2.

55. This and all other quotes about the house, from Broadus, "Little Brown House," *Saturday and Sunday.*

56. Lovat Dickson, *The Ante Room: Early Stages of a Literary Life* (Toronto: Macmillan, 1959), p. 220. It is Rache Dickson, in *The Ante Room,* who tells about Broadus's car, Hotspur.

57. Broadus, "Small Beginnings," *Saturday and Sunday,*" p. 20.

58. Early Calendars included readings required for matriculation in English and for junior and senior courses. Copies of examinations were also included in the Calendar. A copy of one of Broadus's exams has been included in Appendix 2.

59. Bowen, 10-7, quoting R.K. Gordon.

60. Orally to the author, 2002.

61. Bowen, 8-4, quoting Cecil Burgess.

62. Bowen, 15-2.

63. Donald Cameron, *Campus in the Clouds* (Toronto: McClelland and Stewart, 1956), p. 1.

64. Bowen, 5-3.

65. Dickson, *The Ante Room,* p. 220.

66. Esther Miller (BA '27) retired in 1965 after 37 years of service with the University in the Registrar's Office. She wrote a 20-page memoir, UAA 69-23, cited hereafter as Miller, with a page number.

67. Miller, pp. 4–5.

68. Bowen, 10-3, quoting R.K. Gordon.

69. Miller, p. 5.

70. Bowen, 15-7, quoting Agnes Wilson.

71. Dickson, *The Ante Room,* pp. 220–21.

72. Dickson, *The Ante Room,* pp. 229–30.

73. Orally to the author from Mrs. Bowker, 2002.

74. *The Gateway,* February 18, 1936, Letters Column.

75. Orally to the author from Mr. McTavish, 2002.

76. Al Ottewell, *The Gateway,* October 4, 1940, "University Had Very Modest Beginning...," pp. 10–11. Ottewell noted in this article that the yell used at the original convocation was still in use in 1940.

77. The story of the origin of the crest can be pieced together from many sources. *Sons of Martha* is the best.

78. Edith Rogers, *History Made in Edmonton* (Edmonton: The Author, 1975), p. 172. When Marion checked with "the girls," she likely meant the Wauneita Society, comprising the women students, and the Academic Women's Association, forerunner of the Canadian Federation of University Women (Edmonton).

79. Senate minutes October 13, 1908, as quoted in *The University of Alberta, 1908–1983* (Edmonton: University of Alberta Press, 1982), p. 7. The book was published to commemorate the 75th anniversary of the University).

80. Orally to the author from Will Alexander, grandson of Marion Alexander, 2002.

81. In 1910, the *Universities Act* was rewritten, separating the financial and academic powers of governance, with a new Board in charge of finance and management and the Senate in charge of academic affairs. Stuart retained the chairmanship of the Senate. O.M. Biggar and W.D. Ferris are referred to in the Bowen files as Board Chairs, although the first recorded Board Chair was Edwin C. Pardee, serving from 1911–1917. Tory was instrumental in rewriting the *Act,* and the new *Act* gave the government the power to appoint the

president, not the Board. This would make Tory's continuation as president dependent on the premier and not on a multi-member Board. In 2004, the *Universities Act* was replaced by the *Post-Secondary Learning Act*.

Dr. Walter Johns was the last president appointed by the Government, and Dr. Max Wyman was the first president appointed by the Board of Governors. Dr. Johns, however, said that the Government had never appointed a president who had not been informally recommended by the Board (orally from Myer Horowitz to the author, 2002).

82. Ethel Anderson and Agnes Wilson both make this point in Bowen, files 5 and 15.

83. Bowen, 6-1, quoting Tory.

84. The "finally" ended reference is in Corbett, *Tory*, p. 97. The "first Faculty," Arts and Science, is occasionally spelled with an "s" at the end of the word "Science." See Maureen Aytenfisu, *The University of Alberta: Objectives, Structure and Role in the Community, 1908–1928* (Unpublished Master's Thesis, Department of History and Classics, University of Alberta, 1982) concerning Tory's resistance to public pressure to establish a Faculty of Agriculture. Our sister institution, the University of Saskatchewan, established Agriculture as their first Faculty. See Corbett, *Tory*, pp. 5–97 and Johns, *History*, pp. 14–21 on the first two meetings of Senate.

85. MacDonald, *Historic Edmonton*, p. 83.

86. R.K. Gordon, in "Assiniboia Hall, 1913–1919," *New Trail*, October, 1946, p. 174.

87. Corbett, *Tory*, p. 100.

Chapter 3

1. Agnes Wilson used the title "Small Beginnings" for two talks she gave about early life in Strathcona and at the University. Dr. Broadus, the first English professor, also used this title in an essay about early university life in his book, *Saturday and Sunday*.

2. The October 1908 convocation program states that 37 students attended the first day of class.

3. University promotional calendar for 2000 and Alexander, *Retrospect 1908–1929*, p. 9. In *My Forty-Five Years on the Campus*, p. 17, Reg Lister reports that he carried notes between Jennie Carmichael (secretary to the registrar by 1914) and Mr. Howson, who in 1936 was named as a Justice. Jennie and the Judge later married. Howson was also an MLA and Leader of the Liberal Party.

4. Bowen, file 15, quoting Agnes Wilson.

5. All quotes from Ethel in this chapter, including those about SIS, the AWA and initiation, are from Bowen, file 5. Ethel described Tory's history lectures as "awful."

6. MacDonald, *Historic Edmonton*, p. 173 has reproductions of invitations to "Conversats" and freshmen receptions. Libby Lloyd (BA '12) also saved many of these invitations (UAA 69–82-3).

7. Mr. Justice L.Y. Cairns, Chancellor Emeritus, was a 20-year old graduand when he wrote a poem characterizing his 1912 classmates. The characterization of students in this section quotes from that poem. Classmate Libby Lloyd, 1912 class historian, kept a copy of it (UAA 69-82-3).

8. There is more information about Albert in the Prologue and also in chapters that cover through to the 1940s, when he died. All Ottewell's quotes in this chapter are from articles he wrote in two editions of *The Gateway*: October 4, 1940, "University Had Very Modest Beginning," and December 19, 1940, "In Retrospect."

9. Tory persuaded Strathcona high schools not to offer Grade 12 in 1908 so that it could be taught at the University, thus boosting the enrolment.

10. Alexander, *Retrospect 1908–1929*, p. 9 and Bowen, 15-8, quoting Agnes.

11. Sources include Ethel Anderson in Bowen, file 5; Rogers, *History Made in Edmonton*; Johns, *History*; and the first three editions of *The Gateway*. Early Calendars list the names of presidents of the student organizations, but this information is not included in the first Calendar. It is Agnes Wilson who tells us that Mr. Cairns was the first president of the Literary Society (Bowen, file 15). Ethel Anderson is the one who tells us that Laurence was the class humorist and could play piano by ear (Bowen 5-10). Also see *The Gateway*, November 1910, "The Literary Program."

12. Bowen, file 15, quoting Agnes Wilson.

13. The other two are Robert Greenhill and Garett Poston. Stacey McCall served on the Board of Governors from 1939–1945.

14. The main source on Jimmy is *Sons of Martha*. Professor Sheldon's speech is in *The Gateway*, December 1910. I edited his speech. In the original, all the references were to male students only. He was speaking at Alberta College.

15. The quote about seven new women coming each year is in Bowen, 15-5, quoting Ethel Anderson, and is also referred to by Libby Lloyd (UAA 75–68). Women in this era are hard to track because, when they married, both their first and last names disappeared. Stella Ruttan, for instance, became

Mrs. R.J. Russell. The married names of these women, if known, are in the text. Mary Elizabeth (Libby) Lloyd's married name was Elsey. A.J. Johnston is listed in the first Calendar, but not in the graduation program.

16. Second University Calendar. SU Executive members were called the Students' Council, and what we know as today's Students' Council was a "committee of 6." As noted earlier, Agnes was the "first white child born in Strathcona" and the first woman to register at the University." Bowen, file 15.

17. Bowen, 15-11.

18. Bowen, 11-6, quoting John MacEachran. The men also had a short-lived fraternity, Pi Sigma Phi, UAA 86–41, box 19. The 1911–1912 Calendar, p. 20, describes the AWA scholarship.

19. Bowen, file 5, quoting Ethel Anderson.

20. Stella's BA parchment still hangs on the sixth floor of the Humanities Centre.

21. Ethel Anderson in Bowen, 5-2, and Agnes Wilson in Bowen, file 15. York Blaney was the third student who lived on the north side. He would sometimes join Ethel and Decima on their walk over to Edmonton. York was a star athlete.

22. Bowen, 5-2, quoting Ethel Anderson. Mr. Rutherford did not know how to drive, and usually one of his children drove him to work. Orally to the author from Eric McCuaig, Mr. Rutherford's grandson.

23. Byfield, *Alberta in the 20th Century*, pp. 332–33.

24. Bowen, file 15, quoting Agnes Wilson.

25. Bowen, file 15, quoting Agnes Wilson.

26. Alexander, *Retrospect 1908–1929*, p. 10 and Ethel Anderson in Bowen, 5-10. One suspects that Ethel and Doc Alik, who both describe the wasted dance music, were in cahoots to bring dancing to the U of A.

27. Bowen, 10-5, quoting R.K. Gordon.

28. "The information about Lee Carr comes from his son Douglas, orally to the author, 2003.

29. *The Gateway*, November 1910, p. 18. The Wauneita Club sewed all manner of U of A crested items and held a sale, their first fundraiser. *The Gateway*, December 1910, p. 17.

30. The eight new professors and lecturers are listed in the 1911–1912 Calendar as follows: John Malcolm MacEachran (Philosophy); Adolph Lehmann (Chemistry); Ernest Wilson Sheldon (Mathematics); Barker Fairley (Modern Languages); Allan Chester Johnson (Classics); Edouard Sonet (French); James Adam (Drawing); and Cecil Race (Registrar and Librarian).

31. With respect to the date of MacEachran's appointment as provost, what the students really remember, as noted

in the 1948 *Evergreen and Gold* (p. 21), is that before his formal appointment as provost he was the disciplinarian in Athabasca. All MacEachran quotes are in Bowen, file 11, pp. 1, 2, 5, 7 and 10. The comment from Hugh Morrison was made orally to the author in 2002. Reg Lister called MacEachran's future wife, the dietician Miss Russell, "the first woman of any ability that the University had employed" (*My Forty-Five Years on the Campus*, p. 13). In MacEachran's later life, he was vilified for his participation on the provincial eugenics board, which he chaired from 1929–1965.

32. Bowen, 13-2.

33. Bowen, 13-5, quoting Helen Sheldon.

34. Bowen, 13-10, quoting Helen Sheldon.

35. Sources for information on Margaret are *Barker Fairley Portraits* (source of the words "fiery and persuasive teacher"), *Barker Fairley* (source of the words "strong social conscience"), and UAA 2315-2. When Barker was in his 40s, he tried his hand at painting. His portraits now fetch thousands of dollars at Canadian art auctions, and bidding on Group of Seven canvasses runs over the one-million-dollar mark. The Group of Seven members were Frederick Varley, A.Y. Jackson, Arthur Lismer, Lawren Harris, Frank H. (Franz) Johnston, J.E.H. Macdonald, and Franklin Carmichael. In one of their most famous photographs, taken in the Toronto Arts and Letters Club in the early 1920s when the Group was a band of poor and unpopular artists, there is only one other person sitting with them: Barker Fairley.

36. See Alexander, *Retrospect 1908–1929*, p. 11; MacDonald, *The History of the University of Alberta*, p. 11; Johns, *History*, p. 37. The fourth Calendar, p. 67, shows Decima Robinson's exam results. It was the *Strathcona Plaindealer* that reported "a large crowd" and which summarized the convocation program, May 16, 1911, front page. There are two other descriptions of this ceremony. Dean of Arts and Science John Macdonald, looking back to 1911 on the University's 50th anniversary, had this to say: "In 1911 convocation exercises were held for a few students, but it was in 1912 that the first formal convocation ceremony took place. The class of 1912 thus properly regards itself as the first authentic product of the new institution." Walter Johns's description is even shorter: 1911 "saw the first graduates to receive their degrees in course—two the BA, one the BSc in Arts, two the MA, and three the MSc in Arts. These students had, of course, done work previously in other universities or in Alberta College." Dr. Tory's annual report for 1911–1912

states that the five who received graduate degrees had all previously received degrees "at Eastern universities," and "first fruits from our endeavors" is from the same source, p. 8. The Ottewell quotes are from *The Gateway*, October 4, 1940 and are gently edited.

37. Dr. Dyde's son became the first Rhodes Scholar from the University of Alberta.

Chapter 4

1. Bowen, 8-1, quoting Cecil Burgess.

2. Bowen, file 11. It is difficult to tell if the phrase "farm in the bush" is Bowen's or MacEachran's.

3. There are many descriptions of River Lot 5. The quotes here are from *Evergreen and Gold*, 1948, p. 24; Bowen, 11-4 (for Provost MacEachran's first impression); Johns, *History*, p. 6; Corbett, *Tory*, p. 93 (which describes the river frontage); Macdonald, *History of the University of Alberta*, p. 2; Alexander, *A Retrospect 1908–1929*, p. 5. The "farm in the bush" quote has been slightly edited. It is in Bowen, 11-4. Concerning the division of River Lot 5, Nobbs is quoted in Bowen, 5-1 and the original is in Dr. Tory's papers in the UAA. The Reg Lister quote is in *My Forty-Five Years on the Campus*, p. 14. Some of these quotes are slightly edited by, for instance, adding an indefinite article.

4. MacDonald, *The History of The University of Alberta*, p. 2.

5. Today's McKernan area was first settled by James McKernan and his family. James first came west from Ontario with the RCMP. He maintained the first telegraph line in Alberta and was one of the earliest farmers in Edmonton. Over the years, "McKernan's Lake" became simply "McKernan Lake." It was drained to make way for the McKernan housing subdivision.

6. Gordon, "University Beginnings in Alberta," p. 487.

7. All quotes are from *My Forty-Five Years on the Campus*, pp. 10–16 and p. 67, unless otherwise noted. "Dancing endlessly" and "boisterous behaviour" are from Burgess, 8-1, 2. The information about Agriculture students using a Ring House near where the Faculty Club now stands comes from Ken Nicol, a U of A graduate and former leader of the Provincial Liberal Party. The *Strathcona Plaindealer* reference is in the May 16, 1911 edition, front page. Tory's reports to the Board are in the UAA reference area and describe student self-government. The list of names students gave their rooms is from Ethel Anderson in Bowen, 5-11. It should be noted that, in the early years, Athabasca was spelled "Athabaska."

I am indebted to Rob Lake and Keith Smillie in Computing Science for sharing information about Athabasca. Their excellent history of Athabasca can be viewed on the plasma screen in the foyer of the renovated building. In their research file is a description by Tubby Thornton, SU president in 1921 and later professor of Dairying, concerning the acceptable dress for meals. Slippers and a sweater were all right for breakfast, "you had to look half decent for lunch," and dinner was formal, with Provost MacEachran saying grace in Latin through ill-fitting false teeth. No one could hear MacEachran, and so the students timed the actual grace and as MacEachran mumbled, they checked the time. When the time was up, the students sat down.

In contrast to the early appearance of residences on the U of A campus, a residence for men was not built at UBC until 1944, and the first UBC women's residence opened in 1951.

8. The Athabasca ghost story is in *The Gateway*, October 10, 2001, "A Ghost Among Us: The Boy with the Blue Lips," by Dave Alexander. The story was reportedly told to Mr. Alexander by an anonymous woman whose husband encountered the ghost boy in the 1940s.

9. Lister, *My Forty-Five Years on the Campus*, p. 70.

10. Bowen, 11-8 and 11-9, quoting John MacEachran.

11. Orally to the author, 2003, from President Emeritus Myer Horowitz.

12. Information on the University's motto appears in Bowen, 11-9, and also in an undated brochure issued by the Convocation Office of the Register's Office entitled "Emblems of the University."

13. Frances Cruden, "Discovering the Roots of Garneau's Past," UAA 2315-5.

14. Hugh Morrison (BA '30) and his family lived in the Garneau mansion for many years, including Hugh's undergraduate years. The photo of the Garneau mansion was given to the author by Hugh Morrison.

15. The quotes in this section are from Babcock, *Rutherford*, p. 97.

16. Babcock, *Rutherford*, p.97.

17. St. Stephen's College is now home now to Alberta Culture's Historical Resources Division. Sources for this section include Alex Mair, *Gateway City: Stories from Edmonton's Past* (Calgary: Fifth House, 2000), "A Skill Testing Question," and Jac MacDonald, *Historic Edmonton* (Edmonton: Lone Pine & *Edmonton Journal*, 1987). I am grateful to

Christopher Lind, former president of St. Stephen's College, for telling me stories about St. Steve's, including the story about former Premier Aberhart. The 1910 *Gateway* includes an advertisement from Alberta College describing its matriculation program, a full course in music, and a business program. As of 2004, St. Stephen's offers 10 courses for transfer credit. St. Steve's records show that the Bachelor of Divinity degree was last awarded at the University of Alberta in 1975.

18. Sources include Tory's papers as quoted in Bowen, file 4; MacEachran in Bowen, file 11; Burgess in Bowen, file 8; the 1948 *Evergreen and Gold,* p. 25; Johns, *History*; Cashman, *The Best Edmonton Stories*, p. 113; and Lister, *My Forty-Five Years on the Campus*, p. 10. Reg Lister says the original sod-turning occurred in 1908, not 1909. The original name of the Arts Building was "The Main Teaching Building." There is an early reference to an "Arts and Science" building or Building A on "the plan." But after it opened, everyone just referred to it as "The Arts Building." The description of Burgess as shy is in Bowen, 4-2, and it is Reg Lister who describes Burgess as a quiet and constant presence wherever new buildings were going up. In the famous photo of the original sod-turning, the premier is pictured holding the plough. He had been raised on a farm in Ontario, but had never learned to handle a team of horses. Mr. Ferris and Mr. Biggar are referred to as Board Chairs, or members of the Board Executive, before there was a legal entity called the Board of Governors.

19. The description of Reg's years on campus is in *My Forty-Five Years on the Campus*, p. 72. The two parenthetical additions are mine and are based on other parts of Reg Lister's book. The words "guide, counselor and friend" is from the certificate of honorary membership in Convocation. The Chairman of the Men's House Committee was Alan Armstrong. Reg Lister lived in the residences from the day Athabasca opened in 1911 until the University built the Lister family a house in 1930, right behind Athabasca Hall. In 2003, Lister Hall became "The Lister Centre."

20. Henry Marshall Tory, *Going West: Autobiographical Material, 1907–1915* (Ottawa: The National Archives of Canada, MG 30, series D115, volume 27, file 277, 1915), p. 48. It should also be noted that one of the four districts in the old Northwest Territories was named Athabaska.

21. Burgess in Bowen, 8-1, gently edited. All Burgess quotes are in Bowen, file 8. Percy Nobbs was one person who called Burgess "shy." The student who remembers the curfew is Hugh Morrison. The ghost story has been told in a number of university publications, including the 2005 university telephone directory, in an article by Stacey Bisell, p. 2 of the directory.

22. Sources include *New Trail*, 1974, "Pembina: Is That All There Is?" by David Norwood; *Folio,* November 27, 1975, "Pembina Re-opening 1975," "by David Norwood (source of the quote concerning the propeller, p. 3); and Burgess in Bowen, file 8.

23. All Sonet quotes by or about Sonet, including descriptions of his teaching, are in Bowen, file 14. Sonet sitting with hands "palm to palm" is Ruth Bowen's description. E.A. Corbett also tells the story about Killam dressing up as a woman of the night in *Tory*, p. 7.

24. The program is in Libby Lloyd's memorabilia, UAA 75–68. A description of freshman initiation is in *The Gateway*, vol. 4, bound edition for 1913-14, UAA.

25. Ethel Anderson in Bowen, 5-12, Agnes Wilson in Bowen, file 15 (un-numbered), 15-11 and Libby Lloyd, 75-68. I have combined information from their documents and gently edited the tense. There is also information from Ethel Anderson in Bowen, 5-12. Tory's Board reports for 1911 and 1912 were also a source.

26. The Ottewell quote is from *The Gateway*, October 15, 1937. The "pleasure and sustenance" and "warm geniality" quotes are from Gordon, "University Beginnings in Alberta," p. 491. The estimate of Albertans reached in 1913–1914 is taken from *The Gateway,* vol. 4, bound edition, UAA, in an article written by Acting President Kerr. Another source for this section is Aytenfisu, *Objectives, Structure and Role*. In contrast to the U of A's early start in extension activities, an Extension department at UBC was not begun until 1936.

Chapter 5

1. Jack Granatstein, quoted in *The Edmonton Journal*, April 9, 2002.

2. Alexander, *Retrospect, 1908–1929*, p. 13.

3. Desmond Morton and Jack Granatstein, *March to Armageddon: Canadians and the Great War 1914–1919* (Toronto: Lester and Orpen Dennys, 1987), describes the level of mechanization in World War I.

4. Pierre Berton, *Vimy* (Markham: Penguin Books, 1987).

5. Reg's stories about World War I are in *My Forty-Five Years on the Campus*, chapter 5. On a furlough from Vimy Ridge, Reg Lister travelled to Norwich, England, and married his hometown sweetheart.

6. www.historylearningsite.co.uk/somme.htm.

7. To determine that the rest of the class made it back, I compared the names on the memorial plaque in Convocation Hall with the list of medical students printed in the Calendar.

8. Alexander, *Retrospect 1908–1929*, p. 14.

9. Arthur Deitz was killed by the "first shell…on [his] first day in the line…." Johns, *History*, p. 54.

10. All quotes from Charlie Reilly are from his front-page article in *The Gateway*, October 15, 1925. I changed the spelling of Ernie Parsons's first name from "Erny" to "Ernie" to accord with the spelling used in the *University Weekly Newsletters*.

11. Broadus, "At the End of the Line in Wartime," *Saturday and Sunday*, p. 52. There are two existing photos of the 1914 rugby team, each composed of different team members. Presumably, one of the photos depicts the 1913–1914 team and the other the 1914–1915 team. As a result, there is some discrepancy between the photographic image of the team presented here and the names of the team members given in the text.

12. *University Weekly Newsletter* #12, June 24, 1916, gently edited and combining letters from Galbraith and Loptson (UAA 69-82-12) about the death of Ernie Parsons and Norman McArthur.

13. Information about Alex McQueen is from Mr. Reilly's article, the *University Weekly Newsletters* (UAA 69-39, 69-82), and Ken Tingley, ed., *The Path of Duty: The Wartime Letters of Alwyn Bramley-Moore, 1914–1916* (Calgary: Historical Society of Alberta, 1998.), p. 87. I am grateful to Myer Horowitz and Doug Burns for talking with me about Gladys Bramley-Moore, Alwyn's daughter. Gladys Bramley-Moore attended the U of A in the 1930s.

14. Information about Barmey Loptson is from Mr. Reilly's article and the *University Weekly Newsletters* (UAA 69-39, 69-82). The words "somewhere in France" are from the *Weekly Newsletter* # 14 (UAA 69-82-12).

15. Berton, *Vimy*, p. 291.

16. Gord Henderson, "Vimy Ridge Battlefield: Still Haunted by the Ghosts of the Brave," *Edmonton Journal*, November 11, 2004, A16.

17. The Bennett quote is in Newton, *I Passed This Way*, p. 280. The Tory quote is in Corbett, *Tory*, p. 111. Tory's promise to Alberta's farmers that the university would relate its research to practical problems and to social and economic problems of farmers is from Corbett, *Tory*, p. 111. Tory has written about keeping all disciplines under one roof and not "distributing" them across the province in his *Going West*, pp. 19–20.

18. By 1929, the Wauneita Council no longer held disciplinary powers. In an overhaul of the SU constitution, both a men's discipline committee and a women's discipline committee were set up.

19. The quote is from the U of A's 2003 Human Ecology exhibit, curated by Dr. Anne Lambert.

20. UAA 2315-2.

21. Person and Routledge, *Portrait*, p. 138, gently edited for tense.

22. It is Hector who characterizes Tory as "demanding." All quotes from the MacLeods are in Bowen, 12.

23. If you are curious about the one-step, here is a website that contains a video clip of the banned dance: http://memory.loc.gov/ammem/dihtml/diessay7.html. The fourth paragraph has information on the one-step, as well as link to a video clip of the dance. Jane Parkinson, the archivist at the Banff Centre, tracked down the website information on the one-step.

24. Helen Montgomery MacLeod in Bowen, 12. Helen's full description of the plaque was, as she says, originally in "an Edmonton newspaper": The students who signed the plaque were G. Roy Stevens, N. McArthur, F.P. Galbraith, R.M. Martin, J. Buckley, L.G. Simmonds, A.T.M. Glanville, F.G. Day, Chas. F. Reilly, J.W. Lewis, J.B. McCubbin, A. Peart, J.A. Gordon, Arthur Carswell, Ernest Parsons, D.S. Edwards, A. Hutchinson, S. [B.] Lopston, A.R. McQueen, and F. Reg Henry.

25. See Corbett, *Tory*; Johns, *History*; Newton, *I Passed This Way*; and Burgess in Bowen, 8. The quote concerning the numbers educated at Khaki University is from Corbett, *Tory*, p. 156.

26. Newton, *I Passed This Way*, p. 289. It is ironic that the McGill gold medal in math was named after a woman, Ann Molson. And at the University of Toronto, in 1884, when women were first admitted, they were sequestered in a waiting room when not in class, and forbidden to stand in front of the hallway bulletin boards to read messages. See Martin L. Friedland, *The University of Toronto: A History* (Toronto: University of Toronto Press, 2002), p. 92.

27. Sources include *Evergreen and Gold*, 1947, section titled "Faculty and Campus." Alexis Pépin told me about the ghost in November 2004.

28. Sources on Wop May include Person and Routledge, *Portrait*, p. 150; Lister, *My Forty-Five Years on the Campus*,

p. 28; Sheila Reid, W*ings of a Hero: Ace Wop May* (St. Catherine's: Vanwell Publishing, 1997); Patrick Watson, *The Canadians: Biographies of a Nation* (Toronto: McArthur and Company, 2000); Philip H. Godsell, *Pilots of the Purple Twilight: The Story of Canada's Early Bush Flyers* (Toronto: Ryerson Press, 1955). Wop May's partner in the mercy mission was Vic Horner.

The student who remembers Wop May flying under the High Level Bridge is Anne Evans Crofton. Wop May had the mayor in his plane, and they were on their way to drop the ball in an opening baseball game.

And as for who was actually responsible for the Red Baron's death, there is no definitive answer. Wop May thought it was his friend Roy Brown, but it could also have been Australian gunners on the ground. The story is still legendary, as is the mercy flight and the Mad Trapper adventure.

29. Alexander, *Retrospect 1908-1929*, p. 24. The Boyle quote is in Johns, *History*, p. 55.

30. It was "Doc Alik" who chose the heading for the World War I memorial plaque. Orally from Hugh Morrison, July 2003. Albert Robinson, whose name is on the plaque, was Mrs. Tory's nephew.

Chapter 6

1. Bowen, 12-3, quoting Hector MacLeod.

2. *The Gateway,* graduation number, 1920.

3. Bowen, 9-7, quoting Ethel Fenwick Cooper. Miss Fenwick was Superintendent of Nursing. She did not make the rules about bobbed hair. In fact, she bobbed her own hair, making a wig from her cut tresses.

4. *The Gateway,* January 12, 1928.

5. Alexander, *Retrospect 1908-1929*, p. 24.

6. Lister, *My Forty-Five Years on the Campus*, p. 29.

7. Quoted in Tingley, ed., *Strathcona Plaindealer*, pp. 190–92, and gently edited. According to Hugh Morrison, the *Plaindealer* was founded and edited by L.W. Brockington, afterwards the City Solicitor of Calgary and first Chairman of the CBC.

8. Burgess and MacLeod in Bowen, 12-3, 4. The Mayfair, at the time, was not open to Jews or, according to Hugh Morrison, women—except for the wives of members.

9. Ned Corbett, *We Have With Us Tonight* (Toronto: The Ryerson Press, 1957), p. 44, and Ken Dyba, *Betty Mitchell* (Calgary: Detselig Enterprises Limited, 1986), p. 44.

10. Bowen, 6-4, quoting Perrin Baker, gently edited.

11. Marylu Walters, *CKUA: Radio Worth Fighting For* (Edmonton: University of Alberta Press, 2002), p. 12. Al Ottewell wrote a number of articles over the years about the U of A's history in *The Gateway*. One of his articles about CKUA was in the October 15, 1937 edition of *The Gateway*.

12. Barbara Villy Cormack, *Beyond the Classroom: The First 60 Years of the University of Alberta Department of Extension* (Edmonton: Faculty of Extension, University of Alberta, 1981), p. 5. CKUA was taken over by the provincial government in 1994 and headed down the road to privatization. CKUA was pulled off the air in 1997 by its provincially-appointed board for financial reasons. Fans came to the rescue. By 2004, CKUA had 160,000 listeners a week.

13. Cormack, *Beyond the Classroom*, p. 5. The official record concerning CKUA shows Tory and Ottewell requesting funds for the radio station through the appropriate channels, with the Board and Senate giving their approval. But in an early history of CKUA, published to commemorate the station's 40th anniversary (Joe McCallum, *CKUA: 40 Wondrous Years of Radio* [Edmonton: CKUA, 1967]), it is said that, in the budget presented to the provincial government in 1927, there was a $7,000 request for a new lecturer. But instead of the lecturer, what arrived on campus were two 100-foot radio towers, south of Pembina Hall, apparently built by engineering students. Starting with the windmills, so the story goes, the students attached 25-foot iron poles and topped them with antennae.

The first class of electrical engineers had graduated in 1924. After CKUA was on the air, it was their department that "changed the circuits" over the summer months. Working with CKUA guided many electrical engineering students into graduate studies in electronics and communication. Perhaps engineering students were involved earlier than that with the new technology of radio.

The electrical engineering department chair was Hector MacLeod (MSC '16), the former student who, in 1916, had led U of A troops into World War I. Hector now had a Master's and a PhD from Harvard. He also had a good relationship with the University Machine Shop. "It was my nature to be on friendly terms with the University workmen—the men in the Power Plant, the machinists, the electricians...and by kind permission of MacFarlane, the Machinist, I had the privilege of using the University Machine Shop." (Bowen, 12-3, 4, quoting MacLeod.) And so perhaps there was some unsanctioned help in getting CKUA underway.

14. Newton, *I Passed This Way*, p. 164.

15. Newton, *I Passed This Way*, p. 285. The following story about Leone McGregor was told to me orally by Dr. Tyrell in 2004.

16. *New Trail,* January 1943, article by M.D. Skelton.

17. Myrna Kostash recalls this memory on p. i of the introduction to Jon Whyte, *Mind Over Mountains: Selected and Collected Poems* (Calgary: Red Deer Press, 2000).

18. Letter to the editor from Don Cruden in the *New Trail,* Spring/Summer 2002.

19. St. Joseph's College Prospectus, 1927. The *Trail* in 1920, p. 8, noted that St. Joe's was being built "in the angle formed by Eighty-ninth Avenue with the lane leading to the University farm...." St. Joseph's College, which does not receive government grants or University funds for capital costs, plans to raise $1 million to modernize its 77-year-old landmark building.

20. *New Trail*, Winter, 2001–2002, Jacqueline Jannelle, p. 31.

21. Bowen, 8, quoting Cecil Burgess.

22. Bowen, 6, quoting Baker and Chittick. Some of Baker's and Chittick's recollections have been combined into a composite quote.

23. 1929 *Calendar,* p. 49.

24. This is Bowen describing herself, 14-1.

25. "She Brought Us Music" is taken from *Gateway City,* p. 167. The 1925–1926 *Evergreen and Gold*, p. 35, is the main source on Mrs. Carmichael, and source of the quotes. There is also a brief piece about her in Kay Sanderson's *Remarkable Alberta Women* (Calgary: Famous Five Foundation, 1982), p. 66. Vernon Barford directed the first opera in Edmonton in 1904.

26. See Lovat Dickson, *The Ante Room*, p. 216. The quote about the French Club is from Elise Corbett's *Frontiers of Medicine: A History of Medical Education and Research at the University of Alberta* (Edmonton: University of Alberta Press, 1990), p. 70. Information and quotes about Mark's medical career are also from her book, pp. 70-71. Johns, *History,* also has a reference to Mark's medical career. The Faculty of Medicine and Dentistry display on 2G2 of the Walter MacKenzie Centre has an information panel on Mark Marshall, and this is the source for the quotes on the Mark as Chair of Otolaryngology and on the "Marshall Plan." Professor Emeritus of Medicine Dick Sherbaniuk says that Mark changed his name because his son, who was in the US at the time, was having a difficult time because he was Jewish. Orally to the author in 2003. The information about Alfred Bader is taken from *The National Post*, June 5, 2003.

Bader later donated a castle to Queen's University, which admitted him when McGill and the U of T did not.

27. Glenbow Museum, Calgary, Alberta, promotional material written by curator Catharine Mastin for the show "The Group of Seven in Western Canada, 2002."

28. Cashman, *The Best Edmonton Stories*, pp. 199-120. Vernon Barford is a U of A honorary degree recipient.

29. Elise Corbett, *Frontiers of Medicine*, p. 44.

30. Johns, *History*, p. 96.

31. Hugh Morrison (BA '30), a president of the Literary Society, was the first person to tell me about Elizabeth Sterling Haynes. One source for Mrs. Sterling Haynes is a booklet of remembrances produced for a 1974 Elizabeth Sterling Haynes Theatre Event, Paul Fleck Archives at the Banff Centre, accession 80.9, cited hereafter as "Remembrance Booklet." Other sources are cited below in notes concerning her students. I am grateful to author Moira Day for corresponding with me about Mrs. Haynes and for many discussions I had about Mrs. Haynes with staff at the Banff Centre. There is a short piece about Mrs. Haynes in Kay Sanderson's *200 Remarkable Alberta Women*. An article regarding Mrs. Haynes also appeared in the *Globe and Mail*, April 25, 2004, Section R5.

32. "Remembrance Booklet."

33. "Remembrance Booklet" and Leighton, *Artists, Builders and Dreamers*, chapter 6.

34. The first quote is from the "Remembrance Booklet." The description "theatrical sodbuster" is from a book review about Mrs. Ringwood published in *Alberta Report*, June 21, 1982, p. 41. The first four quotes are from a 1978 interview with Mrs. Ringwood by Reevan Dolgoy, provided to me by the Paul D. Fleck Archives at the Banff Centre, accession 1990-442. The last quote ("the strongest influence on me") is from Anton Wagner, ed., *Women Pioneers: Canada's Lost Plays*, vol. 2 (Toronto: Canadian Theatre Review Publications, 1979), p. 15.

35. Elsie's husband also got involved in drama productions as a Physics student. He was later named a Rhodes Scholar and then became a professor at the U of A. Elsie said she married him because he was the "only man I had ever met who was willing to let me go as far as I could." Mrs. Gowan was interviewed in 1980 by Peggy Leighton. The transcript was provided to me by the Paul D. Fleck Archives at the Banff Centre, accession 1990–442. All quotes are from that transcript. The description of the Empire Theatre is drawn from Person and Routledge, *Portrait*, p. 154. Gwen

Pharis's description of Mrs. Gowan is from her interview with Reevan Dolgoy, cited above.

36. Gowan interview, as cited above, and orally to the author from Hugh Morrison, 2001.

37. Hugh Morrison saw *Shall We Join the Ladies* staged at the Stratford in Niagara-on-the-Lake in 2000. It was touted as the first production of Barrie's play in Canada. Hugh made sure he went backstage to let them know that the University of Alberta had beat them to the punch six decades earlier.

38. Orally to the author during interviews conducted in accordance with university ethics guidelines between 2000 and 2006, and in correspondence and phone calls. The quote about Ma Brainard is from Sanderson's *Remarkable Alberta Women*, p. 29. There is an excellent description of initiation in *The Gateway*, October 14, 1926, p. 3. The October 21 issue covers the 1926 debate about modifying, or abolishing, initiation. Hugh's descriptions of "Canadian football" relate to what was sometimes called rugby, not, it should be noted, what we know of as British rugby, but rather a Canadian version akin to football. The information on the two fraternities that were banned in 1909 can be found in UAA 86-41, box 19.

39. The Baker quote is in Bowen, 6-3 and the quote from Tory to his faculty is from Helen Sheldon in Bowen, 13-11.

Chapter 7

1. The alumni quotes are all from interviews referenced elsewhere in this chapter, except for the MacLeod quote (Bowen 12-5) and the "cocoon" quote, which is from a conversation in 2002 with Marion Crosby McGill, (BSC '38 HEC).

2. Ivan Glassco, *Bigwigs: Canadians Wise and Otherwise* (Freeport: Books for Libraries Press, 1968), p.13.

3. Newton, *I Passed This Way*, p. 280.

4. The story, which I have condensed slightly, is titled "A Freshman's First Three Days at the U of A," *The Gateway*, vol. XXVI, no. 1, October 11, 1935, p. 8.

5. From Dr. Stelck's convocation address, 2003, as published on the Senate's website. Also see *The Edmonton Journal* article on Dr. Stelck, May 13, 2001.

6. Lister, *My Forty-Five Years on the Campus*, pp. 39–40. The words are all Reg Lister's, but I have condensed the story and not shown ellipses. Reg has many amusing stories to relate about liquor. On the question of approval by the University of fraternities, they were approved quickly after Tory left for the NRC. Tory apparently opposed fraternities because of their secret initiation rites and exclusivity. He

was supported in this view by Provost MacEachran, but MacEachran threw his support behind the students once Tory left the University.

7. *Edmonton Journal*, article by Jac MacDonald, no date. The article is part of a research file loaned to me by Rob Lake in Computing Science.

8. Mrs. Marjorie Bowker notes that the proper pronunciation of Mr. Powlett's name is 'Paw-lette," with the accent on the first syllable. The Reg Lister quotes are in *My Forty-Five Years on the Campus*, pp. 46–47. Johns, *History*, pp. 139–43, recounts this story and is the source for the quote "a nervous, highly strung boy...." David Hannah, *Postsecondary Students and the Courts in Canada: Cases and Commentary from the Common Law Provinces* (Asheville: College Administration Publications, 1998), pp. 233–38, is the source for quotes related to the court case. Both the institutional history and the legal issues of this case are fascinating. Some of the issues were these: Did the University turn a blind eye when it came to initiation? (Yes). Did the University owe a duty of care towards Mr. Powlett? (Yes). Who was responsible to exercise that duty? (The Board). Did negligence on the University's part cause Powlett's mental collapse? (Yes). Could the Board, the Senate, and the University be sued? Hannah reports that "neither the Board nor the Senate was immune from liability but the University was" (*Postsecondary Students*, p. 235). The Senate resolution is in the 1934–1935 Calendar at p. 65. In Provost MacEachran's interview with Ruth Bowen, MacEachran says he thinks initiation "got all that nonsense out of their systems and then they settled down," Bowen 11-8. MacEachran thinks the University should have appealed and lifted itself "out of the mud." He maintains that Wallace was more easygoing than the steely Tory and that Tory would have appealed (Bowen, 11-8).

9. Apparently local printers gave the SU excellent rates for producing the yearbooks during the Depression because they wanted to keep their artists and technicians fully engaged during these lean years as a bulwark against the day that the economy would pick up. They did not want to lose such skilled workers. Enrolment figures are taken from MacDonald, *The History of the University of Alberta*, pp. 34 and 45.

10. Sources include Newton, *I Passed This Way*, chapter 12; *The Gateway* March 15, 1957, p. 12, "Banff School of Fine Arts Celebrates 25th Years"; Johns, *History*, p. 124; Sanderson, *Remarkable Alberta Women*, p. 61; *New Trail* October 1945,

pp. 252–53; Leighton, *Artists, Builders and Dreamers*; Cameron, *Campus in the Clouds*; information files at the Paul D. Fleck Archives at the Banff Centre, especially 1994 80.9, 13–03–05 and 13a–03–05; and Brian Brennan, *Alberta Originals: Stories of Albertans Who Made a Difference* (Calgary: Fifth House, 2001), pp. 71–74. The quote from Corbett, *We Have With Us Tonight*, p. 97.

   I am grateful to author and researcher Moira Day for corresponding with me about various aspects of the Centre's beginnings.

11. The original Carnegie Library in Calgary was until 1915 the site of Calgary College, which failed as a private university. Strathcona refused a Carnegie grant because the prescribed building size was too small. The grant to the U of A was $50,000 and it was the University that decided to use the money for a library.

12. Stuart E. Ross, *History of Prairie Theatre: The Development of the Theatre in Alberta, Manitoba and Saskatchewan 1833–1982* (Toronto: Simon and Pierre, 1984), p. 101. Ross says that in 1936 Elizabeth assisted 11 theatre groups in Calgary, 12 in Edmonton, four in Lethbridge, "and was teaching or adjudicating plays in two dozen small towns."

13. Leighton, *Artists, Builders and Dreamers*, p. 18.

14. Ross, *Prairie Theatre*, p. 132.

15. Sanderson, *200 Remarkable Alberta Women*, p. 61.

16. Dr. Newton's story about Tory's dismissal from the NRC is in *I Passed This Way*, p. 290. The reference to "that man Tory" is in Corbett, *Tory*, p. 179.

17. Johns, *History*, p. 132; *The Gateway*, January 11, 1935; and *Edmonton Bulletin*, January 5 and 7, 1935.

18. Some of *The Gateway* titles have been shortened and some passages have been gently edited by, for instance, adding pronoun references. Information on the *Cheer Song* is from the October 24, 1939 *Gateway*. Information about the genesis of SUB was drawn from the *Gateways* of October 3, 1930 and August 2, 2001.

19. Information on Ken comes from a meeting with Ken and his wife Marilyn shortly before Ken passed away; from correspondence afterwards with Marilyn; and from interviews with Hugh Morrison. Yearbooks, issues of the *Trail*, and *Evergreen and Gold* were also sources. The information that the High Level Bridge crossing was the highest for many years is from *The Edmonton Journal*, Letters to the Editor (J.A. Kernahan), 2003. The *Globe and Mail* article that referred to Mr. Conibear as the "Kipling of the North" was written by Tom Hawthorn and appeared in the November 6, 2002 edition on page R7.

20. Hugh Morrison was the first person to tell me about these famous columns.

21. Hugh Morrison, sports editor for *The Gateway* in 1929, notes that "Canadian football differs from American football in that it is played on a longer and wider field; twelve men on the field instead of eleven; three downs instead of four to gain ten yards. English rugby, while played on this larger field, has fifteen men on the field at one time and no downs to gain yards, and no forward pass." The *Canadian Encyclopedia*, under the heading "football," has further explanation.

22. UBC students financed a gym in 1929.

23. The information in this section ws compiled from interviews with Mrs. Bowker.

24. Tingley, ed., *The Best of the Strathcona Plaindealer*, pp. 81–82, contains a marvellous story describing how Dr. Broadus fought against the end of the money-losing Toonerville Trolley. Back then, this was the only means of public transportation in the area, and so Broadus and his lobby group "flooded the newspapers with letters to the editors about the loss of quality in their lives, promises by politicians past, and increased usage statistics. The latter was partly due to the free tickets they gave away to patrons along the line. Each time a challenge arose to remove their beloved streetcar they managed to beat it down. In August 1948, this civic war finally ended quietly when buses replaced the aging Toonerville Trolley.... Somehow it would never be the same."

25. All interviews were conducted in accordance with university ethics guidelines.

26. Sources for the family history include John W. Chalmers and John J. Chalmers, eds., *Niddrie of the Northwest: Memoirs of a Pioneer Canadian Missionary* (Edmonton: University of Alberta Press, 2000) and Johns, *History*, p. 117. I am grateful to Mrs. Chalmers for letting me use the 1956 speech she gave at Mabel Patrick's retirement. The speech, gently edited and condensed, forms the basis of this "interview." Her son Ron, an editorial writer for *The Edmonton Journal*, provided a copy of the speech.

27. *New Trail*, Winter 2001–2002.

28. 1935 Garneau yearbook. The students from Garneau High School, in 1935, moved to the Normal School (now Corbett Hall). The retrospective article was written by an unnamed Garneau graduate.

29. Fraser reports that his instructor, a woman, was let go by the University just before she reached the pensionable age of 65. There was, Fraser says, a public outcry. The woman was the first female professor, Geneva Misener. See the Misener biographical file in the University of Alberta Archives.

30. Information on Mr. Taylor was drawn from the US Opera website and related links, and from liner notes by Michael Keith from a 1999 CD recording of Taylor's music.

31. Mrs. Bowker wrote much of the text for this section. I edited it, broke it into sub-sections, and supplemented it with information from personal interviews and conversations with Mrs. Bowker. Mrs. Bowker's most recent interview about free trade was in the context of a G-8 meeting (*Edmonton Journal*, July 2002). Mrs. Bowker's uncle, Lee Carr, attended the U of A in 1908, graduating with the first class in 1912.

32. UBC was established by an act of the provincial legislature in 1877 but never got off the ground because of political rivalry over the location of the campus. Henry Marshall Tory, then from McGill, became involved in organizing the school, and in 1906, McGill College of British Columbia was formed. The Act establishing UBC was passed in 1908, and the temporary campus downtown was nicknamed the "Fairview Shacks." There was no Point Grey campus (UBC's current site) until 1925, and even so, except for the Library, power plant, and Science Building, many of the buildings were "semi-permanent." In 1935 UBC's government grant was cut from $626,000 to $250,000. UBC didn't really 'take off' until the 1940s, when the first residences were built and professional Faculties like Medicine and Law were established.

33. Margaret Matheson, *A Passion for Music: A Biography of Richard S. Eaton* (Edmonton: Spotted Cow Press, 2001), p. 120.

34. I am grateful to Kristen Olson of the Legal Archives Society of Alberta for this information.

35. Harry Evans was mayor of Edmonton from 1917–1918.

36. Nick became head of Canadian Intelligence during World War II. Orally from Sylvia Evans to the author, 2002.

37. Bob Hesketh and Frances Swyripa, *Edmonton: The Life of a City* (Edmonton: NeWest Publishers, 1995), p.102.

38. Hugh Morrison notes that Mark, after "serving in the Navy during World War II, became a high-level civil servant. During the Cold War, he served in the special branch of the RCMP (Secret Intelligence) from 1952–1961."

39. Orally to the author, 2002.

40. When I first saw Priscilla's photograph in the 1933 year-book, her face captured me in a way no other photograph has. I asked Hugh Morrison if he knew this young woman, and thus Hugh became the first person to tell me the story of Priscilla and Sammy. There were several other graduates who later told me this story, including Anne and Sylvia Evans. I am grateful to Priscilla's sister Edith Hilda Millar for telling me about Priscilla's last hours and for sharing with me the photograph taken when she, Priscilla and Agnes went on that last horseback trip up to Mount Edith.

Priscilla's Delta Gamma sister, Nancy Wynn Fairley, told me in 2002 that Priscilla's photograph of her presentation at court hangs today in the fraternity house. When Priscilla died, her mother Edith had a room at the DG house decorated in her daughter's honour and in that room hung the "presentation" photo of Priscilla. The Delta Gamma emblem is engraved on Priscilla's gravestone.

41. My thanks to Edith Hilda Millar for sending me a copy of this poem and to her neighbour, researcher Karen Clark, for finding a copy.

Chapter 8

1. Ringwood was interviewed by Peggy Leighton in 1981, and this is the source for the quote about Gwen's marriage. Paul D. Fleck Library and Archives, accession 1990–44.2.

2. Not only was the Covered Rink turned into a drill hall, but a separate structure (called the Drill Hall) was also built. L.G. Thomas, *The University of Alberta in the War of 1939–1945* (Edmonton: University of Alberta, 1948), p. 13.

3. Reg Lister, "Reg Lister relives 50 Years Recalling Residence Life" in *The Gateway*, February 15, 1957, 8.

4. *New Trail*, Spring/Summer 2002, p. 4.

5. Joseph Boudreau, *Alberta, Aberhart and Social Credit* (Toronto: Holt, Rinehart and Winston, 1975), section 3, items 15 and 41. This book is a collection of newspaper articles about the Aberhart era. The "running wild" quote is from the *Calgary Herald*, August 12, 1937. The quote concerning the Pulitzer prize is from *The Edmonton Journal*, May 2, 1938 (section 3, item 44). The "Running Wild" reference is from the *Calgary Herald*, August 12, 1937.

6. PAA 70.427, Box 127 for all quotes in this section. This box contains the order-in-council and related documents.

7. According to Francis Winspear, Senate had come to play out partisan politics on the floor of the Senate. Mr. Winspear recalled that before the re-vote was taken, there was a recess, and Senators were sending their emissaries down-

town to round up absentees Senators—but only those who would vote the right way. Mr. Winspear served on the Survey Committee that changed the face of post-secondary education in Alberta. Orally to the author in 1996.

8. The marked-up draft of the acceptance speech was provided to the Students' Union in 1996, and in turn provided to me. A copy is on file with the UAA.

9. Newton, *I Passed his Way*, p. 274, gently edited.

10. Newton, *I Passed his Way*, pp. 325–30 ("rich Americans," "end of his tether," "Mrs. Woods").

11. *The Gateway*, February 11, 1947, gently edited.

12. Corbett, *Tory*, p. 235.

13. Some of the headlines have been shortened. The quote "Television should arrive in Edmonton this fall" is from the March 15, 1958 edition, p. 12.

14. Maimie Shaw Simpson, "Taking a Backward Look: Memoirs of a Dean of Women." University of Alberta Archives, Edmonton, UAA 69–55, pp. 4–5.

15. All interviews were conducted in accordance with university ethics guidelines.

16. I have gently edited Ms. Miller's memoir. Ottewell's colleague who describes him as "gargantuan" is Ned Corbett, in David and Peggy Leighton, *Artists, Builders and Dreamers: 50 Years at the Banff School* (Toronto: McClelland and Stewart, 1982), p. 13.

17. Dr. Hardy's quote is from the 1927 *Evergreen and Gold*, p. 6.

18. The recollection of Dr. Sandin is from Walter Harris, *The Department of Chemistry: History and a Memoir, 1909–2003* (Edmonton: Department of Chemistry, University of Alberta, 2003), pp. 8–9.; Dr. Lemieux's recollection is from Association of Professors Emeriti of the University of Alberta, *Echoes in the Halls: An Unofficial History of the University of Alberta* (Edmonton: University of Alberta Press and Duval Publishing, 1999), p. 285.

19. This document was provided by Pat Scott Schlosser from her U of A memorabilia.

20. Johns, *History*, p. 294.

21. Newton, *I Passed This Way*, pp. 349–50.

Chapter 9

1. Johns, *History*, p. 300.

2. *1959–1960 Calendar*, p. 78.

3. . Simpson, "Taking a Backward Look," pp. 47–49, gently edited. The SU president in question was Peter Lougheed.

4. *Evergreen and Gold*, 1956, p. 30. The locations and uses of the offices and lounges changed over the years. For instance, at one point, the SU offices were on the third floor of SUB/University Hall.

5. Orally to the author in 2003 from Librarian Jeanette Buckingham.

6. Bruce Peel, *The University of Alberta Library 1908–1979* (Edmonton: University of Alberta Press, 1979), p. 11.

7. All interviews were conducted in accordance with university ethical guidelines.

8. Both quotes are from Aunger, "Legislating Language Use in Alberta," pp. 473–74.

9. France Levasseur-Ouimet, *D'Hier à Demain: Connaître l'histoire de Saint-Jean, C'est Savoir Qui Nous Sommes* (L'Institut du Patrimoine Faculté Saint-Jean, Edmonton, 2003), pp. 3–6.

10. Ouimet, *Saint-Jean*, pp. 2–3.

11. Ouimet, *Saint-Jean*, p. 12.

12. Ouimet, *Saint-Jean*, p. 17.

13. Aunger, "Language Use in Alberta," p. 477. See also Ouimet, *Saint-Jean*, p. 18. In 1971, as Professor Aunger notes, the *School Act* was amended to allow other "heritage languages" to be taught in the schools on the same footing as French.

14. Ouimet, *Saint-Jean*, p. 16.

15. Quoted in Bowen, 1–19.

16. *The Gateway*, November 9, 1945, "Calgary branch U of A Enthusiastic—Report On Southern Meeting Indicates Willingness To Joint Gateway, Yearbook."

17. 1958 *Evergreen and Gold*, p. 17.

18. Johns, *History*, p. 302.

19. 1959 *Evergreen and Gold*, p. 250.

20. 1959 *University Calendar*, p. 48. Walter Johns describes the development of affiliation agreements in his history of the University of Alberta.

Chapter 10

1. Orally from Brian Peel, 2003.

2. Larry McKill's description of mealtime in Athabasca is drawn from a series of emails written in 2004.

3. *The Gateway*, January 8, 1960, front page.

4. *The Gateway*, January 30, 1970.

5. *The Gateway*, September 30, 1960.

6. *The Gateway*, January 31, 1964.

7. *The Gateway*, February 16, 1968.

8. *The Gateway*, January 19, 1960, October 30, 1961, September 22, 1964, and September 30, 1966.

9. *The Gateway*, September 23, 1960.

10. *The Gateway*, November 30, 1962 and February 16, 1968.

11. All quotes concerning this section are from *The Gateway*, November 5, 1965; September 16 and 25, 1969, October 1, 8, 9, and 23, 1969; and November 7, 1969. The CUS vote is described in Johns, *History*, p. 425.

12. *The Gateway*, September 25, 1967, September 12, 1969 November 27, 1969. The founding of the CFS is described in *The Gateway*, October 27, 1981.

13. *The Gateway*, November 4, 1960.

14. *The Gateway*, December 15, 1961 and January 31, 1964.

15. *The Gateway*, September 25, 1962. Report 150, available through Strategic Planning and Capital Services, lists the dates of all building construction.

16. *The Gateway,* February 27, 1969, p. 1 and p. 5, and March 26, 1969, p. 6.

17. All interviews were conducted in accordance with university ethical guidelines.

18. Myra Davies's website can be found at www.m-enterprise.de/miasma.

Chapter 11

1. Wyman's presidency is chronicled in *The Gateway*.

2. *Echoes in the Halls*, pp. 204–08. See also Harris, *Department of Chemistry*, pp. 62–64 and *The Edmonton Journal*, Dec 10, 2002, "Life and Times" article by Jegg Holubitsky.

3. *The Gateway*, February 13, 1970, p. 3; article by Elaine Verbicky, p. C3 (Christian) and p. C5 (Wyman); and Tim Christian's election pamphlet (Private Collection).

4. The section on Bub Slug was written by Scott Davies, and edited by the author. The quotes, "The four-frame strip...", "The more I think about it...", and "We found out that..." are from *The Gateway*, March 20, 1986, pp. 10–11.

5. *The Gateway*, February 4, 1971, and *Evergreen and Gold*, 1983 edition.

6. All interviews were conducted in accordance with university ethical guidelines.

Chapter 12

1. Personal recollections and interviews with Dr. Horowitz.

2. Personal recollections. General Faculties Council completely revamped the student advisory system in the mid-1970s, establishing the position of dean of students.

3. Information regarding developments in computing on campus was taken from various editions of *The Gateway* and also from the website of the U of A's Computing and Networking Services (www.ualberta.ca/CNS/hyperdis-patch/HyperDispatch19/timeline.html). This section was researched and written by Scott Davies.

4. *Evergreen and Gold: The Year in Review 1983–1984,* Special Anniversary Issue, vol. 52 (Evergreen and Gold Foundation, Edmonton, 1984).

5. The anniversary issue of the *Evergreen and Gold*, p. 33.

6. Information on WISEST was taken from www.wisest.ualberta.ca.

7. In addition to sources cited below, further information on this tragic event was taken from the *CAUT Bulletin*, January 1990, vol. 37, p. 1.

8. *The Edmonton Journal*, December 9, 1989, p. D1.

9. *The Edmonton Journal*, December 8, 1989, p. A1.

10. *The Edmonton Journal*, December 8, 1989, p. 1.

11. *The Edmonton Journal*, December 7, 1989, p. 1.

12. *The Edmonton Journal*, December 7, 1989, p. 1.

13. The *Globe and Mail,* December 7, 1989, p. A2.

14. *The Edmonton Journal*, December 7, 1989, p. A2.

15. The reaction of the female academic engineering community can be seen in a speech delivered to the University Women's Club on December 6, 2004 by Dr. Indira V. Samarasekera, then vice-president (research) at the University of British Columbia. The speech was entitled "The Calling of an Engineer."

16. *Folio*, December 10, 2004, p. 6.

17. *The Edmonton Journal*, December 8, 1989, p. A18.

18. Stories about events at Engineering Week were featured in a number of editions of both *The Gateway* and *The Edmonton Journal.*

19. Troy Roberts, *The Gateway*, January 23, 1990, p. 2.

20. Information regarding campus construction and expansion projects in this period was taken from various editions of *The Gateway* and also from Report 150, released by the Office of Strategic and Capital Planning for this book. Additional figures were provided by the Office of the Vice-President (Facilities and Operations).

21. All interviews were conducted in accordance with university ethical guidelines.

Chapter 13

1. Personal papers. Dr. Davenport's presidency is well-chronicled in *The Gateway*, *Folio,* and the public governance record. I served part-time as Dr. Davenport's executive assistant from 1990–1994. My thanks to Dr. Davenport for reviewing this section.

2. Statistics on Dr. Fraser's accomplishments were gathered from various university offices by Courtney Thomas and reported in *Folio*, May 27, 2005. I served part-time as Dr. Fraser's executive assistant for the first months of 1995 until the position was made full-time.

3. Information regarding developments in computing on campus was taken from various editions of *The Gateway* and also from the website of the U of A's Computing and Networking Services, which can be reached via this link: www.ualberta.ca/CNS/hyperdispatch/HyperDispatch19/timeline.html. This section was researched by Scott Davies.

4. Hannah, *Postsecondary Students*, pp. 24–25. Mr. Hannah's quote is gently edited, and I have omitted ellipses.

5. Hannah, *Postsecondary Students*, pp. 26–27.

6. Information regarding campus construction and expansion projects in this period was taken from various editions of *The Gateway* and also from Report 150, which was released by the Office of Strategic and Capital Planning. Additional figures were provided by the Office of the Vice-President (Facilities and Operations). This section was researched and written by Scott Davies.

7. All interviews were conducted in accordance with university ethical guidelines.

Epilogue

1. My thanks to Dr. Bob Church for reviewing this section.

2. All interviews were conducted in accordance with university ethical guidelines.

3. See the official website of the Department of Tourism and Commerce marketing.

4. Alberta Historical Resources Foundation historical marker located just outside of Camrose.

5. This quote is taken from the 2004–2005 Augustana Calendar, p. 4. This section closely follows the wording of the Augustana Calendar.

6. My thanks to Drs. Taylor and McMaster for reviewing their biographical information.

7. *The Edmonton Journal*, June 25, 2000.

Note on Sources for Timelines

For "Beyond Our Borders," the main source was *The Timelines of History*, compiled by Bernard Grun. Many of the short snippets in the Timelines are from this book.

For information about Canada, the primary source was Mark Kingwell's and Christopher Moore's *Canada: Our Century*.

For the Province of Alberta, the main source was James MacGregor's *A History of Alberta*. *The Alberta Trivia Book* contained some gems, including the information that "Edmonton has more live theatre per capita than any other city in North America" (69).

For Edmonton and Strathcona, *The Best of the Strathcona Plaindealer* and *Edmonton: Portrait of a City* were the main sources. Occasionally I drew from *The Edmonton Journal* and *Examiner*.

For information about the University, Calendars published before 1941 described in detail the history of the University. I would like in particular to acknowledge these Calendars as rich sources for the Timelines.

For the construction dates for early buildings, I depended on Reg Lister's book, *My Forty-Five Years on the Campus*. The list of buildings constructed in the 1940s and 1950s is copied from Macdonald, *The History of the University of Alberta 1908–1958*. Walter Johns's book *A History of the University of Alberta, 1908–1969* was the main source for the list of buildings constructed and renovated in the 1960s. For buildings constructed after 1969, I drew from sources available from the Capital and Strategic Planning department at the University. Construction dates vary as some authors cite the date ground was broken, others cite the date a building was partially occupied or fully occupied, while others cite the date a building was officially opened.

With respect to graduate scholarships, the Tegler scholarship is cited as the first research scholarship in A.G. McCalla's book on the development of graduate studies at the U of A. There was, however, an earlier graduate fellowship, named in honour of E.T. Bishop (1920 Calendar).

For the enrolment, finance, and student fee information, various annual reports were used, along with the University Calendars for each session, as detailed below.

The "Fall Student Head Count" attempts to show approximately how many students were taking U of A classes during each September to April session. This figure includes those in full- and part-time study, graduate students, special students, and auditors. It also encompasses those in correspondence courses, diploma/certificate courses, visiting students, probationary students, and those in the evening credit program, reported variously over the years.

It should also be noted that the 1949–1950 and 1950–1951 numbers include students at the Calgary branch of the Education Faculty, and the 1959–1960 and 1960–1961 numbers include all those studying at the Calgary campus during the Fall session. Extension numbers are not included in any of the figures.

Thanks to Carl Betke (Director, Strategic Analysis) for guiding my use of these numbers.

Like many other figures over the years, the 1908–1909 head count is problematic, because in the *President's Report* for that session, Tory indicates that "forty-seven students registered for full or partial courses during the year." At the same time, the October, 1908 Convocation booklet states that only 37 students attended the first day of classes (see chapter 3 endnotes). The number 45 appears in future annual reports which report previous years' enrolment (such as the 1913–1914 *Report of the Board of Governors*), and so this number is used in the timelines.

Beginning with the 1910–1911 session, the head count is derived from the annual *Report of the Board of Governors*. My figures represent data as reported in the various registration tables, omitting only the numbers of those in the summer session. For 1979–1980 and 1980–1981, figures are derived from the tables of enrolment in the *Report of the Governors*, excluding those registered in spring and summer sessions. For 1999–2000, 2000–2001, and 2004–2005, I have used the enrolment figures as reported in *Summary of Statistics*, again only excluding those in spring and summer sessions.

The "Operating Budget from Province of Alberta" figures are drawn from various financial statements of revenue and expenditure over the years. In particular, the 1908–1909 figure appears in the *President's Report* for that year, and, beginning in 1910–1911, the figures are from each year's *Report of the Board of Governors*. The 1979–1980 and 1980–1981 figures come from the *Report of the Governors* for those years. The 1999–2000, 2000–2001, and 2004–2005 figures are taken from each year's *Financial Statements and Supplementary Schedules* booklet.

These figures are intended to represent the contribution of Alberta Learning to the delivery of teaching, and so the most recent numbers also include the conditional and access grants from the Province of Alberta.

Special thanks go to Debbie Quigg (Manager, Budget Planning) for explaining what these numbers mean and how to compare them over time.

The "Full-Load Undergraduate Arts Tuition" figures are drawn from the University Calendar for each session, and represent the cost of instruction for "one year" of undergraduate study in Arts. The Calendar for many years uses the term "per session." Walter Johns' book makes it clear that a "session" is "one year" (p 123). The figure does not include other significant fees which have been charged over the years.

The "Students' Union Membership Fee" information was also drawn from the Calendars. "Dedicated" fees are those that were created by a referendum stating a specific use for the funds collected, and are listed separately.

SELECT BIBLIOGRAPHY

In addition to the sources listed below, a number of periodical materials were also consulted. The *Edmonton Bulletin*, which was published from 1880 to 1951 and restarted in 1996, provided excellent information regarding the early history of Edmonton and the University of Alberta. This resource was further augmented by *The Edmonton Journal*, which began publishing in 1903, and The *Calgary Herald*, which was founded in 1883. For information that specifically dealt with the University of Alberta, *Folio*, founded in 1964, *The Gateway* (a publication variously of the "undergraduates of the University of Alberta" and the Students' Union which began in 1910), the *Trail*, which began publishing in 1920 and changed its name to the *New Trail* in 1942, and the various editions of the *Evergreen and Gold* (1921–1972) were also consulted. For expediency, the University of Alberta Archives is cited as UAA.

About the University of Alberta

Alexander, William Hardy. *The University of Alberta: A Retrospect 1908–1929*. Edmonton: University of Alberta Press, 1929.

Association of Professors Emeriti of the University of Alberta. *Echoes in the Halls: An Unofficial History of the University of Alberta*. Edmonton: University of Alberta Press and Duval Publishing, 1999.

Aytenfisu, Maureen. *The University of Alberta: Objectives, Structure and Role in the Community, 1908–1928*. Unpublished Master's Thesis, Department of History and Classics, University of Alberta, 1982.

Bowen, Ruth. "Interviews and Draft Stories, 1969." University of Alberta Archives, Edmonton. AA 79-112 MG.

Broadus, Edmund Kemper. *Saturday and Sunday*. Toronto: Macmillan, 1935.

Campbell, Duncan D. *Those Tumultuous Years: The Goals of the University of Alberta President During the Decade of the 1960's*. Edmonton: University of Alberta Press, 1977.

Corbett, Elise A. *Frontiers of Medicine: A History of Medical Education and Research at the University of Alberta*. Edmonton: University of Alberta Press, 1990.

Corbett, E.A. *Henry Marshall Tory: A Biography*. 1954. Edmonton: University of Alberta Press, 1992.

———. *We Have With Us Tonight*. Toronto: The Ryerson Press, 1957.

Cormack, Barbara Villy. *Beyond the Classroom: The First Sixty Years of the University of Alberta Department of Extension*. Edmonton: Faculty of Extension, University of Alberta, 1981.

Elizabeth Sterling Haynes Theatre Event. *1974 Remembrance Booklet*. Paul Fleck Archives, The Banff Centre, Banff. Acc. No. 80.9.

"Emblems of the University of Alberta." Edmonton: University of Alberta Convocation Office of the Registrar's Office, n.d.

Ford, George. *Sons of Martha: University of Alberta Faculty of Engineering 1913–1988*. Edmonton: Faculty of Engineering, University of Alberta, 1988.

Gordon, R.K. "University Beginnings in Alberta." *Queen's Quarterly*, no. LVIII (1952): 487–96.

Graham, Shirley. *Mayfair—75 Years*. Edmonton: Mayfair Golf and Country Club, 1997.

Harris, Walter E. *The Department of Chemistry: History and a Memoir, 1909–2003*. Edmonton: Department of Chemistry, University of Alberta, 2003.

Johns, Walter H. *A History of the University of Alberta, 1908–1969*. Edmonton: University of Alberta Press, 1981.

Levasseur-Ouimet, France. *Connaître L'histoire de Saint-Jean, C'est Savoir qui Nous Sommes*. Edmonton: L'institut du Patrimoine Faculté Saint-Jean, 2003.

Lister, Reg. *My Forty-Five Years on the Campus*. Edmonton: University of Alberta Press, 1958.

MacDonald, Jac. *Historic Edmonton*. Edmonton: Lone Pine & Edmonton Journal, 1987.

Macdonald, John. *The History of the University of Alberta 1908–1958*. Edmonton: University of Alberta Press, 1958.

Matheson, Margaret C. *A Passion for Music: A Biography of Richard S. Eaton*. Edmonton: Spotted Cow Press, 2001.

McCalla, Arthur G. *The Development of Graduate Studies at the University of Alberta 1908–1983*. Edmonton: University of Alberta Press, 1983.

McCallum, Joe, ed. *CKUA: 40 Wondrous Years of Radio*. Introduction by Jack Hagerman. Edmonton: CKUA, 1967.

McLeod, Norman Leslie. *Calgary College 1912–1915: A Study of An Attempt to Establish a Privately Financed University in Alberta*. PhD Thesis, The University of Calgary, 1970.

Miller, Esther. *Thirty-Seven Years, 1928–1946*. University of Alberta Archives, Edmonton. UAA 69-23.

Newton, Robert. *I Passed This Way*. University of Alberta Archives, Edmonton. UAA 71-87.

Peel, Bruce. *The University of Alberta Library 1908–1979*. Edmonton: University of Alberta Press, 1979.

Smillie, Keith. *Computing Science at the University of Alberta 1957–1993*. Edmonton: Department of Computing Science, University of Alberta, 1993.

These Twenty-Five Years: A Symposium. Toronto: Macmillan, 1933.

Thomas, L.G. *The University of Alberta in the War of 1939–1945*. Edmonton: University of Alberta Press, 1948.

Turtle, Gordon. *Dear Editor: Selected Letters to the Gateway, 1908–1982*. Edmonton: University of Alberta Press, 1983.

The University Of Alberta, 1908–1933. Edmonton: University of Alberta Press, 1933.

The University Of Alberta, 1908–1983. Edmonton: University of Alberta Press, 1982.

The University of Alberta. *Survey Committee Interim Report to the Lt Governor in Council, Province of Alberta*. Tabled in Alberta Legislative Assembly, February 25, 1942. Sessional Paper No. 50 of 1942.

———. *Who's Who at the University of Alberta, 1908–1919*. Edmonton: University of Alberta Archives, 1991.

———. *Who's Who at the University of Alberta, 1919–1939*. Edmonton: University of Alberta Archives, 1993.

Walters, Marylu. *CKUA: Radio Worth Fighting For*. Edmonton: University of Alberta Press, 2002.

About, by, or with a Connection to University of Alberta Graduates and Students

The Androssen Unifarm. *Cherished Memories*. Calgary: D.W. Friesen and Sons, 1972.

Bramley-Moore, Alwyn. *The Path of Duty: The Wartime Letters of Alwyn Bramley-Moore 1914–1916*. c.1997. Introduction by Ken Tingley. Calgary: Alberta Records Publication Board; Historical Society of Alberta, 2005.

Cameron, Donald. *Campus in the Clouds*. Toronto: McClelland and Stewart, 1956.

Chalmers, John W. *Gladly Would He Teach: A Biography of Milton Ezra Lazerte*. Edmonton: The ATA Educational Trust, 1978.

Chalmers, John W., and John J. Chalmers, eds. *Niddrie of the Northwest: Memoirs of a Pioneer Canadian Missionary*. Edmonton: University of Alberta Press, 2000.

Conibear, Kenneth. *Northland Footprints*. 1936. Victoria: Trafford Publishing, 2000.

———. *Northward to Eden*. 1938. Victoria: Trafford Publishing, 2000.

———. *The Nothing Man*. Vancouver: M Conibear, 1995.

Davies, Scott. *Beyond the Bricks: Stories of the Nurses' Residences of the University of Alberta*. Edmonton: Faculty of Nursing, University of Alberta, 2004.

———. *The Life & Times of South Lab*. Edmonton: Unpublished Manuscript, 2004.

Dyba, Ken. *Betty Mitchell*. Calgary: Detselig Enterprises Limited, 1986.

Grey Owl. *Pilgrims of the Wild: His Classic Autobiography*. 1935. Toronto: Macmillan, 1990.

———. *Tales of an Empty Cabin: Stories of the Early Days of Canada's North*. 1936. Toronto: Stoddard Publishing, 1992.

Lovat, Dickson. *The Ante Room: Early States of a Literary Life*. Toronto: Macmillan, 1959.

———. *The House of Words*. Toronto: Macmillan, 1963.

———. *Wilderness Man: The Strange Story of Grey Owl*. Toronto: Macmillan, 1973.

Reid, Sheila. *Wings of a Hero: Canadian Pioneer Flying Ace Wilfred Wop May*. St. Catherine's: Vanwell Publishing, 1997.

Rogers, Edith. *History Made in Edmonton*. Edmonton: The Author, 1975.

Sanderson, Kay. *200 Remarkable Alberta Women 1880–1980*. Calgary: Famous Five Foundation, 1982.

Simpson, Maimie Shaw. "Taking a Backward Look: Memoirs of a Dean of Women." University of Alberta Archives, Edmonton. UAA 69-55.

Taylor, Deems. *The Well-Tempered Listener*. New York: Simon and Schuster, 1940.

Tory, Henry Marshall. *Going West: Autobiographical Material, 1907–1915*. The National Archives of Canada, Ottawa. MG 30, series D115, volume 27, file 277, 1915.

Whyte, Jon. *Mind Over Mountains: Selected and Collected Poems*. Ed. Harry Vandervlist. Calgary: Red Deer Press, 2000.

About Edmonton and Strathcona

Babcock, D.R. *Alexander Cameron Rutherford: A Gentleman of Strathcona*. Calgary: University of Calgary Press, 1989.

Cashman, Tony. *The Best Edmonton Stories*. Edmonton: Hurtig Publishers, 1976.

———. *Edmonton: Stories from River City*. Edmonton: The University of Alberta Press, 2002.

———. *The Edmonton Story: The Life and Times of Edmonton, Alberta*. Edmonton: The Institute of Applied Art, 1956.

———. *More Edmonton Stories: The Life and Times of Edmonton, Alberta*. Edmonton: The Institute of Applied Art, 1958.

Edmonton '83: A Pictorial Record of the 1983 World University Games. Edmonton: The Executive Sport Publishing Company, 1983.

Edmontonians of the Century. Edmonton: Corporate Identity Consulting, 2004.

Farnell, Peggy O'Connor. *Old Glenora*. Edmonton: Old Glenora Historical Society, 1985.

Hesketh, Bob, and Frances Swyripa. *Edmonton: The Life of a City.* Edmonton: NeWest Publishers, 1995.

Ivany, Kathryn. *Historic Walks of Edmonton*. Calgary: Red Deer Press, 2004.

MacDonald, Jac. *Historic Edmonton: An Architectural and Pictorial Guide*. Edmonton: Lone Pine & *Edmonton Journal*, 1987.

MacGregor, J.G. *Edmonton: A History*. Edmonton: M.G. Hurtig, 1967.

Mair, Alex. *Gateway City: Stories from Edmonton's Past*. Calgary: Fifth House, 2000.

Millar, Nancy. *The Famous Five: Emily Murphy and the Case of the Missing Persons*. Cochrane: The Western Heritage Centre, 1999.

Person, Denny, and Carin Routledge. *Edmonton: Portrait of a City*. Toronto: McClelland and Stewart, 1981.

Tingley, Ken, ed. *The Best of the Strathcona Plaindealer 1977–1998*. Edmonton: Pioneer Press, 1999.

About Alberta

Aunger, Edmund. "Legislating Language Use in Alberta: A Century of Incidental Provisions for a Fundamental Matter." *Alberta Law Review* no. 42 (2004): 464–97.

Blake, Don. *The Alberta Trivia Book*. Edmonton: Lone Pine, 1990.

Bowker, Wilbur. *A Legal History of Alberta, 1670–1905*. University of Alberta Archives, Edmonton. UAA 2001-165.

Brennan, Brian. *Alberta Originals: Stories of Albertans Who Made a Difference*. Calgary: Fifth House, 2001.

———. *Building a Province: 60 Alberta Lives*. Calgary: Fifth House, 2000.

Brewster, F.O. (Pat). *They Came West*, Banff: Crag and Canyon, 1979.

Byfield, Ted, ed. *Alberta in the 20th Century: A Journalistic History of the Province in Thirteen Volumes*. Edmonton: United Western Communication Limited, 1998.

Holmgren, Eric, ed. *Alberta at the Turn of the Century*. Edmonton: Provincial Archives of Alberta, 1975.

Leighton, David and Peggy. *Artists, Builders and Dreamers: 50 Years at the Banff School*. Toronto: McClelland and Stewart, 1982.

MacGregor, J.G. *A History of Alberta*. Edmonton: Hurtig, 1981.

Rennie, Bradford J., ed. *Alberta Premiers of the Twentieth Century*. Regina: Canadian Plains Research Center, University of Regina, 2004.

Stuart, E. Ross. *History of Prairie Theatre: The Development of Theatre in Alberta, Manitoba and Saskatchewan 1833–1982*. Toronto: Simon and Pierre, 1984.

About Canada and the World

Banner, Lois W. *Women in Modern America: A Brief History*. New York: Harcourt, Brace, Jovanovich, 1974.

Berton, Pierre. *Vimy*. Markham: Penguin Books, 1987.

Bramley-Moore, Alwyn. *The Path of Duty: the Wartime Letters of Alwyn Bramley-Moore*. Calgary: Historical Society of Alberta, 1998.

Doyle, Kevin, and Ann Johnston. *The 1980's: Maclean's Chronicles the Decade*. Toronto: Key Porter Books, 1989.

Duffy, John. *Fights of Our Lives: Elections, Leadership and the Making of Canada*. Toronto: Harper Collins, 2002.

Duval, Paul. *Barker Fairley*. Toronto: Marianne Friedland Gallery, 1980.

Fairley, Barker. *Portraits*. Dault: Methuen, 1981.

Gilmour, Don. *Canada: A People's History, Vol. 2*. Toronto: McClelland and Stewart, 2002.

Godsell, Philip. *Pilots of the Purple Twilight: The Story of Canada's Early Bush Flyers*. Toronto: Ryerson Press, 1955.

Granatstein, J.L., and Paul Stevens, eds. *A Reader's Guide to Canadian History, Vol. 2: Confederation to the Present*. Toronto: University of Toronto Press, 1982.

Grun, Bernard. *The Timetables of History: A Horizontal Linkage of People and Events*. New York: Simon and Schuster, 1991 [1946].

Hannah, David A. *Postsecondary Students and the Courts in Canada: Cases and Commentary from the Common Law Provinces*. Asheville: College Administration Publications, 1998.

Kingwell, Mark, and Christopher Moore. *Canada: Our Century*. Toronto: Doubleday, 1999.

Kostash, Myrna. *Long Way From Home: The Story of the Sixties Generation in Canada*. Toronto: James Lorimer and Company, 1980.

Morton, Desmond. *A Short History of Canada*. Toronto: McClelland and Stewart, 2001.

Morton, Desmond, and J.L. Granatstein. *March to Armageddon: Canadians and the Great War 1914–1919*. Toronto: Lester and Orpen Dennys, 1987.

Owram, Doug. *Born at the Right Time: A History of the Baby Boom Generation*. Toronto: University of Toronto Press, 1996.

Porter, Anna, and Marjorie Harris, eds. *Farewell to the 70's: A Canadian Salute to a Confusing Decade*. Don Mills: Thomas Nelson and Sons, 1979.

Varley, Christopher, org. *F.H. Varley, A Centennial Exhibition*. Edmonton: Edmonton Art Gallery, 1981.

Varley, Peter. *Frederick H. Varley*. Toronto: Key Porter Books, 1983.

Vining, Charles. *Bigwigs: Canadians Wise and Otherwise*. Freeport: Books for Libraries Press, 1968.

Wagner, Anton, ed. *Women Pioneers: Canada's Lost Plays, Vol. 2*. Toronto: Canadian Theatre Review Publications, 1979.

Watson, Patrick. *The Canadians: Biographies of a Nation*. Toronto: McArthur and Co., 2000.

INDEX

court case on increases in, 627–628
for international students, 638–639
negotiations on increases in, 633–634
protests to increases in, 456, 467, **471**, 487, 513, 527–528, **552**, 553
Turc, Jean-Michel, 547
Turner, Terry, 483
Tuttle, Mr., 337
Tweddle, Eleanore Griffith, 417
Tweddle, John, 417, 421
typhoid epidemic, 50, 85–86
Tyrrell, Lorne, 178

UAC
    See Calgary Campus of U of A, Calgary
United Church, 110
United Farmers of Alberta (UFA), 147–148
Universaide Pavillion
    See Butterdome (Universiade Pavillion)
University Act (1906)
    amendment (1965), 456
    Charter Day as celebration of, 235
    provisions in, 21–22, 60–61, 76, 367
    tuition fees under, 627–628
University Bookstore, 390–391, 694
University Cup, 703
University Farm, 248–249
University Hall (first Students Union Building)
    as building, 326, **326**, **386**, 386–387, **486**
    funding for, 248, 257, 328, 386
    student life at, 385–387, 481, 484
University Hospital, 248
University of Alberta, early years
    about first year, 67–80
    as non-sectarian education, 21–24, 30, 37
    Calgary/Edmonton rivalry over, 28–31, 39, 231, 246, 428
    landscaping, 121, 146

site of (Simpson's farm), **19**, 30, 47, 98–101, **99**, **108**
temporary early sites, 67, 67–68, 84
transfer of students from Alberta College, 8, 68
women's right to attend, 21–22, 76
See also academic staff, first; Lister, Reg; Rutherford, Alexander Cameron; Tory, Henry Marshall
University of Alberta, main campus
    aerial photos of, **158**, 159, **225**, **413**, **506**, **565**, **669**
    buildings and plans, **174**, **520**, 520–521, 706
    maps, **99**, **344**
    size in 1960s, 460
    See also individual buildings
University of Alberta, budgets
    See budget for U of A
University of Alberta, campuses of
    See Augustana Campus of U of A, Camrose; Banff Centre; Calgary Campus of U of A, Calgary; Campus Saint-Jean
University of Alberta, convocations
    See Convocation at U of A
University of Alberta, enrolment
    See enrolment at U of A
University of Alberta, student publications
    See *Evergreen and Gold* yearbook; *Gateway, The*
University of Alberta, traditions
    See traditions at U of A
University of Alberta, tuition
    See tuition for U of A
University of British Columbia, 37, 41, 507
University of Calgary, 430, 434
    See also Calgary Campus of U of A, Calgary
University of Lethbridge, 450
University of Ottawa, 399, 402
University of Saskatchewan, 25
University Orchestra, 188
University Secretariat, 387

University Women's Club, 79, 467–468
Upsilon Upsilon, 79, 214
Urion, Carl, 490–499, **496**

Van Dusen, Fran
    See Olson, Fran Van Dusen
Van Loon, Beatrice
    See Carmichael, Beatrice Van Loon
Van Stolk, Mary, 484
Van Vliet Centre, 384, 444, 459, 460, 518
Vargo, Jim, 578, 616
Varley, Frederick
    portraits by, 49, 62, 63–64, 93, 146
Varscona Theatre, 354
Varsity Arena
    See Clare Drake Arena
Varsity Guest Weekend, 369–370, 393, 464, 522
Varsity Rink (Covered Rink)
    early years, 178, 182, **182**, 191
    in 1930s and 1940s, 242, 253–254, **254**, 307, 322, 325, 345
    demolition of, 458–459, 518
Varsity Tuck Shop
    See Tuck Shop
Varsity Varieties, 199, 324, 367, **368**, 370, 390, 393, 464
Vegreville, 10
veterans at U of A
    See World War I; World War II
Vetsch, Cathy, 421
Vietnam War
    impact on U of A, 469, 471, 514, 553–554, 597
Vimy Ridge, Battle of, 136, 137, 138–139, 144–145
violence
    against men, 637
    against women, 574–576, 578
Von Zabhensing, Dr., 125
Vriend, Delwin, 637

Waggett, J.M., **6**
Walden Pond technology, 634
Walker, Ross, 418